Sixth Edition

Human Variation

Races, Types, and Ethnic Groups

STEPHEN MOLNAR

Professor Emeritus
Washington University

PEARSON

Prentice
Hall

Upper Saddle River, New Jersey 07458

Library of Congress Cataloging-in-Publication Data

Molnar, Stephen, 1931–
  Human variation: races, types, and ethnic groups / Stephen Molnar.—6th ed.
    p. cm.
  Includes bibliographical references and index.
  ISBN 0-13-192765-5
    1. Physical anthropology. 2. Race. I. Title.
    [DNLM: 1. Anthropology, Physical. 2. Variation (Genetics)
    3. Continental Population Groups. 4. Ethnic Groups. QU500M727h 2005]

  GN62.8.M64 2005
  599.9—dc22

                                                          2005032627

Publisher: Nancy Roberts
Editorial Assistant: Lee Peterson
Marketing Manager: Marissa Feliberty
Marketing Assistant: Anthony DeCosta
Production Liaison: Marianne Peters-
Riordan
Manufacturing Buyer: Ben Smith
Art Director: Jayne Conte
Cover Design: Patricia Kelly

Cover Art: Todd Davidson/SIS/
Images.com
**Manager, Cover Visual Research &
Permissions:** Karen Sanatar
**Composition/Full-Service Project
Management:** Satishna Gokuldas,
Integra Software Services Pvt. Ltd.
Printer/Binder: Courier Companies, Inc.

Credits and acknowledgments borrowed from other sources and reproduced, with permission, in this textbook appear on appropriate page within text.

Pearson Education LTD.
Pearson Education Singapore, Pte. Ltd
Pearson Education, Canada, Ltd
Pearson Education–Japan
Pearson Education Australia PTY, Limited

Pearson Education North Asia Ltd
Pearson Educación de Mexico, S.A. de C.V.
Pearson Education Malaysia, Pte. Ltd
Pearson Education, Upper Saddle River,
New Jersey

10 9 8 7 6 5 4 3
ISBN 0-13-192765-5

To IVA

who worked so hard to make this book possible

Contents

Chapter 6   Traits of Complex Inheritance and Their Adaptations: II   215

Chapter 7   Human Variability, Behavior, and Racism   269

Chapter 8   Distribution of Human Biodiversity   309

Chapter 9   Perspectives of Health and Human Diversity: Influences of the Race Concept   343

Chapter 10 Changing Dimensions of the Human Species   370

FIGURES

TABLES

Preface

The mapping of the DNA sequences of the human genome has been completed and our knowledge of genetic diversity increases daily. It is now possible not only to differentiate between individuals, but also to offer predictions of susceptibility to specific diseases and response to drug treatment at a personal level. New terms such as genomics and proteomics are now commonly used to define individual responses to diseases and drug treatment. At this primary level, a new focus is on a patient's genetic makeup to guide in treatment selection. A promising approach, to be sure, with many possibilities for the future, but one handicapped by a continued use of the race concept. One reads of "Race and Medicine" or "The Genetics of Race," implying that the classic subdivisions of the last two centuries were meaningful biologic subdivisions. This adherence to such partitioning of our species ignores that these divisions are largely determined by sociocultural factors with a mix of complex traits of size, form, and color. Neither the understanding of health and disease nor the explanation of human biodiversity is aided by such a theoretical focus. This expanded sixth edition explores these conflicts and problems as the origins and distributions of human diversity are discussed.

The book has been reorganized and expanded to include two new chapters. A chapter on adaptation of complex traits describes nutritional influences, and the effects of high altitude on human growth and form have been added. The second new chapter explores how the race concept shapes our perspectives of health and disease and describes the effects of environmental changes on epidemiological transition.

This chapter raises the question of "What Is a Race" in the context of its modern, twenty-first century application. The chapter on the distribution of human differences has been expanded and placed after traits of complex and simple inheritance have been discussed. Chapter 7 on human variability and behavior has been expanded to include examples of inheritance of several major mental abnormalities. Other chapters have been rewritten and updated to encompass the more recent studies. As in previous editions, the traits of simple inheritance are discussed, not only from the perspective of their distribution but also with the view of natural selection. The complex traits of size, shape, and skin color are divided into two chapters with an explanation of their adaptive significance.

Much of what I said in prefaces to earlier editions remains relevant today, unfortunately. Antiquated, outdated race concepts continue to guide both social and biomedical research. Race, ethnic group, and class are commingled, and the heritability of numerous behavioral attributes is offered as an explanation for major social issues. The argument that there is evidence for inherited inequality continues. But the major problem for the study of our species diversity remains—the mixing of biological and social explanations, which continues despite the advances that have been made in the field of genetics. In fact, it is the very growth of knowledge about our genome that has, in some ways, supported a renewed confidence in biological determinism. In this edition, as in previous editions, I shall continue to explore the scope of our knowledge of human diversity and criticize the reliance on racial labels. The mass of new data on genetic markers should underscore the weaknesses of these "classic" race divisions. I shall remind the readers of these problems and try to guide them past the major pitfalls of nineteenth-century thinking as the recent data on "gene geography" and human adaptation are discussed. These pitfalls are often obvious as in the case of the Food and Drug Administration's urging researchers and clinicians to record the race or ethnicity of their subjects or patients. The classifications to be used are those established for the last census—a list of classifications that mix geographical origins with skin color, with ethnicity, and all based on personal identification. Such a scheme is far removed from genetic reality, as we shall see.

For years I have benefited from the inquiring minds of the students I have had the privilege to teach as well as from the comments of my colleagues. I gratefully acknowledge their input as well as the thoughtful analysis of the reviewers of the original manuscript, though the errors and omissions of the final book product are my responsibility. I would also like to thank John Zimmerman and Tracy Molnar for their technical assistance in navigating the maze of Web sites of the modern computer systems. A note of appreciation to Charles Hildebolt for the many hours of conversation discussing some of the mysteries of human biology. The editorial staff of Prentice Hall has been most helpful in guiding this revision through all of the many steps leading to publication and have my appreciation. A special acknowledgement to my wife, Iva, who has continued in her support and encouragement, even for this sixth edition. As always, she has been a partner, often a senior one, in all phases of the research and writing of the many revisions.

chapter

1

Biological Diversity and the Race Concept: An Introduction

The concept that humans can be divided into neat categories labeled races, differing in physical form or by language and color, is a very old idea and has been used again and again throughout history to discriminate between peoples. With the wealth of new genetic information and the expanding record of biological diversity, it has become harder to maintain the older boundaries around the "classical" races or to establish new ones. One would suppose that a newer worldview would have emerged allowing us a different, scientifically based perspective. Such is not always the case, however. We still frequently revert to old stereotypic views and use racial labels as kind of a shorthand code or proxy for explaining biological as well as behavioral differences. A simple visual appraisal of appearances related to size, form, and color of individuals is used to place them into one of several races or ethnic groups.

Skin color is one characteristic that seems to be most significant, and it is frequently used to identify people. We read again and again about black and white peoples, "people of color," and the "dark skinned races" as if such divisions of humans can define a range of biological or behavioral differences. Color has been and is still used for political purposes; the population census continues to use black and white classifications. The health sciences rely on racial categories to guide treatment choice for individuals despite the fallacy of the concept of primary races. The Food and Drug Administration, encouraging studies of individualized medicine (pharmacogenetics), urges researchers to identify their patients' race by one of five categories: two are by color (black or white), two by geographic region (American Indian/Alaskan Native or Asia/Pacific Islander), and one by ethnicity (Hispanic). Such labeling may work for political or social purposes, but it ignores the historical and biological diversity within each group. Racial classification of people based on a few anthropometric traits may offer an illusion of scientific objectivity, but simple visual perception of these traits or self-reporting of one's race is not enough.

The development of twentieth-century biomedical technology with all its sophisticated laboratory methods has revealed a greater biochemical diversity among humans than previously recorded. Such traits are not easily determined but require special techniques for their detection. The blood types, enzymes, and numerous other inherited biochemical factors differ in a range of frequencies among the various human groups studied. The list of these traits is increasing rapidly as newer and more efficient methods are employed. The most important addition has been techniques that permit a precise record of DNA. Certain regions of our DNA show so much variability that distinctions may be made between populations, families, or even at an individual level, as in the use of DNA "fingerprinting." With a combination of the newer methods of biochemical and DNA analysis, a whole new dimension of study has been opened up.

This newly acquired ability to study human biology forces us to reject perceptions of superficial differences, many of which may be due to factors of nutrition, child growth, and climate. But even simple appraisal suggests that *Homo sapiens* consists of many diverse population groups whose range of variability is enormous. Such variety causes one to ponder the composition of our species and casts doubt on any scheme that attempts to divide humanity into a few definite categories we call race. Just why is *Homo sapiens* such a polymorphic, polytypic species? That is, how can we explain the individual variability within a population (*polymorphic*) or the many distinctions among the human groups (*polytypic*)? Why are characteristics of skin, hair, body size, blood factors, or DNA fragment types distributed among the world's peoples in the way they are?

Biological variability appears to result from the combined influences of human behavior and natural forces that have been at work throughout evolution. The size of populations, their isolation, and their adaptation to environmental stresses contribute to, or detract from, the survival of individuals or of an entire group. Each population also reflects, to some degree, the experiences of its ancestors and gives evidence of elements in its environment that have been shaping it through time. This modification over the course of generations is still proceeding and will contribute to future population diversity. No matter how we may define or classify races today, their composition will undoubtedly change over future generations as a result of alterations in evolutionary forces through human adaptation and because of continuing migrations and interbreeding. These and other factors cause changes in population sizes and boundaries and require new definitions and identity labels.

Immigration has accelerated over the last few decades in the Western world, causing us all to become students of human variation to some degree. National population composition—that is, the percentages of minorities—is quite different from that of previous generations and is continuing to change, both here in the United States as well as throughout Europe. This change has frequently been noted in the popular press under news headlines heralding "The Changing Face of America" or "The Browning of America." Such articles, with or without implied value judgments about socioeconomic or cultural differences, outline some of the sources of this change. All too often, traditional racial classification is revived along with a version of nineteenth-century racism, the false notion of "inherited inequality of races." Concepts of national inequality based on race/ethnic difference have also resurfaced with recent and ongoing armed conflicts and terrorism. For example, an international news magazine commented that to reach a peaceful conclusion, we must be willing to "bear the white man's burden." Such a comment recalls an old colonial racial bias out of the past.[1]

Such racism, together with simplistic race labels held over from centuries past, have no place in the twenty-first century. Our forebears' ignorance of the causes and meanings of human differences may be excused because of their lack of knowledge of biology, but today we can claim no such excuse. Many discussions of race, races, and ethnic groups today, however, reveal an appalling ignorance of basic biology and are guided by an ancient folk taxonomy.

Reliance on folk taxonomy as a guide prevents an understanding of the range and degree of human biological variability though much of this variability is readily apparent. For example, skin pigmentation extends from a very pale color among northern Europeans to an extremely dark brown among the peoples of central Africa or New Guinea. Such a distribution is easily identified by casual traveler and scientist alike. In addition, human body size varies widely from a thin and linear build to a shorter and heavier one, but these features of the human anatomy may change readily with dietary habits and child growth rates. Face form and head shape are other distinguishing characteristics that differentiate between populations; compare European with Asian, for example. Hair form, another trait that has attracted a great deal of attention, varies from straight and long to short and spiral shaped. All these obvious features have led, or I should say, misled writers to draw conclusions about the relationships between groups. Look-alikes have been considered to be closely related by common descent, while dissimilar appearances have been taken as evidence of racial distinctions. All other biological traits are assumed to be equally divided, but such is not the case. Race classifications do not work. Look-alikes can have, and often do have, different blood types, hemoglobins, DNA, and physiological traits. In this book I describe these major components of the biological diversity of our species and their distributions and examine the various causes.

HUMAN VARIATION: ITS DISCOVERY AND CLASSIFICATION

How have we become conscious of the varieties of *Homo sapiens* and their place among the living organisms in the world? This awareness developed gradually as a result of extensive explorations of the world by Europeans during recent centuries. Explorers

---

[1]From a poem by Rudyard Kipling, "The White Man's Burden."

brought back specimens of plants and animals unknown in Europe, and these, together with encounters with peoples of the new lands, demonstrated the diversity in the living world—and challenged many of the Europeans' long-established beliefs. The idea that humans descended from an original pair was especially hard to cling to after the discovery of populations differing as much as Africans, Malaysians, and Native Americans. A revival of Aristotle's worldview of idealized living forms scaled to fit within eleven grades of development became the most useful scheme to reconcile such diversity. As expressed by Lamarck (1744–1829), the famous French naturalist whose ideas on the evolution of life forms predated Darwin's, "man represents the type of highest perfection of nature and the more an animal organization approaches that of man the more perfect it is" (quoted in Mayr, 1982:353). With such graded categories, natural scientists were able to reconcile the discoveries of these new peoples with current religious dogma through an arrangement of all living creatures in a scale from lower to higher categories, from inanimate to animate, with humans at the top. This "Great Chain of Being" concept greatly simplified the study of human variability. Europeans were placed at the top of an ascending order, with newly discovered peoples arranged below—an idea that remained popular throughout the nineteenth century.

The "chain" concept fostered the belief that no two varieties of humans could occupy the same developmental level. Later, in the latter half of the nineteenth century as Darwin's evolutionary theories were gaining acceptance, the human varieties were thought to represent several past stages of development. But even before Darwin, there was a firmly held belief that many ancestral human pairs had been created, each differing externally and internally in a way that suited them for a particular environment. These arrangements of our species into varieties were frequently complicated by the scientists' personal biases. Many believed that certain groups had been retarded in their progress toward civilization by environmental conditions. Naturally, these schemes placed Europeans as the superior group and as being thousands of years ahead of other races. This idea of the superiority of one race over another persisted well into the twentieth century, as illustrated in Carleton Coon's *Origin of Races*: "As far as we know now, the Congoid (Negroid) line started on the same evolutionary level as the Eurasiatic ones in the Early Middle Pleistocene and then stood still for a half a million years, after which Negroes and Pygmies appear as if out of nowhere" (1962:659). It is, perhaps, ironic, that forty years later a reverse order is generally accepted.

These issues of racial origins and rates of development were secondary to the major problem confronting scientists two hundred years ago: what to do with the overwhelming quantities of data accumulating from the discoveries in the recently explored world. Their problem was not whether humans varied in their biological makeup; they could see that with their own eyes, although the variation was not always what they supposed it to be because of the impressionistic means used to perceive human differences. But what were the boundaries of these differences, and how might these boundaries relate to humans' past and to human survival?

The modern systematic study of human diversity begins with an attempt to place all living organisms in a classification system established by the Swedish botanist

Carolus Linnaeus (1707–1778). Linnaeus based his classification system on the assumption, current in his day, that species had been of a fixed type and number since creation. Species were regarded as units of organisms that could interbreed only among themselves; an earlier description noted that "a species could not spring from the seed of another, different species." This sharp distinction between species would assist the process of classification. Furthermore, Linnaeus and other natural scientists believed that the number of species was limited, fixed, and unchanging. All one had to do was to collect and classify samples of the various life forms. As his collections increased, Linnaeus was confronted with increasing numbers and variety of organisms, however. The categories had to be expanded and modified with each new edition of his *Systema Naturae*, first published in 1735.

Encounters with humans on other continents presented special problems because of belief in special creation and the fixity of species. Explorers, including Columbus, brought back a few of these exotic people discovered during their travels to display before curious European audiences. The differences in appearance, language, and customs of these strange people increased the questions about the classification of humankind.

The discovery of monkeys and apes in Africa and Southeast Asia presented a special challenge. Where should these humanlike animals be placed? After much consideration, apes, monkeys, and humans were given a shared classification in an order of mammals, the primates. Monkeys and apes were separated into different divisions (superfamilies); apes and humans shared *Hominoidea*, while monkeys were placed in the superfamily *Cercopithecoidea* (Figure 1-1). Though recognizing similarities between humans and apes, Linnaeus ignored the evolutionary implications of his classifications throughout several editions of his work and continued to maintain that species were fixed in number. However, overwhelmed by the increasing evidence of nature's diversity, he gradually altered his position and allowed that certain varieties were

FIGURE 1-1 A Classification of Apes and Humans.

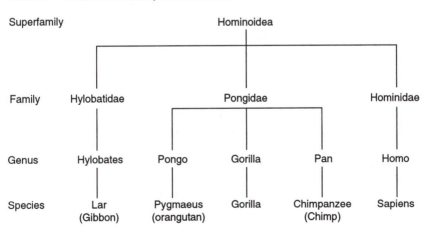

unstable—a conclusion that suggested change over time. Today, of course, biologists no longer consider special creation or the fixity of species but instead consider the fossil record and the natural diversity of biological organisms as evidence of evolutionary change that contributes to the formation of new species or to species extinction. Not only do we view species as dynamic units of the natural world, but we also consider each species in its environmental context, as shown in this definition by Mayr (1982:273): "A species is a reproductive community of populations (reproductively isolated from others) that occupies a specific niche in nature." However, population groups within a species are another matter and may change rapidly even within a single generation, since they can freely interbreed. The rate of interbreeding or degree of isolation can lead to wide-ranging diversity, resulting in a need for further classification into subspecies or groupings into lineages, as in the case of humans.

Linnaeus dealt with the growing awareness of human diversity by using subspecies categories he called human varieties, listed in Table 1-1, which includes some of those offered by other eighteenth-century naturalists as well. These early categories, later called races, were largely determined by comparisons of skin color, face form, and skull shape. Measuring the form and size of the skull was an especially popular method for racial studies, because it allowed the study of ancient populations and enabled determination of their supposed racial affinities. Among the living, the traits of stature, hair form, and shape of the nose were used in combination to distinguish between populations more precisely. Hence, nose form and shape of the midfacial region could distinguish between several of the east and central African people. However, the arbitrary selection of traits and doubts about a fixed number of races led some early workers to suggest that racial classification was unimportant. Also, the fact that all humans could freely interbreed made it clear that no group could be very far removed from the original form of the species and that all peoples shared close common ancestors.

The boundaries for these racial divisions were established as much on the basis of geographical distribution as on biological differences, and behavioral attributes of language and social customs were often associated with biological criteria. Linnaeus attributed behavioral as well as biological characteristics to each group. He defined

TABLE 1-1   Examples of Early Racial Classifications

LINNAEUS (1735)	BUFFON (1749)	BLUMENBACH (1781)	CUVIER (1790)
American (Reddish)	Laplander	Caucasoid	Caucasoid
European (White)	Tartar	Mongoloid	Mongoloid
Asiatic (Yellow)	South Asiatic	American Indian	Negroid
Negro (Black)	European	Ethiopian	
	Ethiopian	Malay	
	American		

Examples of attempts to divide mankind into discrete divisions according to their physical characteristics. These four foremost natural scientists of the eighteenth century agreed with the major divisions of Europe, African, and Asian peoples, but there was some difficulty in placing Native Americans, Southeast Asians, and Pacific Groups.
Sources: Slotkin, J.S. 1965, and Montagu, A.M.F., 1960.

Europeans as fickle, sanguine, blue-eyed, gentle, and governed by laws; he described *Africans* as choleric, obstinate, contented, and regulated by customs; and he characterized *Asians* as grave, dignified, avaricious, and ruled by opinion. These personality profiles that Linnaeus offered together with physical traits are illustrations of biodeterminism: the attribution of types of behavior to certain racial groups. Although this practice may have been understandable in the eighteenth century, given the primitive state of biology and psychology of the day, such confusion of cultural features with biological traits is inexcusable today. Though there has been little or no evidence to support correlations between behavior, character, and skin color since those offered by earlier writers on human diversity, we still read descriptions that claim to demonstrate correlations between race and a whole range of native abilities.

Following Linnaeus, other natural scientists turned their attention to classifications of human varieties. A German physician, Johann Friedrich Blumenbach (1752–1840), the reputed "Father of Physical Anthropology," listed five races whose names are still in use today (see Table 1-1). To the usual criterion of skin color Blumenbach added hair form and facial characteristics, with special attention to the shape of the skull. Skull shape was considered most significant and was regarded as a trait highly resistant to environmental influences. Blumenbach amassed a large collection of human skulls from all over the world for study and, in keeping with the eighteenth-century belief in ideal types, he searched for and found one that represented his ideal of beauty, a perfect specimen. The skull that came closest to fitting this image of perfection was one that had been recovered from the Caucasus Mountains in an area near Mount Ararat. *Caucasoid* eventually became a term commonly applied as a major category that encompassed Europeans, North Africans, and Middle Easterns.

During this period of studies of human variety, our affinity to the lower primates did not go unnoticed. Peter Simon Pallas (1741–1811), a German naturalist and a student of Linnaeus, provided the first family-tree diagram used in biology. In a communication with Blumenbach, Pallas described a diagram depicting degrees of morphological affinity between several animal groups. This tree, or "biological pedigree," implied organic evolution since its arrangement depicted a close affinity between *Homo sapiens* and the lower primates, because of anatomical similarities. Another naturalist, Buffon (1707–1788), noted a greater resemblance between humans and orangutans than between humans and baboons (see McCown and Kennedy, 1972). His conservatism, however, prevented him from accepting human and primate affinities; humans were set apart on the grounds that only *Homo sapiens* had a soul.

Blumenbach, Buffon, Linnaeus, and others in the eighteenth century were handicapped in their attempts to work out a classification more reflective of the actual nature of human variability. They lacked the insights possessed by later generations of scientists who had additional evidence and a clearer understanding of evolution. In addition, Blumenbach and his contemporaries assumed that races of humanity were fixed and unchanging, as they believed species to be. There were, accordingly, distinct boundaries between races, established at creation, and any biological diversity within a race was presumed to be a variation around an ideal type. The characteristics of a European, whose features and skull shape differed from the ideal Caucasoid type, were explained as the result of climate, diet, or even social class. Such concepts of racial types provided a foundation for modern studies of human diversity throughout the nineteenth and twentieth centuries.

As descriptions of additional human populations were offered, explanations of the origins of their diversity were sought. Climate was most often described as a significant influence (the Ethiopian, blackened by the sun, was the usual example offered), but this oversimplification ignored the influence of heredity. As far back as the sixteenth century, Leonardo da Vinci had observed that the black races of Ethiopia could not be the product of the sun's effects, because black parents produce offspring who are black (Slotkin, 1965:91). "Domestication of mankind," a process that supposedly accompanied the development of civilization, was presumed to be another influence on race formation and was described by James Cowles Prichard (1786–1848) in *Researches into the Physical History of Man* (1813). However, in the second edition, published in 1826, Prichard rejected this domestication theory and described the environmental influences and the close correlations between climate and physical type.

In addition to the question of origins or causes of racial variation, the classification of races itself was called into question. Prichard recognized early the problems imposed by dividing humanity into only a few fixed species, and he rejected attempts to divide the human species into "principal families," which was a common practice when divisions were made on the basis of skull shape. "It is by no means evidence that all those nations who resemble each other in shape of their skulls, or in any other peculiarity, are of one race, or more nearly allied by kindred to each other than to tribes who differ from them in the same particulars" (Prichard, 1826:28). Though he did reject such divisions, Prichard described major types of *Homo sapiens* based on head form and coloration. He argued that this was done only to facilitate comparisons independent of any design to ascribe common origins. He suggested that there was no such thing as a Negro race in the customary sense: "Among those swarthy nations of Africa which we ideally represent under the term negro, there was perhaps not one single nation in which all the characters ascribed to the negro are found in the highest degree" (quoted in Stocking, 1973:48). This insight, though strikingly modern, is seldom recalled today. Nor do we recall that some forty-five years later Charles Darwin (1809-1882) described similar doubts about race taxons. In his book *The Descent of Man* (1871:529) he observes, "It is not my intention here to describe the several so-called races of men; but I am about to inquire what is the value of the differeces between them under a classificatory point of view, and how they have originated." Measurements and searches for typical race specimens went on, however.

ANTHROPOMETRY: THE MEASURES OF HUMAN VARIATION

During the nineteenth century, numerous attempts were made to introduce scientific method into the analysis of measures of human diversity. For example, statistical methods were applied to the interpretation of variation in size, and the concept "average man" was introduced as a scientific way of establishing types. Such "ideal types" or averages work well for sorting out widely differing species, but matters become more difficult when investigators are dealing with closely related organisms, and "type" becomes a mere abstraction for comparisons of subspecies (or races). This difficulty increases when we search for forms that match notions of the ideal specimen, a factor that has caused many problems in studies of human evolution. Often the investigator starts with an image of a type and searches until an ideal specimen is found, neglecting those that deviate from this image. Such a simplified view of the natural world has been applied many times well into the twentieth century. For example, Kretschmer (1888–1964), who studied human body form (constitutional types), emphasized in 1930 that this typological system was based on the most beautiful specimens, the rare and happy finds.

Such subjective imagery impedes the understanding of the scope of human variation and serves only to contribute to increase the number of types. These types could, in turn, be used to divide our species into a few "basic" races actually obscuring individual diversities. Any group, large or small, could be said to vary around some ideal or average, and with an increase in the knowledge of human biology more reference points or types would be used to establish new divisions.

There was a further development of *anthropometry*—the physical measurement of human body form—with special description of several cranial features. The major reason that the size and shape of the skull were given so much attention in anthropometric studies was the assumption that skull form was the feature of the anatomy most resistant to change and, hence, cranial form was considered a good measure of one's ancestry. In addition, because the skull housed the brain, the head's shape and contours were supposed to be indicative of the brain's characteristics and even a measure of its quality. The belief that a person's character and intelligence were indicated by the morphology of his or her head has a long history. The study of these supposed interrelationships expanded and developed into a "science" at the beginning of the nineteenth century through the efforts of two German physicians, Franz Joseph Gall (1758–1828) and Johann Kaspar Spurzheim (1776–1832). Their work provided the basis for *phrenology*, a widely popular pseudoscience of the nineteenth century that examined and recorded the skull's contours, supposedly a map or diagram of an individual's latent abilities and talents.

Later, in 1842, Anders Retzius (1769–1860) added a new index to cranial studies that described the general shape of the cranial vault. Retzius divided the maximum breadth of the skull by its maximum length, which gave a ratio known as the *cephalic index* (see Figure 1-2). This index became an important element in cranial studies and was widely used after Retzius reported that European populations could be divided into three types based on their head shapes: *dolichocephalic* (long, narrow head); *mesocephalic* (intermediate shape); and *brachycephalic* (round headed or short and broad shaped). The cephalic index, together with the two types of face form, *orthognathic* (straight faced) and *prognathic* (projection of midface), provided another set of criteria for racial studies. Face form together with cephalic index provided Retzius with a means to divide European populations into four possible groups. Comparing cephalic indices between populations, Retzius reported differences between the skulls of Finnish and Swedish populations. The round-headed Finns were considered an

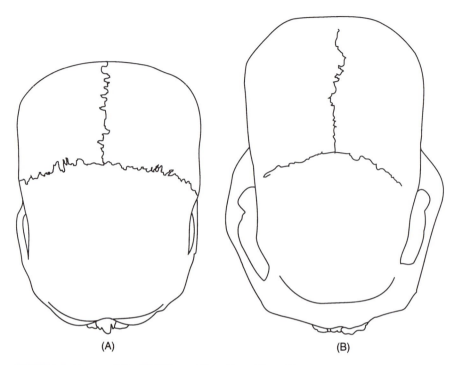

(A)   (B)

FIGURE 1-2   Representative Skull Shapes Viewed from Above. The broader skull (A) is classed as *brachycephalic* in contrast to the long and narrow shape of the *dolichocephalic* skull (B).

indigenous race, whereas the long-headed Swedes had supposedly descended from Indo-European Aryans who invaded Europe thousands of years ago from western Asia. Overall, the cephalic index has been a frequently used measurement in studies of human variation even into the mid-twentieth century.

One of the leading scientists of the day who took a keen interest in Retzius's work was Pierre Paul Broca (1824–1880), a famous French neurosurgeon and founder of the first anthropological society in Europe (1859). Broca applied his training and experience in comparative studies of craniology to provide further support to those who endeavored to relate human behavior to a particular head form. He was convinced that the measured shape of the skull was the best indicator of the quality of the brain. The concern with brain contents, and hence craniology as Broca developed it, was based on an interest in racial differences that he believed to be primordial. Broca worked with great care and treated his measurements with a fine precision. He did not stop with a mere numerical descriptive system but deduced from his measurements the racial history or even the social status of the group under study. He translated skull dimensions into a series of mathematical indices and then deduced the personality and social attitudes of the long-dead individuals, together with their supposed biological affinities. However, after years of such efforts Broca admitted that no single criterion was sufficient to separate the races of humanity (see Gould, 1983).

Though Broca contributed much to neuroanatomy and anthropology in the mid-nineteenth century and introduced several new analytical techniques, his achievements have been overshadowed by the erroneous generalizations he made about social class and intelligence that were very similar to the imaginative speculations of the phrenologists. His attempt to associate lumps or prominences on the skull with various activity centers of the brain may be understood within the intellectual perspectives of nineteenth-century neuroscience. However, the correlation of character, race, and social class to skull form is more difficult to understand, especially since Broca admitted that several organic diseases contracted during childhood could cause deformation of the skull. Despite the efforts of Broca and many others, phrenology passed from scientific acceptability by the end of the nineteenth century. As one author writes, "Phrenology died a pauper's death in the late nineteenth century, victimized by the vicious ostracism of the period's most reputable anthropologists" (Haller, 1971:17). Though this pseudoscience disappeared quietly, the racial classifications begun or supported by phrenologists, which relegated Mongolians, Malayans, Indians, and Ethiopians to inferior positions below Caucasians, were seldom criticized or attacked. In fact, attempts to relate brain size and morphology to race and behavior intensified and continues (see Chapter 7).

While Retzius, Gall, and Broca were developing theories of craniology, several scientists in America were occupied with similar studies. Samuel Morton (1799–1851), a distinguished physician of his day, is best remembered for the thousands of skulls he collected; many were from Native American remains, but a sizable number came from other parts of the world. Morton believed, as did his European colleagues, that skull shape and size indicated race and character. They equated size of skull with intelligence and often reported smaller average cranial volumes for non-Europeans. Morton showed by his measurements that Native Americans had a much smaller cranial volume than did the Caucasoid skulls in his collection. Typological concepts, biased samples, and probably a confusion of data caused his conclusions to be far off and, in fact, there were no significant differences.[2]

Because the European skulls in his collection had the largest cranial capacity, Morton concluded that Caucasoids were the most intelligent of the races—a contention brought up repeatedly in the century following Morton's studies. Therefore, the discovery of skulls of reportedly Caucasoid type in several of the large earth mounds located in the Ohio and Mississippi valleys of the midwestern United States were taken as proof that a vanished race of ancient Caucasian people was responsible for the construction of the vast and impressive earthworks rather than the Native Americans who were seen by the earliest European colonists in the eighteenth century.

Morton's work influenced many others, notably George Gliddon (1809–1857), a famous Egyptologist. Gliddon eagerly and uncritically applied Morton's methods to

---

[2]A careful examination of Morton's measurements and his use of arithmetic means by Gould (1978 and 1983) showed that there were, in fact, insignificant differences between the racial groups. The large differences reported by Morton could be demonstrated only if there had been a bias in the selection of the measurements and skull samples.

cranial studies of the skeletal remains he recovered from Egypt to prove that the pharaoh and the pyramid builders were, in fact, members of the Caucasoid race. This conclusion gave added support to the conviction held by scholars of the day that only the Caucasoids were capable of building higher civilizations. The large mounds and urban centers in the midwestern United States, the Mayan pyramids of Guatemala and Mexico, and the highly developed civilizations of the South American Andes were all presumed to be a result of Caucasoid influence. This is a myth that will not die but keeps reappearing, as for example in the recent arguments over the "racial origins" of the ancient Egyptians (reviewed critically in Brace et al., 1993). These kinds of studies intermingling ancient history and biology continued for many years through to this century. Though now thoroughly discredited, this misuse of craniology was once accepted as scientific proof of the racial composition of ancient populations.[3]

Throughout the development of anthropometry there has been an assumption that if only enough measurements were taken, facts would emerge that would clear up the mysteries surrounding human origins and variations. Numerous select groups were measured throughout Europe, with schoolchildren and military personnel the most frequent subjects. Given the vast number of measurements made during the course of anthropometric studies, a means of analysis had to be devised, and several mathematicians developed statistical methods. Foremost among these early statisticians was Lambert Quetelet (1796–1874), an astronomer and mathematician interested in social statistics. He gathered anthropometric measurements from a large number of military conscripts, university students, and prison convicts, and comparisons were made with a broader sample of European populations. Statistically significant differences of height, weight, and several body proportions were reported between the samples—differences that were attributed to environment or heredity. Most important, these studies established the concept of the "average man" that continues to influence our perspective on human diversity (Stigler, 1986:170).

Especially influential were the measurements of convicts and Belgian army conscripts that provided the raw data for many of the correlations of behavior with body form Quetelet described. These materials permitted the application of probability statistics to predictions of behavior, a method that became widely accepted in both Europe and North America. The statistical methods provided a seemingly scientific basis for investigators who attempted to identify criminal types from a few physical characteristics. Quetelet's statistical work and his descriptions of the "average man" also gave support to those searching for the ideal of beauty and perfection in humans and seeking broader meanings in anthropometric dimensions. The use of such standards or types as predictors of behavior or intelligence was not, however, without its critics, as illustrated by Ambrose Bierce (1842–1914), an American journalist known for his wit and sarcastic pen. "Physiognomy," he wrote, "is the art of determining the character

---

[3]Unfortunately, determination of racial origins by skull morphology has been revived by the argument over the ancestry of a recently discovered 9,000-year-old skull in eastern Washington called Kennewick Man. Claims have been made that the skull has European characteristics and is, thus not an ancestor of contemporary Native Americans but instead represents an ancient population of non-Asian origin.

of another by resemblances and differences between his face and our own, which is the standard of excellence" (see Bierce, 1978).

Among the many major effects that Quetelet's statistics had was his influence on population studies of groups like the Sanitary Commission, organized in the United States during the Civil War. This group of physicians, clergymen, and women nursing volunteers was originally established to inspect camps and hospitals, to advise on the living facilities for the rapidly growing army, and to aid in the treatment of the sick and wounded. From this early beginning, the group went on to establish hospitals, convalescent homes, and organize an ambulance service. As the Civil War continued, the Sanitary Commission's role expanded to include collection of statistical data with a special concern for the health and fitness of recruits.

The Sanitary Commission examined and measured thousands of men, including many recently freed slaves and Native Americans inducted into the army during the Civil War. The results provided an unparalleled opportunity for comparing anthropometric traits of the males of these three groups. Though the stated purpose of these examinations was the practical goal of determining fitness of individuals for army duty, the commission's efforts provided a major study of human variability and was perhaps one of the earliest applications of anthropological theory to practical problems relating physique and endurance to job performance. Generally, the thrust of the study was to determine which physical types or races were most suitable for military service, and for which job. Practical military goals aside, the commission did generate large amounts of anthropometric data collected from a variety of distinct population groups.

Though the anthropometric data collected by the Sanitary Commission are scarcely remembered today, it convinced scientists of the usefulness of such racial variation studies. Joseph Le Conte (1823–1901) wrote in *Man's Place in Nature* (1878) that scientists held the keys to proper race relations in America: "The scientist's methods and his understanding of evolution provided the basis for sorting mankind into a hierarchy of abilities" (Haller, 1971:35). These and many similar statements were merely a reaffirmation of beliefs held by the general public based on simple personal experience—prejudices that accumulated for generations on both sides of the Atlantic. From such works, inspired by "what everyone knows about race," there developed firm beliefs in "racial purity" and a solid conviction that a nation's strength depended on the maintenance of its pure stock (read "Caucasian"). But, though supposedly based on a firm scientific foundation, such beliefs were seriously challenged by the end of the nineteenth century as new data accumulated and a clearer understanding was gained of the mechanisms of inheritance and evolutionary processes.

Race differences were not the only focuses of nineteenth-century anthropometry. With the expansion of measurement techniques to include many features of the living human form, anthropometry was used for standard identification techniques in criminology. As the anthropometric record expanded, comparative studies of the physiques of convicted criminals were inevitable. The increase in crime during the urbanization of Europe spurred the search for specific answers to many of the social problems of the day. The newly accumulated data on a particular segment of society led to the assumption that many crimes were committed by biologically inferior persons. This school of thought was founded on several comparative studies, principally the work of an Italian physician, Cesare Lombroso (1836–1909), who expounded the theory of the "born criminal." He was convinced that the presence of certain physical traits that deviated significantly from the general population norm were atavistic remnants of our "ape" past and that these traits were indicators of a "savage" form of behavior. Through his extensive publications Lombroso cited a long list of "abnormalities"—such characteristics as receding forehead, large ears, square and projecting chin, broad cheekbones, left-handedness, deficient olfactory and taste organs, and exhibitionism evidenced by addiction to decorating the body with tattoos. Persons displaying five or more of these conditions, according to Lombroso, could be considered a type with a hereditary propensity toward sociopathological acts.

For a time this new school of *criminal anthropometry* enjoyed wide popularity because of its seemingly quick and simple answers to what ailed society. Moreover, it reinforced popular perceptions about family lineages and inherited abilities. Studies were expanded to include more of the general population, and large numbers of people were examined in an attempt to establish a relationship between behavior and physique—an early form of *somatology*. This concept of biologically determined criminal tendencies tends to linger on, and from time to time there is a resurgence of interest when identification of pre-delinquents by their body types are proposed as a solution to the reduction of crime. Though simple causes for complex social problems were often sought, there was no evidence to support Lombroso's basic assumptions and there is still none today. Lombroso himself began to express doubts about the significance of his findings and eventually allowed that only 40 percent of crimes were committed by persons with these atavistic traits. Criminal anthropometry was dealt a severe blow by the publication of Charles Goring's *The English Convict: A Statistical Study* (1919) that refuted many of Lombroso's conclusions. Goring stated that if there were any associations between physical character and crime, they were likely to be too microscopic to be revealed. Goring argued instead that criminality was not restricted to particular racial stocks or sections of the community. Nevertheless, the idea of a *class* or *stock* in society with peculiar tendencies was one of the guiding influences within the Galton Laboratory for National Eugenics.

The founder of, and major contributor of, the work that led to the establishment of this laboratory was Francis Galton (1822–1911). As a mathematician, Galton was keenly impressed with the ideas of Quetelet and applied them to develop the field of biometrics. Standardized measurements were collected from thousands of British citizens, and these measurements were presented in mathematical form to identify the norm and distributions of traits within population samples. A graphic depiction of the norm and distribution is given by the Gaussian, or bell-shaped, curve, with the most frequently occurring measurements clustered in the middle portion, or highest point of the curve. For example, there was a calculated norm of body height for the male population of London, and the majority, or approximately 65 percent, clustered about this central point, while shorter or taller individuals were fewer and fell below or above this norm. These were distributed along the smaller, trailing edges of the curve, some distance from the norm, or arithmetic mean. Through this work, mathematical procedures for comparing individuals or samples from entire populations were established.

Galton and his students expanded the scope of their studies and sought to determine the degree of hereditary influences through analysis of several characteristics shared by twins and their families. The investigators attempted to demonstrate through measurements and tests the degree to which inheritance or environment influenced a person's physique, mental ability, and behavior. If parents passed on traits or abilities to their offspring, each family lineage would contain a group or pattern of numerous physical and mental traits of their earlier ancestors. Interpretations of genealogies showing that traits seemed to run in families were lent an aura of scientific support with rediscovery of the particulate inheritance of Mendelian genetics (see Chapter 2). Broad, sweeping generalizations were reached concerning a variety of human traits from health and body size to education and achievement in a social hierarchy.

EUGENICS

What was of particular interest to researchers of the period was a search for evidence of innate behavioral differences among social classes, especially mental ability. Galton outlined a hereditarian position in detail in his influential book *Hereditary Genius* (1869). In it he traced the genealogies of many of Britain's leading families and noted the frequencies of individuals in each lineage who had distinguished themselves as scientists, lawyers, members of Parliament, literary figures, and so on. This book was used as the source of scientific support for a concept of racial and national inequality for the next half century (see Stepan, 1982). In any consideration of the relative influences of environment (*nurture*) and heredity (*nature*) on the determination of mental ability, Galton would be placed on the nature side of the nature–nurture argument, so confident was he in the proof of inheritance of intelligence and behavior.

Deeply embedded throughout this book as well as in Galton's other writing is the theme that the progress of civilization was threatened by high reproduction rates among the poor, weak, or sick, who, he claimed, were allowed to live and reproduce rather than being eliminated in the struggle for survival. Such a theme was not too different from the beliefs held by many of Galton's contemporaries. Most notable was Herbert Spencer, called the "distorter" of Darwinian evolution theory (Stepan, 1982). Spencer misapplied the concepts of "struggle for existence" and "natural selection" to the social issues confronting Victorian England. The growing gap in education, health, and behavior between the classes could be explained, he said, in biological terms. Put bluntly: People in a social hierarchy rise to the top because of superior heredity, while people less well endowed fall behind; nurture could not overcome nature.

Galton stated firmly that, given the scientific fact that intelligence was inherited, the only remedy was to alter the relative fertility of the good and bad stocks in the community. Galton's solution for overcoming this misperceived threat to the nation was to found an organization dedicated to working toward ending the haphazard marriage customs that allowed or encouraged the reproduction of those deemed unfit. He named his organization the Eugenics Society, after the Greek word *eugenes*, meaning "good birth." He proposed that the organization encourage the mating of talented men with talented women, a plan that he concluded would increase the number of eminent men more than tenfold and improve the race. Though Galton planted the idea of eugenics, which gained wide acceptance in the United States and western Europe, it was left to his famous student and later colleague Karl Pearson (1857–1936) to carry on the work attempting to demonstrate hereditary influences on a wide range of behaviors. With the convening of eugenics congresses (the first one held in 1912) and prolific publication in periodicals such as the *Eugenics Review* and *Biometrica*, Pearson expanded the work of the Galton laboratory. These publications, and the guiding philosophy behind them, had, and continue to have, a profound influence.

The eugenics movement grew worldwide during the early decades of the twentieth century, but most rapidly in the United States where the leading advocate, Charles Davenport (1866–1944), established the Station for Experimental Evolution at Cold Spring Harbor, Long Island in 1904. At first this laboratory was concerned with studies of nonhuman species, but by 1910 a second division was organized to do eugenics research. This Eugenics Record Office, as it was called, directed its efforts to gathering census and family data of many types. Davenport, a zoologist, was most interested in applications of Mendel's laws of inheritance to humans. Anthropometric traits of size and shape were considered fixed by the genes one inherited and were listed in endless detail. Records of behavioral and emotional traits were also made. Davenport's reasoning, as well as that of other scientists at the time, was that if blood types and certain metabolic defects were passed between generations, then Mendelian inheritance would apply to other mental traits as well (Chase, 1977).

The Eugenics Records Office intensified the research on behavioral attributes. Family pedigrees were combed for evidence of criminality, alcoholism, feeblemindedness, and moral degeneracy, but more attention was directed toward mental ability following the introduction of intelligence tests (from about 1912). It was but a simple step from this level of family studies to an expansion encompassing whole national groups and races. Family bloodlines and races were seen as predestined for certain roles in life or had certain limitations. Though acceptable to many scientists and popular among the lay public, this effort to demonstrate a range of unchanging, immutable family attributes did not go unchallenged.

The major handicap to Davenport's studies, as well as to those of other eugenicists of the day, was a lack of understanding of gene functions and environmental interactions. The careless and vague use of the race concept common at the time was another problem confounding Davenport's human variation research. These weaknesses were pointed out early in the twentieth century by Franz Boas (1858–1942), one of the founders of American anthropology, who stated

> If the defenders of race theories prove that a certain kind of behavior is hereditary and wish to explain in this way that it belongs to a racial type they would have to prove that the particular kind of behavior is characteristic of all the genetic lines composing the race. (Boas, 1911:253)

In another words if one were to postulate genetic influence as an explanation for a trait, than one could not ignore some populations while accepting the results from related lineages. Unfortunately for social and biological research over the next five decades, this observation was too often ignored.

An additional problem was that many physical traits were treated as if they were permanent and unchanging throughout generations. Boas, in a series of studies of children and adults of immigrant populations, showed the plasticity or changeable nature of these supposed permanent characteristics, such as head or body form. He observed that the many constitutional types of which a race (or ethnic group) is composed cannot be considered absolutely permanent. His Report on *Changes of the Bodily Form of Descendants of Immigrants* (1911) stands as a landmark study of interactions between environments and inheritance. This report compared body form and size of children of immigrants with their parents. Children who were born in America significantly differed from their foreign-born parents in body size and form. They were larger and heavier than their parents—changes that were attributed to improved living conditions, especially nutritional (Boas, 1940a). Interestingly, head shape was one of the more changeable traits: American-born children had longer, narrower heads compared with their parents, hence raising serious doubts about the use of the cephalic index as a "racial" characteristic.[4]

The concept of eugenics was even more strongly attacked from a different perspective. Alfred Kroeber (1876–1960), one of the most brilliant of Boas's former students, wrote early in his distinguished career that "If social phenomena are only or mainly organic, eugenics is right, and there is nothing more to be said. If social is something more than the organic, eugenics is an error of unclear thought" (Kroeber, 1917:175). He hurled a further challenge at those who argued for heredity as a "mainspring" of civilization. "The reason why mental heredity has so little if anything to do with civilization is that civilization is not a mental action but a body or a stream of products of mental exercise. Mentality relates to the individual. The social or cultural, on the other hand, is in its essence non individual. Civilization, as such, begins only where the individual ends" (Kroeber, 1917:180). Considering such observations, it is impossible now, as it was then, to evaluate nation, state, or race on the basis of heredity.

In sum, ignorance about environmental influences on mental attributes or on body form led to many misconceptions about human diversity and its origins and meaning. In addition to the grievous social costs stemming from the misunderstanding of human biological diversity, one of the greatest errors has been made in various schemes of classification. These schemes err when they (1) expect all characteristics to be shared by all members of the same group; and (2) mix unrelated characteristics, as did Lombroso in describing his criminal types. Such "types" are no more real than the "average man." However, simple visual appraisals of human populations other than our own often involve this sort of error. These distinctions, based on limited information, lead us to make faulty groupings of humans and erroneous assumptions about the social quality or worth of these groups. The criteria we may use are not as interrelated as we imagine. Nose form and head shape or stature, for example, have small correlations with one another, and

---

[4]Recent attacks on Boas's original data have been made in attempts to bolster the concept of craniometrics as unchanging and reflective of certain racial types. (See Growth and Adaptation in Chapter 6)

the skin color of the world's peoples has its own special relationship to the environment. Measures or scaling of group behaviors are even less meaningful and reveal few if any heredity correlations as discussed in Chapter 7.

RACIAL BOUNDARIES: FACT OR FICTION?

The mass of accumulating genetic data and historical records document many contacts among peoples throughout the world. The frequent and free interbreeding of these populations, whether European and African, African and Native American, or Polynesian and Chinese, to mention a few examples, is a matter of record. Such evidence has long established that we all belong to the same species and has destroyed many of the racist myths of past centuries. The evidence from paleontology and archeology suggests that this fluidity of breeding boundaries has probably existed ever since ancestral humans' mobility overcame geographical barriers. Despite this evidence, misunderstanding and confusion still occasionally arise over what races are and how racial boundaries, if they exist, can be identified.

The term *race* was applied to varieties of *Homo sapiens* in the middle of the eighteenth century by Buffon, the French naturalist mentioned earlier. Prior to that time, race described breeds of domestic animals—their group membership or descent from a common ancestor. Since then, the term has been used in numerous social and biological contexts and has become encumbered with contradictory and imprecise meanings. The definition of race identity by genetic traits rather than anthropometric characters has done little to clear up this imprecision.

Many people take it for granted that they know what race means and assume that scientific investigation has long ago proved the significance and reality of racial classification. Demographers, historians, politicians, and even human biologists frequently use race terms, but often in different contexts. The various usages require that each time the term is applied, however, a definition must be provided so the reader will know what concept it represents. Does the term refer to the "Chinese race" as opposed to a "Malayan race," or "Hispanic race," the "human race," or the "sturdy British race," a famous phrase used often by Winston Churchill. There is even confusion over the number of divisions that should be identified: As few as three and as many as thirty-seven races have been described, and even more are listed by some authors when they add language and cultural criteria. Two carefully argued papers published in 1950 listed six and thirty races respectively (Boyd, 1950; Coon et at., 1950).

The number of races, especially their boundaries, remains a subject of dispute partially because of the lack of agreement on which traits identify a person's race. Further, just what constitutes a race is a hard question to answer because the definition, or label, depends on the purpose; various approaches to the science of classification (taxonomy) have a built-in bias, especially when applied to humans. It is usually assumed that there is an actual stock or collection of organisms in the natural world awaiting classification—the concept of a real, natural unit (race concept). But, race is not something absolute or "fixed," but rather the product of a set of dynamic equilibrium conditions between genes and environment. Furthermore, social/poltical conditions determine race definitions as explained by Saller, in 1934, who advocated a theory of social races rather than geographical (see Proctor, 1988:253). The samples of definitions that follow give some idea of the vagueness surrounding the race concept over the past fifty years in biology as well as anthropology.

Definitions of Race

DOBZHANSKY:

Races are defined as populations differing in the incidence of certain genes, but actually exchanging or potentially able to exchange genes across whatever boundaries (usually geographic) separate them. (1944:52)

Race differences are objectively ascertainable facts; the number of races we choose to recognize is a matter of convenience. (1962:266)

GARN:

At the present time there is general agreement that a race is a breeding population, largely if not entirely isolated reproductively from other breeding populations. The measure of race is thus reproductive isolation, arising commonly but not exclusively from geographical isolation. (1960:7)

MAYR:

A subspecies is an aggregate of local populations of a species, inhabiting a geographic subdivision of the range of the species, and differing taxonomically from other populations of the species. It is a unit of convenience for the taxonomist, but not a unit of evolution. (1982:289)

VOGEL and MOTULSKY:

A race is a large population of individuals who have a significant fraction of their genes in common and can be distinguished from other races by their common gene pool. (1986:534)

These definitions attempt to treat human diversity with a scientific objectivity. The multiple and varied use of the concept has often resulted in an arrangement of races in a descending hierarchy with its implied racism, however, the resulting prejudice surrounding the term caused an argument for its elimination and a substitution of *ethnic group* instead.

MONTAGU:

An ethnic group represents one of a number of populations, comprising the single species *Homo sapiens*, which individually maintain their differences, physical and cultural, by means of isolating mechanisms such as geographic and social barriers. These differences will vary as the power of the geographic and social barriers acting upon the original genetic differences varies. (1964:317)

This broader, more descriptive attempt to define human groupings on an objective basis without regard to the biases of the day was a reminder of an earlier effort to treat human diversity and its allied social problems from the scientific basis of degree of genetic differences. Populations differed from one another only in the relative proportion of genes for given characters. Accordingly, Huxley and Haddon argued that the concept of race is almost devoid of biological meaning and the word race should be banished and replaced by a more descriptive and noncommittal term—ethnic group (1935:144).

These definitions, though they may appear quite diverse, emphasize certain common factors. The first is an assumption about the role of geographic distribution in race/ethnic group formation. Primarily, the divisions are based on the sharing of a common territory or space and on the assumption that geography played some role in establishing boundaries until recent times when the major migrations occurred (Figure 1-3). The second factor is that all agree on the importance of breeding populations that possess a collection of traits that sets such a group apart. Beyond these two factors, there seems to be little agreement especially when dealing with contemporary populations on the number or divisions to be made.

FIGURE 1-3   Polar-Projection Map of the World Showing the Limits of Nine Geographical Races Described by Garn (1961). Geographical barriers set off the race collections (From Garn, S.M., *Human Races*, 1961. Copyright © 1961 by Charles C Thomas, Publisher, Springfield, Illinois. Reprinted by permission of the publisher.)

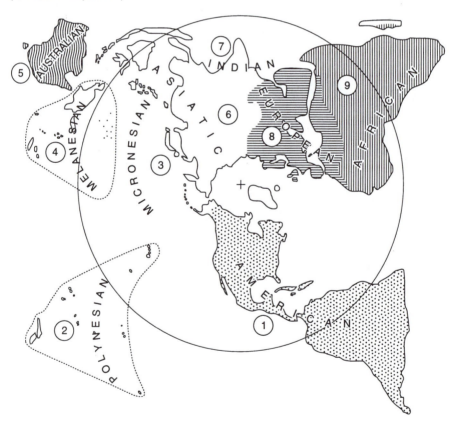

There is some risk that dividing humanity into racial groups distorts the facts and forces the investigator into erroneous channels of thinking, and that the purpose for classification is unclear. As emphasized by Dobzhansky, "The reliability and usefulness of racial classification have often been exaggerated" (1968: 166). But regardless of the numerous ways of looking at human diversity or the evaluation of the utility of race groupings, the fact remains that many biological differences are real and cannot be described or explained away by simple statements about types. The concept of race is not merely a taxonomic problem about which group of populations is related to another or fits together within a certain classification. It is a problem about the ways in which one views *Homo sapiens* through the perspective of time and space. In short, our conception of biological diversity and its origins have been changing and are too often mixed with the social implications of biologial differences.

The more we learn about the variability of population groups, the more difficult it is to fix boundaries between them. The numbers of races and local types of *Homo sapiens* have simply been increased to encompass this expanded knowledge. This may be illustrated by the way in which European populations divided as a more thorough study showed an increased number of contrasts. From southern to northern Europe and from eastern to western Europe, body form and size were seen to differ significantly, as did hair and even skin coloration. In order to encompass this newly recognized diversity, several authors simply added new racial subdivisions. For example, Ripley (1899) determined that European populations consisted of three races: *Nordic*, *Alpine*, and *Mediterranean*. The Nordics were tall, fair-skinned people with large dolichocephalic heads who made up the majority of the northwestern European population. The southern European Mediterranean race were short, brachycephalic people with dark complexions in stark contrast to the Nordics. The Alpine race, the majority of the occupants of central and eastern Europe, possessed average head size and shapes intermediate between the two. Unfortunately for this study, individuals as well as whole population groups possessed mixtures of these traits and could easily be classified into one or another of the races of Europe, and they also could be influenced by environmental changes. This concern with the biological identification of groups continued into the middle of the twentieth century, when more thought was given to what constitues a race and the purpose of classification. The following descriptions show this changing concern.

Earnest Hooton in *Up From the Ape* (1946) defined race as a group whose members present individually identical combinations of specific physical characters that they owe to their common descent. He divided *Homo sapiens* into three physical groups or main races and subdivided these into an array of subcategories. His sorting criteria were primarily skin color, hair color, eye color, and hair form. Similarly, Coon, Garn, and Birdsell in *Races* (1950) used several subdivisions to encompass an expanding knowledge of diversity as they described race as a population that differs phenotypically from all others. They distinguished six racial "stocks" that encompassed thirty races. These races were determined on the basis of evolutionary status as reflected in certain features of the skull and body and special surface features, such as dark skin and face form, that appear as special adaptations to the environment. In 1960 Garn offered a classification differing somewhat from that constructed in his work with Bird-sell and Coon. He described nine races, that were geographically delimited collections of local races. The local races were defined as breeding populations, the numbers of which in any geographical race were very large. A sample of thirty local races was listed as representative (Tables 1-2a, 1-2b). Both the 1950 and 1960 publications emphasized that race divisions were not static and would change over time.

Boyd, in *Genetics and the Races of Man* (1950), defined six races on the basis of certain blood-type frequencies. By 1963 the distribution of the different blood types throughout the world became better known, causing Boyd to increase his original six races to thirteen. The major increase was in the European group, from two to five. This

TABLE 1-2a   Racial and Ethnic Classifications: Two Perspectives[1]

Negroid	**Caucasoid**
African Races or Ethnic Groups	*European Races or Ethnic Groups*
Forest Negro	N.W. European
Bantu	Nordic
Bushman	N.E. Europe
Hottentot	East Baltic
Nilotic	Mediterranean
Pygmies	Dinaric
Oceanic Races or Ethnic Groups	*Irano-Afhan Mediterranean*
Papuans-New Guinea	Armenoids (Asia Minor)
Melanesians	Hamites (North African)
Negritos	Hindu
Asiatic Negritoes	Turkic
Mongoloid	*Oceania*
	Polynesian
Classic Mongoloid	
N. Chinese	*Australoid or Archaic Caucasoid*
S.E. Asiatic	Australian Aborigine
Tibeto-Indonesian Mongoloid	Vedda (Ceylon)
Arctic Mongoloid	Ainu (Japan)
Eskimo	
Evenki, Tungus	**"New Races"**
Samoyedes	Neo-Hawaiian
New World	Ladino
Am. Indian Marginal	Mestizo
Am. Indian Central	N. American Colored
	S. African Colored

[1]The authors tried to arrange human populations into groups that made some order out of the mass of biological data that had accumulated by the 1950s. The results are a series of overlapping terms and classifications called either ethnic or race that relate to some geographic boundaries. Both authors noted, however, that race/ethnic is not a static unit and "new" groups are being formed and old ones vanish as people move about changing population boundaries. It is important to note that this list does not exhaust the number of possible groupings and recombinations of the diverse populations of mankind.

Source: After Coon et al., 1950; Montagu, 1960.

TABLE 1-2b   Major Racial Stocks

1. *Negroid:* All peoples showing special adaptation to bright light and intense heat, wherever found.
2. *Mongoloid:* The same for adaptation to intense cold.
3. *White:* Peoples of the Old World, excluding Australia and the southeastern fringe of Asia, who possess neither of those two kinds of adaptation. Overseas settlers of the same origin, and similar phenotypical form.
4. *Australoid:* The native inhabitants of Australia, whom one of us (Birdsell) has shown to belong to two distinct races and to include one other type, Veddas of Ceylon, and possibly some other remnant populations in Malaysia.
5. *American Indian:* The descendants of the pre-Columbian inhabitants of North, Central, and South America.
6. *Polynesian:* The inhabitants of the outer islands of the Pacific, from New Zealand to Hawaii to Easter Island. While moderately variable, they show resemblances to Mongoloids, white Australoids, and possibly Negroids.

Source: After Coon et al., 1950:140. Copyright © 1950 by Charles C Thomas, Publisher. Reprinted by permission of the publisher.

expansion of the number of categories was clearly a result of the increased knowledge about the distribution of blood types among the world's peoples (see Table 1-3).

Another author, Carleton Coon, combined evidence from the paleontological record with classifications of living *Homo sapiens*. By using a mixed criteria of morphological traits, blood types, and skin color, he divided our species into five races. The Causcasoid, Mongoloid, and Australoid races were no different than those divisions used many times before, but the peoples of Africa were separated into a Congoid race, which included a majority of populations of sub-Saharan Africa, and a Capoid race, consisting of the Khoisan in the southern Africa (including groups formerly called Bushman and Hottentot). According to Coon, these five races were modern descendants

TABLE 1-3   Racial Taxonomy of *Homo sapiens*

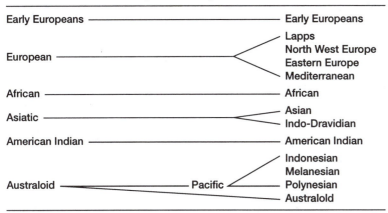

Source: Based on the frequencies of blood types in major groups of *Homo sapiens*; from Boyd, 1950, 1963a.

TABLE 1-4   Classification of Modern Races

Caucasoid	
Mongloid	
Australoid ——————————————————	< Negritos / Full Sized
Congoid ——————————————————	< Negroes / Pygmies
Capoid ——————————————————	< Bushmen / Hottentots

Source: After Coon, 1962, 1965.

of ancient lineages that could be traced back to ancestors hundreds of thousands of years old and were represented in the fossil record. These lineages evolved separately and at different rates, with the Eurasian lineage of the Caucasoid reaching the level of modern *Homo sapiens* earliest while the others arrived later at the sapiens level of development, implying an inferiority of races other than Caucasoid. Coon's intermingling of fossil and living evidence was roundly criticized for misinterpretation of the fossil record and for the racist implications of his conclusions. His descriptions of the living did, however, recognize the difficulties of human classification. These "racial stocks" contained local races of considerable diversity, as in the case of the Capoids and the pygmoid people, who did not quite fit the general category label (Table 1-4).

RACE, GEOGRAPHY, AND ORIGINS

The origin and evolution of human diversity may be traced by the hominid fossil remains, but the fossil evidence is not sufficiently complete to fill out an adequate record despite the many new discoveries in recent years. Neither do these fossils establish a direct line of evolution leading to any particular modern group. We can say with confidence, however, that the earliest fossils to clearly establish an origin of our ancestral lineage (Family Hominidae), four to five million years ago, have been found in Africa. These large faced, small brained, bipedal creatures are distinguished from apelike forms by their dental arcade which, though containing large teeth, have smaller nonprojecting canines in contrast to other primates.

Since the first discoveries in South Africa (the Australopithecines), fossils have been found over broad areas of East and South Africa and encompass a range of variability of body sizes and differing degrees of robusticity. One group of hyperobust forms—those with largest faces and relatively smaller brains—persisted with little change, while another lineage evolved into a more advanced hominid form by 1.5 to 2 million years ago.

This lineage can be traced through a phase of anatomical transition to *Homo erectus* with smaller teeth and face and larger brain, near human but not quite. By this point, a little over a million years ago, these early hunters and users of fire left evidence of their occupation in Africa and Southeast Asia, then in China, and later in Europe. With the spread of *Homo erectus*, the pace of human evolution accelerated, giving rise to an archaic form of species sapiens whose populations left a more complete archaeological record. The boundary between archaic and modern sapiens is ill defined—paleontologists vigorously disagree on the specific anatomical criteria to separate one group from another. Brain size, dento-facial size and form, and cultural artifacts are often used. Mostly it has been a selective bias that determines evolutionary classification of a fossil specimen; European Neandertals are rejected frequently because of their contrast to a concept of an idealized *Homo sapiens* appearance.

Despite disagreements over identity, populations of anatomically modern *Homo sapiens* were established in much of the world (Western Hemisphere excepted). It is within this period, around 200,000 years ago, that some anthropologists have tried to identify origins of the geographical races recognized today. Carlton Coon, mentioned earlier, argued that the lineages of modern races (his group of five) could be traced back through about 500,000 years of time. But, he contended, the earliest to advance to the level of modern *Homo sapiens* were the ancestral Caucasoids in the Mideast and Europe, some 200,000 years before the other lineages. Some authors have excluded Neandertals as mentioned above, while others exclude Asian fossils from *Homo sapiens* claiming they belong in *Homo erectus* instead despite their more recent dates of 40 to 50,000 years ago.

The wealth of additional fossil evidence discovered over the last thirty years has not resolved the arguments over region of origin and rates of evolution. What the more recently discovered fossils have done is extend the antiquity of the human genus, *Homo*, back in time to nearly two million years ago. The fossils have been grouped into two polytypic species encompassing diverse populations. It has also identified Africa as the homeland of the earliest ancestors and this record underscores Africa's broad range of environments requiring differing adaptations within this lineage. This new time frame of human evolution has become something of a mixed blessing for students of human paleontology and biological variation. Numerous controversies have erupted over the place in the human ancestral lineage of each new discovery, and the nineteenth-century habit of an excessive use of new taxons has been revived. The arguments and disagreements among human paleontologists have focused on which newly discovered fossil could be the earliest *Homo sapiens* or which is the more recent of the Australopithecines. What has unfolded within this past decade has been a complete reevaluation of the record of the more recent fossils of genus *Homo* and the contributions of Asian (Peking Man, Java Man, et al.) and European and Mideastern fossils (Neandertals) to the evolution of modern sapiens (Figure 1-4).

The earliest skeletal evidence of *Homo sapiens* is considered to be found in East Africa. This is a complete reversal of the theories of human origins advanced up until thirty years ago, theories that claimed the Middle East as a homeland for humans. This new "out of Africa" or "replacement" theory has relegated many of the hominid fossils, including the later ones from Europe, Asia, and even the Middle East, to an evolutionary side branch (Stringer and McKie, 1996). The Neandertals, Australoids, and *Homo erectus* outside of Africa have been excluded from the mainstream of human evolution. While these groups (considered lesser evolved or archaic forms) were living

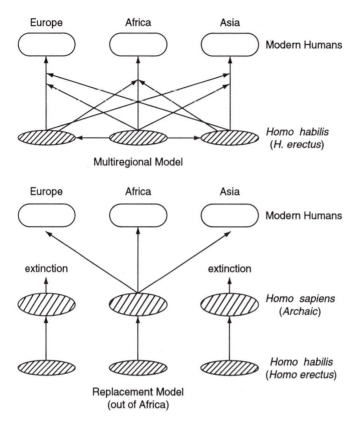

FIGURE 1-4   Models of Human Origins. The "out of Africa" replacement model describes an origin of the earliest representatives of genus *Homo* in Africa evolving from ancestral stock of Australopithecines to more advanced hominid forms. These forms gave rise to *Homo habilis* (*Homo erectus*), who populated broad regions of the old world from about two million years ago. The replacement model postulates that evolutionary advancement to archaic *Homo sapiens* continuing to anatomically modern humans occurred only in Africa about 200,000 B.P. Asian and European archaic sapiens did not advance further, became extinct, and were replaced by modern *Homo sapiens* moving out of Africa. The "multiregional model" explains the fossil record as part of a continuum of evolution, all lineages leading to modern *Homo sapiens*, sharing a common gene pool through a continuous exchange of genes.

in a broad range of environments from subarctic in Eurasia to tropical grasslands of Southeast Asia 50,000 to 200,000 years ago, anatomically modern *Homo sapiens* is said to have evolved in Africa. These humans then migrated out of Africa throughout Eurasia, replacing, or as one theory describes, interbreeding with the less evolved forms to produce the founders of modern populations.

For example, the modern sapiens populations, arriving in western Europe, encountered the Neandertals who could not compete wih this superior species (commonly called Cro Magnon) and thus became extinct. Such an evolutionary model discounts the possibility of any genetic contribution by the Neandertals. A modified concept of European origins considers that the invading Cro Magnon peoples could have interbred with the aboriginal Europeans (Neandertals). This is an oversimplified summary, of course, and the time estimates of migrations out of Africa have varied (from 180,000 to 250,000 years ago or even earlier). The major point is not that reconstructions of human racial origins have shifted geographic locations, but that such reconstructions are still attempted after all the years of genetic research and all the criticisms of the basis for racial taxonomy. This view of superior versus inferior peoples with survival of one and extinction of the other borrows from the typological concepts of an earlier era described previously. A certain skull form and size, for example, is claimed to define modern sapiens in contrast to archaic or earlier ancestral forms. This exclusion of some fossils as human ancestors because of certain skeletal features is puzzling given the variability of many of these same traits found among humans living today. It is also a mystery that the issue of population extinction by a "superior group," in this case African instead of Middle Eastern, should be raised anew.

The twists and turns of the various interpretations of hominid fossil remains have a long history of controversy too intricate and detailed to enter into here. The reader should consult some of the major review articles or recent books for a full and balanced coverage (see Brace, 2000; Stringer and McKie, 1996; Wolpoff, 2000, 1999). It should be noted that the revival of the extinction or "hominid catastrophy" theory coincided with the introduction of a technique to analyze extranuclear DNA of the mitochondria, which is explained in the next chapter. The temptation to apply a new and sophisticated laboratory method to an old question of human origins has proved too much for some writers. They have rushed to criticize interpretations of the fossil evidence for human evolution while at the same time relying on these very fossils for the data necessary to calibrate rates of genetic change.

Counter to what could be called a migration–extinction model or an "Out of Africa" theory of *Homo sapiens* evolution, a multiregional hypothesis offers an alternative explanation that includes all of the fossils of genus *Homo* from the several regions of the inhabited world. It argues that geographical varieties have existed since about 1,000,000 years ago, at least. Basically, the multiregional hypothesis posits that hominids left Africa during the middle Pleistocene and small colonies of these hunters occupied broad regions of the Old World. In Asia, the Middle East, and Europe, they became the founders of lineages that evolved, each contributing to modern *Homo sapiens* descendants (Wolpoff, 2000). Rather than a parallel evolution of these geographically separated lineages, migrations and intermingling of populations were most probable. Similarities, that is, common traits, were maintained by gene flow between groups and all retained the same species identity. Because of the multiple causes discussed in Chapter 2, smaller more isolated populations would have developed some collection of unique traits as in the examples we see in living people today. Population groups would expand or contract over time because of the harshness of the environment, their small population sizes, and the degree of gene flow among them.

Similar rates of evolution appear to have been maintained across these regional population groups and none more or less advanced than others. This multiregional theory is not too different from Carleton Coon's reconstruction, but without the implied racial inequality, of course. Both the multiregional theorists and Carlton Coon have acknowledged Franz Weidenreich as the originator of the concept; the hominid fossil record, at any one time, showed no distinctions above the subspecies (race) level. However, the fossil record has often been used too selectively to bolster one's own hypothesis and human paleontologists frequently ignore Franz Weidenreich's warning, "Any theory of origin of *Homo sapiens* has to be based on paleontological facts and only on them. It is a contradiction to logic and scientific reasoning to eliminate first all recovered fossil hominids from the line of man's ancestry and then give play to one's fantasy to build this line again by free invention of new forms" (Weidenreich, 1947:148). This caution applies especially to those who use limited genetic samples of the living or fossil remains and then examine evidence of hominid evolution in light of this genetically derived reconstruction.

Given the wide dispersal throughout many diverse environments since the time of early *Homo erectus*, from Africa to Asia and to Europe, it is not surprising to find diverse morphological traits in these and more recent fossils of ancestral *Homo sapiens*, just as there are many differences seen today. If morphological characteristics of living humans were to be examined as they are in human fossils, we would then find not four or five geographic lineages, but many, and even these would change over the generations for the several reasons described in the balance of the book. The overinterpretation of these data, that is, the reading of too much into morphological differences found in fossil ancestors or in ourselves, leads to major errors.

CONFUSIONS AND CONTRADICTIONS OF HUMAN CLASSIFICATION

> No argument has ever been advanced by any reasonable man against the fact of differences among men. The whole argument is about what differences exist and how they are to be gauged. (Jacques Barzun, 1965:201)

Confusion of biological and cultural traits has often misled us as we seek to understand human diversity. In the eighteenth and nineteenth centuries, physical traits were often confused with cultural habits of dress or language, or technological adaptations such as hunting, farming, or pastoralism. A classic example is the term "Aryan," which originally identified a group of languages (Indo-European) related to Sanskrit, the language of ancient populations of northern India. Many writers have persisted in using this linguistic classification as if it were a biological unit, even though Aryan included groups as diverse as Iranians, Europeans, and the Singhalese of Ceylon (Sri Lanka). Labels like Celtic, Teutonic, or Slavic are used also to describe a biological unit, though these terms more accurately distinguish between language groupings that include a large number of populations occupying broad geographic ranges. Another example of the misapplication of a cultural attribute is the classification that early European colonists used to distinguish between southern African Khoisans. Those people observed herding cattle were labeled "Hottentot" and the hunting nomads were called "Bushmen" without regard to the fact that the two groups were closely related and would, and often did, shift from one economy to another as environmental resources changed.

Similar distinctions were also made between eastern African groups, and, in fact, are still being applied. Witness the continuing confusion over populations of Tutsi and Hutu in Ruanda and Burundi, East Africa. The Hutus have been described as descendents of the indigenous agriculturists of the area, the Tutsi as a pastoral people descended from nomads who moved southward from Ethiopia between four and five hundred years ago. These distinctions between the two groups are not as clearly defined as the names imply and have remained confused ever since the German and Belgium colonists imposed an arbitrary division between the people.

Even though these groupings may be just as real to the observer as any based on genetic traits, explanations of biological variability should not and cannot be offered on the basis of these classifications. Nevertheless, racial divisions are often described by such popularized terms as White, nonwhite, Asian, Indian, Hispanic, or Jewish; each includes many populations of numerous diverse characteristics. This mixing of units—the confusion between biological, linguistic, and social traits—posed a major problem for anthropologists and still adds confusion today. In large, this is because race studies have been founded on the assumption that there are basic units of humanity of great antiquity. That is, our folklore leads us to the belief that "pure races" existed in earlier times.

Cultural differences are still confused with biological diversity in group labeling. Social behavior and linguistic ability are used to identify groups, as in the example of Mexico. In most of Latin America, differences between "Indio" (a person of Indian ancestry) and "Mestizo"(a person of mixed European–Indian ancestry) are a simple matter of language and clothing. A person may be identified as Mestizo in Mexico if he or she speaks Spanish and wears shoes, ignoring the degree of Indian or European ancestry. In the United States, recent Latin American immigrants as well as U.S. citizens who are descendants of Spanish colonists in the Southwest and California are lumped into the Hispanic category. This is without regard to their complex genetic heritage. Likewise, persons from several of the other Latin American countries are merged into the Hispanic category over the objection of Brazilians. The term Hispanic is derived from a sharing of the Spanish language but should not include Brazilians, who speak Portuguese. Such casual uses of classification obscures the biological diversity while not revealing much about population ancestry.

We use such labels so commonly and carelessly in our daily lives that we have come to assume that they are meaningful. To some degree classifications can have a biological component: Many Jamaicans are dark skinned, unless, of course, their ancestry is more European than African. Likewise, a majority of migrants from Mexico are expected to have certain facial features and relatively small body size, unless they are descendants from several Spanish ancestors. These illustrations could be extended to include contrasts among Europeans as well—the distinctions between northern and southern Europeans, or eastern and western Europeans, for example.

Classification in the United States Census

For social or political purposes, race or ethnic identification may serve a purpose, but these identities change over time and can often confuse more than they enlighten about the composition of the national population. The difficulty encountered by the U.S. government in collecting vital statistics, especially data on disease incidence, illustrates this confusion. To record race or ethnic group for the purpose of collecting infant mortality statistics, infants of "mixed" parents are classified by these rules: "(1) If one parent is white, the fetus or infant is assigned to the other parent's race; (2) when neither parent is white, the fetus or infant is assigned to the father's race." The exception is that if the mother is Hawaiian, the infant is classified Hawaiian (see U.S. Department of Health and Human Services, 1989). This follows a long tradition that has treated children of ethnically mixed marriages as if they possess traits, especially behavioral traits, of the parent who is from a socially disadvantaged ethnic group.

Assignment of a child's race can be even more confusing under changing sociopolitical conditions as illustrated by the experiences of three brothers in DuLac, Louisiana, once an isolated county near New Orleans. All three were descendents of Houma Indians, Native Americans of the Gulf coastal area who had been intermarrying with escaped slaves and with Cajuns (Arcadians, eighteenth-century French refugees from Canada) since the late eighteenth century. The result was a mixed community whose members were classified as "Negro" until 1950. The brothers shared the same parents and had a French surname. Since the state did not recognize the Houma as a tribe, the brother born before 1950 was designated as "Negro" on his birth certificate. The brother born after the Houma were registered as a tribe in 1950, was listed as "Indian." The third, and youngest brother was born in a New Orleans hospital and the nurse, noting the family's French surname, listed him as "White" (Spickard, 1992). So much for the accuracy of official records. A bit of history and social change may have important effects on one's identity.

Racial classification encounters even more problems when census data are collected. The term race has been so misunderstood, and its applications so broad and general, that it is often replaced by the term "ethnic group." Classifications still appear, but it is recognized more frequently that race or ethnic group is defined by society and not by science (Pollard and O'Hare, 1999). Race, historically, has biological roots as described earlier, but ethnic group is a much more difficult to deal with. Language, religion, customs, and national origin provide the basis for defining ethnicity. Categories are broad and change over time as in the case of the Houma brothers. All of these variables cause special problems whenever a government agency seeks to classify the diversity within a national or regional population.

The 1990 census tried to cope by broadening its list of choices by asking each respondent to choose not only a category from among the traditional race types, but also from several new categories of national or ethnic groups (Native Americans, Hispanics, Pacific Islanders, Asians, Chinese, Koreans et al.). The 2000 census was even broader. The old black, white, and Indian categories were retained but a multitude of choices were added; now the respondent was asked to select from a wide range of categories as listed in Figure 1-5.

The number of choices had increased and a separate question asked whether a person was Hispanic or not. A person could also select more then one choice of race—a concession to the objections from people who claimed they could not identify their heritage by a single category type. People of a mixed heritage—Native American, African, and European, for example—could identify their pedigree on the year 2000 census form

→ **NOTE: Please answer BOTH Questions 7 and 8.**

7. **Is Person 1 Spanish/Hispanic/Latino?** *Mark* ⊠ *the "No" box if* ***not*** *Spanish/Hispanic/Latino.*

☐ **No,** not Spanish/Hispanic/Latino   ☐ Yes, Puerto Rican
☐ Yes, Mexican, Mexican Am., Chicano   ☐ Yes, Cuban
☐ Yes, other Spanish/Hispanic/Latino — *Print group.* ↗

8. **What is Person 1's race?** *Mark* ⊠ ***one or more races*** *to indicate what this person considers himself/herself to be.*

☐ White
☐ Black, African Am., or Negro
☐ American Indian or Alaska Native — *Print name of enrolled or principal tribe.* ↗

☐ Asian Indian   ☐ Japanese   ☐ Native Hawaiian
☐ Chinese   ☐ Korean   ☐ Guamanian or Chamorro
☐ Filipino   ☐ Vietnamese   ☐ Samoan
☐ Other Asian — *Print race.* ↗   ☐ Other Pacific Islander — *Print race.* ↗

☐ Some other race — *Print race.* ↗

FIGURE 1-5 Racial Classifications according to U.S. Census of 2000. Questions seven and eight of the census form requests a self-identification of each person in a household. The form attempts to be broad enough to allow for any race, ethnic group, tribe or for various combinations; a respondent may use other labels as indicated by the blank boxes. This census questions whether or not a respondent is Hispanic (question seven) and allows for an indication of more than one race (question eight).
(Source: Extracted from Census Bureau form, 2000; U.S. Department of Commerce.)

more easily than in 1990. Still the golfer Tiger Woods, because of his Asian mother and African American father, would have a difficult time indicating his mixed heritage—1/4 Thai, 1/4 Chinese, 1/8 Native American, 1/8 African, and 1/4 European.

The results of this self-classification may be useful for political or economic purposes (note the inclusion of the Hispanic question), but this classification by itself reveals little about biological diversity, only minority composition of the national population. Racial classification is more poetry than science, more politics than genes, as one writer put it. The diversity of choices certainly suggests the poetry, and the addition of social groups with growing influence acknowledges the politics.

In sum, these examples and contrasts between group labels show that we should not take for granted that the categories into which we put people say much about origins or genetic composition. The expansion of the number of options for self-identification in the last census are no more revealing of America's genetic diversity than the previous one. We cannot consider the old or newer categories as a reality of nature but should recognize them for what they are: a construct, a means of grouping data describing a portion of our species. I shall remind the reader of these problems throughout the book.

HUMAN BIOLOGICAL VARIABILITY: A PERSPECTIVE

We all know what "race" means when used in our daily lives; in the news and in our conversations the labels have meanings. This is largely because of our perception of the obvious physical differences between peoples of different geographic origins, so we can convey meaningful images by labels like Asian, African, or European. But this does not make the division of humans into a few races a useful tool to study our species origins and adaptations. Nor does it enlighten us on the degrees of genetic variability within or between groups. There is no evidence of the existence of pure races now or in the past. The boundaries between the geographic population groups are not absolute nor are they fixed, but the concept of race is fixed in our society, our culture and, our minds so we must deal with it.

What, then, is the reality of human diversity and what are its origins? If race or subspecies is an artificial construct—a device of convenience to enable the human mind to organize information from the natural world—then origins cease to be an important consideration. Rather our concern should be with (1) the possible biological responses to the environment—adaptation, (2) our behavior directing gene flow between generations, and (3) population size or isolation as factors influencing variation between generations and among populations. With these factors in mind, I shall attempt to sort out the various influences on *Homo sapiens*. The term population will be used carefully to refer to that geographically and culturally determined collection of individuals who share a common gene pool. Often ethnicity will define a breeding population since the sharing of a common language, religion, and culture directs gene exchange more within a group than with outsiders. However, "ethnic group" has some special meanings due to its various political and social applications and may or may not affect genetic variability. A label of ethnic group should not be used interchangeably with race since reference to a breeding population is not the same as reference to the inhabitants of a continent, as we shall discover in the following chapters.

The term race will be used sparingly and only within a scientific context to mean a group or complex of breeding populations sharing a number of traits, recognizing that there are no "ideal types." When it is necessary to refer to a broader range of peoples, such as inhabitants of continents, then race will be used in a geographical sense, that is, the "African" or "European" with an acknowledgement that each includes many breeding populations of wide-ranging diversity. But, whatever the application, the intent will be clear—to identify a segment of *Homo sapiens* that differs in some degree from other groups. Each of these labels can be useful in identifying a particular group for the study of genetics or anthropometric traits, with the caution that this is only a first step.

chapter
2

The Biological Basis for Human Variation

The journey from the discovery of particulate inheritance to the definition of gene structure has been a long one, occupying most of the last century. From simple observations of inheritance between generations of easily perceived traits to descriptions of the chemical nature of the gene (DNA), we have witnessed an explosion of biochemical data on cell function and control of metabolic processes. Over this time period, assisted by evermore sophisticated techniques, we are able to view inheritance at several levels: trait transmission between generations, gene and gene combinations, and the molecular or biochemical structure.

With our new-found knowledge it is all too easy to forget or even to ignore some of the key landmarks along the road leading to an understanding of the biological basis for human variation. Many of these landmarks are fundamental for comparisons of population diversity, and it is best to refresh our memory from time to time if we are to appreciate the new molecular genetic discoveries and their meanings for human adaptations to our changing environments.

First, recall that humans share similar modes of reproduction with most other mammals, and inheritance mechanisms are the same—the combination of certain materials from the germ cells of male and female parents to produce a fertilized egg. These mechanisms of inheritance are the source of much of the vast diversity seen in the biological world. For many centuries, natural scientists had sought to comprehend and explain this diversity in the transmission of traits between generations. Explanations varied from a description of a "blending" of parental bloodlines, favored by animal husbandry, to a theory of "preformism," the idea that the individual, in miniature form, existed in either the ovum or sperm awaiting stimulation by fertilization to begin its development. None of these explanations could account for the ranges of individual similarities or differences among offspring and their parents.

Second, keen observers of individuals and their relatives noted that certain traits tended to run in families, that is, the frequency of appearance was greater in some pedigrees than in others. The presence of an unusual form of lower jaw, white forelock of hair, extra fingers or toes, color vision problems, bleeder disease in males, and albinism are some of those traits described hundreds of years ago. A great deal was learned about inheritance by the description of the occurrence of these traits in some family lineages long before modern genetic science.

Third, a comprehension of intergenerational transfer of traits required a thorough understanding of the mechanisms of inheritance. This knowledge has been gained slowly through the accumulated work of many investigators. A significant—and perhaps the initial—advance was made in the middle of the nineteenth century by a botanist experimenting with plant hybridization. The discovery of the laws of biological inheritance by Mendel eventually led to the understanding of these mechanisms and provided a partial answer to the crucial question—the source of individual variation within a population.

PRINCIPLES OF INHERITANCE

Johann Gregor Mendel (1822–1884), often described as the founder of the science of genetics, spent most of his life as a member of the Augustinian order in a monastery in Brunn, Czechoslovakia. He had been an excellent student but had been forced to discontinue his studies because of ill health and poverty. On entering the priesthood he was able to continue his education, in part as preparation for teaching in the local secondary schools. Mendel studied in Vienna under leading natural scientists of the period, and far from being an isolated, obscure, ill-trained monk as has been described, he was well educated for the period. Most important for the future of genetics, Mendel came under the influence of Franz Unger, a botanist whose theory on the importance of varieties in natural populations was probably the stimulus that caused Mendel to begin work on the problem of inheritance (see Mayr 1982).

Whatever the influence, Mendel spent years studying plant hybridization, and he is best known for his extensive experiments on cross-pollination of common varieties of garden pea, *Lathyrus*. Mendel was fortunate in his choice of characteristics because they happened to be traits of simple inheritance: The plants bred true without intermediate traits—that is, each succeeding generation possessed traits like the parental generation. He cross-pollinated these plants for color, shape, size, and form of seed pod. Analysis of these multiple crosses led Mendel to derive the hypothesis that an organism's characteristics were inherited as discrete units or elements and not through a blending of parental traits, as was assumed in Mendel's day.

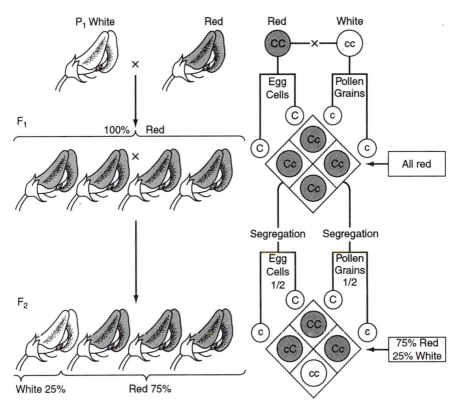

FIGURE 2-1   Independent Segregation: Mendel's First Law.

In some of his earliest experiments Mendel crossed plants that had violet-red blossoms with plants that had white (colorless) blossoms and produced hybrids that all had violet-red blossoms. But when these hybrids were crossed they produced a mix of white and violet-red plants (Figure 2-1). Plants of different stem length were also crossed (tall with dwarf), and the F_1 (first filial) generation were all of the tall variety. Cross-breeding of plants of this hybrid generation (the F_2) produced a mixture of tall and short plants. Mendel sought to explain these results by hypothesizing that these traits were determined by a pair of elements. One of the elements, or heredity particles, was dominant over the other, and they segregated independently in each generation—the *Law of Independent Segregation*. Mendel continued these kinds of experiments many times, and his results were close to a certain ratio of traits in the F_2 generation as diagrammed in Figure 2-1. The relative frequency of these traits is known as the *Mendelian ratio*.

Experiments crossing plants selected for a difference of two traits produced dihybrids with a certain ratio of these traits among the F_2 generation, as was the case with crosses of single traits. These results demonstrated that traits such as seed shape and color were determined by paired elements that independently assorted in ovule and

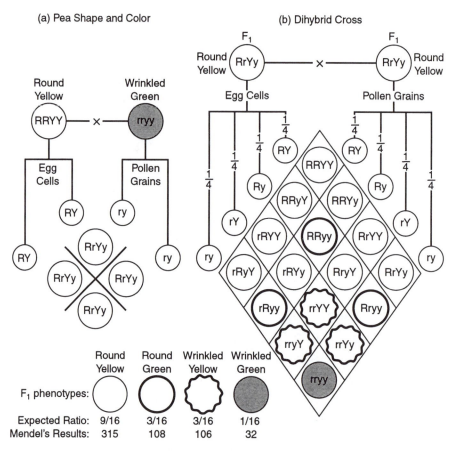

FIGURE 2-2 Independent Assortment: Mendel's Second Law. When Mendel crossed plants, selecting for two characteristics at a time, he found that the paired factors for each character assorted independently. Diagram (a) shows the cross of plants to produce a "dihybrid" generation that, when crossed, produces four different characteristics, shown in diagram (b).

pollen (diagram in Figure 2-2). The repetition of such experiments produced results that could be predicted because they always fell within close range of the expected, establishing the *Law of Independent Assortment*. Thousands of experimental crosses of plants, selecting for single or paired traits, proved the correctness of Mendel's hypothesis and helped demonstrate the mechanisms of inheritance.

Mendel described these results in a paper delivered in 1865 before a local scientific society where it was received with great interest. Though the paper was widely distributed in both Europe and North America, its significance for the understanding of inheritance went unrecognized during Mendel's lifetime. This was probably due, in part, because of his fortuitous choice of true breeding plants; his results were just too good and contrary to results of other plant hybridization studies that did not show such a simple pattern. Also, cellular structures and functions were just being discovered. It was not until 1900 that *particulate inheritance* was recognized as the mode of transmission of characteristics between generations. Three botanical researchers (de Vries, Correns, and Tschermak), working independently on plant hybridization, provided experimental support (Orel, 1984). Within less than a decade other scientists showed that inheritance of traits in animals also followed Mendel's laws. These studies and the thousands of experiments that followed during the early decades of the twentieth century laid the foundation of modern genetics.

The Gene

In 1909, the element described by Mendel became known as the gene, a unit of inheritance—a term derived from the Greek root *gen* ("to become" or "to grow out of"). A most important development in inheritance studies was the recognition that genes segregated just as did chromosomes, the darkly staining, threadlike bodies in a cell's nucleus. This relationship between the theorized unit of inheritance and the nuclear structures also proposed that the units (genes) were arranged along the chromosome body. The locus, or position, of each gene in this linear sequence had a special significance for determination of a trait. For example, the reproduction of dihybrids for color and seed shape, as in Mendel's experiments, suggested that the locus for seed color is on a different chromosome than the locus that carries the gene for seed shape. In addition, there may be more than one form of gene for each locus—for example, one that determines that the seed is green or one that determines that the seed is yellow. These alternate forms of the gene for a particular characteristic were called *allelomorphs*, from which the term *allele* is derived as used today to describe the variety of gene forms of a trait. Again, in reference to Mendel's study, we see that some alleles are dominant to others, as was the case with plant color shown in Figure 2-1. The paired combination of alleles, one carried at a locus on each of the chromosomes of the pair, is called the *genotype*. Hence, the genotype, or heredity type, for color may be CC, Cc, or cc. The trait that is the result of the genotype combination is the *phenotype* (the visible type or trait).

Chromosomes and Cell Division

Each cell of an organism contains several pairs of chromosomes within its nucleus. When the cell grows and eventually divides, as in cell reproduction, these chromosomes undergo several changes that alter their shapes before division. They reorganize from the irregular threadlike bodies of darkly staining material to form shorter, thicker structures. The chromosomes are recognized as independent bodies at this stage and each appears as two joined strands. These strands are called *chromatids* and are held together at a point along their length called the *centromere*. During cell division, or *mitosis*, the chromatids of each chromosome are pulled apart and each is attracted to opposite poles of the cell, which become the center for the formation of the daughter cells (see Figure 2-3). The end result of mitosis is to double the number of cells with an even distribution of chromosome materials between the daughter cells. During the

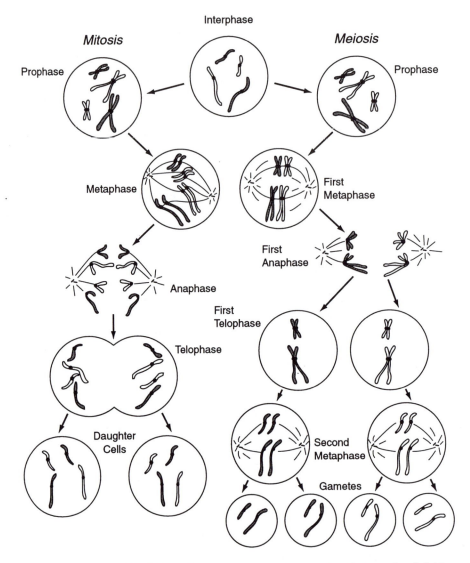

FIGURE 2-3 Stages of Cell Division. These diagrams show the major steps that occur in cell division. A comparison between *mitosis* and *meiosis* illustrates the organization of the chromosomes at each stage.

Mitosis: This simple cell division starts with chromosomes as pairs of chromatids joined at some point along their length by a centromere. Through metaphase and anaphase stages the chromosomes are arranged in the equatorial plane of the dividing cell and, finally, the chromatids are pulled apart by the end of the anaphase. Telophase is the stage during which the cell membrane grows and eventually separates into two daughter cells.

   Meiosis: The major distinction of meiosis is that through a process of reduction and division, daughter cells are produced that have one-half of the chromosomes of the parent cell. The chromosomes are aligned side by side along the equatorial plane in the first metaphase rather than end to end as in mitosis. By the end of the first anaphase the pairs have been separated into cells at a telophase stage, but these cells continue to divide. The second metaphase separates the chromatids into the germ cells called *gametes*.

interphase, or resting stage, the missing halves of chromosomes (the chromatids) are replicated from materials in the cells' cytoplasm, and the chromosomes are then completed and will be ready for the next cell division. The splitting of each chromosome in half and the movement of the chromatids into the daughter cell ensures that each cell has a full and identical complement of genes. Such a process enables tissue growth or replacement while maintaining cell identity and function.

The number and sizes of chromosomes of the body's cells, or diploid number, is fixed for each species. For example, this distinctive array, or *karyotype*, in *Homo sapiens* has forty-six, whereas the chimp and gorilla have forty-eight and the gibbon forty-four. The forty-six chromosomes in our species are arranged as twenty-three pairs, of which twenty-two are known as *autosomes* and one pair, the *sex chromosomes*, are responsible for initiating sex determination. Since the number of chromosomes is critical for normal growth and development and must remain constant from one generation to the next, a basic problem of sexual reproduction is how to ensure that an equal number of chromosomes are passed on to the next generation. Because sexual reproduction involves a combination of materials from two individuals in order to produce the offspring, this problem of the maintenance of a species' chromosome number is solved by a process of cellular reduction and division known as *meiosis*. Meiosis is, to a certain extent, comparable to mitosis of somatic cell division, with several important exceptions (see Figure 2-3). A major distinction is one of chromosome number: The dividing cell during meiosis separates the homologous chromosomes shortly before division. The cells, now with only twenty-three chromosomes, or one from each pair, continue to divide and, during the second metaphase, the chromatids are pulled apart. The final stage produces cells, the gametes, with one half the number of chromosomes, the haploid number in contrast to mitosis where daughter cells maintain the diploid chromosome number.

Chromosomes of the same pair are identical in size. Though there is some similarity between certain pairs, the structural uniqueness of each pair of autosomes sets them apart and prevents the combining of chromosomes from different pairs. Mistakes in meiosis are not uncommon, however. Occasionally a fragment from one chromosome will attach to a chromosome of a different pair (nonhomologous) causing an abnormally long chromosome of one pair while another, with the missing piece, is shorter. This *translocation* frequently causes severe disruption of cellular function that almost always leads to destruction of the cell. If abnormal chromosome form or number occurs, the *zygote* (fertilized ovum) will seldom grow and divide beyond a few divisions and only rarely will it reach the embryo stage. There are, however, some examples when a person survives, as in the case of a part of the twenty-first chromosome attached to the fourteenth which results in a rare form of *Down syndrome*. The person will have a normal number of chromosomes (forty-six) but with a larger chromosome 14. The more common form of *Down syndrome* occurs when the twenty-first pair fails to separate during meiosis and an individual has forty-seven chromosomes, an extra twenty-first chromosome, or *trisomy* (three instead of the normal two). Down syndrome includes a group of abnormal physical traits in addition to a varying degree of mental retardation depending upon the environment of the individual during their childhood.[1] Several other syndromes, described below, are due to abnormal numbers of sex chromosomes or *aneuploidy*.

The *gametes* (eggs in the case of a female or sperm in the case of a male) are formed in specialized tissues found in the gonads and combine with a gamete of the opposite sex in order to form the fertilized egg or zygote. This fertilized egg pairs up chromosomes from each parent in order to duplicate the proper number of chromosomes for the species. This process of sexual reproduction is one of the most fundamental and important factors in the introduction of new varieties because it combines materials from two individuals.

During meiosis each chromosome segregates independently from all of the others. Therefore, chromosomes that were provided to an individual at conception by gametes from the male and female parents are randomly distributed when an individual's own gametes are formed, so it is highly improbable that a person's gametes will contain an even distribution of the chromosomes that were inherited from each of the parents (recall Mendel's law of independent assortment). Of the twenty-three individual chromosomes contained in a particular gamete, for example, fifteen may have been derived from those inherited from one parent and the remaining eight from the other parent. This independent assortment of chromosomes during meiosis is one kind of *recombination* that occurs during meiosis and contributes to diverse combinations of genes in each gamete. The mixing of proportions of one's maternal and paternal chromosomes during meiosis generates a variety of gametes; the total number of gamete types (combinations of paternal and maternal chromosomes) that can be produced by humans is 2^{23} or over eight million.

Another type of recombination, and one that is of primary importance in its influence on gamete diversity, is *crossover* during an early stage of meiosis. Crossover refers to an exchange of parts of nonsister chromatids of homologous chromosomes. The homologous chromosomes align in pairs, or *synapsis*. The chromatids of the pair of chromosomes are closely bound into a tetrad bundle, and when they begin to separate to opposite poles of the dividing cells, there is a swapping of parts of the nonsister chromatids, as illustrated in Figure 2-4. This breakage and rejoining after an exchange of corresponding parts is called *chiasma*, which causes a realignment of the linear arrangement of genes along each chromosome, and the frequency of this occurrence or the chance that it will happen depends on the distance between gene loci (Figure 2-4).

Neither type of recombination adds new genetic information to a population. It merely reassorts the genes so that individuals in each generation will have different gene arrangements and combinations, causing each person to be a unique creation. Because these gene arrangements or genotypes influence the development of characteristics (phenotypes), *recombination* is an important source of individual variability.

---

[1]Langdon Down, a nineteenth-century London physician, described patients with a particular type of congenital deficiency syndrome which affected their growth and development and impaired mental development. Down called this syndrome mongolism because he thought these individuals resembled the mongoloid race due to their general appearance of a broad, flattened face and epicantric eye folds.

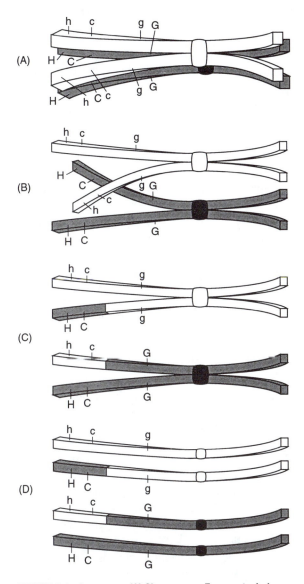

(A)

(B)

(C)

(D)

**FIGURE 2-4 Crossover of X-Chromosome Fragments during
Meiosis.** Occasionally, there is an exchange of fragments between
homologous chromosomes (members of a pair). This exchange may
take place due to breakage of chromatids during the prophase
stage (shown in Figure 2-3). The parts are then rejoined to the other
chromosome. The model of the X-chromosome illustrates the
swapping of the section with the h allele (hemophilia) and c allele
(colorblindness) with the fragment carrying H (normal allele) and C
(normal visual). This event occurs during prophase, steps A and B.
Step C shows a separation of the chromosomes—each is broken
apart into its chromatids, step D. The final result is a realignment
of genes.

The Sex Chromosomes and Sex Determination

Sex determination is a complicated multistep process beginning at conception with the fertilization of the egg by the sperm. If an X-chromosome is provided by the sperm, then the zygote will have an XX pair and will usually possess the genetic equipment to develop into a female. In the early weeks after conception, the embryo tissues begin to differentiate, and the region that will become the urinary tract and reproductive organs reaches a level of development with sex undifferentiated. There is a potential for becoming female should certain conditions continue to prevail—that is, the embryo is a presumptive female. The ducts (Müllerian) that give rise to the ovaries and reproductive organs of the female will develop, while those ducts (Wolfian) that are precursors of male reproductive organs will regress. By the twelfth week the female sex will be established as the embryo enters the fetal stage of development.

If, however, the sperm carried a Y-chromosome the zygote will be XY. A complicated process of differentiation begins, initiating a series of steps leading to maleness of the embryo and hence of the fetus. The short region of the Y-chromosome carries a gene essential for maleness—the *testes determination factor* (TDF) in the sex determining region (SRY). The products of this gene will stimulate the development of testes from the gonadal ridge by the sixth embryonic week. As this development proceeds, a potent form of testosterone is secreted that initiates a series of steps that leads to sex identification. One of the major changes initiated is the alteration of the neural pathways within the hypothalamus of the brain, the controlling center for endocrine function. This pathway regulates ovarian activity and controls menstrual cycling in the postpubertal female. However, the testosterone secretion of the male embryo changes this pathway in the male direction. The testosterone secretions also stimulate differentiation of the Wolfian ducts and formation of the male reproductive system consisting of the prostate gland, seminal vesicles, and vas deferens of the testis; they also organize the shaping and growth of the external genitalia. Another gene (the H-Y), carried on the long region of the Y, has been described as a possible controlling factor in sperm production. In addition, there are controls for cellular receptors of the male hormone, or for maintenance of androgen–estrogen ratios. Other hormones, under the control of genes carried on the Y chromosome, are being discovered even at this writing, and these add to the complexity of biochemical and physical sex identity. In summary, the early embryo stage follows a basic development plan that is female unless altered by the action of the products of certain *Y-linked genes*.

Chromosome determination of sex usually proceeds as expected and sex identity is established, but on rare occasions the opposite turns out to be the case. About once in 20,000 male births, a male is born with a pair of XX chromosomes. What has occurred is that during meiosis in the male parent a fragment of the Y carrying the gene for testes development (the SRY region) breaks and attaches itself to an X, which then is passed on in the sperm that fertilizes the ovum. This means that even though the male offspring has the XX pair, he still possesses the TDF critical for stimulating the products that cause the development of a male embryo. These rare individuals are, however, sterile since they lack the region of the Y-chromosome necessary for sperm production.

By contrast, XY females have occasionally been born, and here the explanation is similar in that the TDF was also involved, but the effect was opposite since it involved the lack of the *TDF gene*. During meiosis in the male parent, the TDF-bearing fragment of the Y was lost and a sperm was produced with this deficiency. Hence, an embryo bearing the X-plus the defective Y-chromosome would develop, following the basic female body plan because it lacked the hormonal stimulation to determine the male sex.

There are numerous other variations in sex determination errors recorded, but these mostly involve differences in the number of the sex chromosomes. Such deviation from the sex chromosome pair usually yields an individual with abnormal developmental characteristics. Occasionally (about once in every 400 male births) an extra X-chromosome is combined with the XY pair. The individual has a diploid number of 47 and is an XXY male with poorly developed sexual characteristics together with some female ones as well (*Klinefelter syndrome*). Males with an extra Y-chromosome (*47, XYY*) have also been recorded. These are normal males, with the exception of their greater-than-average height. Early studies of this condition described a possible association with certain behavioral pathologies and pointed to a supposed high frequency of the XYY condition among mental patients and prison inmates. Subsequent studies, however, found that only a small number of individuals with this syndrome were institutionalized (about 4 percent), whereas the remaining 96 percent of XYY males had normal behavior patterns indistinguishable from those of the rest of the male population. The presence of an extra Y-chromosome does not predispose a male to social pathology, but it has remained a karyotypic curiosity much misunderstood for a long time (Witkin et al., 1976). Another example is the birth of a female with only a single X-chromosome (once in every 3,500 female births). She will have a series of anatomical defects known as *Turner syndrome* (45, XO) and the diploid number will be 45 instead of the normal 46. Such individuals have poorly expressed secondary sexual characteristics and tend to be shorter than normal.

The major significance of the X- and Y-chromosomes, in addition to sex determination, is the influence that the genes that are carried on these chromosomes have on the development of secondary sexual characteristics of form, growth rate, and pattern during adolescence and final adult size. Similar to the distinguishing influences seen during embryonic development, the sex chromosome differences continue to influence child growth. Females reach puberty and pass through their adolescent growth spurt an average of two years earlier than males, and during this growth period they acquire the secondary sexual characteristics that so distinguish male and female. Bodily proportions depart from the childhood form as the pelvic girdle grows more rapidly than the pectoral region (across the shoulders). But linear growth ceases sooner than in the male, resulting in a lower average height. Head and face growth also proceed more slowly, and females retain more of a childlike shape in these two regions. Males in most populations are significantly larger in body size and differ in bodily proportions. They differ also in body hair distribution and density from females, especially in facial hair. These differences, and more (detailed later in Chapter 5), are the result of certain genetic differences in the sex chromosomes, especially the *Y-linked genes*. Many male–female differences are also the result of X and Y size contrasts.

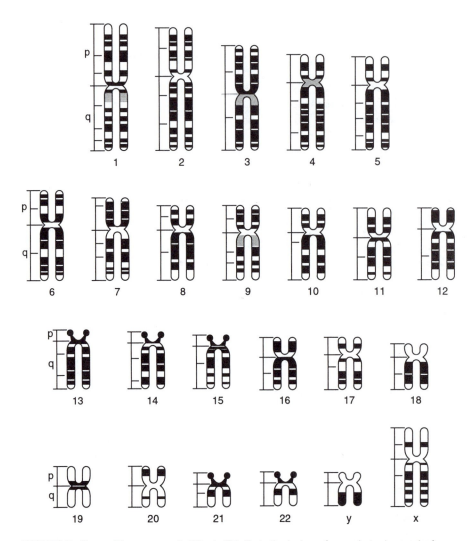

FIGURE 2-5   Human Chromosomes in Mitosis. This illustration is drawn from a photomicrograph of human chromosomes in mitosis. The twenty-two autosome pairs are grouped according to size (karyotype) and the sex chromosomes are placed separately after pair twenty-two. The dark bands illustrate the locations stained by specific chemicals. The short and long arms of each chromosome are designated by *p* and *q* to assist in locating particular sites.

The sizes of the twenty-two autosomes plus the sex chromosomes (the human karyotypes) are diagramed in Figure 2-5. Since the autosomes exist as pairs, each homologous chromosome being identical to its mate in size and shape, only a single member of each pair is shown—the haploid number. There is a comparable region on each member of the pair. For example, certain parts of each chromosome will take up

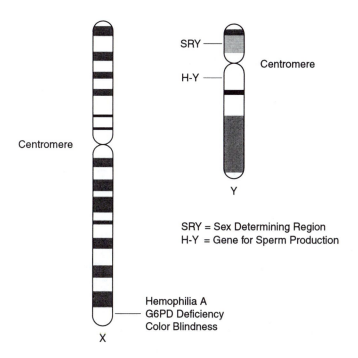

FIGURE 2-6   X- and Y-Chromosomes.

a chemical stain, and these darkly stained areas of one chromosome will have a comparable location on the other one of the homologous pair. These stained regions are grouped on each chromosome into a *p* and a *q* region, the short and long arms above and below the centromere where the chromatids are joined. The X-chromosomes also pair up in a female, and homologous regions exist. A different situation exists in the male, however. There is little homology between the X- and Y-chromosomes.

The Y differs considerably in size and structure from the X. The Y is shorter, so that except for a very small region at the tip and middle of the short arm (*p* region) there is no corresponding region on the X (see Figure 2-6). Any genes appearing on the nonhomologous region of the X-chromosome will not be paired up in male cells, since the male is hemizygous (having only a single X-chromosome). Therefore, genes on the nonhomologous region of the X will express a gene product without any influence from a dominant allele of the genotype that would be present in the female. This causes X-linked, recessively determined traits to occur more frequently in males than in females. The diagrams in Figure 2-6 list some examples. *Hemophilia A* is a rare condition of impaired ability of the blood to clot that has been reported almost exclusively in males; *hemophilia B* is an even rarer form of this defect and still confined to males. The three genes for production of color sensitive pigments of the eye's retinal cones are closely linked, and mutant forms of the red and the green occur in both male and female, but more frequently males. Another X-linked condition is a deficiency of an enzyme of carbohydrate metabolism, *G6PD* (described in Chapter 4).

The ability to perceive the range of colors in our environment is determined by three protein pigments, red, green, and blue. The production of each is determined by genes at separate loci. Certain recessive alleles at one or the other of these closely linked loci will cause defective color vision, mostly in the red-green range. Though defective vision in this range of the color spectrum is commonly called *color blindness*, it is only a partial color blindness with an inability to perceive combinations of reds and greens. A third X-linked gene determines a pigment for blue sensitivity though impairment of color vision in this range is rare. The inheritance of complete absence of retinal cone activity, causing total color blindness (*achromatopsia*) is a rare condition, but several types have been described. Some form of achromatopsia has been reported among most or all individuals in a few inbred island populations. This reflects the population's past history of small ancestral size and breeding isolation over generations as described below.

The influences of X-linkage on the relative frequencies of male and female traits may easily be illustrated by inherited defects of color vision in the red-green range. About 8 percent of males of European ancestry are color blind, that is, they have difficulty in distinguishing between various color hues while there are only one-twentieth as many females with this defect. Persons with an X-linked recessive green pigment gene produce a pigment sensitive to a longer wave length than the normal. This green shift (*deutran*) impairs an individual's ability to distinguish between red and green colors; reds are seen as reddish browns and greens appear as tans. While a red shift in pigment sensitivity (*protan*) is in the direction of shorter light wave lengths, a person is confused by browns and olive greens; they can also perceive fewer colors. The deutran condition is more common (75 percent of the color blind males, for example) while protan individuals account for the rest. Neither can distinguish red and green.

Although major advances have been made in mapping the Y-chromosome DNA and seventy-eight genes have now been mapped, comparatively little is known about specific Y-linked phenotypes. The *p* region carries genetic loci for maleness, as described above, but few other traits have been traced to genetic loci on this short arm of the chromosome. On the long arm (*q* region), there are, as yet, a few ill-defined characteristics that appear to be limited to males. A gene for male pattern baldness is one possibility, and a peculiar hairy growth over the outer edges of the ears, hairy pinna, are two traits that have frequently been mentioned. More recently, studies of nucleotide sequences in several regions, with the aid of restriction enzymes (DNA probes—see below), reported that certain haplotypes are found in males with lowered spermatogenesis (Kuroki et al., 1999). In addition, other Y-chromosome regions (the H-Y included) carry genes that have particular influences on skeletal and dental growth, testes development, and spermatogenesis (see Vogel and Motulsky, 1986; McKusick, 1994, Skaletsky et al., 2003). These and other studies are beginning to define the role of the Y-linked genetic loci in the development of male secondary sexual characteristics.

FORMAL HUMAN GENETICS

Even before Mendel's studies of plant hybridization, astute observations of the transmission of human traits between generations offered an early insight into inheritance.

Studies of human pedigrees and the identification of easily perceived phenotypes, even centuries ago, have added to our understanding of *dominant* and *recessive* characteristics. For example, Maupertius, a French astronomer and philosopher of the eighteenth century, began to satisfy a growing interest in biology by the study of a rare human condition called *polydactyly*, extra fingers and/or toes. He learned of a Berlin family, several of whose members had such a condition. The father of the family had six fingers and toes like one of his parents; the other parent had the normal number. Aided by the father's interest and cooperation, Maupertius traced polydactyly through four generations. Since the condition could appear in some of the children even if one of their parents were normal, he described the condition as a *dominant trait*. What was of special interest was that polydactyly could be expressed differently. One of the two sons in the fourth generation had six toes on his left foot, but the normal five on his right, while his right hand had six fingers and the left hand had only a poorly developed stump for the sixth digit. Maupertius expanded his interest in unique familial traits through study of abnormalities of skin color. Reports of the occasional appearance of nonpigmented skin in African children of dark-skinned parents and among certain Native Americans of Panama (San Blas de Cunha) attracted Maupertius's attention. This abnormal trait was also considered a hereditary condition, but somewhat different in its transmission between generations compared to polydactyly; normally pigmented parents passed on some factor to their children that blocked development of skin color (Glass, 1955). This factor, in light of Mendel's work, could be understood as a *recessive*.

Other scholars of this period and even centuries before made many similar observations on the frequency of rare characteristics occurring in some families. John Dalton (1766–1844), a natural scientist and chemist who developed the atomic theory of matter, and his brother were unable to distinguish reds and greens. This curious coincidence interested Dalton and lead him to trace this visual defect through several family lineages. He concluded that this condition, which became known as *Daltonism*, was hereditary. Later, another scientist, Galton, discussed in Chapter 1 as the founder of Eugenics, showed that Daltonism was more frequent among Quakers than the general population. Galton postulated that the Quaker prescription for black and gray clothing was related to their defective color vision (Darlington, 1969). Another trait that attracted attention down through history was the tendency for certain males to bleed profusely from even a minor skin cut. This "bleeding problem" was recognized at least 2,500 years ago in the Talmud and Bible. Circumcision was not performed on male infants if their mother had born two sons who had been "bleeders". Of particular interest was the knowledge of maternal transmission of this trait at such an early time. If three sisters bore sons who were bleeders, the sons of any other sister were not to be circumcised, but no such prohibition applied to the sons of their brothers (Rosner, 1977).

We now know this condition as hemophilia, mentioned above as a recessive trait determined by genes carried on the X-chromosome: hemophilia A (classic) and hemophilia B (Christmas disease). Males with either trait suffer from lack of coagulating factors so blood clotting is slowed significantly below the normal time. Since European royal family pedigrees have always received careful attention, a great deal is known about trait transmission through the lineages and the most famous is hemophilia among the descendents of Britain's Queen Victoria. This long-reigning monarch probably received the hemophilia gene from one of her parents and passed it on to two of her five daughters (Beatrice and Alice) and one of her five sons. This son, Leopold, lived long enough to father a son and daughter who was, inevitablely, a carrier, while the son was not. Beatrice was a carrier but had no children while her sister Alice of Hesse was the mother of nine, four sons and five daugthers. Two daughters, Irene and Alexandra carried the hemophilia trait and, with dire historical consequences, Alexandra passed it on to her son Alexis, the heir to the Russian throne. This mode of inheritance of X-linked traits is illustrated by the diagrams in Figure 2-7. Carrier mothers may pass on a defect to their sons depending on the type of X-chromosome (X^H or X^h) contained in the ovum that is fertilized. Daughters will not inherit the trait unless the father has the X-linked condition, that is, his X-chromosome carries the recessive allele.

Such keen observations of easily perceived traits distributed through family pedigrees prepared the way for the genetics studies to come. What is surprising was that it took so long (two centuries) for the potential to be fully realized. With the rediscovery of Mendel's work and the recognition of his two principles of particulate inheritance at the beginning of the twentieth century, the search was on for more evidence of human genes. Many new discoveries were made, but the rush to embrace particulate inheritance led some confusion as well. *Mendelian Inheritance* became overly simplified and because many traits, both physical and behavioral, appeared to run in the family, simple genetic explanations were offered. It was an easy step to conclude that one gene determined one trait passed from parent to offspring. The significance of environmental influences over the course of growth and development stages was too often ignored or discounted, especially for certain types of behavior and developmental variability. As we shall see, such simple conclusions of genetic determination were most often applied to behavior.

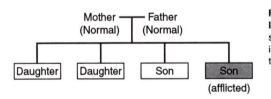

FIGURE 2-7 Example of X-Linked Inheritance. Normal parents can produce a son with an X-linked trait when the mother is a carrier of the recessive (hemophilia in this example).

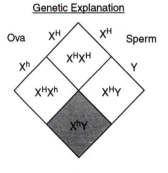

Dominant Inheritance

Mendel used the term dominant to refer to those characters that were transmitted entirely or unchanged in the hybrid (heterozygote). In other words, as we would describe it now, the attribute of character (phenotype) of the heterozygote was the same or differed little from that of the homozygote. According to McKusick (1994:xi), most dominants are incompletely dominant, however. That is, there are few loci where the dominant allele completely obscures any effect of the recessive causing the heterozygote phenotype to be indistinguishable from the homozygote. One of the few examples is *Huntington disease* where the inheritance of a rare autosomal dominant allele predestines the carrier to a severe neurological disease. Symptoms begin to appear in middle age with progressive degeneration of brain cells, causing muscle spasms and personality disorders. Until recently, the presence of this gene could not definitely be established and because of the late onset of the disease, the carrier could become a parent, possibly passing on the gene to his or her children.

A well-studied, but nonlethal, genetic defect called *Achondroplasia*, a type of human dwarfism caused by arrested growth of the long bones due to a defect in cartilage development, offers another example of a phenotype determined by a dominant allele. This dominant allele may appear in a family lineage with no previous history by a mutation (a change in gene structure). Persons who possesses the mutant allele for achondroplasia will be significantly shorter than normal because of a failure of growth of the arms and legs; the trunk is near normal size though with some spinal curvature and the head is larger. This syndrome of abnormal skeletal growth offers the advantage of ease of identification over time across generations. Likewise, the large overgrowth of the lower jaw found throughout several generations of the Hapsburgh dynasty offers geneticists the opportunity to trace patterns of inheritance. These two easily perceived dominant traits express their characteristics each generation, and a simple ratio or proportion exists as shown in Figure 2-8. If one parent has the trait, there is a 50 percent chance that each child conceived will also possess it. However, if both parents have the trait, then the probability that their children will have it increases to 75 percent.

Recessive Inheritance

Unlike simple dominant alleles, the presence of recessive alleles cannot always be detected and sometimes a recessive causes abnormal traits to appear in children of unafflicted parents, often to their dismay. Rather than blame one's bloodlines or one's grandparents, it is best to recognize that humans possess many sets of genes whose actions or potential actions are masked by the expression of the more dominant allelic form. Such genes, called *recessives*, can cause a characteristic to appear in an individual only when they combine as a pair (homozygous combination). A large number of human traits are determined in this way, from conditions of the skin to enzymes, or growth processes to blood types.

One example is a well-known condition that interrupts the synthesis of melanin pigment and causes the individual to be without color in the hair and skin; such an individual is known as an albino. This condition occurs in European populations only about

Occurrence of Abnormal Phenotypes in Parents and Children   Genetic Explanation

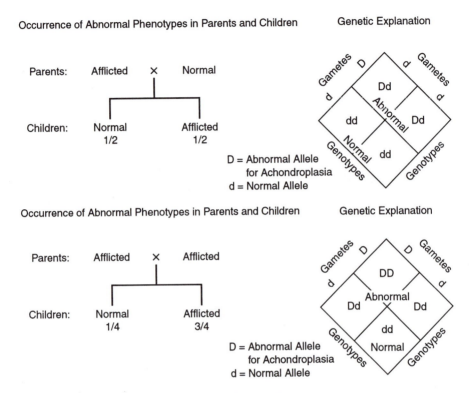

FIGURE 2-8   **Dominant Inheritance: Examples of Abnormal Traits.**

once in 20,000 births, but once in 3,000 births in several Nigerian populations and once in 200 among the Cuna Indians of Panama, mentioned earlier. In a majority of these cases the parents are normal, but each is a carrier of a recessive allele that affects the synthesis of an enzyme essential for the production of melanin; these genes may combine upon conception to produce an offspring who has the recessive pair. There are at least five other albinism types under the control of genes at other chromosome loci, but they are much rarer than this albino type I. There is even a record of two albino parents producing a normal offspring; this led to the conclusion that the parents carried albino genes at different loci (see McKusick, 1994).

Another example of recessive inheritance is provided by the ABO blood-group system. We all inherit a blood type that is of medical importance should blood transfusions be required. Accordingly, the mode of inheritance has been well established. The allele that determines type O blood is recessive to both the A and the B alleles. Hence, it often happens that parents, neither of whom is type O, have an offspring with type-O blood. There should be no immediate question of paternity. The type-O child may simply demonstrate that the parents were carrying the type-O allele, a recessive whose presence is masked by the action of either the A or the B allele (see Figure 2-9). If the genotype is AB, however, both alleles will influence the phenotype. This codominance of the A and

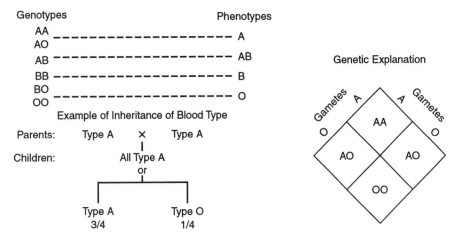

FIGURE 2-9 Inheritance of ABO Blood Types.

B will give a blood type AB, as indicated in Figure 2-9. Codominance, where both alleles contribute to the phenotype, is found to be a condition at numerous genetic loci.

The ratio of recessive trait occurrence in each generation depends on the gene combinations of the parents, of course, and is somewhat more difficult to determine than the simple dominant ratio. If neither parent has the trait, but both are carriers of the recessive gene, there is a 25 percent chance that any child they produce will have the trait. But if one parent is a carrier and the other parent has the trait, then there is a 50 percent chance that their child will have both of the recessive alleles (see Figure 2-10).

Gene Combinations and Interactions

The preceding examples shown in Figures 2-9 and 2-10 illustrate the relationship between genotype and phenotype; a certain allele or pair of alleles will determine a particular trait. Most human traits, however, are of complex inheritance, and several genes may determine the phenotype through their combined action. Such traits are called *polygenic* or *multifactorial* since the products of two or more genes at different loci interact to contribute to the development of a phenotype. Growth processes and body form are under the control of many genes exerting influences during critical stages of the life cycle, for example. The timing of the onset of puberty, development of the several organ systems, and the relative growth of the appendages are regulated by a complex of genes interacting with environments encountered during processes of growth and development (see Chapter 6).

Human skin color, another example, varies over a wide range throughout our species. The synthesis of the melanin pigments of the skin proceeds through several bio-chemical processes, each under genetic control, to produce the brown-black pigment. The hue of the skin, that is, as the color appears to the eye, covers a broad and continuous range from very dark to light and responds to the degree of exposure to the sun's

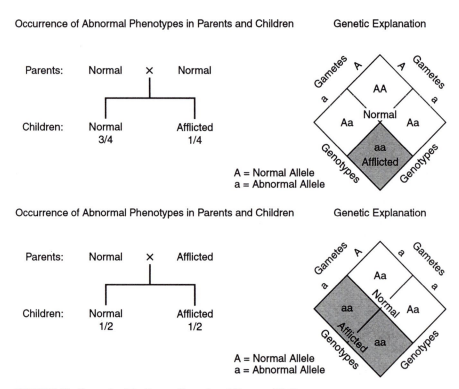

Occurrence of Abnormal Phenotypes in Parents and Children   Genetic Explanation

Parents: Normal   ×   Normal

Children: Normal   Afflicted
             3/4   1/4

A = Normal Allele
a = Abnormal Allele

Occurrence of Abnormal Phenotypes in Parents and Children   Genetic Explanation

Parents: Normal   ×   Afflicted

Children: Normal   Afflicted
             1/2   1/2

A = Normal Allele
a = Abnormal Allele

FIGURE 2-10   Recessive Inheritance: Examples of Abnormal Traits.

ultraviolet rays. Measures made of light-reflectance properties in offspring of one dark-skinned and one fair-skinned parent fall somewhere between the ranges of their parents (Figure 2-11). The degrees of reflectance match closely those predicted by a hypothesis that genes at three or four loci are responsible for the inheritance of skin color. However, the complex of gene interaction is so various that pigmentation of siblings differs and may encompass a broad range. The property of skin color is measurable as a quantitative trait, or described as a multifactorial trait because of the several gene products interacting with environmental factors.

There are numerous other human multifactorial traits that demonstrate a range of environmental and genetic influence. Several congenital diseases (present at birth) and diseases of mature adults seemingly "run" in families (there is a history of congenital disease in one spouse's pedigree). Birth defects like neural tube anomalies (e.g., spina bifida), cleft palate, club foot, and heart defects are examples. The midlife diseases such as hypertension, adult onset diabetes (type II), and coronary heart disease are other multifactorial conditions frequently studied in reference to combinations of familial and environmental influence. The blood pressure of close relatives of a hypertensive person is higher, on average, than for that age group in the general population. Likewise, the relatives of diabetics often show a lessened ability to regulate blood sugar levels and are at risk for developing the disease in later life if excess carbohydrates are consumed.

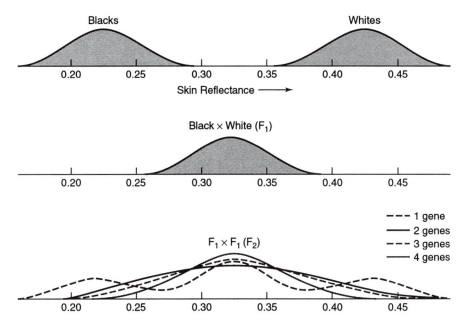

FIGURE 2-11   Skin-Color Distributions in Blacks and Whites. Skin color is measured by the skin reflectance for light of 685 mμ wave length. For the F_2 generation, distributions shown are those expected under various hypotheses about the number of genes involved. Observations on F_2 and backcrosses tend to resemble those expected if the trait is determined by three of four genes. (From Bodmer, W.F., and L.L. Cavalli-Sforza, *Genetics, Evolution, and Man.* Copyright © 1976. San Francisco: W.H. Freeman and Company.)

Furthermore, complexity of the genetic system may cause a trait to vary in frequency or in expression. There are genes that are known to influence more than one trait, and these genes are said to be *pleiotropic*. Because the primary products of gene action are *polypeptides* (chains of amino acids), they may be part of a biochemical pathway leading to the production of several other products. For example, a recessive allele that prevents the production of an enzyme needed in the metabolism of an essential amino acid, phenylalanine, can indirectly cause severe damage to the central nervous system through the accumulation of toxic levels of this amino acid. This condition, resulting from the inheritance of the pair of recessive genes controlling phenylalanine metabolism, is known as *phenylketonuria* (PKU). In addition, persons homozygous for this gene will have paler skin and a reduced thyroid activity because phenylalanine is not converted into a necessary ingredient for the synthesis of another amino acid, tyrosine. This amino acid is the precursor from which melanin, the skin pigment, is made. It is also the basic compound from which thyroxine (the active iodine compound of the thyroid gland) is formed.

Another contributor to phenotypic diversity is the fact that genes do not always cause a character to be expressed in the same way, and sometimes the phenotype does not appear at all, even though the genotype is known to be present. For example, the pedigree of a family that possessed a muscle defect of the small finger that causes the digit to be permanently bent showed a distribution of the autosomal dominant gene through four generations. One of the males in the third generation lacked this inherited defect, though he passed along the gene to both of his daughters in the fourth generation. This skipping of generations is an event that occurs when a gene is partly or *incompletely penetrant*.

In some individuals autosomal dominant traits may be more severe than in other persons. This condition, known as variable *expressivity*, is illustrated by the presence of extra fingers or toes (*polydactyly*). As discussed above, a dominant allele causes the presence of extra fingers or toes, but the trait is not always expressed in the same way. Sometimes an extra digit will appear on both hands and feet, or sometimes only one hand or foot will have an extra digit. These and other traits recorded in family pedigrees illustrate some of the variety of expressions of complex traits. To understand them and their inter-generational transmission, it is necessary to consider the organization and clustering of human populations as they influence future generations.

FACTORS OF VARIATION AND EVOLUTION

Evolution has been described as "descent with modification," a definition that refers to a gradual change of populations of organisms throughout tens of thousands of generations, changes that accumulate and lead to the formation of new species. Such a definition is applicable to studies of paleontological species in comparisons with their modern living descendants who may be diverse in form, as in the examples of the variety of primate species living today. Many of these primate species can be traced through the fossil record to a few common ancestors millions of years ago, as in the example of the ancestral lineage of our species discussed in the last chapter.

This is an abbreviated way of describing one aspect of Darwin's explanation of biological diversity. He emphasized that the world is not constant and that the diverse living forms were connected by descent to a few common ancestors by gradual changes of populations accumulating certain advantageous characteristics over time. This accumulation of favorable variations enhanced populations' survival in the face of local environmental changes. The degree of change and the ability of a population to respond were also affected by their isolation and or competition with other groups.

Since Darwin's theories, the knowledge of Mendelian inheritance, and now the clearer understanding of the nature of the gene, have contributed to a more precise understanding of evolution. Biologists and many anthropologists describe evolution as change in gene frequencies in a population from one generation to the next. This cannot be considered evolution, however, unless these changes persist. The accumulation of these changes, often under the influence of natural selection, is described as *microevolution*. There is an abundance of examples found in simpler organisms, but it is more difficult to demonstrate microevolution among living humans, as we shall describe in the following chapters. Considering the newer knowledge of genetics and the recognition of the significance of a species' environment, about fifty years ago, the concept of *evolution* began to be understood as a change in the adaptation and diversity of populations of organisms. According to Mayr (1982, 1988), this emphasized the dual nature of evolution as a vertical phenomenon of adaptive change and a horizontal phenomenon of diversity among populations. The degree of change and its rate over time were subject to a variety of forces that affected population composition from one generation to the next.

Stability or change within a biological unit (the breeding population) depends on a great many factors. If these factors alter a gene frequency that persists over generations, the result is evolution. If the elements that cause change are counteracted by those that tend to maintain stability, then there will be no net change in gene-pool composition. Such stability is, of course, an ideal situation. Considering *Homo sapiens* for example, the actual condition of a population may be small gene-frequency fluctuation over several generations, partly because each generation appears as a unique unit varying somewhat in number of individuals, age distribution, and sex ratio. This fluctuation in gene frequency likely occurred more in former times when populations were more isolated and suffered higher mortality rates at all ages than today. Treating population gene-frequency equilibrium or disequilibrium of any species has always presented a problem because demographic as well as genetic factors must be considered. An important step was taken with the recognition of Mendelian genetics followed by the development of the foundation of population genetics.

Hardy-Weinberg Equilibrium

Early in the twentieth century, even after particulate inheritance was recognized, there was still considerable confusion over the relationship between dominant and recessive alleles. The question often raised was: If one allele was dominant to another, would not the dominant one eventually, after a period of time, come to be the most frequent allele in the population? The answer is no, of course not. In 1908, an English mathematician, G. H. Hardy, and a German physician, W. Weinberg, independently offered a mathematical formula $(p + q)^2$, which described in simple terms the proportion of a pair of alleles in a randomly mating population living under stable conditions. This formula explained why the dominant allele would not increase.

If the symbols of A and a are used to indicate dominant and recessive alleles, respectively, then the gametes (sperm and ovum) will carry one or the other allele, and recombination through reproduction will occur at a constant frequency. The following combinations are expected in the offspring:

		SPERM	
		A	a
OVA	A	AA	Aa
	a	Aa	aa

This simple diagram shows that one AA genotype is reproduced for every two Aa combinations and every one aa genotype—the *Mendelian ratio*. In the hypothetical situation in which the alleles A and a are present in equal numbers in a population, one-half of the gametes carry the A allele and one-half carry the a. Let p equal the frequency of A and q equal the frequency of a; then the allele frequencies of all combinations within a population can be derived from the following table:

		Frequency of Sperm Alleles A or a	
		P (0.5)	P (0.5)
Frequency of ova alleles A or a	p (0.5)	p^2 (0.25)	pq (0.25)
	q (0.5)	pq (0.25)	q^2 (0.25)

Adding up the frequencies of all combinations to derive a total for the population we get

$$p^2 + 2pq + q^2$$
$$(0.25) + 2(0.25) + (0.25)$$
$$p^2 + 2pq + q^2 = 1$$

Then $(p + q)^2 = 1$ because it is the binomial expression of the quadratic equation. Taking the square root of the equation we get

$$p + q = 1$$

which is a mathematical way of saying that, in a population of sexually reproducing organisms, the total number of alleles at any locus is equal to unity. Therefore, if we know the frequency of one, then the other can be determined (expressed as $p = 1 - q$, or $q = 1 - p$). This should be easy to comprehend if one recalls that only a single allele is present at a locus on a chromosome (though the other chromosome of the pair may carry another allelic form of the gene). In our example of two allelic forms, it is an either–or situation; the A or a is present. Given the random mating conditions, each type of sperm has equal opportunity to fertilize each type of egg, so the 1:2:1 Mendelian ratio of the genotypes AA, Aa, and aa will be maintained throughout the generations and there will be no change in gene frequency. The *Hardy-Weinberg equilibrium* states that the frequencies of p and q will remain the same throughout any number of generations given a stable, random-breeding population isolated from other populations.

An example can be made of the number of individuals who are taste sensitive to a chemical, *phenylthiocarbamide* (PTC), a substance that is bitter tasting to a majority of persons, but tasteless to about 25 percent of Europeans tested. It was found some years ago that this tasting ability is inherited as a dominant allele (T). So a person either TT or Tt was a taster whereas the homozygous recessive tt was a nontaster. If a random sample of a population shows that there are 250 nontasters out of 1,000, then 25 percent have the genotype tt. The gene frequency of the recessive allele (q) in this example can be calculated: $q^2 = .25$ and $q = \sqrt{.25}$, which is equal to .5, or one-half of the alleles for the PTC locus are the recessive form. The frequency of the dominant allele (T) would then be .5 or $(1 - q)$. Nevertheless, even though the alleles are of equal frequency in the population, three-quarters or 75 percent of the individuals have the taster phenotype. This is simply explained by reference to the ratio of the genotypes previously shown. One-half of the recessive alleles (t) are combined with the dominant alleles to form the heterozygote who is a taster (Tt). Throughout future generations, assuming random mating with respect to taste sensitivity, the gene frequencies of these alleles will remain the same and there will be the same number of individuals who are tasters (see Table 2-1).

The Hardy-Weinberg formula assumes, in addition to random mating (genotypes do not influence mate selection), that certain conditions exist that contribute to population stability, and if these conditions are maintained, gene frequencies will remain invariable throughout any number of generations. Few natural populations fit this model situation exactly, but the basic formula established a reference against which change can be measured, and it provides a useful tool in studies of variation and evolution. The forces for change in a population's gene frequencies are *mutation, natural selection, genetic drift* (a sampling error), and *gene flow.*

Mutation

As discussed below, the change in a genetic code results in an alteration in its action and introduces a new variety of allele. The net result is to increase the number of different genotypes within a population. Mutation, then, is the ultimate source of all genetic variation in a population and may provide a species with an ability to respond to a variety of environmental conditions. Some mutations, however, cause such a radical metabolic disturbance that an organism cannot survive; many more are detrimental but

TABLE 2-1   Frequencies of Offspring from All Types of Matings

GENOTYPES OF PARENTS	FREQUENCY OF MATINGS	FREQUENCY OF OFFSPRING			NUMBER OF INDIVIDUALS		
		TT	Tt	tt	TT	Tt	tt
TT x TT	p^4	p^4	—	—	625	0	0
TT x 2 Tt 2 Tt x TT	$4p^3q$	$2p^3q$	$2p^3q$	—	1,250	1,250	0
TT x tt tt x TT	$2p^2q^2$	0	$2p^2q^2$	—	0	1,250	0
2 Tt x 2 Tt	$4p^2q^2$	p^2q^2	$2p^2q^2$	p^2q^2	625	1,250	625
2 Tt x tt tt x 2 Tt	$4pq^3$	—	$2pq^3$	$2pq^3$	0	1,250	1,250
tt x tt	q^4	—	—	q^4	0	0	625
All Types	1	p^2	$2pq$	q^2	2,500	5,000	2,500

Adding up each column gives a total of $p^2 + 2pq + q^2 =$ (all types of matings) and the numerical example adds up to a total of 10,000. This table shows, in a randomly mating population of this size with p of .5, that the numbers of individuals with the three genotypes will be distributed 1/4 TT (2,500), 1/2 Tt (5,000), and 1/4 tt (2,500) each generation. Under conditions of stability, as described earlier, this distribution will remain unchanged throughout any number of generations.

are not lethal. Still other mutations may affect changes in the way organisms metabolize certain substances, resist parasites, or produce antibodies against infectious diseases. A question frequently raised in the past was whether or not all mutations are "bad". The changes in gene structure are seen now as an error in DNA coding with a greater or lesser effect on protein synthesis, depending on the amino acid substituted. If the substitution occurs in a polypeptide position that reduces or eliminates the protein's function to a level that places the individual's survival at risk, then it may be considered bad. In certain environments, however, the mutant allele, though depressing some metabolic processes, may convey a survival advantage to the carrier of the allele. The influence on survival of such an error, or change in code, will be taken up in the following chapters. Here, mutations, without evaluating effect (lethal mutations excepted) may be considered one of the sources of disturbance of genetic equilibrium between generations as measured by the Hardy-Weinberg Equilibrium.

In *Homo sapiens,* mutations apparently occur at a low rate, though this rate may be influenced by ionizing radiation from natural or human-caused sources. The results from exposure to radiation cannot be predicted—that is, which genes will mutate or how often. Some human mutation rates that occur due to unknown causes have been measured in family lineages and are listed in Table 2-2. As shown, the rates are very low and can be calculated by recording the frequency per live births. If, for example, 8 infants out of 100,000 newborns suffer from the effects of a mutant dominant allele then the rate (μ) could be calculated as

$$\frac{8}{2 \times 100,000} = \frac{8}{2 \times 10^5} = .00004 = \mu$$

or the formula:

$$\mu = \frac{M}{2T} \quad \begin{array}{l} \text{(total mutants)} \\ \text{(all births)} \end{array}$$

TABLE 2-2   Estimated Human Mutation Rates for Selected Traits

AUTOSOMAL DOMINANTS	MUTATION PER MILLION GAMETES
Achondroplasia (dwarfism)	10–14
Retinoblastoma (eye tumor)	6–18
Huntington's disease (progressive degeneration of central nervous system)	1
Neurofibromatosis (tumors of nervous system)	13–25
Marfan's syndrome (disorder of connective tissue)	4–5
X-LINKED RECESSIVES	
Hemophilia A (bleeder's disease)	20–30
Duchenne's muscular dystrophy	30–100

This is only 40 mutations per million gametes and such low rates in human populations will disturb gene frequencies only slightly from one generation to the next. Rarely, a mutation may convey an advantage and contribute to increased fitness in certain environments. Carriers of these mutant alleles may survive longer and contribute more offspring. Under such conditions the frequency of the allele may increase rapidly within just a few generations.

Natural Selection

Though chance plays a role in the production of variation within a population of sexually reproducing organisms, the range of variability and composition of a breeding population is limited. All possible genotypes are not represented in each generation with equal frequency. There are factors that limit the extent of population diversity and determine the gene frequencies from generation to generation. A major factor that acts to limit and stabilize genetic diversity is called *natural selection.*

Some individuals, because of one or several genotype combinations, have characteristics that are adaptive in certain environments that enable them to live longer, with an extended reproductive period. They reproduce at a higher rate and, thus, contribute more offspring to the next generation. Such persons, by definition, are the fittest in the sense of Darwinian fitness (those who produce the most offspring). Even slight inherited differences among individuals can be important factors leading to changes in gene-pool composition. Those genotypes that confer reproductive or survival advantage, no matter how small, will increase over generations.

Numerous studies of insects, bacteria, and fast-breeding mammals offer some excellent examples of mutations increasing survival and reproductive rates. There are well-established records of an increase in insect species' resistance, or even immunity, to the effects of frequently used insecticides. Resistant strains of the common housefly began to appear throughout the world within two years after the insecticide DDT was introduced in an effort to control this and other insect pests. It appears that fly larvae of the resistant strains develop faster and survive better in a crowded environment than the DDT-susceptible strains. More of a danger to humans has been the proliferation of resistant strains of malaria-carrying mosquitos. These insects likewise included groups of resistant and nonresistant individuals until the introduction of insecticides reduced the numbers of those susceptible.

Other examples of natural selection are seen in the rise of bacteria strains resistant to several of the commonly used antibiotics, Such resistance has proved to be more and more difficult to control as each new antibiotic enhances the multiplication of resistant strains while destroying the susceptible microbes. Each of these examples shows the effects of environmental changes caused by human intervention and is an excellent demonstration of the operation of natural selection on simpler organisms. Many populations of complex organisms also provide evidence for the action of natural selection, but the changes are less dramatic because the generation time is in weeks, in the case of rodents, or years in humans rather than hours and days in bacteria.

In sum, natural selection refers to all those features of a population's environment and behavior that influence reproduction and survival of individuals over the generations who, as Darwin described, have some reproductive advantage. When a homozygote recessive's fitness is zero and thus eliminated each generation (Selection = 1), then the effects on gene frequency (q_0) change after n generations is represented by the formula

$$\frac{q_n}{(S=1)} = \frac{q_0}{1 + nq_0}$$

Because of our learning capacity and technological achievements, natural selection influences on human gene frequencies are much more complicated, as will be discussed in the following chapters. Diseases, once a deadly menace, have been all but eliminated partially due to the successes of modern medicine and because of public health practices. New diseases have appeared, however. Several strains of infectious organisms resistant to antibiotics are an increasing threat as illustrated by the rising numbers of cases of multiple-drug-resistant tuberculosis. Within the past two decades, mortality from a previously unknown disease, acquired immune deficiency syndrome (AIDS), has increased dramatically. Other, even more lethal viruses have appeared in what were remote regions, but now with a rapidly growing population, migration, and increased travel the barriers of distance have fallen. The results are seen in more frequent interpopulation contact and a multitude of opportunities for natural selection to act as described in the following chapters.

Gene Flow

In addition to increases in the number of people, there has been considerable population movement throughout human history, and much of this migration has occurred over the past few centuries. The migration and mixing of peoples increase genetic exchange, and populations that were once isolated have undergone a considerable change in gene frequencies. Interpopulation contact through migration, trade, or warfare has had a major influence on the genetic variability of many populations; the arrival of Europeans and Africans into the Western Hemisphere is a major example.

This *gene flow*, as it is often called, refers to exchanges between different population gene pools so that the next generation is a result of admixture of the parental population. The admixture in the hybrid population (q_h) depends on the gene frequencies of the parental populations (q_1 and q_2) and rates of intermarriage overtime and is expressed by

$$M = \frac{q_h - q_2}{q_1 - q_2} = \text{admixture for allele frequency } q$$

A higher rate of admixture, or outbreeding, has been an important factor that has countered the influence of isolation, reducing the chance of development of unique gene combinations. Furthermore, it has the potential for introducing new gene combinations, causing the population to be more heterogeneous. The relative influence of gene exchange between breeding populations depends, of course, on the size and length of time in contact. Invading armies, colonists, travelers, and traders have all had an effect on genetic dispersal throughout our species. The geographic distribution of gene frequencies today and in the recent past is quite different from what it had been before the major colonial expansion of western Europe beginning in the fifteenth century, and it is continuing to undergo changes.

Genetic Drift

A critical factor influencing gene frequencies from generation to generation is the total number of individuals who make up the effective breeding population (males and females in their reproductive years). When this number is very small, there is the possibility that not all gene combinations will be represented in the next generation. This may be described as a *sampling error* or *genetic drift*. The chance distribution of the genotypes of offspring from the mating of heterozygotes can serve to illustrate the influences of population size on sampling error. When there is a mating of heterozygotes (Aa × Aa), there is a probability of 25 percent that the offspring will be AA. If the couple produces four children, then the probability is less than 0.4 percent that they all will be genotype AA, while there is 1.5 percent chance that three children will have this genotype (see Table 2-3). Should either of these unlikely events occur and more AA genotypes be produced than either Aa or aa, the frequency of the recessive allele, a, would decrease through chance alone in a population with only a few matings in each generation. The larger the number of matings, the greater the probability that all genetic combinations will be reproduced, so the gene frequencies will remain stable from one generation to the next. By contrast, the fewer the matings each generation, the smaller the sample of the total gene pool. Under this condition there will be a greater chance that certain genes will not be passed on because of the small size of the sample.

There are a number of examples where genes have become fixed at high frequencies in human populations within just a few generations. Island populations throughout the Pacific, as well as religious colonists whose beliefs have resulted in

TABLE 2-3   Distribution of Offspring of Two Heterozygous Parents (Aa × Aa)

GENOTYPE OF FIRST OFFSPRING	PROBABILITY OF FIRST OFFSPRING	GENOTYPE OF SECOND OFFSPRING	PROBABILITY OF SECOND OFFSPRING	TOTAL PROBABILITY
AA	1/4	AA	1/4	Both offspring AA, 1/16
AA	1/4	Aa	2/4	AA followed by Aa, 2/16
AA	1/4	aa	1/4	AA followed aa, 1/16
Aa	2/4	AA	1/4	Aa followed AA, 2/16
Aa	2/4	Aa	2/4	Both offspring Aa, 4/16
Aa	2/4	aa	1/4	Aa followed by aa, 2/16
aa	1/4	AA	1/4	aa followed by AA, 1/16
aa	1/4	Aa	2/4	aa followed by Aa, 2/16
aa	1/4	aa	1/4	Both offspring aa, 1/16

self-imposed breeding isolation, document the influence of population size on gene frequencies. The smaller the size of the *effective breeding population* (N_e) (ratio of males and females of reproductive age to total population), the greater the chance of gene frequency change between the generations:

$$N_e = \frac{4N_f N_m}{N_f + N_m}$$

The influence of the founders' gene combinations is another form of sampling error and is referred to as *founders' effect*, described by Mayr (1963). Because of the improbability of a small group of colonists representing all of the variety of the parent population, this initial error in sampling will have a major influence on future generations of descendants from the founding population. This restricted sampling, or "bottleneck" effect, may be repeated in future generations if, through natural catastrophe or disease, the population loses large numbers of its people over a short period. Consider the example of the small South Atlantic island of Tristan da Cunha, midway between South America and Africa. The 270 persons occupying the island in 1961 could trace their ancestry back to the original 15 colonists consisting of soldiers, shipwrecked sailors, and a few women who arrived in 1816.

The lonely, isolated island has no natural harbor to shelter ships from the rough seas and its environment is harsh, so, except for an occasional individual, there has been no immigration. Despite these restrictions the population had grown to 103 by 1855, when it suffered a setback with the departure of all but 33 persons. A second bottleneck occurred when a small boat, with 15 males aboard, capsized, leaving no survivors. Following this disaster many of the widows and their offspring emigrated, reducing the island population from 106 to 54. The population recovered to reach 270 by 1961. The events that caused this small founding population to undergo an expansion, followed by severe reduction, and then expansion again have caused some rare genetic recessive traits and unique gene frequencies to exist among the modern-day descendants.

Even larger populations, descendants of a few founders, will often contain a high frequency of rare genetic defects. An example of such detrimental genes reaching high frequencies is the inherited defect porphyria. This metabolic disorder prevents chemical conversion of the porphyrin compound, the iron-bearing pigment of hemoglobin, and results in the excretion of excessive amounts in the urine. Persons with the South African type of porphyria, inherited as an autosomal dominant, are ultrasensitive to sunlight, which produces severe skin lesions. The accumulation of porphyrin in the blood leads to a number of symptoms of the digestive tract and nervous system disorders, and persons with the affliction are sensitive, as well, to certain types of drugs like barbiturates. This metabolic defect is rare throughout the world, with most cases reported in the Afrikaans population. The gene responsible for this affliction has been traced through genealogies back to 1688 to a young girl from Rotterdam and her spouse, another immigrant from the Netherlands. The 8,000 carriers of this autosomal dominant allele today are descendants of this marriage. These findings are not surprising, considering that an estimated one million of three million Afrikaans are descendants of forty original couples settling in the Cape area (see Dean, 1963; Jones, 1992).

Random Mating

The Hardy-Weinberg equilibrium assumes that matings take place without regard to genotype; that is, they are random. Persons marry without considering the blood group genotypes; for example, persons do not select a mate of type-A blood and reject one of type B. Therefore, calculations for many of the human gene frequencies will not be disturbed by a nonrandomness of breeding. However, random breeding in another sense does not usually apply in the choice of mates because a number of social as well as biological criteria are considered. In human populations all males and females do not have an equal chance of mating, and there are a number of barriers that reduce random mating. One is *positive assortative mating*, which describes a tendency for "like" to marry "like." Tall people tend to marry tall people and short people tend to marry short people. Also, there is a high positive correlation between the IQs of husband and wife. Persons frequently marry those within their social circle and, until just a few generations ago, geographic distance played a major role in mate selection; marriages took place most often between individuals who lived near each other. Though the distances between prenuptial households is steadily increasing, marriage to "the boy or girl next door" was more fact than fiction until quite recently. Another factor that has affected random matings is society's rules that prohibit matings between close relatives, but these rules may be suspended when small community size limits mate choice, as described in Chapter 8.

Society's rules governing marriage have influenced a degree of outbreeding, or population *exogamy*, where mates are selected from outside of one's extended family or village, reducing homozygosity while increasing heterozygosity. Population *endogamy*, or inbreeding, causes the reverse—an increase in homozygosity. The consequences of the degree of inbreeding may be in evidence in health, growth, and genetics. Children of *consanguineous matings* (marriages of relatives of some degree) are smaller in body size, have a higher frequency of congenital abnormalities, and exhibit greater mortality during the first six years of life (Morton, 1958, 1961; Schull and Neel, 1965). The degree of genetic relationship of the parents increases the chance of pairing deleterious recessives in the offspring because of a higher probability that the parents may be carriers of the same recessive alleles, due to their sharing of a close common ancestor. This increased homozygosity of recessives is shown by higher incidence of genetic diseases in certain populations. There is a greater frequency of consanguinity among parents of affected offspring than among the general population (see Table 2-4).

THE GENE, DNA, AND THE "CODE OF LIFE"

Knowledge of the gene as a unit of inheritance underwent a slow, but steady, advance over the first half of the twentieth century after the rediscovery of Mendel's experiments. The earliest and perhaps the most important of these advances was an understanding of the intergenerational transmission of traits; an information base, not the trait itself, is passed from parents to children. The association of such information

TABLE 2-4   Percentages of Affected Offspring of Cousin Marriages

TRAIT	% CONSANGUINITY[a]
Albinism	19–24
Alkaptonuria	30–42
PKU	5–15
Tay-Sachs	27–53
Xeroderma pigmentosum	20–36
Ichthyosis congenita	30–40
Congenital total blindness	11–21

[a]This indicates the frequency of consanguinity of those parents who produced affected offspring. This should be weighed against the average for the general population, which is less than 1 percent.

Source: Data adapted from Stern, 1973; Vogel and Motulsky, 1986.

with the darkly staining material in a cell's nucleus was made early in the twentieth century, about the time the term "gene" was used to designate the hereditary unit of information. This was followed by a recognition of chromosome pairs, where the genes were thought to occupy a position or *locus* on each. The further advancements made in studies of cell structures and how they divide clearly demonstrated the basic mechanisms of particulate inheritance.

The understanding of gene function, and how mutations occurred, had to wait until the structure of the nucleic acid components within the cell's nucleus could be defined more clearly. Though nucleic acid had been long suspected to be the hereditary material within the cell's nucleus, a direct connection could not be made with cellular processes and growth. These processes were thought to be dependent on the chromosome's involvement in the synthesis of products necessary for the cell's metabolism. The composition of the nucleic acids seemed to be the key to understanding not only the nature of heredity, but also the products regulating the functions of the entire organism as well.

This led to a search for these products, and for many years investigators worked, with some success, to describe the structures of complex molecules, like proteins, that were believed to control cellular metabolism or, in some cases, formed the basic components of body tissues. But the structure of the nucleic acids and their relationship to protein molecules escaped definition until mid-twentieth century. In 1953, James Watson and Francis Crick offered a model to explain the molecular structure of a compound, deoxyribonucleic acid (DNA), whose existence in the nucleus had been known for years. The model proved to be an accurate description of this complex structure, and their discovery had a momentous impact on biology and was just the type of breakthrough that the field needed to start a new phase of genetics research. The discovery was so important and basic to the understanding of the genetic code of life that Watson, Crick, and Wilkins were awarded the Nobel Prize in 1962.[2]

---

[2]Many researchers in several fields laid the ground work for molecular genetics, and Watson relates a very interesting and personal account of the events leading to the discovery of the DNA structure. He also describes the fierce competition among scientists to be the first to identify the functioning of this key molecule (see *The Double Helix*, 1980).

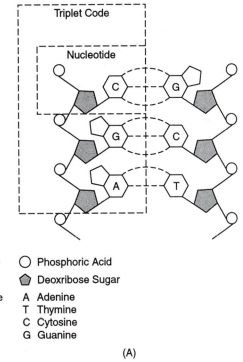

FIGURE 2-12a
Nucleotide Structure, the Basic Unit of the
DNA Molecule. A nucleotide is composed of a
molecule of phosphate and a deoxyribose sugar
to which is attached any one of four types of
organic bases: adenine (A), thymine (T), cytosine
(C), or guanine (G). This basic unit is attached to
an adjacent nucleotide by bonding between
phosphate and sugar molecules as shown. Three
nucleotides, taken together, provide a particular
triplet code because of the combination of the
three organic bases they contain, and this code
specifies a particular amino acid as discussed
in the text.

○ Phosphoric Acid
⬡ Deoxribose Sugar
A Adenine
T Thymine
C Cytosine
G Guanine

(A)

DNA is a long, repetitive, chainlike structure made up of alternating phosphate and sugar (deoxyribose) molecules to which are attached one of four kinds of organic bases (thymine, adenine, cytosine, or guanine). The sugar-phosphate molecules form a basic backbone structure of DNA. The unit composed of sugar, phosphate, and base molecules is called a *nucleotide* (Figure 2-12a), which is joined with the next nucleotide, and this process is repeated over and over until a long chain has been formed. The bases of the nucleotides are attracted to other bases on a complementary DNA strand and the two are held together by a weak hydrogen bond. Each base attracts only one other type; thymine (T) is bonded to adenine (A) and cytosine (C) to guanine (G). The length of the two chains can be diagramed as a ladderlike structure; the long parallel structures are formed by the sugar and phosphate backbones while the connecting rungs are the complementary base pairs (Figure 2-12b). The DNA strands are actually rotated about each other to form the double helix described by Watson and Crick.

The importance of the base-to-base attractions is well illustrated when a cell divides to form two new cells. The DNA strands pull apart and the unbonded bases attract new nucleotides and bond with complementary bases. These nucleotides attach over the length of the original strands, forming two new double helical molecules, as illustrated in Figure 2-12c. This DNA replication at cell division is described as semiconservative; one of the old strands is joined with a newly formed strand so each of

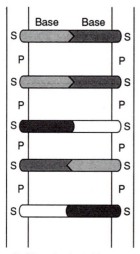

P Phosphoric Acid
S Deoxribose Sugar

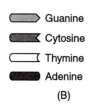 Guanine

Cytosine

Thymine

Adenine

(B)

FIGURE 2-12b
Schematic Diagram Depicting the Ladderlike Arrangement of DNA.
The organic bases of opposite DNA strands are attracted and bound together by a weak hydrogen bond that causes DNA to be a double-stranded molecule. Because of their chemical structures, adenine will bind only with thymine and guanine with cytosine. These base-to-base bonds form the "rungs" of the "ladder" while the series of sugars and phosphates are long side pieces to which the rungs are attached.

the daughter cells will end up with its proper DNA complement. This process occurs repeatedly during cell divisions to produce new tissue and, provided that all replication is correct (no mutations), the daughter cells will be identical to parental cells.

The Gene: Structure and Function

Once the nature of the nucleic acids of the cell nucleus was described, the search was on for an explanation of how they related to cellular functions and division, and what relation these acids had to the transmission of traits throughout generations of cells. The search was directed to protein molecules because of their multiple functions. They provide support (structural proteins), as in the example of *collagen*, an important protein of skin, bone, and many other tissues in the body; regulate metabolic processes (*enzymes*), as in digestion, body temperature control, and production of skin pigment (*tyrosinase*); and influence gene expression through the action of thousands of enzymes in a cell or by hormones like growth, pituitary, and insulin.

Proteins constitute a class of chemical compounds made up of chains of smaller molecules (amino acids) linked together by peptide bonds.[3] The total of these linkages is

---

[3]The major organic molecules of living organisms are classified into four categories: carbohydrates (sugars and starches), lipids (fats), proteins, and nucleic acids.

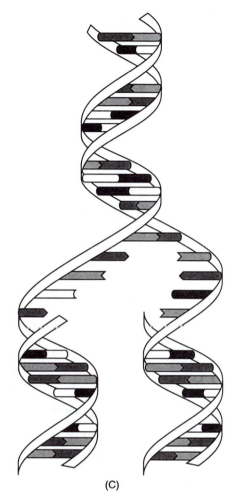

FIGURE 2-12c

Helical Shape of DNA Molecule and Semiconservative Replication. DNA molecules are rotated so they form a double helical structure; the sides formed by the sugar and phosphates and weakly bound bases are connected as shown in Figures 2-12a and b. When a cell divides the DNA molecules must be duplicated in such a way that the new cells will have the exact quantity and sequence of nucleotides. This is achieved by a process of separation of part of the molecule at a time and bonding the complementary nucleotides to the exposed unpaired bases. When completed, this process has created two daughter helixes, each composed of one of the original DNA strands bound to a newly synthesized one, a process called semiconservative replication.

(C)

described as a polypeptide chain. The proteins are composed of varying combinations of 20 kinds of amino acids arranged in a linear chain. The chain may be a few dozen amino acids long, as in human insulin, which has 51 arranged in 2 tightly bonded chains, or a protein may contain 100 or more amino acids, as in globin of human hemoglobin, with 574 organized into 4 polypeptide chains, 2 alpha and 2 beta. The sequence or linear arrangement of the amino acids is critical and provides the protein molecule with a specific identity and hence its function. In Figure 2-13 the normal sequence is shown for the first 6 positions and for position 26 of the 146 in the beta chain of human hemoglobin. A substitution of amino acid, valine, for glutamic acid changes the identity from hemoglobin A to hemoglobin S (sickle cell type), and under certain conditions its function (oxygen transport) is radically altered. Other substitutions also change hemoglobin type as shown. This importance of amino acid sequence raises the question of how cells and structures that synthesize proteins direct the correct organization of the polypeptide chains.

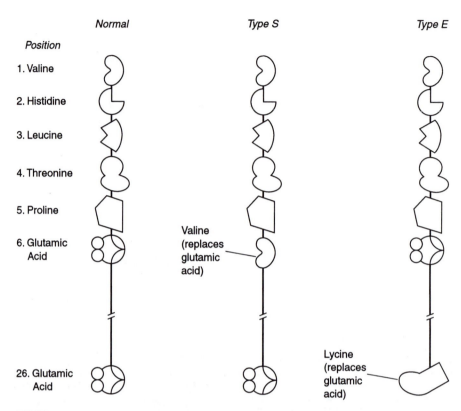

FIGURE 2-13   Amino Acid Sequences of Three Types of Beta Globin. These diagrams depict the amino acids at the first 6 and at the 26th position. Normal, type S, and type E hemoglobin have the same sequence of amino acids at all 146 positions of the beta globin chains with two very important and specific exceptions. Type S has a substitution of valine for glutamic acid at position 6 while type E is the same as the normal for that position but has a replacement of lycine for glutamic acid at position 26.

Because of a pattern of inheritance of different forms of proteins observed in family lineages over the years, protein synthesis was thought to be under genetic control. But the genetic material, though considered to be in the nucleus, was not identified until after mid-twentieth century. The major compounds within the nucleus, the nucleic acids, were at first ignored as the genetic code because their chemical composition, analyzed long before the Watson and Crick discovery of their structural arrangement, showed a presence of only four organic bases. Any hypothesis that these bases existed in a regular structural sequence made it difficult to understand how nucleic acids containing combinations of only four bases could determine the linear arrangement of twenty types of amino acids into a string of dozens or more. Also, the proportions of the bases varied between the two kinds of nucleic acids, DNA and RNA. The major work after 1953 provided many of the answers and opened up the era of *molecular genetics*, which has enormously expanded the understanding of cellular function and its inherited basis.

The Genetic Code

Considering DNA as the genetic code, the problem of amino acid identification is solved when the nucleotides are "read" three at a time as a group instead of individually. Since each nucleotide is identical (phosphate and sugar) except for one of the four types of organic base attached, a group of three nucleotides gives the probability of 4^3 or sixty-four different coded combinations (three positions at which one of four kinds of organic bases may occur). This code then could account for more than twenty amino acids with a number of "codes" left over. After much research, different DNA triplets were shown to code for particular amino acids, and some amino acids could be coded for by any one of several triplets; the DNA code was said to be redundant (see Table 2-5). The problem that remained to be solved was how the DNA code in the nucleus could control synthesis in the cell's cytoplasm where the structures (*ribosomes*) and raw materials needed for the protein synthesis were located.

A second nucleic acid compound, *ribonucleic acid* (RNA) proved to be the transporting agent or messenger that copied the code and relayed it to the sites of protein synthesis, the ribosomes. Figure 2-14 diagrams the basics of this process. It starts in the nucleus when an enzyme, *RNA polymerase*, causes the double strand of DNA to

TABLE 2-5   Genetic Code[a]

AMINO ACID	DNA (TRIPLET)	mRNA (CODON)
Alanine (ala)	CGA, CGG, CGT, CGC	GCU, GCC, GCA, GCG
Arginine (arg)[b]	GCA, GCG, GCT, GCC, TCT, TCC	CGU, CGC, CGA, CGG, AGA, AGG
Asparagine (asn)	TTA, TTG	AAU, AAC
Aspartic acid (asp)	CTA, CTG	GAU, GAC
Cysteine (cys)	ACA, ACG	UGU, UGC
Glutamic acid (glu)	CTT, CTC	GAA, GAG
Glutamine (gln)	GTT, GTC	CAA, CAG
Glycine (gly)	CCA, CCG, CCT, CCC	GGU, GGC, GGA, GGG
Histidine (his)[b]	GTA, GTG	CAU, CAC
Isoleucine (ile)[c]	TAA, TAG, TAT	AUU, AUC, AUA
Leucine (leu)[c]	AAC, GAA, GAG, GAT, GAC, AAT	UUG, CUU, CUC, CUA, CUG, UUA
Lysine (lys)[c]	TTT, TTC	AAA, AAG
Methionine (met)[c]	TAC	AUG
Phenylalanine (phe)[c]	AAA, AAG	UUU, UUC
Proline (pro)	GGA, GGG, GGT, GGC	CCU, CCC, CCA, CCG
Serine (ser)	AGA, AGG, AGT, AGC, TCA, TCG	UCU, UCC, UCA, UCG, AGU, AGC
Threonine (thr)[c]	TGA, TGG, TGT, TGC	ACU, ACC, ACA, ACG
Tryptophan (trp)[c]	ACC	UGG
Tyrosine (tyr)	ATA, ATG	UAU, UAC
Valine (val)[c]	CAA, CAG, CAT, CAC	GUU, GUC, GUA, GUG
Terminating triplets	ATT, ATC, ACT	UAA, UAG, UGA

[a]Symbols for bases in nucleic acids: A (adenine); C (cytosine); G (guanine); T (thymine); and U (uracil), used as a substitute for T.

[b]Essential in diet of young child.

[c]One of the eight amino acids that humans cannot synthesize and therefore must obtain from the diet.

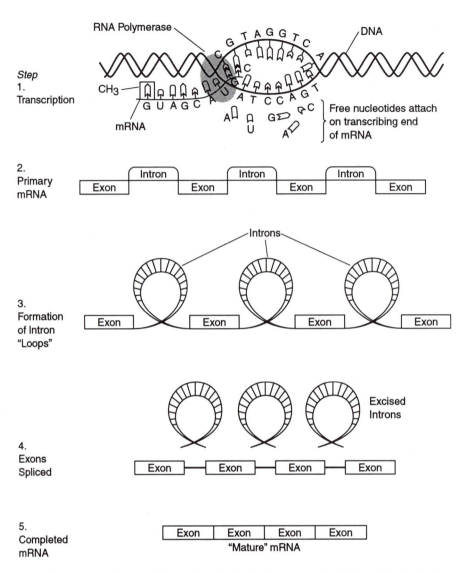

FIGURE 2-14 Transcription of DNA and the Synthesis of Messenger RNA (mRNA). The five basic steps in the process of synthesizing mRNA to transcribe the DNA code are illustrated in this diagram. *Step 1* begins by the separation of a segment of the double helix by the enzyme, RNA polymerase. The exposed bases of one of the DNA strands attract free nucleotides which become bound to one another, forming the single-stranded mRNA, which is a process similar to the formation of complementary daughter strands of DNA during replication. However, the major exception is that the mRNA soon separates, remains single-stranded, and uses the base uracil to bind with adenine instead of thymine. The enzymes move along the DNA and the process is repeated, and when a length of DNA has been "read" the strands rebind to one another. *Step 2* is reached when the transcription is completed and the primary mRNA is separated. At this step the mRNA contains a copy of all of the DNA, both exons and introns. *Step 3* is a maturing process that causes the introns, noncoding portion, to contract and form loops that result in shortening the mRNA, bringing the exons closer together. *Step 4* excises the intron loops and splices the exons together. *Step 5* produces the now shortened and completed strand of mature mRNA that contains the code to direct the production of polypeptide chains of amino acids.

separate along a few triplets beginning at a promoter region of seven bases, TATAAAT (the TATA box). The unbonded bases of one of the strands are temporarily bonded to complementary bases of RNA triplets (codons) that are formed into a chain as the polymerase moves along the DNA. Once a transcription has been made, the mRNA chain segment separates from the DNA. This process is repeated until a terminating triplet is reached (ATT, ATC, or ACT in Table 2-5). At this point a single-stranded mRNA (*messenger*) has been produced; it separates from the sense strand and the strands are rejoined into the double helix as before.

The mRNA is only a primary messenger, however, because it includes a number of noncoding sequences of the gene, the introns. The primary mRNA undergoes a process of maturation that causes a looping of the strand over the intron area, which is then cut and discarded. The remaining ends are joined, linking together those segments of DNA that code for proteins, the exons. The finished mature product of mRNA then moves out to the ribosomes in the cytoplasm, the site of protein synthesis. This single chain of a series of triplets (*codons*) provides an attraction for the bases of short strands of *transfer* RNA (tRNA) to attach temporarily. Each tRNA or *anticodon* (because its bases are complementary to mRNA) carries a particular amino acid. When the codon–anticodon bonds are established, the amino acids, carried by the tRNA, form peptide bonds, and the process is repeated until the stop signal is reached. The completed protein molecule is thus produced (Figure 2-15). The tRNA are free to pick up more amino acids and the process begins again. The triplets (codons) of mRNA are listed with the corresponding DNA triplets and the amino acids in Table 2-5.

This code is nearly universal; that is, in all living organisms, messenger RNA codons specify and the anticodons of the transfer RNA attract the same amino acids. Codon AUG specifies methionine whether in bacteria, amoeba, or human; likewise for the other nineteen amino acids that are used to form polypeptide structures of proteins. Such universality of the code provides strong supporting evidence for the unity of life from the simplest to the most complex. The only exceptions are found in cells' mitochondria where four codons determine different amino acids (UGA specifies trp, AGA specifies stop, AGG specifies stop, and AUA specifies met).

To summarize, a single-stranded nucleic acid (RNA) is transcribed from one strand of the DNA molecule, the sense or template strand. This mRNA is complementary to all those triplet regions between a start-and-stop triplet sequence and includes the coding (exon) and noncoding (intron) regions of a gene complex. The introns are excised from the primary mRNA and the exons are joined before the mature mRNA is released to the site of protein synthesis, the ribosomes. The mRNA begins to attract a tRNA that carries one amino acid specified by the codon–anticodon sequence. A series of these are attached along the strand, and the adjacent amino acids react to form peptide bonds resulting in a long chain that becomes the protein. The mRNA normally replicates from the DNA, a complementary chain of triplets that must be modified by removal of those noncoding portions, the introns, since the DNA carries many more triplet units than are used in the protein synthesis process. The discovery of this excess of noncoding nucleotide material leads to a reexamination of chromosome structure and, together

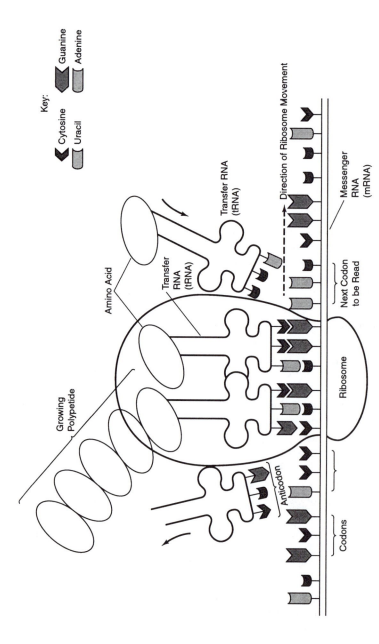

FIGURE 2-15 Formation of Polypeptide Chains. This drawing illustrates the roles played by messenger and transfer RNA in directing the orderly arrangements of amino acids to form polypeptide chains that make up proteins. The *ribosomes*, small granular bodies in the cell's cytoplasm, move along the mRNA and bring the anticodon of the tRNA into contact with the complementary codon of the mRNA. The amino acids carried by the tRNAs form peptide bonds linking together in a chain until the protein is produced. As the process proceeds, the tRNA is released and free to attach to another amino acid.

with the other chromosomes, the basic nature of the human genome (the total complement of genes).

CHROMOSOMES AT THE MOLECULAR LEVEL

The human genome contains enough DNA for over one million genes, but the real number of genes is closer to thirty thousand or even less. This means that a large excess of DNA is replicated and transmitted between generations of cells but is not used in the coding of protein synthesis. This excess, or actually most of the DNA, has more than genetic functions, since DNA fragments may be regulatory, provide start-or-stop signals, or function simply as spacing devices as in the case of the introns. Variation in transcription of the DNA code by cutting and splicing of primary RNA at different base sequences of the introns and exons results in a great variety of mature RNA. This process of alternative splicing enables the coding of hundreds of thousands of proteins from the few thousand genes (Freeland and Hurst, 2004).

The scope of this excess quantity of nucleotides may be appreciated by some comparisons. If stretched out to full length, the DNA equivalent in the total haploid genome in a gamete is a molecule one meter long that contains about one billion triplets. But all of the DNA must be contained in a cell nucleus with the dimensions of 10 μm by less than 1 μm. This placement of such a large mass in a restricted space is made possible by compaction due to "supercoiling" of the helical structures of special proteins called histones (Travis, 2004).

The total DNA of the human genome is divided into chromosomes, and each is a long, continuous chain of DNA coiled and compacted; the longest is 82 μm and the shortest, the Y-chromosome, is 2.15 μm. At the beginning stages of mitosis or meiosis (discussed above) a chromosome is composed of two chromatids held together by a centromere somewhere along its length. A visualization of this arrangement is provided by the drawing in Figure 2-16, which compares components of a chromosome at the structural, microstructural, and submicroscopic level. This knowledge of the fine structure of the chromosome, together with knowledge of the nucleotides and triplets of the gene, has contributed to a clearer understanding of genetic loci and has permitted the mapping of the genome. The human genome project (HUGO) announced on April 14, 2003, the completion of a map of the DNA sequences we carry. The implications of this study for our understanding of human biological variability and disease susceptibility are enormous and will be considered throughout the balance of the chapter.

Regions along the DNA strand of a chromosome have certain noncoding functions or contain codes for particular gene products. The region or locus for certain genetic traits, identified earlier by linkage studies in family lineages described above, has been confirmed and is now being clearly established by investigations of chromosome structure at the molecular level. This advance in our knowledge of inheritance has been made possible by the discovery of a class of bacterial enzymes that can cut the giant DNA molecule into shorter strands at specific base-pair locations. These enzymes, endonucleases, have opened up a whole new frontier for genetic studies.

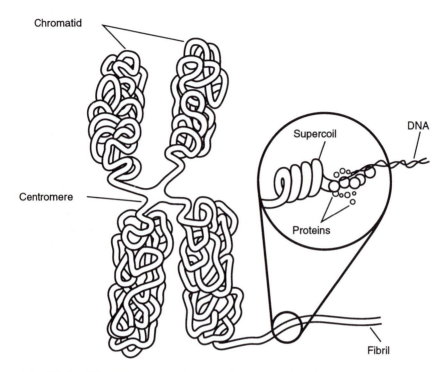

FIGURE 2-16   DNA and Chromosome Structure. This diagram illustrates, at several microstructural levels, the relationship of DNA strands to the chromosome. The *chromatids* are shown as densely compacted DNA linked together at a point near their centers, the *centromere.* The lower-right chromatid shows a section of a fibril that is further magnified to illustrate the supercoiled DNA structures it contains. Further expansion of this segment reveals the particles of proteins and an individual DNA molecule. (Source: Modified and redrawn from Vogel and Motulsky, 1986.)

Endonucleases.   These restriction enzymes, so-called because they cut the DNA molecule at specific points along the chain, have enabled investigators to separate much of the entire one-meter length of the human genome DNA into many shorter fragments. These fragments are of varying lengths (number of base pairs or Bp) and each has a specific triplet sequence at the point of cleavage; the triplet sequence plus one or two other nucleotides provide a point of attraction for one of these enzymes. Cleaving the entire human genome can produce about 500,000 fragments of from 100 to 10,000 Bp in length. These fragments can be separated by the *Southern blotting* method, a technique that separates the different fragments in an electric field and preserves them on a nitrocellulose filter (Southern, 1975). Basically, the technique takes advantage of the fact that fragments differ not only in size but in electric charge as well, a characteristic that will cause the fragments to move at different rates of speed through an agarose gel plate when an electric current is applied (electrophoresis). Once the fragments are separated, the fluid medium, a buffer solution, is blotted out

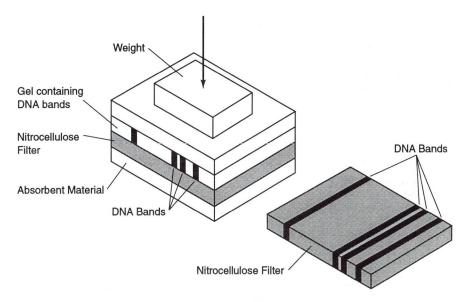

FIGURE 2-17   DNA Fragment Separation by the Southern Blotting Technique. The weight in the drawing compresses the gel layer and squeezes the buffer fluid onto a nitrocellulose filter. The porous filter allows the fluid to pass through to the absorbent material while retaining the DNA fragments. These fragments are positioned as bands relative to one another as they were on the gel.

by squeezing the gel between a weight, blotting paper, and the filter (Figure 2-17). This removes the fluid and leaves the fragments trapped and dispersed on the nitrocellulose filter as they were in the gel.

The hydrogen bonds of these DNA fragments are broken by treatment with an alkali solution separating the double strands. The now single-stranded fragments with specific base sequences can be examined individually by special chemical staining or by use of a radioactive probe. This probe is a short strand of DNA of known base sequence labeled with a radioactive isotope of phosphorus (^{32}P). The DNA probe combines with the complementary DNA strands and forms a double helical structure on the filter. A piece of photographic film is exposed to the radioactive labels over a period of several days. The result is a series of dark bands on the film that identifies the positions of those fragments that had combined with the probes. Because 500,000 fragments are an impossible number to deal with at one time, the chromosomes are first separated and then examined individually. The chromosome DNA may be cut by one or more restriction enzymes[4] and the resulting fragments are then treated by the Southern blotting method (Mange and Mange, 1990).

---

[4]There are hundreds of restriction enzymes (endonucleases) known at this time, with more being added to the list as the HUGO project proceeds.

TABLE 2-6   Examples of Genetic Diseases Detected by Gene Probes

Disease
Achondroplasia
Alpha1-antitrypsin deficiency
Diabetes mellitus (type 1)
Globin gene cluster (alpha)
Globin gene cluster (beta)
Growth hormone deficiency
Hemophilia A
Hemophilia B
HLA genes
Immunoglobulin genes
Lesch-Nyhan syndrome
Osteogenesis imperfecta (type II)
Phenylketonuria
Prealbumin (amyloidosis)
Sickle cell anemia
Thalassemias
Thrombosis III deficiency

Source: Selected from various sources. For a complete listing, see Cooper and Schmidtke (1986).

DNA Probes.   A large and ever-growing library of probes has made it possible to pinpoint the location of a gene on a particular chromosome. These DNA probes are radioactively labeled single-stranded DNA, which attach to the complementary fragments forming a hybrid double helix on the filter as described above. This allows for identification of specific genes or gene clusters because of the way in which the DNA probes are produced, by a method called reverse transcription. Where mRNA is available for proteins of known amino acid sequence, as in the case of the hemoglobins, insulin, and so on (see Table 2-6), an enzyme, reverse transcriptase, assembles DNA nucleotides complementary to the mRNA chain. This process is, as the name signifies, the reverse of the transcription process that occurs in the cell nucleus to produce the mRNA. The difference is, of course, that the molecular geneticist assembles complementary DNA (cDNA) in the laboratory using mRNA material as a template. The cDNA, when treated, becomes a probe to hybridize with the DNA fragments produced upon cleavage of the chromosome DNA by restriction enzymes.

Briefly, a gene product of interest is identified (enzyme, structural protein, etc.), and the mRNA is obtained from a cell or assembled in a test tube, which is possible when the amino acid sequence of the gene product is known. The mRNA provides a template for the synthesis of cDNA. The cDNA is used as a probe to locate the gene sequence on a chromosome fragment. A similar method, in situ hybridization, also uses a radioactive DNA strand but adds the probe to chromosomes in their metaphase of division. The probe hybridizes with the intact chromosome DNA at a specific segment. These methods have permitted many highly imaginative genetic studies and, as investigation of human chromosomes expands at an accelerating rate, the number of useful probes and their applications increase rapidly. Some examples of the locations

TABLE 2-7　Sampling of Human Genes Identified by In Situ Hybridization

GENE AND BASE PAIR (BP) LENGTH	LOCALIZATION CHROMOSOME AND REGION
Beta globin (4,400 BP)	11 *p*
Alpha globin (800 BP)	16 *p*
Insulin (900 BP)	11 *p* 15
LGH (550 BP)	17 *q* 22–24
Interferon	9 *p* 2.1-pter
IFN alpha + beta	12 *q* 24.1
Ig (6600 BP)	14 *q* 32
Ig Kappa (10500 BP)	2 *p* 12
Alpha-fetoprotein (380 BP)	4 *q* 11–22
Serum albumin (1600 BP)	4 *q* 11–22
Ig C lambda (203 BP) (gene family)	22 *q* 11
Myosin MHC (2200 BP)	17 *p* 1.2-pter
Collagen-gene	7 *q* 22

IFN-Interferon, gamma or immune type.

Ig-Immunoglobins.

LGH-Growth hormone (Lactogenic gene cluster).

Source: Selected from Vogel and Motulsky, 1986.

of genes for specific traits are given in Table 2-7. The location is listed by chromosome number, the area (*p* or *q* arms) and the site on the arm. For example, a collagen gene is located on the long arm (*q*) of chromosome 7 at the twenty-second site. Development of these processes has taken place over years of intensive biochemical work, and many are highly sophisticated, so much so that no brief description can do them justice. For more details and elaboration of additional investigation to identify or map the human genome, the reader is directed to a description of "unraveling" the human genome by Davies (2001).

GENE CLUSTERS AND RESTRICTION FRAGMENT LENGTH POLYMORPHISMS (RFLPS)

The various means of identifying gene location and the gene's finer structure have revealed some complications. The studies documented many more polymorphisms of DNA than were expected, but, at the same time, there has been some clarification of the excessive amounts of DNA present in the human genome as noted above. Because of the intensive study of human hemoglobin over the last forty years, the genes, gene clusters, and RFLP of this protein may be used to illustrate some recent discoveries.

　　The genes that regulate synthesis of the alpha and beta globin genes have been located on two different chromosomes: the alpha globin gene of 800 base-pair units on the sixteenth, and the beta gene, 4,400 base pairs, on the eleventh. The identification of the beta globin gene offered some unexpected results. In the process of

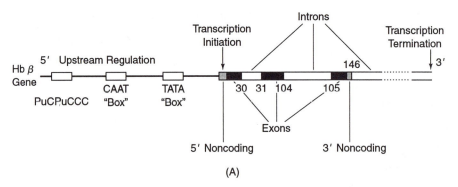

FIGURE 2-18a   Diagram of the Beta Globin Gene of Human Hemoglobin. The *introns* (noncoding) and *exons* (coding) regions of the gene are shown as well as the transcription initiation and termination "boxes." The numbers indicate the location of the codon for a corresponding amino acid position of the beta globin.

hybridization of beta globin DNA with complementary DNA (cDNA), some loops of unpaired nucleotides were produced on the beta globin strand that were visible under an electron microscope. These were segments of DNA not present as complementary regions on the cDNA. The explanation of the results was straightforward. Since the cDNA was a true copy of the mRNA made by reverse transcription, and since the mRNA represented the amino acid sequences of beta globin, then the unpaired DNA sequences were regions that were not transcribed into the completed mRMA. The unpaired regions were introns, as described above, and three are shown in the beta Hb gene diagramed in Figure 2-18a. The Hb gene is actually a cluster of three groups of nucleotide triplets (the black boxes) separated by noncoding units, the introns (white boxes). The gene is transcribed, and in step 1 all groups are represented. Then the introns are excised, the three exons are joined, and the mRNA is complete.

These interesting findings opened up a new realm of investigation. First, the search is on for the function, if any, of the introns. The second area of interest is the evidence that a gene exists "in pieces" as a cluster of nucleotides along a portion of the chromosome 11 DNA. There are, in addition to the Hb gene, several other genes (embryonic globin, for example) in this cluster, and a *pseudogene*, a DNA sequence similar to the functional gene[5] but not transcribed (Figure 2-18b). Additionally, the wide use of several restriction enzymes revealed a great diversity in the size and triplet sequences in the noncoding regions near the beta globin gene.

RFLP. Because of the attention directed to the study of abnormal hemoglobins, a large amount of information has been derived about the restriction fragment length

---

[5]After consideration of units of nucleotides called exons, introns, and even pseudogenes, it is necessary to reconsider the term "gene." It may be best defined as that region of the DNA that contains the nucleotide sequence code for the production of a polypeptide chain through the vehicle of an mRNA chain.

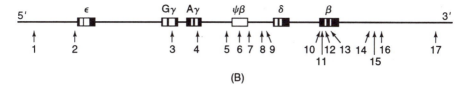

(B)

FIGURE 2-18b   Diagram of the Beta Globin Gene Cluster. The coding parts of DNA are frequently linked to other DNA clusters that play no role in the production of the protien—in this case, globin. However, the thousands of base pairs of this cluster may be cut at specific sites by selected enzymes. The resulting fragments can be used to distinguish between populations and sometimes even individuals. The numbers in this diagram represent sites that are cut by the endonucleases corresponding to those listed in Table 2-8.

polymorphism (RFLP). Table 2-8 lists some of the major restriction enzymes used to cut the beta globin gene cluster at different points. These sites, or points of cleavage in the DNA molecule, are illustrated in Figure 2-18b. The considerable variation between individuals is due to single substitutions of nucleotides, or point mutations. Because much of the DNA between gene clusters is noncoding, these substitutions causing sequence variation have no known functional consequences—at least not at this stage of our knowledge. Some of these variations in cleavage sites produce fragments of different nucleotide sequences, and this series or cluster of nucleotides is called a

TABLE 2-8   Frequency of DNA Polymorphic Sites in the Beta Globin Gene Cluster in Selected Ethnic Groups

POLYMORPHISMS	GREEKS	AMERICAN BLACKS	SOUTHEASTERN ASIANS
Taq I (1)[a]	1.00	0.88	1.00
Hine II (2)	0.46	0.10	0.72
Hind III (3)	0.52	0.41	0.27
Hind III (4)	0.30	0.16	0.04
Pvu II (5)	0.27		
Hinc II (6)	0.17	0.15	0.19
Hinc II (7)	0.48	0.76	0.27
Rsa I (8)	0.37	0.50	
Taq I (9)	0.68	0.53	
Hinf I (10)	0.97	0.70	0.98
Rsa I (11)			
HgiA (12)	0.80	0.96	0.44
Ava II (13)	0.80	0.96	0.44
Hpa I (14)	1.00	0.93	
Hind III (15)	0.72	0.63	
Bam HI (16)	0.70	0.90	
Rsa I (17)	0.37	0.10	

[a]Numbers in parentheses refer to the sites illustrated in Figure 2-13b, which are cut by the restriction enzymes.

Source: Modified from Vogel and Motulsky, 1986.

haplotype. They occur in greater frequency in one population compared to another and even among individuals. As shown in Table 2-8, the RFLP produced by PVUII (number 5 in the diagram, Figure 2-18b) occurred only in the DNA sample obtained from the Greek population. The Hine II restriction site is recorded at high frequency in Greeks and Asians but is low in African Americans.

The nucleotide sequences (RFLP) vary in length and are repeated many times throughout the DNA. The larger ones, called variable number of tandem repeats, or VNTR, are from seven or more nucleotides in length and have a high mutation rate of up to 7 percent. A shorter sequence, the short tandem repeat polymorphism, or STRP, has from two to five nucleotides and is more stable with a lower mutation rate (a tenth of a percent or lower). A third type is now identified, the SNP or single nucleotide polymorphism, that has a lower mutation rate still. All three of these forms of nucleotide sequences are interspaced among structural genes as seemingly useless satellites of DNA.

The continued application of different endonucleases has revealed numerous polymorphisms of satellite DNA (VNTR, STRP, and SNP). By mid-year, 1995, there were at least 20,000 DNA markers identified (Kidd and Kidd, 1996), and this number increased rapidly over the next five years as more laboratories analyzed the human genome. Now there are several hundred thousand polymorphisms recorded on Web site data bases (Roberts, 2000). New methods of identification of these satellites by fluorescent dyes and automated computer-driven readouts are rapidly expanding population data. This has been especially true for the single nucleotide polymorphisms that may mark differences between people (Couzin, 2004). The studies of DNA polymorphisms sampled from populations around the world have opened up a whole new frontier in the study of human genetic diversity, as explored in the following chapters. Since most of these polymorphisms have no apparent functional significance, the RFLP as well as the SNP may serve well as population markers suggestive of a common history, of isolation, or interpopulation relationships. The problems yet to be resolved are twofold: first, the selection of relevant markers, and two, the sampling of populations. These problems and their relevance to studies of human variation and evolution will be taken up in Chapter 4. Finally, variations of the RFLPs, STRP, and SNP are the result of changes in the base sequences or mutations, but these occur in noncoding regions flanking the the gene sites and probably do not influence survival. Polymorphisms in certain regions have been used for forensic purposes for over ten years; guilt or innocence in criminal cases has been resolved and questions of paternity have been settled. The Y-chromosome has become especially useful because of its father-son transmission.

Y-CHROMOSOME DNA POLYMORPHISMS

Application of restriction enzymes to the DNA of this small chromosome has identified numerous nucleotide substitutions on the nonrecombinant part. Some sites are in the SRY region on the short arm while many more have been found on the long arm.

Of particular use are the biallelic polymorphisms (single-base substitutions) that have occurred frequently around the site of cleavage by a particular restriction enzyme. Many of these are population specific and, since they are transmitted only through the male lineage, the Y-chromosome polymorphisms can be used for study of ethnic origins and extended patrilineages, and they are believed to be useful in tracing human evolutionary history (Underhill et al., 1997).

Considering polymorphisms at several sites as a *haplotype* or group, comparisons may be made between widely dispersed populations. For example, base substitutions at nine biallelic sites were identified on Y-chromosomes sampled from Africans, Europeans, Asians, Australasians, and Native Americans. Combinations of these polymorphisms could be grouped into ten different *haplotypes,* which were unevenly distributed among the populations sampled. The African sample exhibited a greater diversity with eight of the ten represented while, in contrast, Native Americans had only two. Europe and Africa shared two of the types that were lacking in the rest of the world. Two haplotypes are found in all populations sampled. These data on Y-chromosome polymorphisms showed statistically significant associations among haplotypes and geographic distribution. Africa appeared to be the most ancient population that expanded its range into Eurasian, replacing Y-chromosomes of the local population with African (Hammer et al., 1998). Such interpretation of Y-haplotypes is consistent with the "Out of Africa" theory of modern human origins, a theory that is not without controversy as explained earlier.

MITOCHONDRIAL DNA

In addition to the DNA in the nucleus, there is a quantity of DNA contained in small subcellular structures, the mitochondria, within the cell's cytoplasm. A typical cell contains about 100 of these mitochondria, whose main function is oxidation of carbohydrate, protein, and fat molecules to provide energy for cellular metabolism. These largely self-sufficient organelles, on average, replicate and divide with each division of the host cell and thereby continue a lineage of coded information contained within this special faction of DNA. This mitochondrial DNA (mtDNA), together with nuclear DNA (nDNA), codes for the production of polypeptide units that regulate the functioning of the oxidative processes of the mitochondria. In a sense, the coding and synthesis proceed very much like that described above for the transcription, translation, and protein synthesis from the nDNA. What sets the mitochondria apart is their number (there are about 100 per cell versus only a single nucleus), their variation in rates of growth and division, and the replication of mtDNA. What is most extraordinary and most useful is the small size of this mtDNA.

Mitochondrial DNA forms a circular single double-stranded helix only 16,569 base-pair units long. Most of these 5,523 codons serve a coding function with no intervening sequences, unlike the nDNA coding units that are separated by noncoding units (introns). Each mitochondrion contains several of these circular DNAs, and they are easily extracted and examined in the laboratory. A single messenger RNA transcript has been made of the entire mtDNA and cleaved by endonucleases into significant coding regions.

As a result, the locations of all of the thirty-seven closely linked genes have been mapped and the nucleotides have been sequenced for each. The functioning of most mitochondrial genes is well established, and certain mutant forms have been related to several disorders of the neurological sensory and neuromuscular systems (see McKusick, 1994).

This cytoplasmic inheritance, as it was once known, offers many opportunities for studies of gene influence on cellular functions. An equally valuable purpose has been suggested for the study of human evolution. Because of mtDNA's high mutation rate (about ten times the mutation rate of nuclear DNA), mtDNA sequences may evolve rapidly. What is most significant is that since the mitochondria are dispersed in the cytoplasm, it is generally believed to be inherited only through the maternal line; the ova contain hundreds of them while those few clinging to parts of the sperm do not enter the fertilized ova. It is this factor of unilineal inheritance and the high rate of genetic variation of the thousands of mitochondrial DNA that offer an opportunity to compare population relationships and origins by comparing estimates of times of divergence of ancestral groups. However, establishing phylogenetic, or family tree, relationships between contemporary populations by use of DNA polymorphisms (the RFLPs) depends on some broad assumptions about origins and time calibrations that have become a center of controversy over the use of "molecular clocks." The usefulness of mitochondrial DNA for establishing degrees of relationship also depends on the assumption that it is distributed only through the maternal lineage. Recently a report described mtDNA crossover that could have come only from an inclusion of paternal mitochondria into the ova (Awadalla, Eyre-Walker, and Smith, 1999).

Comparisons of RFLP data taken from 147 people assumed to represent five population groups (African, Asian, Australian, Caucasian, and New Guinean) offered a reconstruction of human ancestry that started a controversy that has continued over the past decade (see Templeton, 2002). Briefly, researchers using RFLPs of mtDNA offered data that traced all geographic populations back to African origins. Their hypothesis was that modern *Homo sapiens* evolved in Africa approximately 200,000 years ago and expanded in numbers, migrating into other parts of the Old World. As these populations moved into other geographic areas they replaced the archaic forms of genus *Homo* (*H. erectus*). Furthermore, since the mtDNA is inherited through the female line, all living humans could trace their mitochondrial DNA back to a female (or females) living 200,000 years ago on the continent of Africa (Cann, 1987, 1988). This phylogenetic reconstruction gave rise to numerous imaginative, and sometimes illogical, interpretations; descriptions of an "African Eve" appeared in popular science and news magazines that explained that all of humankind could be traced to a single woman. The authors of the original theory of an "Out of Africa" origin did little to slow this trend toward ever-broader speculation and continued to expand descriptions of origins to include other populations like Native Americans, Australians, New Guineans, Pacific Islanders, and so on. (Wilson and Cann, 1992). Wilson, Cann, and their co-workers argued that all these geographical groups were of recent ancestry, an argument quite contrary to much of the archaeological record (Thorne and Wolpoff, 1992; Frayer et al., 1993). The stage was set for confrontation with paleontologists over theories of human origins when molecular biologists applied their many laboratory skills to anthropological questions.

There are several technical points to consider, however, when population RFLPs are compared. The first is that some regions of the mtDNA are less susceptible to change, while others fix mutations at higher rates (Jeffreys, 1989). This means that changes in base sequences occur at varying rates, contributing to high variability of mtDNA within a population. Second, the fact that all thirty-seven genes are closely linked limits the usefulness of the mitochondria for evolution studies (Spuhler, 1988). Third, and most important, is the difficulty in calibration of this molecular clock. Some calibrations assume a steady mutation rate (i.e., a constant change in base sequences) at 2 percent per million years, while others argue for a slower rate of less than 1 percent. These calibrations are obtained by comparisons of living human and ape mtDNA, mainly chimpanzee. The faster rate assumes that chimps and humans diverged from a common ancestor some five million years ago, a time estimated by an earlier molecular-clock application of nuclear DNA data (see Templeton, 1985). The slower rate is obtained because paleontological evidence places the time of chimp and human divergence much earlier, approximately nine million years ago. This slower rate of mutational change pushes the "Out of Africa" date back hundreds of thousands of years and is more compatible with the fossil record. Regardless of which date one chooses to accept, or how one may view the "Eve" theory, molecular genetics, with its new and efficient methods, has provided anthropology with an exciting way of measuring human variability. How this variability is to be interpreted and what the results mean have yet to be decided.

GENES AND POPULATIONS: A SUMMARY

Mendel's experiments laid the foundation for modern genetics. The significance of these experiments was that they clearly demonstrated, for the first time, particulate inheritance, and the concept of inheritance by a blending of traits was at last put to rest. There are several points that should be emphasized. The first is that genes are transmitted in groups because they are a part of the chromosomes that exist as paired structures except when separated at meiosis to form the gamete. At this point in cell division, each chromosome goes its own way; there is an independent assortment that takes place, as Mendel showed with his experiments with dihybrid plants. Another way of describing this chromosome assortment is to consider that in humans, who have forty-six, one-half of the chromosomes are provided by each of the parents. However, this is not necessarily the same order in which they, in turn, will be passed to the next generation. As our gametes develop they will contain some mixture of chromosomes from each of our parents so it is highly improbable that any person will possess one-fourth of his or her genome from each grandparent. Our gametes contain a haploid number made up of a mix of paternal and maternal chromosomes. Recall Mendel's second law, the law of independent assortment, which contributes to a large number of possible gamete types—over eight million.

A second point to consider is that a crossing of heterozygotes produces results that will usually differ somewhat by chance alone from the Mendelian ratio (1:2:1). This is to be anticipated, though, and simple statistical tests can show whether this deviation significantly differs from the expected or if it differs simply due to a chance variation. If the difference is statistically significant, then one of the conditions of the Hardy-Weinberg equilibrium may have been violated.

In considering a Mendelian population (breeding population), those sources of variation and the forces for stability will have to be identified and compared in order to understand any change in gene frequency throughout the generations. Sources of new genetic material (mutations) cause small, minor changes in gene frequency in contrast to migration, which can disturb equilibrium in a single generation. If the mutation is one that conveys an advantage, then natural selection can cause a rapid rise in the frequency of the new allele. Mutations, as discussed, play the role of supplying new genetic material and, considering the complexity in the copying of the genes at meiosis, it is surprising that mutation rates are so low. It is likely that many more mutations occur than have been measured, and that these mutations are responsible for the wide range of biochemical variability that we are beginning to recognize in the human species. Most of these deleterious mutations are, fortunately, masked by the normal allele except in those rare cases when they are combined in the homozygote. We now know of the many variations in DNA fragment lengths, recently described, that frequently occur from either crossovers or from base-pair changes.

Population size is a critical consideration in any study of human variation because of the possibility of loss of alleles through chance alone. The effective breeding population consists of those in their reproductive years (generally considered to be between 15 and 44) and is, on the average, roughly one-third of the total population. Add to this the restrictions imposed by society's rules dictating the matings allowed, and chance can be seen as a major factor in gene-frequency change. Also, chance plays a role in reproduction (the variety of gametes is an example), but human behavior channels a good bit of genetic variability along a certain course, as we describe later.

chapter
3

Traits of Simple Inheritance I: Blood Groups and Proteins

With the rise of molecular biology, analysis of DNA structure, and the mapping of the human genome, more and more is learned about the many human phenotypes of simple inheritance determined by a dominant or recessive allele. Some of the better known traits controlled by genes at a single locus (monogenic) include the various blood-group systems, hemoglobins, enzymes, and numerous serum proteins. This list of specific gene traits is continuously growing as improved techniques permit the identification of polymorphisms at more chromosome loci. The expression of these monogenic phenotypes is influenced relatively little by the environment, in contrast to the wide ranges of variation seen in polygenic traits (multiple gene loci). These monogenic traits are described as discontinuous; each trait is either present or absent, in contrast to the broad ranges of the polygenic traits discussed in later chapters. In the study of population genetics and of those factors that cause changes in gene frequencies, monogenic traits are most useful. Some of these simply inherited traits have also been used as markers to estimate the degree of genetic distance between populations and their probable ancestral relationships. Recently, the use of restriction enzymes to "cut" the DNA molecule at precise locations has added considerable knowledge of the restriction fragment length polymorphisms (RFLPs) in many population groups, and it has added an important method of studies of human biological variation, as discussed in Chapter 4. Before discussion of the precise DNA markers, this chapter will take a more historical view and examine those traits of the blood and enzyme systems identified since 1900. The vast amount of data accumulated is useful in comparing populations and their environments.

BLOOD COMPONENTS AND INHERITED TRAITS

Blood serves the vital functions of transporting oxygen and nutrients throughout the body and removing the waste products of metabolism. Blood consists of specialized cells, *erythrocytes* (red blood cells), whose function is to transport oxygen to the tissues, and a yellowish fluid, the plasma. This fluid part of the blood contains a variety of substances vital to the metabolism. Major plasma constituents are *albumin*, a group of large protein molecules that combine with and transport a number of substances; blood-clotting agents—*fibrinogen*, several clotting factors, and small granular bodies called *globulin* fractions (see Figure 3-1). Another type of cell—the *leukocytes* (white blood cells), mainly granulocytes and lymphocytes—is also found in the blood. Normally there are few of these cells in circulation, but during infection their number rises dramatically as the body's defense against invading organisms.

In our discussion of inherited polymorphisms of the blood we are especially interested in the gamma globulin fraction, including *immunoglobulins*, antibodies that attack the foreign substances entering the body, usually bacteria or proteins. These *antibodies*, our main line of defense, are protein molecules that have the ability to attach to certain other chemical molecules on the surfaces of microorganisms. This attachment causes a group of these organisms to cling together (agglutinate). Many foreign substances such as pollen, mold, virus, or bacteria may stimulate the synthesis of *antibodies* in the host's body; substances with this property are called *antigens*.

The antigen is often a complex molecule with multiple combining sites or locations where antibodies can attach but may be viewed as a simple model shown in Figure 3-2. The antibody, however, is a simpler structure and has fewer combining sites. When the antibody connects with an antigen, there are still sites available to connect with other antibodies and antigens until all combining sites are full. The result is a linkage that ultimately makes it possible for the body's defense to destroy foreign substances or to render them

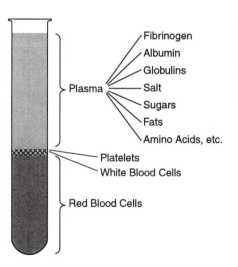

FIGURE 3-1
Blood Components. When a sample of blood is placed in a test tube and spun in a centrifuge the heavier components settle to the bottom with the lighter products and fluids at the top. The diagram lists these major components, the types of cells, and the products in the plasma.

Fibrinogen
Albumin
Globulins
Plasma — Salt
Sugars
Fats
Amino Acids, etc.

Platelets
White Blood Cells

Red Blood Cells

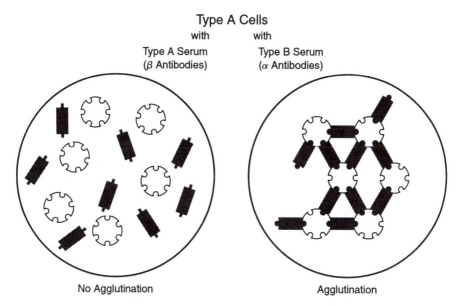

FIGURE 3-2   Diagram of Antibodies–Antigen Reactions. These diagrams show the relationships between red blood-cell antigens (type A) and the two types of serum. No agglutination will occur when type-A cells are mixed with serum from a type-A person. The antibodies are anti-B type (β antibodies) and are not attracted by the combining sites of the type A (left diagram). When type-A cells are mixed with serum from a type-B person, the anti-A antibodies (α antibodies) combine with the cells and agglutination occurs, causing the cells to cling together in a group (right diagram).

harmless by preventing their multiplication. The efficiency of this system depends on the ability to produce antibodies of the right kind and in sufficient quantities.

THE BLOOD GROUPS

There are antibodies in each person's system that are, of necessity, compatible with the individual's own circulatory system. But if blood from one person is mixed with blood from another, then a reaction may occur between the antigens and antibodies of the two individuals. Before 1900, transfusions were used only as a last resort in an attempt to save the patient's life. Often the transfused blood would cause shock and even death because, as we now know, of agglutination of the incompatible antibodies and red cells. At times, though, transfusions were successful, because some blood combinations were compatible.

In 1900 Karl Landsteiner, an Austrian immunologist, began to systematically analyze the pattern of agglutination between the blood donor and recipients. Tests were made by mixing the blood serum from one person with red blood cells from another. Only certain combinations caused an agglutination of the red cells. If a reaction occurred between serum from person A and red cells from person B, Landsteiner found the reverse was also true; serum from B would agglutinate cells from A. Throughout thousands of tests Landsteiner found these results to be consistent, but there were some individuals whose cells could not be agglutinated by either anti-A or anti-B serum. With identity of type, transfusions could now be made safely if the donor and recipient bloods were matched.

Since this original discovery, a number of other major blood groups have been identified by cross-reaction between red blood cells and serum from different individuals and also by reaction of blood cells to specially prepared antiserum. Such antiserum is prepared by injecting human cells into laboratory animals—rabbits, for example—and extracting samples of antiserum made by the animal. This antihuman serum is then tested against a variety of human blood samples and the reactions tabulated. In testing blood cells taken from numerous individuals, agglutination reactions are noted with some antiserum and not with others. Plant extracts have also been applied in this way. Table 3-1 lists several of the more clinically important blood groups, including those useful today in the study of human genetics.

TABLE 3-1   Major Blood Group Systems

SYSTEM	ANTIGENS	GENOTYPES	PHENOTYPES	DATE OF DISCOVERY
ABO	A_1, A_2, B	OO, AA, BB, AB	O, A_1, A_2, B, AB	1900
Lewis	Le^a, Le^b	Le^aLe^a, Le^bLe^b, LeLe	Le (a + b −), Le (a − b +), Le (a − b −)	1946
Rh	(see Table 3-6a)			
MNSs	M, N, S, s	MS/MS, MS/Ms, Ms/Ms, MS/NS, MS/Ns, Ms/NS, Ms/Ns, NS/NS, NS/Ns, Ns/Ns	M, N, MN, S, s, Ss	1927
P	P_1, P_2	P_1P_1, P_1P_2, P_2P_2 P_1p, P_2p, pp	P_1, P_2, p	1927
Lutheran	Lu^a, Lu^b	Lu^aLu^a, Lu^aLu^b, Lu^bLu^b	Lu (a + b −), Lu (a − b +)	1945
Kell	K (Kell) k (cellano)	KK, Kk, kk	K + k −, k + k +, K − k +, (K − k −)	1946
Duffy	Fy^a, Fy^b	Fy^aFy^a, Fy^aFy^b, Fy^bFy^b, FyFy	Fy (a + b −), Fy (a + b +), Fy (a − b +), Fy (a − b −)	1950
Kidd	Jk^a, Jk^b	Jk^aJk^a, Jk^aJk^b, Jk^bJk^b	Jk (a + b −), Jk (a + b +), Jk (a − b +), Jk (a − b −)	1951
Diego	Di^a	Di^aDi^a, Di^aDi, DiDi	Di (a +), Di (a −)	1955
Sutter	Js^a	Js^aJs^a, Js^aJs, JsJs	Js (a +), Js (a −)	
Auberger	Au^a	Au^aAu^a, Au^aAu, AuAu	Au (a +), Au (a −)	1961
Xg	Xg^a	Xg^aY, XgY, Xg^aXg^a, Xg^aXg, XgXg	Xg (a +), Xg (a −)	1962

Source: Based on Giblett, 1969; Mourant, 1983, and Race and Sanger, 1975.

The ABO Blood Group

The ABO blood group is the best known of a long list of the red-cell antigens because of its medical importance, and, since its discovery, millions of people throughout the world have had their blood types recorded. Analysis of these data and comparison of ABO types in families has shown that the type was passed on by Mendelian inheritance. The antigens are under the control of at least three alleles at a locus on *chromosome 9*; the alleles A and B are codominants whereas the type-O allele is recessive. The genetics of the ABO system become more complex as additional alleles are detected. For example, there are actually two types of A (A_1 and A_2) that increase the number of alleles at the ABO locus to four.

Within the blood plasma of each person there are antibodies related to the type of red blood cell antigen. The antibody type as well as the antigen type are under genetic control, and the pattern of inheritance is listed here.

GENOTYPE	PHENOTYPE	ANTIBODIES
	(Blood Type)	
AA } AO }	A	anti-B
BB } BO }	B	anti-A
AB	AB	none
OO	O	anti-a, b

This diagram illustrates that the genotypes AA and AO determine the same blood type (the type of antigen carried by the red blood cell). Persons of this type will have anti-B antibodies in their plasma, so blood from a type-A person cannot be donated to a type-B person. These antibodies are "naturally" occurring, that is, compatible antibodies are normally present in blood serum; their production need not be stimulated by an antigen from external sources. The antibodies (a and b) in a type-O person are somewhat different from those in A or B types; they are smaller in size and their reactions are weaker.

Soluble ABO Antigens and Modifying Genes

When the ABO group was first studied, it was assumed that type O was simply the absence of antigens A and B, and a type-O person's blood would not react to either antiserum. Further study showed that certain other antisera could be found to react with type-O blood cells. The reaction indicated the probability of an antigen on type-O cells and was designated *type H*. The antigen is a molecular fragment on the surface of the blood cell that is common to both the A and B antigens, because type-A and type-O blood cells will also react with the anti-H serum. The reaction is weaker than that of the cells from a type-O person. However, the order of strength of reactions is $O > A_1 > B > A_2$. This H substance may be identifiable in the saliva and other bodily fluids just as the antigens of type A and B of most persons may be present in soluble form (around 75 percent in the British Isles and higher in other regions).

The presence of soluble ABH antigens in bodily fluids, such as saliva, tears, semen, milk, gastric juice, and other watery secretions, is determined by a dominant allele at another locus, and the person who is homozygous or heterozygous is described as a secretor. The inheritance of the ability to secrete the ABH antigens in soluble form is shown by the following genotypes:

GENOTYPE	PHENOTYPE
Se Se >————————————————————>	secretor
Se se >————————————————————>	secretor
se se >————————————————————>	nonsecretor

The existence of these water-soluble forms throughout the body tissues has made it possible to study the structure of the ABH antigens because they can be analyzed chemically. The antigen's molecular structure consists of a chain of simple sugar molecules linked to protein or lipid compound. The A and B antigens are alike except for a different sugar at the terminal end of a common chain forming the H antigen, as shown in Figure 3-3. Without one or the other of these sugar molecules (2 or 3), the molecular structure determines a type O (Race and Sanger, 1975). Since this structure was identified by analysis of the soluble antigens, the antigen on the red-cell surface has been described and confirmed this basic structure (Yamamoto et al., 1990). In Figure 3-4, the process of forming the completed structure is by synthesis of a precursor followed by the formation of a longer intermediate chain in which, if an H gene is present on chromosome 19, an H antigen is completed (shown as step 3). If the individual lacks an A or B transferase enzyme, no further synthesis takes place and the chain of sugars stops at step 3. However, if an A or B allele is present, then an additional sugar is added as in step 4. The differences between the blood type antigens appear to be only simple base substitutions in a segment of DNA at the ABO locus on chromosome 9. These base substitutions determine if an enzyme (A or B transferase) will be present to complete the change from step 3 to step 4. The DNA for allele O is identical except for a single base deletion which prevents coding for the enzyme transferasee. This simple change blocks step 4 and prevents the addition of a terminal sugar. A critical point to consider is that the intermediate chain must be converted to the H antigen before the A or B antigens can be produced.

Bombay Blood Type

The complexity of the ABO system was underscored by the discovery of persons in India whose red blood cells did not agglutinate when mixed with anti-A, anti-B, or anti-H serum. This added evidence that another genetic locus influenced the expression of the ABO blood types. These persons should have had an ABO type given the data from studies of their family pedigrees, but they did not. Further surveys showed that this rare condition is seldom found in any population except among Mohorati speakers in and around Bombay, India, where the frequency is about 1 in 13,000, and on Reunion Island in the Indian

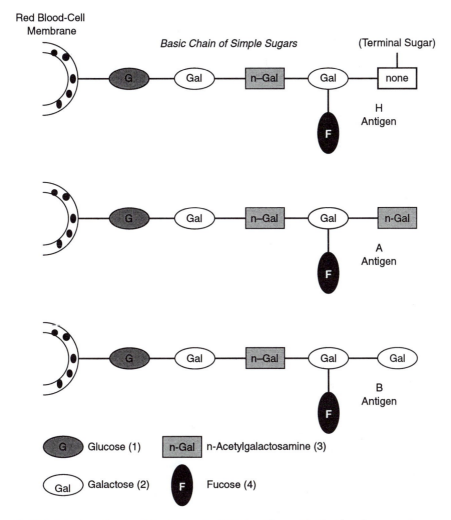

FIGURE 3-3   **Basic Chemical Structure for the ABO Blood Group.** (Modified from Ganong, 2003.)

Ocean (see Gerard et al., 1982). Such persons are said to have the *Bombay* blood type and lack ABH antigens on red blood cells or the soluble form in the serum. This condition, the Bombay blood group, is inherited as a simple recessive and may be understood as the lack of a substance that is essential as a precursor for the structure of the A or B antigen (see Figure 3-4). This process of an intermediate step (step 2) to H antigen is under the control of another locus on chromosome 19, where two alleles have been identified, a dominant and a recessive. Without a dominant allele (H), step 2 to 3 cannot be completed, and a person with such a genotype (hh) would have neither A or B antigen. The recessive (h) is rare and a homozygous genotype (Bombay type) is seldom found, but when it occurs, the person will not type as A or B and his or her blood plasma will contain anti-H antibodies.

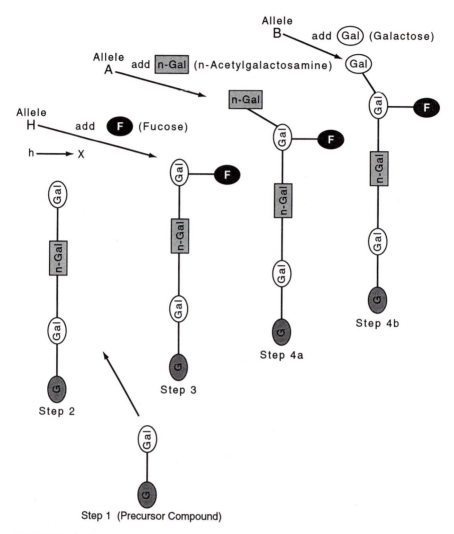

FIGURE 3-4   Synthesis of ABH Chemical Structure. (Data from Hakomori, 1986; Mange and Mange, 1990.)

The Significance of the ABO Blood Group

The importance of the ABO blood type for many forms of medical treatment is beyond dispute; it is essential to identify a person's type so a proper match can be made between donor and recipient. The question of what physiological functions this genetically controlled trait may have is another matter. Also, what, if any, is the significance of the pattern of geographical distribution among the world's people? Since the initial discovery of the ABO system in 1900, many millions of persons around the world have been typed and explanations have been sought for the uneven frequencies found among

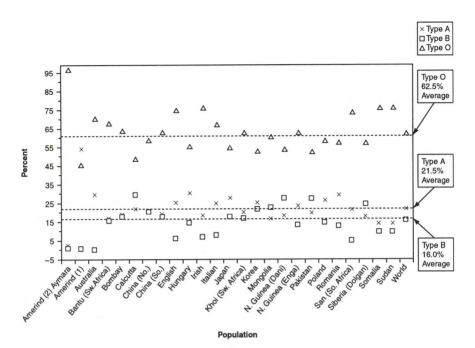

FIGURE 3-5 **ABO Blood Group Distribution.** These twenty-six populations show an uneven distribution of the three types of ABO blood. Most fall at or near the 65 percent world average for type O, the most common. The exception is found in some Native Americans whose type O reaches nearly 100 percent. Type A, the second most common, ranges from near zero to 55 percent. By contrast, the rarest, type B, is significantly below the average of 16 percent, and it is at or near zero in numerous populations. (Data selected from Boyd, 1963a; Mourant, 1983; Race and Sanger, 1975.)

the world's populations. The average frequencies of the ABO alleles for the entire species may serve as a baseline against which individual populations or population complexes may be compared. Allele O (62.5 percent) is the most frequent and the B (16 percent) the least, with allele A (21.5 percent) slightly higher. Populations in many parts of the world deviate widely from these averages, but, with a few exceptions (Australian Aborigines and Native Americans in particular), alleles A and B are usually greater than zero and seldom rise above 25 percent.

Figure 3-5 plots several large populations selected for divergent frequencies of their ABO types. Type-O frequencies fluctuate widely about the world average as does Type B; where type B is highest, type O is lowest. Type A ranges about the world average from 2.4 to 54 percent; this range changes to 14 to 29 percent if the Native American samples are excluded. These differences are unlikely to have arisen by chance alone, though genetic drift played some part earlier in human prehistory because of small founding populations. The key question is: Are different environments influencing survival? A complex of several disease organisms may be acting on different genotypes of blood components. Though the nature of the selection has yet to be fully understood, a number of possible explanations have been offered that relate to differential fertility and variations in mortality rates throughout the life cycle.

Differential Fertility

Differences in the rate of live births of type-O mothers indicates some type of incompatibility; type-O women produce fewer children than expected when the fathers were either type A or B. In addition to reduced fertility in cases of incompatible matings, if the male parent is heterozygous AO or BO, then there is a significantly greater number of OO children produced by a type-O mother (Matsunaga and Hiraizuma, 1962). On the other hand, type-B mothers were reported to have a significantly higher average number of offspring than type-O mothers for all male parent blood types (Kelso et al., 1995). These seemingly contradictory results may be because of the heterozygosity of the parents' genotypes that were not reported.

The differential fertility may act in the following ways. First, there is a selection at the *prezygotic* stage (prior to fertilization of the ovum). In a type-O female there appears to be a greater chance of fertilization by the sperm carrying the type-O gene, so genotypes of the children differ significantly from the expected as in the following:

Parents   AO (male) $\times$ OO (female)

Children   AO   OO   (>50 percent)

With the parental AO and OO genotypes, there are two possible genotypes of the offspring as indicated. The chance of either occurring is 50 percent (the Mendelian ratio is 1:1), but, in fact, a statistically significant greater number of OO offspring are produced. This apparent selection may be due to the antibodies in vaginal secretions that react with sperm specific for type A, thereby reducing the probability of fertilization. Sperm have been shown to possess specific antigen reactions, as in the example of a decrease in number of males produced in later birth order (parity) due to an increase in maternal antibodies against the Y-chromosome bearing sperm.

A second reason for reduction in fertility of incompatible matings is fetal loss due to antibodies A and B in the type-O mother. The naturally occurring A and B antibodies in the O mother do not readily cross the placenta, but some mothers make an anti-A and anti-B that can easily diffuse through the placenta membranes and enter the fetal bloodstream. Once there, they can disrupt development and may even cause fetal death. Overall, several studies show that women who carry fetuses with ABO blood types incompatible with their own have a greater risk of spontaneous abortion. The ease with which some antibodies from the maternal system can pass into the fetal bloodstream can be a danger similar to that known to exist for Rh hemolytic disease (see below).

In sum, fetal–maternal incompatibility may contribute to a reduced fertility rate, increased spontaneous abortion early in pregnancy, and hemolytic disease of the

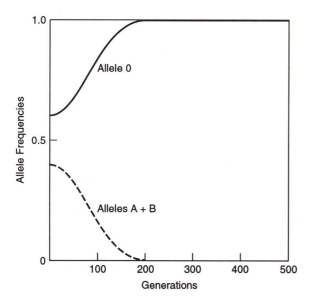

FIGURE 3-6   ABO Incompatibility Leads to Fixation of the O Allele.
Fetal–maternal incompatibility of ABO type contributes to reduced
fertility in the type-O mother. The maternal antibodies select against
a type-A or type-B fetus while favoring a type O. The result is that the
allele O would become fixed in a population within about 200
generations if no counterselective forces are involved, that is, neither
type-A nor type-B persons have an advantage in certain
environments. (Source: Etkin and Eaton, 1983.)

neonate (once in a thousand pregnancies). These are strong selective forces favoring
the increase in the frequency of the O allele over A or B and should lead to rapid fixation. In other words, all populations with such incompatible matings would eventually contain only persons of blood type O (Figure 3-6). With the exception of many
Native Americans, most of the world has populations with a mixture of all three alleles
(see Figure 3-5). Such a mixture suggests other factors have prevented fixation of the
allele O. The question is: What factors favor a preservation of A and B alleles?

Disease Incidence and the ABO Blood Groups

The association between ABO blood types and certain diseases was considered early
in the study of red-cell antigen systems. Namely, was there a significant correlation with
a specific disease? Analysis of thousands of hospital records compared the blood types
of patients with the disease for which they were treated. In this way a wide variety of
diseases were listed for many thousands of patients, but the early results, because of
statistical errors, were disappointing and discouraged further investigation for nearly

twenty-five years. Later these errors were corrected and the search for disease correlations was renewed.

A study of the frequency of stomach cancer in England revealed a difference between regions: The mortality rate was higher in the North than in the South. Aird and associates (1953) at first thought the difference might be due to some environmental factor, and there did prove to be a difference in water hardness; a higher calcium concentration was found in those areas with the lowest stomach cancer rate. The correlation was slight, but when the ABO blood types were compared, there was a higher number of type-A persons with this type of cancer. These results encouraged numerous investigators to expand studies of this medically important blood group. Significant associations were found with a number of tumors as well as with several other metabolic diseases (see Table 3-2). Interestingly, correlations continued to identify gastrointestinal type disorders, from duodenal ulcers to stomach and colon cancers and cancer of the pancreas. This turned attention to the soluble form of the ABH antigens and their function in the digestive tract.

Though the distribution of secretors and nonsecretors throughout the world's populations is not as well recorded as that of the ABO red-cell types, the soluble antigens in tissues and fluids throughout the body of secretors may be a significant factor in our response to foreign chemicals or microrganims. The presence of soluble antigens (ABH) in a majority of people, plus the fact that many food substances, once broken down into their molecular constituents, have specific reactions with the ABH substances, make it highly probable that there is a complex series of reactions between antigens, antibodies, and macromolecules within the gastrointestinal tract. Many of these reactions may enhance digestion or retard it, depending on the substances involved, or there may be chronic irritation of the fine mucous linings of the intestines. At any rate, it is more than a coincidence that a number of the diseases associated with the ABO system are localized within the digestive system. This area of research has not been fully explored, but immunological studies point out the likelihood of gut flora, similar to the blood-group substances, stimulating the production of antibodies appropriate to the individual's RBC antigen. Hence, a type-A person will make anti-B antibodies in response to stimulus by substances in the gut flora and will tolerate antigens similar to type A (Roitt, 1988). Given the wide variety of foods that omnivorous *Homo sapiens* can and has subsisted on for ten of thousands of years, the digestive system would be an area subject to natural selection.

The chronic diseases listed in Table 3-2 have been used in support of the original hypothesis that selection has been acting to influence polymorphisms of the ABO system. Note, however, that these diseases are of the type that usually afflict an individual later in adult life, near the end of the reproductive period. It is unlikely, then, that ulceration, diabetes, or cancer would influence a person's reproductive fitness. However, dietary–antigen relationships should be considered because of strong environmental and cultural influences.

Infectious diseases offer several interesting possibilities for explanation of the adaptability of blood groups. Certain blood types may cause an individual to be more or less susceptible to disease-causing organisms, and several relationships between blood type

TABLE 3-2   Significant Associations between Blood Groups and Noninfectious Disease

DIAGNOSIS	NO. OF SERIES	NO. OF PATIENTS	CONTROLS	COMPARISON	
Neoplasias of the intestinal tract					
Cancer, stomach	101	55,434	1,852,288	A:O	1.22
Cancer of colon and rectum	17	7,435	183,286	A:O	1.11
Malignant tumors of salivary glands	2	285	12,968	A:O	1.64
Cancer, pancreas	13	817	108,408	A:O	1.24
Cancer, mouth and pharynx	2	757	41,098	A:O	1.25
Other neoplasias					
Cancer, cervix	19	11,927	197,577	A:O	1.13
Cancer, corpus uteri	14	2,598	160,602	A:O	1.15
Cancer, ovary	17	2,326	243,914	A:O	1.28
Cancer, breast	24	9,503	355,281	A:O	1.08
Multiple primary cancer	2	433	7,823	A:O	1.43
Nonmalignant tumors Nonmalignant salivary tumors	2	581	12,968	A:O	2.02
Other internal diseases					
Duodenal ulcers	44	26,039	407,518	O:A	1.35
				O:A+B+AB	1.33
Gastric ulcers	41	22,052	448,354	O:A	1.17
				O:A+B+AB	1.18
Duodenal and gastric ulcers	6	957	120,544	O:A	1.53
				O:A+B+AB	1.36
Bleeding ulcers (gastric and duodenal)	2	1,869	28,325	O:A	1.46
				O:A+B+AB	1.51
Rheumatic diseases	17	6,589	179,385	A:O	1.24
				A+B+AB:O	1.23
Pernicious anemia	13	2,077	119,989	A:O	1.25
Diabetes mellitus	20	15,778	612,819	A:O	1.07
				A+B+AB:O	1.07
Ischemic heart disease	12	2,763	218,727	A:O	1.18
				A+B+AB:O	1.17
Cholecystitis and cholelithiasis	10	5,950	112,928	A:O	1.17
Eosinophilia	3	730	1,096	A:O	2.38
				A+B+AB:O	2.13
Thromboembolic disease	5	1,026	287,246	A:O	1.61
				A+B+AB:O	1.60

Source: Examples selected from Mourant et al., 1978; Vogel and Motulsky, 1986.

TABLE 3-3   ABO Blood Groups and Infectious Diseases

DISEASE	REPORTED GREATER SUSCEPTIBILITY (TYPE)
Paratyphoid	O
Cholera	O
Plague	O
Scarlet fever	O and B
Escherichia coli (some strains)	B
Smallpox	A
Bronchial pneumonia	A
Rheumatic heart disease	A

Source: Examples selected from Mourant et al., 1978; Vogel and Motulsky, 1986.

and diseases are listed in Table 3-3. Type O is recorded most frequently in disease associations, which would explain, in part, the balancing effect countering the fertility advantage of the type-O mother noted above. The second most frequent association is type A, with three important infectious diseases, in contrast to the seldom involved type B.

Some of the organisms that cause these diseases have been demonstrated to be similar, antigenically, to either the A, B, or H antigens; that is, they have chemical structures on the coatings of their outer shells that are very similar in form to the antigens on the surface of the red blood cells. The explanation follows that the more similarity between the chemical structures of disease organisms and ABH antigens, the less likely is the individual's defense system to make antibodies against the disease organism. Thus the smallpox virus has a chemical specificity similar to type-A antigen. A person with type-A blood would be more susceptible to smallpox than would an O or B type. The findings of Vogel and his associates (Vogel, 1975) described a mortality of 50 percent in type-A persons (approximately four times higher than in B or O persons) among populations in India, the region that suffered from the world's last smallpox epidemic. As a matter of fact, the frequency of A is much lower among populations of the Indian subcontinent than among Europeans, perhaps a reflection of India's long history of smallpox epidemics.

Another organism, the plague bacterium with its H antigen specificity, appears to be more lethal to type-O individuals. During the Middle Ages and later, plague epidemics were recurrent, with enormous loss of life. In Europe, the first and most lethal pandemic of 1345 caused up to 50 percent mortality in the cities. In wave after wave, this disease passed through the population, but with decreasing fury, until the last reported epidemic of 1645. If one considers the high rate of mortality even in the later periods, then the effectiveness of the disease as a selective agent can be appreciated. Any advantage of inherited resistance, no matter how slight, would be passed on to future generations. This seems to be the case for the blood groups. Those regions of the world where plague has the longest history are the very regions where type O is found at the lowest frequency today. Areas that had suffered through many outbreaks of the epidemic over the centuries have a proportionately higher A and B frequency today than regions where plague had never been reported.

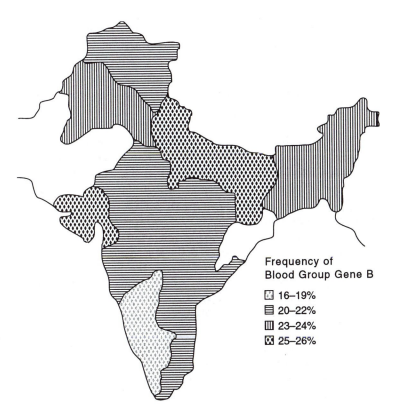

FIGURE 3–7   Distribution of Blood Type B in India. Plague and smallpox have been
major causes of death at all ages throughout India well into the twentieth century. These
diseases were likely sources of natural selection at the ABO locus and are probable
causes of the high frequency of type B. (Based on Buchi, 1968.)

Vogel (1975) points to central Asia, India, and Mesopotamia as major plague centers, areas where populations have the lowest frequency of O. The selection against a
type-O person in populations with a long history of plague would, over the generations, decrease the frequency of this allele. If in the same populations there was also
selection against type-A allele because of smallpox, then both the A and O alleles
would be present in low frequencies. In such populations suffering from the double
threat of smallpox and plague, type-B allele would occur at high frequencies, as it
does in India, where B frequencies are among the highest in the world (Figure 3-7).

Another possible source of natural selection is the peculiar behavior of insects.
Some species of insect vectors appear to prefer one particular host over another.
The temperature or color of the skin, or the chemical compounds excreted, may
influence choice (Wu, 2000). Some studies have demonstrated that mosquitoes have
preferences for the type of blood they choose to feed on. How the insect choice is

made or what chemical substance attracts them is not known, but type O was the most frequent preference. Volunteers were used to record the frequency of bites, and those persons with type-O blood were bitten more often than those with type A or B. Should subsequent studies support these preliminary results, then malaria and other mosquito-borne diseases may be added to the list of disease selection at the ABO locus (Wood, 1974).

Population size is another factor that can influence the course and intensity of natural selection. A glance at the list of infectious diseases in Table 3-3 shows that many are of the type commonly found in larger populations. One is tempted to speculate that only in relatively recent times has selection operated to produce the ranges of ABO gene-frequency variation. Since the Neolithic, 10,000 years ago when *Homo sapiens* developed agriculture and adapted to settled village life, people have lived in close contact within dense settlements, exposed to food and water pollution throughout their lives. Supporting evidence is provided by the fact that the more isolated groups, especially those that have been involved with the development of dense, sedentary lifestyles only in the last few hundred generations, are the ones with the highest type-A and -O frequencies—groups such as the northwest Europeans. The Basques of northern Spain, Sami (Lapps), Australian Aborigines, and Polynesians are some examples of isolation and high A frequencies. Type B is consistently low except in a few isolates in or near Europe (Table 3-4).

By contrast, the populations whose ancestors established the earliest large, densely populated, agriculturally based communities are those with the lowest A frequencies (Native American groups excepted). A majority of India's populations, Thailand, and many Middle Eastern groups illustrate this relationship. This hypothesis is based on

TABLE 3-4   Blood Group Gene Frequencies in Isolates in and near Europe

	GENE PERCENTAGES					
ISOLATES	A	B	O	M	d	K
Icelanders	20	5	75	58	37	5
Irish (Republic)	17	7	76	57	43	4
Lapps	37	9	54	52	16	1
Basques	24	2	74	54	56	5
Béarnais	24	4	72	49	59	3
Corsicans	22	3	75	65	35	4
Sardinians	20	7	73	75	22	3
Walsers	21	5	73	51	41	8
Bergamasques	24	6	70	56	43	5
Valle Ladine	20	3	77	78	56	
Svani (Caucasia)	23	7	70	65	41	
Saudi Arabians	16	11	75	72	25	6
Towara Bedouin	16	9	74	52	31	13
Jebeliya Bedouin	12	26	62	66	54	18
Ait Haddidu Berbers	7	5	89	24	23	4

Source: Selected from A.E. Mourant, 1983.

the diverse data of the reactions between the red-cell antigens of the ABO and several diseases. The problem is a highly complex one; some selective forces may be acting in opposition to each other, as in the case of smallpox and plague, but the net effect is to alter a breeding population's gene combinations.

With all the information that we possess on the blood groups, confirmation of adaptive significance still escapes us, but a range of possibilities exist as human adaptations to their environments change over time. As Vogel stated, the blood-group antigens probably played an important role in *Homo sapiens* evolution and adaptation:

> In earlier centuries, infections have killed a high percentage of mankind before reproductive age. Hence, selective pressure was very strong, and genetic adaptation to infections must have strongly influenced our present gene pool. (1968: 366)

Such influence is especially strong during infancy, that time of the life cycle when selection can be most influential in shaping the gene pool of future generations. High infant mortality, of 50 percent or more of live births, was once the norm and, even in the twentieth century, rates of between 10 to 25 percent have been reported. Often these deaths were due to various forms of gastrointestinal ailments, or infant diarrhea, which is especially severe in those populations that must rely on a polluted water supply. This continues to be a problem in many underdeveloped countries today where life expectancy is short, and infant and childhood mortality remain high while the developed world's mortality has declined (see Chapter 10).

Because diarrheal disease once was, and continues to be, a major cause of mortality today in many parts of the world, blood type has probably been a significant influence on survival. A high rate of infant infectious diarrhea caused by various strains of *E. coli* bacteria is frequently reported, and often the ABO antigens are implicated. The shifting of A- or B-type antigen specificity in *E. coli* strains during the epidemics in eastern Europe in the 1950s alternately caused more frequent episodes in type-B or in type-A infants. In both examples, the infectious diarrheal disease was more acute in both than in type-O infants (Vogel and Motulsky, 1986). Such a recent episode of selection due to infectious disease underscores the probable influences over the last few thousand years of human history as we became more sedentary with increasing population density.

Differences in reactions of the ABO antigens with several kinds of intestinal bacteria have been noted previously, and, as a result, the severity of the diseases that the organisms cause may be expected to vary with blood type. There is no more critical period than when infants are adjusting to the microbial groups common to their environmental setting. This period, and the period of stress on the young child's system during weaning, are times of extreme selective pressures. Adding to this all the parasites and microbes encountered in many tropical regions, marginal diets, and the lack of suitable weaning foods, one can easily see that any difference in susceptibility to infection, even though slight, will lead to extensive differences in mortality rates.

The Rh Blood Group

Another antigen group on the red blood cell surface is a complex polypeptide structure that can cause multiple reactions to several antisera. This *Rhesus system* is second only to the ABO in clinical importance and is the one most often involved in a hemolytic disease of the new born (HDN). In this disease, many red blood cells of the developing fetus and newborn are destroyed by maternal antibodies attacking the fetal cells. Though the disease was known for many years, no explanation could be offered until 1940, when Landsteiner and Weiner showed that anti-Rhesus serum[1] agglutinated red cells of about 85 percent of New York patients tested (see Mourant et al., 1978). The 15 percent of the individuals who did not react to the serum were identified as Rhesus (Rh) negative. The research continued and, about a year later, the investigators discovered that mothers who had given birth to infants with HDN were Rh negative; their blood cells did not react to the anti-Rh factor, but the blood cells of their infants did. These Rh+ infants' RBC had stimulated production of maternal antibodies (see Figure 3-8).

Since the 1940s numerous studies of the Rh system have revealed a large number of Rh antigen types that are inherited as a Mendelian trait. The multiple reactions or potentials for reactions are inherited as if they were determined by three closely linked loci, each with two alleles (each allele determines one antigenic response to an antiserum). The notations Cc, Dd, Ee represent the pair of alleles at each locus; the lower case does not indicate recessivity or dominance, since each allele determines the presence of an antigen, though an antibody for d has not been discovered yet. Because the three loci are so closely linked that crossover rarely occurs, the loci are written together as a combination (haplotype) to represent the genotype. A common genotype might appear as

$$\frac{CDE}{cde}$$

which shows that all antigens in the systems are represented and would interact with the antiserum especially prepared for these tests.

Each parent with the genotypes in Table 3-5 would test positive for C, but, because they are heterozygous for the alleles, the probability is that one out of four offspring would be negative for this antigen. The female, according to her genotype, is homozygous for gene d. She would not react to the anti-D serum test (this individual would be considered Rh negative). However, because her husband has both d and D, there is a 50 percent chance that a child produced by this mating would have the D allele and would be Rh positive. There is also a possibility, in this case,

---

[1]Anti-Rhesus serum was made by injection of rhesus monkey red blood cells into rabbits who then made anitserum specific for the rhesus. Testing against human red cells showed that most people had blood cells that would react with the Rh antiserum.

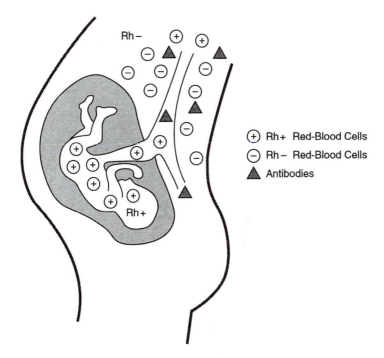

Rh−

(+) Rh+ Red-Blood Cells
(−) Rh− Red-Blood Cells
▲ Antibodies

Rh+

FIGURE 3-8 Reaction of an Rh-Negative Mother to Her Rh-Positive Fetus. If the fetus of an Rh-negative mother and Rh-positive father is Rh positive there is the risk of the mother becoming sensitized by the fetal red-blood cells. A few of these cells may enter the mother's bloodstream and, because they are Rh+, they will stimulate the production of antibodies. These antibodies can freely cross the placenta and destroy the fetal red-blood cells.

of the fetus's stimulating anti-D antibody production in the maternal system.[2] The anti-D antibodies from the mother's bloodstream easily cross through the placenta into the fetal circulation, where they agglutinate and then destroy the blood cells (see Figure 3-8). When such an event occurs, there is the risk of the fetus developing the hemolytic disease. The risk increases with each pregnancy as the mother's system becomes sensitized from carrying previous Rh negative fetuses and her anti-Rh antibodies reach a high level. Naturally, if the genotype of the fetus is negative for D, there would be no danger. Though most of the incompatibility problem is caused by the D allele (about 90 percent), there are some cases due to the E and C alleles and other rare antigen reactions.

---

[2]Blood cells rarely cross the placenta to exchange between maternal and fetal circulation. At birth, however when the placenta is separating from the uterine wall, a few fetal cells can enter the maternal circulation. If the mother's blood type is different from the fetus's, then her system will make antibodies. The antibody level will rise with each pregnancy and so increase the risk of hemolytic disease.

TABLE 3-5   Mode of Inheritance of Rh System (Fisher-Race Notation)

MALE GENOTYPE			FEMALE GENOTYPE
CDE			Cde
cde			cdE

GENOTYPES OF OFFSPRING		
gametes	Cde	cdE
CDE	$\dfrac{\text{CDE}}{\text{Cde}}$	$\dfrac{\text{CDE}}{\text{cdE}}$
cde	$\dfrac{\text{cde}}{\text{Cde}}$	$\dfrac{\text{cde}}{\text{cdE}}$

Over the decades since the discovery of the Rhesus system, treatments have been developed that reduce the risk of erythroblastosis. If the woman is identified as Rh− and there is a possibility of an Rh+ fetus, then some way must be found to prevent her immune system from making antibodies against the antigen D (Rh+). This may be accomplished shortly after the first pregnancy (usually right after delivery) by injection of antiserum (anti-D). This antiserum will attack any fetal blood cells that may have crossed into the mother's bloodstream during labor. Since antibody production does not begin until after 72 hours from delivery, this prevents her immune system from becoming sensitized and thus reduces the risk for each succeeding pregnancy. As an additional protective measure, since fetal blood cells may rarely cross the placental boundary during pregnancy, some antiserum (anti-D) may be injected after the twenty-eighth week of gestation. Since such medical treatment has been available only since the middle of the twentieth century, the question is how allele d could be maintained at such a high frequency in parts of the world when it can cause such problems in pregnancy (Vogel and Motulsky, 1986).

The answer to this riddle has been sought for decades, with no satisfactory answer, nor is there any explanation of a selective value for the Rhesus negative. Clues may be found eventually in the frequencies of the alleles throughout the world's populations. The distribution of the Rh alleles shown in Figure 3-9 provides evidence that strongly supports the argument that selection may have acted on this locus also, though the only disease association thus far reported has been a higher than expected *type D* among patients suffering from rheumatic fever. The most frequent explanation offered for the Rh system is that hemolytic incompatibility serves to regulate the frequency of d(r). This allele, responsible for approximately 90 percent of the hemolytic disease in the newborn, declines to near zero in a population within a few generations when selection is most intense. Yet, despite the selection against offspring of Rh incompatibility matings, a high frequency of d has been maintained in several populations throughout the generations; it is greater than 50 percent in the Basque of northern Spain. These high frequencies suggest that natural selection is operating to maintain a deleterious allele, probably through selection for the heterozygote as we have seen

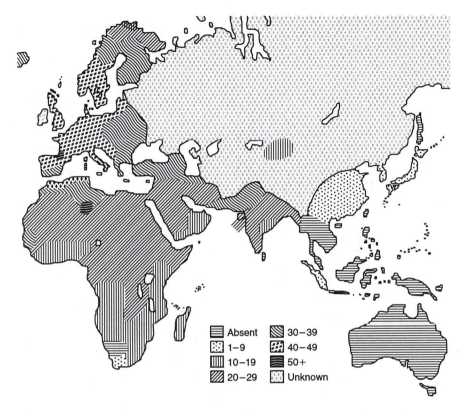

FIGURE 3-9   Percentage Frequency of Blood-Type Allele r (Rh negative). (After Hulse, 1971.)

in other examples. We do not know what the heterozygote Dd advantage may be, but whatever it is, a balance has been maintained and the allele persists at high frequencies in several European and African populations (Mourant, 1983).

Some Minor Blood Groups

In addition to the systems already considered, there are a number of less well known antigens on the surface of the RBC surface. These blood groups are discovered, often by accident, when a patient has an unexpected reaction to a blood transfusion or gives birth to an infant with hemolytic disease even though the mother was Rh+. Careful immunological studies of such cases eventually identify the particular antigen involved. Tests of family members with the new antisera often show a variety of responses and a new antigen system is then established. Often these systems appear to be under the control of a single pair of alleles and some of these new antigens have proved useful in population genetic studies because of an uneven distribution. Such systems have relatively little clinical importance but can be valuable as genetic markers.

The MN System.   The MN system was first discovered in 1927 when Landsteiner and Levine were able to prepare two types of antiserum against human red cells that would identify three types of individuals.[3] The symbols M and N were used to describe the genotypes of this new system. Inheritance of MN type appeared to be of this kind:

MN	X	MN	genotypes (parents)
MM	MN	NN	genotypes (children)
M	MN	N	phenotypes (children)

These alleles are codominants and each determines a characteristic response to an antiserum. The heterozygote (MN) individual would react with both antisera and this would distinguish this individual from the persons who react only with anti-M or anti-N. Unlike the ABO or the Rh systems, the MN system does not appear to have any medical importance—probably because no antibodies are known to occur in humans. Antibodies neither occur naturally nor are induced (as in the Rh system).

Another antigen, determined by a gene at a locus closely linked to the MN locus on the fourth chromosome, is referred to by the term S. There appear to be only two alleles at this locus, Ss, with S dominant, so there are three genotypes: SS, Ss, ss. Both SS and Ss give a positive reaction to the anti-S test, whereas s does not react to the antiserum. The S and the MN loci are linked so closely that there are no known cases of crossover. This means, as in the Rh system, that the genes are transmitted as a unit, a haplotype: MS, NS, and so on.

The seemingly neutral selection of the MNS system results in an even distribution among most of the world's peoples. There are some notable exceptions, however. Native Americans have a high frequency of the haplotypes MS and Ms, in contrast to Australian Aborigines, who have extremely high frequencies of N, reaching from 65 percent to a high of 95 percent. Such highs of this allele have also been reported for certain populations of New Guinea, which is to be expected due to shared origins with Australian populations some 40 to 60,000 years ago when the island was linked to the continent. The total lack of the S allele among Australians, while it is high among New Guineans, is a puzzle, though.[4] Adding to the question are reports of an excess of MN genotypes (greater than expected by the Hardy-Weinberg equilibrium) reported in some populations. These population distributions of the MNS system may be added as one more bit of genetic evidence to aid population studies.

---

[3]Many of the blood group systems have been discovered by mixing blood cells with antiserum made from plant extracts or with antihuman serum made from injecting human red cells into certain animals, usually rabbits. This results in the production of antibodies against a variety of proteins on the red blood cell surface.

[4]Some clues may be found in the diversity of New Guinea populations. Their linguistic diversity (over 700 languages) is nearly matched by their genetics. For example, the Gerbich blood group exists only in a few New Guinea and nearby Melanesian populations. The extreme ruggedness of their environment, causing near complete isolation of numerous populations until late twentieth century, is a likely cause as will be discussed in Chapter 8.

The Duffy Blood Group.   There are three types of antisera of this blood group, designated anti-Fy^a, anti-Fy^b, and anti-Fy^4. A majority of people from around the world have red blood cells that will react to either one or the other of the first two types, and many react to both. However, most people in central and west Africa and many African Americans are negative for both Fy^a and Fy^b but will react to the third type, Fy^4. Given these data, together with numerous family studies, it appears that there are three alleles at this blood type locus on the first chromosome, codominants that determine the presence of a red blood cell antigen (see Table 3-6).

In persons of European descent the frequency of Fy^a reaches a high of 90 percent; the balance are Fy^b, and rarely some have been reported with Fy^4. Throughout central Africa, Fy^4 reaches 100 percent and a high frequency is seen in populations on both sides of the Red Sea and among Kurds of Iraq and Iran. Except for Africans and Europeans, the Duffy blood group has not been widely studied, and a summary of these allele frequencies are listed for several African populations in Table 3-7. Because antigens Fy^a and Fy^b are virtually lacking in most of these populations, these types have proved to be a useful genetic marker for determining the degree of European admixture in African Americans.

One of the interesting aspects of the Duffy system, however, is the probable role these antigens played in the survival of African slave populations when they were brought to the Western Hemisphere. Africans and their descendants possess a degree of immunity to certain forms of malaria, a disease responsible for widespread illness and for mortalities reaching into the millions, even today. Most malarial infection in the Western Hemisphere is caused by the *vivax* parasite, one of the four species of malaria-causing protozoan, but differing somewhat from the other three types, as discussed in the next chapter. *Vivax* malaria is widespread from tropical to temperate regions of the world, once extending as far north as the midwestern United States. It has been brought under control in North America by mosquito eradication, but it was once a major problem for early settlers and proved to be deadly to the Native American populations. The resistance of the African populations, in contrast to Europeans and Native Americans, is one of the explanations offered for their survival and expansion. This resistance is hypothetically due to the nature of malarial infection: Once the parasite is injected into the bloodstream by the bite of a female Anopheles mosquito, it must enter a blood cell to begin its life-cycle phase in the human host. The red-cell antigens of the Fy^a and Fy^b provide attachment points

TABLE 3-6   Duffy Blood Group

GENOTYPE	PHENOTYPE
Fy^{a}Fy^a	Fy (a + b −)
Fy^{a}Fy^b	Fy (a + b +)
Fy^{a}Fy^o	Fy (a + b −)
Fy^{b}Fy^b	Fy (a − b +)
Fy^{b}Fy^a	Fy (a + b +)
Fy^{b}Fy^o	Fy (a − b +)
Fy^{o}Fy^o	Fy (a − b −)

TABLE 3-7   Frequency of Duffy Allele Fy^a in Select Populations

POPULATION	PERCENT OF FY^a
West Africa	
Upper Volta	0
Ghana	0
Nigeria (pooled)	3
Central West Africa	
Giryama	9.9
Kamba	0
Central Africa	
Bantu	7.8
Pygmoid	8.2
Southern Africa	
Bantu	11.8
Khoi	17.6
San	21.6
Sansawe	9.0
North Africa	
Algeria	29.3
Berber	22.7
Europe	
English	41.6
Greek	45.7
Italian	40.4
North America	
EuroAmerican (White)	43.0
AfroAmerican (Black)	21–26

Source: Hiernaux, 1966a; Reed, 1969; Cavalli-Sforza et al., 1994.

for the *vivax* parasite and facilitate entry. The Duffy Fy^4 does not, as demonstrated by laboratory experiments mixing parasites with red-blood cells of differing Duffy type. Type Fy^4 were highly resistant, which explains the immunity of individuals of African descent from this form of malaria. These laboratory results, the epidemiology of *vivax* malaria, and the distribution of the Duffy types offer one of the important examples of the functioning of natural selection in humans (Livingstone, 1984; Mourant, 1983).

THE BLOOD GROUPS: AN OVERVIEW

Studies of the red-cell antigen systems may distinguish individuals on the basis of their reactions to several antisera. These responses, as we have discussed, are determined by complex sugar-protein or sugar lipid molecules coating the surface of the blood cell that have a certain specific identity (antigen) inherited as a Mendelian trait. For most blood groups, the ABO, Rh, and MN, for example, a majority of our species respond in predictable ways. For the rarer systems, reactions to the antisera tests have been recorded less frequently, and relatively little is known about their population distribution. There are many more systems (the "private" antigens) that describe rare cross-reactions with antisera in a single family lineage.

The complexity of the red blood cell antigens need not concern us, nor should the student become dismayed at the large variety of human blood types that have been identified. This variety merely demonstrates the range of genetic polymorphisms of our species. They also provide a vital tool for the study of human genetics, identifying paternity, and distinguishing a monozygous (single-egg or identical) twin from a dizygous (two-ova or fraternal) twin. Population studies also show that the red-cell antigens offer a means for analysis of population migration, admixture, and, perhaps, for study of the forces of natural selection, since many distributions may vary more than expected.

A major question is why we possess this complex of inherited antigens: Just what are their functions? Furthermore, is there any advantage of one type over another under certain environmental conditions? These are hard questions to consider here. Most of the evidence of natural selection has been indirect, as explained previously for the ABO system. The Duffy does offer an example of the antigen function. This and other antigen systems are closely related to cell membrane functioning and probably influence the transport of various molecules, impeding some and facilitating others. At least that is what seems to be the case with the ABO that leads to a reaction of gut bacterial flora of specific types (see Roitt, 1988). As more is learned about the chemical composition of the red-cell antigens, comprehension of their functioning will grow. For the time being, the several blood types continue to be a useful example of human polymorphism.

WHITE BLOOD CELL (WBC) ANTIGENS

Another major cellular component of blood, the *leukocytes*, has become an increasingly important focus for the study of inherited antigens. The leukocytes or *white blood cells* (WBC) are a group of cells whose function is to protect the body against infectious organisms, and, normally, they are present in small numbers; there are between 4,000 and 11,000 compared with about 5,000,000 red blood cells in a microliter of blood. The WBC number rises dramatically when the body is challenged by invading organisms. Unlike the red blood cells, the WBC are not confined to the blood vessels. The WBC can move freely through blood vessel walls and enter spaces throughout the body, circulating not only by way of the blood vessels, but also through the lymphatic system, a series of nodes and ducts containing plasma. This brings them into close contact with nearly all other tissues.

There are several types of WBC, but granulocytes and macrophages are the most numerous (about 50 percent of the total). These are large cells that play a key role against infection as they engulf virus, bacteria, and foreign proteins. Through a complex process in reaction to infection, the granulocytes release peptide particles (chains of amino acids) that stimulate the activity of other types of WBC, the *lymphocytes* (T- and B-cells) that are found mostly in the lymph nodes, thymus, and spleen. The effectiveness of these immune responses, including the activities of the other WBC, depends on the antigenicity of the invading organisms and the degree of similarity or dissimilarity to the host's tissues. In other words, the functioning of the WBC in their protective role depends on their antigen types and the antigen identity of the foreign substance, a recognition of "self" or "nonself."

A key process in the recognition and memory of foreign substances and subsequent immune response is the action of T- and B-lymphocytes. There are several varieties of T-lymphocytes; one is a cytotoxic form that destroys foreign cells, either transplanted, inhaled, or ingested. A second T-cell type serves as a memory to recognize a previous contact with certain foreign substances; consider as an example the lifetime immunity one retains once exposed to childhood diseases like measles. The third and fourth varieties are inducer or suppressor cells that regulate the antibody production of the B-lymphocytes. These inducer T-cells do not make antibodies but communicate by chemical messenger to the B-lymphocytes to stimulate their antibody production. The B-cells will also divide rapidly and differentiate into antibody-producing plasma cells as a response to particular bacterial surface antigens. Through this complex of cellular interaction outlined in Table 3-8, the human immune system is able to respond to literally millions of "nonself" substances over the course of a lifetime (see Ganong, 2003). This scope of protective response is even more impressive when the underlying genetic mechanisms are considered.

After years of research on the immune system, skin grafts, and organ transplants, the WBC are recognized as having a highly variable antigen system, even more complex than that described for the red blood cell (RBC) antigens. There are many differences of the WBC in comparison with the RBC. The WBC are found not only in the blood

---

TABLE 3-8   Immunity and Lymphocyte Cells

BONE MARROW LYMPHOCYTE PRECURSORS

---

give rise to

T-Lymphocytes
    derived cells:
        1. cytotoxic (T_8) — — — → cellular immunity
        2. memory
        3. inducer or helper (T_4)—act on B-cells
        4. suppressor (T_8)—act on B-cells

B-Lymphocytes
    derived cells:
        1. memory
        2. plasma types — — — → humoral immunity
        immunoglobulins Ig G, A, M, D, E

---

serum within the blood vessels but are also distributed throughout most tissues of the body in virtually every fluid surrounding the somatic cells. This wide distribution and their anti-body functions explain, in part, the rejection of skin grafts and organ transplants. Attempts over the years to graft skin from one person to another have failed because the recipient's system rejected the graft as material foreign to its own immune system. How-ever, grafts between identical twins proved to be successful. This success of twin grafts suggested that the immune-rejection process was genetically determined.

Further evidence was provided by studies of the blood serum from patients who had received multiple transfusions; their serum contained a variety of agglutinins (antibodies). Tests of these antibodies against blood samples taken from the general population resulted in the agglutination of WBC in 60 percent of the cases (Dausset and Colombani, 1972). That is, some of the WBC "types" introduced into the patient through transfusion stim-ulated antibody production and some did not. However, the individual's WBC were not affected by the antibodies in his or her own serum. Following this evidence of individual differences in the ability to produce a variety of antibodies of specific identity, family and twin studies were conducted. The results obtained by cross-typing and matching blood cells of close relatives established the mode of inheritance of WBC antigens. These ear-lier studies were followed by many others over the next three decades and have identified a large complex system of WBC antigen types (human leukocyte antigens or HLA).

The Histocompatibility System (HLA)[5]

There is a series of glycoproteins (antigens) on the surfaces of the WBC that function as a part of the antibody processing during the immune response outlined earlier. These antigen types of the WBC form are so diverse that they constitute the most polymorphic system of inherited traits known, thus far, in humans. The antigens are, like the RBC antigens, molecules of sugars linked to a protein as part of the cell's sur-face membrane, and their presence is detected by a reaction with specific antibody form. In addition to their location on the WBC, these antigens are also found widely dispersed throughout tissues of the body and are attached to all other cells except RBC, sperm, and certain placental cells.

The antigen types are determined by several closely linked loci on chromosome 6 and designated HLA-A, HLA-B, HLA-C, HLA-D, HLA-DQ, and HLA-DR. Since there are from eight to forty alleles at each locus, the resulting multiplicity of allelic combinations of these loci make any simple designation impossible. Normally, a per-son's HLA system is expressed as a haplotype, the listing of the allele present at each of the loci. For example, in a study of 334 people in England, the haplotype HLA A1-B8-DR3 was found among 10.4 percent, which was a world high for this particular haplotype while it was only half as frequent in most other western Europeans. By

---

[5]The system of WBC antigens exists in most vertebrates and is referred to by the general term major histocompatibility complex or MHC. In humans, the more specific term, human leucocyte antigen or HLA is used.

TABLE 3-9 Major HLA Haplotypes of Selected Populations

			POPULATIONS*												
			1	2	3	4	5	6	7	8	9	10	11	12	13
HLA HAPLOTYPES			(Percent of Total Sample)												
A1	*B8*	*DR3*	10.4	5.1	5.1	7.1	8.9	9.1	12.1	5.3	—	1.5	3.7	3.6	2.2
A2	*B35*	*DR4*	0.1	—	0.4	0.1	—	—	—	—	1.9	—	14.8	3.6	—
A2	*B35*	*DR5*	—	0.4	0.7	0.4	—	—	—	5.3	0.6	—	—	—	—
A2	*B35*	*DRW8*	0.3	0.4	0.4	—	—	—	0.8	2.6	0.9	—	7.4	—	—
A2	*B44*	*DR4*	4.0	1.8	1.1	1.2	3.6	1.5	2.7	—	—	—	—	—	—
A24	*B35*	*DR4*	—	0.2	—	0.1	—	—	—	2.6	0.9	0.8	14.8	—	—
A24	*B7*	*DR1*	—	0.4	—	0.2	—	—	—	—	4.5	—	—	—	—
A24	*BW52*	*DR2*	—	—	—	—	—	—	—	—	7.8	—	—	—	—
A24	*BW54*	*DR4*	—	—	—	—	—	—	—	—	6.2	—	—	—	—
A26	*B38*	*DR4*	0.1	0.1	—	0.1	0.6	—	—	7.9	—	—	—	—	—
A28	*BW58*	*DRW6*	—	—	—	—	—	—	—	—	—	—	—	—	6.7
A3	*B7*	*DR2*	4.5	2.9	1.1	3.7	5.3	3.0	6.6	—	—	—	—	—	—
A30	*B13*	*DR7*	0.8	0.9	0.4	0.6	2.4	3.0	1.2	5.3	—	11.3	—	3.6	—
AW33	*BW65*	*DR1*	0.1	0.5	0.4	0.5	—	1.5	—	7.9	—	—	—	—	—

*Populations: 1. English, Celtic, Dutch, Scandinavian; 2. German, French, Italian, Spanish, Swiss; 3. Austrian, Yugoslavian, Czech, Hungarian; 4. American, Canadian; 5. Australian; 6. South African Caucasoids; 7. Other Caucasoids; 8. Jewish-Ashk; 9. Japanese; 10. Chinese (including Chinese subsets); 11. American Indians; 12. Mexican; 13. Black Africans.

Source: Modified and selected from Bodmer et al., 1987.

contrast, the most frequent haplotype found among Japanese populations was HLA A24-BW52-DR2, which occurred in 7.8 percent of the sample. Table 3-9 summarizes a variety of HLA haplotypes distributed among several population groups (see Bodmer et al., 1987). With a clearer understanding of the antigenicity of the HLA system, close tissue matches may be obtained by identifying the haplotypes of close relatives, a procedure that is a vital step in the preparation for organ transplants.

Because of the protective function of the WBC in the immune system, disease–HLA type correlations have been sought. Over the past fifteen years frequent associations have been reported between HLA types and specific diseases. Eighty-nine percent of the patients with a chronic inflammation of tendons and ligaments at specific skeletal joints (ankylosing spondylitis) had the B27 antigen. Celiac disease, a type of chronic inflammation of the intestinal tract, is another association with the HLA system; 68 percent had HLA type B8. Rheumatoid arthritis, type I diabetes (juvenile), and multiple sclerosis also show a significantly higher frequency of certain of the HLA types. Such associations between disease and the HLA system do not prove cause, however, but do provide a reference point to study a chain of genetic–environmental interactions that may result in a disease state. Others types (BW53, DRB1, DQB1), common among West Africans, provide a degree of immunity from malarial infection endemic to the region (Hill et al., 1992). The resistance to malaria possessed by carriers of these HLA antigens is probably as great as that conveyed by hemoglobin S described in the next chapter.

In addition to its clinical significance and because of its diversity throughout the species, the polymorphisms of the HLA system provide another set of genetic markers of human variability. Several geneticists and anthropologists have used such data to trace population migrations and to reconstruct ancestral relationships on the basis of HLA haplotype similarity or dissimilarity. The number of loci and the variety of alleles provide a means of gaining a closer perspective on interpopulation relationships. Peopling of the Pacific and relationships between Melanesian, Polynesian, Australian, and New Guinean populations have been postulated on the basis of similarities or differences in their HLA types (Ohashi et al., 2000; Serjeantson, 1984). The HLA antigens are also useful in calculationing degrees of admixture as in examples of African-European-Native American hybrid populations.

POLYMORPHISMS OF SERUM PROTEINS

In addition to the diversity of red and white blood cell antigens, there are numerous proteins in blood plasma that function as antibodies or as carriers of nutrients. Some are large and complex while others have a smaller, simpler form. These differences in protein form can readily be identified by several methods of electrophoresis, which separates protein fractions into various groups by molecular sizes, as sketched in Figure 3-10. Because of their differing mobility in an electric field, each of the major groups—albumins, groups specific (GC), globulins, lipoproteins, transferrins, and haptoglobins—separate at a certain point along the starch gel strip.

Each of the several globulin fractions are under genetic control and show a range of alternate forms. For example, the albumins, once thought to be a protein of little variation, are now also known to be highly polymorphic with eighty known genetic variants (see Szathmary, 1993). Likewise, transferrins and haptoglobins are polymorphic, though in a more restricted range. In addition, the more recently discovered apoproteins involved in transport of lipid components are under the control of a least a dozen genes. These polymorphisms of protein carriers in blood serum are distributed among different regional populations in some interesting ways. The meaning of this serum protein polymorphism is not always apparent, but some clues are provided by the following examples.

Immunoglobulins (Gamma Globulins)

The immunoglobulins are a group of antibodies specific for certain foreign antigens introduced as mold, pollen grains, or the proteins of an infectious organism. Each person has the capacity to synthesize an enormous number of different antibodies, and this synthesis takes place within the B-lymphocyte cells in circulation, as outlined above. Only a small part of our antibody production capacity is ever realized, however, since it depends upon a specific stimulation of the T- and B-lymphatic cells. Once stimulated, the B-cells begin to divide, producing identical cells that secrete the antibody specific to the antigen. The result is a group of slow-moving globulins, whose

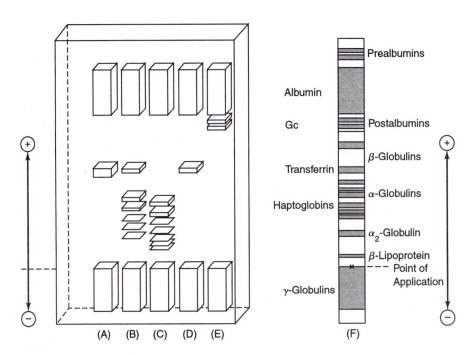

FIGURE 3-10   Relative Electrophoretic Mobilities of Protein Constituents of Human Serum. These diagrams show the relative positions of the various components after electrophoresis in alkaline starch gels; variations in conditions of electrophoresis lead to changes in resolution of some of the proteins. (a), (b), (c) Haptoglobins, phenotypes Hp 1-1; Hp 2-1, Hp 2-2, respectively; (d) transferrin, TfC; (e) group-specific component, phenotype Gc 2-1; and (f) composite showing relative electrophoretic mobilities of important constituents of serum. (From Buettner-Janusch, J., *Physical Anthropology: A Perspective*, 1973. Copyright © 1973 by John Wiley & Sons, Inc. Reprinted by permission of the publisher.)

variety is the result of a combination of an individual's genotype and environmental experience. This causes a difference from individual to individual while maintaining some shared types within each family or population. Pastoral people, like the Turkana of Kenya, share numerous immunoglobulin types with their neighbors in contrast to those found among native Australians. Likewise, Inuit (Eskimo) hunters in the Canadian Arctic possess a composite of immunological types that differ from other Arctic people like the Saami (Lapps), reindeer herders in Scandinavia.

The combinations of the HLA genes of these and other populations contribute to such differences, of course. But the immunological genes at several loci determine the potential of response to certain environmental stimuli (in the form of foreign antigens), and the diversity of these stimuli further adds to population contrasts because of the nature of the formation of the gamma globulin types. These globulins (20 percent of all plasma proteins) consist of highly variable and complex protein molecules composed of four polypeptides, a pair of heavy chains, each linked to a smaller or light chain (Figure 3-11). Most of the heavy chain is a constant

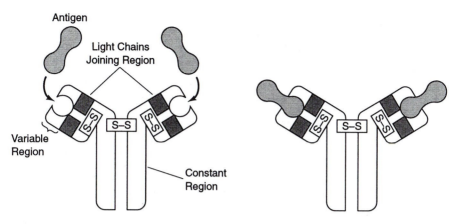

FIGURE 3-11   Diagramatic Representation of Antibody Structure. The antibody is a complex of light and heavy chains of polypeptides linked together by two sulfur atoms (S-S). They consist of a basic constant chain linked to a variable region that has a structure specific for a particular antigen. This recognition site binds and inactivates the antigen as illustrated.

region, a stable amino acid sequence, while the part that is linked to the light chain is highly variable. The amino acid arrangement of the light chain varies to conform with the identity of the foreign antigen that had stimulated antibody production. The antigen is then attached to this region rendering it inactive, thereby protecting an individual's system against a disease or a debilitating allergic response. Comparisons of the constant heavy-chain regions among the immunoglobulins reveal five classes whose functions vary as shown in Table 3-10.

The IgG group of immunoglobulins is the most plentiful and has been extensively studied. The constant parts of the heavy chains show a great deal of genetic polymorphism and are described as the *GM system*, which has at least twenty specific antisera reactions. Though some of these reactions show Mendelian inheritance as simple codominant alleles and each region of the chain has a amino acid sequence under control of a separate locus, it is not clear how many genetic loci are involved. The loci do appear to be closely linked on the fourteenth chromosome, each with several codominant alleles and classified by type of antisera.

There is a variation in the frequency of occurrence of several of the *GM types* among the world's populations that have been tested. These types appear to be inherited in groups referred to as haplotypes, or clusters of specific GM antisera reactions, for example, haplotype {1,17,21} is most common. Numerous other haplotypes appear in some regional populations more frequently than in others. Eighty-six percent of West Africans tested have GM{1,5,17} in contrast to the San of southern Africa with only 28.2 percent; they have mostly {1,5,15,17), a rare type found in few other people. Europeans, GM types encompass a broad range, perhaps due to so much mixing of people throughout history. Asians likewise have diverse GM types, but Africans appear to be most diverse of all. Realization of African genetic diversity is increasing as more samples

TABLE 3-10   Types of Immunoglobulins

TYPE	PLASMA CONCENTRATION (μ/ml)	FUNCTIONS
IgG	12,100	Inactivates bacteria and virus
IgA	2600	Neutralizes toxins
IgM	930	Inactivates bacteria and virus
IgD	23	Unknown
IgE	0.5	Activates allergic responses

are collected from well-defined populations as we will discuss in later chapters. On sum, this distribution of our antibody system's polymorphisms suggests varying levels of ability to react to certain classes of disease-causing organisms. Diversity and higher concentration of one haplotype over the other suggest that natural selection has been operating together with the other factors that influence gene frequencies.

Haptoglobins

The haptoglobins are group of serum proteins that are of particular interest. They are part of the alpha$_2$ globulins and have the capacity to combine with the oxygen-carrying pigment-protein complex, hemoglobin, when it is released into the plasma upon the destruction of old red blood cells because of disease or age (RBC has a life span of about ninety days). This combining with haptoglobin prevents a loss of hemoglobin through excretion by the kidneys. The haptoglobin-hemoglobin complex is carried through the circulatory system to the liver, where it is separated into its iron-bearing heme group and protein (globin) portions. The heme is converted to bilirubin and then to bile in the gallbladder, while the atoms of iron are recycled in the production of new red blood cells in the red bone marrow. The globin chains provide a resource of amino acids for protein synthesis. The preservation and transport of the free hemoglobins are vital and are influenced by haptoglobin's binding power.

    Three types of haptoglobin have been identified, each under genetic control through the action of a pair of nondominant alleles at a locus on chromosome 16. The genotypes and phenotypes would appear as

GENOTYPES	PHENOTYPES
Hp^1Hp^1	Haptoglobin 1–1
Hp^1Hp^2	Haptoglobin 1–2
Hp^2Hp^2	Haptoglobin 2–2

The global population distribution of haptoglobin frequencies varies widely, from less than 20 percent to more than 80 percent for one or the other allele. The highest frequency of Hp^1, for example, appears in numerous tropical populations who, typically, have high parasite loads. Most of these parasite are the types that attach to red blood cells, increasing the rate of red blood cell destruction. Because Hp^1 has a greater affinity for hemoglobin and hence a higher binding capacity, possession of this haptoglobin type would be an advantage in populations where hemolytic anemia is very high and quantities of free hemoglobin must be conserved.

Transferrins

Another protein variant is a beta-globulin (transferrin) that binds atoms of iron and transports them to the tissues as needed, especially to the bone marrow where hemoglobin is formed. Transferrins also assist in the absorption of iron through tissue membranes, especially dietary iron through the gut wall. The necessity of this protein for iron transport is best documented by examples of persons with a rare recessive allele that results in a total lack of transferrin in their plasma. Such persons suffer from severe iron deficiency anemia, despite an excess of the mineral, due to the failure of absorption and transport (McKusick, 1994).

Transferrins exist in at least seventeen forms as identified by electrophoresis methods, and each seems to be under genetic control of an autosomal nondominant allele. The several variants fit into one of the three groups; the majority are in group TfC and a slower group, TfD, whereas only a few variants occur in group TfB. These polymorphisms are distributed unevenly throughout the species and numerous populations have only a single type. The TfC type is the most common; populations in Africa and India have 80 to 100 percent while TfB and TfD variants are rare. The significance of polymorphism of the alleles for this iron-binding protein is not certain, but there may be some relationship to a variation in iron-binding capacity. Such a difference would make certain forms more efficient in populations suffering from a high rate of red-cell loss, as was suggested for haptoglobins. An increase in combining capacity would be advantageous to populations in which a large percentage of the people were subject to chronic anemia. Any advantage, no matter how slight, in the absorption and transport of this vital element would contribute to survival.

Lipoproteins

Apoproteins are a class of proteins that combine with triglycerides and cholesterol to form lipoprotein complexes. These complexes are transported in blood plasma and through intestinal and cell membranes; the structure of apoproteins influence attachments to combining sites on cell membranes. Such attachments either facilitate or retard the absorption through the membranes and affect the actions of the several enzymes of fat metabolism. Because of this close interaction with lipids and because the apoproteins mediate the transport and breakdown (catabolism) of cholesterol, these proteins have been closely examined since their discovery.

There are three major apoproteins designated APO B, APO C, and APO E, each coded by genes at a different locus. Each varies in combining capacity for triglycerides and cholesterol and play a more or less active role in the formation and transport of lipoproteins. The two forms of APO B, molecular weights 48 and 100, are active in different circulatory regions; B-48 transports exogenous ingested fat from intestines to liver, and B-100 is involved with the endogenous system transporting very low density lipids from liver into the circulation. APO C is involved with both areas of the lipid transport (Ganong, 2003). Because of its correlation with abnormal lipid profiles and possible influence on coronary heart disease (CHD), the APO E has received close attention.

Apoprotein E gene is represented by three alleles in the general population: APO E-2, E-3, and E-4, coding for an apoprotein with varying combining capacities. E-3 is the most common accounting for 67 to 87 percent of APOE proteins and E-2 is the least common, 1.6 to 10 percent. E-4 has an intermediate frequency of 10 to 25 percent and carriers of this allele express abnormal lipid profiles, especially higher cholesterol levels. This suggests that the E-4 is one of the genes involved in CHD, so extensive population surveys are in progress to trace the distribution of the E-4 allele. The results thus far have been inconclusive despite the known involvement with lipid metabolism but may be one of the factors that increase risk of heart diseases. The surveys do show a wide variation from a high in New Guinea of 36 percent to a low of 14 percent in Euro-Americans and less than 2 percent in Native Americans. Africans (Nigeria) had a frequency of 31 percent, Afro-Americans recorded 26 percent as did native Australians, and Greenland Inuit were close with 23 percent (Gamboa et al., 2001; Wu et al., 2002). This distribution, while interesting as one of many genetic markers at the APO loc; (APOB and APOC vary as well), does not establish a definite link with diseases of the heart and circulatory system.

INBORN ERRORS OF METABOLISM

Some of the more interesting and useful of the genetic markers in the study of human populations are various types of inherited biochemical defects. Many of these defects are due to a lack of enzymes that regulate important steps in our intermediate metabolism. Because of these deficiencies, proteins are not synthesized, carbohydrates are not converted to energy, lipids (fats) are not properly utilized, or other essential substances are not transported or stored. Examples of all these problems have been identified in the human genome, many of which are due to a recessive allele. Fortunately, most of these inherited conditions are extremely rare, with only a few cases identified in the medical literature. A catalog of Mendelian traits in humans has been prepared that lists these genetic defects together with all known traits of the human genome; it is updated periodically and has been entered since 1994 on the Internet (see "Morbid Anatomy of the Human Genome," in McKusick, 1994).

Since Garrod's classic paper in 1902 describing an inherited biochemical defect, *alkaptonuria*, there has been a continuous search for other such disorders, and many inherited enzyme defects have been reported. A majority of these traits result in a pathology of the metabolism that may be more or less lethal. Some manifest themselves as a lack of a single enzyme that results in an interruption of a biochemical pathway and are easily identified, such as phenylketonuria (PKU). Other types of inherited defects may cause the individual to be more susceptible to certain environmental conditions. An example is provided by the degenerate lung disease (emphysema) that occurs more frequently in susceptible individuals (persons inheriting ineffective forms of alpha antitrypsin, the inhibitor of the digestive enzyme, trypsin) when they are exposed to air pollution. A partial list of the incidence of more common types of recessive diseases in *Homo sapiens* is provided in Table 3-11. These examples all suggest the extent of the possibilities of error in a complex metabolic system like our own. All population groups have their share of inherited diseases, though there is considerable variation because of a past history of natural selection, genetic drift, isolation, or gene flow.

Phenylketonuria

Phenylketonuria (PKU) is a disease caused by the inheritance of an autosomal recessive gene on chromosome 12 that prevents synthesis of the enzyme phenylalanine hydroxylase (PAH). Individuals homozygous for this allele are unable to metabolize an essential amino acid, phenylalanine, which occurs in most dietary proteins. In homozygous normals and heterozygous carriers, the excess phenylalanine not used for protein synthesis is oxidized into tyrosine. The homozygote recessives lacking PAH enzyme have a block in their metabolic pathway (see Figure 3-12), and the phenylalanine amino acid is metabolized more slowly through an alternate pathway. This slower conversion

TABLE 3-11   Common Recessive Diseases

DISEASE	INCIDENCE PER MILLION BIRTHS[1]
Cystic fibrosis	800
Duchene's Muscular Dystropy (x-linked)	200 (males)
Homophilia A and B (x-linked)	100 (males)
Albinism	100
Congential adrenal hypoplasia	100
Phenylketonuria (PKU)	100
Aminoacidurias (excluding PKU)[2]	50
Mucopolysaccharidoses (all forms)[3]	50
Wilson's Disease[4]	30
Tay-Sachs disease	10
Galactosemia	5

[1]Estimated average incidence for all populations combined.

[2]Blockage of amino acid metabolism resulting accumulation similar to PKU

[3]Diseases resulting in defects in the metabolism of complex sugars whose accumulation cause a variety of developmental abnormalities.

[4]Block of copper metabolism

Source: Bodmer and Cavalli-Sforza, 1976; Mange and Mange, 1990.

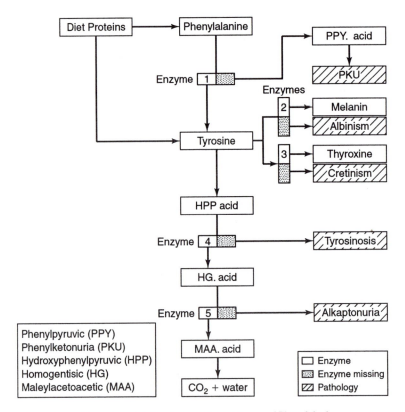

FIGURE 3-12   Normal and Abnormal Metabolic Pathways of Phenylalanine and Tyrosine.

process results in accumulations of phenylalanine in the blood of up to fifty times the normal levels. The excess levels of phenylalanine are toxic to the developing central nervous system in most infants and young children. If the toxic levels persist in the bloodstream over time, brain damage will result. Untreated, the PKU individual will suffer severe mental retardation and that person's mental capacity, as measured by IQ tests, will be significantly lower than normal; a victim's usual IQ range is from 20 to 80 (Figure 3-13). Note also the lower range of head size and differences in reflectance properties of the hair; the PKU infant tends to lighter hair color due to lower amounts of melanin. All represent the pleiotropic effects of the PAH allele. It is important, therefore, to identify those infants at risk as early as possible.

The Guthrie test for PKU in newborns was begun in the 1960s in Europe, North America, and Asia, and since then millions of infants have been examined. Europeans and Americans of European descent had the highest frequencies, from 1 in 6,000 to about 1 in 20,000 births. It is extremely rare among Japanese, African Americans, and Ashkenazic Jews. Even among Europeans the gene frequency for

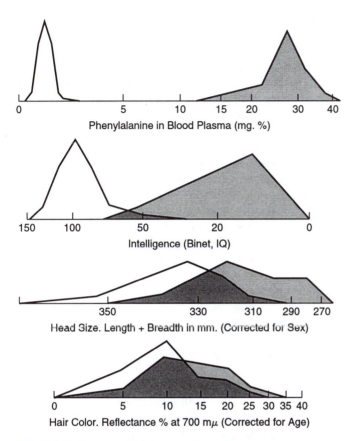

FIGURE 3-13 **Frequency Distributions of Some Characteristics of Phenylketonuria in Phenylketonuric Patients (Shaded) and in Control Populations.** Hair color and head size show pronounced overlap, and intelligence shows some overlap. The level of phenylalanine in the blood, however, is higher in all phenylke tonurics than in controls. If intelligence were the only phenotype used in the analysis, the genotype would be said to be nonpenetrant in a small proportion of cases. When plasma level of phenylalanine is the phenotype, the genotype is found to be fully penetrant. (From McKusick, Victor A., *Human Genetics*, 2nd ed., 1969. Copyright © 1969 by Prentice-Hall, Inc. Redrawn from Penrose, *Ann. Eugenics*, 16 [1951], 134.)

the PKU recessive is highly variable; eastern Ireland has about 1 PKU infant per 7,000 births (a calculated gene frequency of 0.014) in contrast to 1 in 18,000 births in London (a gene frequency of 0.007). Scandinavian populations have even lower frequencies (0.0038) while in several eastern European populations the PKU trait is nearly as high as in eastern Ireland. These tests have proved to be very useful in the identification of those infants at risk, and if the PKU condition is identified at birth, treatment begins immediately. By careful management of the dietary levels of the amino acid phenylalanine, the infant can grow and develop normally. After childhood, a person can return to a standard diet, suggesting that additional factors affect the control of the amino acid level. This is an example of the "dependent gene"—the expression gene products depend upon gene environment and phase of life cycle (Moore, 2003).

Since the wide-scale measure of blood levels of phenylalanine was instituted, individuals have been identified with abnormally high levels of phenylalanine, but without the symptoms of the PKU disease. These persons developed normally and appeared to tolerate the abnormal levels by some unknown mechanism. The metabolism of the amino acid turned out to be more complex than first thought, and several pathways have been defined, each with some degree of partial deficiency in metabolism. Different types of PKU have also been defined in different family kindreds (see Mange and Mange, 1990). This increase of diversity in the genetics of an amino acid metabolism is to be expected as a more thorough analysis has been made of the DNA region at the PAH locus on chromosome 12. Several alleles of the PAH genes have been identified and, considered with the diverse flanking sequences of the non-coding DNA, they are grouped into about fifty haplotypes. The fact is that individuals vary in their effectiveness in converting an essential amino acid, and the resultant pathological conditions vary among populations due to the presence of one or another of the haplotypes (Weiss, 1993).

Consider the biochemical pathway in Figure 3-12 and note the range of steps beginning with the conversion of phenylalanine. There is a succession of conversions, each leading to a variety of products, and all are affected by the efficiency of the first conversion. Defects at this stage actually affect the subsequent series of biochemical conversions. At certain of these steps other enzyme defects, inherited as recessives, may occur. Note the alternative pathways indicated by arrows from the shaded blocks to labels of abnormal, relatively benign conditions compared to PKU. One of these is alkaptonuria, which causes excretion of an acid, alkaptone, that causes an affected person's urine to turn black when exposed to the air, as first described by Garrod in his paper on inborn errors of metabolism (1902). The condition is rare and no severe health effects result. However, darkly pigmented granules appear in the afflected person's cartilage, and occasionally symptoms of arthritis result.

What is of special interest, though, is the reduced quantity of the amino acid tyrosine in persons of impaired phenylalanine metabolism. Because tyrosine is a precursor for biochemcial processes that lead to the production of melanin, these persons tend to have fairer skin, light-colored hair, and blue eyes. The effects on the production of thyroxine, a hormone of the thyroid gland, are not recorded, but there may be differences between those persons of normal and subnormal levels of tyrosine due to the lack of its synthesis. Since some tyrosine is obtained through food proteins, persons with reduced synthesis of this amino acid are still able to produce the melanin pigment, unlike those persons with total or near total impairment of melanin production.

Albinism (Oculocutaneous Type)

Many of the inborn errors of human metabolism require sophisticated biochemical methods to identify, but a few traits result in obvious, easily recognized phenotypes. The most striking and highly visible of these phenotypes is *albinism*—total or near total lack of melanin, the pigment of skin, hair, and the iris of the eyes. Albinism has been recognized for many centuries, as far back as biblical times (Noah was reputed to have been an albino). The albino phenotype varies in frequency from 1 in 20,000 births among Europeans to 1 in 1,100 among the Ibos, a large ethnic group of West Africa. In several small, isolated, inbred populations the frequency is reported to be as high as 1 in 146 live births; the Cuna, a Carib Indian group occupying islands off the Caribbean coast of Panama, and the Hopi of Arizona are populations with such exceptionally high frequency of albinos.

There are several autosomal recessive alleles at loci on chromosomes 9, 11, and 15 that affect the synthesis of melanin. Two major types of albinism have been defined: type I, where the afflicted person lacks tyrosinase, the enzyme needed to convert tyrosine to a precursor compound for melanin production; and type II, where the afflicted person tests positive for tyrosine enzyme but is still unable to synthesize melanin. The type II tyrosinase positive form accounts for the majority of albinism and it is the type seen most frequently in Africans and Native Americans. In contrast, type I occurs less frequently and is the type usually responsible for albinism among Europeans (Witkop et al., 1989). Numerous other inherited defects in melanin synthesis have been identified, and this raises doubts about any single model of explanation; fourteen types of albinism have been defined and at least sixty alleles at the tyrosine locus are known. The complexity of the pigment system is underscored when albino parents give birth to normally pigmented children. This phenomenon of *complementation* (the additive effect of gene products from different loci) was offered to explain how a male and female, apparently with the same defect, produce phenotypically normal individuals. Though both parents lacked pigmentation, mother and children tested positive for tyrosinase. The father tested negative for this enzyme, as expected for an albino (type I). The explanation is that the parents were albinos due to different metabolic defects and there were at least two genetic loci (A and B) involved in the production of melanin. This is illustrated in the following way:

Albino parents' genotypes   aaBB × AAbb

Children's genotypes   all AaBb (normal pigmentation)

Some Variations in Sugar Metabolism

The major source of energy for the metabolic processes of the body is a simple sugar, glucose derived from several kinds of complex carbohydrates of the diet. These complexes of starches or sugars must first be broken down into simpler structures in the small intestine so they can be absorbed into the bloodstream. This hydrolysis or cleavage into smaller molecular structures is mediated by enzymes for that particular carbohydrate compound. For example, amylase is the enzyme that brings about the hydrolysis of starches, sucrase the enzyme for sucrose (cane sugar), and lactase the enzyme that causes hydrolysis of milk sugar, lactose. There are many more enzymes that play essential roles in the digestion, energy conversion, or storage of carbohydrates that are ingested by the human diet. A reduction or an absence of certain of these enzymes is known to be inherited as autosomal recessives.

Deficiency of the Lactase Enzyme.   As in the case of other mammals, the newborn human's source of food for the first few months or even years is the milk secreted by the mother's mammary glands. In addition to protein and fat, the secretion contains an important carbohydrate, lactose, the principal source of energy for the growing infant. This milk sugar is a large, complex molecular structure that cannot be absorbed directly into the bloodstream. It must first be split into its simpler components, *glucose* and *galactose*, which are then absorbed through the upper intestinal tract. The enzyme *lactase* catalyzes this breakdown of the lactose sugar, and this enzyme is secreted in large quantities by the cells lining the walls of the upper intestinal track through-out infancy and early childhood, diminishing in adolescence. Following the weaning period as individuals change their diet to solid food, the lactase enzyme reduces to 10 percent or less of the level present in the infant. This level and activity of the enzyme may be maintained into adult life in some individuals, depending, perhaps, on the continued use of fresh milk from dairy herds. A majority of people, however, do not maintain lactase into adult life and hence lose their ability to digest fresh milk.

Adults and adolescents rarely consume fresh milk; even many pastoral peoples with a ready supply of this rich food source ferment the milk into some form before consumption and seldom use it fresh. In its fermented form, bacteria do the job of the lactase and split the milk sugar into digestible products. A majority of human adults are lactase malabsorbers (LMAs) and most tend to avoid milk. This group includes virtually all Asians and Africans as well as many Europeans (see Table 3-12). There are populations, however, where a large percentage of adults maintain an ability to digest lactose and are classified as absorbers (LAs). Such individuals are found mainly in northern Europe and among a few pastoral tribes in East Africa. All have had a long history of direct consumption of fresh milk from their cattle, goats, or reindeer. This experience over the centuries may have contributed to a population with a high rate of lactose digestion, though note the variability and the large percentages of adults who are LMA despite the reliance on milk as a food source. Analysis of family pedigrees in Finland, for example, showed that those adults who were unable to digest lactose had inherited the lactase deficiency as an autosomal recessive; adults who were absorbers were either homozygous dominants or heterozygotes, while the malab-sorbers were homozygous recessives (see Sahi, 1978a, 1978b; Flatz et al., 1982).

Avoidance of fresh milk is the major indicator of malabsorption (LMA) because of the gastrointestinal distress caused by undigested lactose, which is converted to lactic acid, carbon dioxide, and hydrogen in the colon. The continued use of fresh milk into adulthood is considered an indication of effective digestion. Anecdotal description

TABLE 3-12   Frequency of Lactase Deficiency

POPULATIONS	% LACTOSE MALABSORPTION (LMA)
African Ancestry	
Watutsi (EA)	17
Baganda (WA)	94
Bantu (WA)	89
Nilotic (Sudan)	61
No. Nomads (Sudan)	38
African American	70–74
Asian Ancestry	
East Asian	80–100
SE Asian	70–80
Chinese	85
Native Americans (NA)	50–70
Native Americans (SA)	100
Inuit (Greenland)	72
European Ancestry	
Austria	20
Poles (Canada)	28
France	37–41
Finland	18
Saami (Lapps)	17–36
Germany	12–21
Italy	30–51
America	20

Source: Data from Bayoumi et al., 1981; Flatz et al., 1982; McCracken, 1971.

of milk use among many of the cattle herders of East Africa is considered evidence of a high frequency of the lactase allele. For example, among the Orma, a cattle-herding people of Kenya, fresh milk is frequently consumed, especially during the dry seasons. All adults and children partake without the distressful symptoms of the malabsorption syndrome, except for the story of one 12-year-old male of mixed parentage who suffered distress when consuming fresh milk; his mother was Bantu, an agricultural group living nearby (Ensminger, 1990). A more precise way of determining lactose tolerance is by measures of hydrogen (H^2) in a breath test; an individual's malabsorption of lactose results in higher levels of H^2 in expired air. Applications of this test to Sudanese populations revealed much the same relationship between a dairying economy and lactose absorption as seen among the Kenyan populations. Sudanese from tribes of pastoral nomads had a higher percent of lactose-tolerant individuals (62 percent) than did the agriculturists (36 percent) living on the Sudan–Egyptian border (Bayoumi et al., 1981).

Similar observations have been offered for Europeans where the observed differences in use of milk by adults have been confirmed by laboratory tests for lactase phenotypes (see Flatz et al., 1982). Milk-using experience and lactose-tolerance correlations vary somewhat, however. Among the Saami (Lapps) of Finland, groups with many centuries of experience in fresh milk consumption, the range of LMA among adults varies from 25 percent to as high as 60 percent. Rural populations of southern Finland, with 3,000 years of milk consumption, have as few as 17 percent LMA individuals (Sahi, 1978a). In sum, milk-using experience has contributed to a high frequency of the gene for adult lactase persistence in some peoples of the world.

Those persons able to digest lactose have an advantage in their ability to use a rich source of carbohydrate, but they may also be endowed in another way. Since lactose sugar facilitates the absorption of calcium through the gut membranes, those consuming and digesting milk on a regular basis may be at an advantage in the far northern temperate zone. In the higher latitudes, the short hours and weak sunlight reduce the synthesis of vitamin D, a vitamin necessary for calcium absorption and the growth and maintenance of skeletal tissue. Hypothetically, then, in areas where people are deprived of adequate vitamin D, anyone who can compensate by increased calcium intake may be at a selective advantage. Such a hypothesis overlooks, however, the experiences of lactose absorbers in Africa, where sunlight and vitamin D sufficiency are not a problem. The hypothesis is worthy of consideration within a broader context of skin pigmentation, diet, and evolution as discussed in Chapter 5.

Galactosemia.   There are a number of other inherited abnormalities of carbohydrate metabolism. One of the better known defects is *galactosemia*, which is the inability to convert galactose to glucose. This metabolic defect is inherited as an autosomal recessive trait. Persons homozygous for the allele lack the enzyme (galactose-1-phosphate uridyltransferase) necessary to convert galactose, one of the sugars produced when a molecule of lactose—milk sugar—is split during digestion. Heterozygotes have quantities of the enzyme that are intermediate between normals and the afflicted person.

Within a few days or weeks of birth, the afflicted infant begins to show signs of distress and an impairment in its ability to digest milk. If allowed to go untreated, the accumulation of galactose in the blood leads to several serious conditions: stunted growth, enlarged liver, mental retardation, and cataracts. Fortunately, galactosemia is rare (from 1 in 65,000 births in Europe to 1 in 118,000 reported in the state of Massachusetts), but the several known cases may be due to a recessive at different loci. The galactosemia cases do provide, however, another example of inherited defects in metabolism that result from the lack of a single enzyme (Vogel and Motulsky, 1986).

Some Other Metabolic Defects

In addition to inherited disorders of carbohydrate metabolism, there are a number of examples of enzyme deficiencies that affect metabolism of the organic bases of the DNA or partially block synthesis of the lipid (fat) coverings of nerve fibers. Most are quite rare, occurring only in a few inbred lineages, while some are present at distressingly high frequencies. McKusick (1994) lists several thousand for which the mode of inheritance is known. A few disorders are described below as examples of those genetic defects that are of anthropological interest.

Errors in Purine Metabolism.   Whenever there is an excess of purines like the organic bases of the DNA and RNA nucleotides, adenine and guanine, for example, the compounds are converted through several steps to an ultimate end product, uric acid. A normal person excretes a soluble form of excess uric acid through the urine. There are several metabolic abnormalities, however, that cause uric acid to accumulate in the tissue in crystalline form, causing much pain. *Gout* is a common term for one disease that occurs in a number of forms and more often in males than in females. Some individuals have a tendency to develop this disease because of an inherited enzyme defect, an X-linked recessive. Overeating, especially a diet high in proteins, increases the uric acid produced and can bring on the symptoms of joint pain and swelling.

Another form of purine acid metabolism deficiency is accompanied by an elevated uric acid excretion and a peculiar form of self-destructive behavior. The afflicted child, always male, chews off his lips and if not restrained will bite off the ends of the fingers. This *Lesch-Nyhan* syndrome has attracted much attention since its description in the 1960s, and biochemists have identified an enzyme deficiency in the pathway of conversion of the purine nucleotides. The deficiency is inherited as an X-linked recessive and, though the female carrier can be identified, she does not show any of the disease symptoms.

Errors in Pyrimidine Metabolism.   The end products of pyrimidine (organic bases like cytosine, thymine, and uracil) metabolism are highly soluble, unlike the products of purine metabolism. Thus, an overproduction of pyrimidines does not cause any pathological symptoms to appear, but there are certain enzyme deficiencies in pyrimidine metabolism that are inherited as a recessive trait and that result in certain detectable compounds. One such compound is beta-aminoisobutyric acid or *BAIB*. This substance is formed by the breakdown of pyrimidines and is further reduced to carbon dioxide and ammonia by the action of a transaminase enzyme. High rates of excretion have been measured in some people who are homozygous for this recessive allele. Their metabolism is otherwise normal except for the excretion rate of BAIB. In addition, persons undergoing radiation treatment for cancer excrete large amounts because of the high rate of destruction of DNA in the cancer cells.

There appears to be no pathology associated with high excretion of BAIB. Persons who are low excretors (less than 40 mg/day) appear to be no more or less fit than high excretors (300 mg/day). With the exception of a correlation with radiation treatment for cancer just noted, there appears to be no disease correlation for BAIB excretion. However, there is a significant geographic distribution of populations who are high excretors (see Table 3-13). Large numbers of excretors are seen among Asians; in contrast, Europeans and Americans of European descent tend to be low in number (only 10 percent are high excretors). Among African Americans, excretors are more frequent, but they still number far below the percentage of high excretors in Asian populations. Though the meaning of this most common metabolic variant is not clear and fitness does not appear to be influenced, the phenotype provides another interesting marker for the study of human polymorphisms.

TABLE 3-13   Distribution of BAIB Excretors

POPULATION	NUMBER TESTED	FREQUENCY OF HIGH EXCRETORS
North America		
European descent		
Michigan	71	0.03
Texas	255	0.10
New York	218	0.10
New York	148	0.11
African descent		
Michigan	25	0.20
New York	38	0.15
Indians		
Apache	110	0.59
Apache	113	0.42
Eskimo	120	0.23
Chinese	33	0.45
Japanese	41	0.41
Central America		
African descent (Black Caribs)	285	0.32
Asia		
India	16	0
Thailand	13	0.46
Marshall Islands		
Rongelap	188	0.86
Utirik	18	0.83

Source: After Buettner-Janusch, J., *Origins of Man*. Copyright © 1966 by John Wiley & Sons, Inc. Reprinted by permission of the publisher.

Tay-Sachs disease.   There are numerous disorders of the metabolism of lipids (fats) and associated complexes formed with sugar molecules. Such disorders are inherited as recessives that occur at very low frequencies so the chance of a homozygote recessive is very remote, somewhere in the range of once in a million conceptions. In certain populations, however, a recessively inherited disease may occur at high frequencies even though the homozygous recessive is a lethal combination. There are several diseases of this type, but one of the best known is *Tay-Sachs*, a neurodegenerative disorder that causes death before two years of age. Despite its mortality, Tay-Sachs occurs among the Ashkenazic Jewish populations of eastern Europe and the United States once in every 2,500 births. This frequency contrasts to 1 in 500,000 non-Ashkenazi births (Ludman et al., 1986). Given these relative frequencies, one in twenty-five persons in the Jewish population is a carrier but shows no signs of the disease.

Tay-Sachs disease is caused by the accumulation of a lipid-sugar molecule, ganglioside, an important constituent of cell membranes. Synthesis of this molecule occurs by a regular and continuous process as sugar molecules are linked to a type of long-chained lipid molecule. Excesses that are produced beyond the normal cell membrane requirements are degraded by removal of sugar molecules from the lipid portion of the chain, thus maintaining a balance of gangliosides in cell cytoplasm. This is an especially important process in the fast-growing and dividing cells of newborns and infants. In Tay-Sachs individuals, this regulation process is interrupted and excess gangliosides accumulate in neuronal cells, causing the brain to become swollen and distended. Brain functions are severely impaired and the infant fails to develop normal neurological responses; muscular control degenerates, followed by paralysis, and loss of hearing and sight occurs by the end of the first year.

Excess gangliosides are degraded by two enzymes called hexoaminidase A and B. Because of inheritance of recessive alleles, Tay-Sachs victims lack hexoaminidase A (Hex A) and hence are unable to normally metabolize ganglioside molecules. The recessive allele has been localized to the short arm (region p) of chromosome 15, and the mutation is a single-base substitution (G to C) in intron 12 of the DNA sequence. Other mutation forms have also been identified, most resulting in loss of the ability to synthesize the enzyme. In another population with a high frequency of Tay-Sachs, French Canadians of Quebec, a different mutation has been identified (Myerowitz and Hogikyan, 1987). The phenotype of both groups, however, is the same: They lack the enzymes necessary to process the ganglioside molecules. Measurements of the Hex A enzyme levels can identify newborns or fetuses who are at risk. Parents of such infants would be carriers of the defective allele (heterozygotes) who, though they show no symptoms of the disease, have less than normal levels of the enzyme. The measurement of the Hex A enzyme level can identify the carriers and can assist in genetic counseling for prospective parents whose families have a history of Tay-Sachs disease.

The persistence of the high frequencies of this detrimental gene has perplexed scientists for years, and thus far only two explanations have been offered. The first relates to the effect of population size and isolation. The Ashkenazi Jewish populations today probably descended from between 1,000 and 5,000 people who migrated from the Middle East about 1,000 years ago. This small founder size, followed by generations of near isolation and inbreeding, would be in the range for genetic drift to be effective. However, since there are at least two abnormal Hex A alleles now known, genetic drift seems less likely as the cause of Tay-Sachs frequencies. A selection favoring the heterozygote is an alternate explanation (Chakravarti and Chakraborty, 1978). Arguments have been advanced that the crowded ghetto environments fostered the persistence of typhoid and tuberculosis diseases at high levels. Continued exposure acted as selective forces that favored certain genotypes; infections were less acute and mortality was lower. In this case, the argument continues, carriers of the Hex A deficient allele suffered lower mortality rates, survived longer, and had higher fertility rates that compensated for the loss of Tay-Sachs infants. Thus far, family studies over several generations in Poland support this hypothesis; families with a history of Tay-Sachs produced more living children in the tuberculosis–typhoid environment. The exact mechanisms involved in this hypothetical relationship of Hex A levels and infectious disease have not been demonstrated, but it is founded on similar hypotheses of balanced polymorphism in the persistence of other lethal recessives in certain disease environments—for example, the high frequency of the cystic fibrosis gene in certain populations.

Cystic Fibrosis.   The most common lethal genetic disease in European and European-derived populations is cystic fibrosis (CF), inherited as an autosomal recessive. The disease is a disorder of the exocrine glands, those glands that excrete their products into tubules (pancreatic enzymes or parotid salivary glands, for example) in contrast to endocrine glands (pituitary, thyroid, or adrenal are three examples) that release their hormone products directly into the blood. The CF patient suffers from respiratory and digestive problems due to secretions of thick, viscous substances that block tubules and do irreversible damage to several organs, the lungs and pancreas in particular. By blockage of the pancreatic ducts, the enzymes are prevented from reaching the digestive tract, and accumulation of the thick mucus in the smaller air passages of the lungs impairs respiration. This deadly combination of respiratory and digestive problems causes cystic fibrosis to be one of the leading causes of childhood mortality. Before 1950 few survived past infancy, and even today with treatment available, life expectancy is still only twenty-four years. The disease prevalence is from 1 in 500 to 1 in 3,800 births in those of European ancestry. It is extremely low among Africans (1 in 17,000) and rare in Asians (1 in 90,000 births of Asians in Hawaii). The high overall rate among ancestral Europeans in the United States gives a carrier frequency of one in twenty (Weiss, 1993).

The location of the CF gene and identification of its product represents one of a growing number of success stories in genetic research. For years the search was handicapped by incomplete understanding of the physiology of the disease; a high rate of excretion of sodium chloride in the sweat (about five times normal) was recognized, but the connection with some gene product was not established. The locus was isolated to chromosome 7 by 1985, but it was several years before the gene structure was described. The DNA sequences of 500,000 base pairs were finally established as the code determining a large, complex protein called the cystic fibrosis transmembrane conductance regulator (CFTR). This complex unit encompasses a number of cell membrane functions, mainly ion transport (see Ganong, 2003). Thus far, twenty-four different mutations have been identified with CF disease. The high frequencies of several of these mutations in certain populations raise the question of the maintenance of a lethal recessive just as in the example of Tay-Sachs. If the homozygous recessives die before the age of reproduction (as was the case prior to the 1960s), and if those that survive now have such low fertility rates, then what accounts for the one in twenty carrier frequency among many European populations?

The CF allele is correlated with the distribution of tuberculosis, which occurred in epidemic proportions in England during the sixteenth century. It then spread to the Continent with the expansion of the Industrial Revolution, which contributed to concentrations of growing European populations in urban centers. Eventually, by the late nineteenth century, this "white plague" or "consumption" became a major cause of death on both sides of the Atlantic. Any individual who had a resistance to this disease, no matter how slight, would enjoy a longer life and a higher reproductive rate. A convincing case is made for carriers of the CF allele in this kind of environment (see Meindl, 1987). The heterozygote (carrier of the mutant allele) had an increased capacity to secrete highly viscous fluids containing large amounts of mucopolysaccharides in the lungs and could more rapidly repair cellular tissue damage caused by invading tubercular bacteria. In sum, the carrier's elevated levels of secretions, while not as severe as in the homozygous recessive, conveyed an advantage in certain disease environments. This is an interesting hypothesis that offers to explain the high rates of CF in tubercular-exposed populations, but it does not consider the CF rates among the Ashkenazim. It is comparable to the hypothesis for Tay-Sachs persistence in eastern European Jewish populations but does not consider ethnic groups exposed to the same disease environments. These disease–genetic associations should be analyzed among a broader range of peoples but, unfortunately, there are few published data on CF or Tay-Sachs outside of those populations mentioned.

OTHER POLYMORPHISMS OF ANTHROPOLOGICAL INTEREST

Taste Sensitivity

There is a wide range of taste sensitivities in humans. Some of us detect certain chemical compounds more easily than others. Hence, detection of levels of saltiness, bitterness, or sweetness in foods and beverages differs among us all (Williams, 1956). There is good evidence that some of this sensitivity is inherited, as has been thoroughly demonstrated by at least one substance. Perhaps no other polymorphism is so easily detected by a simple test as is taste sensitivity to a substance called phenylthiocarbamide or *PTC*. In high concentrations this substance tastes bitter to some people, but not to others. Since the accidental discovery of this condition over fifty years ago, millions of people have been tested and the frequency of tasters and nontasters has been calculated.

This ability to detect the substance PTC is determined by a dominant allele (T): Persons who are TT or Tt can detect a bitter taste. In almost all populations tested there are tasters and nontasters, but as more careful tests have shown, there are various degrees of sensitivity. The homozygote dominant individual (TT) is more sensitive than the heterozygote (Tt) or the homozygote recessive (tt) and can detect the bitterness in more dilute solutions. The frequency of nontasters covers a broad range among a sample of ethnic groups. We can see a range of variation of nontasters (tt) from a low of less than 2 percent in aboriginals of Taiwan (Formosan natives) to a high of over 40 percent in residents of the city of Bombay, India. As described in Chapter 2, given the percent of homozygous recessives, frequencies for both dominant and recessive alleles can be calculated. These calculations give frequency ranges of 0.134 to 0.652 for the recessive (t) and 0.865 to 0.342 for the dominant (T), comparing Taiwan to Bombay. Most European and European-derived populations have frequencies within the middle of these ranges. A sample of English in London showed a gene frequency of 0.57, Belgians, 0.48, and Finns, 0.54 for the recessive t allele.

The significance of this taste polymorphism is not certain, though it may be widespread among primates. Studies of chimpanzees and rhesus monkeys revealed taste sensitivity variation over a broad range (Eaton and Gavan, 1965). The question of the significance of this polymorphism becomes more difficult when we recognize that the substance, PTC, is a synthetic compound not found in nature. However, the whole chemical compound does not cause the bitter sensation: It is a small cluster of atoms, a carbon, nitrogen, and sulfur tightly bound and acting as a single unit (a radical, in chemical terminology) that causes the bitter taste. This radical of carbon–nitrogen–sulfur (CNS), or thiocyanate, is widely distributed in nature and occurs in many commonly used food plants. Several plants of the Cruciferae family (cabbage, turnips, mustard greens, and so on), as well as cassava (manioc), a tropical root that is a dietary mainstay for millions of people, contain this thiocyanate group. There is some evidence that avoidance of the bitter-tasting foods containing CNS may be an advantage enjoyed by the taster.

Nontasters are more susceptible to thyroid deficiency, and a higher frequency of nodular goiter is found among them than in people who are tasters. This is due to a depression of iodine uptake by the gland because CNS is a component of a class of chemical compounds, thioglucosides, that can block iodine absorption under certain conditions. Reduced thyroid function results from lowered iodine levels that, in turn, affect lowered metabolism, particularly in child growth or in lowered fertility in adults (Jackson, 1993). One hypothesis explaining taster polymorphism is that persons able to reject CNS-bearing plants would reduce the degree of thyroid interference in contrast to nontasters. This could be a major advantage among those populations in iodine-poor areas of the world. Food avoidance, special food preparation, as in the case of cassava from which most CNS is extracted, or use of high iodine content salt all contribute as adaptive mechanisms to maintain normal metabolic levels.

Cerumen (Ear Wax)

The waxy substance that accumulates in our ears has two different types that are under the control of a pair of alleles. The wet, sticky wax is determined by a dominant allele whereas the wax of dry, flaky consistency is determined by a recessive. In addition to the stickiness or dryness, the waxes differ in their lipid (fat) content and in the quantity of antibodies that they contain.

The ear wax types vary throughout the world's populations. A majority of Asians (80 to 90 percent) have the dry type, in contrast to Europeans and Africans, who usually have the wet ear wax. Among Asians and populations of Asian descent, though, there is a cline of variation that correlates with temperature. Dry ear wax is frequent in northern Asian populations while the wet type is found more often among tropical populations in both Asia and the Americas. For example, 93 percent of Mayan Indians in the Yucatan of southern Mexico have the wet type of ear wax. Because of this clinal distribution and because of lipid and antibody differences, there is a probability that wet ear wax may serve some protective function in hot, humid climates. However, there is no conclusive evidence. The distribution of cerumen alleles provides another example of a long list of polymorphisms that require further study before their adaptive significance can be understood (Ibraimov, 1991; Petrakis et al., 1967).

TRAITS OF SIMPLE INHERITANCE: SOME CONCLUSIONS

The advances in human biology have been rapid and remarkable over the past thirty years. Not only have many new genetic markers been reported, but their chromosome loci have been noted as well. Additional population data have also been obtained, and frequency distributions are more readily available for many simply inherited traits. Blood components and enzyme systems for numerous non-European populations are being published more frequently. In addition, one of the greatest single achievements has been the study of the finer structure of genes and those numerous strands of noncoding units that separate the functional segments. The use of DNA fragments has aided in describing human diversity, and these DNA pieces of varying lengths have been added to a growing list of polymorphisms. The study of human biological diversity has moved from an examination of the end product of gene action, the phenotype, to the recording of the actual genetic code itself. However, these developments have not been an unmixed blessing; they have revealed an enormous range of variability right down to the level of an individual's identification by nuclear DNA polymorphisms. The comparisons of populations must now take into account this new information, and anthropological explanations of population structures, their history, and gene flow become evermore important.

4

Traits of Simple Inheritance II: Hemoglobin Variants and DNA Markers

Polymorphisms of many traits such as blood groups, enzymes, and proteins differ markedly in frequency among populations and the several factors that contribute to gene-frequency change offer a way of explaining these trait differences. Influence of such factors as population size, migration, or gene flow can often be well documented by reference to historical events, linguistic similarities, or archaeological evidence. It has been and is still difficult, however, to demonstrate natural selection in humans, and there is little direct evidence of superior fitness of heterozygotes for one or another polymorphism. The hypothesis of phenotype fitness in certain environments, such as the relative immunity of heterozygote carriers to a particular disease, is difficult to test. The postulated fitness of heterozygous carriers of lethal genes described in the last chapter offers some explanation for the persistence of high frequencies, but there have been few direct links made between genotype and disease. Much of our data is more indirect and is derived from epidemiology and demography, comparisons of differential survival or fertility rates of normal homozygotes and carriers of a lethal or near-lethal gene. However, more complete evidence for disease selection is offered by human hemoglobin variants in malarial environments. This chapter describes these hemo-globin variants, their distribution, and probable disease relationships and considers the use of DNA markers for population comparisons.

HEMOGLOBINS: NORMAL AND ABNORMAL

The red blood cells contain a variety of proteins, the largest percentage being hemoglobin, approximately 85 to 90 percent. Hemoglobin is a large, complex molecule composed of four long chains of amino acids (polypeptide chains). Each polypeptide encompasses a heme group, a large molecule (porphyrin ring) containing an atom of iron that binds with a molecule of oxygen (O_2) and, incidentally, gives blood its red color when oxygenated. These iron atoms, within the center of the heme groups, combine with two atoms of oxygen in the lungs and then transport the O_2 throughout the circulatory system, releasing it as needed by the surrounding tissues. This uptake, transport, and then release of oxygen is a complex process dependent on several characteristics of the enzymes within the RBC, the structure of the heme groups, and the oxidative state of the atoms of iron they contain. In addition, another significant factor influencing red blood cell function is the structure of the globins, that is, the amino acid composition of the alpha and beta chains.

The structure of hemoglobin is the most thoroughly studied of any protein, and its large size enables ready comparisons of electrophoretic mobility, a technique applied by Linus Pauling for comparative studies of proteins (Figure 4-1). Since the 1940s, when Linus Pauling showed the molecular differences of hemoglobin of persons with sickle cell disease (Pauling et al., 1949), samples of this blood protein have been examined for millions of people from around the world. Hundreds of hemoglobin variants have been detected. Most are rare variants, occurring only in a few families, and some are polymorphic, reaching frequencies of greater than 1 percent (see Livingstone, 1985). Many

FIGURE 4-1   Separation of Hemoglobins by Electrophoresis.

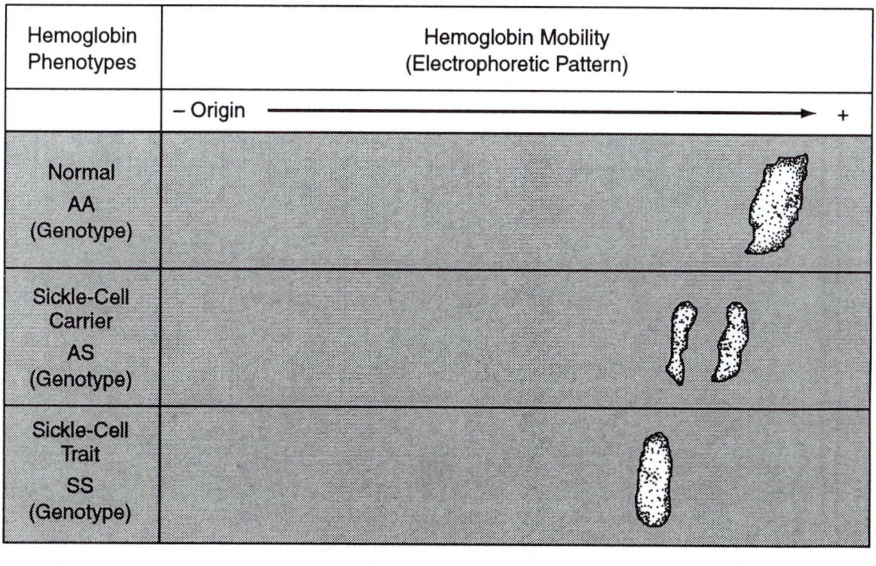

Hemoglobin Phenotypes	Hemoglobin Mobility (Electrophoretic Pattern)		
	− Origin ⟶ +		
Normal AA (Genotype)			
Sickle-Cell Carrier AS (Genotype)			
Sickle-Cell Trait SS (Genotype)			

of these variants differ by only a single amino acid in the entire polypeptide sequence of either the *alpha globin chain* (141 amino acids) or the *beta globin chain* (146 amino acids). A sample of these changes in amino acid sequences is listed in Table 4-1. Note the substitution of *histidine* (His) by *tyrosine* (tyr) at position 58 in a variant of the alpha chain called IIb M Boston, named for the city where it was first discovered, or consider the Honolulu

TABLE 4-1   Major Alternation in Amino Acid Sequences

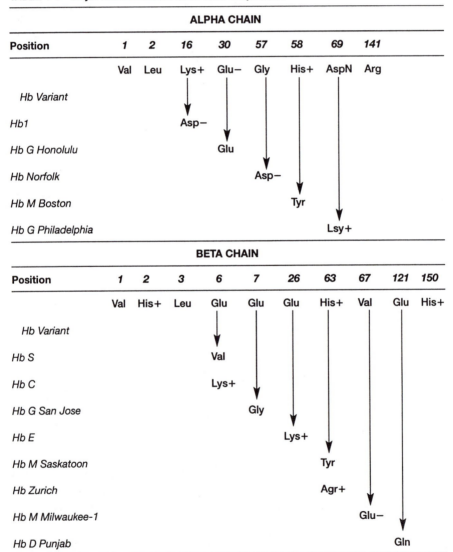

ALPHA CHAIN

Position	1	2	16	30	57	58	69	141
	Val	Leu	Lys+	Glu−	Gly	His+	AspN	Arg
Hb Variant								
Hb1			Asp−					
Hb G Honolulu				Glu				
Hb Norfolk					Asp−			
Hb M Boston						Tyr		
Hb G Philadelphia							Lsy+	

BETA CHAIN

Position	1	2	3	6	7	26	63	67	121	150
	Val	His+	Leu	Glu	Glu	Glu	His+	Val	Glu	His+
Hb Variant										
Hb S				Val						
Hb C				Lys+						
Hb G San Jose					Gly					
Hb E						Lys+				
Hb M Saskatoon							Tyr			
Hb Zurich							Agr+			
Hb M Milwaukee-1								Glu−		
Hb D Punjab									Gln	

Source: Reprinted by permission from Watson, James D., *Molecular Biology of the Gene*, 4th ed. Menlo Park, Calif.: The Benjamin/Cummings Publishing Company, Inc., 1987, Figure 8-8, p. 193.

G variant at position 30. Position 6 of the beta chain shows two variants; if *valine* (Val) is substituted for *glutamic* acid (Glu), then Hb S is produced, but if *lysine* (Lys) is the substituted amino acid, then Hb C is produced. Most substitutions appear to have little or no effect on hemoglobin function and hence red blood cells and health are normal. But changes of amino acids at certain critical positions, Val or Lys at position 6 and Lys at position 26 of the beta chain, for example, may reduce or radically alter hemoglobin shape and interrupt the normal RBC function of oxygen transport. The Hb S variant can result in a high rate of blood cell loss followed by severe anemia (sickle cell anemia), contributing to a host of circulatory problems and early death.

These sequences of amino acids in hemoglobin are inherited as simple Mendelian traits. If the symbol of normal hemoglobin is Hb^A, and Hb^S signifies the abnormal sickling type, then the mode of inheritance can be written

Parents' genotypes: $\qquad\qquad Hb^AHb^S \times Hb^AHb^S$

Children's genotypes: $\quad Hb^AHb^A \quad Hb^AHb^S \quad Hb^SHb^S$

The expected ratio of these will be 1:2:1, the Mendelian ratio of offspring produced from the mating of heterozygous parents. The individuals with the Hb^AHb^A hemoglobin will produce beta globin strands with a particular sequence of amino acids and, since this is the most frequent type, it is considered the normal form. However, the Hb^S allele codes for a single amino acid substitution as noted above. The alleles Hb^A and Hb^S are nondominant, that is, a heterozygote person's blood-forming tissues will produce normal and abnormal hemoglobin. Their red blood cells will then contain mixtures of molecules of both types, but a larger proportion will be of the normal hemoglobin A. The homozygote recessive person (Hb^SHb^S, or simply SS) can produce only hemoglobin molecules with the valine substitution in the beta chain.

If all hemoglobin has this simple change in amino acid sequence, the cell may undergo a deformation in shape when oxygen is taken up by the surrounding tissues. As oxygen is released by the hemoglobin molecules, the polypeptide chains begin to alter their spatial orientation and will change to a series of helical-shaped fibers. The more oxygen removed, the more the hemoglobin molecules will alter until enough of these long fiber bundles have formed, and subsequently they stretch to deform the blood cell. As this process proceeds, the shape of the deformed cell becomes crescent or sicklelike in appearance instead of its normal round shape; hence the term "sickle cell" (Figure 4-2).

Persons with the SS hemoglobin may develop what is called sickle cell disease (SCD). They can survive for long periods without clinical symptoms of the disease, and few of their cells will undergo the sickling process, depending on the rate of oxygen consumption. When, however, there is a greater demand for oxygen, which would occur during vigorous exercise, surrounding tissues take up more oxygen from the RBCs as they pass through the peripheral blood vessels. This causes more of the molecules to become deoxygenated; shape change follows, which brings on a sickling

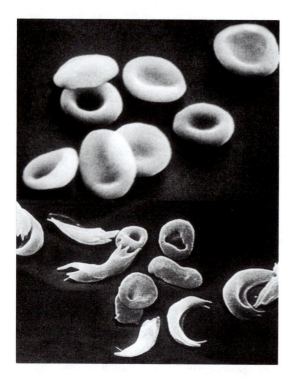

FIGURE 4-2   Normal and Sickled Human Red Blood Cells.(Photo Researchers, Inc.)

crisis. The distorted cells lose flexibility and clog smaller blood vessels, especially in the peripheral circulatory system. To remove this blockage, the body's immune system responds by attacking and causing the cells to *lyse* (break apart). Hemoglobin is released from the red blood cells as they rupture and, because of a reduction in cell number and increased free hemoglobin, anemia and a whole host of associated afflictions will result (Figure 4-3). The SS homozygote person may be at greater or lesser risk depending on age, disease, work habits, diet, and geography. A manual laborer is at greater risk of sickling than a person who has a sedentary occupation, for example. Exercise in the thinner atmosphere in the mountains, or flying in planes with unpressurized cabins could bring on a crisis.

Though sickling crises vary among individuals, the SS genotype is considered a near-lethal combination with a high mortality rate. Average life expectancy is about forty years in African Americans, but much lower in Africa where few live to adulthood. There are reports, however, of some adult homozygotes leading normal productive lives in Ghana, West Africa, though the odds weigh heavily against the survival of individuals with SCD (Konotey-Ahulu, 1982).

By contrast, heterozygote carriers of the sickle cell trait (SCT) enjoy a high degree of protection because a majority of their hemoglobin is normal and the Hb^A molecules combined with the Hb^S prevents the abnormal hemoglobin (Hb^S) from forming fibers distorting blood cells. The heterozygote's red blood cells function

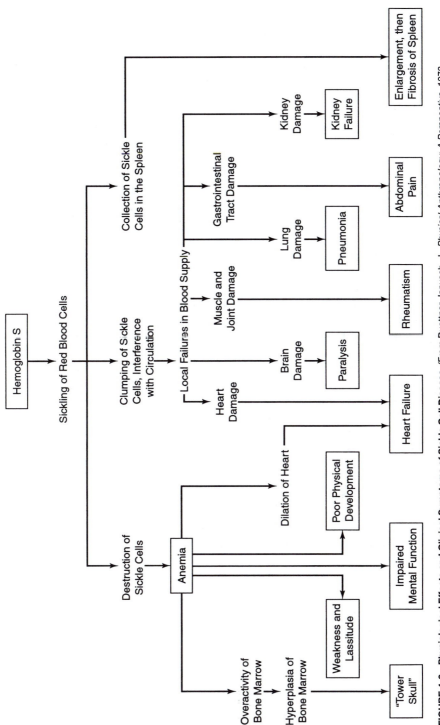

FIGURE 4-3 Physiological Effects and Clinical Symptoms of Sickle Cell Disease. (From Buettner-Janusch, J., *Physical Anthropology: A Perspective,* 1973. Copyright © 1973 by John Wiley & Sons, Inc. Reprinted by permission of the publisher.)

normally under most circumstances, and only very rarely do these cells, with a mixture of hemoglobin types, sickle (Edelstein, 1986). However, there has been considerable confusion over the relative health risks faced by heterozygous persons (AS) compared with homozygous normals (AA). This has been especially true in the United States, where about 10 percent of African Americans are carriers. A carrier (SCT) has been thought to be at greater risk when exercising heavily or when working at altitude, and flying in planes was thought to be beyond their physiological capability. Throughout the 1970s the Navy tested recruits and nearly all officers coming on active duty for the presence of the sickle cell trait. Army personnel were also screened, but only those applying for airborne duties were examined. Major commercial airlines also joined this confusion by grounding or even firing personnel with the SCT (Bowman, 1977). Such misunderstanding had been grounds for rejection of African Americans with SCT from the Air Force and was the cause of at least one forced resignation from the Air Force Academy in Colorado Springs (see Duster, 1990). By 1981, the ban on cadets with SCT was ended, but several major corporations have continued to test prospective employees (see Kevles, 1995).

Since these biased reactions thirty-five years ago to a trait common in African Americans as well as in several other ethnic groups, the issue or nonissue of physical disability of heterozygotes has diminished. But the confusion can still occur, and there are groundless fears over blood transfusions, misunderstanding of genetic counseling, and confusion of SCT with SCD. What concerns a carrier more than the risk of disease or shortened life expectancy is the probability of producing a child with the sickle cell disease (SCD). If both parents are carrying the S allele, there is a 25 percent chance of producing a child with genotype SS (recall the Mendelian ratios). Then, if the frequency of carriers is considered, the chance of producing a sickle cell child can be calculated for an entire population group. African Americans may be used as an example.

Given that the Hb^S gene frequency averages about 5 percent in the entire African American population of about 33 million and, of this number, 10 percent are carriers (heterozygotes; AS genotypes), there is a probability of 1 in 100 that the mating of heterozygotes will occur (or 0.10×0.10). This assumes that matings are random in regard to the hemoglobin locus. The probability of producing an SS child from such matings can be calculated from the Hardy-Weinberg equilibrium:

African Americans
0.10 (AS) × 0.10 (AS) = 0.01   (mating probability)

The probability of SS newborns from any mating of African Americans is then calculated by

0.010 × 0.25 = 0.0025   (homozygote probability)

This is about 1 in every 400 births in the entire African American population, given that the average of SCT individuals is about 10 percent. Actually, the frequency of newborns with SS genotype varies by region; it is higher in parts of the southeastern

United States, where there are about 15 percent heterozygotes (SCT), and lower in northern cities like New York, with the gene at only about 3 percent.

The probability of heterozygote matings is much higher among African populations since the gene frequency of S is between 10 to 20 percent, or even higher in some parts of the continent. If the frequency of heterozygotes is considered to be 20 percent in central Africa, and matings are random in regard to the hemoglobin locus, the following probability of can be calculated:

$$0.20 \text{ (AS)} \times 0.20 \text{ (AS)} = 0.04 \quad \text{(heterozygote mating)}$$

Then the probability of producing an infant with SS is

$$0.04 \times 0.25 = 0.01 \quad \text{(or 1 in 100 births)}$$

The chance of infants with SCD living to the age of reproduction is low; their fitness relative to the other genotypes ranges from zero to about 10 percent. These differences of genotype fitness have raised many questions, and the answers have offered an excellent model of natural selection operating on the human species. Despite the Hb^S (or S) allele being near lethal, it still exists at high frequency (from 10 to 20 percent) in numerous populations, especially in central Africa. With few if any homozygotes living to adulthood and reproducing, there is a high loss of S alleles each generation. A decline in frequency over the generations would be expected, but such has not been the case. This question of the persistence of the S allele despite selection against it was addressed in the 1950s by Allison (1954). He considered and then discarded the possibility that mutations (A to S) replaced the lost alleles, since a rate 100,000 times higher than any known human mutations would have had to be maintained (Livingstone, 1958 and 1989). With replacement by mutation ruled out, relative fitness of the genotypes was considered in those African populations with the highest S frequencies. In these populations, compared to the heterozygotes (AS), 15 percent more of the homozygous normals (AA) and 90 percent more of the homozygous abnormals (SS) died between birth and the age of reproduction. This relationship may be presented as genotype fitness:

$$AA = 0.85; \quad AS = 1.0; \quad SS = 0.10$$

DISTRIBUTION OF HEMOGLOBIN S

These relative fitness values favor the carrier and maintain a balance of the two alleles (A and S); in other words, some environmental factor or factors selectively favored the heterozygotes. They lived longer and reproduced at a higher rate, compensating for the lost S alleles, which maintained a balanced polymorphism in the population. Malaria, because of its high mortality and concordant geographical distribution with certain abnormal hemoglobins, was considered as a likely selective force. Just as Haldane had suggested in the case of thalassemia (another hemoglobin variant), the AS heterozygote was probably more resistant to the mosquito-borne disease malaria. This possibility of

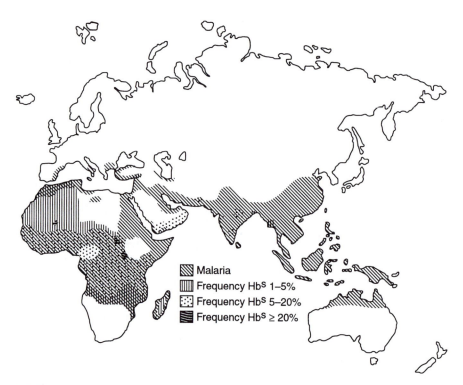

FIGURE 4-4   Distribution of Malaria and Sickle Cell Anemia. (Redrawn from Buettner-Janusch, 1966.)

the relative resistance of the genotypes stimulated data collection on malarial epidemiology and evidence for the distribution of abnormal hemoglobins (Figure 4-4).

The highest frequencies of Hb^S occur in central Africa, northeast and northwest India, and Arabia. High levels are also found around the Mediterranean, especially in Greece and Turkey (Table 4-2). Such a distribution in some countries bordering the Mediterranean results in cases of SCD reported among Europeans, much to the surprise of physicians trained to think of sickling as an African disease. This expectation of "race limited disease" is well illustrated by an inquiry to the editor of the *Journal of the American Medical Association* by a writer who wanted to know if there were any documented cases of SCT or SCD occurring in persons of European extraction. Powars (1994) replied in a short review of Mediterranean population movements that, yes, it was possible to be blond and blue-eyed (look non-African) and still have the trait. The brief summary offered by Powars, however, did not mention Arabia or India and so left the impression that Hb^S was a gene of African origin. The response, by use of terms of nonblack and black, also confused perception and physical appearances (i.e., skin color) with genetics without questioning traditional racial typology; such confusion of race and disease will be explored in Chapter 9.

Explanations for this distribution outside of Africa have often been related to the history of the area, which experienced an ebb and flow in the migration of diverse

TABLE 4-2   Some Examples of Populations with Sickle Cell Trait (SCT)

NATION OR REGION	SCT %
Africa	
Senegal	5–12
Guinea	8.5–20
Liberia	.07–28
Nigeria	18–32
Zaire	4–36
Angola	4–35
Kenya	0–25
Mediterranean	
Sicily	2.0
Greece (Orchomenos)	23.0
Turkey (Mersin)	13.0
Saudi Arabia	5–12.0
India	
Madras	14–17.0
Nilgiri district	8–31.0
Baster district	16–38.0
*Americas**	
United States	3.2–15.1
Panama	5–14.0
Brazil	3–8.6

*Populations sampled had African ancestors.

Source: Erhardt, 1973; Livingstone, 1985; Schroeder and Munger, 1990.

peoples, resulting in the establishment of colonies and the importation of slaves from sub-Saharan Africa, beginning probably as early as 2,000 years ago in the Mediterranean. Much of the distribution of the Hb^S alleles probably occurred during the years of Islamic rule from about A.D. 825 to 1060. These events of conquest plus widespread trade continued to disperse the S allele over the course of hundreds of years. The more recent importation of African slaves into the Americas, however, was condensed into a period of less than four centuries, bringing people from several African regions to the New World. The history of the slave trade offers a special case of distinctive environmental variables acting within a limited time frame, as will be considered below.

In India, trade and some colonization from Africa are also known to have occurred, events that offer a possibility of introduction of the Hb^S allele. It is difficult to explain the presence of such a high frequency in several parts of India, however, solely on the basis of the importation of slaves or the establishment of colonies (Figure 4-5). There is a possibility that an allele such as Hb^S, which is advantageous under certain conditions, appeared in several populations throughout human history by random mutations. The allele would then become fixed at high frequencies. Such occurrence of spontaneous mutations would rule out the need to associate a gene with a particular ethnic group (Das, 1995).

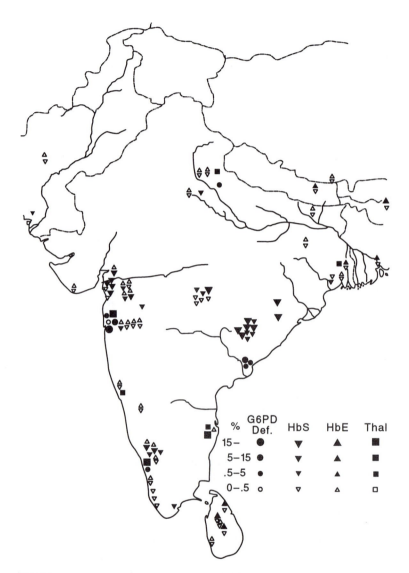

FIGURE 4-5   Hemoglobin S and Other Red-Cell Defects in India. (Reprinted from Livingstone, F.B., *Abnormal Hemoglobins in Human Populations,* 1967. (Chicago: Aldine Publishing Company, 1967; copyright © 1967 by Frank B. Livingstone. Reprinted by permission of the author and Aldine Publishing Company.)

Though the question is far from settled, there are supporters for both sides of the argument: For gene distribution by migration or by independent mutation. One group of scholars explains that a few mutations in a central area could have resulted in a gene, such as Hb^S, advantageous in certain environments. From that area, probably in eastern Nigeria, the gene spread by population migration and interpopulation contact, increasing in frequency because of its selective advantage. This spread has classically been associated with the expansion of populations of Bantu speakers, early agriculturists who successfully exploited tropical rain forests because of their possession of iron tools and an efficient food crop, the yam. Such a reconstruction, however, would make it difficult to explain how the gene arrived in more remote areas noncontiguous with the main African homeland and outside of the ancient trade route networks—areas such as northeastern India, for example.

Significant clues to understanding the occurrence of the SCT are not found simply in histories of population movements but are also found in the nature of the environments in several areas where SCT is frequent. Because of the concordant distributions of malaria and Hb^S, we have an important example of genetic adaptation of *Homo sapiens*. Populations with long histories of contact with the disease malaria usually exhibit the highest frequency of SCT (and also other hemoglobin abnormalities). The apparent relationships between these abnormalities and malaria are explained by a hypothesis that states: An individual who is a heterozygote (a carrier of the abnormal gene) enjoys a relative degree of immunity to infection by the malarial parasite in comparison with a person with the normal genotype.

MALARIA AND NATURAL SELECTION

The highly lethal mosquito-borne disease malaria is endemic in many tropical regions, where people are continuously infected throughout the year. In subtropical regions infection is more cyclical, following the rainfall patterns and increases in mosquitos. Malaria was once more widespread, occurring in much of the eastern United States and even in parts of Europe well into the twentieth century. Continuous efforts to eradicate the malaria-transmitting mosquito have eliminated the disease as a major problem in these areas. The disease remains the number one cause of sickness and death in many developing countries in the tropics, however. There are between three to five million new cases each year and approximately two million deaths (Starke, 1996). If deaths owing to complications arising from malarial infection are added, then the death rate is actually greater. The influence of malaria is illustrated when stringent control efforts are made by developing countries; total mortality rates are reduced by one-third to one-half. This experience among contemporary populations illustrates the significant influence malaria has had in modern times. Before mosquito control and drug treatment, it had likely been an even stronger selective force effecting humanity. The negative effects of malaria, however, are seen in other ways besides death rates. The endemic malarial conditions that exist among tropical populations mean that individuals carry a quantity of parasites in their bloodstream from time of birth, and, in many areas, are reinfected year round. This, together with the burden of other parasites common to the tropics as well as limited nutrition, lowers general health, reduces energy levels, and increases susceptibility to other diseases. All these factors affect life expectancy, but malaria appears to be the major selective force.

The disease we call malaria is caused by several protozoan species of the genus *Plasmodium*. Humans are hosts to four species of *Plasmodium*, each of which causes a different type of malaria: *vivax*, the most common form and with a wide geographical distribution; *ovale*, the rarest form native to West Africa; *malariae*, a broadly but unevenly distributed parasite causing a mild form of the disease; and the fourth and most deadly type of malaria, *falciparum*. This species requires a warm climate to flourish, and its distribution is largely limited to the tropics (Harrison, 1978). These single-celled parasites have a complex life cycle, part of which is spent in the body of a mammalian host, where it enters the red blood cell and, using the cell's energy supply, multiples until the RBC is destroyed. The released parasites accumulate in the larger blood vessels, especially those in the liver and spleen.

Malaria is transmitted to humans by the bite of a female *Anopheles* mosquito infected with the parasites, or an uninfected mosquito may suck up the parasites when biting an infected human. Either way, the mosquito is an important link in the distribution of the disease and can deposit malarial organisms in uninfected persons. Since mosquitos are carriers or *vectors* for malarial transmission, the distribution and spread of the disease depends on the habits and life cycle of the particular *Anopheles* species. Of the two hundred species known to function as a vector of the *Plasmodium* parasites, there are only about twenty important ones, because the parasites develop better in some species of mosquitos than in others. In addition, each world region provides an environment that favors certain mosquitos; for example, the species *A. gambiae* is the major vector for distribution of *falciparum* malaria in Africa and Arabia; *P. falciparum* accounts for 80 to 90 percent of the malarial infections found among the populations in these regions. Throughout India, Southeast Asia, and New Guinea, other species, requiring different habitats, are important vectors of *vivax* and *falciparum* malarial parasites.

The part humans play in this host-vector disease organism scheme is important and complicated because of the specific habitat needs of the major species of mosquito. These needs are often provided by human disruption of a natural environment, a disruption that creates expanded breeding places for the insect. Such environmental changes are evident in the example of slash-and-burn techniques of the tropical rain forest horticulturists, who radically alter the flora and drive away many mammals that might have been hosts to the mosquitoes. This style of agriculture involves the cutting and then burning of trees, and the removal of the tropical rain forest cover exposes the thin tropical soils to rapid erosion in high-rainfall areas. Stagnant pools of water collect and provide mosquito breeding places; furthermore, humans locate their dwellings in groups where numerous families live in close contact. All of these conditions provide an ideal situation for the transmission of malarial parasites on a continuous basis, causing up to 100 percent of the population to be infected. For example, the *A. gambiae* mosquito, the efficient vector for the most lethal malaria, *falciparum*, is best adapted to those conditions that exist around human habitations in tropical rain forests with village clearings, stagnant pools of water, and open sunlit garden plots. In contrast, it does not breed well in thickly forested areas with few open areas; other mosquito species predominate but are less effective vectors (Livingstone, 1958).

Primitive agricultural activities and adoption of sedentary village life not only caused many environmental changes but also contributed to a significant increase in human population, accompanied by a decline in the number of wild mammals in the vicinity of the settlements. In the past, the *Anopheles*, or their ancestral forms, may have preyed on other mammalian hosts, just as many mosquito species still do. Through the development of human sedentary life since the Neolithic, several mosquito species have come to depend on humans as their major host. Also, sedentary human populations provide many more hosts than did wandering bands of nomads. This has allowed our species to increase with the expansion of agriculture, which offered somewhat conflicting life-support conditions in prehistory and early historic times. As humans gained skills in plant domestication, a surplus of food was produced that supported larger populations, but food production and the settlement patterns in turn altered the environment, favoring an increase of malaria. This disease caused a high mortality, but the losses of human life were more than balanced by gains made with the adoption of agriculture.

Under these conditions of early agricultural life, any degree of immunity that some people may have had because of their genotypes would contribute to their longevity and an increased reproduction rate. Since malarial parasites depend on red blood cells for nutrients during part of their life cycle, red blood cell metabolism under disease conditions has been studied for years (Edelstein, 1986). The results show that red blood cells containing some types of abnormal hemoglobin are less able to support malarial parasite growth. These red blood cells are also more fragile, with a shorter life span, and have a lower energy level. These factors reduce the multiplication of parasites and result in a smaller number of cells in circulation. The most clear-cut relationship between malaria and all of the red-cell variants appears in the case of Hb^S; in endemic malarial areas, persons with SCT have lower parasite counts than do normals.

In areas where *falciparum* is endemic, there are several examples of natural selection favoring the survival of individuals with SCT. They are less likely to die from *falciparum* malaria than persons with all normal hemoglobin. There is a significantly greater number of heterozygotes in the 45-plus age group, which indicates a longer life span compared with homozygous normals. In addition, fewer die in infancy and more reach adolescence. Also, fertility is higher among female carriers; they have a higher live birthrate and lower parasite counts than do women with all normal hemoglobin. Though untested, fertility is likely to be higher among heterozygous males due to fewer episodes of high fever associated with malarial attacks, since spermatogenesis is impaired by prolonged elevated body temperature. Table 4-3 lists a summary of the evidence for differential fitness of the heterozygote (AS) in malarial environments. The combined data gained from laboratory tests and demography make a strong argument, but more convincing are the distributions of the S allele and malaria (see Figure 4-4). The hypothesis that the concordant distributions of gene and disease are the result of natural selection is reinforced by the evidence of several other inherited hemoglobin defects.

TABLE 4-3   Malaria as a Selective Force

	HETEROZYGOUS AS	HOMOZYGOUS AA
Fertility		
Female	Higher	Lower
Male	Higher sperm count	Impaired spermatogenesis(?)
Demographic		
Child	More children (age 1–4 yrs) Highest frequency among juveniles	Fewer adolescents
Adult	Greater number with SCT	
Morbidity		
Parasite count	Lower	Higher
Cerebral malaria	Less frequent	A major cause of adult mortality
Epidemiology		
Frequency of Hb^S	Highest in areas of endemic malaria	No correlation

OTHER ABNORMAL HEMOGLOBINS

Several inherited abnormal hemoglobin types exist at polymorphic frequencies and have wide geographical distributions. Most of these types do not cause disease in the homozygote as serious as sickle cell, though some may result in anemia under certain conditions. Distribution of these hemoglobins is concordant with malaria of the *falciparum* and *vivax types*. Though not as well tested as in the case of Hb^S, the same hypothesis may be offered: There is probably a higher survival rate of the carrier of one of these hemoglobin types.

Type E Hemoglobin.   This major hemoglobin is also the result of a point mutation in the beta globin gene (amino acid lysine for glutamic acid; refer to Table 4-1). Hb^E, the third most frequent hemoglobin type (after Hb^A and Hb^S), has a more limited distribution that begins approximately where Hb^S distribution ends. It occurs in very high frequencies (0.15 percent) among populations extending from India, through Southeast Asia, to New Guinea. The homozygote EE does not suffer as severely from acute anemia as does the SS nor is there cell distortion, but there appears to be a difference in fitness between the genotypes that favors the heterozygotes. The distribution in New Guinea demonstrates this well; the hemoglobin E is most frequent among populations living on the coastal plain, where vast, swampy low-lying areas sustain hyperendemic malaria. Away from these areas in the highlands of greater population density, malaria disappears as a health problem (until recent times), and frequencies of Hb^E diminish to zero.

Other hemoglobin abnormalities with polymorphic frequencies are found in a more restricted range of populations; examples are Hb C in a limited area of West

Africa and Hb O_{Arab} in the southern part of Arabia. Hemoglobin D_{Punjab} is another, named for the region of India where it was found. No hemoglobin abnormalities are known to exist among native peoples of the New World. Those abnormal hemoglobins that are found among populations in the Americas today occur in those persons who are descendants of African slaves or in samples of Europeans who had migrated from malarial areas where certain hemoglobin abnormalities were present in high frequencies (as noted above).

The Thalassemias.   The abnormal hemoglobins listed above are due to a single nucleotide substitution (point mutation); alpha and beta globins are still produced, but with a different amino acid sequence. In the case of *thalassemias*, complete synthesis of either the beta or alpha globin chains is interrupted. This large variety of abnormal hemoglobins result from point mutations that cause a shift or a deletion in entire DNA sequences of either the exons (the part that carries the code) or introns (the noncoding, intervening sequence) of the alpha or beta globin genes. Instead of single amino acid substitutions in the globin chain as described above, DNA transcription is interrupted or shifted so the codons of mRNA are not produced in a correct sequence or are even eliminated (see below). In some types, the globin chains may have a normal sequence but are produced in reduced amounts, or a chain may be shortened, and, in some cases, the alpha or globin chain is totally absent. These numerous variants of globin chain syntheses can result in severely handicapped hemoglobin function followed by a frequent loss of the red blood cells. The individual with such an affliction may have a life-threatening anemia, depending on the type of the inherited abnormality. These defects of globin chain production, or *thalassemias*, are among the most commonly inherited disorders in *Homo sapiens*, they may account for an estimated 100,000 child deaths per year.

The first disorder to consider is *Thalassemia major*, originally described as a form of inherited anemia found among populations of several countries bordering the Mediterranean Sea. This condition is determined by an autosomal dominant in part of the beta globin gene cluster on chromosome 11. This mutant allele (beta thalassemia) decreases or halts the synthesis of the beta-Hb chain. A reduced amount results in an imbalance of the quantity of alpha and beta chains in the completed hemoglobin. Red blood cells with this imbalance are unstable and are lost through hemolysis at a rapid rate in the homozygous person. A total lack of beta globin chains, as in the case of the $beta^0 39$, the most common type in Sardinia and other Mediterranean areas, causes the cells to be even more unstable.[1] Homozygotes for this allele will suffer a severe form of anemia (thalassemia major), and few will survive adolescence. The heterozygotes (thalassemia minor) may have a milder form and usually live free of symptoms, since the reduction of beta-Hb production in the heterozygote is somewhat compensated for by a continued synthesis of fetal hemoglobin well into adult life.

---

[1]There are now at least thirty-seven different mutations that affect the beta globin chain synthesis, and some cause a more critical disruption of globin synthesis than others.

TABLE 4-4   Beta Thalassemias of Selected Ethnic Groups

ETHNIC GROUP	BETA THAL MUTATIONS	TYPE	FREQUENCY
African American	TATA box (29)	$\beta+$	39%
	Poly A site	$\beta+$	26%
Mediterranean	Intron (110)	$\beta+$	38%
	β 39 term	βo	29%
Indian	Intron 1(5)	$\beta+$	36%
	Deletion (61)	βo	36%
Chinese	Frame shift (71/72)	βo	49%
	Intron 2 (654)	βo	38%

Source: Data selected from Vogel and Motulsky, 1986; McKusick, 1994.

Comparisons of beta thalassemia occurrance among several populations are made difficult by the fact that thirty-seven genes around the DNA of the globin gene affect rates of synthesis. Various mutations of these genes have been found distributed unevenly around the Mediterranean; one predominates in the western region while another is more common in countries along the eastern shores (see Table 4-4). Each affects a thalassemic condition resulting in anemia, but with varying degrees of severity. In fact, each ethnic group appears to have its own mutation in some of the genes that regulate hemoglobin production. Thalassemia of the $beta^0 39$ type accounts for 95 percent of thalassemias in Sardinia, but only 65 percent in Spain. In Greece and other countries of the Eastern Mediterranean, intron 1, a $beta^1$ type, is in the majority. Despite severe selection against the homozygote of some types, beta thalassemias are widespread throughout much of the Old World. In certain regions of Italy, for example, 35 percent of the people are carriers of alleles for some form.

Similar high frequencies of beta thalassemia alleles are seen in many African populations, especially in North Africa and in certain pastoral tribes in Sudan. Beta thalassemia is also frequent in Thailand, Southeast Asia, and parts of China (Chan et al., 1987). The severity of the disease varies from lethal to mild depending on the site of the mutation. Considering only those mutations that result in a complete absence of beta globin production, $beta^0 39$ and 6 are the principal mutations in the Mediterranean, $beta^0 17$ and 41 in south China, and $beta^0 15$ and 8 in India. As investigations of the thalassemias broaden, additional mutation sites are being discovered in specific ethnic groups that range at this time from Europe and Africa, through the Middle East to India and Thailand, with South China and Taiwan included on the far eastern edge of this distribution (refer to hemoglobin section in McKusick, 1994). From these eastern outliers in China with beta thalassemia genes to New Guinea, a new group of mutations appear as the predominant form of hemoglobin variants.

Alpha Thalassemia.   Deficiencies of alpha chain production are highly variable, resulting in a greater variety of clinical expressions than reported for beta thalassemia. This is due to a more complicated mode of inheritance; there are two loci on chromosome 16 that carry the structural genes for alpha globin. Mutations at one or

TABLE 4-5   Alpha Thalassemias of Selected Ethnic Groups

ETHNIC GROUP	ALPHA THAL MUTATIONS	TYPE
	Chain Termination	
African American	UAA to GAA	Seal rock
Mediterranean	UAA to AAA	Hb Icaria
Indian	UAA to UCA	Hb Koya Dora
Southeast Asian	UAA to CAA	Hb constant spring
	Other Types	
Arabian	RNA cleavage (α2 gene)	α2 gene
	Frameshift codon 14	α1 gene
Sardinian	AUG to ACG	α2 gene

Source: Data selected from Vogel and Motulsky, 1986; Oppenheimer et al., 1984; Hill, 1986.

both of these loci, usually gene deletion types, cause clinical thalassemias that vary from mild to severe to lethal. Homozygotes for mutant genes at two loci are unable to produce any alpha globin, while in contrast, a carrier of a single affected gene has less than a normal amount, but the hemoglobin remains functional (see Table 4-5). Between these two extremes are carriers of a mutant at two loci, or homozygous at one locus and a carrier at another. Such individuals will produce varying amounts of alpha globin, and since the hemoglobin varies in stability, suffer different rates of hemolysis.

The alpha thalassemias are some of the more common inherited disorders, but the deletion mutation combinations vary among the ethnic groups, just as noted above for the beta thalassemias. Deletions at one alpha gene are common worldwide with the highest frequency (33 percent) in East Africa and the Mediterranean. In contrast, deletions at both alpha loci are the most frequent types in Southeast Asia. Mutations of the nondeletion type that interfere with mRNA also show wide ethnic variation. Different ones are reported for populations in Greece, Sardinia, India, China, Southeast Asia, and Melanesia.

Some thalassemia types appear in high frequencies despite the homozygous disadvantage. This is explained by the hypothesis that selection favors the heterozygote in malarial environments, as in the case of sickle cell anemia. The majority of the alpha thalassemias are milder, especially those expressed in Southeast Asian and Melanesian populations, but the frequencies still follow the distribution of malaria. A case in point is New Guinea, where a study was made in populations of the coastal areas to test the malarial hypothesis. Frequencies of alpha gene deletion-type mutations ranged from 22 percent to 68 percent in coastal areas. In the central highlands, an area of greatest population density, the deletions drop to between 2 and 5 percent. Malaria is endemic in New Guinea, where both *falciparum* and *vivax* types are present in particularly virulent strains that are resistant to antimalarial drugs. Its incidence is highest in the marshy coastal areas and drops appreciably with altitude; the highland areas are believed to have been malaria-free before European contact. The distribution of the thalassemia mutations likewise falls with increasing altitude and diminished risk of malarial infection. Hill (1986) showed a high correlation between the mutations and malaria, and he also recorded a clinal variation from New Guinea through the Solomon Islands to New Caledonia, as malaria and alpha thalassemia decline. He argued that selection favors the heterozygote of even this mild form of thalassemia when malaria is present. Thalassemia mutants are low or absent in the Fiji Islands, which are free of malaria. This distribution of hemoglobin mutants is similar to the relationship in the Mediterranean areas and also relates to a malarial parasite's survival and growth in red blood cells with defective hemoglobin.

THE ENZYME G6PD (GLUCOSE 6 PHOSPHATE DEHYDROGENASE)

While considering hemoglobin variants and their influence on survival, an enzyme, G6PD, should be noted because of its many inherited forms. The enzyme is present in all cells of the body, where it catalyzes a variety of functions, but one of the most essential of these functions is performed in the red blood cells. The enzyme initiates a step in a biochemical pathway, a chain of conversions that enables the red blood cell to reduce harmful oxidative products of cell metabolism (hydrogen peroxide, for example), and thus protect the cell membrane. These processes and the stages of chemical conversion are too complex to consider here (see Ganong, 2003 for specific details). It is sufficient to say that G6PD is a vital substance for red blood cell function, and the cell's life span is directly related to the quantity of the enzyme present. This is especially true when red blood cells are under oxidative stress from either chemical or parasitic sources. Nevertheless, enzyme function varies over a wide range because of different G6PD polymorphisms.

The G6PD enzyme is under control of a gene on the X-chromosome as described in the discussion of sex linkage in Chapter 2. There are a number of alleles of this gene, and some code for the production of an enzyme form that operates less efficiently. Many altered forms of the G6PD enzyme have a lower level of activity, and these variants are described as deficient (G6PDD or Gd−). Under most circumstances this does not pose a health problem for the individual. However, even mild infections will increase the level of oxidative products in cells and will depend on an active series of reducing agents to render these waste products harmless. Under such conditions, the level of G6PD activity is important; in cases of serious infection or parasitation, effective G6PD may be critical. In Gd− persons, when confronted with such oxidative stress, blood cells increase in fragility and frequently lyse. This results in hemolytic anemia of varying levels of severity depending on the acuteness of the disease. Certain toxins in drugs or in plants can have a similar effect and can cause a transient form of anemia—that is, the production of new red blood cells will bring cell concentration back up to normal when the oxidative substance is removed. Recognition of the effect of these toxins eventually led to the discovery of the inherited defect in the red blood cell enzyme system.

The drug sensitivity of the red blood cells of some people has been recognized since the 1920s, when synthetic antimalarial drugs were first introduced as substitutes for quinine, the natural product used for centuries in the treatment of "fevers." The earliest use of the synthetic antimalarial drugs was in the British army, whose widespread occupation of many tropical areas placed tens of thousands of personnel at risk of malarial infection. Adverse responses to the drugs were soon reported among many of the Asian troops. Later, in World War II and during the Korean War, sensitivity was again noted. About 10 percent of African American soldiers suffered from anemia following administration of drugs such as primaquine; later, anemias were also recognized among those of southern European ancestry. This repeated the experience of the British army earlier; some ethnic groups suffered from a debilitating level of anemia when given certain drugs to prevent malaria. Though the genetic connection had not yet been made, doctors recognized that some deficiency condition existed in the RBC of these patients that caused cell destruction on exposure to these drugs. The anemia diminished when the source of the irritant was removed, and cell count gradually returned to normal.

The exact nature of the cell deficiency was determined in the late 1950s through laboratory tests devised to identify the susceptible individuals. It was found that these individuals had lower G6PD activity in their RBC than those persons whose cells did not hemolyse (burst apart) under the test procedures (Beutler et al., 1955). Once these test procedures were refined and proved effective in identifying afflicted individuals, many thousands of blood samples were examined. Deficiencies were found to occur more frequently in males than in females, suggesting that G6PD synthesis is under the control of an X-linked locus, which is now mapped to the same region as the colorblindness and hemophilia loci. Males with normal G6PD have Gd A or B, the most common types, whereas the deficient males have either Gd A− or Gd B−. Females who are G6PD deficient would be homozygotes for the defect Gd A− or Gd B− alleles. Heterozygote females tend to have a mixture of normal and abnormal RBC because only one of their X-chromosomes is active in each of the cells of the blood-forming tissues.

Since these original studies, 325 other variants of G6PD have been reported. Fortunately, most of these are quite rare and only a few of the variants appear to be malarial-drug sensitive. The major variants exist in numerous populations from New Guinea to India, Italy to Africa, and throughout the Middle East (Table 4-6). The highest frequency of Gd− is found in countries around the Mediterranean, particularly among Egyptians and populations on the island of Sardinia. The variant Gd A− is frequent—about 20 percent among Africans. The more severe variant form, Gd B−, is found in frequencies of 15 to 20 percent in Greece, Sardinia, and the Middle East. China and Thailand also show high frequencies of variants with low activity levels (Beutler, 1983).

A surprising relationship exists between several of these Gd− variants and a widely used food plant, the fava bean (*Vicia faba*). It has long been known that some people had a hemolytic response following consumption of these beans or even upon exposure to its pollen. Such sensitivity is referred to as *favism*. Very much as in the drug-induced reaction, there is a recovery from the anemia when exposure ceases. Yet these fava beans have been a dietary staple of many populations of the Mediterranean region for centuries, and it is these same populations that have the highest frequency of the Gd B− allele, coding for the most deficient enzyme form. Also,

TABLE 4-6   Classes of Some Common G6PD Variants

CLASS	POPULATION	ENZYME ACTIVITY
Gd B	Majority	Normal level
Gd A+	African	Near normal
Gd A−[b]	African	10–60% of normal
Gd B−[a, b]	Mediterranean	0–5% of normal
Gd Canton[a,b]	Chinese	4–25% of normal
Gd Anant[b]	Thailand	Near normal
Gd Mahidol[b]	Thailand	5–16% of normal
Gd Mahidol[b]	Thailand	5–16% of normal
Gd Hektoen	Thailand	Above normal

[a]Sensitive to fava bean.

[b]Sensitive to certain oxidizing drugs.

Source: Data selected from McKusick, 1994; Vogel and Motulsky, 1986.

southern China, the largest producer of fava beans in the world, has populations with high frequencies of the more severe form of G6PD deficiencies.

The explanation for this relationship between such a potentially harmful plant and an inherited defect relates to the malarial environments in which these people live, as considered earlier for the abnormal hemoglobins. The plant toxins (divicine and isouramil) place an oxidative stress on the red blood cells, so in Gd− persons many more of their RBC are prone to lyse, especially in the case of the older blood cells. The rate of destruction is a function of the quantity of the plant toxins ingested. The RBCs maintain a very narrow or precarious balance, and any additional oxidative stress can increase hemolysis rates; cell life span is shorter and a greater number of immature cells enter circulation. The intake of malarial parasites tips this balance and hemolysis increases, thereby reducing parasite multiplication rates. The blood cells are sustaining activity within a narrow level between the oxidative stresses and the parasite load. Assisting in this balancing act the blood cells must endure is probably a taste sensitivity to the fava bean that limits consumption, thereby reducing the hemolysis rate until challenged by parasites. Though not identified yet, this taste sensitivity is hypothetically an adaptation that assists in resistance to malaria. Possibly there are other common food toxins as well that work as low-level hemolytic agents, but the fava bean is the only one studied for this property (Greene, 1993).

Finally, these red blood cell variants, the abnormal hemoglobins, G6PD deficiency, and thalassemia are not confined to a single geographical area nor are they unique to a particular "racial" group. The genes for these variants are widespread among many populations and closely follow the pattern of malaria distribution. No simple explanation of population migration and admixture has been able to account completely for these distributions. Major migrations of the world's peoples have undoubtedly been involved in the dispersal of these mutant genes, as in the case of African Americans, but selection in a malarial environment remains the most important factor. Several studies of the concordant distribution of the genes and disease support this conclusion, and one of particular interest is on the isolated island of Sardinia.

DISTRIBUTION OF RED-CELL VARIANTS IN SARDINIAN POPULATIONS

The island of Sardinia lies 126 miles (200 kilometers) off the Italian coast. Its mountainous terrain isolates many of the towns and villages that are home to 1.5 million people (1993 census) who trace their ancestry to several European and Muslim invaders. Until modern times, the islanders have been relatively isolated from the mainland, following each of the periods of colonization by Spain, France, Italy, and North Africa. Though these ancestral groups left limited genetic traces, according to Cavalli-Sforza and co-authors (1994), gene flow tends to be directed and limited by the geography and history of the island, so gene frequencies of certain markers today vary significantly from area to area. The populations of coastal communities differ in many ways, linguistically, historically, and genetically, from villages above the coastal plain. One of the most notable of these differences are the genetic markers that relate to a malarial environment. Until 1944, when a major mosquito-control effort was begun, parts of Sardinia were among the worst malarial areas in the Mediterranean, and the island is an extensive source of epidemiological data.

Studies of Sardinia offer substantial evidence to support the hypothesis of relationships between thalassemia, G6PD deficiency Gd B−, and malaria. Most significantly, a clear inverse correlation was found between altitude and frequency of thalassemia and G6PD deficiency (Figure 4-6). At higher elevations, as one moves away from the coastal plain, the rate of malarial infection decreases because the environment is less favorable to the mosquito vector. Changes in gene frequencies are also seen; there are fewer carriers of the genes for Gd B− and thalassemia among the populations of villages in the mountains and foothills (note the major drop in G6PD deficiency above 400 meters). Thalassemia also declines, but at a lower rate. These declines with altitude offer a successful test of the malarial hypothesis—the carriers for these defects are favored at lower elevations. Where the risk of malaria is less, however, the frequency of thalassemia and Gd B− decreases.

Some Sardinian villages, however, do *not* fit the correlations. In other words, the selective force (malaria) is present, but there are few people who are carriers of the genetic traits (G6PD and thalassemia) that would provide them with a degree of immunity; an explanation must be sought elsewhere. The villages of Carloforte and Usini, both in a malarious area, were settled in the last 200 years by immigrants from other regions, Spain (Usini) and Genoa (Carloforte). These founders did not possess the Gd B− or thalassemia genes. This reconstruction is further reinforced by the genealogical evidence; the few individuals with these traits can trace their ancestry to an earlier Sardinian origin (Siniscalco et al., 1966, Piazza et al., 1985).

If the malarial hypothesis is accepted, then the genes for such variants as Hb^S, Hb^E, thalassemia, and G6PD deficiency are an advantage for populations living in the area where malaria is endemic. The survival value of being a carrier living under malarious conditions outweighs the disadvantages of the genetic variants. The selection for the heterozygote establishes a balanced polymorphism that maintains the abnormal gene at high frequencies. These relationships have probably existed for as long as humans have practiced agriculture in the tropics—about 3,000 to 4,000 years. The situation in the subtropics is more complex, and the insect vectors are different, as are the types of malarial disease that they transmit. The association between agriculture, settled

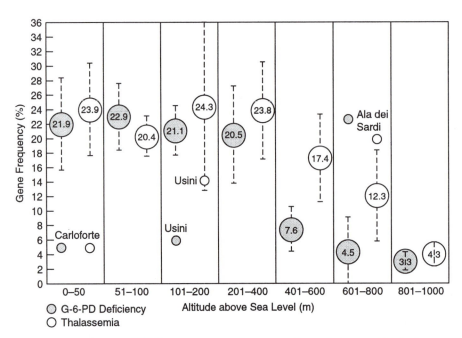

FIGURE 4-6   Incidence of G6PD Deficiency and the Thalassemia Trait in Relation to Altitude above Sea Level. The figures in each of the large circles are the averages of the gene frequencies found in the villages that fall within the ending altitude groupings (0–50 meters, 51–100 meters, etc.). (From Siniscalco, M., et al., "Population genetics of hemoglobin variants, thalassemia and glucose-6-phosphate dehydrogenase deficiency, with particular reference to the malaria hypothesis." Copyright © 1966 by World Health Organization. Reprinted by permission of the publisher.)

village life, and malaria is probably the same, however. Skeletal remains from Greek Neolithic and later Bronze Age sites show signs of bone modifications associated with chronic anemia, similar to that caused by thalassemia (Angel, 1966). Because recent descendants of these populations were those who suffered from a high incidence of malaria, it is assumed that the early agriculturists brought about environmental changes that contributed to a persistence of malaria down through the ages.

The linkage between human action, disease, and natural selection continues to this very day, as will be explored in later chapters. The numerous polymorphisms of the globin genes remain the best illustration of this linkage, as is further illustrated when a major selective force is reduced or removed entirely. Such a condition of rapid and radical change was created when hundreds of thousands of people were transported as slaves from their African homelands.

GENE FREQUENCY CHANGES AND AFRICAN AMERICANS

The discovery and occupation of the Americas by Spaniards and Portuguese starting in the fifteenth century opened up a dark page in human history. Not only were death and destruction wrought on native peoples of the New World, but also about ten million

Africans were enslaved and transported to North and South America. From about A.D. 1502 until the 1860s, slave ships landed their human cargos in ports stretching from Virginia in the north through the Caribbean to Brazil in the south. The sugar plantations of the Caribbean, with a high mortality and a need for a large labor force, absorbed most of the slave imports. About 51 percent of the total of the slave imports over the three-and-a-half centuries was divided between the Caribbean colonies of Spain, Britain, and France. The second largest number of slaves, 38 percent, were imported into the Portuguese colony of Brazil. The southeastern parts of North America imported only 6 percent, and a majority were landed between 1720 and 1820.

Conditions were harshest, and mortality was highest, on the sugar plantations, requiring a continuous replacement of the losses with new slaves. It was many years before natural increase (an excess of births over deaths) began to stabilize populations in these areas. In contrast, the working conditions and less severe disease environments in the North American colonies (later the United States) fostered a rate of natural increase that gradually reduced the proportion of African-born slaves. Even during the peak of slave imports (1780 to 1800), those of African birth accounted for only 20 percent of the slave total (Fogel and Engerman, 1984). This uneven distribution of founders, and the varying rates of survival in the different colonies, contributed to the genetic diversity we find among African American descendants today.

Most notable are the differing frequencies of the sickle cell trait. As noted above, African Americans in the United States have, on average, less than one-fourth to one-half of the Hb^S found among West African populations today (5 to 10 percent versus 20 percent). Assuming that the West Africans had this same frequency of Hb^S centuries ago when the slave trade began, then the reduction among their American-born descendants is highly significant. This reduction, occurring over the three-and-a-half centuries of their occupation in the New World, was rapid and may be accounted for either by admixture with Euro-Americans or by an elimination of the selective advantage of the carrier of the sickle cell trait. First, it should be noted that there is a considerable variation in degree of European ancestry recorded among African American communities; admixture is higher in large urban areas of the North and West, while it is much lower among populations in the southeastern United States, especially along the Atlantic coast (Pollitzer, 1994). Admixture alone could account for some reduction in Hb^S, since it is those very populations with fewer genes of European origin that retain the highest frequencies of African-derived genes. That is, hemoglobin C and S are more frequent in Charleston, South Carolina, than in Pittsburgh, Pennsylvania.

This brings up the second possibility for explaining the decrease in hemoglobin S— the selection favoring the carrier. Malaria is probably not indigenous to the New World, but it spread rapidly, mainly in South and Central America, since its introduction at the time of colonization. The major types, *vivax* and *falciparum*, have adapted to indigenous mosquito species and remain a major problem in many tropical areas. Malaria was also once common in the southeastern United States. Since the late nineteenth century when mosquito eradication programs became widely applied, it has disappeared from North America except for an occasional outbreak of "traveler" or "airport malaria" when the travelers return infected with malarial parasites, or mosquitos survive transport in aircraft wheel wells and fly off to infect persons near airports.

During earlier centuries the disease was a major health problem, rising to epidemic levels at times in some southern areas. Nowhere in North America, however, was malaria mortality comparable to the West African experience. In addition, the malaria was probably *vivax*, since this is the most frequent type found outside of the tropics (Harrison, 1978). There is a possibility that some *falciparum* appeared in the extreme southern fringes of the country, as suggested by the symptoms described in health department reports. The coastal regions of South Carolina, for example, probably experienced this type because of their climate and environment (Pollitzer et al., 1966).

The question of malarial type is an important consideration because of the difference in mortality of each, *vivax* being least deadly. Most important, though, Africans appear to have an immunity to *vivax* because of their Duffy blood group type, discussed in the last chapter. Such a resistance would mean that, in areas where *vivax* was predominant, malarial infection would not have acted as a selective force favoring the carrier of the sickle cell trait if that person also had the Duffy blood group type Fy^0. With mixed parasite types (*vivax* and *falciparum*) and climatic differences, malaria, as a selective force, diminished over the generations since arriving in North America. Declines in the Hb^S frequencies would be slow in the earlier generations, but the rate of decline would accelerate rapidly into the early twentieth century as mosquito control programs became effective and there were fewer outbreaks of malaria. The area where malaria persisted the longest, South Carolina, is home to African Americans with the highest Hb^S frequency today—the residents of the offshore Gullah Islands (Pollitzer, 1958). They are also one of the few groups in America with significant amounts of Hb^C, the allele otherwise restricted to a region around northern Ghana and Volta in West Africa. Questions of the distribution of sickle cell hemoglobin, both here and in the Old World, have become even more important with the rise of the newer genetic technology.

DNA MARKERS OF HUMAN VARIATION

With the use of endonucleases (restriction enzymes), an enormous amount of knowledge has been gained about the nucleotides of the noncoding sequences flanking the exons of the hemoglobin gene. This rapid advance in biotechnology has provided us with an ever-growing record of diversity at the DNA level, measured by the strings of base sequences cut into various lengths. These restriction fragment lengths vary from person to person, identifying a uniqueness of our individual genome, the so-called DNA fingerprints. Some, however, occur more commonly and are present at polymorphic frequencies which, in turn, differ among populations. Many RFLPs have proven useful as a type of genetic marker, particularly those in the noncoding DNA sequences in the region of major structural genes. Identifying and locating a major gene with its surrounding RFLPs provide a means of recording population distributions and origins. Most useful have been the genes for hemoglobin, especially the beta globin gene on chromosome 11 that shows seventeen sites of cleavage in the globin gene cluster. The degree of RFLP variation among several ethnic groups illustrates one of the earlier applications of restriction enzymes as discussed in Chapter 2 (refer to Table 2-8).

Markers of the Globin Gene

Following the report by Kan and Dozy (1978) that there were at least two different RFLPs in the globin gene sequence of persons carrying the sickle cell trait, the search was intensified to discover other restriction sites that might be common to this gene sequence. Samples were taken from a broad spectrum of peoples from Africa, Arabia, India, and the United States. Numerous RFLPs were discovered in flanking sequences around the Hb gene, but certain combinations of these polymorphisms appeared more frequently than others. Several restriction sites (usually eight) were considered together in what is called haplotypes because of their close linkage (recall the blood group haplotypes). Many of the RFLP haplotypes occur only rarely, but there are four frequently found in populations with a high frequency of the sickle cell gene. These haplotypes are named after the ethnic group where they were first discovered: the African types of *Senegal, Benin,* and *Bantu,* and an *Asian* type (distributed among populations from Arabia to India). Another African type, *Cameroon,* has recently been described. Table 4-7 lists these haplotypes for eight restriction sites indicated by a plus if the fragment is cut at that point or minus if it is not.

With this record of haplotypes associated with the sickle cell gene a number of new questions emerge that relate to population movements, the spread of the gene, natural selection, and the possibility of independent mutation in the different populations. Considering the question of population movements first, we may look at the origins of Hb^S and its frequency among modern-day African Americans. Reviews of their African origins (Curtin, 1969) show that regions within a 2,000-mile range from north to south supplied differing proportions of slaves for the North American market (Figure 4-7). The majority (70 percent) came from an area defined by the borders of modern-day Ghana and Nigeria, the area where the *Benin* type predominates. The balance came from the Senegal region to the northwest and the Bantu area in the south. The result is that most African Americans with SCT have the *Benin* type (Antonarakis et al., 1984). The exception is South Carolina, because Senegal was the major supplier of slaves so the *Senegal* haplotype is found more frequently there than in Virginia (Labie et al., 1986). By contrast, the *Bantu* or Central African haplotype is the predominant type among

TABLE 4-7   Restriction Site Haplotypes for the Beta Hemoglobin S Gene

HAPLOTYPES[a]	RESTRICTION SITES[b]	
Senegal	− + − + +	+ + +
Benin	− − − − +	+ − +
Bantu	− + − − −	+ + +
Arab-Indian	+ + − + +	+ + −

[a]Haplotypes found in populations in three African regions, Arabia, and India.

[b]Combinations of DNA sites cut by restriction enzymes above and below the beta hemoglobin gene S. The + indicates a fragment cut at this site and − no reaction to the enzyme.

Source: Data selected from Livingstone, 1989, and Williams, 1985.

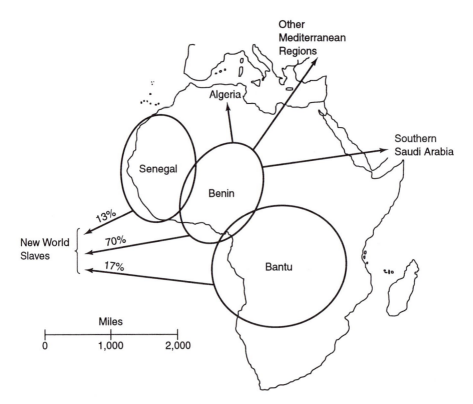

FIGURE 4-7   African American Origins of Hemoglobins. Origin and migration of African groups carrying three different Hb^S chromosomes (area of origin indicated by ellipses). Each chromosome, or haplotype, is defined by a distinctive pattern of RFLPs in the 60-kb length of DNA surrounding the β-globin locus. A separate mutation of Hb^A → Hb^S occurred in each background haplotype sometime in the past and is detectable today by restriction enzyme analysis. (From Mange and Mange, 1990, Sinauer Assoc. Reprinted by permission.)

sickle cell carriers in Brazil, reflecting the region of African origins of modern-day descendants because of the trade routes established by the Portuguese between their colonies in Africa (Angola) and Brazil (Zago et al., 1992). Comparisons of three national groups of African descendants in Caribbean and Brazilian populations show contrasting frequencies of sickle cell haplotypes because of these differing histories (Table 4-8).

A second major question relates to the origin of such haplotype diversity; there are over twenty for the restriction sites along the sixty-eight kilobases of the beta globin gene cluster. Most Hb^S haplotypes are rare, present in less than polymorphic frequencies in a few populations, but the wide distribution of the four major types, three African and one Asian, raises the possibility of differing genetic histories and perhaps contrasts in the expression of the sickle cell trait. The existence of these RFLPs in the beta-Hb cluster have been explained by independent mutations. That is, the Hb^S allele arose by mutation in each of the four geographic regions at different times (Hill and Wainscoat, 1986). There was the same substitution in the globin gene DNA sequence (valine for glutamic

TABLE 4-8 Haplotypes of the Sickle Cell Trait among People of African Descent (in percent of those with SCT)

HAPLOTYPE	JAMAICA	UNITED STATES	BRAZIL
Senegal	10	15	1
Benin	72	62	26
Bantu (CAR)	17	18	73

acid at position 6), but different replacements occurred in the noncoding flanking sequences. The carriers of the sickle cell gene benefit from a degree of resistance to the malarial parasite, as explained above, regardless of restriction site haplotype.

The homozygotes differ, however, in the severity of sickle cell disease (SCD) that they suffer. The time when a sickling crisis occurs and the clinical course of the disease vary significantly between the haplotypes. The Asia (*Arab-Indian*) type is a milder form, with fewer sickling crises and a longer life span, probably due to a retention of fetal hemoglobin gene activity. The persistence of fetal hemoglobin into adulthood moderates the influence of Hb^S molecules. Red-blood-cell-carrying fetal hemoglobin reduces the rate formation of the stiff fibrous bundles when oxygen is taken up by the tissues from the globin S strands, thereby preventing distortion of the cell. The *Senegal* S haplotype also has a milder form of SCD, particularly in comparison to the *Benin* type; *Senegal* S homozygotes retain a higher percentage of fetal hemoglobin, as do the Asia types, and they also have a lower sickle cell count. These differences in the expression of SCD, along with the retention of a resistance to malaria, tend to support an argument for independent mutation having occurred in each of the four major areas.

The question of sickle cell origin is by no means settled. But one explanation is that, because the beta globin gene region is subject to high rates of recombination and given that the Hb^S gene is under intense selection favoring the heterozygote, the beta globin underwent only a single mutation somewhere in the Middle East. It then spread rapidly with the advance of agriculture. Through population movement into new areas and diffusion between adjacent populations, Hb^S became established at high frequencies following the increase in malaria as a major disease. The various haplotypes we record today may be the result of recombinations from the original haplotype, probably the Asian (*Arab-Indian*) type (Livingstone, 1989). This explanation of the rapid spread of an advantageous gene in malarious environments offers a plausible counterargument to the multiple mutation hypothesis, and only additional studies may offer a test of the hypothesis. But the evidence we have to date does illustrate the importance of recording RFLP haplotypes around major genes and opens the way for new applications of genetic data. In addition to the genetic code of the structural genes we now have markers that can broadly describe population migrations and histories.

Gene Geography

Technology has been advancing rapidly since the earliest applications of restriction enzymes to the studies of human DNA sequences. The formation of the Human

Genome Project (HGP) in 1990 with the goal of identifying each gene location on its chromosome and then sequencing the entire three billion nucleotide base pairs of the human genome is an example. This project merged advanced biochemical methods with sophisticated data analysis by high-speed computer (Brown, 2000). From a slow start in 1990, the sequencing process accelerated with one after another of the chromosomes defined by their base-pair sequences. On June 26, 2000, the two independent research groups announced that sequencing of 85 to 95 percent of the human genome had been completed.[2] Both groups claimed success through their different methods, but gaps in the list of the three billion bases remained (Pennisi, 2000). These gaps had been filled by April 19, 2003, and the sequence of bases for the entire human genome was recorded with a low error rate of only one per 100,000 bases. Not only do we now know the DNA complement of our species, but also that automation has advanced to a level where luminecence of short base sequences can quickly identify unknown samples.

The general and scientific press has been filled with enthusiastic descriptions over the past decade of the biomedical potentials of this newly acquired record. Most articles emphasized three points: First, 97 percent of the over three billion bases were "junk," in that the base sequences did not code for a protein product; second, we had fewer than the 100,000 genes previously estimated—the number of 30,000 was established; and third, the enthusiastic recounting of the advantages conveyed by this genetic knowledge. Writers dwelt on the hopeful application to an individualistic medical treatment—a sizable minority of patients do not respond to many pharmaceuticals as they are expected to, for example. With the knowledge of a person's genes, appropriate treatment could then be selected. This emphasis on individuality or *genomics* contrasted with statements that a person's genome was 99 percent identical to all other humans. The 1 percent difference expressed our individuality for innumerable traits (Cohen, 2000). This realization of human similarity, but yet uniqueness at a certain level, causes one to wonder about the nature of the genome composition reported.

The Human Genome Project offered "model genomes," a composite of DNA gained from chromosome samples of a few individuals. The HGP mixed together chromosomes taken from twelve donors and the Celera research group selected five from thirty volunteer donors acquired through newspaper advertisements. We are told that they included three females and two males of diverse ethnic backgrounds (Pennisi, 2000). This sampling process of a limited number may be appreciated for the purpose of establishing the technical methods and providing the world with the first human genome sequences. When comparisons are made for purposes of understanding diverse reactions to medical treatment, susceptibility to disease, or statements about 99 percent similarity, however, a different and broader sampling should be expected. A study of sequence variation at the population level that reveals differences in the

---

[2] One group consisted of a public consortium of universities working with the National Institutes of Health. This group used a method of fragmenting DNA from one chromosome at a time for analysis. In 1995, a private research lab (Celera) introduced a method of separating the entire human DNA complement into tens of thousands of base strands and then proceeded by computer-driven automated analysis to identify the sequences of the bases. This set up a competition, and a race was on to see which group could reach the goal of defining the human genome first.

frequency of occurrence of certain DNA polymorphisms becomes necessary if we are to fully comprehend human diversity.

At this point in time, 150 years after Mendel's discoveries, we should not have to be reminded that there is a broad range of genetic variation throughout the species and across generations. Whether this is at the exon level or in the flanking sequences of introns, we, as individuals are not variants of some "standard" type of *Homo sapiens* genome (see Kidd and Kidd, 1996; and Weiss, 1993). Recall the range of genetic markers described in the last chapter and the hemoglobin polymorphisms discussed above. Given the data we now possess, it appears that two to three-fifths of the world's population have been excluded from the sample pool. The composite genome produced the HGP from several U.S. individuals could more aptly be called, "the Western nation genome project" (Smagilk, 2000).

Considering that much of this genetic diversity may be under represented or even lost if sampling is limited to persons of European descent, it is essential to broaden the genome record to include representative samples of non-Europeans.[3] Furthermore, anthropological studies over the last century have identified many small, relatively isolated indigenous populations that have maintained unique languages and cultural traditions. Groups scattered about the vast Amazon basin of South America are examples, as are people living in the more remote parts of New Guinea. In more accessible areas there are many small populations that have managed to retain an ethnic identity despite sustained contact with the influence from larger national communities. Tribal groups in Africa and hunter–horticultural groups in Southeast Asia are other examples of indigenous people who come to mind. But this only notes the "exotic" populations who are rapidly being absorbed; the millions of people divided by language and custom into ethnic groups within Asia are also an important source of information on population diversity. Such groups must be considered as breeding populations if any human genome study encompasses questions of genetic variability distribution.

To meet this requirement, a group of anthropological geneticists have come together to plan a program to collect and disseminate knowledge of DNA diversity. This program, the Human Genome Diversity Project, has as its goal the collection of blood samples for genetic analysis from a wide range of indigenous peoples. The focus is on geographically isolated people of distinct cultures and languages who, it is expected, will yield more information about diversity than large genetically admixed urban communities. Europeans, Euro-Americans, and African Americans are well represented in samples and are under study in numerous laboratories, but most indigenous peoples are fast disappearing as distinct populations. The goal is to add them to the DNA record to broaden the sample for the human species, a kind of "gene geography."

Since as early as 1984, several laboratories have been collecting blood samples from numerous indigenous groups of Africa, South America, and New Guinea. Blood

---

[3]I use "non-European" here to contrast the data sources of the ongoing genome research since it is difficult to select an unambiguous name or label to identify populations. Ethnic group, indigenous, aboriginal, exotic peoples, or a geographic label are terms that have been used by different authors, but these have been applied inconsistently. I avoid racial classifications for the reasons discussed in the first chapter.

cells, usually lymphoblasts, are grown in specially prepared cultures and multiplied many times, forming perpetual cell lines to serve as a resource for present and future DNA analysis. This DNA resource provides a data bank of genetic markers of significantly different population clusters around the world (Cavalli-Sforza et al., 1986; Cavalli-Sforza, 2004). New blood samples are being added each year, in addition to the expansion of the number of DNA markers that are recorded, increasing our knowledge of human polymorphism. With systematic analysis of RFLPs (restriction length polymorphisms) of these DNA samples it is now possible to discuss global patterns of DNA marker variation. Differences in short fragment sequences, deletions, or even single nucleotide changes in the intron regions offer an excellent data resource for population comparisons. As new genes are mapped to their chromosome loci, the surrounding noncoding base sequences are recorded, revealing that many are present at polymorphic frequencies.

A study of three Native American populations typed by thirty RFLPs of nuclear DNA is an example. Compared with a mixed sample of Europeans, these Native Americans showed a range of differences and less average heterozygosity (Kidd et al., 1991). A broader study of 100 DNA polymorphisms, gained from five populations on four continents, demonstrated emphatically the need for spreading the human genome study more widely across diverse populations. Bowcock and associates started with 47 markers and then expanded the number to 100 four years later (Bowcock et al., 1987, 1991). A majority of the markers (86) were bi-allelic and 14 were multi-allelic. These RFLPs were taken from clusters about the loci of well-studied genes that code for a variety of proteins from hormones and haptoglobins to enzymes and receptors. Table 4-9 offers a selection of ten DNA markers as examples.

The gene abbreviation and product are listed as is the gene's locus; for example, TH, the gene coding for an enzyme, tyrosine hydroxylase, is located on position 15.5 of the short arm (p) of chromosome 11. The restriction enzyme, Taq 1, cuts the DNA flanking this gene into three fragments, 4.3, 2.3, and 2.0 kilobases long (see Alleles column). The next five columns list the frequencies with which these restriction fragments occur in each of the five population samples. The 4.3 fragment was found in 11 percent of the Pygmies of the Central African Republic, 45 percent in Melanesia, and 5 percent in the Chinese sample, for example. Considering the RFLPs at all ten loci, some alleles (fragments) occur at nearly 100 percent or are absent altogether.

What this means is that mutations, probably deletion types, arose in certain base sequences within the noncoding flanking sequences of a gene. When a restriction enzyme (the Taq 1 of our example) is applied to a sample of DNA, three different bp lengths are cut, because the 2.0 and 2.3 bp alleles are so close their frequencies are counted together as a single allele. This allele is the most frequent type found in four of the five populations, ranging from 0.84 to 0.95. In the Melanesian sample the alleles are nearly equal, 0.45 and 0.55. The other RFLPs also show differences among the five populations. The explanation for allele diversity may relate to a long history of population isolation and variable mutation rates; selection can probably be ruled out since these flanking sequences of DNA may not influence the gene expression. Comparisons of RFLPs, then, offer an important series of markers for use in the comparison of population relationships. Comparisons of all 100 markers by genetic distance formula enable the construction of

TABLE 4-9 Frequency of Ten Selected DNA Markers

GENE	LOCUS[1]	ENZYME[2]	ALLELES[3]	CAR PY[4]	ZAIRE PY[5]	MELANES[6]	CHINESE[7]	EURO[8]
APOB (apolipoprotein)	2p24	EcoRI	14	0.18	0.07	0.00	0.32	0.20
			12, 2.1	0.82	0.93	1.00	0.68	0.80
sample sizes				38	59	23	44	40
SST (somatostatin)	3q28	EcoRI	12	0.60	0.76	0.41	0.84	0.91
			6	0.40	0.24	0.59	0.16	0.09
sample sizes				35	51	22	51	360
ADH2 (alcohol dehydrogenase)	4q21	Rsal	1.25, 1.5	1.00	1.00	0.70	0.18	0.67
			0.58, 1.5	0.00	0.00	0.30	0.82	0.33
sample sizes				17	22	23	67	36
GHR (growth hormone receptor)	5p13	BstN1	1.4, 2.1	0.15	0.35	0.03	0.06	0.00
			0.6	0.85	0.65	0.97	0.94	1.00
sample sizes				88	91	32	62	66
TH (tyrosine hydroxylase)	11p15.5	Taq1	4.3	0.11	0.07	0.45	0.05	0.16
			2.0, 2.3	0.89	0.93	0.55	0.95	0.84
sample sizes				37	57	22	60	92
APOA1 (apolipoprotein A-1)	11q23	XmnI	8.3	0.40	0.43	0.52	0.59	0.82
			8.1	0.17	0.03	0.10	0.08	0.00
			6.6	0.42	0.54	0.38	0.33	0.18
sample sizes				40	35	21	83	78
IGF1 (insulin–like growth factor 1)	12q23	HindIII	6.3	0.00	0.00	0.07	0.18	0.20
			5.8	1.00	1.00	0.93	0.82	0.80
sample sizes				43	49	27	17	174
RB1 (retinoblastoma)	13q14.2	BAMIII	4.4	0.96	0.79	0.50	0.37	0.23
			2.3, 2.1	0.04	0.21	0.50	0.63	0.77
sample sizes				53	57	32	106	48
HP (haptoglobin)	16q22	BamHI	9.2	0.62	0.55	0.56	0.64	0.57
			7.5	0.38	0.45	0.44	0.36	0.43
sample sizes				47	55	32	88	58
GH (growth hormone)	17q22	BglII	13.0	0.04	0.09	0.31	0.54	0.32
			10.5	0.96	0.91	0.69	0.46	0.68
sample sizes				47	81	32	87	111

[1]Chromosome and locus.

[2]Restriction enzyme.

[3]Kilobases of fragments cut by enzyme.

[4]Biaka Pygmies of Central African Republic.

[5]Mbuti Pygmies of Zaire.

[6]Nasioi Melanesians from Bougainville, Solomon Islands.

[7]Chinese residents of San Francisco born in mainland China.

[8]Europeans or Euro-Americans (northern or central European origins).

Source: Data selected from Bowcock et al., 1991.

a tree of descent leading back to a hypothesized common lineage (Felsenstein, 1973). As expected, Melanesians are further removed from the European branch than Chinese, and the Pygmy sample is at a greater distance still (Figure 4-8).

Still another set of nuclear DNA markers is provided by the variable number of tandem repeats (VNTR) in the noncoding flanking sequences. They may vary at polymorphic frequencies and, if considered together with adjacent markers within the gene cluster, are useful for postulating population origin and dispersal. The gene CD4 that encodes for a glycoprotein on the surface of the T-lymphocyte, essential for proper immune function, offers such an example. Located on the short arm (p) of the twelfth chromosome, the CD4 has two polymorphic regions of interest (Figure 4-9). The first is a series of short tandem repeats of the bases *TTTTC* located before exon 1. This string of bases is repeated from 4 to 15 times, which, with flanking sequences, results in 80 bp for a tandem repeat of 4. For 15 repeats, there are 135 bp and there are 10 other base-pair lengths recorded between these two extremes. Counting the number of base pairs as alleles, there are as many as 12 found among 13 African populations; fewer alleles are found in the Native American, Asian, and European samples (a total of

FIGURE 4-8   Tree Diagram Estimating Genetic Distances between Five Population Groups. (Data from Bowcock et al., 1991.)

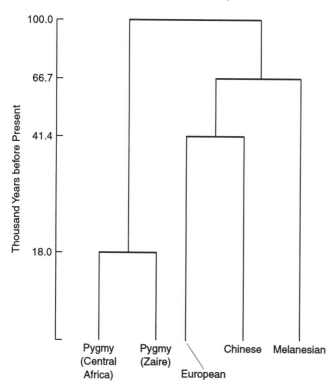

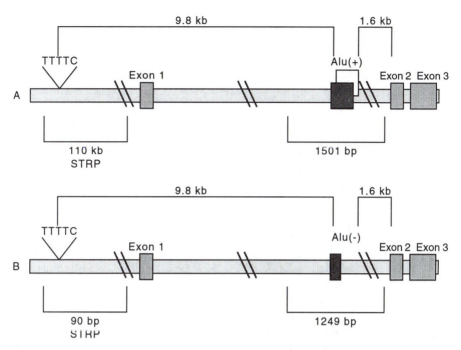

FIGURE 4-9 **Two Polymorphic Markers in the Noncoding Region of the CD4, Chromosome 12.** This schematic diagram represents a segment of chromosome 12 that carries the exons (1, 2, and 3) of the CD4 gene. Also shown is the noncoding region that contains a region of short tandem repeats of the TTTTC base series and the Alu series, a string of 285 bp.

Polymorphism 1
The TTTTC is a base sequence that is repeated from four to fifteen times. Adding the products of flanking sequences and those from amplification by PCR (polymerase chain reaction), the total base pairs will vary from 80 bp for a *four repeat allele* to 135 bp for a *fifteen repeat allele*. These short tandem repeat polymorphisms (STRP) vary widely among populations tested.
   Part A shows a STRP of 110 bp in contrast to a STRP of 90 in Part B.

Polymorphism 2
The Alu, a string of from 250–300 bp repeated up to 500,000 times throughout the human genome, has a deletion type mutation at the CD4 locus on chromosome 12. This results in deletion of 256 bp from the more typical 285 bp represented by Alu(+) In Part A and Alu(−) in Part B representing the deletion. (Data from Tishkoff et al., 1996.)

32 non-African populations). These data are used in conjunction with a second polymorphism, the Alu deletion in the flanking sequence before exon 2 of the CD4 gene.

   The Alu cluster (named for the Alu 1 enzyme) is a fragment of 250 to 310 bps in length repeated throughout the human genome about 500,000 times and widely dispersed among all autosomes plus the sex chromosomes. In the case of the flanking sequence of the CD4 gene, there has been a mutation that deleted 256 bp (Alu2) of the 285 bp (Alu1). Because this 256 bp deletion has not been found in the great apes, the Alu1 is considered the ancestral type, and the mutation is likely to have occurred after the divergence of the human ancestral lineage from the chimps, some five to six million years ago, plus or minus a million years (Wolpoff, 2000). Such a time frame for the divergence of human ancestors from the great apes has also been used to estimate a time of modern *Homo sapiens* migrating out of Africa, as described in Chapter 1, and it is applied here with the use of the two polymorphisms of the CD4 gene cluster.

Both markers (haplotypes of the STRPs and the Alu2) were identified in unrelated individuals of forty-two geographically dispersed populations, and the frequency with which the different STRPs occurred with the Alu1 or Alu2 were recorded (Tishkoff et al., 1996). The deletion Alu2 rarely occurs in Asians, Pacific Islanders, or Native Americans (less than 2 percent), and when it occurred there was the 90 bp STRP. The Alu2 is frequent among Europeans (25 to 30 percent) and Africans (7 to 28 percent) and appeared most often with the 85 bp STRP. Considering all haplotypes, Africans have a greater variation than all other populations. Because of this haplotype variation at the CD4 locus, the explanation of recent origins of non-Africans was proposed as the most acceptable by Tishkoff and associates. They offered an estimate of 120,000 years before present (YBP) for the earliest modern humans in Africa. The appearance of Alu(−) outside Africa range from 200,000 to 300,000 YBP depending on calculations used. These estimated dates coincide with those derived by mtDNA analysis and relate well to a presumed appearance of modern human fossilized skeletons in Africa and the Middle East. However, such a reconstruction of human ancestry is not universally accepted, as noted earlier, and depends on many assumptions discussed below.

Ancestral origins and times of migration aside, these data support several observations of African genetic diversity. Even without the use of DNA markers, McKusick (1994:714) noted that regions of the HLA system were most variable among African populations; the polymorphism of the DR and DQ regions are twice as extensive as that of Northern Europeans. The use of sequences of noncoding DNA as RFLPs, STRP, deletions, or combinations as haplotypes can extend our knowledge and are useful markers of population relationships. Even the uniqueness of certain of the VNTRs can identify individuals.

DNA Fingerprints

The use of various radioactively labeled DNA probes (short segments of single-stranded DNA) has provided an even finer focus of our view of DNA polymorphisms.[4] These probes will bind with the other DNA wherever there are complementary base sequences in the noncoding regions or minisatellites around the structural genes. Each chromosome has many repeats of these minisatellites, and mutations, unequal crossovers during DNA replication, contribute to polymorphisms as we have described above. Because of the thousands of repeats, the Alu for example, and the variations in base-pair spacing, it is highly improbable (once in tens of millions) that any two people will have the same sequences. This means that when a sample of DNA is chemically extracted from cells, treated, and subjected to electrophoresis, the smaller fragments move more rapidly than the larger ones and after a time lapse all fragments will be separated according to

---

[4]Nucleotides with a phosphorus 32 (a radioactive isotope) are added to short segments of complimentary DNA (ᶜDNA).

size.[5] These fragment groups are fixed in place on a paper or membrane, ready for analysis, and each individual's DNA will produce a unique pattern.

A final step is to render the strands radioactive. Radioactive DNA probes are washed over this paper and the probes will attach to every fragment where there is a complementary base sequence. This hybridization of probe and satellite DNA results in differing radioactively labeled fragment lengths. These are then detected by exposing film over several hours to the radioactive labels. This results in a series of dark bands on the film very much like the bar codes seen on almost all items on sale in stores today. The band positions of the hybrid DNA fragments on the film have the same relationships as the fragments on the electrophoresis gel plant. Figure 4-10 diagrams this process, with person A showing only a single DNA fragment repeat between the enzyme cuts in contrast to persons B, C, and D. The DNA fragment of A will migrate furthest in a given time.

These regions, repeat sequences or "minisatellites" in the noncoding regions (introns), are hypervariable and will result in unique "bar codes." Jeffreys, a British geneticist studying restriction enzymes and DNA probes, recognized the potential applications for human identification (Jeffreys et al., 1985). Jeffreys and his colleagues isolated a fragment of DNA near the myoglobin gene containing a 33 base sequence, which was repeated more than twenty times within the fragment. The repetitiveness of this minisatellite attracted their attention and, after cloning, a probe specific for the region was produced. Applying the probe by methods described in Chapter 2 to other DNA sequences, they found that the minisatellite was repeated frequently throughout the entire genome. Comparison of samples taken from several people showed a pattern of hypervariable regions specific to the individual (Figure 4-11). That is, the alignment of the pattern of dark bands on the film, the regions of hybridization with the radioactive probe, differed for every person tested except in the case of monozygotic (identical) twins (Gill et al., 1985). There was nearly 100 percent heterozygosity in small populations, and a study of four generations of an inbred lineage demonstrated that the bands followed the laws of Mendelian inheritance, but new bands frequently appeared in children because of crossover during replication (Vogel and Motulsky, 1986). This work opened up an entirely new avenue of human identification we now call DNA fingerprinting.

The DNA identification method has been applied many times since it was first used by Jeffreys to settle an issue of maternity in Britain in 1985. A young Ghanaian boy, living with his father in that country, wanted to migrate to Britain to live with his mother. His plans were blocked by immigration officials, who claimed that the woman reputed to be his mother was, in fact, his aunt. Imposing new restrictive immigration policies that allowed admittance of only the biological children of parents in legal residence, the officials refused to grant a visa. Jeffreys was asked to help settle the issue of the mother or aunt relationship. DNA samples were taken from the undisputed offspring of the woman who were living with her in Britain, and these were compared to the boy in Ghana. The closeness of the hypervariable regions studied demonstrated that all of the children had the same biological

---

[5]The process is multistaged: (1) DNA is chemically extracted and cut at various sites by a selected enzyme; (2) these short segments are separated into single-stranded units; (3) the DNA single strands are subjected to electrophoresis.

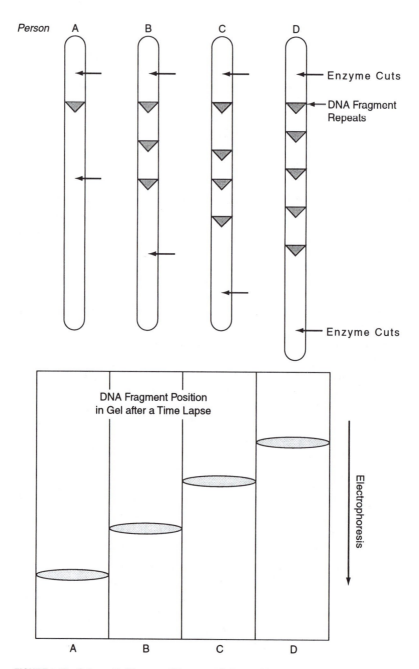

FIGURE 4-10   Schematic Diagram of Fragment Polymorphism.

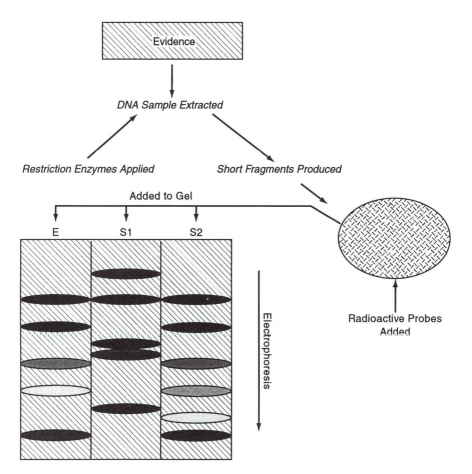

FIGURE 4-11   DNA Fingerprints: A Schematic Illustration.

parents. The woman was, in fact, the mother, as she had claimed, and the visa was granted so that the boy from Ghana could be reunited with his mother in London.

   This case gained considerable publicity and drew the attention of the police in Leicester County, England, who had tried in vain to solve a series of brutal rapes and murders of young girls. The police had samples of the murderer's semen from the girls' clothing and thought that it might provide evidence to help convict a confessed suspect. When blood and semen were compared in what was the first application of DNA fingerprinting to forensics, Jeffreys showed that the suspect could not be the killer, but that the same man had killed both girls. Still without a solution, but with a growing confidence in this new technology, the police proposed to collect blood samples from every male within the districts surrounding the locations where the bodies had been discovered. This makes for a very unusual crime story, related in all its police and forensic details by Joseph Wambaugh in his novel *The Blooding*. The blood tests could only be voluntary, since, under British law, testing could not be compulsory. Most males cooperated; eventually over 5,000 were eliminated as suspects, and in the process DNA fingerprinting acquired the image of an infallible tool of science. It was this image of scientific infallibility that eventually gave the murderer away; his fear of the test was so strong that he paid a friend to assume his identity and take the test for him. When this deception was revealed months later, the police had their suspect and an eventual conviction. Since then, DNA has been more and more widely applied to convict the guilty or exonerate the innocent—but not without some mistakes and errors along the way, as labs struggled to improve techniques and develop standards.

Comparisons of VNTRs between samples can rule out identity—the possibility that they came from the same person—because of a broad difference in banding patterns in the gel. However, establishing that a single individual's VNTRs are present in both samples is a matter of probability—the chance that two individuals could have the same banding pattern. Frequently, this probability is stated in terms of one in ten million or a hundred million—very long odds that have had impressive impacts in criminal cases. Such probabilities depend on the data base from which sample VNTR banding patterns are taken. The frequencies of the occurrence of DNA fragments, produced by restriction enzymes, are measured in several population samples. Usually four or five enzymes are used, and averaging the results provides a reference base to calculate probabilities. The problem is which populations to select and how they should be grouped in a society of such diverse origins as ours. The establishment of data bases—Caucasoid, African American, Asian, and Hispanic—are assumed to provide representative samples, adequate for forensic comparisons. If a suspect is identified as Hispanic, then the DNA sample refers to the Hispanic data base, Caucasoid to Caucasoid, and so on. The assumption is that the data base is derived from a homogeneous, randomly mating population and that such randomly selected samples share close common ancestry and are representative of the whole. Furthermore, the biological relevance of such classification is questionable, as in the "Caucasoid" versus "Hispanic" data bases, or when considering the diverse and broadly admixed group we call African Americans.

DNA fingerprinting has come a long way since Jeffreys first applied VNTR to identification of individuals. Laboratory standards have improved and a field of forensics DNA has become an important part of criminology. Florescent detection of DNA markers by automated machines has made individual identification faster and more accurate. The FBI and crime bureaus of several states have established data banks of DNA profiles of convicted felons. The rush is on to compare these samples with DNA extracted from evidence collected from the scenes of unsolved crimes and new matches are being reported frequently. But even more important, convictions have been overturned by DNA evidence, and prisoners, sentenced to be executed for murders they did not commit, are set free. Applications of DNA markers to legal questions as well as solutions of historical mysteries—such as the identification of the skeletal remains of the Russian Czar Nicholas II and his family, or Thomas Jefferson's fathering the children of his slave Sally Hemings—are outlined by Kevin Davies (2001). Davies, in his review of the cracking of the DNA code, details some of the enormous potential for individual and population identification that the human genome code provides.

GENETIC MARKERS AT THE DNA LEVEL: SOME CONCLUSIONS

The development of technology to identify the finer structure of DNA has led to a multitude of population studies. Distinguishing between populations on the basis of various markers within the noncoding regions has added a new dimension to recording human diversity. Before conclusions are reached about origins and ancestral relationships, caution is warranted, however. The high mutation rates of VNTR (variable numbers of tandem repeats), about 7 percent, and the frequency of crossover and recombination contribute to an uncertainty and can lead to erroneous conclusions. The lower mutation rates of short tandem repeat polymorphisms (STRP), 0.12 percent, cause them to be more useful in cross-population comparisons; that is, these markers of shorter DNA repeats are applicable to a longer time depth, while the VNTR are limited to a more recent time frame. The 15 to 20,000-year separation of Native Americans from eastern Siberian origins may be measured by STRP in contrast to the few generations that separate Euro-Americans from their European ancestors. The increased use of single nucleotide polymorphisms (SNP) for population comparisons has added a new dimension in the study of identity by descent. These three types of nuclear DNA markers, together with an increasing variety of restriction enzymes, provide anthropology with a rapidly expanding store of data on human biological diversity. There are 20,000 markers recorded for Europeans, the most thoroughly studied of any regional group. As more laboratories become involved, the store of data is growing for other ethnic groups as well.

Laboratories are studying different sets of markers, resulting in little population overlap, however. If such a situation continues to exist, there will be a vast store of knowledge about human nuclear DNA variants, but scant basis for population comparisons. It is comparable to a hypothetical example: If, over the last fifty years, one lab had recorded only the ABO blood group in Britain while another lab recorded the Rhesus types in eastern Europe, the result would be knowledge of the ABO in one area and Rh types in another. Considerable detail on blood types would have been accumulated, but there would be insufficient data for comparison between populations. A more relevant example is the paucity of information on the haplotypes of the HLA system among people of African or Asian descent in contrast to the wealth of information that exists for Europeans. Such an information gap has impeded the search for suitable transplant donors. News accounts appear frequently describing the plight of some ethnic minority family seeking bone marrow or organ donors. Georgia Dunston, a geneticist at Howard University, is seeking to fill the genetic gap for African Americans by collecting samples from 25,000 volunteers over the next five years. This would establish a data base for use in medical treatment, thereby evaluating the relevant genetic verus social influences on disease. This is a difficult task given the genetically diverse ancestry and the high degree admixture in modern African Americans, but the data base is an essential first step for defining the genomics of this large minority group. Data bases have likewise been proposed for other ethnic groups, for example, Hispanic, but progress has been slow, especially given the confusion of social and biological definitions.

Because of this problem of investigative diversity, there has been an appeal for marker standardization (Kidd and Kidd, 1996), though there is no reason for preference of one marker over another, except for ease of typing and utility for population studies. They suggest three markers (PLAT, HOXB, and DRD2) that have already proven useful in population studies, in addition to the CD4 described above. These markers, together with those for the alpha and beta globin chains, provide an excellent start in standardization. The authors conclude their appeal with a warning that "Our history as a species is written in our DNA sequence and in the distribution of variation in that sequence within and among human populations. However, we need a concerted, coordinated effort to study enough of that message that we truly understand it and are not led astray by fragments read out of context" (Kidd and Kidd, 1996:12).

That such an appeal is necessary after more than a decade and a half is, I believe, a testimony to the rapid application of a new, complex technology and the confusion that has been generated. It is a prime example of technology outrunning interpretive frameworks. We have simply acquired so much data on human biological diversity that we cannot place it within a frame of historical reference—the record of species origin and dispersal gained from the fossil and archeological record. At least, not yet. We are trying to survey the human landscape at the submicroscopic level, nearly an atom at a time. Imagine doing a survey of a forest for marketable timber content by counting leaves instead of whole trees. In the process, the intervening sequences (the noncoding regions where the markers are identified) had been assumed to be neutral in that they do not contribute to the expression of the gene sequences. The neutrality of the noncoding DNA now proves to be incorrect; the flanking sequences of the structural genes influence transcription and expression of its products.

The DNA-based studies, to date, document the depth of similarities among peoples of the entire planet—we differ by less than 1 percent of our total genome. These studies emphasize the shallowness of our perceived differences based on simple visual appraisals of skin, hair, size, and shape. The record of DNA markers tells us little about how we gained certain of these complex traits—how we acquire a certain size and appearance, a skin color, or rates of growth. Simply, the environmental influences on expressions of DNA codes are little known, with few exceptions. We explore these influences on human diversity in the next chapters.

chapter
5

Traits of Complex Inheritance and their Adaptations: I

In the preceding chapters I have described some traits of simple inheritance, phenotypes of blood types, enzymes, and hemoglobins that are determined by single genes. Also, several types of DNA markers were added to the list of genetic polymorphisms. Though such polymorphisms are now known to vary widely among population groupings, they have seldom been applied as identity labels for ethnic groups or races. Rather, the classic race labels continue to be used to identify a group of individuals from which blood or tissue samples are collected for genetic study. Differences in gene frequencies are then compared on the basis of such race/ethnic group labels.

The inherent inconsistencies of such a method are many. Besides the application of a discredited classification system, the major problem is that the use of easily perceived traits ignores the broad and continuous variability of those traits that are strongly influenced by environmental factors. Traits such as skin color, face form, body size, and head shape have all been applied to the classification of races, but similarities do not necessarily denote common ancestry or membership in a so-called racial stock. Similarities or dissimilarities among populations, however they may be classified, mean much more.

One of the first considerations of similarities is an apparent "fit" between a people and their environment. Arctic peoples seem to share certain characteristics of body form, inhabitants of arid lands likewise appear to be similar, and as noted in the first chapter skin color correlates closely with latitude. Early explorers and naturalists made such observations of geographical distribution of traits of size, form and color, but explanations were hampered by limited scientific resources. Now we can describe adaptation due to genetic differences and physiological variability.

Adaptation may be defined as an adjustment or modification made by individuals or populations in response to environmental stresses encountered during the human life cycle. These adjustments may be either long term or short term, biological or behavioral, or both. Considering the complexity of cultural, the behavioral component is broader, with endless variety. We find a diversity of people surviving (adapting) in almost all environments of the natural world. The biological component consists of short-term adjustments, or *acclimatization*, that our physiology allows us to make to climate variables of temperature or solar radiation, for example. A second component, *genetic adaptation*, is made over generations as frequencies of certain favorable genes increase, for example, the hemoglobins or HLA antigens mentioned above. In some environments, certain alleles reach polymorphic level in the populations because of the adaptive advantage the alleles convey to the carrier.

Our size, form, or color that we perceive as significant labels are anatomical traits determined by a complex of factors interacting with the products of several genes over the course of one's lifetime, especially during growth. Such traits are described as multifactorial or polygenic and, under environmental influence, produce continuously varying phenotypes, as is well illustrated by the diversity of human body form and size. Factors of climate and diet affect development and growth. Though a person may inherit clusters of genes that could promote rapid development leading to a tall, proportionately large adult, poor nutrition or disease encountered at critical growth stages would limit size below one's maximum potential. Also, there is individual variation in size and form even among siblings because of unique individual responses to similar conditions. These and other phenotypes of complex inheritance vary over a continuous broad range, and there is a great deal of overlap within and between population groups. The same applies to that trait most frequently used to classify *Homo sapiens*, skin color. A number of enzymes and hormones affect the synthesis of *melanin* (skin pigment); that, in turn, is affected by energy in the ultraviolet range of the solar radiation spectrum. There are numerous widely dispersed populations in, or originating from, Africa, India, and Australia with darkly pigmented skin. While they differ in frequencies of many genetic markers, skin pigmentation is one of the few phenotypes that they share in common. This chapter will describe the range of variation of such complex traits and will explore their origins and adaptive significance.

THE STRUCTURE AND FUNCTION OF SKIN

We humans are visually oriented, so it is not surprising that we tend to view and classify our world in terms of color. This is especially true when categorizing ourselves. There-fore, we continue to classify by labels of black and white or brown and yellow, as if nature has "color-coded" our species for ease of identification. So ingrained is this color concept in our thinking that we are surprised upon discovery that no such divisions of mankind exist. Imagine all of world's six-plus billion people lined up side by side and arranged according to the degree of light or darkness of their skins. We would find that from one end of the line to the other, color would gradually change without major gaps from one degree to another. Any categorical divisions made would be strictly arbitrary and ignore the ranges of variability. Skin pigmentation, regardless of how it is labeled, is the result of a complex interaction of cell functions, biochemistry, and geography. To understand this complex we have to first consider skin and its functioning under various environmental conditions.

The human body is clothed in a protective covering of a renewable, elastic tissue that is continuously worn off as it is replenished throughout our lifetime. Skin's functions are varied: from protection of underlying muscle tissue, glands, and blood vessels to containing a large lymphatic system that plays a major role in immunological response to invading microbes and insects. Skin also functions in thermal regulation (maintenance of body temperature within its normal range), through surface radiation aided by the rich network of blood vessels just below the surface. These subcutaneous vessels can quickly dilate, increasing the blood flow to aid metabolic heat loss, an important function during heavy work in hot climates. Constriction of these same vessels conserves body heat under cold conditions, maintaining skin temperature lower than that of the core body. Assisting in thermal regulation through the skin are sweat glands distributed in varying densities over the body. These glands are capable of excreting large amounts of water that evaporate, cooling the body; heat of evaporation requires 600 calories per gram of water. In addition to this heat loss, the sweat glands excrete metabolic waste products, minerals, and some vitamins, so sweating can have both a positive effect (cooling) and a negative effect (water, mineral, and vitamin loss). Another function, and an extremely important one at higher latitudes (further from the equator), is the synthesis of vitamin D (the vitamin essential for calcium metabolism). A final function is protection against the harmful effects of the ultraviolet rays (UVR) of the sun, a function that involves both skin color and structure.

Skin consists of several structures organized in two major layers, the *dermis* and *epidermis*. The innermost, or dermal layer, consists of thick collagenous fibers and contains the blood vessels, nerves, hair follicles, and gland cells (sweat, sebaceous, and apocrine). This layer is covered by a thinner protective sheath of epidermis, a tissue with very active keratinocytes (basal cells). These basal cells or keratinocytes divide frequently and migrate upward. They gradually lose their vitality until they form flattened *squamous* cells consisting mostly of *keratin*, a dense inert protein, the major constituent of nails, hair, and outer skin. This outermost skin layer of keratin is that part that wears away or flakes off.

An important component of skin structure, and the major contributor to its color, are specialized cells called *melanocytes*, located in the lowest level of the epidermis. These cells have long, fingerlike projections, or dendrites, that are spread out from the cell body and come into close contact with the newly divided basal cells. The major function of these melanocytes is the synthesis of a substance called *melanin*, a pigment widely dispersed among vertebrate species. As the pigment granules are formed, they are concentrated into packets, or *melanosomes*, that are dispersed into the dendrites. From there, the melanosomes are injected into the basal cells

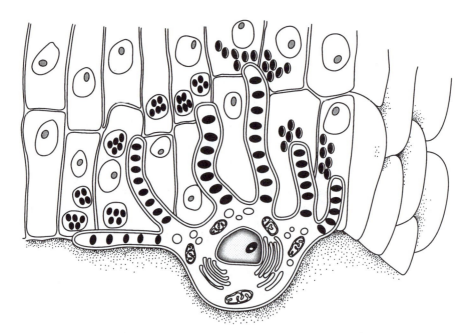

FIGURE 5-1   Epidermal Unit: Pigment and Basal Cells. Epidermal melanin unit, showing the structural and functional relationship between melanocyte and surrounding cluster of keratinocytes to which it transfers melanosomes. (Source: From A.H. Robins, *Biological Perspectives on Human Pigmentation.* Copyright © 1991 Cambridge University Press, with permission of the publisher.)

(Figure 5-1). These cells then carry the melanosomes as they migrate outward from the lowest layer of the epidermis, distributing the melanin throughout the upper layers of the epidermis. The skin color of all of us depends on how much of this pigment is distributed in our skin, which, in turn, depends on the rate of melanin synthesis.

What is especially significant to our investigation of human variability is the considerable range of difference in melanin within and between populations. The number of melanocytes is approximately the same in all people (even albinos have a normal number), but the degree of melanin density varies widely. Color differences must be due, then, to a difference in the activity of melanocytes. In dark-skinned peoples, the cells function at a high level, synthesizing large quantities of melanin, whereas in fair-skinned northern Europeans, the cells make very little melanin. This activity is influenced by several genes, as suggested by comparisons of parents and their children. Offspring of a fair and a dark parent will produce melanin at an intermediate level (Figure 5-2). Though this figure shows only the averages of reflection characteristics (ranges among family members are not indicated), the comparisons do suggest significant genetic factors. What these genes are and how many are involved is a matter of dispute; a number from four to six genes has been proposed. This number of genetic loci seems to be too small, however. Consider the complex processes of pigment production in humans. For example, there are fourteen different types of albinism known, each under control

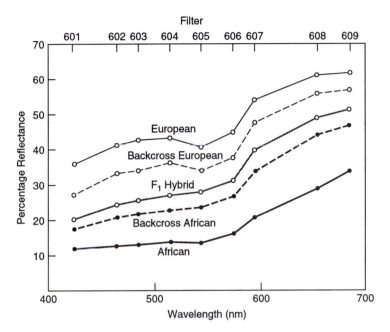

FIGURE 5-2 Mean Reflectance Curves of European, African, and Various Hybrid Groups. (Source: G.A. Harrison et al. 1988. *Human Biology*. Oxford: Oxford University Press.)

of different genetic loci, each with multiple alleles (McKusick, 1994:1605). One group of ten albino types lacks the tyrosinase enzyme because of any one of sixty mutations, and the other four are tyrosinase positive but are still unable to make melanin because of one of twelve mutations of a P gene on chromosome 15. The biological product of this gene has yet to be identified (Spritz and Hearing, 1994).

There are multiple mechanisms involved in synthesizing pigment. The amino acid tyrosine is the starting point for all these processes, and we all, even albinos, have large amounts concentrated in our melanocytes. The key to conversion of *tyrosine* is the enzyme *tyrosinase*, but the amounts of melanin produced are not related to the quantity of this enzyme. Even fair-skinned northern Europeans have sufficient quantities that could make them very dark. But there are inhibitors of tyrosinase that function more in some people than in others, and these inhibitors are likely regulated by several gene products that vary from group to group. Australians and pygmoid peoples of Southeast Asia are dark because of processes different from those of sub-Saharan Africans, and Asians are different still in their melanization. What these processes are exactly and how many genes are involved are now being described. Several genes are involved in the function of a melanocyte-stimulating hormone, its receptor site, or some stage of conversion of the amino acid, tyrosine, to its derivatives. For example, the MC1R locus that codes for proteins that affect melanocyte stimulating hormones vary in diversity among populations; sub-Saharan Africans have the least in comparison with

Asian or European populations who have numerous alleles at this locus (Rogers et al., 2004). The variation of human pigmentation can be appreciated if the processes of melanin synthesis are considered.

The conversion of tyrosine to melanin pigments can be summarized by the steps listed in Figure 5-3. First, note that the bulk of the amino acid is provided by hydroxylation of another amino acid, phenylalanine, and only about 5 percent comes from the diet. Tyrosine serves as a major component in hundreds of proteins, while another pathway leads to the formation of hormones of the thyroid gland, *thyroxine*. Tyrosine is also the starting ingredient for important hormones, the neurotransmitters: dopamine, noradrenaline, and adrenaline. The DOPA compound in pathway A (see left side of figure) is converted to a dopaquinone, which is then converted to either a brown-black melanin (eumelanin) or, if the amino acid cystine is added, a phaeomelanin (red-yellow) is formed. These processes occur in the melanocytes, and the several stages of chemical conversion are catalyzed by tyrosinase. The chemical derivatives at several steps have been identified as well as certain of the enzymes, but those that regulate the processes or inhibit the tyrosinase effects are not well established.

One likely inhibitor is *glutathione*, a ubiquitous compound that functions as a co-enzyme for many chemical reactions in several types of cells, from blood to skin. In the process, glutathione is changed from the oxidized state (GSSG) to the reduced state (GSH) and back again by inflammation or UVR, giving up or taking on a hydrogen atom. The reduction of GSSG to GSH is mediated by an enzyme, GSH

FIGURE 5-3   Biochemical Pathways of Melanin Synthesis.

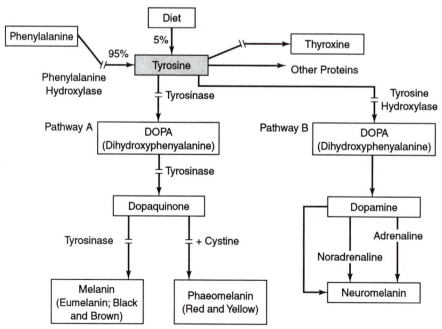

reductase, and this reduced form inhibits the conversion of tyrosine to its derivatives. To simplify, the more GSH present the less melanin will be produced by the melanocytes. The opposite will occur upon oxidation of GSH to GSSG by UVR; melanin will increase (Halprin and Ohkawara, 1967; Prota, 1989).

This inhibiting effect on melanin synthesis may be seen by the influences of ultra-violet radiation (UVR) in fair-skinned persons. UVR exposure reduces the level of GSH in circulation, melanin increases, and after a period of time, skin tanning becomes notice-able. Further support for the relationship between GSH and pigmentation is provided by normally dark-skinned persons who have less GSH. Such a comparatively lower level is likely due to a less effective form of GSH reductase than that found in fair-skinned per-sons. A few studies have shown that people of African descent have the least active form of the three variants of GSH reductase (McKusick, 1994:576). Hence, the biochemical pathway converting tyrosine to melanin seems to be modulated by GSH levels diverting all or part of the conversion of dopa-dopaquinone-eumelanin to the phaeomelanin, lighter form of pigment, by addition of amino acid, cystine (Dolphin and Poulson, 1989). The actual biochemical interactions will likely prove to be more complicated, but, for now, this model offers a way of explaining the control of melanin production, response to the UVR environment, and population diversity of skin pigmentation.

Another important pathway, pathway B as shown in Figure 5-3, also begins with the conversion of tyrosine to DOPA, but there is a different enzyme, tyrosine hydroxy-lase, which is not present in melanocytes but is found in those tissues that produce several *neurotransmitters* (stimulants of neural tissues). This pathway B is of interest because of its end product, neuromelanin, a pigment that appears in parts of the brain. Neuromelanin is formed in cells in the brain stem by auto-oxidation of some of the neurotransmitters, and it has been mistakenly related to skin melanization. The two melanins are not related except for starting from the same amino acid, tyrosine. Most importantly, each melanin is the product of a different biochemical pathway (Ganong, 2003). We all have neu-romelanin regardless of how much skin melanin we may produce; even albinos who are tyrosinase negative synthesize neuromelanin.

This brief overview underscores the complexity of the melanization process, and this complexity is extended further when external factors are considered. Certain hormones, some diseases, and perhaps mineral deficiencies (copper or zinc, for example) influence melanocytes, but the greatest stimulus is provided by the energy of UVR. Increased melanin production following Ultra Violet (UV) exposure explains the ability of most lighter skinned people to tan during the summer months with more hours of sunlight. There is a wide range of individual tanning ability, however, from slight among northern Europeans to a rapid buildup of melanin among peoples native to the Mediterranean area. Even among people who are normally dark skinned, their melanin density increases upon prolonged exposure to the sun. Sex and age also influence melanin density and sensitivity to the effects of UV rays. Newborns of dark-skinned parents are lighter in color, sometimes even pink, and as they grow older their skin darkens until it reaches, by adolescence, an intermediate range between their parents. In addition, females of any population average less melanin than males. These factors of age and sex may have relevance to health and protection from disease or even survival.

The ability of humans to endure periods of direct exposure to solar radiation for prolonged periods varies and depends largely on the concentration of melanin that functions as a filter blocking the ultraviolet portion of sunlight from penetrating through the epidermis to the dermal layer where blood vessels, nerves, and gland cells are located. Heavily pigmented skin filters out about 95 percent of the ultraviolet, whereas fair skin blocks only about 50 percent (Quevedo et al., 1985). UVR can also be blocked by keratin, which is quite dense in thicker corneum layers, and this could play an important protective role. Albinos in West Africa develop thick, callused pads on the backs of their necks, for example (Harrison, 1975). The dense, near-inert keratin no doubt aids in filtering UVR, but melanin is more effective.

SKIN COLOR, GEOGRAPHY, AND NATURAL SELECTION

Before the major migrations brought on by colonization, the darkest skinned people inhabited a region defined by the Tropics of Cancer, 22 degrees north, and Capricorn, 22 degrees south of the equator (Figure 5-4). This tropical zone has the longest, most intense daily solar radiation, with little seasonal variation. The distribution of dark-skinned peoples coincident with solar radiation intensity has caused scientists to argue for centuries that skin color was adaptive and equipped people for the climatic conditions under which they lived. Such an argument has often been countered by observations that several of these populations live in humid tropical rain forests where little sunlight reaches the ground, and these tropical peoples (Pygmies, for example) still had some of the darkest skins found anywhere. By contrast, some desert dwellers, like the !Kung of southern Africa, had skin with much less melanin. Other doubts about the correlation of skin color and latitude have been raised by Arctic and sub-Arctic peoples—Inuit and Siberian reindeer herders, for example—who have a considerable amount of melanin though, given their environment, they would be expected to be pale like the Saami (Lapps) of Scandinavia. Add to this list dark-skinned Tasmanians, who had lived at high latitudes (the island of Tasmania, 42 degrees south, is as far from the equator as is Boston, Massachusetts) for at least 20,000 years.[1]

Despite these and other exceptions, there is a close positive correlation between latitude and light reflectance of the skin for most populations. Relethford (2000) reported that skin reflectance of males increased 8.2 percent for each ten degrees north latitude and females increased 8.1 percent. A lower correlation was reported for the Southern Hemisphere; male relfectance increased only 3.3 percent per ten degrees south and females 4.7 percent. The darker skin of native peoples of the southern latitudes, and hence a lower reflectance correlation, may be explained by the history of migration patterns. The later arrivals, like the Zulu in southern

---

[1]The degree of pigmentation of the Tasmanians depends on anecdotal descriptions from the nineteenth century and cannot be confirmed by modern measurements since the last Tasmanian had died by the end of that century. Any survivors today claiming Tasmanian descent are of mixed European ancestry.

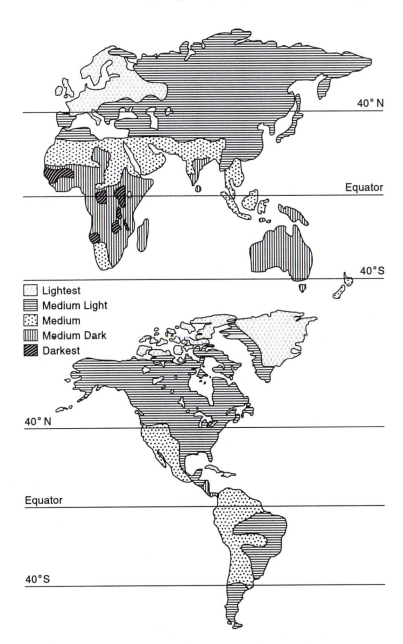

FIGURE 5-4   Distribution of Human Skin Color. (From Frisancho, A.R., *Human Adaptation*, 1979, St. Louis: The C.V. Mosby Co.; modified from Brace, C.L., and A. Montagu, *Man's Evolution*, 1965, New York: Macmillan.)

Africa about 1,000 years ago, had a more heavily pigmented skin than the local populations of Khoisan. Hence, measurements of their descendents are responsible for the mixed pattern of medium and medium-dark distributions shown in southern Africa (Figure 5-4).

Ultraviolet Radiation (UVR)

Ultraviolet rays represent a portion of the sun's electromagnetic energy below the wavelength band for visible light. A large fraction of ultraviolet, in the range of 290 to 320 millimeters (mm) (2,900 to 3,200 angstroms) wavelength, is absorbed by the ozone layer surrounding the earth. Little reaches ground level, but there is a sufficient amount of this energy to affect many life forms, and it is this part that is of most concern. Table 5-1 lists the three components of UVR, their degree of penetration, and biological effects. These shorter wavelengths are also influenced by the angle between the sun's rays and the earth's surface; time of day as well as season of the year causes a reduction of radiation penetrating the atmosphere. The sun is most intense at midday on the equator and declines with the hour. The higher the latitude, the lower the solar radiation and the greater will be the seasonal variation, as shown by the diagram of the daily UV radiation count in Minneapolis over the year (Figure 5-5). The change between midwinter and midsummer is about 1,800 percent. By contrast, little seasonal change occurs within the tropical zones, and these differences between tropical and temperate zones in amounts of UVR have profound biologic effects. In Boston and other cities at the same latitude, for example, there is

TABLE 5-1   Solar Radiation and the Ultraviolet Spectrum

WAVELENGTH[1]	BIOLOGICAL EFFECTS[2]	PENETRATION[3]
Ultraviolet-C 190–290 mμ	Germicidal; little skin penetration	Scattered and absorbed by dust, water vapor, and ozone; little or none reaches earth's surface
Ultraviolet-B 290–320 mμ	Sunburn, cancer, tanning, and vitamin D synthesis	More energy reaches earth's surface
Ultraviolet-A 320–400 mμ	Same as above but less effective; the additional influence of photolysis on some vitamins	More energy reaches earth's surface than above

[1]The units of measure of solar spectrum are given in millimicrons (mμ), which are equal to 10 angstroms.

[2]The biological effects vary according to wavelength and have greater or lesser effect on different cell structures or chemical compounds; e.g., the 290–320 range stimulates the production of melanin and also provides the energy for vitamin D synthesis from its provitamin. The higher range UVA also has some of these effects.

[3]The penetrating power of the UV energy spectrum is a function of its wavelength; the shorter wavelengths are absorbed and scattered by more substances and little or no energy reaches the earth's surface. Likewise, the longer wavelengths penetrate the skin more deeply; e.g., at 360 mμ the penetration is twice as deep as it is at 240 mμ (see Faber, 1989).

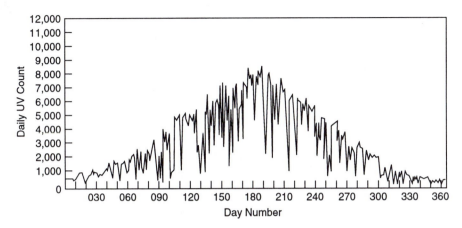

FIGURE 5-5   Daily-Total of Ultraviolet Radiation for 1974 in Minneapolis. The record of UV measured in this North American city at 44.58° north latitude illustrates the broad range of difference between midsummer (day 185) and midwinter (day 350). (Source: From Faber, 1982. "Ultraviolet radiation." In *Nonionizing Radiation Protection*, 2nd ed., M.J. Suess and D.A. Benwell-Morison, WHO Publication, No. 25.)

enough UVB to stimulate vitamin D production only after the middle of March (Jablonski and Chaplin, 2003).

Human Skin and Solar Radiation

The effects of solar energy on the skin vary considerably, depending on wavelength. There is a deeper penetration of the skin by energy at the near infrared range (1,000 mμ), but little ultraviolet (290–400 mμ) reaches the lower layers of the epidermis (stratum germinativum where the basal cells are most active). The thickness of the corneum, or outer layer, and melanin pigment have significant effects of blocking and scattering UVR: Darkly pigmented skin is penetrated much less deeply than fair skin. The shortest wavelength, UVC, has the least penetrating power; besides, little energy from this range reaches the earth's surface. The longer part of the ultraviolet spectrum, UVA, will reach further down into the epidermal layer, but with seemingly less biologic effect, harmful or beneficial. UVA does stimulate the melanocytes to some degree and provides energy for vitamin D synthesis. The middle range UVB, however, has the greater influence. Penetration is less, and it is more readily blocked by melanin, but its biologic effects are greater, with more vitamin D synthesized and more melanin produced (Faber, 1989). These varying characteristics of UVR are important factors in our adaptation to geographic regions with variable degrees of solar radiation, as described later.

First, because we judge skin color by the visible part of the spectrum, the differences in the reflective properties of human skin should be noted. We may measure differences by beaming a quantity of light on a section of untanned skin and then

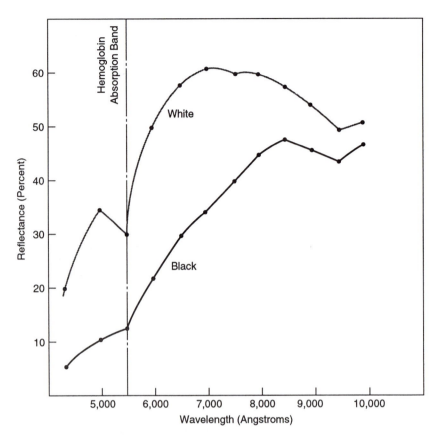

FIGURE 5-6   Skin-Reflectance Characteristics of a Sample of American Blacks and Whites.
Average reflectance characteristics of black and white skin on the flexor surface of the forearm.
Measurements made from visible light to the near-infrared range with marked absorption Indicated
in the white sample at approximately 5,500 angstroms (the absorption for hemoglobin). (Redrawn;
based on Barnicot, 1957.)

measuring the amount reflected. This method gives an accurate method of detecting
relative degrees of melanization. Figure 5-6 shows comparative skin-reflectance properties of Africans and Euro-Americans. The curves indicate greater reflectance by
"white" skin over the entire spectral range tested. These curves, however, were
constructed from average values of all subjects tested and obscure ranges of reflectance
variation. Figure 5-7 illustrates some of this variation of reflectance characteristics of
several populations that vary in pigmentation (see also Figure 5-2). In this study,
reflectance was measured at the upper end of the visible range. The Euro-Australian
(whites) reflected roughly 50 percent of the light, and Native Australians (Aborigines)
only reflected about 10 percent; other groups showed reflectance properties between
these two extremes. The two groups that recorded male and female reflectance values
showed males lower on the scale, a result of darker male skin.

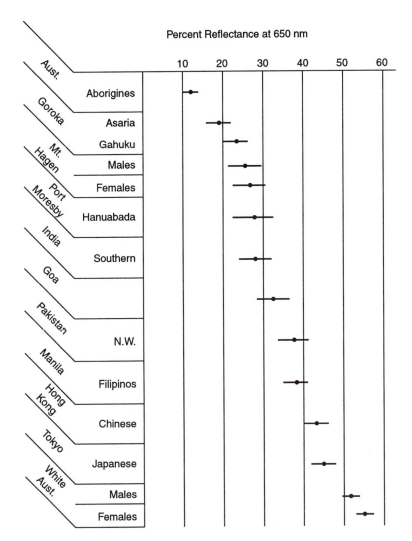

FIGURE 5-7 Skin-Reflectance Characteristics of Several Populations. The mean percentage of reflectance from the foreheads of samples of several populations is indicated by the dot, and the range of plus or minus one standard deviation is indicated by the line. (Source: After Walsh, R.J., "Variations of melanin pigmentation of the skin in some Asian and Pacific peoples." Copyright © 1963 by the Journal of the Royal Anthropological Institute. Reprinted by permission of the publisher.)

Natural Selection and Skin Color

The simple distributional evidence of skin color is not a sufficient explanation of its adaptive advantage; consider some of the probable mechanisms that may be operating. If we regard the epidermis as a filter that reduces the amount of UVR penetrating the skin, we may establish the relative advantages or disadvantages of high melanin content of the skin in various environments. Comparisons of environmental effects are aided by the colonization of tropical regions by fair-skinned people over the past four centuries.

Sunburn: If we consider the reddening of the skin, we can see many advantages enjoyed by people who naturally have dark skins or who can make melanin quickly, especially if they work outdoors. Depending on the degree of exposure, sunburn causes congestion of the subcutaneous capillaries, destruction of cells at several layers, and edema (collection of fluids under the skin's surface). Besides being painful, sunburn can be very dangerous. Rapid cell destruction followed by peeling of large sections of skin can open the way for infection. Another effect is the reduction in ability to regulate body temperature, because sweat gland function is reduced to the point where internal body temperature buildup leads to heat exhaustion. Prolonged exposure to the sun can also cause permanent damage to underlying tissues. Premature wrinkling of the skin due to a destruction of the elastic collagen fibers is another effect of long-term exposure. Darkly pigmented peoples are less prone to this solar radiation damage because of the filtering effects of the melanin, and hence such people appear to age more slowly.

Cancers: Overexposure can result in more permanent damage, as in the example of skin cancer, where some of the cells' DNA is altered. There are three types of skin cancer: basal cells in the lowest level of the epidermis; the flattened squamous cells near the outer layer; and malignant melanoma, a cancer of the melanocytes. The first two types are the most common of all human cancers but have a low mortality rate because they do not metastasize and spread to other tissues. Melanoma, because it does grow and spread if not treated early, is one of the deadliest forms of all. The incidence of these skin cancers is highest among fair-skinned persons who are exposed to the sun for prolonged periods. Persons whose occupations keep them outdoors have a greater chance of developing skin lesions, usually on the face or on the backs of the hands. The highest frequencies of skin cancers in the world are among Euro-Australians living in Queensland—about 265 cases reported per 100,000 males and 156 per 100,000 females. The incidence among whites living in South Africa is much lower—133 per 100,000 males and 72 per 100,000 females. By contrast, British populations have a low of only 28 per 100,000 males and 15 per 100,000 females. In the United States the rate of new skin cancer cases has radically increased—up to 1,000,000 new cases per year, and some 38,000 of these are the most lethal type, *malignant melanoma*, that accounts for 7,000 deaths (Leffell and Brash, 1996). The relation to sunlight is clear; Tucson, Arizona, has seven times the number of new skin cancers than Minneapolis or Seattle. Even more confirmation of cancer risk is provided by the fate of thousands of albinos in Nigeria; virtually all have skin cancer or precancerous lesions by age 20 (Faber, 1989). Among the darker skinned populations, problems related to solar radiation are minimal, and skin cancers rarely, if ever, occur. Recently, skin cancers have received more attention because of an increase during the past two decades, and the number of cases are expected to rise further because of ozone layer depletion, thereby allowing more UVR to penetrate the atmosphere.

The Photochemical Effects

Besides the damage caused by UVR there are *photochemical* effects, the changes of chemical bonds when certain compounds are exposed to sunlight. Several chemicals essential for our metabolism have this sensitivity and will undergo decomposition (photolysis) under the influence of UVR. Among these sensitive chemicals are several vitamins: folic acid, riboflavin, and vitamin E. The photosensitivity of these substances suggests that dark skin may protect certain critical metabolites in the blood and dermis from the photo decomposition effects of UVR. Several experiments have shown that levels of folic acid in the blood were depressed by ultraviolet light; such was the case with patients of Scandinavian descent undergoing treatment for certain skin ailments by exposure to ultraviolet light. Branda and Eaton (1978) reported that folic-acid levels in such patients dropped significantly during the course of their treatment. Though no comparable study has been reported for vitamin E or riboflavin in humans, these substances are known to be photosensitive as demonstrated by laboratory experiments.

UVR also has a positive photochemical effect. Vitamin D, essential for skeletal growth and absorption and transport of calcium, is synthesized by the action of UVR on a sterol compound, 7-dehydrocholesterol, an oily substance found in the lower layers of the epidermis. Because the amount required for proper maintenance of calcium levels is small (only about 300 to 400 units per day), an exposure of a small area of the body to the sun for a short period is sufficient. It has been estimated that 20 cm^2, or about the area of the skin covering a human infant's face, is sufficient. Any interference with this amount of exposure (by reduction in time, ultraviolet light, or in surface area) correspondingly diminishes the amount of vitamin D synthesized. Dark skin requires six times as long to make the same amount of the vitamin as light skin, and the time will also vary by latitude; synthesis is more rapid in the tropics and takes longer in the northern temperate zone. Since vitamin D is scarce in most foods except fish oils, it is usually difficult to get through dietary sources. The synthesis in the skin can then be very important when the results of a vitamin D deficiency are considered.

The effects caused by a reduction in the vitamin vary between individuals, depending on their age. Rickets, once a frequent disease in northern Europe, will develop in children deprived of vitamin D. Their rapidly growing bones will fail to mineralize properly and the weight-bearing parts of the skeleton, the legs and pelvis in particular, will become distorted and misshapen as the infant begins to walk. In its severest form, rickets can even result in death. One of the clearest examples of the course of rickets and the influence of diet and lifestyle comes from well-documented medical records of the last two centuries. Children living in crowded slums of industrial cities of eighteenth- and nineteenth-century England suffered from a high frequency of rickets. The smoke-laden air and the crowded streets with no open space and little sunlight reduced the chance of satisfying the body's requirements for the vitamin. Given the environmental influences, rickets has been called the first air-pollution disease (Loomis, 1970). Diet was an important factor also, because fresh milk and fish were expensive and scarce in the diets of factory workers. Adults did not escape this problem of vitamin D deficiency and low calcium; they suffered from osteomalacia, the adult form of poorly mineralized bone.

In addition to this example, these vitamin-D deficiency diseases have occurred in a wide variety of environments, even in the tropics. Women of some cultures suffer more frequently because of a tradition that causes them to be confined to the household from early childhood and allowed in public only if they are completely covered. The restriction on their daily activities and their required clothing reduce the amount of exposure to sunlight. For example, Bedouin women in North Africa and the Middle East remain inside the family's tents most of the day, and if they venture outside they must clothe themselves completely with skirts and veils. Only the small area of skin around their eyes is exposed to sunlight. This seclusion of women indoors also affects the health of infants and children. Infants in Muslim cultures and among high-caste Hindus frequently develop rickets during infancy, but many recover as young children when they are allowed to play outdoors. Females, often married at 12 years of age and then forced into the seclusion of the home and veil, frequently develop the disease again.

Rickets can also occur in modern urban populations even today. For example, among the large numbers of East Indians and Pakistanis who have settled in the British Isles during the last fifty years, cases of rickets and osteomalacia have made their appearance. The combination of low incidence of sunlight in these northern latitudes, deeply pigmented skin, and dietary customs significantly reduces the chance of the synthesis of an adequate amount of vitamin D. The pathological results—skeletal malformations—have been reported in several clinical studies. This is similar to the experience of African American populations living in North American cities. Before the widespread use of vitamin D supplements, mainly in fortification in milk, rickets was suffered by many children, but most frequently among those with dark skins.

Surprisingly, over the last decade there has been an increase in the number of children suffering from vitamin D deficiency. In addition, the blood levels of the vitamin are too low in many older adults and even in adolescents. The causes relate to more indoor activity with less exposure to sunlight and the tendency to avoid fortified milk. But the overall problem is complex and has several ramifications. People have frequently been warned of the dangers of overexposure to UVR and advised to use sun screen. Following this advice to the extreme, many are deprived of sufficient quantities of vitamin D. Unless they consume vitamin and calcium supplements, they run the risk of poorly mineralized bones. Mothers, especially, are at risk; more cases of rickets have been diagnosed in infants who have been breast fed, without vitamin supplements, and who are kept out of the sunlight. Again, latitude and skin pigmentation are important variables; the majority of new rickets cases have been among African Americans living in the northern cities (Stokstad, 2003).

Rickets and osteomalacia, in severe forms, can shorten life span and are most effective as selective forces among females because these diseases can lead to distortion of the pelvis. Figure 5-8 compares a normal and distorted pelvis inlet, showing the serious influence that rickets can have on female growth. Even a slight deformation of the pelvis reduces the birth canal and interferes with normal childbirth, increasing the risk of death of the mother or the fetus during childbirth. The effects of the disease can be measured by the frequency of deformed pelvis among females; only 2 percent of white women had a deformed pelvis compared with 15 percent of black women.

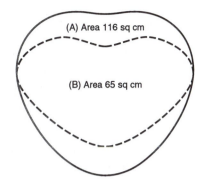

FIGURE 5–8   Outline of normal pelvic inlet (solid line) and contracted pelvic inlet due to severe childhood rickets (broken line). (Source: From Frisancho, A.R., *Human Adaptation and Accomodation*, *1995.* Ann Arbor: The University of Michigan Press.

Since the near-universal addition of vitamin D_2 to milk in the United States and most European countries, however, rickets has been nearly eliminated as a childhood disease, except for some Asian migrants to northern Europe and now a resurgence among certain groups in North America.

Despite the disadvantages of dark skin in the temperate zone, it can be advantageous to be deeply pigmented in the tropics when overexposure to ultraviolet rays could cause not only sunburn and skin cancer, but also hypervitaminosis (an overproduction of vitamin D). Too much vitamin D is harmful and causes calcification of many soft tissues throughout the body and impairs kidney function. The toxic level may be as low as 40,000 international units (IU) for infants to 100,000 IU for adults (normal individual needs vary between 400 and 1,000 IU per day). Whole-body radiation has been estimated to produce upward of 120,000 units per hour, which is well above the toxic level (between 10,000 and 100,000 IU per day). Clothing, of course, reduces the amount of skin exposed, but the reader should remember that tropical peoples wear relatively little clothing. Besides, during the first few years, children in tropical climates seldom wear any clothing at all and during the day are much more active than adults. This would add to the degree of their exposure and hence the potential for producing toxic levels of vitamin D unless protected by skin pigmentation.

SKIN COLOR AND EVOLUTION

The preceding discussions of the harmful and helpful effects of solar radiation provide some evidence of the direct effects on human survival. Considering all those factors that relate—skeletal structure, calcium metabolism, skin pigmentation, and incidence of UVR—we now ask: How have they affected human evolution? Is the color of *Homo sapiens* naturally dark and, if so, what accounts for the relative depigmentation of the Europeans and the medium pigment of Asians?

The wealth of accumulating fossil evidence supports earlier hypotheses that our immediate ancestors evolved in the tropics and spread into, and permanently occupied, the northern latitudes relatively recently in time. This was probably not before the third interglacial period, about 120,000 years ago. At this time these prehistoric populations were probably dark skinned and suffered the detrimental effects common to deeply pigmented peoples living in regions of low UVR. The selection for peoples who could thrive under such conditions—that is, relatively depigmented fair-skinned peoples—has lasted until the present century. There is evidence that the adjustment to these selective forces must have taken thousands of years. Even during the Mesolithic period, between 10,000 and 15,000 years ago, northern European populations suffered from poor mineralization. Skeletal remains from Sweden and other areas of northern Europe dating to this period show many signs of poor calcification of their teeth and bones. Likewise, similar evidence is seen among skeletal materials dating from medieval times.

Two things made possible our continuous survival in the northern latitudes. The first is the steady decline in pigmentation throughout hundreds of generations or, rather, selection favoring the survival of individuals whose genes influenced lesser melanization resulting in lighter skins. The second is the increased use of fish in the diet during the past 6,000 years—particularly herring that is rich in vitamin D-bearing oils. Eventually, though no one knows where the practice began, a home remedy for rickets was introduced: the use of fish liver oils to cure this childhood disease. There also developed the practice of placing infants outside, even during the coldest months, to be exposed to "fresh air and sunshine." Both of these measures have the same end results and have helped our species to sustain life and maintain large populations in northern Europe.

A discussion of the protective effects of melanin must also consider the changes of photolysis (light-caused chemical breakdown). Experiments with human and laboratory animals, noted previously, have shown that photolysis reduces folic-acid levels. If individuals live on diets marginal in folic-acid content, they will be particularly susceptible to a reduction in vitamin action owing to the destructive effects of the sun. Impaired growth in children and low reproductive capacity are a result of folic-acid deficiency and would be a strong selective influence for dense pigmentation as protection against photodecomposition of this essential vitamin. A similar argument could be made for protection of riboflavin and vitamin E. The probability that melanin functions to reduce photodecomposition of certain vitamins and prevents overproduction of vitamin D argues strongly for natural selection of dark-skinned peoples in areas of intense solar radiation. Add to this the tests that show immunity depressed by UVR and the argument for the protective effects of melanin is strengthened (Robins, 1991).

If another feature of human skin is considered, its tanning ability, then evidence can be added to that already discussed. Selection appears to have been for skin that will vary in pigmentation according to the incidence of ultraviolet light. The best adapted, then, would have skin that tanned well in the summer (reducing vitamin-D synthesis as exposure to sunlight increased with the long summer days) and lightened during the winter to take all possible advantage of the weak winter sun. Europeans native to southern Europe, North Africans, and western Asian populations have skins with a higher degree of melanin content than their northern neighbors, so they tan much better—a feature that is a significant advantage in their climates.

Any classification based on degree of pigmentation, real or imagined, as an identifier of population or ancestry can be misleading. Skin coloration happens to be much more complex and variable than is usually appreciated, and it requires far more discussion of pigment biochemistry and genetics; however, many of the interrelationships between sunlight and physiology have been clearly established. One final consideration, we should note, is the difference between the skin color of males and females in the same populations. As stated earlier, females have lighter skin, which, given their need for a more carefully regulated calcium metabolism, makes good adaptive sense. Children are also much fairer than their parents; often the infants of dark-skinned parents are pink, and their skin steadily darkens throughout childhood. This is another factor that shows the interrelationship between the human skin pigmentation system and solar radiation, demonstrating again the advantages that variable skin pigmentation can confer on a human population.

CRANIOFACIAL TRAITS

The facial and cranial components of the human skull form an anatomical complex that develops at different rates under the control of numerous genes. As the brain expands, especially during infancy, the cranial bones increase in size to provide adequate space, changing the shape of head. Likewise, dental development proceeds, altering the facial configuration from the midface to the lower face. This alteration to accommodate dental development proceeds over a period of years until early adulthood. The muscles that control mandibular movements expand to meet the requirements of mastication—the jaw movements and bite forces. As this complex of muscles enlarges, the points of muscle insertions on the bone also increase in robusticity. Another factor contributing to face form is the opening into the upper respiratory tract. Seen in the bare skull, this opening is pyriform or pear shaped and varies greatly in width near its base which is just above the root tips of the anterior dentition. Taking into account the space needed for this nasal opening, mechanical support of the dental arches and masticatory muscles and the space requirements of the brain, the human head is formed as a compromise to meet all these needs.

Between the processes of growth of the neurocranium and the dento-facial changes, the human cranium of the child, adolescent, and adult differs in proportion and size at each growth stage. The final product—the adult cranium form—is the result of the complex of all of these growth processes and mechanical forces interacting over a period of years. Comparisons of family members show strong resemblances, and members of the same population also share some similarities. Beyond small population groups, ranges of variability of distinguishing features increase and labeling or classification become more difficult.

Head Size and Shape

The shape and size of the head have been under intense study by generations of anthropologists, and numerous descriptive measurements have been devised. The human head has been of special interest because it houses that most important and mysterious part of our anatomy, the brain, and because of the wealth of well-preserved skulls from prehistoric times. Representative skulls from these extinct ancient populations often possess a unique combination of characteristics that have been used to suggest relationships between past and present populations. Ancestral origins, migration routes, and ethnic identity have been postulated. As described in the introductory chapter, certain cranial characteristics were, unfortunately, also presumed to be indicative of certain behavioral attributes; hence the profound interest in the morphology of our skull.

Among the many skull features examined, the one most frequently used in the past for establishing the classical racial groups has been the shape of the head, defined by the *cephalic index*, as noted in Chapter 1. This index, the ratio of the breadth to the length of the skull, provides an approximation of shape without regard to size. The skull of our species varies from long and narrow to short and broad—a variation of cephalic index from 70 (breadth = 70 percent of length) to about 90. Certain populations tend toward one or the other end of the range; Australian Aborigines have the narrowest, in contrast to the Saami (Lapps) of Scandinavia who have the broadest head shapes. The rest of us range somewhere in between.

Despite its frequent use in the past, this index has to be discounted as a racial criterion because of its broad range and because there are similar indices found for such disparate groups as Quechua of the Andes and central Europeans (brachycephalic) or Africans and Australian Aborigines (dolichocephalic). If several cranial and facial dimensions, describing face and head shape, are taken in combination and examined by modern statistical techniques, however, then distinctions are found between many populations. Degrees of relationships—that is, relative distances from a common ancestor—have been estimated in this way. The average cranial–facial morphology of northern Europeans differs significantly from that of southeastern Europeans, for example. The cranial remains of ancient peoples who overran central Europe throughout recorded history have also been identified by this method (Schwidetzsky and Rösing, 1982). The peopling of the Pacific and the Americas presents a challenge to prehistorians, but their studies are aided by extensive comparisons of cranial–facial shape of recent and prehistoric populations (Brace et al., 2001; Pietrusewsky, 1990).

Such studies may be possible if care is taken in selecting dimensions of various features; body size, age, and dental use are among those factors that influence dimensional change. The overall rate of growth and body size also influences shape because there is a positive correlation between stature and skull length; an average, taller individuals have longer heads. Because of these factors, plus the pattern of distribution of cranial shape, cephalic index remains an element of interest in the study of bodily proportions. However, it should be considered as a part of the overall growth and development pattern influenced by environmental factors. Recall the changes in growth and head form among American-born children of European immigrants reported by Boas, as discussed in the first chapter. These and later studies proved that head form could significantly change in a single generation as living conditions improved. Facial as well as cranial changes, between 1909 and 1935 among New York Jewish children, were also described (Boas, 1940b:67).

Climatic conditions can also exert influences. For example, Beals and co-workers (1984) made a comparative study of 20,000 skulls from populations around the world and found a close correlation between environmental temperature and head shape. Populations in colder climates had, on the average, rounder heads than peoples in the tropics, a characteristic that is likely to be of adaptive significance. The relationship of surface area and mass of parts of the mammalian body form influence the radiation of metabolic heat and affect temperature regulation. The closer a structure approaches a spherical shape, the lower will be the surface-to-volume ratio. The reverse is true as elongation occurs—a greater surface area to volume is formed, which results in more surface to dissipate heat generated within a given volume. Since up to 80 percent of our body heat can be lost by radiation from our heads on cold days, one can appreciate the significance of shape. The relation between surface area and volume is a critical factor in heat radiation to regulate body temperature.

Cranial Capacity and Brain Size

Perhaps more speculation and nonsense have been written about the size of the human brain and its relationship to intelligence than about any other aspect of our anatomical variability. This is probably because the size of the cranial vault differs so much among peoples today and has increased throughout much of the fossil record of human evolution. The estimated volume of the cranial vault or cranial capacity increased from a low of 450 cubic centimeters (cc) among the earliest hominids, the Australopithecines, to the highest in archaic and modern *Homo sapiens*. This high brain volume, estimated from cranial capacity, was achieved relatively early in human evolution, approximately 100,000 years ago, among the Neandertals of Europe. In fact, the estimated mean size of their cranial capacity (1,450 cc) is actually higher than the mean for modern humans (1,345 cc).

The increase of brain size during the last two or three million years of evolution was an extremely important event for paleontological studies, and comparisons of cranial capacities of the different fossils can be useful to some extent. When comparisons are made between fossils over broad time spans, some conclusions may be made about intelligence if advances in technologies are also considered. The brain, represented by estimates of gross size, can then be said to have evolved, say between the earliest hominids (Australopithecines) and *Homo erectus* some two million years later, but note that brain size reached its modern range about 100,000 years ago (Neandertals). Since then there has not been an increase in brain size means and the curvature and proportion of the frontal lobes have remained the same throughout hominid evolution (Allen et al., 2004). What is especially notable is the wide range in size variation among contemporary populations, and the lower end of this range extends well below some of the volumes of many of our earlier hominid ancestors.

Should we conclude that some of our fossil ancestors were more intelligent because of a larger average cranial capacity? Of course not! There is no evidence that individuals with small cranial capacities, and hence small brains, are any less intelligent than persons with larger cranial vaults housing larger brains. The differences among modern populations' brain sizes do not have any relevance to mental ability. As von Bonin (1963), a foremost neuroanatomist, once stated, the correlation between brain size and mental capacity is insignificant in modern *Homo sapiens*. Brain scans by MRI (magnetic resonance imaging) in recent years have supported von Bonin's earlier observation. Though correlations between IQ-test scores and brain size have been reported in some studies, the correlations were low—accounting for 16 percent or less of test-score variance. The size of the brain is but one of the factors related to human intelligence (Andreasen et al., 1993).

The MRI scans of a few subjects that yield a low correlation are less impressive than the wide range of brain size among members of the same population where no correlation to intellectual attainment is found. There are abundant examples of extreme differences in brain size in all populations that have no bearing on ability or achievement. Many famous statesmen, scientists, and literary figures had cranial capacities at either end of the range—from Anatole France and Turgenev (1,100 cc) to Oliver Cromwell and Lord Byron (2,200 cc), while the great poet, Walt Whitman and Albert Einstein had to get along with even less, only 1,282 cc and 1,230 cc, respectively.

Brain and body size is closely correlated; most studies, especially the earlier ones that are often used for comparison, seldom considered the overall size of the individual. Also, females average 10 percent smaller cranial capacities than males—a difference that is related to the smaller average female body size. Taller individuals have larger brains, as documented by numerous studies; brain weight is positively correlated with height (Pakkenberg and Voigt, 1964). Simply stated, larger people have larger brains. In addition, brain volume or weight is difficult to measure, either by estimation from cranial capacity of the dry skull, from the head of the living individual, or from the brain at autopsy, where age and cause of death are important influences. The methods used to remove and separate the brain from the spinal cord, as well as the skill of the investigator, will influence the results increasing or decreasing weight.

Nevertheless, there are authors, even today, who insist on recording and emphasizing so-called racial difference in cranial capacity as if it were meaningful. See, for example, Burnham (1985), who argued that brain size is a significant indicator of intelligence, or Rushton (1992), who has revived the old argument of "inherited inequality" (see Chapter 7). Because of this persistent use of estimated brain size for such purposes, measurements drawn from a number of populations illustrate the broad range (Figure 5-9). Before the reader draws any conclusions, two important points should be noted. First, note that the range from the highest to the lowest is only 263 cc. Second, there is a variation of more than + or − 100 cc about the mean of most populations; this would place many in the highest or lowest of the range as shown by the three European samples. Also note the high and midrange means for Native Americans. In short, there are people with small heads and some with large heads; differences of 200 cc or more of cranial capacity within the same population are not unusual. In sum, individuals with larger or smaller cranial capacities are normally

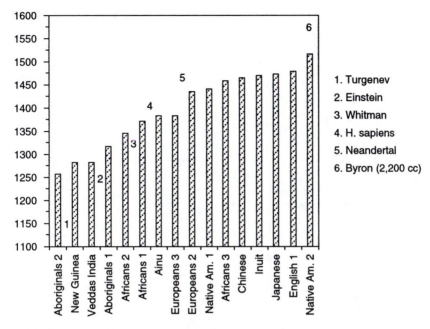

FIGURE 5-9   Ranges of Average Cranial Capacity. The average male cranial capacities have been selected to illustrate the ranges of cranial volumes found in modern human populations. There has been no correction for body size, but note that those at the lowest end of the range are also those with the smallest average body size. Six famous people are included for comparison. (Source: Data selected from Montagu, 1960; Tobias, 1970; Ricklan and Tobias, 1986.)

functioning and intellectually competent individuals, and neither individuals nor groups can be sorted by such a highly variable measurement as cranial capacity. If these data had been corrected for body size the outcomes would likely have been different. Similarities or differences become understandable when growth processes and body size are considered.

Face Form

The human face is highly variable in its shape and size, and there are distinctly individual forms. We can easily recognize our friends by their facial appearance, and we automatically, and even subconsciously, group people according to their expressions or the dimensions and proportions of the face. One worker went so far as to divide faces into ten different categories or types, from elliptical to oval, including such classifications as rectangular and pentagonal. Even with many gradations among these categories, it was still impossible to apply them to all members of a population. Any scheme devised to describe facial characteristics of certain populations is just a rough approximation that will include only a portion of the individuals in the group. The form of the mouth, prominence of the chin or nose, and the position of the eyes are visual clues that enable recognition. We all tend to group people into broad general categories, and

FIGURE 5-10   Faces of *Homo sapiens*. This composite photograph illustrates the range of variability of our species. (Source: Courtesy of United Nations.)

we see these groupings as related to what we have come to accept as the classic racial or ethnic divisions of our species; the terms Eskimo, Aborigine, or Chinese project a mental image of what a person in that category looks like before we ever see the individual. The composite photograph in Figure 5-10 offers an example of the diversity of face form.

Little is known about the causes of such diversity or about the degree of genetic influence. The soft tissues of the face are arranged in any number of ways and change with age; family resemblances may vary from slight to strong and population affinities are usually clear. Also, there appears to be a geographical distribution of face form that suggests some adaptation to climate; the flat, broad face of northern Asian peoples has been described as an adaptation to cold ever since the earliest days of anthropology, while at the same time the large, probably bulbous nose and the expanded maxillary sinuses of the European Neandertal were also considered cold adapted. There are few physiological studies to support such an explanation, however. A clearer understanding of facial structures is provided by studies of the facial skeleton.

Human face shape is complex and is the result of several large and small bones organized about three basic structures; the eyes, the nose, and the mouth.

The development and placement of these structures must be coordinated to provide sufficient space and symmetry to enable the functions of sight, respiration, and alimentation, each with special requirements of shape, size, and position in the overall facial arrangement. The spacing of the orbits of the eyes, for example, influences the visual field and affects appearance to a large extent, while the size of the nasal aperture allows for inhalation through the upper respiratory tract and is related to the bony structures of the roof of the mouth and the midface. The mouth, in turn, has a size and shape closely related to the size and spacing of the teeth in the dental arcade.

The shape of the human face has changed a great deal from the heavy *prognathic* structure possessed by our fossil ancestors to the reduced structure in modern *Homo sapiens*, which is rather small in proportion to our large head. This change has come about over a long period of time as our ancestors relied less on their jaws and teeth for procuring and manipulating food and more on hand-held implements and cooking. The stresses on dento-facial use declined and large teeth and their supporting bones were no longer as important for survival as they had been. These bony structures are primarily the brow ridges (the ridge of bone over the eyes), the cheekbones (or zygomatic arches), and of course the upper and lower arches of bone that support the teeth. With a reduction in these elements, the human face began to acquire a new look, and size proportions were drastically altered (Brace, 1962). All of the world's populations did not undergo exactly the same pattern of change, however, nor were their faces altered at the same rate. Many of the facial features have maintained large sizes in some populations, such as the Inuit (Eskimo) and Australian Aborigines who have continued heavy dental use well into the twentieth century.

One rather distinctive facial characteristic clearly involved in the evolutionary process is *prognathism*, the forward protrusion of dental arches. A comparison of modern humans with recent or ancient and fossil Neandertals illustrates the reduction in the lower face of modern humans (Figure 5-11). Many modern populations today have prognathic profiles, yet this does not indicate a closer affinity with fossil ancestors; rather, it is often a result of the presence of large teeth in broad dental arches. Because the major purpose of the bony structures in this part of the face is the support of the dentition, the bone arches of the maxilla and mandible are correspondingly large.

Teeth have proved to be significant in the study of human variability because of their importance as evidence in evolution and adaptation to environmental conditions. Teeth served *Homo sapiens* well as cutting, grinding, and shearing implements in past times, as the heavily worn dental remains of prehistoric and earlier historic humans demonstrate (Brace, 1962; Molnar, 1971). In fact, human survival up until recent times depended a great deal on a sturdy dentition and a heavy, well-formed skeleton, as illustrated by the robust dental arches in Figure 5-12. With the rise of technological efficiency to process the raw materials necessary to sustain life, however, there was less reliance on the dental arches as implements, so in modern times our teeth are often looked on as annoying items of our anatomy that frequently require dental treatment.

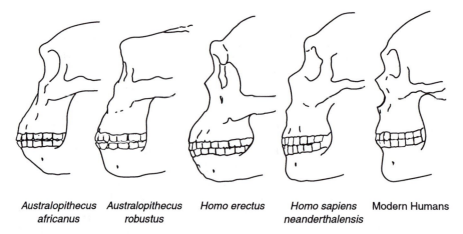

| Australopithecus africanus | Australopithecus robustus | Homo erectus | Homo sapiens neanderthalensis | Modern Humans |

FIGURE 5-11   Alveolar Prognathism. These sketches diagram the facial distinctions of several phases of human evolution. In contrast to the modern profiles, the lower face—mainly the anterior tooth row and chin—was much more robust and the teeth protruded further forward. The cheekbones (zygomatic arches) and brow ridges were also larger in earlier human ancestors.

Teeth have characteristics of shape and size that increase the dentition's utility as a chewing implement—extra molar cusps and reinforced enamel ridges are examples. Throughout evolution these characteristics varied from population to population so that, today, the many ethnic groups show considerable diversity in these dental features because of the differences in selective forces for sturdy teeth that have been operating on each group. Tooth size, especially the diameter of the molar crown, shows great variation. From the large crowns of the Australopithecine molars (approximately 15-mm diameter in the cheek-to-tongue direction) to the small sizes of many European populations (11.5-mm diameter of the first molar), the dentition of humans and their ancestors has steadily reduced in size over time. This reduction has not been equal nor has it been constant in all of the world's peoples; today some people, such as the Australian Aborigines, still possess large teeth, well within the range of those found in European fossils of the mid-Pleistocene.

Shovel-shaped incisors are another dental feature that occurs more frequently in certain populations than in others. This term describes an incisor tooth that has thickened enamel margins on the lingual surface (tongue side of the tooth). These raised surfaces provide structural reinforcement that prevents or reduces the possibility of breakage. In many Asian peoples—Chinese, for instance—most individuals have these types of incisors, and Asian children suffer far less from breakage of the upper central incisors in childhood accidents than do European children.

Several other features of the dentition also show a great deal of variability and, in some cases, have been grouped according to ethnic group. More often, though, there is only a variability in the frequency of the occurrence of the particular trait; most, if not all, groups of humanity possess the trait to some degree. The molar cusps are an example,

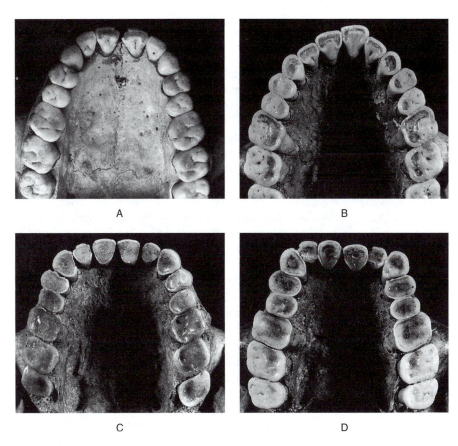

A   B

C   D

FIGURE 5-12   Examples of Worn Teeth in Prehistoric Populations. The upper dental arch is shown at several stages of wear. The unworn teeth of a 16-year-old (A) are compared to three adults who have suffered various degrees of tooth loss because of a tough abrasive diet requiring heavy chewing. A younger adult, about 25 (B), shows less wear than C, a 35-year-old, and D, a 45-year-old. (Source: Iva M. Molnar.)

because their number and arrangement on the molar crown have often been used to identify racial affinity. Some groups frequently do tend to have one or another pattern; for example, there are very seldom fewer than five cusps on the lower first molar of the Australian Aborigines, whereas the first molars of many Europeans tend to be reduced in size with only four cusps. Many individual Aborigines differ from this typical pattern, however, and often have a sixth cusp. So it is with other racial characteristics of the teeth; though members of a group may have a higher frequency of one or more dental traits, they are seldom unique possessors, and others may have the same traits (as in the case of shovel-shaped incisors found in 10 percent of Europeans). To sum up, the range of variability of the dentition of modern *Homo sapiens* is so great that several characteristic features must be considered together before population group affinity may be described.

Nose Form

The nose dominates the midfacial region and contributes a great deal to a person's distinctive identity. Form and size vary over a wide range; there are people with short, broad, or long, narrow noses, and all combinations in between. The linear measures are easily made on either the living or the dry skull, and many thousands of measurements have been recorded. Nasal index (width/length × 100), an approximation of shape like the cephalic index, is also easily derived and has received a great deal of attention. Nose shape appears to have a pattern of geographical distribution and was once thought to be a distinctively racial trait. In some ethnic groups a certain shape does appear more frequently. An index of 104 describes a nose that is slightly wider at the nostrils than it is long; such high indices are found among the Pygmies of the Ituri Forest area in central Africa and Aborigines in central Australia. Narrower noses, represented by low indices (85 and below), are found among numerous groups throughout the world—in many Native Americans, North and East Africans, Europeans, and Eskimos. The contrasts in nasal breadth—narrow to broad form—encompass the spectrum of human diversity without regard to racial classification.

Because the nose performs vital functions of the upper respiratory tract—filtering, warming, and moistening the inspired air—the adaptive significance of its size and shape variation has been examined closely. The nose is lined with mucosal membranes covering a dense bed of fatty tissues through which a rich supply of blood flows. These membranes can secrete large amounts of water, up to 1 liter per day, which moistens the inspired air. The moistening function serves to help maintain the inspired air at the relative humidity of 100 percent required by the lungs. Other structures of the respiratory track contribute moisture, but the lining of the nose serves most effectively in this function. This means that the amount of total surface area of the internal nose and adjacent structures become more important in drier areas. Natives of arid regions of the world then would be expected to have a nasal geometric shape that provides the greatest surface area per unit size. Among desert and mountain peoples the narrow nose is the predominant form, and it is true for people in the colder and drier climate of the Arctic. A narrow nasal aperture provides an efficient mechanism for warming in addition to moistening the inspired air. It is a simple matter of geometry that a high, narrow nasal opening can warm and moisten air more efficiently than a short, broad one because of its greater surface area to volume ratio (Franciscus and Long, 1991; Wolpoff, 1968). In climates where the moisture content of the air is very low, whether the dryness is due to intense heat or intense cold, the greater surface area of nasal membranes offers a conditioning effect of the inspired air and reduces stress on the tissues of the bronchial tubes and lungs. It may be argued that this is a survival advantage—natural selection favors a certain shape and size.

Since face form, as noted above, is a result of a complex of the growth of several facial bones, any single feature is the result of several interacting processes. This is especially true of nose form, whose width is related to the size and proportion of the upper dental arch. Wider palates are necessary to accommodate large teeth, and the roots of the anterior teeth require robust bony support resulting in a broader nasal aperture. The indigenous peoples of Australia, whose teeth are the largest of any modern people, offer a good example of this relationship between several facial structures. Though most Australians live in some of the driest areas of the world, their noses are extremely broad, much more than predicted by the moisture–shape relationship model. This greater breadth dimension is related to the large anterior teeth and to the heavy chewing forces exerted on the dental arches during childhood that stimulates the palatal growth. Also, their prognathism tends to be associated with a short, broad nose, and a significant correlation has been found between the length of the skull base and nasal width.

These factors of climate influence and structural interrelationships suggest that numerous variables are involved in shaping the face during growth and development to achieve a certain adult form. Conclusions, therefore, should not be drawn too quickly about relationships between any two populations solely on the basis of a similarity in structure. Face form, like other bodily dimensions, develops according to environmental factors acting on the gene products that regulate growth. It is not necessary to postulate migrations and interbreeding populations to explain similarities, as was once done for the Nilotic face form found in groups like the Nuer, Watusi, and other East African pastoralists. At one time their long, narrow noses were believed to be one of the features resulting from admixture between African and western Asian populations. Subsequent genetic studies have not supported this explanation. No doubt, during a period of thousands of years, contact with western Asian populations may have occurred and some interbreeding was most likely. The Nilotic face can be the result of local selective forces (hot, dry air) and the size and shape of the dental arcade; it is not merely a matter of interbreeding between peoples of differing face forms. Human face forms do show a geographic distribution pattern, but this is the result of much more than the migrations and interbreeding of peoples in the past. To speak of African, Asian, or European faces ignores the range of variability found within each continental group.

EYE COLOR AND HAIR COLOR

Melanin granules also determine the various shades of eye color by the distribution and density of the pigment in the iris. Blue eyes occur when there is little melanin scattered throughout the iris structure. The light reflected from the relatively depigmented upper layer is in the blue range of the visible light spectrum. So blue eyes occur most often in fair-skinned persons. Variations in the density of the pigment and its distribution cause a graded color series from pale blue to brown. Though eye color tends to be related to the degree of skin melanin, darker eyes do occur in individuals with fair skin. This suggests that different gene loci control the production and distribution of eye pigment. The genetics of eye color has not been worked out, but it is likely to be the result of several loci, which would account for the range of individual differences seen even in the same family.

Hair color is also determined by the degree of melanin present and generally correlates with skin color. Most humans have darker hair, ranging from brown to black. There appears to be growth factor involved as well; many children of European ancestry are fair haired until late childhood or adolescence, after which hair darkens. In some, there is a persistence of fair hair throughout adolescence and adult life, associated with fair skin that is especially notable in northern Europe. Aging also effects hair for as we grow older there is a graying of the hair in all people. The age of onset is highly variable, of course, regardless of degree of skin color.

However, the association with fair skin is not universal; some deeply pigmented peoples have light-colored hair. In central Australia, for example, many Aborigines have blond hair as children, a feature that appears in stark contrast to their dark skin. As they reach adolescence, their hair usually darkens to match their skin, but some maintain light hair color throughout their lives. The reason for this blondness among the Aborigines of central Australia is still open to speculation and is a lively topic for discussion. Blondness of the Australians is apparently due to a gene or genes for the trait and not because of some European admixture, since those individuals with the blond trait have all Aboriginal characteristics, and the evidence for a lack of European genes is reinforced by carefully collected genealogies (Birdsell, 1981). The peculiar example of the contrasts between hair and skin pigment raises the question of the complex inheritance of pigmentation of hair, skin, and eye color and suggests the possibility that the dark skin of Pacific peoples may be due to genes different from African populations.

Hair Form

When the skin of our species is compared with that of other mammals, the first distinction noticed is the near hairless, naked appearance. On closer inspection, however, the skin is not hairless; even apparently naked areas have about the same number of hair follicles as do our furrier primate relatives. Human hairs are finer, thinner in diameter, shorter, and most are relatively colorless. The distribution, density, and color of body hair, though, are subject to vast individual differences, and some ethnic groups have denser body hair than others. For example, there is a relative lack of facial hair among male Asians and Native Americans, in contrast to the heavy beards of many European males and the beards and dense body hair of the Japanese Ainu. Body hair distribution also shows significant sexual dimorphism, with females having less hair, and a near total lack of facial hair.

The hair on the head also varies considerably in length and form, from straight to wavy or curly and the spiral "peppercorn" shape. Asians have straight hair that is thicker than the wavy or curly hair of many Europeans. Frizzy or woolly hair is the form of most Africans, and the San or !Kung are noted for their short, spiral-shaped hair. The adaptive significance of hair form is not understood, but it is likely that certain forms, woolly or spiral, allow for an air space between the scalp and outer edges that insulates the head from the intensity of the sun's heat in the tropics. Such an insulating mechanism would be an advantage to the !Kung hunters of southern Africa or to Melanesians in New Guinea. As is the case with the other polygenic structures we have discussed, the distribution, form, and color of hair are inherited. The number of genes involved, though, is not known, but some inherited defects of hair structure have been reported. One rare form that is of special interest, "woolly" hair, was discovered in a large family kindred living in an isolated region of Norway. Their hair grows to only a short length before the ends break off and gives the appearance of the frizzled or woolly hair form seen in some Africans. The "woolly" hair condition is different from that of Africans, however, and is inherited as an autosomal dominant trait (Stern, 1973).

HUMAN FORM AND ITS VARIABILITY

The human body form varies over a wide range of sizes and shapes, and there is considerable difference among populations. In fact, contrasts in size and shape happen to be one of the more striking of human diversities. From pygmoid peoples, tall, slender East Africans, and the tall robust northern Europeans, or from Arctic peoples to southeastern Asians, we find that the ratio between stature and body weight differs in ways that may reflect environmental conditions of climate, diet, and disease acting on the genome. In other words, many traits of our body shape and size are the result of adaptation during growth and even later in the lifecycle.

Body Size

The height of normal adults in our species ranges from around 150 to well over 185 centimeters (cm). This range in human stature is distributed among the world's peoples in some very interesting ways. There is a clinal distribution related to latitude; the further from the equator, the greater the average height, as in northwestern Europe and China. Nearer the equator, in the tropics, the shorter the people. Such a latitude-height cline is not without exceptions, however. There are many examples of tall people living close to very short or even pygmoid groups. For instance, the Mbuti Pygmies of the Ituri Forest in the Congo live just a few hundred miles from a group, the Tutsi, considered to be among the tallest people in the world. Another contrast in body size is seen among Native Americans of the Southwest; Hopi of northern Arizona average 10 to 12 cm shorter than the Tohono Otam (Papago) who live about 200 miles to the south. In fact, there is a confusing array of sizes distributed over continents and islands without regard to former racial classifications. Every geographical or ethnic grouping has tall and short people, and stature covers such a broad range that general statements are precluded such as, "Europeans are tall"—note the difference between northern and southern Europeans. Figure 5-13 offers diagrams depicting mean statures for several population groups. Though African Pygmies are at the lowest end of the range, many other geographical populations have groups with comparably short stature.

In all populations there is a range of sizes—people who are taller or shorter than average—just as there are differences of sizes among siblings. These differences

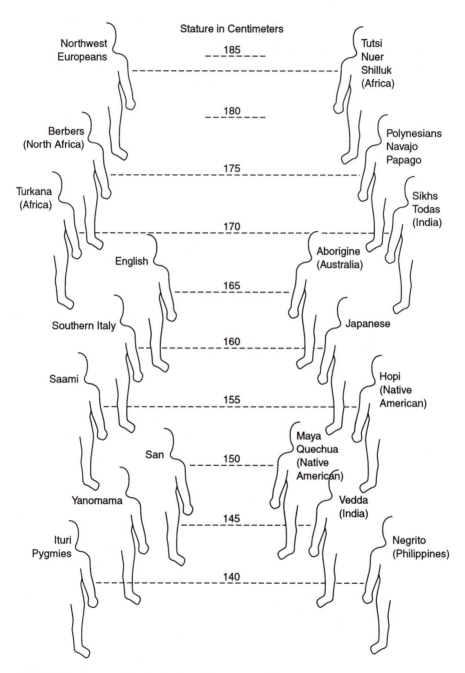

FIGURE 5-13 Diagram of Stature Variation between Populations.

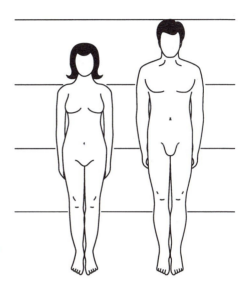

FIGURE 5-14
Sexual Dimorphism: Differences in Size, Shape, and Proportion of Male and Female Body Form. This drawing depicts the average 5–10 percent difference between male and female. Some populations show a greater or lesser dimorphism. Shape and proportions also vary due to secondary sexual characteristics and differences in the relative widths of the pectoral and pelvic girdles.

reflect interactions of environment with the genetic component as described later in this chapter under variations in growth. One of the most clearly defined contrasts of size and shape attributable to genetic influence is seen when comparisons are made between adult males and females; one or more genes on the Y-chromosome influence a slower rate of male maturation and the eventual attainment of a greater size (Hauspie and Susanne, 1998; McKusick, 1994:2563). Males tend to be larger than females in any population, and though there are often taller females and shorter males, average male size exceeds female body size by 5 to 10 percent (see Figure 5-14). This difference between the sexes is referred to as *sexual dimorphism* and refers to the many other contrasts in body size and proportions, as well as to stature.

Body Form

A relatively simple way of determining body proportion is to compare a person's standing height with his or her sitting height. The cormic index[2] or ratio between the two measurements indicates proportion of stature owing to the legs or the trunk. In populations with relatively short torsos and long legs, such as the Australian Aboriginals and many Africans, the cormic index is less than 50 (a ratio of 50 would indicate the legs and trunk plus head were approximately the same length). The tall stature of Nilotic groups in East Africa north of Lake Victoria (Tutsi, Dinka, Shilluk, Nuer) is due more to their very long legs than to trunk length, whereas most descriptions of the Pygmies note their elongated trunks and short legs and long arms. Many

---

[2]Proportions of body length are easily measured by dividing sitting height by standing height. This gives an index that describes the contribution of the head and trunk length to total body height, which ranges around 50 percent.

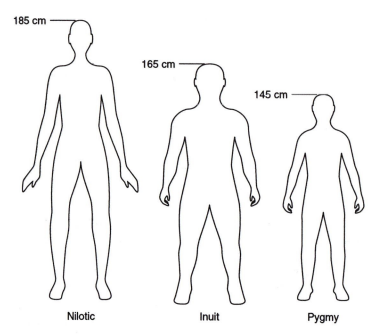

185 cm

165 cm

145 cm

Nilotic

Inuit

Pygmy

FIGURE 5-15   Drawings of Three Distinct Body Forms: Nilotic, Inuit, and Pygmy.
Three distinct body forms are represented in this drawing. The Nilotic form illustrates a
tall, slender shape found among many of the pastoralists of East Africa (Watusi, Masai,
and Turkana). The Inuit (Eskimo) shape is in stark contrast, with shorter stature and
heavier body. By comparison, the Pygmy is not only the shortest and lightest human
but has a relatively long torso with short legs.

Chinese populations, as well as groups of Native Americans, have cormic indices as
high as 54 percent, which indicates rather long trunks and short legs (Figure 5-15).

Likewise, the ratio of arm-to-leg length (intermembral index) indicates another
bodily proportion and shows some population differences. Though many populations
show a tendency toward a particular body form, characteristics of shape are not reliable as a marker of a geographic population/ethnic group. A case in point is provided by the results of an extensive anthropometric survey of Australian Aborigines.
Abbie (1975) reported extremes in adult stature of 146 cm to 190.6 cm for males and
137.6 cm to 174.3 cm for females; the cormic index ranged from 40.8 cm to 53.4 cm
for males and 41.3 cm to 54.3 cm for females. Despite the perception of a casual
observer, some persons had very long legs while others had very short ones. Another
example is the short legs and long torsos of Japanese populations, a characteristic
described for many Asian populations. This high average cormic index is changing as
Japan's children have accelerated in their growth rates since the 1950s, a trend
described in the next chapter.

Pygmies. These central African populations are exceptional for their small
size and are, in many ways, in stark contrast to neighboring groups. The general

relationships between body size, diet, climate, and growth seen in many of the world's peoples do not seem to apply to these dwarfed peoples. They are short in stature (under 144 to 145 cm), well below the mean for most other populations, but they have a long torso with short appendages. Most of their cranial and facial dimensions are near "normal," within 95 percent of the means for other African populations of the region. Pygmy faces are broad and marked by exceptional nasal breadth, well above the African average (Cavalli-Sforza, 1986). Such characteristics are more typical of some Pygmy groups than of others, as in the case of those in the western and central areas of the Pygmy range. According to Hiernaux, people called Pygmies are those below 150 cm, while others up to 160 cm are properly called pygmoid (Pygmy-like). He notes that applying this label based on body length is difficult and can be misleading, since many agricultural populations are shorter than some groups called pygmoids (Hiernaux, 1977:189).

Today, approximately 150,000 Pygmies live in small groups scattered throughout the tropical rain forests of central Africa, from near the Zaire–Uganda border in East Africa to the Central African Republic and Cameroon in the west. These groups are believed to be descendants of prehistoric hunters who have been progressively reduced and thinly scattered over the area, as early agriculturalists began to occupy portions of the tropical rain forest approximately 2,000 years ago. The Pygmies have been pushed farther and farther into the more remote, agriculturally less desirable regions until, today, the largest numbers of Pygmies in Africa are concentrated in central Africa around the Congo basin and along the tributaries of the Congo River. In these areas the Pygmies have established a close trading relationship with the agricultural groups, trading labor or the proceeds of the hunt for cultivated foods. Many have become highly acculturated, integrated into farming villages and seldom follow their former nomadic ways. The best known are the Efe, Batwa, and Bakanga who live in the regions east of Kisangani (Stanleyville) in Zaire. A few groups, such as the Babinza, however, live in the western region of central Africa; these western groups are far less numerous and more widely dispersed. It is interesting to note that the shortest people in the world, the Mbuti of the Ituri rain forests in Zaire, live within two-to three-hundred miles of the world's tallest and thinnest people, the Tutsi of Ruwanda, referred to as "elongated Africans" (Hiernaux, 1977).

Pygmoid populations called Negritos, sometimes referred to as Oceanic Pygmies, are dispersed throughout many of the more remote areas of South Asia, the Philippines, and New Guinea. They are found in the jungles of the Malayan Peninsula and on the island of Sumatra; these are the Semang and the Senoi (Sakai), who are only slightly taller than the average African Pygmy, with a mean stature of 152 cm (5 ft.). Off the west coast of the Malayan Peninsula are the Andaman Islands, inhabited by three distinct groups of Negritos: the Minicopies, the Onge, and the Garawa. They are all similar in features and a bit shorter than the Semang, 149 cm (4 ft., 10 in). The Onge are quite fat, and the women develop large fleshy buttocks, similar to the steatopygia of many San and Khoi females of Southern Africa (Figure 5-16). On the Philippine Islands of Mindanao, Palawan, and the northern part of Luzon are a few remnants of pygmoid populations. Among the best known are the Aetas, whose

FIGURE 5-16   Steatopygia of a !Kung female. Steatopygia is one of the characteristics for which the Khoisan people of south Africa are famous. It is an enormous increase in the size of the buttocks by an accumulation of fatty tissue. The shape is maintained and the weight is supported by an addition of fibrous tissue. The condition is most accentuated in females.

mean stature has been given as 147 cm (4 ft., 9 in). Other Negrito groups are found in the remote parts of the mountains of western New Guinea; the Tapiro tribe, with a mean stature of 144 cm (4 ft., 7 in), is an example.

The general characteristics of the Negritos, besides small stature, are very dark skin color, woolly hair, scant body and facial hairs, broad nose, and slight to moderately developed brow ridges. All groups do not share equally in these features, and there is a considerable variation between certain populations. In the case of skin color, some Negritos, as in the Philippine populations, have lighter brown or even yellowish skin, whereas the Andaman Islanders have very dark brown to black skin. Facial features also differ considerably, from smooth, rounded foreheads to heavy brows (usually in New Guinea groups) that match well the facial features of many Australian Aborigines.

A major problem that has long puzzled students of human variation is the question of the origins of these dwarfed peoples. What, if any, is the relationship between African Pygmies and pygmoid peoples of Southeast Asia, New Guinea and the Philippines? Casual visual comparisons suggest that they are descendants of the same ancestors because of their comparable size, skin color, and hair form. In the past, Pygmies and Negritos had been classified as a single race, and certain anthropologists even suggested elaborate migration routes to get the ancestors from an African homeland to the present-day distribution. Comparative studies of several genetic markers show, however, that the African Pygmy and Southeast Asian pymoids (Negritos) are unrelated, independent groups with only their short stature and certain other physical features in common. Negrito populations shared blood types and serum protein polymorphisms with their normal-sized neighbors (Boyd, 1963b; Omoto, 1987). In fact, dwarfed peoples, in general, may be no more than local inbred populations (Abbie, 1967). The question of the cause of the pygmoid condition is still unresolved, however.

Some clues may be provided by the extensive studies of genetic and physiological characteristics of the African Pygmies. During six expeditions over a ten-year period, teams of experts collected a broad spectrum of biological and anthropometric data from western Pygmy groups (Cavalli-Sforza, 1986). A great deal was learned about their physiology and certain genetic markers, but the most relevant to understanding their small size were the studies of growth hormone secretion. Though Pygmy size suggests a deficiency in human growth hormone, the tests revealed that they secreted an amount within the normal range. Further tests showed, however, that they were relatively unresponsive to the effects of growth hormone. This was due to low levels of two of the protein groups essential for growth, a growth hormone receptor (GHR) and somatomedin, an insulin-like growth factor (IGF). The IGF, a short polypeptide chain that is essential for cartilage and bone growth, has been thus far identified in two forms, an IGF_1 and an IGF_2. Type 2 is present at normal levels, but type 1 is abnormally low in the Pygmies tested and appears to be genetically determined (Merimee and Rimoin, 1986). Such studies of growth hormone responses have yet to be performed on Negritos and the specific gene or genes are still not identified, but it is likely that there are additional factors that modify tissue response to growth stimulation.

In addition to their short size, the Pygmies differ in body form from their neighbors, a form that reduces the efficiency of heat radiation, even though they are seemingly well adapted to hot, humid conditions. Because of the near 100 percent relative humidity of their environment, heat loss due to sweating is not useful in dissipation of body heat and is not a possible compensation for lack of radiation heat loss. Pygmies may compensate through a reduction of internal heat production through a reduction of basal metabolism or of muscle mass, which can be accomplished with weight reduction. A 25 percent decrease in total body weight lowers metabolic heat production by 18 percent, but if weight reduction is in muscle mass, metabolic heat is lowered as much as 23 percent. This is a possible explanation for Pygmy heat tolerance. Cavalli-Sforza (1986) describes the relative lower muscle mass of Pygmies as represented by their thin calves, upper legs, and arms. Comparisons of these dimensions with those of other Africans place Pygmies in the lower end of the range. This hypothesis of muscle mass and heat tolerance has yet to be fully tested, but muscle/metabolic activity is probably an explanation for survival under conditions that challenge the major mechanisms for maintaining a thermal balance as an individual goes about a routine of work.

Body Weight

Body weight also varies over a wide range as does size and shape. Adult weights vary from about 32 kilograms (kg) (70 lbs.) to more than 90 kg (200 lbs.), but numerous individuals exceed these values. Also, weight does not correlate closely with stature. Some tall people are very thin for their height, as in the example of the Nilotic form in Figure 5-15. By contrast, there are numerous examples of heavier, but shorter people populating the colder regions of the world. There seems to be little ethnic variation in a tendency of fat storage. We all gain weight when we consume more food calories than our body uses for its metabolic energy, though some of us have higher or lower metabolic rates depending on age, gender, and physical activity.[3] Intriguing exceptions have been reported where certain populations of Native Americans, Pacific Islanders, and Australian Aborigines become extremely obese when they change to the refined high-carbohydrate, high-fat foods typical of American diets today. These groups apparently have a genetic propensity to obesity, which may relate to the conditions of their aboriginal past as considered the next chapter.

Though dietary quantity and quality (carbohydrate, fat, protein combination) affect bodily proportions and weight, there is a close correlation with mean annual temperature. Generally speaking, in colder climates people are much heavier for their height than people in warmer regions, and the ratio between height and weight of the individual may be even more significant than limb ratios or trunk–limb proportions. Table 5-2 lists some representative populations selected for variation in size and for the extreme temperature of their habitats. The body mass index (BMI) of several

TABLE 5-2   Body Mass Index and Mean Annual Temperature

POPULATION	WEIGHT (KG)	HEIGHT (M)	HT^2	BMI	TEMP
Turkana	55.0	1.77	3.133	17.555	70–80
San	50.8	1.60	2.560	19.844	70–80
CAR Pygmies	41.5	1.44	2.074	20.010	80
Australia	60.0	1.73	2.993	20.047	70–80
CAR Farmer	54.6	1.61	2.592	21.065	80
Japan	61.0	1.70	2.890	21.107	50–60
Yanomama	50.0	1.53	2.341	21.358	70–80
Quechua	58.5	1.63	2.657	22.017	40–50
U.S. (EA)	69.1	1.76	3.098	22.305	—
Saami	66.1	1.71	2.924	22.606	30–40
Evenki	59.8	1.61	2.592	23.071	20–30
U.S. (AA)	72.2	1.76	3.098	23.305	—
Xavante	69.8	1.70	2.890	24.152	70–80
Inuit	66.7	1.64	2.690	24.796	10–20
Samoa	81.2	1.72	2.958	27.451	70–80

BMI: body mass index (Wt/Ht^2).
CAR: Central African Republic; EA: Euro-American; AA: African American.
Source: Data selected from Eveleth and Tanner, 1976 and 1990.

[3]The recommended intake of food calories is about 2,000 calories per day and females require 20 percent less. This amount may be adjusted up or down depending on age, health, and physical exertion. If the food consumed exceeds caloric needs, the body stores the surplus as fat. There have been extensive arguments among diet experts, but the fact still remains unchanged: Energy in exceeding energy expended equals weight gain.

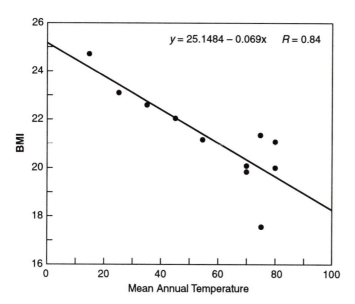

$y = 25.1484 - 0.069x$ $R = 0.84$

FIGURE 5-17   **Body Mass Index versus Mean Annual Temperature.**

populations is plotted against the mean annual temperatures of their environments (Figure 5-17). Among those in the warmer regions, particularly the wet tropics, there is a tendency towards a lightweight, slender body form, whereas by contrast, native inhabitants in the temperate or arctic regions are heavier for their stature. These examples of body form and size variability under differing environments demonstrate the great plasticity of human development reflecting varying conditions of climate, diet, and disease encountered at various growth stages.

BODY SIZE AND FORM: PERSPECTIVES OF HEREDITY

Our genes play a role in the development of size and form and the proportions of the craniofacial region which explains, to some degree, our resemblance to parents, siblings, and other relatives. But which genes are involved and how they work through their products is still hard to define. Genetic influence is firmly established, however, by the different effects of the X- and Y-chromosomes resulting in sexual dimorphism. In addition, there are several chromosome abnormalities that effect size and form, for example, Turner's syndrome (XO), Down's syndrome, and the XYY male, or single-gene mutations like achondrodystrophy, as described in Chapter 2. There is also a long list of hormonal deficiencies and variants of cellular receptors that affect growth as outlined in the next chapter. Few direct links have been made to the genes that are involved. There have been reports of numerous cases of growth failure because of low levels of growth hormone, thyroxine, and insulin to mention a few. Some of these cases have been traced through family linages, but none have been extended to a population sample except for the abnormally low levels of the insulin-like growth factor reported in African Pygmies.

Records of correlations between close relatives, especially twins, may compensate for the lack of data on the gene products affecting complex traits. A perfect correlation ($r = 1.0$) would indicate that the trait was under close genetic control without establishing which genes were involved. None of the traits of size and form reach this high level even in the case of monozygotic (MZ) twins (single ovum) who have identical genomes. Their correlations are close to one if they were raised together, but lower if raised apart. Dizygotic (DZ) twins (separate ova) and siblings have nearly the same correlations. What these correlations tell us is that close relatives share a number of genes in common that elicit products (hormones, cell receptors, and so on) influencing growth. But the wide range indicates a significant variance due to environmental factors.

Our adult size is close to that of our parents' size. Simply, we will probably be tall if we have tall parents or short if they are short if our growth environments are similar. However, there is a wide range of factors that influence growth outcome. As described above, children of immigrants tend to be larger than their parents when migration has improved their socioeconomic status—higher income, more food, better housing, and less disease. The key to understanding these factors and their diverse influences is a close examination of child growth under various conditions as described in the next chapter.

chapter
6

Traits of Complex Inheritance and Their Adaptations: II

Man can long resist conditions which appear extremely unfavorable for his existence.
(Charles Darwin, 1871: 542)

With these few strokes of his pen, Darwin summed up his observations of human adaptability made over the course of his five year around-the-world voyage. The thousands of scientists and explorers who followed over the generations, likewise expressed a wonder over our species' ability to cope with, and even thrive and multiply, in some of the most stressful of environments. Whether through behavioral adaptation or by acclimatization through physiological adjustment, humans have been able to endure nearly every climate encountered on this planet. We can cope with high or low temperatures, survive erratic weather patterns, and endure the rigors of stress at high altitudes. We can obtain essential nutrients from a variety of plant, animal, and marine life and cope with scarcity when a preferred food is in short supply.

Such ability to adapt to various stresses does not come without costs, however. Costs can be measured in metabolic energy expended to maintain body temperature in cold environments, and resultant changes in bodily proportions, or a conservation of energy when confronted with food shortages and rapid response of certain hormones to food excess. Differing patterns of child growth can provide a record of these episodes of adaption.

CHARACTERISTICS OF GROWTH AND DEVELOPMENT

The shape and size an adult acquires are results of a complex of processes that occur during infancy and childhood. Over a span of our first dozen or so years of life we pass through several stages that affect the size and function of our bodies. The growth and development of the body's organs and structures are under control of a complex of genes whose products interact with the environment to produce the various dimensions and proportions discussed above. Nutrition, climate, and disease all act to regulate how we grow and at what rates. We resemble our parents, of course, but with improvements in environments seen in succeeding generations over the twentieth century, we have often exceeded our parents in growth rates and attainment of adult height. Genetic influences are hard to define, and ethnic variations in body form and size tend to diminish as more diverse groups come to occupy similar growth environments. Responses are much the same in most groups for which there is comparative date. In effect, we are the products of our growth experiences. From the !Kung of southern Africa to Australians and Arctic Inuits, all children respond to favorable conditions in the same ways in their growth. Puberty is reached earlier than in a stressful environment, final adult height is greater, and body shapes become more similar. Children throughout the developed world are achieving their genetic growth potential. There are still short and tall people, fat and thin, and some proportionate differences, but not as broadly expressed as in previous generations. By contrast, the socially disadvantaged groups in the developing countries lag behind. Though conditions favoring growth are improving and are better understood, genetic influences have not been identified. We must rely on comparative studies of people of diverse origins.

What has been clearly established is that there are several markers or way stations that may be used to measure the relative quality of human growth. All humans pass through these well-defined periods during which growth may accelerate or slow down in response to environmental stressors, mainly nutritional, reflecting a major means of human adaptation. The age or timing of certain growth periods—the onset of puberty, for example—varies from group to group. The passage through these stages is relatively similar, however; all humans spend approximately one-third of their lives preparing for the remaining two-thirds. These growth periods are listed in Table 6-1. Note that male and female timing is nearly the same except for an earlier onset of puberty and adolescence in the female.

The normal birth weights of full-term infants range around 3,200 grams (gm); poorly nourished mothers give birth to infants averaging about 10 to 15 percent lower. To achieve this size during the 270 days of gestation, the original weight of the fertilized ovum must be increased several billion times. From conception to birth the single cell is transformed into a complex organism consisting of billions of cells divided into numerous specialized tissues. Growth and development must occur at varying rates so that each unit will have its correct functional proportion by birth. The embryo grows at a linear rate of 1.5 mm/day during the second month, which is an enormously rapid growth rate; for example, if this rate were continued after birth, a 914 cm (30-foot)-tall adult would be produced. From about the eighth week, growth slows until the sixth and seventh months,

TABLE 6-1   Classification of Growth Periods

PERIOD	MALE	FEMALE
I. *Infancy (neonate)*	Birth–1 year	Birth–1 year
	(First 4 weeks)	(First 4 weeks)
II. *Childhood*	*1–16 years*	*1–16 years*
early	1–6 years	1–6 years
mid	6–9 or 10 years	6–9 or 10 years
late	9 or 10–16 years	9 or 10–16 years
III. *Puberty (in late childhood)*	13–14 years	12–13 years
IV. *Adolescence*	14–18 or 20 years	13–18 or 20 years
V. *Adult*	20 years +	20 years +

Source: After W.M. Krogman, *Child Growth*. Ann Arbor: University of Michigan Press, 1972, Copyright © The University of Michigan Press, Reprinted by permission of the publisher.

when fetal growth begins to accelerate. After this peak during the fetal stage, infant and child growth slows, but it begins to accelerate again in late childhood to another peak in adolescence (the growth spurt) when 6 to 8 cm of height may be gained in a single year.

Different body regions grow at varying rates at each stage, as in the example of the head, which accounts for a major proportion of growth during the fetal and infancy stages. This emphasis on cerebral development, one of the hallmarks of our species, is illustrated by the body-weight and brain-weight changes from the second month of gestation through the child's seventh year (Table 6-2). The brain weight accounts for 93 percent of the total weight, until the last four months of fetal development, when other parts of the body begin to enlarge rapidly; then the brain is only approximately 10–12 percent of total weight at birth. This appears to be the maximum size that can be maintained during fetal growth because of the brain's high energy requirements;

TABLE 6-2   Age Changes in Brain Size

AGE	BODY WEIGHT*	BRAIN WEIGHT*	% OF BODY SIZE	VOLUME OF BRAIN	CRANIAL CAPACITY	PERCENTAGE
Newborn	3,100	380.0	12.3	330	350	94.3
3 months	—	—	—	500	600	83.3
6 months	—	—	—	575	775	74.2
9 months	—	—	—	675	925	73.0
1 year	9,000	944.7	10.5	750	1,000	75.0
2 years	11,000	1,025.0	9.4	900	1,100	81.8
3 years	12,500	1,108.1	8.9	960	1,225	78.4
4 years	14,000	1,330.1	10	1,000	1,300	76.9
6 years	17,800	1,359.1	7.6	1,060	1,350	78.5
9 years	25,200	1,408.3	5.6	1,100	1,400	78.6
12 years	37,100	1,428.0	3.8	1,150	1,450	79.3
18 years	59,500	1,444.5	2.4	1,200	1,500	80.8

*Weights in grams. Volumes in cubic centimeters.

Source: Based on Tobias, 1971; and Young, 1971.

it consumes about 20 percent of total body energy. From birth until the seventh year the brain grows much more rapidly than other tissues (except for the lymphoid tissues). By age 7 a person has about 95 percent of his or her adult brain weight and the remainder is acquired slowly over the next decade.

By comparison, after the first year of life, other tissues become slower in their growth until adolescence, when body size increases rapidly and the reproductive organs mature. The weights of several organs at various growth stages show a linear increase from birth to adulthood (Table 6-3). By the time puberty (adolescence) is reached, the brain is very close to its adult weight. The thymus gland, a lymphoid organ in the lower neck that functions as part of the immunological system, decreases in size by contrast. Size and proportions of head, trunk, and legs also change.

Growth Rates

The several growth processes that occur at varying rates are influenced by genetic and environmental factors. The interplay of these factors may retard or accelerate growth. At each point in time we are expected to be at a particular stage of development, but many of us deviate from this established norm. We may be taller or shorter than our classmates, reach puberty earlier or later, or our skeletal system may develop at other than expected rates. In other words, our developmental age will often not coincide with our chronological age. One good measure of our progress is the degree of skeletal development or "skeletal age" as compared to chronological age.

Skeletal maturation.   Most bone development begins during the embryonic period when the bones' characteristic shapes are formed in cartilage; the exceptions are cranial bones and the clavicle, which are developed from membranous tissues. During the latter part of the embryo state, mineralization of the cartilage starts from ossification centers and progressively increases until major portions of the bones have calcified. Bones continue to grow by this process of cartilage formation and then mineralize with calcium phosphate throughout childhood and adolescence. Throughout childhood the

TABLE 6-3   Average Weights (in Grams) of Organs at Different Ages

	NEWBORN	% OF ADULT WEIGHT	1 YEAR	6 YEARS	PUBERTY	ADULT
Brain	350	26	910	1,200	1,300	1,350
Heart	24	8	45	95	150	300
Thymus	12	80	20	24	30	0–15
Kidneys (both)	25	8	70	120	170	300
Liver	150	9	300	550	1,500	1,600
Lungs (both)	60	5	130	260	410	1,200
Pancreas	3	3	9	—	40	90
Spleen	10	6	30	55	95	155
Stomach	8	5	30	—	80	135

Source: Reproduced with permission from Lowrey, G.H., *Growth and Development of Children*, 7th ed. Copyright © 1978 by Year Book Medical Publishers, Inc., Chicago.

secondary centers of ossification become established and contribute to growth. The ends of the bones, or *epiphyses*, remain separated from the *diaphysis* by a cartilage plate late in adolescence when they fuse. It is through this process of cartilage formation, followed by mineralization, that growth occurs. The active bone formation at the epiphyses contributes to an increase in length. Each bone of the skeleton has a characteristic growth rate, and skeletal age or maturation is based on the degree of ossification of these centers and on their ultimate fusion with the main shaft (Figure 6-1). For example, the epiphysis that will form the head of the femur (the long bone of the upper leg) appears between the second and tenth month of infancy. Its ultimate fusion with the main shaft occurs between age 13 and 20.

In young children many bones of the skeleton remain unfused, and some bones (in the wrists, for example) have not yet begun to form. Radiographs of the hands of a child from the fourth to the seventh year show the development of the wrist bones (carpals), which begin to develop at different times during early childhood. Their relative sizes and degree of calcification show quite clearly (Figure 6-2). The fingers

FIGURE 6-1   Skeletal Development. First appearance of the shafts (diaphyses) and joint ends (epiphyses) of the appendicular skeleton (f.w.: fetal weeks; f.m.: fetal months; m.: months; y.: years). (From Robertson, G.G., "Developmental Anatomy," in *Morris's Human Anatomy*, 12th ed., ed. B.J. Anson. New York: McGraw-Hill Book Company, 1966. Reproduced by permission.)

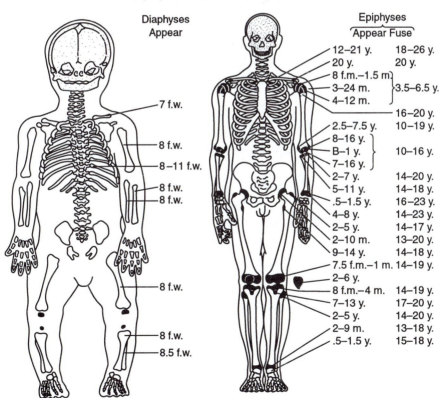

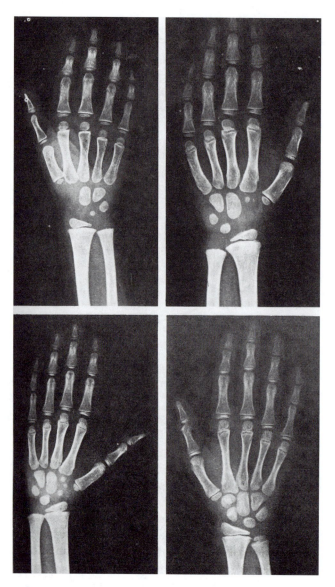

FIGURE 6-2   Radiographs of Hands of Children. The development of the carpal bones (wrist bones) and the appearance of the epiphyses of the metacarpals and phalanges at ages four (top left), five (to right), six (bottom left), and seven (bottom right). (Reproduced with permission from Lowrey, G.H., *Growth and Development of Children*, 7th ed. Copyright © 1978 by Year Book medical Publishers, Inc., Chicago.)

(phalanges) and the adjacent metacarpals (wrist bones), which grow in a pattern similar to the long bones of the arms and legs, show up clearly in this radiograph. The details of the diaphyses and associated epiphyses are shown at various stages. Thousands of individuals of many populations have had their hands radiographed, and standards of skeletal age have been established relative to chronological age.[1] In this way, individuals with retarded growth may be identified early and, if owing to dietary or hormonal deficiencies, corrective measures can be taken.

There are many examples of deviation in skeletal development and epiphyseal fusion rates that are due more to general health and nutritional status than to ethnic differences. The timing of skeletal growth is much the same in all children given equivalent environmental quality, though Asian children are slightly more advance (Ulijaszek, 1998). Where major contrasts exist due to socioeconomic standards, disparities between groups appear. Developmental age, as measured by skeletal maturity, may lag from several months to as much as a year behind chronological age. This variation cuts across all ethnic boundaries and is class related as discussed below. In addition, there is a clear sexual dimorphism; females are between one to two years earlier in their skeletal development.

Skull.   At birth, the bones of the cranium are separated by unossified membranes that allow great flexibility and permit the passage of the infant's head (averaging 35 cm in circumference) through the birth canal. Starting from birth, there is considerable activity at the ossification centers, and the cranial bones increase in size until they meet and eventually fuse later in adult life. Certain cranial bones, however, fuse soon after birth. For example, the halves of the mandible fuse at the mandibular symphysis (the chin region) during the first year, and also the left and right halves of the frontal bone of the skull fuse along a suture through the middle of the forehead. Other cranial bones remain separated for many years and are joined at an irregular unmineralized junction (the sutures). These sutures gradually calcify with age, and the adjoining bones eventually become fused together. The older the individual, the less distinct will be the cranial sutures. This process of cranial bone mineralization covers a broad time range because each suture fuses at a different rate (Figure 6-3).

Dental maturation.   At birth, the deciduous teeth are nearly complete, and some are ready to erupt within the first few months. Below their roots, buried deep within the jaws, are the developing permanent teeth, which gradually replace the deciduous teeth as the individual grows (Figure 6-4). This process of dental development is long and complicated; starting at about the sixth week in the embryo and continuing until the sixteenth year, there are some teeth in various stages of development while other teeth are fully formed.

The first teeth (deciduous incisors) erupt during the sixth to ninth month, while the crowns of the permanent first molars, incisors, and canines are just beginning to

---

[1]Radiographic atlases of children have been in use for decades as standards against which development may be measured. The two best known are Greulich-Pyle, produced by a study of Cleveland schoolchildren, and the Tanner-Whitehouse, complied from x-rays of British children (see Eveleth and Tanner, 1990).

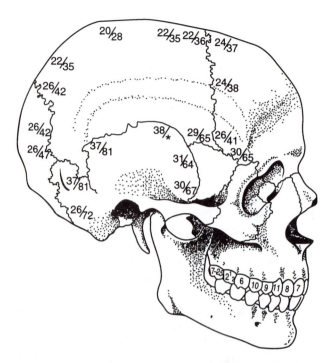

FIGURE 6-3   Suture Closure of the Skull. The superior figures indicate the age at which the portion of the suture begins to obliterate; the inferior figures, the age at which obliteration is completed. The * indicates that the suture never completely closes. The figures on the upper teeth give the usual ages in years of the eruption of each permanent tooth. Owing to the great variability involved, these figures must be used with caution. (From Montagu, M.F. Ashley, *An Introduction to Physical Anthropology*, 3rd ed., 1960. Courtesy of Charles C Thomas, Publisher, Springfield, IL.)

form. This process of development and eruption continues until the twenty-first year (an average among Euro-Americans), when the third molar (wisdom tooth) erupts, if the person is fortunate. Frequently, the third molar is malformed, malpositioned, or is impacted within the bone and must be removed surgically. The timing of dental development is listed in Table 6-4. Note that the crowns are completed and eruption occurs before the roots are fully formed.

Tooth-calcification sequences are fairly regular and provide a good indicator of age analogous to the skeletal ossification centers. Eruption times, however, can be quite variable. Diet and disease are strong influences; earlier eruption appears to be the rule among higher socioeconomic groups. Also tooth eruption is, on the average, a few months earlier in females. No definite genetic pattern has been established, though there have been several reports of ethnic differences. Tooth eruption among Europeans and Euro-Americans is later than among Native Americans, Asians, and African Americans. Australian Aborigines, along with their large dental arches, appear

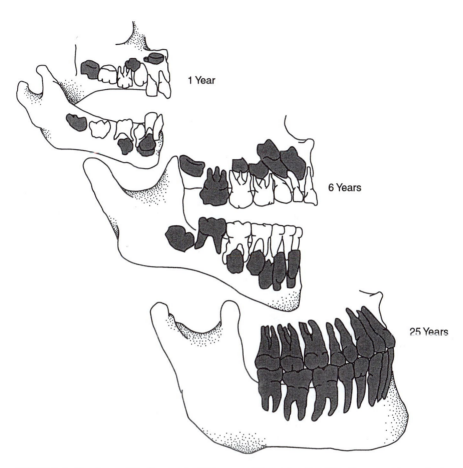

FIGURE 6-4   Eruption and Replacement of Primary and Secondary Dentition. Permanent (secondary) teeth are shaded. (From Harrison, R., and W. Montagna, *Man*, 2nd ed., 1973. Reprinted by permission of Prentice-Hall, Inc., Upper Saddle River, NJ.)

to have the most advanced dental development, especially the third molars, which have been known to erupt as early as 13 years compared to the norm of 18 to 20 years (Brown, 1978).

Growth Spurt.   There are wide individual variations in the time of puberty and the onset of the adolescent growth spurt. The timing of this rapid increase in growth rate depends on the same factors that influence overall growth. In males, the growth spurt may occur anywhere between 12 and 16 years, approximately two years later than in females (whose growth spurt is generally between 10 and 14 years). After a year, the rate decreases, but growth continues slowly into the teens or early twenties. If measurements are taken throughout a person's growth years

TABLE 6-4   Chronology of Human Tooth Development

TOOTH	ONSET OF CALCIFICATION	CROWN (COMPLETED)	ERUPTION	ROOT (COMPLETED)
Deciduous				
Central incisor	4–4.5 months (in utero)	1.5–2.5 months	6–8 months	1.5 years
Lateral incisor	4.5	2.5–3	8–10	1.5–2
Cuspid	5	9	10–20	3.5
First molar	5	5.5–6	12–16	2.5
Second molar	6	10–11	20–24	3
Permanent				
First molars	Birth	2.5–3 years	6 years	9–10 years
Central incisors	3–4 months	4–5	7	9–10
Lateral incisors	10–12	4–5	8	10–11
Canines (cuspid)	4–5	6–7	11	12–15
First premolars (bicuspid)	1.5–2 years	5–6	10	12–13
Second premolars (bicuspid)	2–2.5	6–7	11	12–14
Second molars	2.5–3	7–8	12	14–16
Third molars	7–10	12–16	[a]	18–23

[a]The eruption time of the third molars highly variable, with a range of 16–22 years.
Source: Modified from Logan and Kronfeld, 1933; and Schour and Massler, 1944.

(longitudinal study), then a rapid gain can easily be seen, as shown in Figure 6-5, which plots average height increment gains for early- and late-maturing groups. This acceleration in linear growth can be quite remarkable; some individuals may gain 10 cm or more in a single year. Similar changes occur in weight, fat distribution, and bodily proportions. These changes, however, are more gradual and continue over longer periods.

Sexual Maturation

Toward the end of childhood (8 to 9 years in females and 10 to 11 in males), a series of morphological and metabolic transformations begin that continue over a period of several years, transforming a child into a young adult. The body gradually begins to increase its growth rate with the approach of puberty. Changes occur in hair patterns and bodily proportions, and the sex organs begin to mature and increase in size. Approximately two years after entering this stage, the individual begins the adolescent growth spurt. The voice deepens (in males), breast development begins to be apparent (in females), and other secondary sexual characteristics appear—changes in fat distribution and development of hips (in females), for example, and increase in shoulder girth in males. Pubic and axillary hair begins to appear in both sexes, and males start to show signs of facial hair. The onset of sexual maturity in the male is not clearly defined; the increases

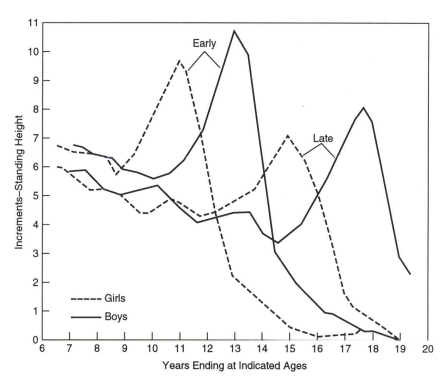

FIGURE 6-5　**Amount of Increase in Height per Year of Early-Maturing and Late-Maturing Girls and Boys.** Although late-maturing girls show the peak rate of growth almost two years later than early-maturing boys, they still reach this stage nearly two and a half years before late-maturing boys reach the same peak velocity of growth. The curves of growth for height and weight are related to the maturation of the skeleton. This, in turn, is related to maturation in general (including the hormonal changes associated with sexual maturation). (From Tanner, J.M., *Growth at Adolescence*, 1962. Copyright © 1962. by Blackwell Scientific Publications, Ltd. Reprinted by permission of the publisher.)

in the sizes of the sex organs and their hormonal secretions are gradual and continue over a long period.

Menarche.　In the female, the first menses, which occurs within a year of the growth spurt, is an excellent marker dividing prepuberty and postpuberty phases. There has been a trend over the twentieth century toward a decrease in age at menarche, especially among children in the developed countries. For example, where records have been kept for one-and-a-half centuries in western Europe, an average age of 17 years was registered in 1840 compared to 12 and 14 in 1998 (Table 6-5). Today, 95 percent reach menarche between 11 and 15 years of age in the United States with expectation that the trend toward earlier menarche has ceased.

Neither racial/ethnic group nor climate appear to be a factor in the timing of female maturity, though both have been examined extensively during the past few decades (Eveleth and Tanner, 1990, 1976). More likely menarche is related to those

TABLE 6-5   Age at Menarche

POPULATIONS	AVERAGE AGE (YEARS)
European	
Various populations	12.5–13.5
Nineteenth century	15–17
New Zealand	
Maori	12.7
European	13.0
United States	
Afro-Americans	12.5
Euro-Americans	11–15
Chinese	
Hong Kong	12.5–13.3
Africa	
Nigeria	14.1
Uganda	13.4
Watusi	16.5
Hutu	17.0
New Guinea	
Bundi	18.0

Source: Eveleth and Tanner, 1976 and 1990; Frisch, 1988.

same environmental factors that contribute to accelerated growth and changes in body composition. During and immediately after the adolescent growth spurt, female body composition changes radically. The rapid weight gain during this time is greatest for body fat—a 120 percent increase as compared with the lean body component (muscle and bone) increase of 49 percent. This significantly shifts the lean body mass-to-fat ratio from 5:1 in the prepuberty years to a 3:1 ratio at menarche, indicating a significant rise of stored energy (male lean body ratios are around 5:1, by contrast). Rose Frisch (1988) has argued convincingly that it is this change in composition that provides the energy requirements of the female reproductive physiology. A minimal amount of 17 percent body fat is needed to initiate menses; in a girl of 165 cm (65 in) tall, a total body weight of 49 kg (97 lb.) is needed, or 38 kg (83.8 lb.) for a person 155 cm (61 in). The earlier attainment of these sizes and of the changes in body composition, as in the case of children in well-off socioeconomic groups with optimum nutrition, contributes to earlier menarche. By contrast, Frisch notes that many adolescent female athletes and ballet dancers experience delays in menarche as their store of body fat falls below the critical level.

Malnourished children are unable to meet the energy demands of optimum growth so their weight gain is significantly lower than in well-nourished populations. Girls grow more slowly, enter their growth spurts later, and slowly accumulate a store of body fat—all factors contributing to a later menarche. Contrasts by socioeconomic class have been reported in all countries. In Europe, urban girls enjoying better economic conditions reached menarche one year sooner than their rural cohorts; Indians of higher social class in the Punjab reached menarche one-and-one-half years earlier than girls from poorer families. The same contrasts are seen between economically well-off urban Nigerians and rural poor; the well-off had a menarchial age closer to the European average. The latest ages that have been reported for any children were found in the Bundi tribe in the highlands of New Guinea. They had the slowest growth recorded in the world today, and girls reach menarche at about 18 years. By contrast, the tribes living on the coastal plains grow faster and reach menarche at 15 despite the location of their homeland in a malarial area. Additional evidence of nutritional influence is provided by European populations who lived through the hardships of two world wars. Many populations subsisted for long periods at or near starvation levels. The average age at menarche during these times increased by two years to age 16, a point not too far from late eighteenth-century levels of their grandmothers and great grandmothers.

The correlation of body weight and menarche is one factor to consider in female growth. Another is the close correlation with pelvis size. The timing of first menses with attainment of adult pelvic dimensions has been used as an example to counter Frisch's adolescent body fat hypothesis (Ellison, 1998:229). Simply, skeletal maturity is a more important measure of female reproductive maturity than body fat/muscle mass ratio. However, consider that growth rates of different systems, body composition and skeletal growth in particular, are interrelated and depend on nutritional inputs.

Growth as Adaptation

Children living in poor environments, suffering from childhood diseases, and deprived of adequate nutrition show signs of growth failure. A major marker of these stressors, often described, is a later and a less-pronounced growth spurt (Figure 6-6a). Poor adolescent boys in London, through the late eighteenth to early nineteenth century, were described as so short that today only two of the eighty-one ethnic groups for which height data are available are smaller. These boys, working in factories or wandering the streets, averaged 6 to 11 cm shorter than boys of the middle class. This average is well below the British standard of 1965 marked by the reference lines from the third to ninety-seventh percentile. Factory girls likewise fell below standards, but not by as much as did the males of the 14 to 18 age groups (Figure 6-6b).

This sorry state of child health was, perhaps, one of the lowest points in modern British social history. Alarms were raised about deterioration of the lower classes, and there were fears that there would not be lads strong enough to carry rifles for the army or man the ships of war. Among the responses were the founding of various charitable organizations and the passage of laws relieving some of the worst aspects of child labor. The Marine Society was founded to provide shelter and training for homeless vagabond boys, and the Factories Regulation Act was passed to try to lessen the harshness of the conditions of child labor; among other things, it required a rest and meal period of one-and-one-half hours each day and prohibited hiring of children under the age of 9.

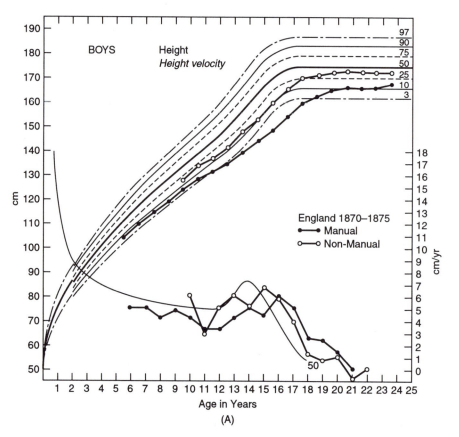

FIGURE 6-6a Heights of boys of the manual worker class and of the nonmanual, mostly professional, class, in about 1870 in England. Values from Roberts (1874-1876). Means are used for the manual group up to and including 15.0; modes thereafter. Means are used for the nonmanual group throughout.

Not much of a difference, considering the typical twelve-hour workday, but it was an improvement and a recognition of the need for social change. Out of the Marine Society effort came further improvements, refelcted in the heights of male adolescents shown in the graphs in Figure 6-7. Between 1770 and 1810 no changes are seen, but thereafter, further advances in child welfare are reflected in the larger sizes recorded for 14 to 16 years of age (Tanner, 1981). The accumulation of these and other data from many studies of the health and welfare of children document some striking contrasts between succeeding generations and point to some significant trends. During the twentieth century, children reached maturity earlier and were larger at all ages than previous generations.

Longitudinal Growth Trends.   Growth data from several European countries and North America show an average gain of 1 cm in adult height per decade during the twentieth century. To a large extent, this is part of a trend toward earlier maturation; individuals obtain their adult height at an earlier age. Males in the United States today

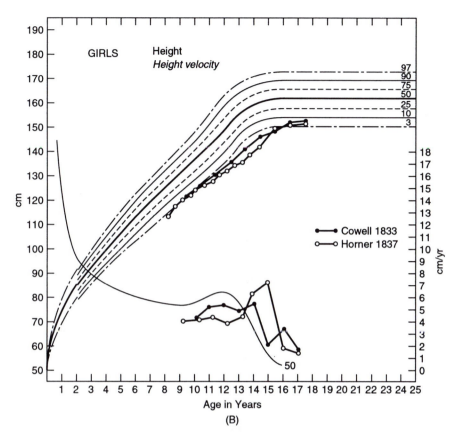

FIGURE 6-6b Mean heights of girls working in factories in the Manchester–Leeds area in England in 1833 and 1837. Means for 1833 have been adjusted by subtraction of 0.5 cm for footwear. (Source: From J.M. Tanner, 1981. *A History of the Study of Human Growth.* Reprinted with the permission of Cambridge University Press.)

reach their adult height at around 18 years, whereas their great-grandfathers did not attain their full adult height until age 26. Improved living standards in many societies have enabled children to grow to their maximum genetic potential; this increase in size during the past several generations is called a *secular* trend (Figure 6-8).[2] The graphs compare average heights of four groups from age 4 to 23 and show a 15-cm increase in adult height since 1833. The group of boys measured in 1833 were factory hands whose growth was retarded in late childhood and adolescence. Their height at age 14 was a full 20 cm less than the standard of 1965, but slow growth over a prolonged

---

[2]Secular trend in this context refers to long-term, or generational, changes in body size that have been observed in many populations over this century. The majority of studies have been made on populations of developed countries where final adult height has increased from 1 to 1.5 cm per decade, especially noted in the United States, western Europe, and Japan. In addition, many indigenous peoples have also undergone an increase in stature following a change in diet and living conditions as noted.

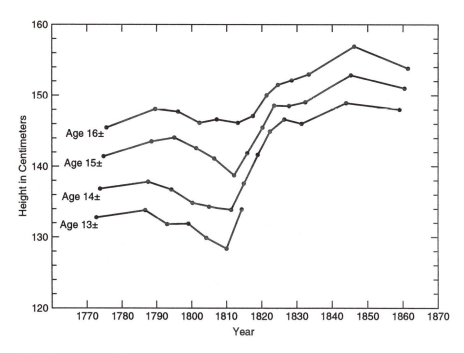

FIGURE 6-7 Heights of Marine Society recruits aged 13±, 14±, 15±, and 16± from 1769 to 1860. Each point represents a 5–15 year cohort. (Source: From J.M. Tanner, 1981. *A History of the Study of Human Growth*. Cambridge, MA: Cambridge University Press.)

period made up for some of this deficit. This catch-up period suggests that depressing environmental effects are more influential on growth rate than on final size.

Environmental Influences and Ethnic Differences

Boys and girls in the developed countries are heavier and taller than their parents. This secular increase in size has caused the height and weight tables of a generation ago to be far outdated. Reasons for this secular trend are often related to a general improvement in nutrition and health care with a reduction of infectious diseases (especially the childhood diseases) and to more adequate housing. To this list of factors should be added the reduction or elimination of child labor. Most of these changes have occurred over the twentieth century. Differences still remain among socioeconomic groups in many countries, but the extremes are less than during the nineteenth century, and these improvements are marked by growth pattern, a record that reflects the social conditions of the times (Tanner, 1986). Furthermore, secular changes cut across all of the so-called racial/ethnic boundaries.

This phenomenon of increased growth and earlier maturity occurs in all groups whose socioeconomic circumstances allow children to be raised at optimum levels of nutrition and health. African Americans, a much studied group, show increases of body size over the past few generations despite their higher morbidity and mortality rates.

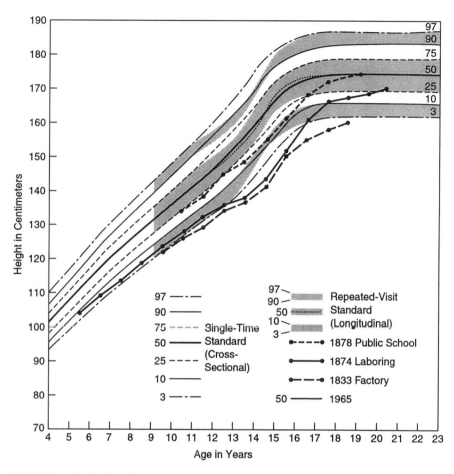

FIGURE 6-8   Secular Trend in Height. Secular trend in height is shown by surveys of the height of English boys in the years 1833, 1874, and 1965. Data are reproduced on a standard growth chart. "Single-time standard (cross sectional)" refers to the average result from cross-sectional surveys. "Repeated-visit standard (longitudinal)" refers to the average result from longitudinal surveys. The numbers 97, 90, 75, and so on indicate percent of the male population shorter than a given height. (Source: From Tanner, J.M., "Growing Up," September 1973. Copyright © 1973 by Scientific American, Inc. All rights reserved.)

They now attain, by age 18, an adult height that places them among the tallest in the world (Tables 6-6a and 6-6b). Broader ethnic group comparisons show that Euro-Americans, Europeans, and Africans who have been raised under similar economically well-off circumstances show few differences, except for the longer legs of Africans, noted in Chapter 5. By contrast, the Turkana, an east African pastoral group, grow more slowly and lag behind the pace set by African Americans. They continue to grow well past adolescence and reach the African American adult level by age 22.

The growth of Africans and Europeans is very similar, but east Asians are shorter at all ages and complete their growth earlier. This is a consideration of Asian averages

TABLE 6-6a Heights (cm) and Weights (kg) of Select Populations (Boys)

GROUPS	3 YEARS		6 YEARS		9 YEARS		12 YEARS		15 YEARS		18 YEARS	
	Ht.	Wt.	Ht.	Wt.	Ht.	Wt.	Ht.	Wt.	Ht.	Wt.	Ht.	Wt.
USA												
NCHS-1a[1]	95.0	14.5	115.4	21.1	133.2	30.2	148.4	41.6	169.2	58.8	176.8	69.1
NCHS-1b[1]	94.6	14.4	116.2	20.5	134.4	29.9	147.6	40.0	171.2	64.2	176.7	72.2
Europe												
Netherlands[1]	98.2	—	118.8	—	136.6	—	152.1	—	173.2	—	180.9	—
Factory Boys[12]	—	—	—	—	122.3	—	135.6	—	151.5	—	160.8	—
Sandhurst[12]	—	—	—	—	—	—	153.0 (13 yrs)	—	160.9	—	174.2	—
England[1]	94.9	14.7	115.1	20.6	131.7	28.4	145.4	—				
Africa												
Hutu[3]	—	—	111.4	18.2	122.9	22.3	137.0	20.2	154.7	41.5	167.1	57.5
Turkana[1]	89.2	11.3	106.2	15.1	122.9	20.2	139.4	26.9	148.1	34.8	162.1	47.0
Asia												
Japan[1]	92.0	14.0	113.0	20.0	130.0	28.0	147.0	40.0	166.0	56.0	170.0	61.1
China (PRC)[1]	95.1	14.0	114.7	19.2	130.6	25.3	144.2	33.0	162.0	46.9	167.7	53.2
Evenki[4]	92.8	14.2	110.5	19.0	123.3	23.6	133.0	27.9	157.1	47.3	160.6	57.3
Amerind												
Inuit (1938)	87.6	15.3	108.7	22.2	123.3	27.7	132.3	34.5	145.3	43.7	158.5	63.6
Inuit (1968)	96.0	16.5	111.5	20.2	128.5	28.6	140.7	36.4	153.2	44.8	163.1	62.3
Quechua[8]	84.5	11.0	104.2	18.7	118.5	24.2	129.5	29.8	144.0	38.0	153.7	48.2
Quechua[7]	88.2	14.0	107.8	19.7	121.6	25.3	133.0	31.7	149.4	44.5	160.0	57.2
Pacific												
Australia[9]	90.2	12.7	114.3	18.2	128.6	24.1	143.1	31.4	163.3	48.1	173.0	60.0
PNG[10]	85.2	11.5	97.0	15.2	110.6	20.4	123.0	25.6	136.7	32.9	149.8	52.0
Fijian[1]	92.0	14.6	112.8	20.1	128.7	26.2	140.0	33.0	157.3	45.0	169.0	62.8
Am. Samoan[11]	—	—	116.9	22.6	131.9	31.6	143.6	37.1	—	—	172.8	88.2
W. Samoan[11]	—	—	115.0	19.8	126.9	28.5	134.5	32.2	—	—	170.4	73.4

TABLE 6-6b Heights (cm) and Weights (kg) of Select Populations (Girls)

GROUPS	3 YEARS Ht.	3 YEARS Wt.	6 YEARS Ht.	6 YEARS Wt.	9 YEARS Ht.	9 YEARS Wt.	12 YEARS Ht.	12 YEARS Wt.	15 YEARS Ht.	15 YEARS Wt.	18 YEARS Ht.	18 YEARS Wt.
USA												
NCHS-1a[1]	93.6	14.0	114.4	20.2	132.0	29.3	150.2	42.1	161.7	55.1	163.8	—
NCHS-1b[1]	93.8	13.9	115.8	20.8	133.1	29.9	154.1	50.1	162.2	57.1	—	—
Europe												
Netherlands[1]	97.3	15.4	117.3	21.7	135.0	29.8	152.9	39.9	165.6	57.1	166.7	69.0
England[1]	93.7	14.1	114.3	20.5	131.8	28.3	146.7					
Africa												
Hutu[3]	—	—	—	—	122.4	22.3	135.1	28.8	149.2	37.6	155.0	—
Turkana[1]	91.2	12.2	105.7	14.4	125.7	21.7	140.1	29.3	152.4	34.8	164.4	—
Asia												
Japan[1]	92.0	14.40	112.0	19.0	130.0	23.0	149.0	41.0	156.0	51.0	—	—
China (PRC)[1]	91.5	12.8	110.0	18.4	123.4	22.9	138.7	31.4	142.9	40.2	151.1	—
Amerind												
Inuit[5]	92.0	16.0	106.0	19.6	119.7	25.5	139.3	39.0	150.8	50.7	149.4	—
Inuit[6]	94.2	16.1	112.2	21.3	128.5	30.3	147.2	45.3	156.8	56.8	158.0	—
Quechua[8]	85.5	11.3	103.9	17.0	119.0	22.4	131.3	30.0	141.6	42.9	147.8	—
Quechua[7]	88.4	13.6	104.8	18.8	120.1	24.8	137.9	35.7	147.0	46.5	148.9	—
Pacific												
Australia[9]	—	—	112.0	18.0	130.0	26.0	148.0	37.5	156.0	47.5	—	—
PNG[1]	85.0	11.6	99.2	15.9	114.9	20.6	123.0	26.8	140.7	37.7	147.5	—
Fijian[1]	89.5	13.5	112.0	20.0	128.0	26.0	143.6	35.2	155.5	49.3	161.5	—
Am. Samoan[11]	—	—	116.0	21.5	133.6	32.3	145.3	41.6	—	—	160.3	78.3
W. Samoan[11]	—	—	111.6	19.2	128.4	29.2	137.5	33.8	158.3	—	158.3	68.4

Source: [1]Eveleth and Tanner, 1990: NCHSla: National Center of Health Statistics-White; NCHSlb, AfroAmerican; other populations as noted.
[2]Hausman and Wilmsen, 1985; Heights ans weights reported for ranges of ages 2–4, 5–9, and 10–16 so a midpoint age is recorded in this table.
[3]Hiernaux, 1964; [4]Leonard et al., 1990; [5]Rode and Shephard, 1984; [6]Auger et al., 1930; [7]Leatherman et al., 1995.
[8]Frisancho and Baker, 1970; [9]Brown and Townsend, 1982; [10]Heywood, 1983; [11]Bindon and Baker, 1985; [12]Tanner, 1981.

and based on a few select populations, for example, Hong Kong Chinese. The reader should be aware that variations can be extreme when broader comparisons are made (note the 7 ft. 1 in. tall Chinese basketball player in the NBA). What is most interesting is the case of the Japanese, whose stature has increased an average of approximately 10 cm between 1932 and 1982, despite a 2-cm decline during the war years of 1939 to 1945. This secular trend may soon cease and will bring the Japanese within 5 cm of British and American averages. Of special note is that sitting height has changed little. The stature gains have been due largely to increased growth of the legs, which will change the cormic index and bring bodily proportions nearer to those of Europeans (Eveleth and Tanner, 1990).

By contrast, groups of similar genetic composition raised under differing social and economic circumstances differ in average body size at all ages. Children, grouped according to socioeconomic class (SES) based on the father's occupation, income, and number of children in the family, show significantly greater growth rates and height attained for age among those of the upper SES levels. Children whose parents are members of the professional or managerial classes mature earlier and are 2 cm taller as adults than children whose father's occupation is unskilled labor; at adolescence, the difference reaches a high of 5 cm. Further evidence of class differences may be offered by studies in Europe and the United States of immigrant populations whose children make gains each generation approching national standards (Bogin, 1999). How well children fare in these new homelands is a good measurement of a family's status.

In sum, the many studies of human growth demonstrate that environmental quality has similar effects whatever the population or ethnic group. The tempo of growth and attainment of adult height provide evidence of social conditions, and, in fact, economic historians have used stature as a proxy for the measurement of economic fluctuation during various periods of recent history (Komlos, 1995). Appreciation of the influences environment has on growth will make it easier to understand human variability of form and size though exceptions beyond populations do raise questions. The Chinese have produced seven-foot-tall basketball players despite their average small body sizes, and though Samoans have sent some very large men to play professional football, the average Samoan is smaller than the average American (refer to Table 6-6a). We are, after all, the result of our growth experiences and there appear to be few ethnic distinctions. Firm evidence of ethnic variations of genetic polymorphisms influencing body form and size is lacking, however. Except for the insulin-like growth factor found in the Pygmies and some rare conditions of hormone deficiencies, there are few data on the genetics of the complex of growth and size attainment. The high correlations of twins and close relatives does not help much except to underscore that growth has a high heritability (genetic variance influence on phenotypic variance), but environmental factors are still responsible for a broad range of variability.

NUTRITIONAL INFLUENCES

The quality and quantity of foods selected determine how well a child fairs during critical growth phases and adult height achieved as described above. Also, the health and work performance of adults reflects their nutritional state. A basic consideration is the satisfaction of metabolic energy requirements measured in calories (kc).[3] Total caloric intake required depends on age, sex and work load. Hence, the "standard" male (70 kg and 172 cm) who is moderately active needs to ingest between 2,500 and 3,000 kc per day to maintain body weight. The "standard" female (58 kg and 162 cm) needs relatively less, 2,100 kc per day with an additional 300 kc during pregnancy and 500 kc during lactation. Additional energy intake of up to 2,000 kc may be required of both male and female when work load increases—farming, chopping wood, carrying, walking long distances, and so on. If these energy expenditures are not meant by increased food intake, the body's fat stores will be consumed.

Children, from ages 1 to 11 years, require between 1,300 and 2,400 kc per day, a proportionately much higher intake than adults. After age 11, boys and girls diverge somewhat in their energy needs; boys require about 20 percent more to maintain growth because of their greater muscle mass. If these energy needs are not met, growth slows and is prolonged. In adults, activity levels decline and fat stores are depleted.

Essential Nutrients

Nutrient needs may be provided by a variety of foods from either animal or plant sources or a combination of both. Humans can grow and maintain health and physical activity if these foods provide the following groups of nutrients in required amounts. Individual requirements vary widely depending on age, gender, and level of physical activity, but basic physiological functions depend on provision of certain quantities of the following food groups.

Proteins. The tissues of the body, the hemoglobin and plasma of the blood, as well as enzymes and most hormones, to name a few substances, are made up of proteins. Throughout our lives, these must be formed, rebuilt, or replaced as our bodies grow or age and damaged tissues are repaired. The turnover rate is about two and one-half grams per kilogram of body weight per day, or about one hundred and seventy-five grams for the average adult male. Thus, there is a continuous need for new protein which requires basic components, amino acids, so synthesis can proceed. During synthesis, these amino acids have to be taken up and arranged in a proper order under genetic control. All but eight of the twenty amino acids can be synthesized in the body from other products. These eight indispensable (essential) amino acids must be obtained from the foods we eat (Table 6-7). During childhood, two additional amino acids (histidine and arginine) are essential, since children are unable to synthesize them in sufficient quantities to meet the demands of their rapidly growing tissues.

Most animal proteins provide the best sources of these essential amino acids since all eight are present. By contrast, vegetable proteins are lacking in one or more of these essential eight. Maize (corn) is deficient in lysine, rice lacks lysine and tryptophan, and most varieties of beans are deficient in methionine. In vegetarian

---

[3]A calorie is a unit of heat needed to raise the temperature of one gram of water one degree Celsius. In measures of metabolic or of food energy, the unit is in terms of a thousand calories, or *kilocalories*.

TABLE 6-7 Required Dietary Amino Acids (Essential)

AMINO ACID	CHILDREN (0–4 YEARS)	ADULTS
Arginine	++	– –
Histidine	++	– –
Isoleucine	++	++
Leucine	++	++
Lysine	++	++
Methionine	++	++
Phenylalanine	++	++
Threonine	++	++
Tryptophan	++	++
Valine	++	++

++ Dietary amino acids required.
– – Adults synthesize these in sufficient quantities,
but children do not.

Source: Adapted from Ganong, 2003.

diets, these missing amino acids of one plant source may be provided by another. A combination of rice and beans is one favorite and maize and beans another.

When sufficient amino acids are ingested and proteins are synthesized to compensate for the wear-and-tear quotient of tissue breakdown and repair, then a person is said to be in *nitrogen balance*. As proteins are broken down, a quantity of amino acids are catabolized—they are separated into the basic elemental units of their composition. Some of these elements, principally nitrogen, are excreted in the urine. When nitrogen intake (as part of dietary amino acids) is equal to the amount excreted, then a balance is obtained. Where more tissue is lost than is replenished, as in starvation, or if there is an increase in hormones like cortisone or insulin, there is a negative balance—more nitrogen is lost than can be replaced by the ingested food components.

In addition to providing for the basic protein synthesis, it is necessary to replace an obligatory loss; there is about 10 percent of protein turnover per day that is lost, mostly through excretion. Any diet should contain proteins beyond a basic level to compensate for this loss as well as provide for new tissue building and to allow a safety margin. Though recommended daily allowances have been adjusted over the years, amounts of between eight-tenths and one gram per kilogram of body weight are recommended at this time. Increased amounts are necessary for children and pregnant or nursing women. The diets of many populations around the world appear to fall far below these protein levels, however.

Fats.   Energy, in excess of daily requirements, is stored in the form of molecular compounds called lipids, or fatty acids. Most lipids are contained in adipose cells congregated into fat layers at several locations throughout the body. This fat tissue, as differentiated from muscle and bone, is a significant part of total body weight that varies with the balance between energy intake and expenditure. Normal, nonobese adult males have 10 to 12 percent of their body weight as fat and females have around

20 or 25 percent.[4] When food intake increases beyond daily energy needs of basal metabolism and exercises, body fat content rises; it declines when the reverse is true.

There are numerous other functions of lipids in addition to energy storage. They are a major constituent of cell membranes, they coat nerve fibers, and they provide chemical precursors for steroids and cholesterol. Lipids are also important for the absorption and transport of several nutrients like calcium and the fat-soluble vitamins, A and D. In addition, of major biological importance is the energy supplied by the fatty acids (triglycerides) to muscle tissue at resting or at low levels of exercise. As exercise increases energy expenditure, the muscle contraction needs are provided by carbohydrates (Ganong, 2003).

Dietary fat is a rich concentration of energy (9.3 kc/g) since it supplies over twice the amount per gram provided by either carbohydrate (4.1 kc/g) or protein (4.1 kc/g). It is then relatively easy to exceed one's energy needs on a diet high in fat content. Dietary fats are grouped into saturated and polyunsaturated, according to molecular structure. Furthermore, fats are chemically identified as Omega 6 and Omega 3, with different effects on the ratio of high-to-low density lipids. The type of fat as well as the quantity have received a great deal of attention because of concerns with health problems associated with diet, obesity, and heart disease. We can subsist on low-fat intakes providing we consume oils or fats that contain the three essential polyunstaturated fatty acids (linolenic, linoleic, and arachidonic). In fact, there are many populations who subsist on less than 6 percent of their total caloric intake (see below). By contrast, there are populations who consume an excess of saturated fats to the detriment of their health.

Carbohydrates. This nutrient category varies from a simple compound such as glucose to complex starches like glycogen. We are most familiar with carbohydrates as starches in potatoes, wheat products, and rice or as sugar, in candies and ice creams. The major physiological role of this class of compounds is to provide energy within the cells (glucose) or to store it in the liver and muscle tissue as glycogen, where it is readily available for quick conversion to glucose. The excess glucose in circulation is converted to triglycerides and stored in adipose cells.

Our carbohydrate requirements are not of the same order as either the essential fatty acids or amino acids. There seems to be no specific type of carbohydrate that our metabolism requires. Most food plants contain carbohydrate starches consisting of long chains of glucose molecules (amylose and amylopectin). These are digestible, but plants also have fibrous structural materials made of cellulose that are not. The ratio of cellulose to digestible starches makes some plants more or less desirable as human food. Many of the tubers that have high starch concentrations can be produced cheaply, and the nutrients are easily obtained. By contrast, grains contain starches wrapped in an indigestible fibrous sheath, costly in time and labor to remove. Nevertheless, grains are a plentiful source of carbohydrate and provide, in various processed forms, the bulk of caloric intake for a majority of humans today.

---

[4]Obesity is defined arbitrarily as body weight greater than 20 percent of the standard weight for height, age, and sex.

Micronutrients.   To enable metabolic processes to proceed within normal body temperature ranges two groups of micronutrients, *vitamins* and *minerals* must be present an essential dietary components to act as catalysts. The *vitamins* serve many vital functions in chemical processes throughout the metabolism, functioning individually or as co-factors with enzymes. One of the earliest demonstrations of vitamin needs was the frequent occurrence of scurvy among sailors on long see voyages. Lacking access to fresh foods for extended periods of time, the early voyagers would slowly weaken, and many died as the soft tissues throughout their bodies slowly degenerated; ligaments lost elasticity and walls of smaller blood vessel ruptured (Carpenter, 1986). The collagenous fibers of these structures could not be maintained or rebuilt in the absence of vitamin C. The first sign of this problem is bleeding of the gums and loosening of the teeth as the supporting ligaments dengenerate. These seafarers expected to suffer from this disease as one of the costs of months at sea without fresh foods. Eventually, they learned that supplements of picked vegetables or small amounts of citrus juice could maintain health and prevent scurvy. Centuries later, the antiscurvy compound in fresh foods (vitamin C) was identified, and many other essential vitamins have been discovered since. The early Arctic explorers also suffered from scurvy until they adopted the food habits of the Inuit. These well-adapted people (the Inuit), though, lacking access to any plant foods for most of the year, gained sufficient vitamin C from undercooked meat, marine mammal skin, and raw fish.

Examples of other vitamin deficiencies are found in the cases of poorly formed and distorted bones (rickets) of poorly nourished children, described in Chapter 5. Rickets was eventually related to vitamin D deficiency, a vitamin plentiful in fish oils. The lack of vitamin A or its precursors (the carotenes) in many fresh vegetables causes various forms of visual impairment, especially xeropthalmia and night blindness. Xeropthalmia is the major cause of blindness in young children of developing countries, especially where rice is their dietary staple with few fresh vegetables. Pellegra, a generalized disorder affecting skin, mucous membranes, and the central nervous system has long been associated with an overdependence on maize (corn). Such a diet, largely devoid of other foods, is niacin deficient which is a key vitamin for the normal functioning of most cells. Thiamin deficiency is another of the vitamins related to a poor diet. Where polished white rice is the diet staple, people are at risk for beriberi, a malfunctioning of the neurological system and of the heart.

Mineral Elements.   As components of our diet, several important elements also serve numerous vital functions. These functions range from calcium and phosphorus providing the mineral structure of bone, to the transport of essential substances as in the example of iron. Bound with a globin protein, iron is the key element in the transport of oxygen. Hormonal functions of trace elements are also important as in the example of iodine combining with molecules of the amino acid tyrosine in the thyroid gland to produce thyroglobins. These thyroglobins, principally thyroxine and thyronine, control metabolic process mainly by regulating cells' oxygen consumption. They influence growth and development, increase absorption of carbohydrates through the gut wall, and help regulate lipid metabolism. These functions ultimately depend upon only a small daily supply of iodine (about 40 micrograms) to stimulate the function of a healthy thyroid gland.

Perhaps the first trace element deficiency disease to be identified was goiter, the hyperactivity and swelling of a thyroid gland that produced too little thyroxine because of iodine insufficiency. Goiter is typically found among those populations subsisting on foods grown on the iodine poor soils found in many parts of the world. Peoples throughout much of Asia and Europe have a long history of this disease. People living in the New Guinea highlands have especially high goiter rates because their low iodine intake is made worse by diets high in substances that inhibit thyroid function. The Yanomama of South America also have low iodine intake but they rarely exhibit goiter symptoms, probably because of their unique ability to absorb and retain the element (Neel, 1994).

These mineral elements of iron, calcium, phosphorus, and several others must be present in fairly large quantities in the body, and they need to be replenished at a high rate. Several other required elements are needed in varying amounts from only a few micrograms to several milligrams. Cobalt, selenium, and magnesium are some examples of this group of elements that function in the body as essential components of certain metabolic processes. Zinc, for example is necessary for normal growth and for tissue repair, as in wound healing. The element cobalt is a key component of vitamin B12, selenium is needed in but a few parts per million for skeletal mineralization and muscle development, as is magnesium, though it is needed in much larger quantities (Fowden et al., 1981).

Considering the multitude of our nutritional needs and the variety of ways we have found to fulfill them, the quantitative and qualitative requirements of the human diet are difficult to standardize. What is the optimum diet needed for good health is a question that has often been asked and is still debated. We know about some deficiencies that cause pathological responses but are unsure of what others may exist. Measurements have been made of the energy needs of the growing child or the working adult, pregnant women or the elderly. So many exceptions have been recorded, however, that references to any single standard or average is of limited value since guidelines have been developed mainly from studies of populations of the more developed countries.

Comparative Diets

The three nutrient categories collectively fulfill our needs for energy and tissue rebuilding. What proportion of carbohydrate to protein or fat to protein continues to be the subject of much debate. There is evidence that a fat-free diet is unhealthy and even lethal; beyond the requirement for the essential fatty acids, lipids are needed to aid the digestion of animal protein. But the optimum amount of fat needed is not known. Recommended protein levels have changed over the last few decades. From a high of two grams per kilogram, protein has been lowered to 0.57 grams and then increased to 0.8 to allow for a lower digestive efficiency of certain protein types. A relatively small amount is sufficient as long as the essential amino acids are provided. No advantage is derived from increasing protein intake. The level of carbohydrates, that cheapest of food sources, is likewise uncertain. In most of the world, a good deal depends upon family income though. The lower the income and the larger the family, the higher the carbohydrate proportion among people of the underdeveloped world.

Diet is a matter of available food varieties, custom, income, and taste. Table 6-8 offers some examples of diet proportions reported for several population groups.

TABLE 6-8 Comparative Diets

ETHNIC GROUP	TOTAL CALORIES	CARBOHYDRATE			FAT			PROTEIN		
		cal	%	gm	cal	%	gm	cal	%	gm
USA(a) (male)[1]	2,860	1066	37	260	1628	57	175	308	10.8	75
Britain[2]	3,016	1619	53.6	400	995	32.9	110	401	13.3	100
New Guinea[3]	1,361	1200	88.2	292	30	2.2	3	131	9.6	32
New Guinea[3]	2,236	1865	83	454	207	9	22.3	164	7	40
African[2] (Kikuyu)	2,182	1579	72.3	390	198	9.0	22	405	18.5	100
Pacific[2] (Tokelauans)	2,350	818	34.8	202	1258	53.5	139	275	11.7	68
Inuit (a)[5]	2,290	41	2	41	1720	60	185	530	32	100
Inuit (b)[5]	2,770	820	32	200	1120	43	120	830	25	156
USA(b) (male)[5]	2,800		50	341		35	50		15	56

Caloric values per gram:

Fat;   9.3 kcal
Carbohydrate (CHO);   4.1 kcal
Protein;   4.1 kcal

Source: 1. National Academy of Sciences, 1980. 2. Harrison et al., 1988. 3. Ulijaszek et al., 1987. 4. Schaefer, 1981. 5. National Academy of Sciences, 1989.

The weight of each category is given in grams and from this the number of kilocalories is calculated. Then its percent of the total energy intake is determined. Hence, the British male daily caloric intake was listed as 3,016 kcal and, of this, carbohydrates contributed 53.6 percent, fat 32.9 percent, and protein only 13.3 percent of the total. Note that protein contributes the lowest energy proportion, fat the second, and carbohydrate the highest. Note also the range in proportions of the fat energy contribution. Though it is difficult to recommend an average diet, nutritionists describe a 50–35–15 percent of carbohydrates, fats and protein as desirable balance. However, these proportions vary widely among peoples with extremely different adaptive strategies as illustrated in Figure 6-9. As customs change and income rises so does diet composition; usually it is the proportion of fat that increases. But humans have always managed to use a diversity of foods to satisfy hunger, if not all of their physiological needs.

A review of the subsistence of small-scale societies during their ecological transition from their traditional lifestyles offers a broader perspective. Comparisons of different groups at several stages of change from their traditional diets should shed light on satisfaction of basic human nutritional needs. The key question is what foods are used, their seasonal availability, and the effects of newly introduced foods as they supplement or replace traditional diets.

Responses to Food Varieties.   Children are more affected than adults by changes in living conditions since their growing bodies are sensitive to even mild fluctuations of the environment. The status of a population's children is thus one of the significant measures of a people's successful exploitation of their environment as we noted above. Specifically, the mortality and morbidity rates from infancy through adolescence says a lot about adaptation when comparisons are made between generations or to other populations. Additionally, since diet deficiencies and disease are closely linked and influence an individual's progress through childhood's stages, growth (the proportionate change in size) can offer an excellent record of a population's adaptation. Simply, if conditions are good and there are adequate food, shelter, and protection, childhood disease and mortality rates will be low. Children will respond by achieving a rate of growth that will enable them to reach a certain size and weight range at each age. Comparatively, then, child growth followed by measures of final adult size become markers of adaptive success.

Starting with simple observations of human growth patterns, that is, a child is so large and heavy at a certain chronological age, we may use these values to compare populations. Height and weight means for male and female children, ages 3 to 18 years from a sample of populations are compared to the National Center for Health Statistics (NCHS) norms (see Tables 6-6a and 6-6b).[5] These populations are representative of a wide range of ethnic groups at different economic levels living in diverse environments.

---

[5]The NCHS is used as a reference standard in the evaluation of the children of many ethnic groups. Though recognizing that genetic influences are important and are responsible for many of factors of growth diversity, the NCHS standards of both Euro-Americans and Afro-Americans offer a benchmark for evaluation of children and the quality of their environments in many nations because the environmental influence vastly outweighs the genetic in most cases. (See Eveleth and Tanner, 1990.)

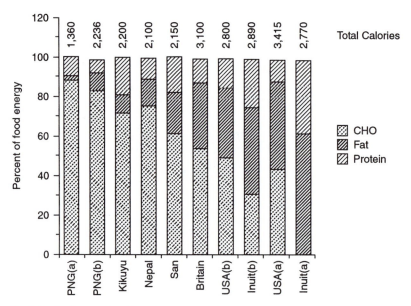

FIGURE 6-9 Comparative Diets. Proportions of three major diet components.
Source: See Table 6-8.

Children in the United States are larger and heavier at all ages with their growth slowing as they near their final adult height at about age 16 (females) or 18 (males). Children of the several indigenous groups lag behind in the attainment of size at each age. Their growth is slower and prolonged, sometimes into early adulthood. Most achieve an adult height significantly lower than the U.S. means except for the Turkana whose males continue to grow beyond age 20, eventually reaching a final adult height slightly exceeding the U.S. standards.

How much these differences are due to an annual average of undernutrition or simply to seasonal food shortages is hard to determine, but there are some clues offered from comparisons of groups before and after nutritional changes. Food supply fluctuation and resultant growth or health changes have been followed more closely in the San and Turkana of Africa than any group. When a more stable food supply becomes available, however, size and weight increase to near the norms for other, more sedentary societies. Though among the smallest and lightest people in the world, adult San have gained 6.6 cm for males and 3.4 cm for females over the last seventy-five years. This increase is attributed to an improvement in the lot of a "disadvantaged people," especially a supplement of foods gained from their pastoral neighbors (see Tobias, 1978).

Among the San, such supplements to their traditional diet tend to level out seasonal effects that, in the past, have caused fluctuation in adult weights, but have especially affected children. This observation is supported by the improved growth response of children in villages where their families work as farm laborers. These children were taller and heavier and fewer fell below the fifth percentile for their age group when compared so NCHS standards. Only 23 percent of 1- to 4-year-olds and 24 percent of 5- to 9-year-olds fell below the fifth percentile in 1970 compared with 65 percent who did so in 1967, but fewer difference were seen in the older age groups (Hausman and Wilmsen, 1985). Further contrasts were shown in a study of children from another settlement, some of whom attended school and some who did not. The children, not attending school, did not differ significantly from the same age groups measured twenty years before; a majority of both groups were below the third percentile. Benefiting from a feeding program, only 29 percent of the school children fell below this level. They were taller and heavier with greater fat stores approaching the quantity of other ethnic groups in the same village, the pastoral Tswana and Herero (Hansen et al., 1993). The transition to sedentary life and a regular food supply increased energy intake and resultant body fat stores, hence their improved rate of growth.

The children of the Turkana pastoralist society have responded in the same way to diet changes. Growth was slow, as noted, for both males and females who remain below the NCHS fifth percentile for African Americans until after age 19 and 16 respectively. A lack of dietary calories depresses weights far below standards, but the high-protein intake sustains a higher linear growth compared with other Africans. With the establishment of a settlement complete with crop irrigation to encourage sedentary agriculture, the growth profile is changing. Children in the 5- to 10-year-old range are taller and heavier than their nomadic counterparts though infants in the nomadic community are heavier probably due to a greater milk intake. The advance in growth of settlement children has been ascribed to the supplemental feeding at nursery and primary schools (Little et al., 1983).

On the other side of the world, in extremely different environments, the native Australians and peoples of Papua New Guinea (PNG) have shared much the same experience as their African counterparts. Children have an accelerated growth pattern in contrast to previous generations as diets have shifted more toward the Western type. The Australian Aboriginal child, however, still lags behind the Euro-Australian. Growth improvements have been noted among Aboriginal children in towns and urban areas, who received supplemental feeding, in contrast to remote out-stations where quantity and quality of diet are more limited. Of the 100 children surveyed in "fringe camps" near the town of Cunnamulla, Queensland, only 10 children were at or above the fiftieth percentile for their age. In contrast, 34 of the 98 "town" children had attained this growth level (Copeman et al., 1975).

Comparisons of Aboriginals, who grew up during the 1930s, with their children and grandchildren some thirty years later showed an increase of as much as six centimeters in adult height for both sexes. This secular increase over about a thirty-five year period may be described as due to improvements in nutrition, health, and general living conditions. The living conditions certainly changed as more Aboriginal Australians became sedentary occupants of government-run settlement or lived in fringe camps around towns, but the improvements in diet and lifestyle may be questioned. There has been a steady increase of refined European foods, mainly flour and sugar, in their diets while bush foods of their traditional diets have declined. This near total reliance on a few refined foods has reduced the variety of nutrients while increasing diet energy intake. The Inuit, though adapting to an extremely different environment, also gained in height when they changed their diet. It may be that an increased energy intake was the primary cause of the secular growth increase (Barrett and Brown, 1971).

Not too distant in miles, but environmentally a world away in contrast to the central Australian desert, are the wet tropics of the mountainous island of New Guinea. The occupants of these rugged highland valleys are among the smallest people in the world (refer to Tables 6-6a and 6-6b). They are smaller at all ages than their Australian neighbors and their children are the slowest growing of any population. This may be considered as an adaptation to the rigors of the wet tropical environment and their high-carbohydrate, low-protein diets (Heywood, 1983). However, over the last few decades with mining developments, the sale of timber, and cash-crop agriculture, Papua New Guinea populations are rapidly moving more into the cash economy of the modern world. Among the many effects of this shifting economy is a greater dependence on imported foods with a concomitant increase in protein and refined carbohydrates.

Such dietary shifts have resulted in greater weight gains at all ages throughout those New Guinea populations participating in this transition. The Bundi, for example, gain more of their subsistence from store-bought Western foods than they did twenty years ago. As a result there has been a significant influence on growth. Adolescents of both sexes grow more rapidly and are heavier than their counterparts of two decades earlier. Despite this increase of growth rate, adults remain short, and lightweight compared to U.S. standards (Zemel and Jenkins, 1989).

Response to changing diets has been most apparent among children of urban areas or in boarding schools where their diets departed significantly from the traditional. The major differences were in the protein content, and an experiment with diet supplements demonstrated the importance of this food component for New Guinea child growth. Over eleven years, one group was given a supplement of ten grams of protein a day while a second group received twenty. The height and weight gain of both groups exceeded that of children on traditional diets. Bone density and maturation rates also were significantly improved in the supplemented groups. Beneficial growth effects of protein were further demonstrated by the differences between the two supplemented groups: Those receiving twenty grams per day exceeded those receiving only ten grams (Lampl et al., 1978).

The health impact of a transformation to a cash economy is clearly underscored by the weight and height gains of people in the OK Tedi region of western Papua New Guinea. Since 1975 when gold and copper mining began providing employment, greater height gains (156.8 cm verus 154.3 cm) are evidenced by a larger stature of the younger adult males in 1984 who had been exposed to Western foods.[6] In addition to

---

[6]Western diet refers to the high-energy protein and fat-rich diets of the developed countries. This highly refined diet, low in natural fiber, does provide the food components for optimum growth. They also contribute to over nutrition, obesity, and ill-health in later life.

increased consumption of imported foods (mainly rice and canned fish), improvements in subsistence farming were made with the shift to a fast-growing variety of sweet potato displacing the taro root as a major food crop of the region. This improvement alone may account for at least some of the growth gains over the decade.

The influence of a cash economy brought on by the mining operations is especially apparent when working and nonworking families are compared. Males employed at the mines are taller and heavier than their nonworking counterparts living a traditional lifestyle (158.1 cm versus 155.4 cm; 58.6 kg versus 51.9 kg) and females of working spouses are also taller and heavier (149.2 cm versus 147.4 cm; 51.1 kg versus 44.6 kg). Interestingly, there is even a difference seen between those living closer to the mines than those further away; individuals living within a day's walk are taller and heavier. Though the children remain below standards for height and weight at all ages, some improvements were seen and food availability due to the mine employment was the likely cause (Lourie and Taufa, 1986; Ulijaszek et al., 1987).

Despite the climatic extremes of tropical and arctic environments, peoples of Alaska, Canada, New Guinea, and Australia all had similar responses to changes in traditional diets. The growth status of the Inuit today has improved over that of their parents and grandparents a half century ago. Comparisons of Cumberland Sound populations in 1938 and 1968 showed children heavier at all ages and a height gain of 5 cm in males over the thirty-year period. This gain was closely correlated with an increase in Western food consumption, an increase which, interestingly enough, coincided with a decline in protein (from 300 grams/day to 100 grams/day per capita). As the people shifted away from their native diet and depended more on imported Western foods, there has been an overall caloric increase. Similar, but less dramatic changes have been seen among the people living at Igloolik, Canada, on the shores of Hudson Bay above the Arctic Circle throughout the 1970s and 1980s. Children under 18 approached the Canadian and NCHS standards (Shephard and Rode, 1996). This relationship of growth pattern to diet adaptation is comparable to that experienced by the western Alaskan Inuit. The Alaskan Inuit were among the earliest to make trade contacts and they achieved growth patterns, comparable to NCHS standards several decades ago. The males reach 171 cm in height and weigh 70.5 kg by age 18.

Secular trends.   The children of the indigenous populations, discussed above, have all attained greater weight and height than those of their parents, especially after 3 years of age. This has come about as the people have undergone a transition from their traditional lifestyles and is most apparent in the examples of hunter and gatherers who have shifted to a sedentary life. The Australians and Inuits have especially responded in a dramatic way to high inputs of refined carbohydrates, mainly sugar, flour and pastry products. Children of both groups have accelerated their growth and gained earlier maturation, but at some cost to their health in later years.

The San and Turkana of Africa have also undergone significant changes, but in somewhat different ways. The San are becoming taller while the Turkana are gaining in fat stores as exhibited by the village children of both groups on supplemental feeding programs. There is a more consistent level of nutrients available throughout the year. Growth and work requirements are met without broad variations in food availability in contrast with the seasonal fluctuations of previous times. But, again, improvements and changes in the diets of these former nomads are not without costs to their health and there have been influences on female fertility.

The agriculturists in both New Guinea and the Andes are experiencing changes as they become more integrated into a cash economy as their nations become involved with the developed world. Social class stratification is a new and major factor differentiating among subgroups within these populations. Those families with the means to purchase store foods tend to thrive as reflected by their children's growth. The seasonal effects related to dependence on traditional foods is lessened in the case of the Quechua. The greater participation in a cash economy by the Papua New Guinea peoples has also improved their protein intake together with the addition of refined carbohydrates.

Considering the examples of these indigenous populations in relationship to their subsistence levels, their responses are very similar in that they grow slowly on their traditional diets. Their growth adaptations have resulted in a secular change in size as economic status improves the food intake and health care. Of course, there are many factors influencing height and weight at each age, but one common factor is shared by all of these populations: the provision of sufficient food energy for both work and growth. Much of this change has been due to importation of high-energy, refined foods, a large component of Western diets.

ADAPTATION TO COLD OR HOT ENVIRONMENTS

Like other mammals, humans must maintain their internal body temperature within a narrow range in order for metabolic processes to proceed normally.[7] These processes generated heat, and this heat may be conserved or dissipated depending on a number of factors including age, gender, physical condition, clothing, and the temperature of the surrounding environment (ambient temperature). Deep body temperature must be maintained close to 37 °C (98.6F) regardless of other conditions. We can tolerate some variation as in the case of vigorous exercise when temperature will rise two or three degrees and then return to normal after resting. Lower temperatures (around 34 °C) are reached during sleep, but as we resume physical activity our internal temperature rises again. Beyond these ranges an individual's metabolism is impaired to various degrees.

Basal Metabolic Rate

At a resting state, after twelve to twenty-four hours of fasting, the lowest rate of biochemical activity constant with life is called the basal metabolic rate (BMR). The

---

[7]Metabolism is the sum total of all biochemical reactions contributing to life of the individual. These include, for example, the chemical processes of muscle contraction, food digestion and its transport, the processes of growth or tissue regeneration, and respiration.

total energy expenditure of these biochemical processes is measured in kilocalories (kcal). While at rest, this energy produces enough metabolic heat to replace body heat lost in a thermal neutral environment. This basal state enables all biochemical reactions to continue with minimal energy expenditure while normal body temperature of 37 °C. (98.6 °F) is maintained. Any activity that requires muscular exertion will elevate the metabolic activity and thus can be measured in reference to the BMR. Varying metabolic rate changes the quantity of heat generated.

The measurement of metabolic rates is made by recording the volume of oxygen consumed per minute, which is then converted to an energy measure; 4.83 kcal are generated for each liter of oxygen. Hence, a person consuming 250 milliliters (ml) of oxygen per minute will have consumed 360 liters (1) over the course of a twenty-four hour period which is equal to 1,734 kcal (360 $\times$ 4.83). Since heat is lost through the body surface area, the rate considers not only energy over time, but body size as well. In practice then, BMR or metabolic rates are given in terms of kilocalories per square meter (M^2) of body surface per hour. An average sized male (176 cm tall weighing 75 kg) has a surface area of 1.91 square meters. His BMR would then be 1,734 divided by 1.91 M^2 divided by 24 hours which equals to 37.83 kilocalories per square meter of surface area per hour of energy expended by this individual.

Thermal Regulation

The control of body temperature is achieved by balancing the heat gained or lost. This balance is achieved through insulation, variation in the blood flow nearest the body surface (subcutaneous circulation), and by varying metabolic processes to increase or decrease the heat produced. Obviously ambient temperature plays a significant role as has been shown by the many thermoregulation studies of human subjects under controlled laboratory conditions. A nude subject, at rest, can achieve a thermal balance (heat gained = heat lost) at ambient temperatures of between 25 to 27 °C (77 to 80.6°F), the thermal neutral range. Below this range, heat-generating mechanisms are increased and the network of blood vessels below the skin constrict, reducing heat loss. Metabolic rate increases to compensate for body heat lost. If ambient temperature continues to fall, muscle contractions of shivering generate more heat, and the more peripheral blood vessels in the arms and legs constrict to aid in conservation of heat energy.

If room temperature rises above the neutral point, the body compensates by reducing heat production and increases heat loss. Vasodilation increases the blood volume in the peripheral circulation bringing more of the deep body heat nearer the surface. This is then dissipated through several mechanisms depending on the ambient conditions. A flow or transfer of heat (radiation) is the principal mechanism and accounts for about 67 percent of the loss, while evaporation of sweat accounts for 23 percent and about 10 percent through convection (flow by air from a warmer to cooler body). If the elevated temperature continues over a period of time, then metabolic rate declines. The relative efficiency of these three mechanisms of heat loss

TABLE 6-9   Body Heat Loss by Three Mechanisms (percent)

BODY MECHANISM	AMBIENT	TEMPERATURE	(C°)
	25	30	35
Radiation	67	41	4
Evaporation	23	26	90
Convection	10	33	6

Source: Adapted from Folk, 1974.

depends on the ambient temperature; radiation losses decline and evaporative loss increases with a rise in room temperature (Table 6-9).

With increased temperature, evaporative heat loss (0.6 kcal/ml) becomes more effective as a mechanism. Sweat increases about 20 ml for each 1°C rise in air temperature. Should there be both a high temperature and a high moisture content of the air, measured as relative humidity, the rate of evaporation declines and the sweat glands reduce in activity. This reduces the efficiency of evaporative heat loss. Consider differences between dry and wet tropics or a temperate zone summer; dry heat is more tolerable than humid heat at the same temperatures because of the cooling effect of sweat evaporation. Thermal regulation of body heat under the conditions of high moisture content of the air (relative humidity greater than 75 percent) then depends more on radiation. The effectiveness of radiation heat loss varies according to body size and shape; the larger the surface area for a given weight, the greater the heat lost through radiation. Blood circulation, subcutaneous fat layers, and bodily proportions are interrelated factors affecting temperature maintenance. These interrelationships of surface area, insulation, and circulation to thermal regulation have been summarized in three different ways to explain mammalian thermal regulation.

Fourier's Law.   This general law as applied to any body with internal heat generation states that the rate of heat loss per unit of time is *directly proportional* to the body surface and to the difference between the internal temperature of the body core and that of the environment. Additionally, the heat loss is *inversely proportional* to the thickness of the shell, simply, the more insulation the lower heat flow. These general principles of heat exchange may apply to mammalian species. Heat loss is hampered by increased subcutaneous fat (thickness of the shell), and with increases in ambient temperature and/or a rise in core temperatures, dissipation of heat becomes more difficult. Since up to 70 percent of metabolic heat may be lost through radiation, the body's surface-area-to-weight ratio is a most significant dimension.

Bergmann and Allen Rules.   Over a century ago a German physiologist, Carl Bergmann, observed that populations of many wide-ranging species of mammals varied in body size relative to mean annual temperature. Those populations inhabiting the colder regions of the species' range tended to be larger and heavier than those inhabiting the warmer areas. The opposite was noted in the tropics, where high environmental temperatures make efficiency in dissipation of body heat an important adaptive characteristic; average body size was smaller. Some thirty years later, an American zoologist, John Allen, also observed that mammalian body proportions were correlated with climate. He proposed a rule that the protruding parts of the body (tails, limbs, ears, face) tend to be shorter at the colder end of a species range. Conversely, these body parts were longer in the warmer regions. Taken together, the two rules offer an explanation of the role that form plays in the maintenance of body temperature under varying climatic conditions.

These rules are based on sound observations of mammalian physiology and on the recognition of simple geometry. First, mammals must maintain body temperature within a narrow range, and second, metabolic heat production is proportionate to body weight, that is, the heavier the individual, the greater the amount of heat produced at rest or during muscle exertion. This metabolic heat maintains the animal's body temperature, and if an excess is produced, it must then be dissipated to prevent raising the animal's temperature, which happens easily on a hot day. On colder days, more heat is lost to the colder air surrounding the body so the metabolism increases, generating more metabolic heat. By small adjustments of metabolic processes, the animal is able to maintain a normal body temperature while at rest. However, this ability depends on the range of ambient temperature of the air surrounding its body. If the ambient temperature is too far below the animal's normal body temperature, then increasing metabolic rate alone cannot compensate. If the temperature is too far above body temperature, then there is a difficulty in dissipating excess heat generated during exercise. Third, and most important, heat lost is directly proportionate to the surface area.

A consideration of simple geometric shapes offers an illustration of the relationships between body surface and weight or mass considered as volume. In the case of a cylinder, the lateral surface area changes linearly while volume changes as the square. This means that volume increases at a higher rate than does area. For the cylinders in part A of Figure 6-10, compare the formulas: Area $= 2\pi rh$; Volume $= \pi r^2 h$. The cylinders with a radius of 1 and lengths of 2 and 4 have a surface-to-volume ratio of 2 to 1. An increase in the radius of the figure from 1 to 2 reduces surface-area-to-volume ratio, critical to thermoregulation, from 2:1 to 1/2:1 while doubling the length maintains the same ratio. In the case of a mammalian body, the longer, narrower-shaped figure will have more surface area to dissipate metabolic heat generated in proportion to weight. A simple exercise can further illustrate this relationship. The cube in part B of Figure 6-10 has a measure of 2 units on a side and a surface-to-volume ratio of 3, while doubling the length of the sides to form a rectangle doubles the volume but the surface-to-volume ratio is reduced to only 2.5. Though mammalian bodies are not geometric shapes like cubes, cylinders, or spheres, they generally do attain shapes with advantageous surface-to-volume ratios.

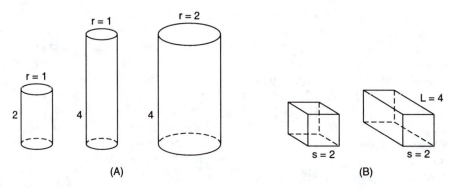

FIGURE 6-10   Changes in Surface Area to Volume.

The question is whether geographic variation in human body shapes conforms to the Bergmann-Allen rules. Do not clothing, shelter, and dietary variations enable humans to grow and achieve a body form independent of climatic influences? The climate effects on human size and shape were described by Roberts (1978), who noted that the geographic distribution of human body form tended to follow the Bergmann and Allen rules for mammals, which relate body-surface area to metabolic heat dissipation or to its conservation. Distribution of stature–weight ratios offers evidence that, despite cultural influences, climate does, in fact, influence body form. People, heavier for their height, are found more frequently in colder areas, which relates to a need to conserve body heat and avoid the risk of hypothermia. Taking body mass index (BMI), or weight (kg) divided by height (m) squared, shows a close negative correlation with temperature; the higher the BMI, the colder the climate (see Table 5-2 and Figure 5-17).

There are several exceptions to these correlations, however. The peoples of the Pacific are the first examples that come to mind. Samoans, though occupants of the warm tropics, have one of the highest BMIs of any population (near arctic populations); Fijians, Hawaiians, and Maori are also large people with high BMI ratings. The explanation for Pacific Islanders' high BMI may be found in their long history of ocean voyaging during which they encountered cold stress (see below).

Heat Stress and Acclimatization[8]

Biological and behavioral factors that enable humans to cope with a range of environmental temperatures are so interrelated that it is difficult to separate the relative influences of each factor. However, the resultant efficiency of acclimatization to heat may be measured in several ways. The first is a comparison of body forms. Residents

---

[8]Heat stress may be defined as that level of ambient temperature that impedes the dissipation of metabolic heat necessary to maintain thermal balance.

of the dry and wet tropics are much alike in that they have a greater surface area to body weight, but shape is a more important mechanism for heat dissipation in the wet tropics since the efficiency of heat loss through sweat is impaired by high humidity. In fact, tests under conditions of air saturation show that some people have a remarkable ability to suppress sweating. Australians in the humid tropical north and New Guineans sweat at lower rates (up to five times less) than European controls.

By contrast, sweating as a cooling mechanism under arid conditions is efficient but expends body water rapidly. Three groups of Australians living in the central desert had a sweat rate of twice that of Europeans; they lost body water at a rate of 13.6 ml/kg/hr versus 6.5 ml/kg/hr for desert-acclimated European subjects. To compensate for this fluid loss the Australians showed a remarkable ability to rapidly ingest water, drinking up to 2 percent of their body weight in 10 to 35 seconds or a rate of 17 seconds per liter while the best rate for European controls was 100 seconds. This consumption was typically in the early morning before the group broke camp prior to their day's foraging. The rapid consumption increased their extra cellular water to 28.3 percent of their body weight compared with 19.8 percent in the Europeans. This overhydration led to a surprising high rate of urine flow of up to ten times greater than the controls (Macfarlane, 1976).

Carefully controlled studies of work effort under heat stress conditions in South Africa documented mine workers' remarkable sweating ability (a volume of 400 to 900 ml per hour) during the first two hours but showed a significant decline in the third and fourth hours of tests (Wyndham, 1966). European and Africans alike were able to maintain body temperatures and heart rates within tolerable limits, but the Africans were able to do so at lower sweat rates. When sweat rate in millimeters per hour was corrected for body size and compared with the Australian results, then similar rates were seen between most subjects.

The San and Australians under hot dry conditions had the highest sweat rates, but people acclimated to these conditions can also reach these levels (see Table 6-10). Even European controls, who were larger, heavier, and with a thicker layer of subcutaneous fat, increased their ability to regulate body temperature through water loss. Marked contrasts are reported, however, for people indigenous to hot humid conditions; New Guineans maintained low sweat rates as did San residents in the humid swampy area of the Okavango delta (Northern Botswana). Their responses to heat stress is similar to test results for Australians in the humid Arnhem land area and the "bagged" tests[9] of subjects in the central desert. The moisture content of the air had a suppression effect as noted above.

In sum, humans have a remarkable ability to endure and acclimate to heat stress, which is not surprising considering our ancestor's tropical origins. We all share this ability, but some of us are better able to cope with thermal loads as suggested by the test results from studies of several indigenous people. However, conditioning, or acclimating to high ambient temperatures over time, improves our capacity to adjust. Do

---

[9]These bagged tests consist of placing the subject's arm in a plastic bag for a period of up to ninety minutes in direct sunlight. The sweat excreted is then measured and the rate calculated.

TABLE 6-10   Sweat Rates as Heat Adaptation (ml/hr)

ETHNIC GROUP	HOUR 1	HOUR 2	HOUR 3	HOUR 4	
So. Africa					
Bantu[1]	405	439	361	289	ml/hr#
	101	102	102	103	temp*
White[2]	593	547	418	446	ml/hr
	102	103	103	104	temp
Bantu[3]	675	938	720	508	ml/hr
	100	101	101	101	temp
White[4]	157	160	227	232	ml/hr
	100	101	101	101	temp
San[5]	593	643	592	481	ml/hr
	102	102	102	102	temp
Australia					
Aborigines[6]	444	468	391	323	ml/hr
	101	102	102	103	temp
Whites[7]	951	823	585	608	ml/hr
	101	102	102	102	temp
Sahara Desert					
Arabs[8]	577	741	571	487	ml/hr
	101	102	102	103	temp
Whites[9]	654	827	705	594	ml/hr
	101	102	102	103	temp

#Milliliters of sweat per hour.

*Rectal temperature in degrees Fahrenheit.

The subjects were all able-bodied, young adult males.

South Africa: 1. Bantu and 2. Europeans unacclimatized to the heavy mine work at high temperatures; 3. Bantu and 4. Europeans after acclimatizing to work conditions; 5. San, the nomadic hunters of southern Africa, tested under controlled conditions of energy expenditure.

Australia: 6. Aborigines and 7. Europeans tested for sweat rates under controlled heat stress conditions.

Sahara Desert, North Africa: 8. Chaamba Arabs and 9. French army recruits tested for sweat rates under controlled conditions of energy expenditure.

Source: Data selected from Wyndham, 1966.

the indigenous people of either Australia or Southern Africa surpass the European in this capacity? Seemly so, given the test results. The ability to accept large volumes of extracellular water in a short period, the maintenance of lower temperatures and heart rates, and the suppression of sweat rates under humid conditions seem to be unique to some people. In addition, such people conserve electrolyte balance; they excrete significantly lower levels of sodium, for example. This is a particular advantage for people in those areas where replacement is difficult as in the case of tropical rain forest people like those in New Guinea. But these contrasts in heat acclimation among indigenous people following a traditional lifestyle and those who are acclimated are difficult to gage.

There are behavioral factors that interfere with direct environmental effects. The use of clothing and shelter or a timing of physical exertion to avoid the hottest part of the day are among the more obvious behavioral responses, just as keeping close to a water source enables desert aborigines to replenish body water losses. Another equally important factor is dietary changes. Most of the indigenous people described above subsisted on a high-carbohydrate, low-fat, low-energy diet and had lower resting metabolic rates. Their caloric intake declined even further during the hottest weather as their need for water restricted foraging of desert peoples. In the wet tropics, water was not a problem; rather it was the need to replenish sodium lost in sweat. Extensive trade routes had been created to distribute salt in the New Guinea highlands as in central Africa. Where this vital substance was lacking an indigenous people would make use of ashes of certain plants as in the case of Yanomama of South America.

All of the tropical peoples possess a marked economy of excretion of salts. But as these people become more acculturated and changed their physical activity patterns and their diets, their physiological responses to heat stress became more like the responses of European controls.[10] On the other hand, the controls benefited from the training to work under heat stress conditions. The exposure to and training in heat conditions brought on an acclimation in all populations. Some reached a higher level than others. The efficiency in control of body water and maintenance of temperatures differ little, though some individuals because of age, gender, weight, and body proportions acclimate sooner and achieve higher levels than other.

Cold Stress and Acclimatization

Some of the best evidence for human physiological adjustments to cold stress come, surprisingly, from studies of desert populations—the Aborigine of Australia and the San of southern Africa. During the winter months, though daytime temperatures usually remain within comfortable range, they plummet below freezing overnight. The people, following their traditional lifestyle, made few concessions to the cold. The Australians did not use clothing, but they might sleep close to a campfire huddled in family groups during the coldest of nights. Sometimes pet dogs would be included in the clutch of bodies for added warmth. The San, likewise, lacked protective clothing except for genital covering and sometimes a skin cape. They also made use of fire, a brush shelter for a wind break, and slept in groups. In neither case was body warmth maintained in what Europeans consider a comfortable zone. Nevertheless, a good night's sleep could be achieved while European subjects who volunteered to try sleeping under the same conditions would remain awake uncomfortably shivering throughout the night. These desert dwellers' endurance of periods of moderate cold stress without ill effects was achieved by their ability to acclimatize.

---

[10]Control is a general scientific term widely used to identify a group of subjects from which baseline comparative data are obtained.

Australians from the central desert were compared to European control subjects over a period of eight hours' exposure to nighttime temperatures of 3 °C as they tried to sleep nude and in the open. The Australians tolerated lower core temperatures of about four degrees without a rise in resting metabolic rates measured at 37 cal/M^2/hr versus an increase in European controls to 49 from 40 cal/M^2/hr at thermal neutral temperatures. They also endured a lowering of skin temperatures over the eight hour period, down from 32 °C at the first hour to 28 °C by the end of the test. Similar cold stress tests of the San of southern Africa produced nearly the same results, a lowering of skin and core temperatures. These desert peoples from both regions endured a mild hypothermia of the outer body by reducing the heat transfer from the body core through vasoconstriction. This conservation of energy was aided further by a lowering of their resting metabolic rate. Because of their small amounts of subcutaneous fat compared with the Australians, the San lost relatively more heat that was compensated for by a somewhat higher metabolic rate. Both groups, however, give an example of energy conservation in the face of moderate cold stress while the Europeans exhibit what may be called an energy wasteful response with a relatively high rate of heat loss through the maintenance of higher body surface temperatures. This loss is compensated by intermittent increases of metabolic rates for short intervals over the test period (Frisancho, 1995; Steegman, 1975).

Another population, the Alacaluf of the southern tip of the South American continent, also showed an apparent disregard for the protective advantages of clothing. Though they lived in a cold land of high precipitation and chilly winds where the sun is seldom seen and winter temperatures hover at or near freezing, little clothing was worn. Aside from genital covering and the occasional use of stiff, poorly preserved pelican skin capes, their bodies were continuously exposed to the weather. They used crudely constructed huts and huddled around open fires for warmth at night, but during the day they suffered from cold stress with a high rate of heat loss. Adding to their cold discomfort was their use of crude canoes for fishing and gathering of seaweed and mollusc. These Alacaluf are the few remaining descendants of the people described by Darwin in his journal when he noted that his ship was met by nearly nude natives paddling their canoes in a snow flurry. He observed snow flakes melting on their bare shoulders that did not seem to distract or discomfort the occupants of the canoes as they looked over the strangers arriving at anchorage in a large and mysterious ship. In sum, the Alacaluf live in a cold and inhospitable land that even today is sparsely populated. One of the still unsolved mysteries of human adaptation is how or why these aboriginal peoples survived with so little technological protection from the elements.

Comparisons of their physiological responses to cold stress with European controls and with other aboriginal peoples show how they acclimatized. Overnight tests of the few surviving Alacaluf under moderate cold conditions (3 °C) showed that they maintained high skin and core body temperatures comparable to the European controls. Vasodilation did not reduce body heat loss as seen in the examples of the desert peoples described above. The Alacaluf compensated for the high rate of heat loss by maintaining a high metabolic rate over the eight-hour period, consistently higher than the controls and without the intermittent declines of the Europeans. A special adaptation of the Alacaluf is their higher foot temperatures and the tolerance of cold pain. In sum, what we find is a humid-cold-adapted people who wastefully expend metabolic energy to compensate for losses as they maintain higher temperatures over the body surface (Dill et al., 1964).

Arctic peoples, confronted with extreme cold stress, must rely on their culture to provide technological means for their survival; they do not live without protective garments and shelter. The Inuit, for example, build shelters of skins alternating with layers of moss stretched over whale ribs or driftwood frames. Away from the coastal areas, caribou hide tents are used part of the year while blocks of compacted snow are used to build the famous igloo that provides effective protection against the subzero temperatures. Except for driftwood along the coastal areas, the only fuel available is oils from the marine mammals (seals, walrus, et al.). The careful use of a small flame from a stone dish of oil in these shelters gives off sufficient heat to keep the interior above the freezing point. The clothing of Arctic peoples, especially the Polar Inuit, is rightfully famous for its efficiency in protecting the wearer. The use of caribou or polar bear skins in double layers enables movement and survival in all weather by creating what has been described as a "microclimate." Nevertheless, despite all this protection, the people still have shown effective acclimatization to the coldest temperatures on this planet.

In general, native Arctic peoples have a higher metabolic rate that is fueled by diets high in protein and fat. The studies of the Inuit record that their metabolic rates are 40 percent higher than European controls; even under warmer conditions, they exceeded the controls by 13 percent. These higher rates enabled the maintenance of higher skin temperatures and there was greater peripheral circulation, especially in the hands and feet. Their higher metabolic rate cannot be explained on the basis of diet alone because acculturated Inuits who have adopted a Western type diet maintained rates higher than even those Europeans who were well acclimated to Arctic conditions (Le Blanc, 1975).

Thermal Stresses: Some Conclusions

Humans have the capacity to endure temperature extremes they encounter in various parts of the globe. Through physiological adjustments, internal homostasis can be maintained. Conservation or dissipation of metabolic heat may be accomplished by finely regulating subcutaneous circulation through alternating dilating or constricting blood vessels. The variation in the metabolism is another basic physiological process; if body heat is lost at a rapid rate, the metabolism can increase, or it may decrease in hot environments to reduce heat load, aiding the dissipation processes. The stresses and the diet encountered during growth results in certain body forms. These variations in form can aid in heat lost or be conserved through radiation. Choices in the use of various technologies like shelter, clothing, timed activities, and dietary selection influence survival in harsh climatically challenging environments. The end result of our physiological acclimatization depends to a large degree on these biobehavioral interactions.

Because body heat loss is proportional to surface area, climate also influences BMR differences among populations even with the traditional variation in clothing use. The higher the mean annual temperature, the lower the average metabolic rates of a population. Tropical populations average lower rates than do temperate or Arctic peoples since less body heat is lost in warmer environments. Some ethnic variation has been reported because Europeans, even after they have acclimatized to an Arctic-type diet, still record a lower metabolic rate than do Inuit, however. Disease states as well as hormonal balances also play a role in varying the metabolism; hypothyroid conditions reduce metabolism, for example, while increases in thyroid activity or disease infections elevate the metabolic rate and body temperature.

Applied to humans, the physics of heat production and exchange lead to an expectation of persons of a certain body form relative to climate, and this is what we find. People inhabiting cold environments tend to be heavier, with proportionate shorter limbs and higher subcutaneous fat; metabolic rates are also higher. Tropical residents are shorter, lighter in weight, and more linear in bodily proportions. Their metabolisms are also relatively lower and they have less subcutaneous fat. However, there are numerous exceptions, and it is difficult to separate diet quality and quantity from climate effects on growth and body form. Malnourished children grow slower and become shorter adults, and their response to energy deprivation is even more pronounced under cold stress conditions.

A notable exception to the correlation of body size with temperature is the Polynesian people who inhabit islands scattered over the wide reaches of the Pacific. As described above, these people, especially Samoans, are noted for their large sizes and high BMI that is comparable to Arctic and sub-Arctic populations. One explanation offered is related to the cold conditions encountered during their voyages in open canoes.

Between 3,000 and 4,000 years ago Polynesians began to extend their voyages farther and farther into the vast Pacific, probably from bases in the western Pacific scattered about the Solomon Islands. The voyages were made in open sailing canoes and extended over several weeks. During this time, the sailors were exposed to the cold, wet conditions found at sea, even in the tropics. The wind-chill factor plus inability to shelter one's body from the sea spray caused body heat loss that could be life threatening. The rate of loss of body heat depended on body proportions. Houghton (1996) graphically describes these conditions encountered by these early seafarers and argues that the largest, heaviest individuals had the best chance of surviving the trip. He noted that some of the largest and most muscular people are found in Oceania, and, far from being an exception to Bergmann's rule, their bodily proportions conform to the expected. The conditions that their ancestors were exposed to during the crossing of open ocean selected for those individuals who could grow large and accumulate body fat rapidly. Certainly, experiences of many modern-day sailors document the conditions at sea, and physiological experiments record the variation in rates of heat loss that closely correlate with body proportion and composition. A thinner individual with higher surface-to-mass ratio will lose heat faster, undergoing a drop in body temperature three times as fast as a larger, heavier person.

This ability of the Polynesians to gain weight rapidly and increase fat stores worked well to enhance survival of their ancestors but is a disadvantage when they shift to a Western diet. They gain weight, become obese, and suffer from one of the highest diabetic rates in the world. Another people who are exceptions to the BMI-temperate climate correlation are the Tohono Otami (Papago) of Southern Arizona. These desert dwellers also have a rapid response to surplus food intake and quickly gain weight to the point of obesity and suffer from diabetes. Though their ancestors did not share cold stress experiences similar to those of Polynesians, the Tohono Otami do have much the same response to overnutrition. The sequel leading to diabetes in both populations suggests similar genetic factors that will be discussed in Chapter 9.

In sum, humans have a great deal of plasticity in their responses to climatic temperatures and these responses are measured by their metabolism, nutrition needs, growth, and body form. Ethnic groups appear to differ in all these factors, but how much is due to acclimatization or genetic adaptation is not known. Unraveling the influences of environment and genes remains a challenge.

HIGH ALTITUDE ENVIRONMENTS: STRESSES AND RESPONSES

The earth is surrounded by an envelope of gases that consist mostly of nitrogen (78 percent) and oxygen (21 percent); this atmosphere is the densest at sea level (barometric pressure, 760 mm). Atmospheric density declines with elevation, the distance above sea level or altitude, and nitrogen and oxygen content decreases though the proportions remain the same. This thinner air has important consequences for plant and animal life, and well-defined environmental zones exist in the mountains because of the lower oxygen pressure. For example, trees do not grow above an elevation of approximately 4,000 meters (m) (13,000 ft.), whereas grass and certain herbaceous plants that are used as pasture can grow up to 5,500 m (18,000 ft.). Some important food plants like grains and potatoes can grow up to 5,000 meters. At these higher elevations, more of the shorter wavelengths of solar radiation (ultraviolet and cosmic rays) penetrate the thinner air. There is also greater radiant energy heat loss so temperatures are colder than at lower elevations of the same latitude. The conditions in an alpine environment that create microclimatological stresses are listed in Table 6-11.

Though the net effect of all of these stresses makes life at high altitudes very unpleasant and harsh, over one hundred million people have been living in these demanding regions since prehistoric times. Humans have developed certain

TABLE 6-11   Environmental Stress at High Altitude

Hypoxia (abnormally low levels of oxygen)
Intense ultraviolet radiation
Cold (greater radiant heat loss)
Aridity (owing to high winds and low humidity)
Limited nutritional base (due to reduced plant and animal fertility)

physiological and cultural means to cope with the stresses of an alpine environment. Cultural adjustments can alleviate the effects of cold temperature and high winds. For example, the use of shelter and dark clothing, which absorbs 95 percent of the sun's radiant heat (versus the 30 percent that light-colored clothing absorbs) are ways of protecting against the intense cold and UVR. The location of dwellings at strategic points in the valleys can compensate to some degree for the rough terrain. Especially adapted food crops and animals are raised on slopes above the villages in the Andes, and combined farming and pastoral nomadism in practiced in the Himalayans. By skillful use of resources and terrain, humans have been able to thrive over the millennia in these geographic regions of limited resources. Adaptation to the low-oxygen pressures of the rarefied air is another matter, however. This requires not only culture adaptation, but also certain physiological adjustments to enable individuals to sustain near-normal activities at higher elevations. Some individuals appear better able to adjust than others as shown by *high-altitude natives* (HANs).

Oxygen Requirements and High-Altitude Adaptations

Human physiology requires a certain minimum amount of oxygen for normal tissue function, approximately 40 mm as measured in terms of barometric pressure.[11] The partial pressure of oxygen (pO_2) in the arteries must be maintained at or near 95 mm for delivery of the 40 mm to the tissues.[12] The respiratory system, hemoglobin (Hb), and circulatory system function to provide the required oxygen. In the dense atmosphere, at sea level, the human circulatory system readily diffuses the inspired air through the lung tissue into the capillaries where oxygen is combined with hemoglobin to an *arterial saturation* (SaO_2) of 98 percent of its capacity. The oxygenated hemoglobin is then distributed by the circulatory system, providing the amounts of oxygen needed. It is more difficult at high altitude, however, as oxygen saturation decreases with a decline in atmospheric pressure.

At 3,000 meters (10,000 feet) elevation, pO_2 in the alveoli (the air sacks of the lungs) declines from 104 to 67 mm and SaO_2 is reduced to 90 percent. Now tissue oxygen supply becomes a critical problem and a person is confronted with *hypoxia*,

---

[11]Atmospheric pressures are measured in terms of the height of a column of mercury, as for example in a laboratory barometer familiar to generations of students. Hence, the air pressure at sea level will force the mercury column to a height of about 760 mm that will fluctuate up or down depending on the air pressures of a passing weather front.

[12]Partial pressure of oxygen is its proportion of air, 21 percent.

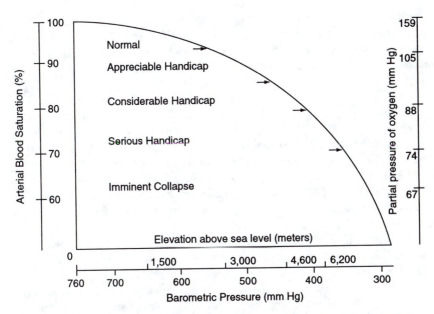

FIGURE 6-11 Oxygen Saturation of Arterial Blood at Altitude. (Source: Adapted and modified from Pace, N., *Man at Altitude*, 1961, Charles C Thomas, Springfield, IL.)

a decrease below normal levels of oxygen. The degree of hypoxia and its effects vary with altitude and work level; exercise or even simple movement may be restricted. Figure 6-11 lists the percent of oxygen saturation of arterial blood and the degree of handicap to human activities at several altitudes. There is sufficient atmospheric oxygen and arterial saturation for normal activity up to about 2,300 m altitude. Appreciable handicap is experienced above that elevation and becomes considerable at 3,000 m where oxygen delivery becomes more difficult.

This major stress at high altitudes, low oxygen pressure, stimulates metabolic changes to maintain a necessary level of oxygen in circulation throughout the body. There are several physiological adjustments to hypoxia that can be made; some are of long-range benefit and require a period of time for the person to acclimate to lower oxygen pressure. Certain adjustments are made immediately when a *low-altitude native (LAN)*, acclimatized to sea-level pressures, moves up to high altitude. These physiological responses are most acute at first, but they gradually decrease as other, more long-term compensations become effective.

Acclimatization to Hypoxia

The immediate reaction to lowered atmospheric oxygen is increased respiration rate that brings larger volumes of air into contact with the lung tissues. The tidal volume (quantity of air per breath) increases as hyperventilation declines over time and returns to near-normal levels after approximately a year as other mechanisms begin to compensate for lower atmospheric oxygen. The lungs begin to function more efficiently; diffusion through the respiratory membrane of lungs become more efficient, easing the exchange of gases at a lower pressure differential. Given the respiratory requirements for acclimatization, lung size and function appear to differ somewhat between HANs and LANs in many respects as described below.

An effect of this hyperventilation is a decrease in the level of carbon dioxide (CO_2) that causes the blood to become more alkaline. This rise in pH must be adjusted by the kidneys through excretion of greater quantities of sodium bicarbonate to maintain an acid-base balance of the blood at near-normal levels. The change in pH affects the hemoglobin's attraction for oxygen. The *oxygen disassociation curve*, the measure of hemoglobin—oxygen affinity, is altered by certain red-cell enzymes and the carbon dioxide in the tissues. This enables hemoglobin molecules to release more oxygen through tissue capillaries or bind more as the red cell passes through lung capillaries, depending on blood pH.

The second hypoxic response is a greater cardiac output to increase blood flow through the blood vessels of lung tissue and throughout arterial circulation. The heart's stroke volume (quantity of blood per beat) will increase and resting pulse rate will rise from 70 to 105 beats per minute. The pulse rate will decline to near-normal levels after a few days, but stroke volume will remain higher than at sea level.

A third adjustment to altitude occurs over several weeks as the blood-forming tissues increase synthesis of red blood cells. The volume of cells (hematocrit) will rise to over 50 percent of total blood volume. This offers a greater quantity of hemoglobin to transport more oxygen. As residence at altitude continues, more capillaries will open up in the lung tissues, further increasing the rate of oxygen diffusion.

Several studies of long-term residents at altitudes above 4,500 meters have confirmed this change in red-cell density. Hemoglobin (Hb) concentration increases from fifteen grams per tenth of a liter of blood to eighteen or more (15 gm/dl to 18 gm/dl), thereby increasing the oxygen-carrying capacity per unit volume of blood. This will increase oxygen delivered to the tissues by about the same amount as it would be at sea level, where people average a lower Hb concentration. This form of response is not without its costs, however, because the greater number of blood cells per unit volume increases blood viscosity, making it more difficult for the heart to pump a given volume. This raises questions about the actual benefit of an increased number of blood cells (Ballew et al., 1989).

Table 6-12 summarizes the various short- and long-term mechanisms involved in human response to hypoxia. Considering all of these factors, especially respiratory and cardiovascular responses, humans have a physiological plasticity to acclimatize to higher elevations. This ability varies, depending on age, health, and physical condition. Trained athletes have an advantage over sedentary persons, and children may grow and become well-adapted adults; their oxygen delivery systems are far advanced over their sea-level peers. Though these adjustments to hypoxia at high altitudes enable relatively normal physiological functions, there are limits. Human activity and settlements extend only to about 5,000 (16,000 ft.) though herdsmen and miners may work at 5,800 m, but at a great cost to their health and with a shortened life span. Bolivian

TABLE 6-12   Human Acclimatizations to Hypoxia

Red Blood Cells
An Increase in number.

Hemoglobin-Oxygen Disassociation Curve
  An increase in an enzyme (DPG) in the red blood cells decreases the affinity of
  hemoglobin for oxygen, which in turn enhances the oxygen release to the tissues.

Circulation
  An Increase in cardiac output during the first days of exposure.

Capillaries
  An Increase in capillary network to aid in oxygen diffusion to the tissues.

Ventilation
  Hyperventilation occurs during the first year of exposure, which increases arterial
  oxygen saturation.

Cellular Metabolism
  Several cellular changes have been reported in LANs that increase tissue adaptation to
  low-oxygen pressure.

tin miners average only about eight years of life after they begin laboring in the mines, for example. Adaptation or acclimatization can be only partial because our species has evolved, and survives best, in the denser atmosphere found below 3,000 m.

Certain populations, however, appear to be more efficient in their responses to hypoxia. They seem to be better able to endure the stresses at a high altitude, because of acclimatization throughout their long history of residence at these higher elevations. The natives of the Altiplano area of the Andes, mainly the Quechua and Aymara, have several characteristics that imply genetic adaptation to such environments. The inhabitants of the Himalayan plateau are likewise well adapted to the rigors of altitude.

Characteristics of High-Altitude Populations

Certain high-altitude environments have been occupied for at least 10,000 years in South America and up to 20,000 years in parts of Asia. Though poor in resources, such areas—the high plains of Ethiopia and the Atlas Mountains in Africa, eastern Turkey, Iran in the Middle East, the Himalayas and Tibetan Plateau, and the Andes in South America—have sustained millions of people. The best known area, perhaps, is the high plateau (Altiplano) of the central Andes, which spreads over 400,000 square miles across parts of five countries, from Ecuador in the north to Chile in the south. More isolates, the Himalayan mountain range encompasses nearly one million square miles of the Tibetan plateau.

Today's residents of the Himalayan plateau (4,000 m average elevation, 13,000 ft.) and the South American Altiplano, especially in Peru, have provided an excellent opportunity for the study of human adaptation to altitude. The question of functional and genetic adaptation has been investigated for more than a half century among the Quechua of Peru who have shown a remarkable ability to sustain life at the greatest limits of human habitation (from 3,000 to 5,000 m). More recently, populations in

Nepal and across the Tibetan plateau (average elevation of 4,000 m) have been added to studies of high-altitude adaptations. In this section we consider some of the findings of these studies and how they may add to our understanding of human adaptability and biological diversity.

Body Size and Growth.   One of the frequently described characteristics of high altitude natives (HANs) is their smaller size for most body dimensions compared to low altitude natives (LANs). Quechua children who have lived all their lives at about 4000 m grow considerably slower than do their "co-ethnics," or Quechua children, living at lower elevation. Both of these groups fared less well than groups of Quechua children measured ten to fifteen years later. All, it must be noted, lagged far behind in their growth than groups of American children except in one dimension, chest circumference.

In the district of Nuñoa, of Southern Peru, the reduced atmospheric oxygen at 3,800 to 4,000 m affects both growth and work performance. Even small altitude differences within the district have effected a difference in adolescence growth (Frisancho and Baker, 1970). Other factors besides altitude affect growth differences as described by comparisons of children measured in 1964 with those measured in 1983. The children of the 1983 group were taller, but with less difference noted in adults as shown in Table 6-13a and b. The size of the Nuñoans, the smallest of any Andean population, is affected by seasonal food scarcity exacerbated by socioeconomic differences (Leatherman et al., 1995). Lower income groups rely more on a traditional diet of locally produced foods whose quantity changes over the course of a year and the people suffer greater seasonal variation. As costs rise, they are able to purchase less of the high-energy processed foods so their caloric intake varies. In contrast, upper-income families make use of a wider variety of nontraditional foods purchased at the markets, and they are able to maintain higher energy intakes throughout the year. The results are seen in their children's growth patterns that exceed those of the lower income groups.

These economic improvements and, hence, higher nutritional inputs caused a secular trend in growth as discussed earlier in this chapter. Such trends have been reported in both Tibetan and Sherpa children. The 5- to 12-year-old Sherpas measured in 1982 were up to 8 cm taller and 5 kg heavier than those measured in 1972. Tibetans, likewise, gained between 6 to 12 cm in height and 3 to 8 kg in weight between 1965 and 1991. The rarefied atmosphere of their environments did not change, obviously, but the economics of both populations did. Over the years there was an improvement in the socioeconomics of both groups, leading to better nutrition and health care that contributed to increased height, weight, body fat (determined by thicker skinfold measurements). Such secular changes suggest that nutrition levels of high-altitude populations may be more significant than low oxygen for growth and development (Weitz et al., 2000). However, Tibetans remain shorter and lighter than Chinese national standards and the Han Chinese living in the general region, but at lower elevations.

Chronological and Developmental Age.   Another growth factor that shows significant differences among high-altitude populations is retarded skeletal development. Compared with U.S. standards, the growth of the skeleton is delayed and the epiphyses

TABLE 6-13a Height (cm) and Weight (kg) of Children at Altitude (Males)

Groups	3 years Ht.	3 years Wt.	6 years Ht.	6 years Wt.	9 years Ht.	9 years Wt.	12 years Ht.	12 years Wt.	15 years Ht.	15 years Wt.	18 years Ht.	18 years Wt.
USA												
NCHS-I[1]	95.0	14.5	115.4	21.1	133.2	30.2	148.4	41.6	169.2	58.8	176.8	69.1
Asia												
China(PRC)[2]	95.1	14.0	114.7	19.2	130.6	25.3	144.2	33.0	162.0	46.9	—	—
Tibetan[3]	—	—	113.8	18.8	121.1	22.3	144.1	34.3	153.7	43.3	165.4	55.7
So. Amer.												
Quechua[4]	88.2	14.0	107.8	19.7	121.6	25.3	133.0	31.7	149.4	44.5	160.0	57.2
Quechua[5]	84.5	11.0	104.2	18.7	118.5	24.2	129.5	29.8	144.0	38.0	153.7	48.2
Aymara[1]	86.4	12.0	111.3	19.7	119.5	22.5			153.0	42.4	155.0	

TABLE 6-13b Height (cm) and Weight (kg) of Children at Altitude (Females)

Groups	3 years Ht.	3 years Wt.	6 years Ht.	6 years Wt.	9 years Ht.	9 years Wt.	12 years Ht.	12 years Wt.	15 years Ht.	15 years Wt.	18 years Ht.	18 years Wt.
USA												
NCHS-I	93.6	14.0	114.4	20.2	132.0	29.3	150.2	42.1	161.7	55.1	163.8	
Asia												
China(PRC)	91.5	12.8	110.0	18.4	123.4	22.9	138.7	31.4	142.9	40.2	151.1	
Tibet	—	—	113.5	19.2	125.0	22.4	146.9	36.4	151.2	42.6	155.0	52.0
So. Amer.												
Quechua	88.4	13.6	104.8	18.8	120.1	24.8	137.9	35.7	147.0	46.5	148.9	
Quechua	85.5	11.3	103.9	17.0	119.0	22.4	131.3	30.0	141.6	42.9	147.8	
Aymara	91.5	13.6	108	18.8	118.5	23.7			144.0	47.7	150.7	56.3

Source: 1. Eveleth and Tanner, 1990; 2. Leonard et al., 1990; 3. Weitz et al., 2000; 4. Leatherman et al., 1995; 5. Frisancho and Baker, 1970.

fuse later than in low-altitude populations. There is a one- to two-year delay in Andean children and two- to four-year delay among Tibetans until the age of 16. The gap between chronological age (CA) and developmental age (DA) narrows through the period of slow prolonged growth of late adolescence until age 20 when both populations approach chronological age standards. In females, the gap between DA and CA is about one year less at each stage. The developmental delays in both sexes contribute to a slower linear growth and a later age for achievement of adult stature, age 22 in males and age 20 in females. This slower development may account for the short stature of HANs (Frisancho, 1995).

In addition, there is a retardation in the development of secondary sexual characteristics; little dimorphism is seen until about the fourteenth year because the onset of puberty is delayed. Growth is slow and prolonged in males, and they experience only a slight adolescent growth spurt. Andean males achieve only about a 5-cm annual increment in height at their peak compared to the 10 or 12 cm gained by U.S. males. Females fare somewhat better at high altitudes than males. Nuño girls experience a moderate adolescent growth spurt, only about 20 percent less than in U.S. populations. This peak in adolescent growth occurs later by two years and is prolonged (Frisancho, 1995).

Menarche occurs, on the average, a year later among Andeans at high altitude than among their counterparts at sea level (13.5 years versus 12.8 years). Delays until between 13.4 years and 14.3 years of age are experienced by Europeans at altitude compared to the 11.9 to 12.7 range at sea level (see Table 6-5). Among Tibetans, menarche occurs at age 18.1; this is one of the oldest ages recorded (Moore et al., 1998).

Reproduction. Because of the difficulty of breeding cattle and horses at altitude, it has long been postulated that temporary infertility occurs when humans migrate to high-altitude regions. Some indications of the human reproductive system's response have been found. Comparisons of testosterone secretions decline by 50 percent or greater over three days but then return to near sea-level values after a week. Sperm counts decrease to approximately 70 percent of their sea-level values, and the frequency of abnormal forms with lower motility increase with altitude. Luteinizing hormones decline and menstrual cycles of LANs are disrupted as well as the delays in menarche cited above. Comparisons of HAN with LAN women show a shorter birth interval among HANs than LANs at altitude (TFR of 8.6 for Quechua women versus 4.5 for Mestizo women). There is also greater risk of fetal loss and a higher incidence of congenital abnormalities (Hoff and Abelson, 1976). The overall effects of high altitude on fertility are reflected in higher infant mortality and lower birth weights which exist to some degree among both high-altitude and low-altitude natives.

Birth Weights. Infants born of healthy, well-fed mothers normally weigh around 3,200 to 3,400 gm (7–7.5 lbs). This weight is significantly lower when the mother is malnourished, ill, or alcohol or drug addicted. There is an influence of altitude also, with a decline in birth weight of about 100 gm per 1,000 meters. Healthy women living at 1,600 to 2,100m in the Rocky Mountains give birth to infants weighing between 3,035 to 3,297 gm and this range declines to 2,655 to

3,065 gm at 3,100 m. In the Andes and Himalayas, birth weights illustrate even more clearly the effects of hypoxia at altitude. At 4,300 m, mothers living in the Nuñoa district give birth to infants weighing between 2,800 to 2,982 gm. This represents a startling difference in fetal growth when compared with their co-ethnics living near sea level whose infants weigh 3,000 to 3,400 gm. In several Himalayan populations significant differences are also seen; birth weights average 3,300 gm at 1,200 m compared to 2,700 gm at 3,600 m (Moore et al., 1998).

Infants of lower birth weight are at a greater risk; their mortality is higher, and congenital abnormality is more frequent. A probable cause is the lowered oxygen levels reaching the fetus when the mother resides at a high altitude. Certain adjustments, however, are made to oxygen deprivation. The placenta is enlarged and has increased vascularization, and the fetus grows more slowly. Females of different ethnic groups, however, have varying success in coping with low-oxygen levels. Mestizo women[13] in Puño, Peru (elevation 3,850 m), have low-birth-weight infants (about 2,500 gm) about 23 percent of the time, whereas highland native women produce only 10 percent low-birth-weight infants (Mazess, 1975). Another response to hypoxia during preganancy is offered by the examples of Tibetan women whose lower extremity circulation is redistributed to increase blood flow to the uterine artery compared with Chinese women living at altitude who do not. Andean women do alter circulation patterns somewhat by increased diameter of the uterine artery to cope with the oxygen needs of the fetus and by a higher ventilation during pregnancy that increases arterial blood saturation.

Himalayan and Andean People at Altitude

The millions living in the valleys and plateaus of these large regions have different histories and prehistoric origins. The Andes were probably occupied within the last ten thousand years while archeological evidence can trace occupation of the Himalayan region back at least twice that long. The millions living in these areas and their long history of acclimatization to hypoxia warrant some comparisons. With increased scientific study of the Tibetan and Sherpa, questions were raised about their responses to altitude stress in comparison with the Quechua of Peru. The first assumptions were that these peoples living tens of thousands of miles apart, but in similar environments, had acclimatized in the same way to the rarified atmosphere of their respective homelands. Though broad similarities were identified, some significant differences began to emerge.

Body Form.   Though Quechua children lag behind in most measures of growth, they show acceleration in growth of the thoracic region. This results in the larger chest circumference and barrel-chested appearance of the Andean native. European children growing up in the Andes also have greater chest dimensions as

---

[13]Individuals of Native American and European ancestry of a degree not specified.

adults after a lifelong exposure to lower oxygen pressures. The European response is developmental, while the Quechua is described as genetic since Quechua children growing up near sea level show a similar growth acceleration though it is not as great as their high altitude relatives. This accelerated growth of the thoracic region had been presumed to be an adaptation, a means of passing a greater volume of air over the lung membranes each breath (Frisancho, 1995).

Interestingly, populations of the Himalayas do not have expanded chest dimensions to the extent seen in Andean populations (Greska and Beall, 1989). Chest dimensions relative to stature are smaller among people of the Himalayan region when compared with Andeans. Differences are seen between HANs and LANs of the Himalayas, however, which suggests a developmental effect similar to that seen among European children raised at altitude. The stimulus of hypoxia to increase respiratory rate could act to increase growth in chest size of LAN children though the extent of response is greater among Andeans.

Ventilatory Response.   Increases in chest size suggest larger lung volumes measured by forced vital capacity (FVC) the largest amount of air that can be expired after maximum inspiratory effort. This FVC is used as an index of pulmonary function in general and has been used to compare HANs with LANs. In addition, the lung tissues of HANs have a greater vascularization and a lower resistance to blood flow in the pulmonary arteries and capillaries, allowing an increased capacity to diffuse gases compared with LANs, even after they have undergone a period of acclimatization to high altitude (Frisancho, 1995).

These relationships between size, structure, blood flow, and efficiency in oxygen transport came under question in later studies of Tibetans. Their adaptation did not seem to depend upon increases in chest size as much as an alteration in respiratory responses. Measured in terms of resting respiration rates, Tibetans maintained a rate one-and-a-half times the Andeans (19.7 L/min versus 13.4 L/min). Their response to hypoxic tests were twice that of Andeans; ventilation was increased by 0.93 L/min with each percentage drop in arterial oxygen saturation compared with the 0.45 L/min change for Andeans. These responses, similar to those of LANs, suggest that Tibetans have achieved successful adaptations to altitude by different means than the Andean natives (Beall et al., 1997). Another factor to consider is that lung volumes of the two groups are not that different and that Tibetan volume is increased with little change in thoracic dimensions by lowering the diaphragm. This and maintenance of higher ventilatory responses enable adaptation with little change in blood cell concentration.

Blood Cell and Hemoglobin Concentration.   There are several differences in oxygen transport and blood cell concentration in Andean and Tibetan populations. The Andeans are known for an increase in red blood cell production in response to hypoxia. Hematocrit rises to over 55 percent in Aymaran males in Bolivian compared with 40 to 45 percent for Tibetan males. The Tibetans will also increase blood cell production, but there must be a stronger hypoxic stimulus encountered at 4,000 m (Beall et al., 1998). As noted above, the greater number of red cells translates into more hemoglobin per unit volume of whole blood, which, in turn, means a greater oxygen-carrying capacity. Tibetans males have hemoglobin concentrations of 15.6 gm/dl (males) and 14.2 gm/dl (females), which is closest to LANs, in contrast with 19.1 gm/dl and 15.2 gm/dl for Andean males and females, respectively.

These differing concentrations of up to 20 percent more hemoglobin in Andeans facilitates a higher oxygen saturation—SaO_2 of 92.1 percent versus 89.4 percent in Tibetans. This supports a conclusion that Andeans are better adapted because of their higher saturation rate aided by higher pulmonary arterial pressures; other cardiovascular functions work for Tibetans' adaptations (Beall et al., 1999).

Andeans versus Tibetans.   Alternative responses to hypoxia have been demonstrated by many studies of LAN migrants at high altitude and a wide individual variation was seen. With the diversity of results it is difficult to partition out a particular trait or traits of the circulatory system or respiratory system and say which are the most beneficial to survival at higher elevations. Comparisons of peoples of the Andes and Himalayas, however, show some advantages of different responses to hypoxia. In broad, general terms Tibetans adapt by *higher respiration rates*, measured by resting rate, and by a high ventilatory response to hypoxia. In contrast, respiratory rates are lower in Andeans, but they increase hemoglobin concentration. Both populations use combinations of heart and lung functions to assist their adaptation to life at altitude. The degree of their success is demonstrated by the survival of large populations over many generations

CONCLUSIONS: COMPLEX TRAITS AND THEIR ADAPTATIONS

Most of the complex traits we possess enable us to adapt to a range of environmental conditions by short-term responses we call acclimatizations, or physiological adjustments, to environmental stresses we encounter at each stage of the life cycle. This plasticity depends on our genome that contains certain genetic components that enable us to resist disease, cope with malnutrition, endure heat or cold, or survive at altitude. It is hard to identify which of these genes enable what response. What can be said, though, is that our genetic combinations and their products make us a kind of physiological "jack-of-all-trades" enabling us to live anywhere and do anything within broad limits, aided by our behavioral/cultural capacity. Figure 6-12 diagrams the interaction of these forces that form our complex phenotypes or traits.

In the measures of adaptation, short or long term, no single trait can be identified as essential to survival under a particular environmental stress. There are several ways that humans acclimate to altitude stress, and people have used all or a combination of means to do so. Thermoregulation—the maintenance of body temperature—is achieved in varying ways by people under cold or heat stress. Likewise, a number of ways have been developed to gain essential nutrients, and no natural diet has been defined. There are no

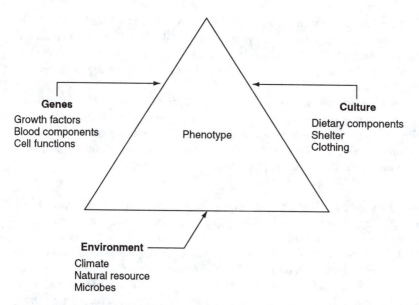

FIGURE 6-12   Model of Major Influences on Phenotypic Expression. Source: Modified and redrawn from Baker, 1997.

people living at a primordial level—a band of primitives—to demonstrate earlier forms of human adaptations. The numerous populations (sometimes called primitives) that have been studied together with people of industrial societies show a species-specific range of responses. Each population can readily adapt to changes of environmental stresses. *Homo sapiens*, in sum, is flexible in biological and behavioral responses. Our perception of easily perceived traits of size and form, of physiological variables, and of custom and tradition often mislead us in our search for type of adaptation.

chapter

7

Human Variability, Behavior, and Racism

Individuals vary considerably in their behavior, as they do in many of their biological traits. One does not have to be an expert to recognize this. Just as we perceive differences in human size, shape, and color, we readily differentiate between persons on the basis of their personality traits. These traits, however, are even more complex than those polygenic traits already discussed. Behavior is influenced to an extraordinary degree by cultural factors. Family, religion, and nation have profound influences that establish lifetime patterns of behavior; even the historic era in which we live shapes many of our behavioral attributes, as any comparisons between generations in the twentieth century will show. A problem arises when we attempt to quantify such attributes and try to draw conclusions about an individual's worth or quality or aptitude. All too often we merely seek an easy answer and rely on group membership as the key to individual evaluation. Just as with characteristics of color, size, and shape, our perceptions are based on ill-founded assumptions about heredity and classification.

The study of human behavioral diversity is further complicated not only by the racism of group identity, but also by confusion of social and biological definitions of race. For example, by the end of the nineteenth century, beliefs in "higher" and "lower" races reached a peak as achievements of entire nations or civilizations were attributed to the "superior germ plasm" of their citizens. Most frequently the Nordic race was described as the bearer of this superior germ plasm. The French aristocrat Count Gobineau dedicated the contents of his four-volume series, *The Inequality of Races*, to an attempt to prove that the Nordics, whom he described as the "bearers of the lamp of civilization," were above all other races. The rest of the species, including the bulk of other Europeans, were grouped into races that were inferior. According to Gobineau, "It was the Nordic who created the high civilizations of the past and who were responsible for the formation of modern states" (Gobineau, quoted in Barzun, 1965:54).

This conviction of racial superiority supported a rationalization for the treatment of the aboriginal peoples whom Europeans encountered during their world exploration and colonization. Confronted with the high mortality and declining populations that they were no doubt responsible for, the colonial government officials talked glibly of "a passing of an inferior race." The attitude was especially evident in New Zealand following the defeat of the Maori armies; these Polynesians, with their highly developed tribal government and efficient use of land, presented special problems of conquest. The concept of inferior race, however, still prevailed as summed up by one official: "Taking all things into consideration, the disappearance of the race (Maori) is scarcely subject for much regret. They are dying out in a quick, easy way, and are being supplanted by a superior race" (Belich, 1986:299). This kind of statement that could have come from officials virtually anywhere in the far-flung European colonies was not surprising because it expressed the sentiment of the time. Even among the medical missionaries, who were charged with tending to the physical and spiritual needs of the colonized people, there was the firm belief that the "race has run out" and, after two or three generations, only a remnant would remain (Fenton, 1859:31). Many other examples were offered from peoples around the world; all non-Europeans, by definition, were incapable of higher development and, confronted with the impact of civilization, the inferior peoples would perish. There was a scaling of inequality even among the Europeans; southern Europeans were placed lower than northern populations, and eastern Europeans were at the bottom of the scale. Such beliefs have persisted even into recent decades, as shown by the dominant theme of a book that revived racism in the 1970s: "It must not be forgotten that certain races of man not only never attained independently to the status of civilization, but never independently reached the intermediate phase" (Baker, 1974:528).

Such brief statements define the direction of writings that sought to understand human societies in terms of heredity. Of course today we no longer speak of "superior germ plasm" as the source of civilization, nor do we define race and national character. Or do we? There has been a resurrection of such beliefs by anti-immigration groups and some social scientists in the last decade. We can now reread the concepts of Gobineau, newly refurbished with the language of modern genetics: The processes by which nations are created are largely biological and America's core comes from European stock. It then follows that admitting large numbers of non-European immigrants will be dysgenic (equivalent to race suicide). Bluntly stated by some writers, people create cultures that express their genotypes (Rushton, 1995). The question of whether superior genotypes are carried by one or another ethnic group is explored in a long, statistically ladened argument by Herrnstein and Murray (1994). They postulate that since intelligence is largely hereditary (their assumption), immigration of those groups with lower intelligence (as scored by standard tests) will put a "downward" pressure on the national average. Since these low test scorers fall within the nonwhite category as defined by the Census Bureau, the threat of passive genocide by immigration is real to those who retain the race-purity myth of times gone by. This concern over passive genocide—the replacement of genes from one group with those of another—is based, however, on many ill-founded assumptions about behavioral genetics and on an unbounded faith in psychological tests. This confidence in testing procedures and in heredity of behavioral traits is but a continuation of a long century of searching for an understanding of the differences among individuals and between societies.

RACE, NATIONS, AND RACISM

The revival of Mendelian genetics in 1900 offered a scientific background to the concepts of inherited inequality. If many physical characteristics were determined at conception by combinations of parental genes, it was then postulated that mental ability, aggression, and various social pathologies were also inherited. Theories of social reform and human behavior were decidedly influenced by this presumed evidence of particulate inheritance. Psychologists in the United States eagerly applied the new genetic theory to explain a host of social problems of the day. Criminality, delinquency, alcoholism, prostitution, and a long list of many other forms of socially deviate behavior were observed to occur more frequently in some families. Certain family lineages seemed to produce more than their share of criminals, alcoholics, and so on. Furthermore, these lineages were clustered into groups, often by nationality and region. These families provided a resource for the newly developing field of behavioral genetics, which in turn, provided a scientific basis for discrimination against groups of new immigrants classed as inferior by recently developed psychological tests.

The interest of authorities in the mental quality of the immigrants at the turn of the century was grounded in a firm conviction that certain racial groups, as well as certain national groups, were biologically inferior. This interest was heightened by the change in country of origin of the immigrants, which had been a worrisome problem for some time to many Americans involved in the eugenics movement that was dedicated to the improvement of the species. Before 1890, most immigrants came from western Europe, but by the turn of the century this source declined, and a so-called new immigration began. Eastern and southern Europe were the sources of this more recent migration, all with populations of non-Nordics. The newly devised mental tests provided a ready means of sorting out the undesirables. The results of comparisons of test scores achieved by the new immigrants with those of U.S. citizens of Nordic descent were interpreted as a decline in immigrant intelligence, which was believed to be a grave threat to Nordic survival. Psychologists like Henry Goddard and Carl Brigham, a participant in the testing program of army recruits during World War I, attributed this decline directly to the change in racial origin of the immigrants. Many writers warned that steps must be taken to preserve America's "precious heritage of germ plasm," and, in 1924, steps were taken in the form of restrictive immigration laws that limited the number of immigrants according to their national origin (reviewed in Cravens, 1978).

The immigrants streaming through Ellis Island during the early 1900s were a target for snap judgments about inferior behavior; if their poor performance on various tests did not give them away, their appearance and language would. They were smaller than the average American, some differed slightly in face form, and of course their clothing was a strange fashion (Figure 7-1). Certainly these were trivial differences, but significant to the scientists and immigration officials of the day. This set the theme— genetic determination of nations and cultures—for social research over the first decades of the twentieth century, and after a seemingly quiescent period, these ideas were revived decades later (Brimelow, 1995)

The modern-day feelings about inequality (now referred to by more subtle terms such as ethnic differences) are dealt with from a perspective of "birth dearth" or the lower fertility rates of peoples of European origins in contrast to "others." Such fertility differences contribute to an imbalance of population growth rates and, together with the high level of legal and illegal immigration, will result in a much lower proportion of western European stock. The implied or implicit concern is that such an ethnic imbalance will contribute to social turbulence (Wattenberg, 2004:18). Though this author discussed the changes of ethnic balances in the U.S. population, the same may be said of the United Kingdom and several other countries of western Europe. This illustrates, in a contemporary context, a growing concern with changes in national origins as industrialized nations become more dependent on immigrant workers.

There is no need at this point to review those strongly held beliefs that associate a particular form of behavior with certain national or racial groups. We have all heard

FIGURE 7-1   Photo of Immigrants on Ellis Island Awating Admission about 1900. (Library of Congress.)

such arguments many times. Consider, though, that if there is a wide genetic diversity within each major geographic unit (race) of the several biological traits that we have previously described, then there should be an equally wide range of those genes that may relate to people's behavior. Simply stated, there is a diversity of innate abilities, no matter how defined, in all groups of *Homo sapiens*. Just as the distribution of easily perceived traits was not understandable by clustering them into major geographical units, it is also impossible to talk of a racial variation of behavior. Never the less, we still do.

Behavioral Stereotypes

Stereotypes of mental ability are easy to imagine and hard to overcome. The categorizing of people according to some real or presumed type seems to offer a shortcut to understanding innate differences. But many of the behavioral distinctions among groups are more often due to cultural influences, socioeconomic status, or the physical environment than to genetic influence. Furthermore, anthropologists throughout the last century demonstrated that an observer's own cultural background greatly influences his or her judgment or perception, particularly if he or she is studying an aboriginal society that lacks a written language and whose people look and/or dress quite differently from members of the observer's group.

The cultural component is responsible for a great deal of variability, and often human societies are evaluated as being modern or primitive, simple or complex. The behavior of individuals participating in a culture other than our own differs from what we have come to accept as "standard" behavior. The contrasts are striking, particularly when the technology is rudimentary or simple, such as in the societies of New Guinea or Australia. The minds of these peoples have all too often been described as "primitive" because we of the Western world mistakenly equate technology with cultural development. Rather than make a value judgment though, it would be more logical and would contribute more to our understanding if each culture were considered an adaptation to the physical environment in which it is found. Whether it be the rigorous environment of the Australian "outback," which nurtured the culture of the Aborigines, or tropical rain forests of nearby New Guinea, the sociocultural framework of each enables the maintenance of human society of great complexity in response to environmental challenges.

Since aboriginal populations declined radically in the twentieth century and are less and less available for study, the attention of social scientists has turned more frequently to minorities defined by economic class and/or by ethnicity. Interpretation of the results of many such studies has frequently been used to argue that there is something innately inferior about an ethnic group. To the biological determinist, this would explain the higher rates of mortality, criminality, teen pregnancy, or the lower income, higher unemployment, and so on. A fact seldom noted by those who would explain social problems by reference to "inferior genes" is that many minorities around the world occupy a similar social position. New Zealand Maoris, Gypsies in Hungary, "guest" workers in Germany, Algerians in France, and Morocans in Spain are among the groups who should be mentioned because they represent a diversity of genetic ancestry but still share a similar relationship to the national majority population among which they live. The same stereotypes have been applied to these ethnic groups: They are lazy drunkards and/or thieves who produce large families of uneducable retarded children who grow up to become a burden on society.

In addition to minority groups, biological determinists have often described national character in a similar way: The antipathy, the hostile acts of aggression, and at times even warfare, between ethnic groups, sometimes even among close descendents, is said to be due to differences in genetic heritage. Darlington, a foremost human geneticist of his day, described the centuries of conflict between the English and Irish:

> This quarrel can be understood only in terms of the profound racial difference between the Gaelic-speaking natives and the English-speaking invaders, a difference which even today, after twenty generations of limited hybridization, is still not seriously blurred.
>
> The English were sober, industrious, mechanical, calculating and ruthless; characteristics invaluable in government. The native Irish by contrast were imaginative, unpredictable and even irresponsible. Their pre-Aryan and perhaps paleolithic speech had died out only in the ninth century and they had more left of their paleolithic instincts. (Darlington, 1969:449–450)

Thus, Darlington appeared to explain away a long and very complex sociopolitical history on the basis of persistence of "paleolithic instincts," whatever they are. The conflict continues in this century, and I am afraid that some fragments of this stereotype persists.

Special attention has repeatedly been directed to stereotypes of African Americans, especially to a supposed innate learning handicap marked by their lower than average performance on certain standardized tests. Of course, the difficulty of attempting to unravel the inheritance of learning ability of this or any group is confounded by the complexity of the learning processes, to say nothing of the lack of data on gene admixture (beyond skin color or self-identification) of the subjects examined by these tests. Even the detection of any genes affecting learning ability in an individual is not possible, as remains the case for many other polygenic traits that have unknown gene combinations. About all that the many studies have shown is that, as a group, African Americans have a lower average IQ, by a few points, than the white (read Euro-American) population. Much more has been made of this small difference than the data permit, especially when discussing genes, behavior, and race or ethnic group, because no control for gene admixture is ever made. That is, the individuals of the sample grouped as "black" in the United States are descendants of several generations of hybridization, and the European admixture varies widely. To expect an even distribution of genes from the African founders to their descendants four-hundred years later is to ignore Mendel's laws and return to concepts from the days of bloodlines and inheritance by blending.

Where do these beliefs in the biological inequality of minorities come from, and why are they so frequently repeated by otherwise distinguished scientists? Well, these beliefs come from personal bias, to begin with—from the uncritical acceptance of broad generalizations reinforced by erroneous data and sanctioned by statistical manipulation of tests designed to measure mental attributes. Writers of novels and travel books also had an influence, one that continues even today. Such influence spreads the stereotypes of cultures, nations, and peoples. It reinforces beliefs in personal perceptions and labels. Despite overwhelming evidence to the contrary, intuitive approaches to the study of human diversity have persisted, as the following quotation illustrates:

> Nature has color-coded groups of individuals so that statistically reliable predictions of their adaptability to intellectually rewarding and effective lives can easily be made and profitably be used by the pragmatic man in the street. (Shockley, 1972:307)

What about this color coding? Are there really such simple ways by which a "pragmatic man in the street" can evaluate the quality of another human being? Is it as easy as identifying a criminal type by the size of the nose or ears, as was proposed by Lombroso a century ago? Is "innate ability" as plain as the nose on your face or the shape of your head, or are many writers today again confusing and mixing traits that bear no relationship to one another? Cranial capacity or brain size is regaining its former popularity as a measure of intelligence, basic racial stocks are still retained as reference points, and testing as a measure of innate differences has undergone a resurgence.

Ethnic Group: Classification and Behavior

Identity of ethnic group membership may be useful for political purposes and necessary for certain government record keeping, and categorizing individuals has certainly been acceptable throughout our history. In any attempt to study trait inheritance, however, the same labels and categories do not apply. A nation's subdivision of its population relies on social and political considerations, as demonstrated by the continuing changes in the choices for self-identification by category on government forms. These are social classifications and bear little resemblance to the actual genetic composition of one's group as discussed in Chapter 1. We have entered a new era of an expanded understanding of our genome, and behavioral as well as biological research should acknowledge this fact. There is no racial behavior any more than there is an ethnic group behavior representative of underlying genetic causes.

Group classification based on some single attribute, such as geographic origin (e.g., Asian), language (e.g., Hispanic), or skin color (e.g., white versus nonwhite), ignores all other attributes and neglects to consider degree of admixture. Furthermore, the ethnic label, Asian, encompasses thousands of populations totaling over a billion-and-a-half people whose territory (17 million square miles) includes virtually every climate and environment on the planet. To assume that a few or even thousands of individuals selected from such a large, diverse group might be a representative sample of "Asians" is totally incorrect. The reader should not have to be reminded that "Hispanic" is also a label devoid of genetic meaning. It has gained prominent political status in the last two decades and includes people of diverse national and genetic origins. "White" or "nonwhite" identity is perhaps the most vague and meaningless of all. Who are included in one or the other group and how white or nonwhite does one have to be? There is considerable confusion over this seemingly simple question. Where, for example, do Hispanics fit in? The census forms allow for a person to identify as "either", but does regional origin (Europe or Mexico) matter? Fernandez reviewed multi-ethnicity and, in trying to unravel some of the complexity of what he calls "the melting pot of La Raza," concluded that region matters: "Mexican Americans make up the second largest non-White ethnic group in the United States" (1992:127). What does the label nonwhite really mean? Non-European, non-Western, or?

The confusion over color, origins, and genetics is even more extensive when the ethnic group African American is considered. Their ancestry is a mixture of African and European with a contribution of Native American genes, forming, in some areas, triracial hybrids (Pollitzer, 1972). The average of European admixture is given as 25 percent, based on comparisons of fifteen polymorphic loci (Chakraborty and Kidd, 1991), but this is only an average. The range of admixture is quite broad across the United States, less in small enclaves in South Carolina, and higher in urban centers of the Northeast. The large and widely dispersed populations of African origin in Central and South America and throughout the Caribbean add to the genetic heterogeneity of those we label African American or black. In addition, African ancestry is anything but homogeneous. African populations are as diverse as any in the world, as explained earlier, and the lineages of their New World descendants lead back to contributions from a variety of these populations. As noted in Chapter 4, slaves were imported into the Western Hemisphere from a broad geographic region. Even at a single port of entry, Charleston, South Carolina, between 1716 and 1807, the slave cargoes came from an area extending from Senegambia to Angola, a distance of about 3,000 miles.

The question of color classification is not answered, but there should be doubts about its use as a meaningful genetic category. If for no other reason, criticism of studies of group differences in intelligence can be made on these grounds: The studies are often carried out on groups whose actual genetic composition is not known. Nor is the group distinguished or identified in any way as a breeding population, and its recent ancestry and history are ignored. The only concern of group identification is with the social definition of race—again highlighting the error of confusing culture and biological variables. It is one thing to discuss genetic potential, gene frequency, or inherited ability within a breeding population whose members share a large number of genes in common. But it is another matter to discuss these variables in reference to a race or an ethnic group (socially, politically, or biologically defined).

Despite these problems, the claim has often been made that an admixture of European genes actually contributes to an increased IQ in African Americans, as if Caucasoids were a homogeneous group all possessing the same gene combinations, regardless of whether northern or southern, eastern or western European in origin. Such claims of effects of admixture on IQ are unfounded; data do not exist to support a contention that intelligence varies with degree of ancestry. In fact, there is no connection between the test performance of an individual and the number of that person's European ancestors. Estimates of the degree of European ancestry of 350 African American residents of Philadelphia were made by careful analysis of blood groups and serum proteins, which is possible because, as we discussed in Chapters 3 and 4, European and African populations differ in average frequencies of certain genetic markers. This method was used instead of asking the subjects to estimate their degree of European ancestry on the basis of known ancestors. With an estimate of their ancestry established through biochemical genetics methods, this group was given a variety of mental tests. Scarr and her associates reviewed the results and demonstrated that those persons with a high degree of African ancestry did no better and no worse than those individuals who had several European ancestors (Scarr, 1981; Scarr and Weinberg, 1978). Simply, genetic admixture did not influence test performance in this study.

Among other things, this Philadelphia study, and the twin studies described later, demonstrate that hereditary influences on behavior can only be studied when the ancestry and genetic admixture of each individual tested are known, and only when breeding population boundaries are established can interpopulation comparisons be made. These are difficult criteria to fulfill, of course, but any study that purports to examine genotypes and the behavioral phenotypes must carefully determine population composition. Anything less produces misleading data. This is particularly true because of the confusion that still surrounds race concepts and especially the identification of an individual's group membership. Is race/ethnic group membership made by self-identification, teacher's identification, or another method, for example? These problems are often ignored even when differences in social and biological classifications are admitted, as the following quotation illustrates:

> Although most of the studies of racial differences in intelligence are based on social definitions of race, it should be noted that there is usually a high correlation between the social and the biological definitions, and it is most unlikely that results of the research would be very different if the investigators had used biological rather than social criteria of race in selecting groups for comparison. (Jensen, 1971:16–17)

Jensen, a leading proponent of the racial inequality argument, knowingly mixed a social classification with a genetic one. I question his assumption that there is usually a high correlation between social and biological definitions. It has not been tested and, given the problems of admixture, self-identification, and the race concept, it is not likely to be. If he wished to argue that "American blacks" (or any group, for that matter) score lower on IQ tests than "American whites" because of some innate difference, then careful account must be taken of the genetic composition of each group. How can genetic determination be studied unless population admixture is known? What about the tests themselves? What do they, in fact, measure?

INTELLIGENCE QUOTIENT: A MEASURE OF MENTAL ABILITY?

The definition of intelligence and how it is to be determined eludes us though intelligence has become fixed in our culture as meaning "innate ability."[1] Since Francis Galton attempted to measure intelligence over a century ago, the argument has raged on endlessly

---

[1]Intelligence is variously defined with little agreement among educational psychologists. General problem–solving ability comes perhaps closest to an acceptable definition. Some psychologists would emphasize the innate quality of intelligence while others take a broader view of environmental interaction with various abilities, expanding over time as child development proceeds.

over what standardized tests actually measure. Despite the millions of tests administered during the twentieth century, no agreement has been reached as to what is actually tested. "Intelligence is what IQ tests measure," states one educator. "IQ tests measure learning experience," declares another. Whatever the test scores reveal about an individual's ability, the tests are widely used in our society and often place individuals within a niche in our educational system, guide employment decisions, and are used by the armed forces for aptitude classification of recruits. Such placement by whatever the institution has far-reaching effects on a person's intellectual development and future achievement. The test scores of an individual may vary 4 to 5 points on retesting over short intervals, but over intervals of several years, variations of 20 to 30 points are known, reinforcing the belief that tests are a measure of one's learning experience (Schiff and Lewontin, 1986:194).

Intelligence Test Origins

Most modern educational psychology testing procedures trace their origins to Alfred Binet, a French psychologist who developed the first usable intelligence test in 1905 (the Binet-Simon test). The purpose of the original test was to identify students with low academic achievement so they might be assisted by special programs. Binet was concerned with the development of therapeutic courses to aid students who had performed poorly compared with children of their age group. Binet did not attempt to describe the source of the problem of those falling below their group nor did he determine whether their poor performance was due to environmental or congenital factors. In fact, he specifically rejected those who described intelligence as a fixed quantity. Nevertheless, subsequent adaptations of Binet's test have often concluded that the results revealed the quality of inherited intelligence.

Rather than attempt to define what intelligence was, Binet took the direct approach of establishing what was "normal mental development" in his society. Normal was simply the performance of a majority of children between 3- and 13-years-old on a series of tests. These tests were constructed from a collection of questions typically used in the classroom, except in the case of preschoolers. The number of items answered correctly by a child was compared to the average of correct answers for the age group. The majority range of children completing tests with the average number of correct answers was set at between 65 to 75 percent, and the lowest 25 percent with the greatest gap between their developmental and chronological ages were defined as backward. Binet, at the suggestion of a German psychologist, William Stern, divided developmental or mental age (MA) by chronological age (CA) to get a quotient of mental development. The children in the majority range would have a quotient of one, those above the 75 percent level would have a quotient of greater than one, and those in the lower end of the range would be below one. The MA divided by CA was multiplied by 100 to give us an intelligence quotient or the well-known IQ. Note two things: First, the range of normals of 65 to 75 percent is arbitrary and based on statistical methods of the day, a fitting of the majority to a normal, or bell curve. Second, because the questions selected were those taken from material commonly taught, it is not surprising that the test performance was highly predictive of academic achievement.

American Intelligence Tests

The Binet-Simon test was imported to this country and became popular among American psychologists even without modification. It was first used by Goddard to test immigrants at Ellis Island, as mentioned earlier, with what was then considered a great success because the tests supposedly weeded out the mentally deficient. When American schoolchildren were tested, however, the results were poor until Lewis Terman of Stanford University adapted the test to American standards. This meant, in effect, that questions were selected that were relevant to the American experience. Terman used groups of California schoolchildren and adjusted the scores of each age group so the average was 100; that is, a person performing "normally" at his or her age level would be expected to score around 100 because this was the majority score fitted to a curve described as a normal distribution with a standard deviation of 15 points. This modified form was published and distributed in 1916 as the Stanford-Binet (or IQ) test, with claims that it would establish the level of a child's intelligence and be an invaluable education tool.

The IQ test was quickly accepted and applied by teachers and American psychologists to thousands of schoolchildren. The extent of these applications and the test interpretations went far beyond the original goals. Binet and Simon designed their test series to identify relative academic achievement and carefully avoided consideration of the results in terms of innate ability. In fact, Simon accused those who treated intelligence as a fixed quantity of having a brutal pessimism (quoted in Chase, 1977:236). Nevertheless, the pioneers of mental testing in America—Terman, Goddard, and Robert Yerkes—readily looked to the test results as evidence of a person's inherited mental ability. Discussions of feebleminded, bright, and dull persons, determined by IQ scores, were repeated frequently in the current psychological publications. Terman's major contribution, according to his biographer Minton (1988), was "to establish a fine gradation of measured ability so schoolchildren could be placed in educational tracks commensurate with their tested level of intelligence." This meant, in practical terms, that Terman's recommendations supported classroom segregation, since most ethnic minorities averaged lower scores. Indirectly, the testing of schoolchildren lent an aura of scientific validity to the folk beliefs of biological determinism. The "mental measuring science" was expanded even further by the approach of America's involvement in World War I.

A short time after its introduction, the modified Binet test was adapted for the testing of recruits inducted into a rapidly expanding army. Eventually nearly two million males were tested by the Alpha test (for literates) and the Beta test (for illiterates and non-English speakers). The results of this mass testing have been described in numerous books and have generated considerable controversy that continued more than two generations later (see Pastore, 1978). This controversy was fired by the psychologists involved in the test design, who presented the results as measures of "native" intelligence and concluded that it would be a fruitless waste of effort to attempt to improve the lot of the low-scoring groups. A continuing exchange of publications followed, arguing over the meaning of testing procedures and native intelligence. Briefly, many writers accepted an interpretation of the test scores that concluded that the average mental age

of American adult males was 14.[2] This led to the common theme that American traditions were at risk. Statements asserting that democracy was threatened because large
numbers of our citizens were of such low intellect, or that "no one of us can afford to
ignore the menace of race deterioration or the evident relations of immigration to
national progress and welfare," continued to appear until the eve of World War II.

Terman, defending test scores as evidence that there was a high frequency of
adults of a low mental age, described the threat to the "welfare of the State" because
of differences in birth rates. He warned that "the propagation of mental degenerates"
must be curtailed. Such strong beliefs expressed in 1917 by a respected scientist immediately gained wide public acceptance (described in Block and Dworkin, 1976:348–49).
The reader today, before accepting this kind of rejection of charitable attempts at
assistance for the more unfortunate, should ask who the feebleminded were to whom
Terman was referring. They were, of course, those who scored lowest on the IQ tests
and on the army tests that were so readily employed by psychologists as a diagnostic
tool of mental ability. Recall that many of the groups who scored lowest were newly
arrived immigrants from eastern and southern European countries, the grandparents
and great-grandparents of so many Americans living today. These Americans, descendants of the immigrants classified as "mentally" deficient, now occupy every profession
and level of socioeconomic achievement. Their test scores are also higher!

The ready acceptance of test scores by psychologists, educators, and the general
public revealed hidden dangers to any society that based government policy on such results
of normal tests. Immediately, there were reactions against the conclusions and the various
applications. Some writers, realizing the problems of the tests and the violation of scientific
method that they involved, reacted with sharp comments laying bare many of the fallacies
underlying the search for a single measure of innate human ability. Most vocal and
eloquent of the critics was the editorialist Walter Lippman, who observed: "The whole
drift of the propaganda based on intelligence testing is to treat people with low intelligence
quotients as congenitally and hopelessly inferior. The prominent testers believe that they
are measuring the capacity of a human being for all time and that this capacity is fatally
fixed by the child's heredity." He continued further in an exchange of letters with Terman
and admitted that he was emotional in his response: "I hate the impudence of a claim that
in fifty minutes you can judge and classify a human being's predestined fitness in life. I hate
the abuse of a scientific method which it involved. I hate the sense of superiority which
it creates and the sense of inferiority which it imposes" (see Pastore, 1978).

IQ Tests and African Americans

Throughout World War II and most of the postwar decade, the mental-testing issue
diminished in importance, and the environmentalists seemed to dominate the heredity–
environment question that had been a battleground for a century. Equal access to
quality education for all children became a central issue. This could not be achieved

---

[2]We should feel indebted to a journalist, Walter Lippman, who pointed out the nonsense of such a
conclusion when scientists of his day (1922) overlooked such an obvious contradiction. Lippman observed
that the average adult intelligence cannot be less than the average adult intelligence no more than the
average mile is three-quarters of a mile long.

without school desegregation, an emotional issue that generated major opposition and resurrected the hereditarians. The acceptance of innate ability as measured by performance on standard tests regained its former scientific aura in the fight against school desegregation. The concept of racial inequality never really diminished; however, some of the "races" were removed from the lists. The former inferiors—Alpine and Mediterranean types, eastern and southern Europeans—were now considered equal to the formerly superior Nordics. Furthermore, many of these "inferior types" were now designing and administering, at all levels of the educational system, the very tests that had labeled their own parents and grandparents as mentally inferior. Americans of African descent continued to be categorized as before, though after 1954 they could not be excluded or limited in educational access except on the basis of test scores.

African Americans' average test scores were at the lower ranges of military aptitude and IQ tests, results which fit with the racist dogma of the day. These results continued to be a prop for the legal fights to maintain separate education, despite the evidence that educational expenditures and school quality had significant effects on test scores. Recruits from urban centers, especially in the North, scored higher on the army Alpha test than did those from rural areas; those from the southern states averaged lower in both categories. Klineberg (1935) pointed to school expenditure per pupil as the independent variable. A most embarrassing fact for the racist, and a fact generally avoided, was that African Americans who had attended schools in the northern cities scored higher than rural southern whites. Despite these data, America's confidence in the predictive value of psychological tests continued, but now with many more test forms applied at all levels of our educational, social, and economic institutions. The results could place us in occupational, educational, or social niches and were eagerly accepted as statements of our innate abilities.

What was said about the IQs of immigrants at the turn of the twentieth century was repeated in reference to African Americans, but with considerably more emotion. "Their intelligence is significantly lower, they lack the ability to handle abstract reasoning" (Jensen, 1969:81), and "test performance of a group improves in proportion to the admixture of Caucasoid genes" (Shockley, 1972:298); "differences in cognitive abilities (IQ) are correlated with differences in brain size, and both brain size and cognitive ability are correlated with age, sex, social class and race" (Rushton and Ankney, 1996) are a few samples. Such repetition of the early misapplication of test scores to another socially disadvantaged group fifty years later is disheartening, especially in light of the mass of work that has gone into development of intelligence-testing programs during recent decades. We still find claims that "intelligence is inherited and relatively unchanged by the environment (education) and IQ tests are a measure of this innate ability." These claims must still be examined and refuted (as described by Weinberg, 1989:98). Though there are many more testing procedures today, there is less support for the argument that performance in relation to some group average is a measure of intelligence.

The variety of tests, including the Stanford-Binet, have all placed African American achievement below a national norm (Euro-American) by 15 points. This distance between groups is an indisputable fact, but note that the range of variation is broad. Some studies report as little as 10 points or as much as 20 between the means (Figure 7-2a). This large study comparing elementary school children from five

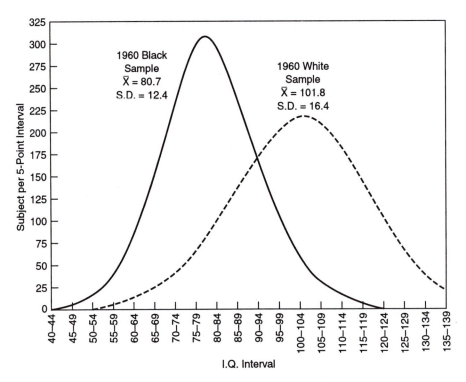

FIGURE 7-2a Comparison of IQ Distributions of American Black and White Elementary Schoolchildren. The distribution of American black I.Q. is taken from a sample of 1,800 children enrolled in elementary schools in five southern states. The mean of 80.7 contrasts with the 101.8 mean of a normative white sample and is the greatest difference reported. (From Kennedy, W.A., V. Van de Riet, and J.C. White, 1963. A normative sample of intelligence and advancement of Negro elementary school children in southeastern United States. Copyright © 1963 by The Society for Research in Child Development, Inc. Reprinted by permission of the publisher.)

southern states encompasses a range of socioeconomic groups living in urban and rural environments. Not incidentally, the IQ mean is below the white norm by 20 points, the largest difference ever reported. Also, the distribution of the IQ values of blacks overlaps that of whites, by a wide margin. More important, however, arithmetic means will vary depending on which group or groups are sampled. Comparisons of Boston, Baltimore, and Philadelphia schoolchildren by race showed the least intergroup difference of any study. These samples were grouped according to socioeconomic status. The Boston sample compared black and white children from the same overall high socioeconomic level. These 7-year-olds performed at a high level with less than 5 points between them and the distributions were nearly identical. No effort was made to evaluate the degree of admixture and simply classed as black or white.[3]

---

[3]The labels of black and white are used interchangeably with African American or Euro-American by many authors and they are so used here. Remember though that such labels rarely account for degrees of ancestry nor do authors note the means by which an individual is labeled, self-identification, or by the teacher.

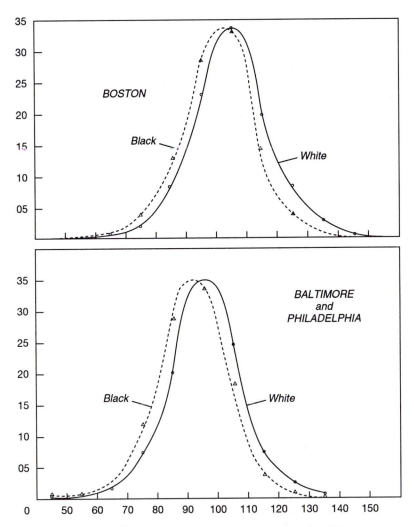

FIGURE 7-2b and 7-2c   Comparisons of IQ scores of Black and White Schoolchildren. Two groups of 7-year-old children were matched for socioeconomic status (parental occupation, education, and income) and their IQ test scores were compared. The black and white children of the higher socioeconomic group from Boston showed nearly identical IQ distribution, the means differing by only 4 points, 104.2 versus 100.0. The IQ means of lower socioeconomic children from Baltimore and Philadelphia at 95.3 and 91.2 were 10 points below the Boston children. The differences between black and white children, however, were still only 4 points, an insignificant difference. (Source: Modified and adapted from Nichols and Anderson, 1973.)

Comparisons of 7-year-old children in Baltimore and Philadelphia produced nearly the same results; only 4 points separated the children, 95.3 versus 91.2 (Figures 7-2b, and 7-2c). These children were from a lower socioeconomic level than the Boston groups and their scores probably reflect educational quality and home environment.

What is notable is that at both levels there is little difference between black and white children in these studies compared to the 20 point difference shown in Figure 7-2a. However, comparing the highest of 104 in the Boston study with the lowest of 91 for the Baltimore black children, there is a difference of 13 points, close to that persistently 15 point lower average that is mentioned so often for African Americans.

It is worth recalling that this average of 15 points is very close to differences recorded between native-born Americans and eastern European immigrants of the 1920s. Given this history and viewed as contrasts between geographic regions or school districts or socioeconomic levels, there is a question of the real significance of scores on standardized tests. Is race or ethnic group a factor as so frequently reported, or are contrasting learning environments the independent variables?

IQ Tests and World Populations

Comparisons of ethnic groups across international boundaries give results similar to those obtained in the United States (Table 7-1). Most groups of northwestern Europe populations scored between 10 and 20 points lower. The exceptions were subjects in Italy and European descendants in New Zealand and Australia, who performed at the mean. The rest of the sample populations averaged IQ scores of about one standard deviation below the mean (100) on the basis of performance on a variety of mental tests that included the Stanford-Binet, Raven, and Catell-Culture Fair tests. These results are summarized by Lynn (1978), who attempted to interpret ethnic group performance on the basis of race, the implication being that the differences were genetically determined. He had trouble, however, explaining the high IQ of Italian subjects (mean = 100) while Spain, Greece, and Yugoslavia had the lowest for Europeans (mean = 87). The European IQ scores had a north–south gradient except for the Italian. He offered the explanation that the gradient was due to the racial composition of the population:

> If these results from Caucasoid, Iranian, and Indo-Dravidian nations are considered in the light of the racial composition of the populations, it is apparent that where the people are predominantly of northern European stock, as in Britain, northwestern Europe, the United States, Australia, and New Zealand, their mean IQs are approximately 100. (Lynn, 1978:278)

This should not be hard to explain considering that the tests were designed by and for northwestern Europeans. The differences all fall within the range reported for minorities in the United States and other countries, which is one standard deviation below the mean. Also, scores from different tests vary, as in the case of the two New Zealand Maori samples—a mean of 84 on the Otis and 94 on the Queensland tests. It should be noted in the table that Australian Aboriginal children varied in test performance depending on the closeness of their contact with European settlements. The aboriginal children far removed and with little contact with Europeans scored the lowest.

TABLE 7-1   Table of Comparisons of IQ in Several Populations

POPULATION	TEST	I.Q. SCORE
Northern Europe		
Scotland	Stanford-Binet and Terman-Merrill	100
Belgium	Cattell's Culture-Fair	104
France	Raven's Progressive Matrices	104
Southern Europe		
Italy	Raven's Progressive Matrices	100
Spain (army)	Raven's Progressive Matrices	87
Yugoslavia	Raven's Progressive Matrices	89
Greece	Wechsler Scale	89
Middle East		
Iraq	Goodenough DAM	80
Iran	Goodenough DAM	80
India		
Univ. of Calcutta	Stanford-Binet	95
Univ. of Calcutta (post-grad. students)	Raven's Progressive Matrices	75
Variety of Indian states	Raven's Progressive Matrices	81–94
Afro-Americans	Shuey (81 different ones)	85
Africa		
Uganda	Raven's Progressive Matrices	88
Uganda	Terman Vocabulary and Kohs Blocks	80
Jamaica	British Intelligence	75
Jamaica	Terman Vocabulary and Kohs Blocks	low 80s
Tanzania	Raven's Progressive Matrices	88
Ghana, Jahoda	Raven's Progressive Matrices	75
South Africa	British National Foundation for Educations Research	87
South Africa—Zulu	Raven's Progressive Matrices	75
American Chinese	Stanford-Binet	97
Asians		
Japan	Wechsler Scale	106.6
Bandung, Java	Goodenough Draw-a-Man	96
Native Americans		
Eskimo	Raven's Progressive Matrices	70–80
Eskimo	Vernon—several	85
Amerinds (Canada)	Coleman—several	91–96
	Vernon—several	79
Australia		
Europeans	American Otis	95
Aborigines (Victoria)	Peabody Picture Vocabulary and Illinois Psycholinguistic Ability	80

(Continued)

Table 7-1   Table of Comparisons of IQ in Several Populations *(Continued)*

POPULATION	TEST	I.Q. SCORE
Aborigines (Queensland)	Queensland	78 in isolation 85 in close contact
Pacific		
Europeans (N. Zealand)	Otis	98.5
Maori (N. Zealand)	Otis	84
Maori (N. Zealand)	Queensland	94
Micronesia	Cattell's Culture-Fair	88
Polynesia	Pacific Infants Performance Scale	88
Southern Africa		
!Kung (Kalahari)	Maze	55

Source: Data selected and adapted from Lynn, 1978; Flynn, 1984.

What Influences IQ Test Performance?

How can this consistently lower performance of ethnic minorities around the world be explained? Some may explain away the differences in terms of genetic variation as outlined by Lynn. Many educators and psychologists, Jensen included, point out the strong role environment plays in academic achievement and IQ scores, however. Jensen (1969:60) noted that moving children from a deprived environment to an improved one can boost IQ 20 to 30 points. In addition, the socioeconomic status of the parents greatly affects the IQ performance of the children; there is also a high correlation between performance and quality of education, as demonstrated by a comparison of the army Alpha tests with the state expenditure on elementary education. Adults who had resided as children in states with lower school expenditures scored lowest on the tests (Table 7-2). Regional disparities in school funding still exist and with the same consequences (Block and Moore, 1986).

Contrary to claims that compensatory education has failed to boost IQ because "intelligence is largely inherited" (Jensen,1969), there are several studies that show the opposite. One of the most successful educational enrichment programs boosted IQs of a group of black preschoolers by 33 points. This project, carried out in Milwaukee by Rick Heber, an expert on mental retardation, provided a major enrichment in the lives of children born to black mothers living in the most impoverished area of the city. The program included extensive training of the mothers in simple skills and offered personal one-on-one teaching for the children from a few weeks old until 6 years of age. The results were astounding. This group, chosen at random from volunteers, achieved skills far beyond those achieved by the control group who were not given the special training (Loehlin et al., 1975:159–160). Likewise, another preschool enrichment program (the Abecedarian project) that continued over fifteen years provided environmental stimulation for children who otherwise would have been deprived. These children gained as much as 20 IQ points over the control groups, and these gains were long lasting, as shown by following the

TABLE 7-2   Median and Mean Negro and White Army Alpha Intelligence-Test Scores
and School Expenditures per Child Aged 5 to 18 Years by State

State (1)	WHITE			NEGRO			School expenditures (8)
	N (2)	Median (3)	Mean (4)	N (5)	Median (6)	Mean (7)	
Alabama	779	41.3	49.4	271	19.9	27.0	1.51
Arkansas	710	35.0	43.3	193	16.1	22.6	3.09
Florida	55	53.8	59.8	499	9.2	15.3	4.68
Georgia	762	39.3	48.3	416	10.0	17.2	2.68
Illinois	2,146	61.6	66.7	804	42.2	47.9	13.46
Indiana	1,171	56.0	62.2	269	41.5	47.6	11.75
Kansas	861	62.7	67.0	87	34.7	40.6	10.58
Kentucky	837	41.5	48.6	191	23.9	32.4	4.57
Louisiana	702	41.1	49.0	538	13.4	20.8	2.52
Maryland	616	55.3	60.2	148	22.7	30.7	8.44
Mississippi	759	37.6	43.7	773	10.2	16.8	2.63
Missouri	1,329	56.5	61.9	196	28.3	34.2	8.54
New Jersey	937	45.3	52.9	748	33.0	38.9	14.04
New York	3,300	58.4	63.7	1,188	38.6	45.3	19.22
North Carolina	702	38.2	45.9	211	16.3	22.1	1.51
Ohio	2,318	67.2	73.0	163	45.4	53.4	12.13
Oklahoma	865	43.0	50.6	98	31.4	35.9	5.50
Pennsylvania	3,280	62.0	67.1	790	34.8	40.5	12.85
South Carolina	581	45.1	51.1	334	14.2	19.2	1.93
Tennessee	710	44.0	52.0	504	29.7	35.9	2.71
Texas	1,426	43.5	50.2	854	12.2	18.2	4.38
Virginia	506	56.3	60.5	57	45.6	52.0	3.39
West Virginia	423	54.9	60.8	67	26.8	28.5	6.79
Subtotal (23 states)	25,774	49.53	56.00	9,399	26.09	32.30	6.91
District of Columbia	77	78.8	85.6	30	31.2	34.3	17.78
Total	25,851	50.75	57.23	9,429	26.43	32.39	7.36

Source: From Spuhler and Lindzey, 1967, "Racial differences in behavior" in *Behavior Genetic
Analysis,* ed. Jerry Hirsch (Copyright © 1967 by McGraw-Hill Book Co.; reprinted by permission
of the publisher); data from Yerkes, 1921; and *Statistical Abstract of the United States,* 1902.

children through their school years (Ramey et al., 1982). Two decades later Head
Start is a proven success.

There have been many other demonstrations of the effects that environment has
on test performance. The frequently cited Coleman report, *Equality of Educational
Opportunity,* described the results of an extensive study carried out on 650,000 schoolchildren in 4,000 public schools. The part of the report that has frequently been seized
on as proof of racial inequality is the achievement test scores showing that white
students scored significantly higher than nonwhites. Any application of these results
as evidence to support a particular brand of racist dogma ignores the bulk of the
report that deals with the wide range of social factors related to the educational process
and student performance. For example, the higher the socioeconomic level of the

entire student body of a school, the higher the test scores of all ethnic groups (see Chase, 1977:498).

In the 1970s, a group of educational psychologists, headed by Mayeske, carefully reexamined the data published in the Coleman report. Their thorough analysis of each section isolated five significant sets of variables influencing test scores. Of these five, racial-group membership was the fourth lowest in its influence on test performance. When the scores are statistically weighted for socioenvironmental differences, the average scores of the several ethnic groups show very little difference. Figure 7-3 plots the percentage of difference between these groups when each of the environmental factors is considered. When adjusted for social background, the differences dropped to insignificant levels.

Health factors can also exert a major influence on test performance. Hearing defects in early childhood can lower IQ by 20 points. Premature and underweight babies have significantly lower scores at several developmental stages; at ages 3 to 5 years, for example, their IQ mean was 94.4. Multiple births are also a significant factor: Twins score 5 points lower on the average than singletons, and triplets score 9 points lower (see Loehlin et al., 1975:196–229). Nutrition also affects test performance; in many studies increases of up to 10 points are reported for children placed on enriched diets provided through school lunch programs. Maternal health, as measured by prenatal nutrition, smoking, alcohol or drug abuse, and birth weights, also shows high correlations with infant and childhood development and with children's test scores during preschool and elementary school years.

What Do the Tests Measure?

Since the earliest introduction of intelligence testing, modifications have been made in an attempt to accurately test groups of diverse social backgrounds, languages, and experiences. The search has been for a culture-free test—that is, a series of questions that will reveal natural ability uninfluenced by a person's past experiences. Dozens of tests have been designed since the early days of the Stanford-Binet, but to date, no culture-free test has been devised despite claims to the contrary. This is not unexpected, because ability to distinguish between objects, identify words, and so forth at any age is determined by a complex of interactions between inherited qualities, development, and experiences. It should have been obvious from the start that children, regardless of their ethnic backgrounds, raised in isolated rural communities will have experiences distinct from middle-class suburban children. This was reflected by the lower scores of certain social groups tested in the 1900s who included such diverse groups as recent immigrants, isolated communities in Appalachia, and Native Americans.

Children, even today, are not participants in an equal homogeneous educational unit. Each state is divided into school districts controlled by local boards with differing budgets, standards, and most important, expectations of achievement. Though several states have made efforts to standardize their school districts, facilities are unequal and teaching qualifications and student–teacher ratios vary. This is

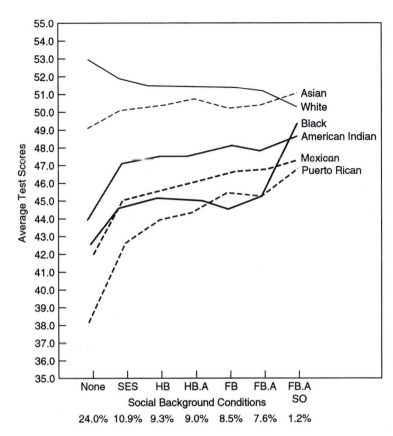

FIGURE 7-3 Racial-Ethnic Group Achievement Means Adjusted for Social Background Conditions. Percent of total difference among students in their achievement that is associated with their racial-ethnic group membership

SES = Socioeconomic status

HB = Home background; this set of variables includes both socioeconomic status and family structure

HB.A = Family attitudes about their ability to influence the course of their lives and the extent to which education benefits them

FB = Family background; educational, social, etc.

FB.A = Family background and area (of residence; regional; urban; rural; etc.)

FB.A = Quality and achievement-motivational mix of school attended

SO

". . . the differences among the various racial-ethnic groups in their achievement levels approach zero as more and more considerations related to differences in their respective social conditions are taken into account" (Mayeske, 1971, p. 112). (From Mayeske, 1971, U.S. Department of Health, Education and Welfare.)

especially apparent in densely populated inner-city communities. Children trained under these conditions develop a vocabulary and language style unique to their experiences, in contrast to children raised in more affluent suburbs or in rural areas. Their sociocultural differences, some argue, affect IQ test performance just as was true in the case of the eastern European immigrants three generations ago. The results are reflected in test scores, school completion rates, and percentage of graduates who are college bound (see *Digest of Educational Statistics*, 1999; Block and Moore, 1986).

Simply put, children from different social environments perform at different levels if given the same test. A case in point is the frequently used Stanford-Binet and Wechsler tests which were first standardized on a sampling of U.S. middle-class white children and adolescents in California. Hispanic, African American, and Native American children all performed below average on such a test. The test and its later revisions have been challenged on the basis that they are "culture bound" and handicap those of different socioeconomic backgrounds and also non-English speakers. Groups out of the cultural mainstream today score lower than the norm. When test content and new norms are established, scores rise accordingly, as did those of the immigrants, whose scores reflected their length of residency in the United States.

To overcome the difficulty imposed on African American children by the Stanford-Binet, Williams, an African American psychologist, designed the Black Intelligence Test of Cultural Homogeneity, the BITCH test (Loehlin et al., 1975:69). Questions were selected to reflect the environment and experiences of these children. The results were normed accordingly, and children who had been classed as low IQ fell well within the normal range of the BITCH test, reflecting the importance of cultural experience in measures of ability. The importance of a culturally relevant test is described from a personal perspective by Williams (1974), who related that his low scores influenced his high school counselor to discourage college and suggested that he consider a manual trade instead. Despite this discouragement he went on to earn a doctorate and achieve distinction as a professor of psychology at a major university.

Similar experiences can be cited for other minority children. In Riverside, California, a sociologist was concerned with the possible mislabeling of intellectually competent people. She formed a research group and began an eight-year-long study of 644 persons selected from over 6,000 in a public-housing project. The results confirmed her fears of mislabeling: A majority of those adults who had been labeled "mentally retarded" as children because their scores had fallen below the 70-point cutoff were filling normal roles expected for their age and gender. They were employed and raising families; over 80 percent had completed eight or more years of schooling, and 100 percent were able to care for themselves, a success rate not predicted by their poor test performance (Mercer, 1972). Given these results from such an intensive study, the fault of mislabeling probably lay with the test itself—the Wechsler Intelligence Scale for Children (WISC). On the theory that a language problem was the root cause, a Spanish-language version was used to retest children throughout California. Their median scores increased by 13 points and some of the children's scores increased by as much as 25. Wider testing across ethnic lines demonstrated that more than language was involved; over a quarter of the variances between Chicanos (Hispanics), Anglos (Euro-Americans), and Blacks (African Americans) were accounted for by sociocultural differences. It was no surprise that income, parental education, and household size headed the list of influences.

Considering these complexes of interacting factors that influence a child's variability in test performance, the tragedy is that test results are too often accepted as a measure of innate potential. The similarity between the lower than average scores of the immigrants fifty to eighty years ago and the lower scores of Hispanics and African Americans today should have warned against such an acceptance. The pattern that was followed by the eastern European immigrants has shown that they and their offspring increased their IQ with residence in the United States and acculturation into American society. There is every expectation that, as more opportunities become available to ethnic minorities and there is a decrease in sociocultural differences, IQ averages will increase among these groups as it has in the past. Such increases, especially given the recently described *Flynn effect*, raise further doubts about what tests actually measure (Ridley, 2003).

Over the last century IQ scores increased an average of 18 points per generation in twenty industrialized countries. Children in the 1970s scored an average 15 points higher than did their parents and grandparents in the 1930s, that is, they were able to answer more of the test questions, pushing the norm to a higher level (Flynn, 1984). Military personnel in World War II likewise showed improvement over their fathers of World War I: The average recruit's IQ, calculated from the Armed Forces Qualifying Exam, was up by 14 points over the previous generation. Dutch army recruits boosted a 20-point rise over their fathers'. But the greatest increase has been reported for 6- to 8-year-old Kenya school children whose IQ increased 11 points between 1984 and 1998, and if continued at this rate would advance 24 points by the time they reached adulthood (Bower, 2003). The reasons for this intergenerational rise in IQ level—the *Flynn Effect*—have not been well established yet, but they are likely to involve differences in test norms, sophistication in test taking, and a general increase in communications technology. In the case of the African children, improved nutrition and health services may be contributing causes along with increased education opportunities compared to their parents' generation. I will leave it to the psychologists to explain why, in only two or three generations, there has been so much gain in a score that is allegedly a measure of an innate ability commonly called intelligence. Whatever the answer turns out to be, it certainly cannot involve genetic change.

Any genetic explanation becomes even more difficult when applied to ethnic minorities, who around the world score below the norm—by the "magical" one standard deviation. The many ethnic groups are not, as some writers continue to imply or even assert, handicapped by their genes. Such an argument rests on three faulty assumptions: First, group classification is equivalent, or nearly so, to breeding population; second, that measurement, however made, determines some innate quality of the individual (i.e., that it is equivalent to a phenotype); third, that mental ability phenotype is largely hereditary. Of these three assumptions, the most problematic is the degree to which heredity influences intelligence, however measured.

BEHAVIOR AND INHERITANCE OR INHERITANCE
OF BEHAVIOR

Studies of human behavior are plagued by a basic problem: We believe in a natural aptitude for a whole series of traits, especially intelligence. Add to this the rapid expansion of data relating genes to mental illnesses and personality traits, and we start with a severe handicap. The problem is further confused by the nature of whatever behavioral traits we identify and treat as biological phenotypes. In addition, specific genotypes are difficult to identify because of the complexity of gene interaction with environmental variables. What we do know is that the uniquely human capacity of language is inherited. This ability enables an individual's mental development to rapidly expand from infancy onward at a rate and scope depending on the range of environmental stimuli. Such stimuli are derived from a wide variety of sources, both behavioral and biological. Also "hard wired" in our genome are our growth sequences, life cycle, and bipedalism, which makes us unique among mammals. The number of genes (about 30,000) we possess do not make us human. It is the way in which the genes are transcribed. These gene transcriptions and then their translation into proteins occur in response to both behavioral and biological stimuli.

The biological sources include those nutrients necessary for normal growth, and certain deficiencies may have profound effects on behavior if they occur at crucial periods of brain development. Substances that affect growth and metabolic rates, hormone action, and, in turn, *neurotransmitters* (chemical compounds that stimulate neural tissues) make up only a portion of biological influences. Behavioral stimuli are received from individuals with whom the infant and growing child interacts, and the circle of influences grows with a child's development, expanding ever outward. Given the breadth of the known stimuli to mental development—biochemical and behavioral—any attempt to categorize or classify human mental capacity or personality into taxonomic subdivisions, as has been done for traits of blood or DNA, is simply beyond any reality.

The question of just how much of our behavior is determined biologically and how much by our experience is still disputed. Some writers claim that behavior is influenced minimally by one's inheritance in contrast to the vast changes that can be made by the environment, as in the example of test scoring for personality or intelligence. Other writers have revived the old nature argument used by the eugenicists of the past century, who argued that a person's biological as well as behavioral makeup is determined by heredity. Few will deny, however, that there are inherited behavioral differences between individuals, and that there is probably a significant biological component underlying many of our behavioral responses. Genes code for polypeptides and influence the production of biochemical components—hormones, enzymes, lipids, and so on—and the effects are expressed in various ways depending on the individual's metabolic environment. The degree of influence of these gene products on human skills or aptitudes is not known except for those examples of inheritance of rare pathological conditions.

An extreme form of biological influence may be illustrated by the mental retardation that often accompanies several kinds of chromosome abnormalities. The Klinefelter (XXY) and Down (trisomy 21) syndromes involve mental impairment along with the physical defects that result from errors in chromosome number. But even then, environments make a large difference as improved treatment of Down syndrome patients has demonstrated. When raised by caring parents in a home environment, they show a marked improvement compared with the institutionalized Down's patients. There are also several possibilities for explaining certain clinically defined mental illness in terms of enzyme variants. The inherited metabolic diseases phenylketonuria, Tay-Sachs, and galactosemia, described in Chapter 3, all have associated effects of mental retardation. Extreme iodine deficiency is another factor, as it severely depresses thyroid function and retards growth with varying degrees of mental impairment (Hetzel, 1993). Cretinism is the most acute form. Beyond such pathological examples, little evidence can be offered for inheritance of mental or behavioral traits. However, there have been several studies that associate certain gene markers with some forms of pathological behavior as summarized below, but environment still remains a major mediating factor in expression of gene products.

Genes, Environment and Mental Traits

After so many decades of emphasis on environment to the near exclusion of inheritance, research now is being directed more toward the identification of gene products as they affect expression of complex traits. This has been especially true in studies of psychological illness. The higher than expected occurrences of several illnesses among relatives and the high correlations found in identical twins suggest significant genetic influences. The specific gene, or gene factors have not been easy to identify, however, except in cases of extreme pathology. Furthermore, not all genes are active at birth but are expressed only under certain environmental conditions. In this age of genomics, behavioral scientists are making a determined effort to establish the biochemical component as well as the actual DNA sequence responsible for so many of our personality traits and neurological functions (Plomin et al., 2003). The association of traits with certain neurochemicals has been a starting point to discover the DNA mutation as it effects the brain.

Alzheimer's disease. This neurodegenerative disorder begins slowly in late middle age with small memory loss and progresses to a major loss of cognitive functions. It is a common dementia of the elderly occurring in 5 percent of those over 65 years of age and is the fourth leading cause of death. This frequency increases with aging until 40 percent of those over 90 years old are diagnosed with the disease. With a growing number of people living beyond age 65, Alzheimer's disease has attracted more attention from genetic researchers than ever with some interesting findings.

There is a familial risk of 50 percent; if a family member has Alzheimer's, there is 50 percent probability of a first degree relative having the disease by age 85 to 90. A high correlation is reported in twins; there is 43 percent probability of both identical twins (MZ) contracting Alzheimer's, but only 8 percent for nonidentical (DZ) twins. Another study reported results of 78 percent for MZ twins and 39 percent for DZ twins, which provides an estimated 0.60 heritability.

The search for genetic factors turned up an apolipoprotein (APOE gene), a transporter of lipids (see Chapter 3). Of the three alleles, E 4 is over represented in Alzheimer's patients and may be a significant influence on both early and late onset of the disease. Plomin and associates (2003:504) note the increased risk for carriers of this allele, but explains that it is neither necessary nor sufficient for developing the disease. The presence of APOE 4 accounts for 40 to 60 percent variance among all populations, however. Determined by studies of white populations, the odds ratio of contracting the disease varies depending on genotype, 2.7 to 3.3 times as likely for genotypes E3-E4; 12.5 to 14.9 times for E4-E4. Japanese odds were 5.6 and 33.1, respectively, while African Americans were lower at 1.1 and 5.7 for the E3-E4 and E4-E4 genotypes. Explanations for these differences are lacking, and there are probably other factors that confound the results. One-third of people with Alzheimer's lack an E4 and 50 percent who have E4-E4 genotype survive to age 80 without the disease (Williams, 2003:13).

Schizophrenia.   This severe chronic mental disorder is one of the most common of mental diseases and accounts for about 50 percent of psychiatric patients. It is characterized by chronic mental disorder, psychotic symptoms involving formal thought disorder, disturbances of perception and feelings, and delusions and hallucinations. Schizophrenia's onset is before age 45 and its symptoms are not due to organic disturbances or mental retardation. The disease has been described as caused by an excess of dopamine, or a dysfunction in serotonin and glutamate transmission systems. An opposing hypothesis, supported by MRI brain scans showing increased lateral ventricle size, explains that schizophrenia is a neurodevelopment disorder (Owen and O'Donovan, 2003:463). If the developmental disorder, probably prenatal, is the sole cause, than no further genetic causes need be explored. Because the disease is complex with diverse symptoms and has a high heritability, however, gene influences should be examined.

First, the disease occurs worldwide, near evenly distributed across all populations. Europe and Asia have an incidence of from 0.2 to 1.0 percent while higher rates are reported for the United States and Russia. In each population where family studies have been carried out, the risk factor or ratio is higher among relatives of a schizophrenic; a lifetime risk of 10 percent for a sibling versus 1 percent across the general population. In twins the risk is much higher. Second, the concordance between MZ twins is 41 to 65 percent compared to 0 to 28 percent for DZ twins. Heritability works out to be 0.8, which is a high influence of genetic variance on phenotypic variance. This suggests a strong genetic component, but 50 percent of MZ twins are discordant; that is, about half the time when one twin is schizophrenic, the other is free of the disease. Such results from twin studies and from analysis of biochemical components of the patients blood lead to a search for genetic factors.

Serotonin, a major neurotransmitter that has excitatory effects, interrupts sleep patterns, and, at certain levels, contributes to anxiety responses. It is described as a therapeutic target for antipsychotic drugs, so serotonin and its receptors were studied for genetic connections to schizophrenia. Associations were found between a single-base substitution in the gene that encodes the serotonin receptor, 5HT2a, and schizophrenia. The samples were small, but the results encourage further study. Likewise, another major neurotransmitter, dopamine, has attracted attention mainly because certain drugs block dopamine receptors and bring on schizophrenic reactions. The disruption of the dopaminergenic system by blockage of D2 receptor as a possible cause of schizophrenia has been a popular neurochemical hypothesis. The genes that encode this and other receptors have been examined for their association with the disease. Weak associations have been found for the dopamine receptor gene (DRD2), but there were more encouraging results for receptor DRD3. Association was found between schizophrenia and Ser9Gly polymorphism on exon 1 of the gene (Owen and O'Donovan, 2003:471).

Though there is evidence to suggest genetic influence on behavior, normal and pathological, specific genes have not been identified. The few examples described above offer clues, but behavioral genomics has advanced slower than expected (Plomin et al., 2003:534). The attempts to merge correlations of relatives, especially twins, with the new genomics have not been successful. To a large extent behavioral genetics research has depended on the heritability quotient as an indication of genetic influence. Searching for correlations among family members for a particular trait has had its reversals and mistakes. In no area of behavioral research is this more clear than in the study of cognition-mental ability.

Heritability of IQ

Many of the assumptions of inherited mental inequality, as measured by intelligence tests, are based on studies of close relatives and MZ twins. The correlations of test scores of these relatives, and especially of twins raised together and apart, range from less than 0.2 to a high of 0.87 for MZ twins. The correlation coefficient of 0.8 has been derived from these studies and has found a prominent place in the literature discussing inherited inequality. This high correlation is interpreted as evidence that the genetic component influences intelligence more than environment (80 percent versus 20 percent) because correlation between subject groups is considered equivalent to heritability. The reliability of this evidence is questionable from many perspectives, but it is weak evidence of genetic influence, mainly because the concept of heritability is often misunderstood and misused. The measure of the genetic component of a trait is not given by the heritability quotient, though many authors still continue to use it to support their arguments over genetic determination of behavior.

Heritability, in the broadest sense, is that proportion of variation of a trait in a population that is due to a variation of genotypes. As discussed in Chapter 5, when a polygenic trait such as stature, for example, is measured in a population, there will be a mean and a range of sizes, tall and short people above or below the average. The total variation, or variance, about the mean is due to the variance in genotypes among the individuals of the population plus the variance of environments they encounter during their growth and development. In other words, the total population variation is due to both variation of genotypes and environment. This relationship can be expressed mathematically: variance in phenotype (V_p) = variance in genotypes (V_g) + variance in environment (V_e). Heritability (H^2), then, is that proportion of variance owing to genotypic variance and can be written as follows:

$$H^2 = \frac{V_g}{V_e + V_g}$$

Phenotypes measured within a population may have a high degree of variance owing to high genetic variance; it will therefore have a high H^2. Likewise, phenotypes with low genotype variance will have low heritability. Those populations with less genotypic difference between the individuals will thus have a lower heritability. If the hypothetical case were considered in which all individuals were the offspring of a single fertilized ovum, their genotypes would be identical copies of the original. Because there would be no genetic variance in our hypothetical population, the V_g would be zero and H^2 would then be zero. Such offspring could still have a high phenotypic variation if environmental variance was high.

Heritability then is not a measure of genetic influence on a phenotype; it is merely a measure of the total effect of the genotype variance on phenotypic variability in a population. The heritability ratio, then, is not a constant value that tells us the degree of genetic influence on a phenotype of any single individual. As stated by Jensen,

> There is no single true value of the heritability of a trait. Heritability is not a constant, but a population statistic, and it can vary according to the test used and the particular population tested. (1971:13–14)

If the example is used of a group of individuals placed on a diet that contains a carefully controlled constant amount of the amino acid phenylalanine (the $V_e = 0$), then any variance of phenylalanine blood levels (the V_p in the population) will be due to V_g or a variance in the genes that affect metabolism of the amino acid. If later the diet is varied between members of the same group, then phenotypic variance will increase. This does not mean that the genetic contribution or the effect of the genes is any less, merely that the relative contributions of V_g and V_e will change. In neither case is the degree of genetic contribution of gene effect known. Recall the discussion of biochemical pathways in Chapter 3.

Another example would be the number of our fingers and toes determined genetically during the late embryonic stage. This number is fixed at five per appendage and varies only in rare cases of dominant genes for a condition, polydactyly, discussed in Chapter 2. The genetic variance for the number of digits is zero in most populations and near zero in those few where polydactyly occurs; this means that H^2 is at or near zero. The zero heritability does not mean that genes do not effect the digit number in each individual, just that population variance is zero, the exceptional populations with polydactyly aside. By contrast, there are broad environmental affects on appendages and digits if embryo or fetal growth is interrupted at crucial growth stages. A mother's exposure to a number of drugs and diseases is known to cause such growth disturbances, which would translate into a high environmental variance for the population.

Comprehension of gene effects and a population ratio, used so often to argue for more or less influence on a trait, is difficult and confusion abounds. How can there be zero heritability if genes still affect a phenotype? This seeming contradiction may be solved and the question answered if one considers a time before Mendel's particulate inheritance. Before genetics, and before modern science, humans became very adapt at manipulating the environment, and without knowing the heritability formula they used its basic principles. Farmers could selectively breed their stock by the simple logic that any variation in animals living under a stable environment (the same food, pasturage, and so on) was due to some factors (bloodlines) that could be passed on to the next generation. In this way, undesirable traits could be selected out and useful traits bred for. Chickens that grew fastest and produced the most eggs, cows that produced the most milk, or cattle that showed the greatest weight gain could be used as breeders. The genetics of these traits were not known (and in many cases are still uncertain), but desirable effects of selective breeding could easily be seen, evaluated, and used to advantage.

Because of the frequent and continuing confusion, it should be restated that heritability describes a property of populations, not of individuals. Heritability is not a measure of genetic determination of a trait. It is a limited piece of information that measures the fraction of phenotypic variance due to genetic variance within a given population, at a particular time, and under specific environmental conditions. Should there be an increase in environmental variance, then the heritability quotient will change. It is a population statistic just as are mortality, birth, and fertility rates. Estimates of heritability derived from the variance of one population cannot be applied to another. Given the difficulty in studying the genetics of human populations, how is the heritability quotient derived?

Twin Studies

Hundreds of studies of monozygous or identical twins offer a source of data for estimates of heritability. The importance of these studies for estimating human heritability cannot be overstated. The significance is that these individuals, conceived from a single fertilized ovum, have identical genomes. It follows, then, that any phenotypic differences are the result of environmental influences. Measurements of traits in samples of both monozygotic (MZ) and dizygotic (DZ) twins have been made, and comparisons of the correlations have given considerable information about the relative influences of genes and environment. The data most revealing of the genetic effects come from studies of MZ twins reared in separate households that are, presumably, different environments. Unfortunately, not many such subjects have been located and carefully studied; there have been only four such studies to date with the recent addition of the Minnesota Twin Project (Bouchard et al., 1986). Before 1974 there was another, and by far the largest study, with fifty-three twin pairs described by an English psychologist, Cyril Burt. The results of a battery of mental and achievement tests in this investigation set the standard for twin studies and provided the basis for a correlation of IQ of twin pairs of 0.771, which was cited in many papers and texts that discussed inheritance of mental ability.

Burt's twin studies began to be questioned critically in the early 1970s, however. His results were just too consistent from the data described in one study to the next as additional separated twins were identified and enrolled in the project. As the number of twin pairs increased, the correlation coefficient remained the same to the third decimal place. The possibility of data manipulation and even scientific fraud, by the outright invention of subjects, was raised. Kamin went through the laborious work of checking the data step by step and noted the statistical impossibility of the correlations remaining the same from 1951, when twenty-one pairs were described, and 1958, when the number was increased to thirty and finally to fifty-three pairs by 1964 (Kamin, 1974). Following Kamin's work, others began to examine Burt's many publications and uncovered numerous flaws, unknown coauthors, nonexistent master's theses, and perhaps manufactured data. At that point the conclusion was inescapable: For several decades, a major fraud may have been perpetrated on the scientific community (Hawkes, 1979; Hearnshaw, 1979).

The effect on educational psychology in general and on twin studies in particular would have been minimal if it had not been for the prestige of Burt among educational psychologists. His conclusions were quoted in many standard texts and even used as a guide to educational policies implicitly influencing the treatment of minority students, especially in their placement in academic tracks. The exposure of the fraudulent data was a major blow to many who maintained that IQ had a high heritability and hence was largely genetic. This hereditarian group soon recovered and argued that the other twin studies supported their position that environment only minimally affected mental ability as measured by IQ tests. These arguments, however, neglected the lack of control for similarities or differences in the environments of twins raised apart. Though the Minnesota study has helped bolster a hereditarian position, the range of heritability quotients for traits other than IQ has been ignored (Table 7-3).

The higher correlations between the identical-twin groups can be taken as a reflection of their genetic likeness and are used to establish degrees of genetic influence. Hence, a correlation of 0.64 to 0.78 between identical twins raised apart is taken as evidence that genes influence the trait by that much. The balance of the difference is assumed to be due to environmental variables because of their genetic identity. Therefore, the proportion of gene influence on the phenotypes is equal to the correlations between twins, or $H^2 = r_{obs}$ derived from the following formula:

$$\text{r observed} = \text{r genetic} \times \frac{V_g}{V_e + V_g}$$

Because r genetic $= 1$ (there is a perfect correlation between MZ twins), then

$$\text{r observed} = \frac{V_g}{V_e + V_g} = H^2$$

Again, the reader is reminded that this refers to a variance observed in a "population" of twin pairs (the number of twin pairs tested) and does not express

TABLE 7-3 Correlations of Identical Twins Reared Together and Apart

	MINNESOTA MZA		MZT	
	R	Pairs (No.)	R	Pairs (No.)
Anthropometric variables				
Fingerprint ridge count	0.97	54	0.96	274
Height	0.86	56	0.93	274
Weight	0.73	56	0.83	274
Mental ability—general factor				
WAIS IQ—full scale	0.69	48	0.88	40
WAIS IQ—verbal	0.64	48	0.88	40
WAIS IQ—performance	0.71	48	0.79	40
Raven, Mill-Hill composite	0.78	42	0.76	37
First principal component of special mental abilities	0.78	43	NA	NA
Personality variables				
Mean of 11 Multidimensional Personality Questionnaire scales	0.50	44	0.49	217
Mean of 18 California Psychological Inventory scales	0.48	38	0.49	99

MZA = monozygotic twins raised apart; MZT = monozygotic twins raised together.
Source: Data selected from Bouchard, T.J., Jr., et al., 1990.

degree of genetic influence in any one individual. In other words, individuals may, and often do, perform quite differently from their twin, while others earn scores close to their twins (Table 7-4). The twins raised apart are treated as separate populations, with mean and variance; the two groups are then compared for covariance (correlation).

The H^2 covers a considerable range, and this single measure depends a great deal on the selection of twins and their environments, both for MZ twins raised apart and for those raised together. The correlations that are used are based on a number of twin studies during the last fifty years, and each study has several inherent problems. First, in the case of twins reared apart (MZA), the age at time of separation varies over a wide range, from a few days to 6 years, which causes a wide variety of environmental influences on the development of the twins and in turn influences the correlations. Second, many of these studies encompass a time span of a half century, dating back to a time when techniques and methods differed considerably from those of today. Also, the twin studies were not standardized for sex and age, both of which are influential on IQ, and improper correction for these factors will produce differing correlation values. The effects of environmental differences are suggested in Table 7-4, which also shows the relative degree of genetic influences. There are numerous other problems encountered when twin studies are attempted; even those MZ twins reared in separate households were often reared by relatives, uncles, aunts, and so forth. There are also recorded cases in which twins had maintained close contact during various stages of their childhood, even attending the same schools, which raises the

TABLE 7-4   Heritability Estimates in Twins Reared Apart and Together

REFERENCE	PSYCHOLOGICAL TEST VARIABLE (P)	NO. OF PAIRS (n)	INTRAPAIR CORRELATION (r_p)	ESTIMATES H^2
Husén (1959) year groups 1949–1952	IQ by I test	MZT 215	0.894	—
		DZT 416	0.703	—
Newman, Freeman, and Holzinger (1937)	Binet Mental Age	MZS 19	0.637	0.637
		MZT 50	0.922	±0.136
		DZT 50	0.831	
	Binet IQ	MZS 19	0.670	0.670
		MZT 50	0.910	±0.126
		DZT 50	0.640	
	Otis score	MZT 50	0.947	—
		DZT 50	0.800	—
	Otis IQ	MZS 19	0.727	0.727
		MZT 50	0.922	±0.108
		DZT 50	0.621	
	Stanford Educat. Age	MZS 19	0.502	0.502
		MZT 50	0.955	±0.172
		DZT 50	0.883	
Shields (1962)	Dominoes	MZS 37	0.758	0.758
	Intell. Test	MZS 34	0.735	±0.070
	Mill Hill Vocabul. scale	MZS 38	0.741	0.741
		MZS 36	0.742	±0.073

MZS = monozygotic twins separated; MZT = monozygotic twins (brought up together); and DZT= dizygotic twins (brought up together).

Source: Adapted from Vogel and Motulsky, 1986.

probability of many shared childhood experiences before they were ever tested as participants in a twin study program (Lewontin et al., 1984).

Many of the differences or variations are even more interesting than the similarities. Some of the twins raised apart have up to 20 points of difference. Another study of 26 pairs showed differences of up to 14 points between the individuals (Vogel and Motulsky, 1986). In examples of adopted children there is an average gain of some 20 points over their biological mothers, and the correlation between parents and children is approximately 0.5, but bright parents usually have children with lower IQs, which is described as "regression towards the mean." These comparisons were taken a significant step further by studies of transracially adopted children (Scarr and Weinberg, 1983). The study tested parents in 101 adoptive families who had 176 adoptive children (130 were "socially" classified as black); the families also included 143 biological children of the parents. Most adoptees (111) were younger than 1-year-old when adopted, and 65 were adopted after their twelfth month. The homes were economically well off, and the parents scored in the bright-average range. Tests of all children were recorded; the black adopted children averaged 110 points IQ or 20 points above comparable children in the black community. The adopted black child averaged

6 points lower than the biological children in the families. Scarr and Weinberg (1983:261) interpreted these high IQ scores as an indication that genetic differences do not account for a major portion of the IQ differences between racial groups. They also concluded that black and interracial children reared in the "culture" of the test design performed as well as other adopted children in similar families. If all of these factors are considered, there is a basic error in the argument that implies lower IQs among certain ethnic or racial groups are due to their "inferior" genes.

In an earlier study of genetic and environmental influences, Scarr-Salapatek (1971) described the results of 992 pairs of MZ twins in Philadelphia. First, and perhaps most important, was that 75 percent of the total variance on test scores of whites was due to genetic variance, whereas the proportion of genetic variance in disadvantaged black populations was less. This provided evidence for the correctness of the statement that studies of twins as a method of obtaining H^2 are not fully applicable to the general population, because twins are a select sample who are frequently treated differently by parents and others who the twins encounter during their childhood.

Scarr-Salapatek also tested the hypothesis that "social class differences in phenotypic IQ are assumed to reflect primarily the mean differences in genotype distribution by social class; that is, environmental differences between social classes (and races) are seen as insignificant in determining total phenotypic variance in IQ" (1971:1286). Scarr and Weinberg (1983) found, through extensive black and white twin comparisons, that the hypothesis was false; the environment played a more significant role in population variance. These results, together with those obtained from later studies of transracial adoptions, provide a solid base from which to reexamine the degree of genetic influence on behavior. The conclusions they reached are clear: The class, or rather the cultural environment, is of equal or greater importance to a child's development than is the genetic component.

> The implications of the differences between race and social class for intellectual achievement is that there are more likely to be genetic differences in IQ scores between social class than racial groups. (Scarr, 1981:79)

It is of interest that these two researchers reached a point where social class is given such emphasis, especially since our racial and ethnic labels have become more of a class designation and less of a biological one.

CLASS AND CASTE

Ogbu in his study of minority education explored the effects of class and caste on IQ differences and described the relative environmental influences within and between populations. Environmental influences are greater between populations than within a population because the two levels of comparison are not the same. Within a population we compare individuals, whereas the intergroup comparisons treat groups (castes or classes) sociologically defined (Ogbu, 1978). Even the perceived differences between black and white Americans are more sociological than biological, as noted above in the discussion of transracial adoptee studies.

According to Ogbu, the social classification of African Americans is a castelike status and suggests that their minority position and achievements are comparable with those of other minorities—Native Americans, Mexican Americans, and Puerto Ricans. Society's expectations, the limited educational opportunities, and lower expectations of economic rewards, together with social barriers, have caused responses of "mental withdrawal," leading to a failure in educational achievement. Whether or not the reader accepts this observation, and, to be sure, the situation has changed somewhat in the last decades, the evidence of lower achievement of these minority groups is there to see. Each of these minorities scores lower on the standard tests by, interestingly enough, 15 points or one standard deviation. They also have the highest school-dropout rate, the highest unemployment, the lowest income, and so on.

When caste boundaries and lower expectations are considered in the social-environmental equation a further weakness of the inherited inequality arguments is revealed. It is interesting to compare again the IQ scores of several ethnic groups as listed in Table 7-1. Northwestern Europeans are at the top with the standardized score of 100, whereas all others, especially ethnic minorities, have lower scores—many about 15 points lower. This says more about social boundaries limiting learning experiences than about innate mental ability.

Every nation has its minorities, relegated to some caste that is considered biologically inferior and socially undesirable as well. India is famous for its elaborate caste system once codified by law and sanctioned by religious beliefs. Still maintained by custom, the castes are arranged in social stratification from Brahmin at the top, with the greatest social prestige, wealth, and political status, to a middle-group "nonpolluting caste" that performs services for the Brahmins, to the lowest level untouchable castes that carry out the least desirable occupations of scavengers, sweepers, washermen, and laborers. Other nations have also established social castes, perhaps not as rigid in boundaries, but still an identification of a minority group, be it the "guest" worker—usually from North Africa, southern Europe, or Turkey in France or Germany—or the historically famous Gypsies, especially in central and eastern Europe. In the United States, of course, African Americans, Hispanics, and Native Americans have occupied these lower caste positions.

Most Asian minorities in the United States have, by and large, fared better, but in their homelands there are numerous and complex caste systems. Even in Japan, there are castelike minorities—the following statement by Nakasone, the former Japanese prime minister, notwithstanding. Nakasone, in a public speech, explained Japan's achievements by referring to the high levels of intelligence of its citizens.[4] "Our average score is much higher than the United States. There are many Blacks,

---

[4]Despite the repeated reports of a higher IQ (102–105) among East Asian schoolchildren (Japanese and Hong Kong Chinese), there is considerable doubt over the test accuracy. The problem of cross-national testing and sample sizes notwithstanding, the tests used and the scoring methods are questionable (see Lane, 1999).

Puerto Ricans, and Mexicans in America. In consequence the average score over there is exceedingly low." Forced later to apologize for what was perceived as a racial slur, Nakasone tried to explain with the observation that Japan was a monoracial society. He added that "there are things that the Americans cannot do because of multiracial nationalities there," a statement that made matters worse.[5]

On the contrary, Japan does have minorities. The best recognized are the Koreans, small in number to be sure (only about 700,000) but forced by discrimination to remain on the fringes of Japanese society. A still smaller ethnic group, the Ainu descendants of the original inhabitants, have suffered considerable economic and social deprivation during the centuries. Though numbering only about 24,000 today, they too took offense at Nakasone's remarks. Another group that definitely disturbs the notion of a homogeneous society is the Burakumin, a social minority caste that has been limited by centuries-old tradition to undesirable occupations (sweepers, slaughter-house workers, and so on). This social caste occupies a position in Japanese society nearly comparable with that of the untouchables of India. Though there has been intermarriage between Japanese and Koreans during past generations, there has been little with the Burakumin caste, who rank lowest on the social scales of Japanese society; in fact, during the prewar era intermarriage was forbidden by law. The purpose of pointing out the existence of this low caste is to note that the school performance of the Burakumin children is well below the national norm; they score, on average, 15 points (one standard deviation) below the Japanese average.

Ogbu suggests that this is evidence of children's reaction to society's expectations and to a teacher's attitude toward low-caste children. He emphasized that when persons of this caste had migrated to Hawaii or the American West Coast, their school performance was equal to that of the other Japanese children, since the American schoolteachers were not aware of the caste differences. The teachers simply dealt with all children of Japanese ancestry, or, for that matter, all Asians in the same way—they had high expectations of school performance. The story could be continued by relating the experiences of minority Jewish groups (Orientals, Yemenites, Ethiopians) in contact with the dominant Ashkenazim, in Israel, but the contrasts are the same as related earlier. The same expectations, stereotypes, and treatment are found in Israeli society (Schiff and Lewontin, 1986).

Castes and Class: Back to a Nineteenth-Century Perspective

While Ogbu views class and caste status as the major factors determining several measures of behavior and socioeconomic status in complex societies, several recent writers consider the opposite to be true: Groups of people become more and more assorted into classes because of inherited ability. Accordingly, in this view, a "cognitive elite" is emerging as

---

[5]Though these remarks by the then prime minister of Japan were later qualified and a sort of apology was published, the initial comment stated his firmly held belief in the inequality of ethnic groups (*New York Times*, 3 January 1986). Several newsmagazines published essays discussing the issues raised and were severely critical of Nakasone (*Time*, 6 October 1986; *Newsweek*, 6 October 1986).

people rise to the top in our egalitarian society because of their inherited ability, leaving behind those genetically less well endowed (Herrnstein and Murray, 1994). They see a nation (the United States) increasingly divided along lines of genetically brighter and duller people. Correlations are then made between these groups and a series of socioeconomic markers: income, education, crime rates, illegitimate births, poor parenting skills, and so on. The correlations with class are then related to average IQs, and the conclusion is drawn that most of the nation's social ills emanate from the lowest of the cognitive classes. The reader should recall that there were similar discussions of class, innate ability, and societal problems 100 years ago: One's rise to the top of the social order was due to one's family lineage. Consider also that correlations between two variables do not prove causation, especially when comparing polygenic traits developing within a network of environmental stimuli. This caution is especially important because Herrnstein and Murray accept numerous statistically weak correlations (in the range of 0.2 to 0.4, a perfect correlation being 1.0) as indicative of cause (i.e., intelligence as the primary determiner of several social factors).[6]

These cognitive classes, so confidently derived on the basis of performance on mental tests, assumed that the tests measure a general factor or g, a concept of mental ability defined by Spearman in 1904. Simply stated, there is a positive correlation of a person's performance on various mental tests. This correlation reveals a g factor that is presumed to be a general innate property of the human brain upon which environmental stimuli would act. Though it has enjoyed a wide popularity, the existence of g has not been proved, and it has been roundly criticized as perhaps only a statistical artifact, or a reflection of the way multivariant data are manipulated.[7] Some psychologists accept and others reject the *general intelligence concept*, or g factor. Those who reject the concept consider it a meaningless statistic without predictive power; mental test scores yield a single g in some studies, but not in others (Bower, 2003). Given these disputes over intelligence, plus the criticisms of the tests themselves, basing a broad conclusion about innate ability on a single score for the purpose of explaining social status and behavior is questionable, to say the least. Nevertheless, IQ is offered as predictor of a range of behaviors, as in such statements as "At the lower educational levels a woman's intelligence best predicts whether she will bear an illegitimate child" (Herrnstein and Murray, 1994:167); further on the authors state that degrees of civility are correlated with IQ and that 8 points below normal is significant.

What is even more questionable is the reliance on heritability; the proof of genetic influence was taken by the authors from a misinterpretation of the heritability quotient. They note that various studies report H^2 ranges from 0.4 to 0.8 so they take a middle range of 0.6 to be what they consider to be the degree of genetic influence on cognitive ability (Yes, heritability is equated with a gene effect in an individual.). This

---

[6]Gould discusses the weak correlations as well as the misuse of statistical methods by Herrnstein and Murray. The assumptions about the meaning of multiple correlations and goodness of fit are examined (Gould, 1994).

[7]Thurstone, in discussing factor analysis, described the ways in which correlation results could be made to vary by rotation of the different dimensions (1940).

reliance on a genetic explanation ignores all of the cautions from behavioral geneticists. Genetic causes of a variety of behaviors have been sought for a long time, and some successes have been recorded, but caution still remains the watchword. Robert Plomin, a behavioral geneticist, noted: "The wave of acceptance of genetic influence on behavior is growing into a tidal wave that threatens to engulf the second message of this research: the same data provide the best evidence for the importance of environmental influence" (1989:105). And again, fifteen years later, he cautioned that, ". . . genetic factors constrain certain outcomes rather than determine a particular trait" (Plomin et al., 2003:xix). These cautions should be heeded given the mountain of new data pouring forth from genetic marker studies in search of genomics of behavior.

A complete summary and criticism of the long thesis of Herrnstein and Murray that class divisions equate to intelligence that in turn relates to behavior cannot be given here. Several books and essays have been written addressing this thesis and the various issues that arise (for example, see Jacoby and Glauberman, 1995; Fraser, 1995; Molnar, 1996). I can, however, note some conclusions drawn by Herrnstein and Murray that are a continuum of the nineteenth-century dogma.

First, that the wrong people are having the most babies is implied by statements about "demographic headwinds." The authors stress that modernization has brought falling birthrates, with birthrates dropping faster for educated women. This introduces a dysgenic effect (a downward shift in ability) and affects the cognitive capital of the country. "Whatever good things we can accomplish with changes in the environment would be that much more effective if they did not have to fight a demographic head wind" (Herrnstein and Murray, 1994:342). Expressing such concerns is reminiscent of Pearson's warning a century ago in his Huxley Lecture in 1903: "England was breeding less intelligence than she had done fifty or a hundred years ago. Given the scientific fact that intelligence was inherited, the only remedy was to alter the relative fertility of the good and bad stocks in the community" (see Kevles, 1995).

Second, the implication that the wrong types of immigrants are arriving on our shores is another echo of an earlier era. According to Herrnstein and Murray's interpretation, a majority of legal and illegal immigrants come from ethnic groups that score well below the white average (see Herrnstein and Murray, 1994:358). This comment sounds very much like some made during the battle to tighten immigration restrictions in the early 1900s. Discussion of the demography of intelligence goes further than repeating earlier warnings; it updates and modernizes them: The percentages of legal immigrants are broken down by ethnic group, the IQs are estimated for each group, the appropriate arithmetic is performed, and then an average of 95 is given for all.

These conclusions about innate cognitive ability and group behavior are surprising, because the authors note that predictions of individual behavior cannot be made from an IQ score. They state that "Cognitive ability accounts for only a small to middling proportion of the variation among people" (Herrnstein and Murray, 1994:117). But, unfortunately, the balance of their long book is about correlations of group behavior and intelligence, and they pay little attention to the overwhelming evidence of environmental factors. Mackintosh (1986), a British psychologist, observed that IQ may have a significant heritable component, but there is little evidence that average differences between ethnic groups are genetic. He emphasized that differences in IQ between white, West Indian, Indian, and Pakistani children in Great Britain are closely correlated with their social circumstances.

Finally, the point emphasized by so many writers since IQ tests were introduced is that no one single measure can represent innate ability, and that the norms are standardized by tests administered to the majority groups and used as a standard against which all others are compared. We are dealing with an unknown number and complex combination of genes when we consider mental ability. The polygenic nature of whatever brain functions are involved means that a considerable number of inter-actions occur between genes, gene products, and environmental stimuli. We know the location and action of the genes that enable us to distinguish or prevent us from distin-guishing color, but we do not know what genes are involved in spatial orientation, reading, or math skills. It is misleading to attempt to partition the relative influence of environment and genetics in such a complex organism as *Homo sapiens*. The nature of much of our genetic system is its potential to interact with environmental stimuli. One's society provides the context and content of this stimuli. The cultural environ-ment, the genes, and stored experience all provide a mental template that will vary from population to population and from generation to generation. A behavior cannot be inherited but must be developed under the combined influence of genetic and environ-mental factors. In general, gene expression can occur only in a certain context, and this is especially true in the case of those involved in neurological functions.

GENETICS, INTELLIGENCE, AND THE FUTURE

Despite warnings since the introduction of intelligence testing that we face a decline in average intelligence, the opposite has occurred. Longitudinal data have shown that there has been no decline in intelligence. In fact, our generation scores higher than previous ones, and this includes minorities as well. The arguments over the reasons for the 15-point gap between minority and majority population scores rage on as they did throughout the past century. But note that the gap is found in minorities wherever the tests have been applied; it is hard to defend the differences between a Maori minority and the New Zealand national norm on the basis of the same genetic argu-ment made for differences recorded in the United States or among minorities in Great Britain and elsewhere.

The differences in measured mental ability or IQ between social groups (or racial groups) have been questioned many times and are often attributed to overall differences involving survival and lifestyles in complex industrial societies. The basis for variance in IQ may lie in discriminatory practices, economics, and language. Groups consistently scoring lower on standardized tests do not necessarily come from inferior environments, but from those that differ from the environment of the group on which the test was originally standardized.

The various tests were designed as predictive devices, and as such they work well to a limited extent in that they are predictive of academic success—but, unfortunately, people have tried to use them for other purposes. Lewontin and many others have raised the question of what these tests actually measure and—what is more important—how the results are applied (Lewontin et al. 1984). In addition, using IQ tests as predictors of competence or success in a vocation after formal training has been seriously challenged (Fallows, 1989). Fallows argued that though the test scores are good predictors of academic achievement, they are poor or useless as an indication of career success. He suggested that opportunity and motivation to achieve are more important. As examples, he listed a variety of occupations and professions where the person's class standing, or grades in college, or training programs had little bearing on professional competence. He cited, among other examples, the success of the G.I. Bill that supported millions of veterans in college—people who would otherwise not have had the opportunity to gain an advanced education.

Careful use of biological or social definitions of race and controlled or modified tests matters little if we simplistically assume that humans are color coded. It is dangerous and inaccurate to assume that, if the variation of trait X in one population differs from the variation of that trait in another population, then all inherited traits differ at the same rate between the two groups. Races are not inferior or superior; there is no gene for slow learning, and the genetics of whatever it is that IQ measures have yet to be determined; if it will ever be possible is another matter. The future may look bleak to some who claim a decline in IQ, but there are no data to demonstrate such a decline. On the contrary, there is every indication that environmental improvement will increase, with an expansion of the opportunities for people to realize their full potential. As Dobzhansky states,

> Correctly understood, heredity is not the "dice of destiny." It is rather a bundle of potentialities. Which part of the multitude of potentialities will be realized is for the environments, for the biography of the person, to decide. Only fanatic believers in the myth of genetic predestination can doubt that the life of every person offers numerous options, of which only a part, probably a minuscule part, is realized. (1976:160)

A personal observation as a conclusion for this chapter is in order. I would like to warn any reader to approach studies of genetics and behavior or behavioral genetics with great caution. Often, and I fear more frequently than not, authors who describe the relationship of genetics to behavior approach the task with some bias. It is to be expected. We are, after all, the product of our experiences and training within a society and, however much we try to be objective, our questions as well as our conclusions are biased to some degree. The revival of the nature–nurture controversy and the development of behavioral genetics in the last decade are good examples. Too frequently, authors will accuse one another of covert or even overt racism or will refer to a political bias (for example, Marxism), and they will then discount the data reported or the criticisms made because of these alleged biases. Without citing specific works beyond those mentioned earlier, I would argue that we are all guilty to some degree. The major sin of writers on all sides of the question is clear, but generally ignored—that is, the sin of omission; too often they avoid a close examination of the concept of race and its validity for the study of human diversity. Nowhere are personal biases more apparent than in the taxonomy of our species. The use of *racial stock, race, hybrid,* or *ethnic group* is too frequently mixed with sociological classification based on a group's self-identification or on the labels imposed by the majority population. This casual use of stereotyping in the name of classification must stop if objectivity is to be introduced to the study of human diversity at any level, but especially in the investigation of behavioral differences and measured abilities.

Consider the following statement:

The human species has a past rich in migrations, in territorial expansions, and in contractions. As a consequence, we are adapted to many of the earth's environments in general, but to none in particular. For many millennia, human progress in any field has been based on culture and not on genetic improvement. (American Association of Physical Anthropologists Statement on Biological Aspects of Race, 1996)

chapter
8

Distribution of Human Biodiversity

The study of *Homo sapiens'* biodiversity depends on an understanding of its distribution and, in previous chapters, I discussed a number of traits whose distributions are well known. Those of complex inheritance are highly visible and provided the foundation for racial classifications. These traits seemed to mark distinct boundaries between people; no one would confuse an African with a European or with a resident of China. Plainly stated, people from distant parts of the world look different, and we may assume a person's region of origin or ancestry by certain physical features that they possess. Yet the boundaries between close geographic regions are not that well defined. What is most important is that however we may draw the boundaries, they do not coincide with the gene frequencies for simply inherited traits. Further, most of our genetic diversity (90 percent) is due to differences among individuals of a group in contrast to the small difference between groups. Any study of human diversity must recognize this conflict between identities and labels. Yet, we still use the race concept in our every day language and in science.

The term race has been applied to units as small as local breeding populations (demes) as well as to large population groups occupying entire continents (geographical race). Race has also been used quite frequently to describe a religious, cultural, or political group (Jewish, Aryan, English, and so on). Another casual use of the term is shown by the phrase "the human race," which has nothing to do with biological classification. Ethnic group is more and more frequently used today as a substitute term for people presumed to be of different ancestral descent, especially as it applies to national minorities—as in the case of Hispanic or Asian ethnic groups in the United States. Though ethnic labels may fit the needs for socioeconomic or political divisions, they can be inappropriate for the study of biological diversity and are often misleading. Furthermore, inconsistent use of biological markers has added materially to the confusion over classification. Comparisons of populations for traits of simple inheritance yield different results than do comparisons of complex traits of these same populations, for example. The geographical distribution of red-cell antigens, histocompatibility (HLA) types, and DNA polymorphisms differ markedly, and none correspond well with classification based on quantitative traits like skin color and body form.

This lack of concordance of trait distribution brings up the question of how the human species may be subdivided into groups for description and study. There is no simple solution, and devising methods of division has always been difficult, particularly because many of the so-called racial differences are trivial in comparison with species differences. Genetic loci are shared by all human populations and, with rare exceptions, none are unique to any one group. It is a matter of differing frequencies of certain alleles that provide markers that may distinguish between populations. Many genetic polymorphisms vary less among the classic geographical races than among populations composing them. Hence, several named tribes of southern Africa differ significantly at several loci (e.g., Rh, GM, and HLA systems) just as they differ from equivalent-sized groups living 2,000 miles to the northwest (Excoffier et al., 1987). Such differences have been also recorded among population groups of the other major geographic divisions. What had once appeared to be a few simple subdivisions of our species turns out to be numerous small and large clusters of genetic heterogeneous groups dispersed throughout the geographic range of human occupation (Cavalli-Sforza et al., 1994).

The growing record of gene diversity and the reality of population variability have caused human biologists to avoid or even to abandon the use of the race concept as a viable tool in the study of human diversity. Over forty years ago, Hiernaux observed that "In my opinion, to dismember mankind into races as a convenient approximation requires such a distortion of the facts that any usefulness disappears" (1964: 43). The facts to which Hiernaux referred are the many types of evidence of human biological diversity, which include the several traits of simple inheritance that I discussed in the preceding chapters. The rapid accumulation of new genetic data over the past decades shows that biological diversity and its distribution is much more complex than formerly recognized. Further, many of these trait distributions cut across population and geographic boundaries and no one group seems to be uniquely endowed with a particular gene. However, some investigators still consider racial classification a useful means of studying adaptation and epidemiology because they view races as "natural units" (Polednak, 1989). Others dismiss race as but an artifact of *Homo sapiens'* past. But writers still lapse into the old tradition of using the Negroid, Caucasoid, and Mongoloid triad even when describing the most sophisticated studies of gene diversity; this often occurs when tracing a population's origins. Such lapses occur despite the tracing of ancestry by DNA haplotypes of the Y-chromosome and mitochondria as well as several phenotypes of the nuclear DNA. Traits should be considered individually and not as a group or cluster unless the resulting classification, based on one character, reflects the variability of others. Recognition of these problems has caused genetic anthropologists to tread carefully around the old race concept and more and more frequently the breeding population has become the unit of study. Humans cannot be classified into discrete categories with absolute boundaries (AAPA Statement on Race, 1996). The study of biodiversity is much more than simple classification; it depends on an understanding of causes of distribution of traits.

SOME FACTORS CONTRIBUTING TO GENE DISTRIBUTION

Human variability as it is distributed through time and space depends on a multitude of factors. Several are the same factors that operate on any biological population of sexually reproducing organisms, and these factors influence gene frequency throughout the generations, as described in Chapter 2. Other influences are uniquely human since we are highly mobile and are able to manipulate the environment at will to affect successful adaptation in a variety of climates. These abilities depend not only on technological achievements, but also on our linguistic skills and the elaboration of complex social systems. These systems control behavior and coordinate individual and group activities. Of particular importance is direction of breeding behavior—the regulation of mate choices. This is accomplished by the establishment of abstract boundaries, or mating circles within a population, that define kinship with genetic implications as well as a social meaning.

Proscribed Marriages

All societies enforce some form of *incest taboo* that forbids or proscribes marriages between relatives of some degree, which always includes the nuclear family—parents and offspring—within this restricted category. Exceptions were brother–sister unions that were favored in several ancient civilizations like the Egyptian, Hawaiian, and Incan in order to maintain the royal bloodline. But beyond the nuclear family, degrees of relationships are defined differently in each society. Many tribal and simple agrarian cultures have preferred certain types of cousin marriages. The selection of a mate from among one's uncles or aunt's children was desired and helped maintain property while reinforcing alliances among family lineages. This practice of marriages between relatives was also followed by several royal families of Europe over the centuries. The goal was to establish political alliances by intermarriages, usually between cousins. The Hapsburg Empire of central Europe was founded on such alliances, for example, and had the effect of uniting a good part of Europe for centuries. Later the children, grandchildren, nieces, and nephews of Queen Victoria ruled throughout Europe. This maintenance of political alliances through royal bloodlines worked fairly well until World War I when empires fell and many national boundaries were drawn or redrawn.

For the majority of humanity, however, the tendency has been to outbreed, depending on availability of potential mates. Marriages between cousins were forbidden in some societies but allowed in others where distribution of property was enhanced by unions between offspring of uncles and/or aunts. A preferred union was between the children of a brother and sister, usually an arranged marriage for a male to marry his mother's brother's daughter as an example. This is described as a "cross-cousin" marriage as compared to a "parallel-cousin" marriage where the union was between the children of brothers or sisters. Both such forms have the same inbreeding coefficient—that is, the likelihood of pairing the same recessive alleles with frequent detrimental effect to the homozygote offspring as described in Chapter 2. During the long periods of human history restrictions on cousin marriages were often waved in numerous smaller populations with limited number of potential mates, as in the case of relatively isolated island communities. The restrictions and permitted exceptions were detailed and carefully codified even in nonliterate societies. Such marriage arrangements have declined in frequency in modern times as socioeconomic structures have changed with the empowerment of women being a most influential force.

Regulation of consanguineous marriages were and still are an important part of the Western legal system.[1] Most state laws in the United States forbid marriages between cousins, always the first cousins, but there are fewer restrictions on second or third cousins. Exceptions are made in some states if the woman is over 50, past her reproductive age. In addition, there were laws that forbid interracial marriages in forty states. These so-called miscegenation laws were gradually repealed until they remained on the legal statutes in only a few states when, thirty-eight years ago, the U.S. Supreme Court ruled these laws in violation of the Fourteenth Amendment.

Religious and Social Barriers and Boundaries

Religious sanctions have played an important role in mate selection. Some marriages are sanctioned while others are prohibited on the basis of either degrees of familial relationship or church membership. The examples of conflict over cross-religion marriages are all too familiar to require detailed examples. What should be recalled, however, is that though sanctions on mate choice have weakened considerably in modern times, they were strong influences in the past. Custom, tradition, and economic class have also been, and in some cases remain, powerful forces in directing mate exchange; a majority of marriages in modern Western society occur between members of the same ethnic group (however defined). A study of mating patterns in San Francisco, California, serves to illustrate this point.[2] Of fifteen ethnic groups compared in this cosmopolitan city of 700,000, a majority of the marriages over several months in 1980 were between group members—Chinese with Chinese, Japanese with Japanese,

---

[1]Marriages between "blood relatives" of some degree is defined by a kinship lineage linking individuals to a common origin.

[2]Ethnic group membership in this study was defined by census records, marriage certificates, and use of surnames. This is an imperfect method, to be sure, for any genetic study. It can suffice to demonstrate how social networks and self-identification may direct mate choice.

Mexican with Mexican, and so on. Family pressure was probably one of the major reasons, but residence patterns and economic and education factors were also influential (Peach and Mitchell, 1988). This study of marriage patterns in a population of heterogeneous origins demonstrates how social forces still are effective in forming mating networks. At earlier times in our history, imagine how much stronger the influences of population size and group identity must have been in directing gene flow and determining the composition of the next generation.

If we consider these social influences on population distribution, then any grouping of human variability, at whatever level, may become a much more viable means of studying human diversity. The way in which we choose to group human populations depends, of course, on our purpose, and we must keep this purpose in mind when working with these groups. For example, one should not classify races or ethnic units on the basis of sociopolitical or religious criteria and then explain or interpret their existence in biological terms. The same stricture applies to groups established on the basis of geographic boundaries. The so-called natural boundaries do not prevent interpopulation contact, though distance does, of course, reduce the frequency of interpopulation matings and, hence, gene flow. Likewise, sociopolitical or religious differences may influence the composition of the next generation, but only to the degree that restrictions are enforced. The significance of this influence is determined by the humans involved and by their society's rules. The religious and often violent political differences in Northern Ireland, for example, have reduced or prevented interbreeding between the Catholics and Protestants, in contrast, say, to the frequent cross-religious marriages in the United States. The net effect is establishment of two breeding populations in Northern Ireland within what would have been a homogeneous group. Similar examples can also be found in many other parts of the world where religious, economic, or political strife has resulted in a degree of isolation between groups (often referred to as ethnic groups). In their various homelands, Sunni Muslims are isolated from Shia, Sephardic Jews from Ashkenazim, and Koreans from Japanese, though they share a close common ancestry and isolation may not be complete.

There are some interesting distributions of the patterns of genetic markers or phenotypes around the world. If we examine a single trait or several together, we find that groups vary widely from one another in the frequencies they possess. The worldwide distribution of traits such as the blood types, abnormal hemoglobins, or DNA polymorphisms shows broad differences among populations. The same applies for any number of complex traits. These distributions are often attributed to evolutionary factors which, of course, do play an important role, especially for those phenotypes under intense selection. The fact remains, however, that populations are socioeconomic units and were established and are maintained because of conditions other than those determined by their biological attributes. The combinations of characteristics and their underlying gene frequencies are often distributed because of social, economic, and political conditions that have contributed to the growth and maintenance of the biological unit, defined as a breeding population. Unique gene frequencies can be found in several island populations because of their small size and geographic isolation, for example. Likewise, members of religious sects differ significantly in many genetic markers from their neighbors as a result of their decision to maintain breeding isolation. This raises the question of the biosocial nature of human populations.

The history of a population—how long it has lived in a given area, what selective forces have been acting on it, and what contacts it has had with other populations—helps to understand the distribution of human variability. The effects of the European colonization of the world dramatize the significance of mass movements of people over the last four centuries. People carrying genomes largely adapted to conditions in a temperate zone environment now reside in tropical environments, and tropical peoples now occupy temperate environments. Over the course of these migrations, many indigenous peoples were destroyed or absorbed into a larger population network.

This describes only a short time frame of human history, however. Our ancestors have always moved about, and over thousands of years there have been numerous major changes of population boundaries—the prehistoric expansion of people out of the Middle East around the Mediterranean and into Europe, for example. The peopling of the Western Hemisphere began about 20,000 years ago with a series of migrations from northeastern Siberia. This entry into a vast uninhabited region spread people of Asian origins over areas with diverse environments, founding the ancestral stock of Native Americans. The landing, about 900 years ago, of founders of modern-day Maori on the unpopulated islands of New Zealand is another case of wide dispersion of humans. Smaller scale, more gradual changes can also occur through interpopulation contact and through the establishment of nearly isolated island populations throughout the Pacific. These changes of boundaries may occur as consequences of the pressure of overpopulation, new technology, and exploration, or as a response to new subsistence patterns such as plant domestication, requiring more land. Whatever the causes, populations rise and fall, expand or contract over time, and change the dimensions of their distribution.

RACES, ETHNIC GROUPS, OR BREEDING POPULATIONS

Explaining the arrangement of the varieties of organisms found in the natural world is as much a problem today as it has always been. With the newer techniques of taxonomy that use computer facilities, investigators can process thousands of bits of information, many more than the naturalists of previous generations could. Rather than establishing and clarifying distinct boundaries between populations, this additional information often raises new questions and casts doubts on the validity of many older, accepted taxonomic units. As noted earlier, anthropologists of the nineteenth century classified Melanesians with Africans because of similarities in skin color and hair. Such classification did not persist for long before anthropologists realized that there were numerous differences between the two groups. Over the decades many distinctive characteristics of cranial facial morphology were recorded that demonstrated that the Melanesians were more closely related to other population groupings of the Pacific region. The similarities and degrees of relatedness are summarized by Howells (1973:40) in Figure 8-1. The "distances" from some presumed common ancestor are indicated

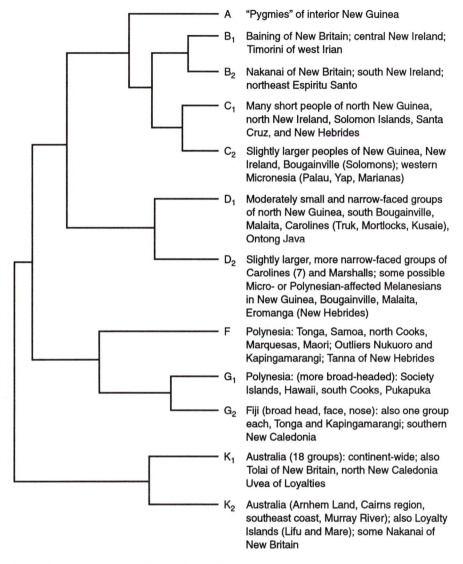

A   "Pygmies" of interior New Guinea

B_1 Baining of New Britain; central New Ireland; Timorini of west Irian

B_2 Nakanai of New Britain; south New Ireland; northeast Espiritu Santo

C_1 Many short people of north New Guinea, north New Ireland, Solomon Islands, Santa Cruz, and New Hebrides

C_2 Slightly larger peoples of New Guinea, New Ireland, Bougainville (Solomons); western Micronesia (Palau, Yap, Marianas)

D_1 Moderately small and narrow-faced groups of north New Guinea, south Bougainville, Malaita, Carolines (Truk, Mortlocks, Kusaie), Ontong Java

D_2 Slightly larger, more narrow-faced groups of Carolines (7) and Marshalls; some possible Micro- or Polynesian-affected Melanesians in New Guinea, Bougainville, Malaita, Eromanga (New Hebrides)

F   Polynesia: Tonga, Samoa, north Cooks, Marquesas, Maori; Outliers Nukuoro and Kapingamarangi; Tanna of New Hebrides

G_1 Polynesia: (more broad-headed): Society Islands, Hawaii, south Cooks, Pukapuka

G_2 Fiji (broad head, face, nose): also one group each, Tonga and Kapingamarangi; southern New Caledonia

K_1 Australia (18 groups): continent-wide; also Tolai of New Britain, north New Caledonia Uvea of Loyalties

K_2 Australia (Arnhem Land, Cairns region, southeast coast, Murray River); also Loyalty Islands (Lifu and Mare); some Nakanai of New Britain

FIGURE 8-1 Relationships of Pacific Peoples by Measurement. Comparisons of craniofacial and body measurements of 151 Pacific populations showed a clustering in three major branches: (1) Melanesian (A–D), with a subbranch of Micronesians (C_2 and D_2); (2) Polynesian (F–G); and (3) Australian (K). The degree of relationship or similarity is indicated by the length of the connecting branches in the diagram; for example, the K branches of the Australian samples are most distant from branch A of the Pygmies of interior New Guinea. (Source: From Howells 1973. Reprinted by permission of George Weidenfeld and Nicolson Limited.)

by the lengths of the branches. These, in turn, show separations of differing degrees between the contemporary peoples; the Nakanai of New Britain, a Melanesian population, are more distant from Polynesian branches than they are from peoples of New Guinea. The populations of these island groups are a diverse lot, the result of generations of "racial churning" by several migrations and mixing of neighboring groups, further varied by social forces of mate selection and genetic drift (Swindler, 1962). Distributions of these traits as well as the recent list of DNA polymorphisms are the results of a long process of human behavior and biological interaction. This forces any classification, no matter its basis, to be an arbitrary means of organizing the data for study—one that is subject to change.

The question is not whether the earlier or later classifications were a true, accurate description of the natural world. The former methods merely had another way of viewing biological diversity, especially through those characteristics that could be measured and compared at that time; grouping of all dark-skinned people together was as logical to the early anthropologists as the use of DNA polymorphisms is today. As additional traits are considered, however, the boundaries of earlier classifications break down. Since the development of genetic theory and description of DNA polymorphisms, life's diversity is now seen somewhat differently. Groups of organisms appear as dynamic units, many of whose identifying traits may change in frequency from generation to generation. Types or averages are no longer considered a sufficient means to describe groups of individuals participating in a breeding population. It is this dynamic condition that makes it extremely difficult to establish any all-inclusive taxonomic unit. The concept of basic racial stocks, or geographic races, becomes more difficult to sustain with the rise of a broader knowledge of our species' genetic composition and the recognition of the influences of social and environmental forces.

The problem that classification offered for biological studies was recognized early, but the labeling of people continued, and it continues to this very day. The study of human biology, especially the attempt to classify, is hampered by a disagreement over several aspects of diversity: its origin, its relation to the environment, and whether basic racial stocks are "real" and of great antiquity. Demographics—that is, the growth and expansion or decline of a population—is a more recent addition to the list of recognized influences on distribution of biological diversity. Considering the growing knowledge of human diversity, it seems best to return to a fundamental statement of biological classification: A species is considered a natural biological unit genetically isolated from other species. By contrast subspecies are arbitrary divisions of a species identified for a particular purpose. The subspecies, or race, forms no such "natural" unit and can freely interbreed with others of the same species. The number of subspecies or the composition of each described depends on the characteristics that the investigator considers important. In other words, whether or not an individual or group of individuals are identified as a particular race is determined by their possession of certain arbitrarily selected traits. More than fifty years ago, in studies of animal taxonomy, there was what was called the 75 percent rule. If 75 percent of the members of one population differed from another, then the two populations were considered to be distinct subspecies. This guideline worked more or less successfully depending on which criteria were used to assign the individuals. Another guideline was the geographical distribution of populations and the history of contact, if any, between them.

The older rules of animal taxonomy are becoming increasingly difficult to apply, and most present-day concepts of race are founded on genetics and emphasize similarity of gene frequencies throughout populations of a geographic region. This collection, or population complex, shares a close common ancestry and has been under the influence of similar selective forces. The existence of such conditions would result in a high degree of similarity of certain genes in these populations. Recall, for example, that malarial environments have been a prime cause of the spread of abnormal hemoglobins. But this distribution of hemoglobin types follows that of malaria and cuts across population boundaries, following geographic environments that support malarial mosquitos. As knowledge of gene diversity and its adaptation increases, the concept of race becomes less useful. For example, the numerous studies today relating ethnic groups and diseases emphasize sharing of portions of their genomes through common descent from recent ancestors. Populations of Africans and Europeans prove to be more similar than Europeans and Asians, or Africans and Native Americans. In each of these broadly defined groups (African, Asians, etc.), there are differences seen at both the phenotypic and the DNA level.

Genomics, the study of an individual's genome, documents the genetic diversity we bear and has become increasingly more important with the expansion of DNA research. Certain components of a genome may increase an individual's risk for some disease. The higher than average incidence of adult diabetes among Native Americans and Polynesians, or the propensity for high blood pressure among African Americans, and differing rates of cardiovascular disease probably have a strong genetic component. But, any race or ethnic labeling of an individual must be made carefully and cautiously. The question may be raised about genetics: Which Native American population or which African American group, since each encompasses a broad, diverse genetic heritage. Arbitrary assignment of an individual to one or another group based on self-identification or racial profiling will not suffice for studies of gene and disease-risk correlations. The means of racial/ethnic classification, the very concept, and its applicability to biomedical studies and patient treatment are still much debated (Fincher et al., 2004; Garte, 2002).

The various definitions listed in the first chapter, however, encompass a broad range of comprehension of the race concept.[3] The definitions of race all share in common a recognition of the importance of geographic history of each group. Dobzhansky (1944:252) stated: "It is recognized that most living species are more or less clearly differentiated into geographic races, each race occupying a portion of the species distribution." Many of the investigators today would likely subscribe to this definition, with the additional qualifier of gene frequency differentiation. Also, most

---

[3]I use the word "concept" as defined in Webster's dictionary: "an idea of a class of objects, a general notion." Most writers do also, I believe, even though they do not state the precise meaning. Used in this way, the implication is that race is a "real" object in nature, waiting to be discovered and labeled.

appreciate the fluidity of boundaries due to human behavior. Few students of human diversity, however, view race as a natural unit existing in nature and awaiting discovery and classification. At least that is the case for anthropologists studying human variation who apply the race concept to aid in communication (e.g., African, Asian, Native American, etc.). But for other professionals it is a different matter. The news media need a convenient label for use in a story about a minority group and politicians cast about for a politically correct term. Law enforcement officials need a quick answer to aid in possible identification of an unknown skeleton. They are not concerned with the nuances of population labels or gene admixtures. All that is required is a simple description that might be useful and answer the question: Do the skeleton's features place the person in one of society's commonly used categories of ethnic group or race? It is the job of the forensic anthropologist to provide such information despite the more complex problems relating to biological diversity. Race or ethnic types as socially defined labels are too convenient for some purposes to discard. It is a problem, however, when such identifications continue to find their place as an orientation for many biomedical studies with a goal of defining genetic characteristics.

Geographic Races

The importance of geography and environment has often been recognized in the definition of races and still remains significant if applied correctly. Garn (1960) used spatial distribution of human varieties as a means of establishing racial groups as he described geographical, local, and microraces. Microgeographical races and local races are smaller, less inclusive groups, comparable with the breeding populations used by many workers who study human variation. These basic units are subject to localized natural selection, and population size also effectively influences differentiation between groups. The numbers and composition of local races are continually changing, with migration and interbreeding forming new ones, as experienced in Hawaii with the encounters among peoples from all parts of the world over the last 200 years. The largest, most inclusive group—the geographical race—includes many diverse local groups. The geographical race conforms most closely to the older description of basic racial stocks or major races (Australoid, American Indian, Mongoloid, Caucasoid, and Negroid). In a way, this category can be misleading, because members of geographical races often share only a few physical attributes. We must consider also that human differences—especially those morphological traits used to establish racial groups—are not as extreme or as great as generally supposed. This is most frequently seen in the case of morphological similarities that lead to the assumption that look-alikes have common ancestry, as discussed earlier. Intraracial variation is extensive in the major geographically determined races and is often overlooked.

Europeans: The Irish example.   Except for a superficial identification of the majority of the inhabitants of a continent, "basic stock" or "geographical race" tells us little about biological diversity or the interrelationships between breeding populations or the effects of the environment, which are the dimensions of the selective forces that act on the populations. Basic stock does not describe gene combinations, but all too often it contributes to stereotypes—the images generated when citizens of nations or regions are mentioned. That individuals seldom conform to our image is too large a disappointment to admit, a sin of which we are all guilty. Ripley's description of races of Europe, mentioned in the first chapter, provided us with images of Europeans that tend to persist to this day, so it is important to recall an exhaustive study of human diversity within one of these so-called races.

Conclusions about similarity or dissimilarity of populations is a matter of focus—at what level will regional populations be studied? If a broad view is taken of a large region, for example northwestern Europe, than a homogeniety of traits will be seen among the people of the region. If a study takes a closer look, however, more detail and greater diversty is revealed.

Hooton and Dupertuis (1955) photographed and recorded several anthropometric dimensions of 10,000 Irish males, residents of more than a dozen counties of Ireland. They found that few subjects fit the Irish stereotype so often used to depict one of the major "local races" of Europe. In fact, the Irish population's range of variability encompassed most of the European race types described by Ripley. In head form, a trait typically used to identify race in the first half of the twentieth century, the males ranged in cephalic index from very narrow to very broad. Likewise in stature, the range included very short men (146 cm) to tall (202 cm); 95 percent of nearly 9,000 males were included in a range between 158 and 186 cm.

This anthropometric survey suggests a modern population descended from multiple ancestors over a long history. Relethford (2003), analyzing this Ireland study by modern statistical methods, described significant differences between eastern and western parts of the country. Closer similarity was found to continental Europe in the eastern counties as would be expected given the recent history of contacts. Scandinavian influence was strongest in the midland counties, probably the result of a ninth-century invasion of a large force of 10,000 who sailed up the Shannon river from Galway bay on the west coast. Relethford suggests that this group who established permanent settlements in the midlands had a more lasting influence than the earlier settlements scattered along the eastern coastal areas around Dublin. Later genetic surveys of blood groups and Y-chromosome haplotypes also show these distinctions between the western and eastern counties. Besides the significance of the midland counties, the links of the eastern parts of Ireland to England and Scotland and continental Europe represent past invasions and colonizations that brought large numbers of settlers to the more desirable farms lands of the region. The result of a long history of people from western Europe and Britain entering Ireland has been a churning of populations, creating a mosaic of diversity among the modern Irish. Traces of this history are seen in the distinctive clustering of counties (Figure 8-2) identified by morphological traits, blood groups, and Y-chromosome haplotypes.

New World Peoples.　　Another example of focus, stereotype, and limitation of geographic labels is the diversity found among Native Americans. Rather than matching

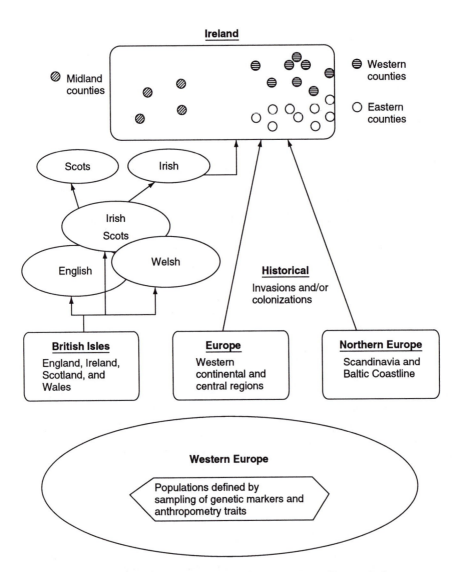

FIGURE 8-2 Population Similarities or Differences: A Matter of Focus. The genetic distance between populations become more apparent with a closer focus, that is, when the sampling is larger and more detailed. Comparisons of widely dispersed populations of western Europe show a breakdown by geographic areas (British Isles, northern and western continental Europe). Further comparisons within the British Isles show divisions between English, Scots/Irish, and Welsh. The Scots/Irish is divided further into two separate populations. Finally, Ireland divides into a cluster of countries as described by Relethford. (Source: Race and Sanger, 1975; Hooton and Dupertuis, 1955; Relethford, 2003; Darlington, 1969.)

TABLE 8-1   Mean Stature of a Sample of Native American Males

TRIBE	LOCATION	STATURE (CM)
Motilon	Brazil	146.2
San Blas	Panama	149.9
Yanomama	Venezuela	153.2
Jivaro	Brazil	154.2
Maya	Yucatan	155.4
Otomi	Southern Mexico	158.0
Quechua	Peru	160.0
Hopi	Arizona	161.1
Zuni	New Mexico	161.4
Navaho	New Mexico	169.6
Aymara	Chile	161.8
Eskimo	St. Lawrence Island	165.0
Yaqui	Sonora	166.7
Papago	Arizona	168.8
Choctaw	Louisiana	171.4
Pima	Arizona	171.8
Blackfoot	North Dakota	177.4

Source: Selected from Comas, 1960; Newman, 1953; and Eveleth and
Tanner, 1976.

any stereotype, they vary greatly in size and form, from tall to very short (Table 8-1). Some populations are composed of people of heavy build who are prone to obesity, like the Toho O'Otam (Papago) of southern Arizona. In contrast are the short, slender people who dwell in the tropical rain forests of Central and South America, like the Yanomama of Venezuela and Brazil. Face form also covers a wide range, from broad, heavy faces to small, gracile faces with long, narrow noses; head shape varies over the range of cephalic indexes recorded for our species. Similar diversity is seen in several of the genetic markers of blood and taste sensitivity. Though Native Americans share a close common ancestry as descendants of populations who migrated from Siberia over the Bering Strait beginning approximately 15,000 to 20,000 years ago, their present-day variability should not be obscured by a broad, all-inclusive classification. This diversity among Native Americans is illustrated further by the tree diagrams in Figures 8-3a and 8-3b. Figure 8-3a is a dendrogram derived from a genetic distance formula obtained from comparisons of gene frequencies at fourteen genetic loci in ten Native American groups with frequencies found in three Asian groups. This depicts the relative genetic distance between Arctic peoples (North American and Siberian) and several sub-Arctic Native American groups. Figure 8-3b is a diagram computing genetic relationships based on thirty complex traits of dental morphology. Many of the same Arctic and sub-Arctic peoples are compared, in addition to representatives of South American populations. Both genetic distance diagrams show a greater similarity between northern Siberian and sub-Arctic peoples of North America than with other Asian groups.

This broad picture of a northeastern Asian connection is supported by four haplotypes of mtDNA (A,B,C,D) which are found in a majority of living Native Americans. The presence of A, C, and D in peoples of northeast Asia suggests a direct ancestral

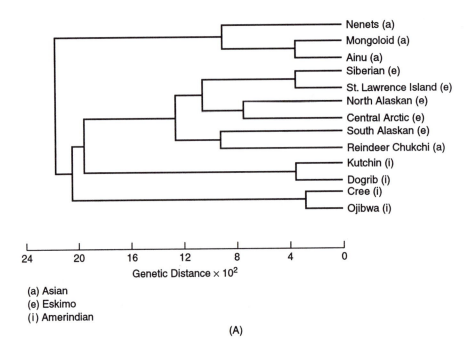

(a) Asian
(e) Eskimo
(i) Amerindian

(A)

FIGURE 8-3a   Dendrogram Showing Genetic Similarities among Asian and American Arctic and Sub-Arctic Populations. (Szathmary, 1985. Copyright © 1985 by The Journal of Pacific History, Inc. Australian National University, Canberra, Australia.)

FIGURE 8-3b   Relationships within and between Native American, Pacific, and Old World Populations. Based on twenty-eight dental trait mean measures of divergence clustered by unweighted pair group, arithmetic averages method. (Turner, 1985. Copyright © 1985 by The Journal of Pacific History, Inc. Australian National University, Canberra, Australia.)

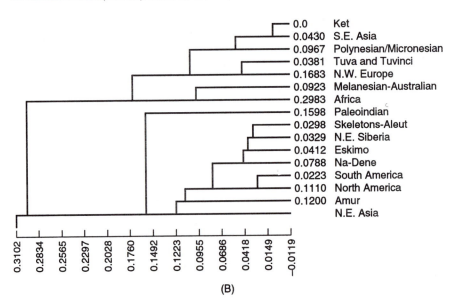

(B)

relationship. Type B has been identified in populations further to the south around Lake Baikal and can be taken as evidence of more diverse founding populations for the Americas (Schurr, 2000). A fifth, and rarer haplotype, X, identified in prehistoric skeletal remains, also points to a wider Eurasian origin. The X haplotype has not been found in Northern Siberians but does occur in Europeans. The presence of this haplotype in prehistoric skeletons rules out admixture and opened the possibility of trans-Atlantic contact as another Native American origin (a persistent and popular, if a speculative theme; witness the attempt to declare Kennewick man as an ancient European). The discovery of the X haplotype in people living in the Altai mountains near Lake Baikal (Relethford, 2003) has laid to rest this popular bit of folk history of pre-Columbian ancestry.

The evidence accumulated to date suggests two or three major migrations from Asia across the Bering straits into the New World, the most recent being the entrance of the ancestors of the Inuit. As new discoveries are made the interpretations vary for time and origins, but it is firmly established that the migrations depended on sea level fluctuations with glacial advances during the terminal ice age. How many people crossed this vast area opened up by the drop in sea level or exactly when are still disputed. But there is no doubt that these early hunters from several Siberian regions entered a resource-rich continent and expanded rapidly in numbers. This expansion from a relatively few founders would have contributed to biological variation of their modern descendants we see today.

African peoples.   Once commonly grouped as a Negroid race, Africans are another example of millions of people being treated as if they were all members of a homogeneous population. North Africa is described as region populated by people more closely related to the Middle East and Europe than to the rest of the continent; they have often been labeled "Caucasoid" despite their darker skin color. Sub-Saharan populations are often lumped together as "Black Africa" with a few recognized subgroups: Pygmies of the central African rain forests, Khoisans of southern Africa, and the tall slender people of the eastern highlands. The balance include most of the African people, west Africans and Bantu (a name of a major language subdivision). The Bantu, as it turns out, encompass a diverse range of peoples, from short, pygmoid farmers of central African rain forests to the large robust Zulu farmers and herders of the southern African grasslands. Far from being homogeneous types, there are wide differences between many of linguistic or tribal units as shown by the frequencies of several common alleles.

The use of alleles of the Rh, HLA, and Gm systems together with mtDNA and beta globin separates African populations south of the Sahara into significantly different clusters (Excoffier et al., 1987). The Khoisans of southern Africa were grouped in one unit, east and west Africans in others, while all differed from Pygmies and another group, the southern Bantu (e.g., Zulu). The major African Gm haplotype (1, 17, 5) varies over a range of 50 percent among these populations. Similar ranges of diversity were reported for the Rh system (cDe, CDe, and cDE haplotypes). Both HLA-A and HLA-B gene frequencies encompassed a wide range, and analysis of ten populations established a significant difference between Khoisan, west African, and southern Bantu. What these comparisons have shown is that there are clear distinctions found among Africa populations, and according to Excoffier and co-workers, these distinctions agree well with linguistic divisions.

These distributions of the gene frequencies are representative of a history of migrations and past contacts among Africans, as well as with groups outside the continent—east Africans with Arab–Asians, for example. In addition to suggesting a history of population migrations and contacts, this record of divisions of gene markers among sub-Saharan peoples cautions against the use of geographic race in human biological studies.

The extensive diversity within each of the classic geographical race divisions is clearly established, whether one examines the complex morphological traits or the inherited phenotypes of the blood. In fact, Lewontin (1974) emphasized that intrapopulation diversity (the diversity among individuals) often exceeds that between populations. As he explained, 85 percent of our species' genetic variability is among individuals within a nation or tribe. This is illustrated by a table of major genetic markers, their diversity within the species, and their proportion in populations or races (Table 8-2). Such variability has been recognized many times by human biologists and anthropologists, but it seldom prevented them from using some form of classification until quite recently. Since the increased use of gene markers and DNA polymorphisms, however, there has been a growing discomfort with the race concept and all of its related assumptions.

TABLE 8-2   Major Genetic Markers in *Homo sapiens*

LOCUS	ALLELE	POPULATIONS AND GENE FREQUENCIES
Serum Proteins		
Haptoglobin	Hp^1	0.09 (Tamils)–0.92 (Lacondon)
Lipoprotein	Lp^a	0.009 (Labrador)–0.267 (Germany)
Enzymes		
Red cell acid	p^a	0.09 (Tristan da Cunha)–0.022 (Australian)
Phosphatase	p^b	0.979 (Australian)–0.91 (Tristan da Cunha)
Phosphoglucomutase	PGM_1	0.430 (Habbana Jews)–0.938 (Yanomama)
Adenylate kinase	AK^2	0 (Africans)–0.130 (Amerinds-Pakistanis)
Blood Groups		
Kidd	JK^a	0.310 (Chinese-Dyaks)–1.000 (Eskimo)
Duffy	FY^a	0.061 (Bantu-Chenchu)–1.000 (Eskimo)
Lewis	Le^b	0.298 (Lapps)–0.667 (Kapinga)
Kell	K	0 (Many)–0.063 (Chenchu)
Lutheran	Lu^a	0 (Many)–0.86 (Brazilian Amerinds)
Rh	CDe	0 (Luo)–0.960 (Papuans)
	Cde	0 (Many)–0.156 (Chenchu)
	cDE	0 (Luo)–0.308 (Dyak-Japanese)
	cdE	0 (Many)–0.174 (Ainu)
	cDe	0 (Many)–0.865 (Luo)
	cde	0 (Many)–0.456 (Basques)
ABO	A	0.07 (Toba)–0.583 (Bloods)
	B	0 (Amerinds)–0.297 (Austr.-Toda)
	O	0.509 (Oraon)–0.993 (Toda)

Source: Selected from Cavalli-Sforza et al., 1994, R.C. Lewontin, 1972; Mouant, 1983.

Throughout the last decade, with each new study a greater variety has been found within than between populations, just as shown thirty years ago by Lewontin. Taking a broad base of comparison with a measure of the distribution by restriction-site polymorphisms on autosomes, mtDNA, and the Y-Chromosome, a greater diversity was found among Africans than Asians or Europeans (Jorde et al., 2000).

Excoffier and co-workers, cited above, proceeded with caution in group identification and relied mainly on language-family affinities and tribal names as ethnic identifiers. Likewise, a recent large compendium that collated frequency data on forty-nine genetic markers reported in 1915 populations depended on ethnic and tribal names as well as classification of language groups. Through multivariant analysis techniques, this study attempted to trace evolutionary history of populations in each of the major geographical regions (Cavalli-Sforza et al., 1994). The resulting estimated distances and calculated degrees of relationship give one pause for acceptance of a simple human taxonomy (i.e., race). Early in their volume, the authors clearly outline the problem with seeking to divide the human species into discrete units. They noted that ". . . we can identify clusters of populations and order them into a hierarchy that we believe represents the history of fissions in the expansion to the whole world of anatomically modern humans. At no level can clustering be identified with races, since every level of clustering would determine a different partition and there is no reason to prefer a particular one" (Cavalli-Sforza et al., 1994:19). Even in their cautious use of tribal or linguistic labeling to designate a group cluster's gene frequencies, there are a multitude of problems that have been pointed out by ethnologists and historians. Many of the tribal units from which blood samples had been acquired did not exist a few hundred years before; language affinities may also not be an adequate label of identity (MacEachern, 2000).

Such problems of group identification for the purpose of comparative study of human diversity have been described earlier in detail by Hiernaux, when he began an analysis of data collected during a biological anthropology field survey in central Africa in the 1950s. He noted that, though it was customary to start a description of survey results with a classification of the groups studied, the use of existing taxonomies, rather than relying on the data collected, was misleading. His observation led to the question, "What do we want to classify?" The answer seems unequivocal: "the gene pools of the breeding population" (Hiernaux, 1966b:289). Most field studies of human diversity have followed this lead ever since.

This and other surveys of local groups using gene markers as well as anthropometric dimensions document that geographical race is merely a convenient label, an abstraction applied in the broadest sense. To describe and study the significance of human variability, we must use a more restricted and precise grouping; otherwise, important interpopulation differences will be obscured.

BREEDING POPULATIONS

Human breeding populations are the result of complex social organization and culturally directed behavior that have created geographical clusters of mating circles with porous boundaries. A complex of social customs and taboos proscribe and prescribe sexual relations and establish the basis for family life, as well as determine family lineages, clans, caste systems, and religious affiliations. These present well-established culturally defined boundaries in turn affect gene combinations of the next generation. But the boundaries are not rigid and enforcement is quite flexible, varying across generations and affected by distance and by demographic structure—the age distribution and the sex ratio of the members of the communities. The result may be a highly variable gene flow within and between populations.

Geographical distance is an important consideration, for it obviously places limits on social contact and may reduce choices of a mate to a local population. In prehistoric times distance between early agricultural villages and between nomadic bands was especially influential in limiting gene flow. Even during fifteenth- to sixteenth-century England, gene flow was spatially restricted and a man was most likely to find his mate within one-half a mile of his residence. Later studies of parish records for residents of Ottmoor villages in Oxfordshire, England, showed that 35 percent of marriages were between partners where at least one spouse came from outside the parish throughout most of the eighteenth and nineteenth centuries. The average distance between prenuptial households was six to eight miles. By the mid-nineteenth century, this interparish marriage rate had increased to 63 percent with average distances of ten miles or more (Tranter, 1985). The net effect was a broadening of the scope of mating circles to encompass a larger number of small local populations, thereby expanding the genetic heterogeneity. Improved transportation, increased nonfarm employment opportunities, and a rise of urbanization with Britain's industrialization not only affected demography (particularly rates of annual increase) but also materially influenced change in the gene pool composition each generation (Molnar and Molnar, 2000).

If these increases in distance between the prenuptial households seem impressive, consider the mobility that was brought about by the railroad, and, more recently in the twentieth century, by the invention of the automobile and its universal use in developed countries. Even so, between 1940 and 1960, more than one-half of marriages were between persons who had lived less than one mile apart. As modern transportation and rural–urban migration has increased mobility further still, a broader exchange of genes is occurring as expected. Whereas formerly, small breeding units were restricted by economics, politics, or geography to a village community, today mating circles have expanded and the gene pool is much broader. In a world undergoing rapid urbanization, defining breeding populations and tracing patterns of gene flow are more difficult.

The effects that mating structures, distance, and population size have on gene frequencies are graphically illustrated by a study of modern Italian populations in the vicinity of the Parma Valley. Located in the north-central part of Italy, this combined agricultural and industrial region contains a scattering of rural villages of various sizes and a few urban centers. In the foothills and surrounding mountains, there are several smaller, relatively isolated villages that can trace their origins back to prehistoric times. For several years, the geneticist Cavalli-Sforza and associates have recorded the frequencies of alleles of the ABO, MN, and Rh blood group systems of these populations. Historical and social factors were also examined, because the sedentary nature of some of these populations, the varying degrees of their isolation, and the availability of marriage records from church archives made these communities an excellent source for the study of genetic variation and mate selection (Cavalli-Sforza, 1969, 2004a).

The results of the study show a close correlation between village size and gene-frequency differences. The villages in the mountains, with populations smaller than those at lower elevations, exhibit a greater degree of genetic drift. This documents the relationship between effective breeding-population size and genetic variation among communities as theorized to be a factor in disturbance of the Hardy-Weinberg equilibrium. This population size–genetic variation of the several communities is illustrated in Figure 8-4a. There is less difference among the larger communities at the lower elevations. In addition to size, genetic variation between villages is also influenced by the relative lack of migration. Most marriages occurred between persons of the same church parish, and the next most frequent matings occurred between persons within eight kilometers (Figure 8-4b). Given these factors, many consanguinial marriages occurred in the mountain communities; more special dispensations, granted by the Catholic Church for cousin marriages (7.13 percent of all marriages between 1640 and 1965), were awarded to residents in these villages than to those in the larger towns (between 0.63 and 1.64 percent over the same period). As expected, the isolation, small population size, and low rate of migration had limited one's choice of a mate, as is reflected in the church records of special dispensations allowing cousin marriages.

In lesser developed societies, a rugged environment together with poor transportation contribute even more to population isolation. People within remote villages

FIGURE 8-4a   Variations in the Frequency of a Blood Type between Parma Valley Valleges. Variations were greatest, as predicted, in the isolated upland hamlets and declined as population density increased farther down in the valley in the hill towns, on the plain, and in the city of Parma. (From Cavalli-Sforza, Luigi Luca, "Genetic Drift in an Italian Population." Copyright © 1969 by Scientific American, Inc. All rights reserved.)

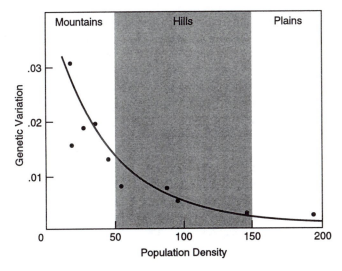

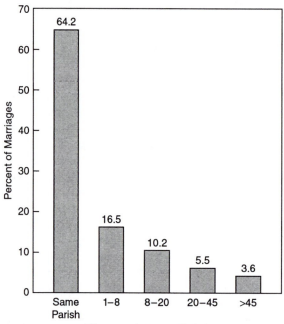

FIGURE 8-4b   Distances between Prenuptial Households in Parma Valley Villages. Migration in the upper Parma Valley has been infrequent, a conclusion drawn from the fact that most marriages recorded from 1650 to 1950 in parish books united men and women who were from the same village. The number falls as the distance separating birthplaces increases. (From Cavalli-Sforza, Luigi Luca, "Genetic Drift in an Italian Population." Copyright © 1969 by Scientific American, Inc. All rights reserved.)

may have scant opportunity to intermarry with others only a short distance away, even if they happen to be members of the same designated tribe, a preferred relationship. The rough, hilly terrain in the west Bengal region of eastern India causes the isolation of numerous groups. One of these groups, the Pahira, provides an example of the effects of this isolation. The 1,400 people of this tribe of food collectors live in small hamlets scattered over 300 square miles. They are clustered into three units or divisions. Each unit forms an endogamous breeding population with little admixture in each generation with other such clusters. For example, considering three generations, the majority of individuals had both parents who were from the same unit. According to Basu (1969), this village endogamy has resulted in significant differences in frequencies of the genes for the ABO blood group and taster phenotypes. Though members of the same tribe, these smaller units of hamlet clusters form distinct breeding populations. Thus, we must be extremely cautious in any statement about the gene frequencies of large groups, whether nations, states, tribes, or races; such groups are often a composite of numerous smaller units.

Reports describing gene frequencies of, say, several African tribes of the Bantu language group, the Saami, the British, or Native Americans can be completely erroneous unless the sample is taken from individuals who are chosen from the same breeding population within the social/political unit—a difficult task, but a necessary one if we are to attempt to understand the genetics of human diversity. An example is the distribution of the blood groups that have been recorded for vast numbers of people. Boyd (1963a) used these traits as sorting criteria in an attempt to differentiate races of humanity, as noted earlier, and the gene frequencies are summarized in Table 8-3. These groups cover large geographic regions and include numerous smaller breeding populations. The blood-group markers listed for the groups tend to describe or imply a homogeneity where little or none actually exists. Even adding additional markers of the numerous protein polymorphisms of the many restriction sites of DNA does not alleviate the basic problem of defining the unit of study. Ethnic and tribal names change over time for various reasons and individuals alter their identity easily, much to the distress of the scientist who is attempting to collect tissue or blood samples for study. Some groups, however, maintain an identity as a well-defined breeding population.

Population Isolates

In more complex societies with caste and class stratification, social distance can play a role in mate choice similar to that of geographic distance. Peasant–aristocracy stratification in medieval Europe tended to isolate breeding populations and cluster multiple genetic units within smaller areas. A similar situation exists even today in Latin America between those classified as Indios (Native Americans), Mestizos, Afro-Americans, and Euro-Americans. Though intermarriage may occur infrequently, the ethnically defined boundaries affect a restricted mating circle. There was a considerable amount of unidirectional mating—upper-class males mating with lower-class females in the past, however.

A recent study of genetic admixture in the population of the large Amazon city of Belem, Brazil, serves to illustrate the dominant social group contribution (Santos et al., 1999). A sampling of Belem's ethnically mixed urban population for five markers on the mtDNA, which define 99 percent of all Native Americans, showed that indigenous women had contributed 50 percent to the formation of Belem's population. This contrasted to the 5 percent contributed by indigenous males, as measured by a Native American specific Y-chromosome marker. The authors explained that historically Europeans had been encouraged to mate with indigenous women and, during the first 200 years of the colony, were rewarded with land grants if they married. The results of this colonial policy are seen today in this genetically mixed population with a predominantly Euro-male contribution. With a gradual relaxation of social sanctions and with the rise of urbanization, intermarriages across caste boundaries have increased as they had in Europe earlier. A few generations from now, the genetic profile of this ethnically diverse population will likely be more balanced with a higher contribution of Native American males.

Another example of unidirectional gene flow measured by Y-chromosome haplotypes is the presence of a high frequency of Middle Eastern (Semitic) haploypes in

TABLE 8-3   Frequencies of ABO Blood Groups

POPULATION	PLACE	NUMBER TESTED	BLOOD-GROUP FREQUENCY			
			O	A	B	AB
Low A, virtually no B						
American Indians:						
Toba	Argentina	194	98.5	1.5	0.0	0.0
Sioux	South Dakota	100	91.0	7.0	2.0	.0
Moderate A, virtually no B						
Navaho	New Mexico	359	77.7	22.5	0.0	.0
Pueblo	New Mexico:					
	Jemez, etc.	310	78.4	20.0	1.6	.0
High A, little B						
Bloods	Montana	69	17.4	81.2	0.0	1.4
Eskimo	Baffin Land	146	55.5	43.8	.0	0.7
Australian						
Aborigines	Southern Australia	54	42.6	57.4	.0	.0
Basques	San Sebastian	91	57.2	41.7	1.1	.0
American Indians:						
Shoshone	Wyoming	60	51.6	45.0	1.6	1.6
Polynesians	Hawaii	413	36.5	60.8	2.2	0.5
Fairly high A, some B						
English	London	422	47.9	42.4	8.3	1.4
French	Paris	1,265	39.8	42.3	11.8	6.1
Armenians	From Turkey	330	27.3	53.9	12.7	6.1
Lapps	Finland	94	33.0	52.1	12.8	2.1
Melanesians	New Guinea	500	37.6	44.4	13.2	4.8
Germans	Berlin	39,174	36.5	42.5	14.5	6.5
High A and high B						
Welsh	North Towns	192	47.9	32.8	16.2	3.1
Italians	Sicily	540	45.9	33.4	17.3	3.4
Siamese	Bangkok	213	37.1	17.8	35.2	9.9
Finns	Hame	972	34.0	42.4	17.1	6.5
Germans	Danzig	1,888	33.1	41.6	18.0	7.3
Ukrainians	Kharkov	310	36.4	38.4	21.6	3.6
Asiastic Indians	Bengal	160	32.5	20.0	39.4	8.1

Source: From Boyd, W.C., "Genetics and the Human Race," *Science* 140:1057–1064, Table 2, 7 June 1963. Copyright © 1963 by American Association for the Advancement of Science. Reprinted by permission of the publisher.

southern African populations. The Lemba, a group of Bantu speakers spread over an area extending from South Africa to Zimbabwe, have an oral tradition that they are of Jewish origin. These people, commonly called the "black Jews" of South Africa, are thought to be descendents of Jewish males from the Arabian peninsula intermarrying with local Bantu women. The cultural evidence supports this tradition up to a point, but certain of their food taboos, religious practices, and male circumcision are also common to other Africans and Middle Eastern Muslims. Strong support for Lemba origin is found in the genetic evidence, however (Relethford, 2003).

Comparisons of the haplotype frequencies of the Y-chromosome by genetic distance maps place the Lemba between Bantu speakers, like the Zulu, and Jews of the Middle East and Europe. These comparisons support a paternal Jewish origin due to the influx of Jewish traders who moved among the ancient Lemba about 2,000 years ago. Counter to this historical reconstruction of ancient population movements is the argument that the male ancestors could have come from a broader contact with Semetic peoples. This argument was answered with the evidence of a particular haplotype, however. Thomas and colleagues identified a Y-haplotype most common among males who considered themselves members of Cohen, one of three traditional Jewish descent groups; Levi and Israel being the other two (Thomas et al., 2000). The presence of this Cohen model haplotype in 9 percent of all Lemba males and as high as 50 percent in Lemba males who belonged to what is considered the oldest of the clans supports their tradition of Jewish descent.

In India, the complex religious and caste system of Hindus, the predominant religion, establishes an immense social distance between several well-defined groups. These groups form endogamous communities isolated along occupational lines that were rigidly maintained until recent times. The Brahmin, the highest caste, are isolated from the lower castes arranged in a descending order with a decreasing degree of social contact. The lowest, the "scheduled" or "exterior" castes, who fill the most menial jobs of sweepers and garbage collectors, are excluded by an even greater distance from contact, except as servants. These "untouchables" have little or no chance of marrying or mating with the higher castes, and to do so was once punishable by death. Though the law has been abolished, occasional violence and even murders still occur. Such social isolation has contributed to some unique patterns of genetic trait distribution over the Indian subcontinent that anthropologists and geneticists have been trying to explain for more than a century. The recent studies of Y-linked and mtDNA traits have not made their task any easier. There is apparently a directional gene flow with upper-caste males carrying more of the markers believed to have been contributed by "Aryan" invaders from the west (Iran) 3,000 years ago. Tracing gene flow by mtDNA shows a different pattern since the mtDNA traces the female lineage and their intercast mobility is less restricted than that of males (Jones, 2003).

What has made such a task even more difficult is that clear trait boundaries are difficult to define due to the sizes of each of the caste groups, numbering in the tens of millions in a nation of one billion people. Comparisons of Hindus from two eastern states (Orissa and Andhra Pradesh) with Rajasthan in the west of India showed significant heterogeneity for several genetic markers. Differences of origins and ancient separations of these groups are also reflected in their language group boundaries—Dravidian and Indo-Aryan (Tartaglia et al., 1995).

Even without as rigid a caste system, religion has proven to be effective in maintaining endogamous communities in Europe as well. By rigorous enforcement of sanctions against interfaith marriages, religious sects have limited mating circles to a very narrow range. During the Middle Ages through to modern times, disputes among religions have contributed to a proliferation of breeding isolates. Catholics, Lutherans, Jews, and several Protestant denominations have all proscribed interfaith marriages down to this very day. The effects are seen in a higher than expected frequency of certain rare alleles. The occurrence of the rare neurological disorder, Tay-Sachs, among eastern European Jews is an example described in Chapter 3. Restrictions on freedom of worship have also forced many groups in recent history to migrate, usually in small groups, carrying but a small sample of the gene pool of their homeland.

The Old Order Dunkers of Pennsylvania provide an example of a small population who migrated but maintained their identity and isolation in their new homeland. This group can trace its origins to 1708 in the Rhineland area of Germany with the establishment of a sect of the German Baptist Brethren. The American colony began in 1719 when twenty-eight persons arrived in Pennsylvania to be joined later by others from the same Rhineland region. The New World colony flourished and grew in size until religious dissent among themselves caused the sect to split into three divisions in 1881. The smaller division retained the original beliefs and practices of the earlier settlers and became known as the Old German Baptist Brethren (or Dunkers). About 1950, there were fifty-five communities spread over the Midwest with a few in California and Florida. Three of these communities remained in the area of Pennsylvania where the colony began and where the communities were examined by a team of medical and genetic experts.

This extensive study by Glass and his co-workers (Glass et al., 1952) focused on several genetic characters, the blood groups of the ABO, Rh, and MN systems, as well as certain complex traits. Their findings showed that the Dunker isolate of 300 persons differed significantly from the average trait frequencies of the U.S. population as well as from populations living in those regions of Germany from which the group's ancestors had migrated. Blood type A and blood type M were much more frequent in the Dunker sample, for example. Other phenotype distinctions were observed in the population that were believed to be due to the small size of the effective breeding population (there were only ninety parents) and because of its isolation over the generations. Though it has been difficult to accurately document sampling error (genetic drift) in humans, this case study provided some interesting data to support population size as a factor in gene-frequency change. In addition, there is the genetic composition of the colony's original founders to consider. Were they carrying a unique combination of these genetic markers or were they a representative sample of the numerous Rhineland populations? Other such religious isolates provide additional clues to the operation of founder's effect and genetic drift.

Another Anabaptist sect, the Hutterites of North and South Dakota, and Sackatchewan, Canada, provide further evidence of human isolates and the genetic consequences of colony isolation and a small number of founders. A majority of the Hutterites today, about 33,000 people living in 300 colonies, can trace their ancestry back to 442 founders. These founders were part of a larger group of German settlers living in Russia, but in 1874 they immigrated to the United States, fleeing from military conscription of the adult males. Over the next five years the balance of the religious sect, some 1,200 people, left Russia to join their brethren in South Dakota (Oved, 1988). Expert farming skills in the northern great plains, using a hardy strain of Russian wheat, earned them rich rewards; the new colonies expanded rapidly and gained a high degree of self-sufficiency. Good health and a high birthrate (an average of eight children per marriage) caused the Hutterites to increase to their present number even without gaining religious converts or new immigrants. As each colony expanded to what the community deemed a critical size, about 150 people, new lands were acquired and certain families were selected to found a new community.

Because of differing origins (mainly between the earlier and later migrants), the Hutterite colonies are divided into three divisions called Leutes, and there has been little interbreeding among them during the last century. This isolation of the Leutes results in some unique gene frequencies when compared with North American and European populations because gene flow into the colonies from outside populations is near zero. As a result, the frequency of type-A blood has increased, whereas type B has decreased to a low level and has even disappeared in some colonies. In addition to the RBC blood types, a recent study of the HLA system (WBC types) showed many of the HLA haplotypes common to Europeans, but the S Leut (Schmiedenleut) had high frequencies for seven HLA haplotypes that have rarely been detected among Europeans. The S Leut also differed significantly from the other two Leutes in the combination of the forty-five haplotypes recorded (Kostyu et al., 1989). This rapid growth from a few founders experienced by the Hutterites illustrates again the effects of breeding-population size and isolation.

Another example is provided by the Amish of Pennsylvania, descendants of 200 founders who entered Pennsylvania between 1720 and 1770; from these few, the population grew to 45,000 by 1960. This growth from a handful of ancestors, with few immigrants added to the colony, resulted in close inbreeding through past generations, as suggested today by the few surnames that account for a majority of the population; 80 percent of the families in two Pennsylvania counties are accounted for by only eight surnames. Consequently, certain rare recessive genetic disorders occur in high frequency (McKusick, 1978). Further waves of migrants, about 3,000 between 1815 and 1865, led to establishment of colonies in Ohio, Indiana, and Illinois. The Amish, because of high fertility, have a population growth of 3 percent per annum, a rate exceeded only by the Hutterites. By the 1980 census there were 80,000 Amish living in twenty states and the province of Ontario, Canada.

In addition to the size factor, founders or original colonists were often a select group, not a representative cross section of the parent population from which they migrated. Hulse (1957) pointed out that a great many immigrants to the British colonies in North America came as a group from one or a few adjacent regions of the British Isles. He also noted that these immigrants possessed certain physical characteristics that set them apart from the general population of their homeland. Differences in body size, proportion, and pigmentation of eyes and hair were easily recognizable among the Scots, Welsh, or Irish from different counties, for example. Additional data of the uniqueness that may be possessed by immigrant groups are provided by Hulse's study of the Italian Swiss; Hulse observed that they were generally taller and heavier than the stay-at-home group. One may suppose that such groups as the Hutterites, Dunkers, and Amish may also have descended from ancestors who were not representative of the general populations. This biased sample of migrants from a parent population can result in some unusual distributions of traits throughout future generations that sets the modern-day descendants apart. Though these factors are lumped under the term founder's effect or principle, they cover a multitude of events, some chance and some intentional. The founding group may also, by chance, have certain recessive genes that give rise to a high frequency of these alleles when the population expands. The growth in numbers of humans has not been evenly distributed, however, throughout the range of time of our expansion nor has it been continuous. Some regional groups experienced rapid growth for a few generations or centuries only to suffer periods of loss or stagnation as described in Chapter 10.

Once a group is established as a breeding population, the size of the reproductive unit plays an important part in determining the composition of each succeeding generation. Genetic drift becomes an increasingly important factor in gene-frequency change with the decline in number of mating partners. The effect may be accentuated because of differential fertility among the matings; fewer individuals contribute to the next generation. In large modern populations, an estimated one-fifth to one-sixth of adults in their reproductive years produce one-half of the next generation. In small, relatively isolated groups, such differential fertility can have an even greater effect on the gene fixation of each generation. This can result in the formation of sharp genetic variation among tribes, villages, clans, or any other socially defined breeding unit for no other reason than limited mate choice.

When the genetic variation of groups such as the Hutterites, Amish, or Dunkers are studied, there are written records available to establish historical origins and family genealogies. For nonliterate peoples such as Native Americans, villagers in New Guinea or Africa, and nomadic bands in Australia, however, information on origins and identification comes from different sources. Researchers must use archeological evidence to establish population contacts or make do with a few accounts provided by travelers, anthropologists, or missionaries. More often, identification is made, at least initially, on the basis of linguistic similarities between groups or tribes and their location. The assumption is that tribes speaking the same language or similar dialects are related and share a close common ancestry.

Often the analogy is made between the spread of language and the spread of genes, assuming parallel patterns of linguistic and genetic variation. Several writers, though recognizing that languages evolve (i.e., change) at a much faster rate than genes, have dealt with language groups, families, dialects, and so on, as if language dialects coincided with breeding-population boundaries (Cavalli-Sforza et al., 1994). At a level of broad surveys, genetic diversity appears to parallel major linguistic boundaries, as in the case of a description of sub-Saharan Africa where a majority, about 200 million people, speak 500 languages of the Bantu subfamily. Placement of a genetic sample of villagers into one or another language unit for comparison of degree of common ancestry sometimes works fairly well, though there have been criticisms of village/tribal designations. Names identifying a population can be quite various at times, depending on who has recorded it and for what purpose. Were the people in question listed by government authorities or by a researcher entering linguistic or genetic data? The outcome can be quite different and confusing when comparisons are made of population boundaries. Further, these boundaries often change over time. Some identified tribal units did not exist a century ago and others have undergone name changes reflecting their sociopolitical status (MacEachern, 2000). Simply, social units identified by the government or private agencies may not be representative of past divisions of ancient populations.

Comparisons of gene-frequency distribution and language boundaries have also been made for many Native Americans, especially among those distinctive linguistic groups widely separated by geographic distance. The distribution of plasma protein GM types was traced throughout North and South America and regional differences were noted (Callegari-Jacques et al., 1993). Further differences within these regions could be defined when the data were grouped by language families. The Inuit and Na Dene speakers (Athapaskans of the Pacific Northwest) differed from all others. Populations of the Southwest, like the Pima and Hopi (Uto-Aztecan speakers), differed from the many tribes of Carib speakers in Central America and the Caribbean areas, and these, in turn, differed from Andean Quechua and the Yanomama of Venezuela. These studies of genetic marker distributions, however, dealt with large continent-wide populations; the data for linguistic-genetic boundary concordance is not as convincing for smaller groupings.

An example is the comparison of blood-group gene frequencies among populations of several villages of the New Guinea highlands. Livingstone, comparing data on the distribution of blood groups with language boundaries, showed significant gene-frequency differences between villages, though all spoke the same language and shared a close common ancestry (Livingstone, 1963). This lack of correlation between the gene markers and language was probably due to a combination of genetic drift and founder's effect, since the villages were highly endogamous, descendent from a small number of founders. By contrast, along New Guinea's north coast, villagers speak seventeen different languages of the two major language groups of the region, Austronesian and non-Austronesian (Papuan). There was a close correlation between language and genetic distance, that is, the amount of gene flow (Serjeantson et al., 1993). The language-genetic distance correlation drops to zero if the geographic effect is removed which is not surprising, considering the isolating effects of the rugged terrain which reduced gene flow. It reinforces observations about the effects of genetic drift on heterogeneity and suggests that language boundaries are not complete or long-term barriers to interpopulation gene flow. The extensive studies of language, anthropometry, and genetic markers conducted in the Solomon Islands, especially on the large island of Bouganville, also identified extensive heterogeneity among people living in relatively isolated villages scattered over the rough mountainous terrain (Friedlaender, 1987). Overall, the Austronesian speakers, though genetically diverse, differed from the smaller numbers of Papuan populations along the coastal regions of the Solomons.

Even the evidence of gene-frequency differences or similarities between populations is not always a reliable means of determining degree of common ancestry. Though small groups may have separated into two different units only within the recent past, they can still have significantly different gene frequencies. Villages of the Xavente and Yanomama, both South American tribes in the upper Amazon basin, will divide into groups to establish new villages when a settlement reaches a certain critical population size (about 150 people), which is surprisingly close to that of the Hutterite colonies noted above. Community leaders determine which individuals will leave to establish the new village, and division is most often made along extended family membership: brothers, their wives and children, as well as cousins of various degrees form the founding population. The net effect, over the generations, is to produce villages whose populations' gene frequencies may differ significantly even though they were closely related through a recent common ancestry. The population divergence that results from this process of population subdivision is described as the "lineal effect" by James Neel (1970:816).

Other examples of gene-frequency divergence are also offered by the Yanomama, described as a "fierce" people who had been continually at war with their neighbors. Raids were often made on nearby villages for the purpose of revenge for some previous attack or simply to obtain captive women (Chagnon, 1983). In one particular example, young women from the Makiritare tribe were brought back from a raid on a nearby village. These women proved to be highly fertile over the years of their captivity and among them produced an average of 7.3 children compared with the 3.8 average for Yanomama women. Chagnon and associates (1970) described the episode—raid, capture, and high fertility of the captive women—as being responsible for an unusually high frequency of the Diego blood group gene among this particular village, in contrast to a low frequency found in other Yanomama villages.

Another influence on "tribal" heterogeneity is polygamy, a preferred form of marriage in earlier human history. It has been, and still may be, an important factor influencing the genetic composition leading to heterogeneity. In some traditional societies in which this form of marriage is still practiced—several South American tribes, for example—70 to 80 percent of the offspring are from polygamous unions. Because some males are able to acquire more than one wife, it is obvious that many other males have a restricted opportunity to reproduce; hence, the genetic contribution to succeeding generations is limited to a very few males. Some males, because of their dominant position as clan leaders or relatives of high-status individuals, contribute disproportionately to future generations. This reduces intergenerational gene flow and acts much like the founder's principle in producing a certain gene combination. Polygamy may have been an important force in human evolution, especially during periods when the strongest, bravest, or best hunter was able to acquire more wives. The Inuit, for example, had a very practical way to care for widows and orphans. The surviving family of a recently deceased hunter of the band was moved into the household of the most successful hunter, whose duty it was to care for them by taking the widow as his second or third wife and her children as his own.

Chance, or "fate," and natural events as well as intentional acts (such as migration) play an important role in determining the growth, size, isolation, and, ultimately, gene frequency of the population. A typhoon may wipe out most of an island population, as on Puka Puka in the South Pacific, where an eighteenth-century typhoon left only seventeen survivors. These seventeen were all from the lower class in the Polynesian

TABLE 8-4   Regional Increases of Populations (in millions)

REGION	A.D. 1	1000	1500	1650	1750	1850
Africa	16	33	46	55	61	81
China	53	66	110	140	225	435
India	35	79	105	150	175	230
Eastern Europe	5	7	20	32	48	100
Southern Europe	18	12	20	28	35	58
Western Europe	10	15	33	50	60	110
North America	1.8	3.5	6	4.5	7	34.25

social structure, and persons of this class throughout Polynesia are, on the average, shorter. Shapiro (1942) explained the shorter stature of today's populations as a consequence of this chance event. Starvation and disease, too, have often decimated populations, leaving only a handful to start a new generation. Descendants often have traits or combinations of traits quite different from those expected. When studying a particular human group, the geneticist should be fully aware of its past history. Gadjusek noted: "The vicissitudes of history caused by social, psychological, and natural events operating on small bands have contributed greatly to the determination of the evolutionary course that has led to man" (1964: 134). They have also added to the characteristics that set many modern human groups apart. Favorable location is another major factor in population diversity and growth; consider the eightfold increase in populations of western Europe—especially those of British origin during the past four centuries (Table 8-4).

In the case of chance events mediated by certain human actions, the founder's principle discussed earlier has been a major factor in the evolution of the human gene pool. When *Homo sapiens*, as a species, was very small in numbers during prehistoric times, the recurrence of the founder's principle would have produced much intergroup variability. The dangers of prehistoric existence probably destroyed many small groups, whereas in others a few hardy and lucky souls were able to survive and reestablish the population. As long as *Homo sapiens* remained at the nomadic hunting and gathering level, a chance fluctuation in population size because of random, natural events would cause the species to remain small. There was little possibility for the formation of large, homogeneous breeding populations.

CLINAL DISTRIBUTION OF TRAITS

In addition to population clusters, any discussion of human biological diversity must consider another concept: the geographical gradients of single traits that seemingly cross population boundaries. If the geographical location of sampled data is marked and those data points of the same magnitude are then connected, the results appear as clines. The connected series of data points (phenotypic traits, gene frequencies, DNA markers, etc.) are distributed on a map in much the same way as barometric pressures or temperatures are plotted to depict weather fronts. This graphic expression of trait values seems to vary continuously by a gradual progression from one geographical region to the next. The apparent regional variation of biological gradients occurs frequently among widely dispersed populations and have been called clines. Such regional dispersion suggests that the distribution is meaningful, the result of either the action of selection or of massive gene flow as in a major population migration (see Birdsell, 1993).

Taking into account genetic markers and morphological differences among adjacent or distant populations, geographical variability of our species is self-evident, as discussed in earlier chapters. A number of gene markers (blood groups, hemoglobins, immunoglobins, and so on) are considered to be distributed in concordance with the selective forces of particular diseases. The concordance of the distribution of malaria and abnormal hemoglobins is the clearest example (see Figure 4-4). In the case of natural selection acting on a trait of complex inheritance, the geographical plot of skin color variation among the world's population stands out as an example (refer to Figure 5-4). The map in Figure 5-4 shows that the density of melanin content of the skin is highly correlated with latitude; the more northerly peoples have a lighter skin pigmentation. Likewise, body form relates to climatic factors of temperature and humidity. To the eye of the observer, as explained earlier, there is an apparent covariation with climatic conditions. Peoples living in colder climates tend to have a larger body size. Nose form is closely related to absolute moisture content of the air (vapor pressure) and, of course, skin color is highly correlated with the quantities of solar radiation striking the earth's surface.

Major migrations or invasions are responsible for massive gene flow and advances of genetic clines across broad geographical regions. Figure 8-5 traces one such advance of type-B blood group frequency throughout modern Europe. The allele decreases along a cline from east to west and is probably a genetic reminder of the invasions of Asian pastoral nomads into eastern and central Europe many times over the last 2,000 years. These invaders came from areas that today have populations of high type-B frequency. This contributed to the foundation of the gene pools of many of the populations of the region today. Clines for other gene markers (Rh and MN) also represent this east-to-west movement but are not as clearly defined.

These distributions pass through many populations as if they were entirely independent of the boundaries constructed by human mating habits. The spatial location of the populations, however, causes the formation of a gradual series of genetic or phenotypic frequencies. The construction of a line through these data points produces the cline. The fact that the location of populations forms the cline makes it difficult to explain the distribution of a single gene, though several workers have used such an approach. Most recently, gene combinations have been used to trace population distributions. The use of several genes, language families, and archaeology has been applied successfully to construct population maps, but not without some of the problems mentioned above (Cavalli-Sforza et al., 1994). These maps produce a clinal complex that can be interpreted as common origins, population movements, gene flow, or simply genetic distances between related groups. As such they can be used to avoid some of the pitfalls inherent in the plotting of single gene traits.

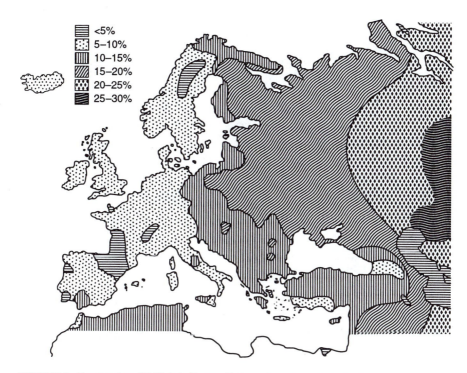

FIGURE 8-5   Frequencies of B Allele in Europe. (Redrawn From Mourant, A., *The Distribution of the Human Blood Groups*, 1954. Copyright © 1954 by Blackwell Scientific Publications, Ltd. Reprinted by permission of the publisher.)

The clines representing distribution of traits over broad areas frequently may obscure sharp differences between adjacent populations. When data from an increased sampling of local populations are added to a broad survey, sharp distinctions between neighboring populations are often identified, and the clinal boundaries of gene frequencies must be redrawn. Figure 8-6 illustrates this point: As a gene-frequency distribution becomes better known, the broader, more encompassing clinal expressions break down. Compare those regions of France and Italy that list the frequencies of the B allele with those noted in the broader clinal distribution plotted in Figure 8-5. Note that the broad overview lists a frequency of 5 to 10 percent while a more comprehensive series of measures shows over 15 percent in certain Italian areas.

In sum, there are several possible explanations for clinal distributions of human traits. The most frequently offered is that clines indicate the effect of natural selection. Livingstone has suggested that clines may be due to recent advances of advantageous genes or to gene flow between populations with different equilibrium frequencies for the gene. The geographical distribution of the hemoglobin S gene, body form, and skin color suggests such advances; gene frequency follows the distribution of selective forces of disease, climate, and UVR. Clines can also reflect the past history of an exchange or flow of genes among populations. The gene flow through interbreeding or migration

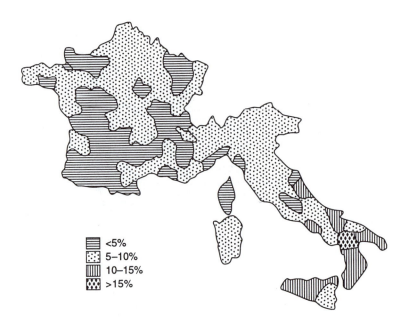

FIGURE 8-6 Distribution of B Allele in France and Italy. (Redrawn From Morganti, G., "Distribution of blood groups in Italy." Copyright © 1959 by Churchill. Reprinted by permission.)

contributes to genetic distribution often far in advance of any selective force that might be operating. The intrusion of Asians into eastern Europe, Middle Easterners into India, and the island-hopping colonization of the Pacific all contributed to the clinal variations of the world, as would have been seen before the fifteenth-century era of European colonial expansion.

BREEDING POPULATIONS VERSUS CLINES

> It has often been assumed that subspecific groupings based on the distribution of one, or at most a few characters will necessarily be concordant with the distributions of other variable characters. This, it seems, may be so for populations isolated in mountains, islands, caves or other restricted and special habitats, but is not usually the case in wider, more continuous regions. (Barnicot, 1964:198)

This quotation expresses another of the major objections to the use of geographic races as units of study. Some students of biological diversity consider that the proper method for studying human variability is the single trait, as it is distributed across population boundaries. In contrast, others focus on the uniqueness of a combination of characters within breeding populations. What we should be concerned with is not labeling of taxonomic units, but the distribution of traits among the world's peoples and the meaning of their variation.

Several examples of this variation at the phenotypic, genotypic, and DNA levels have been offered. Some have distributions that coincide with the distribution of certain selective forces and, in several striking examples, also with massive population movements. The presence of a cline of darkly pigmented skin in North America together with hemoglobin S (Hb^S) and a Duffy blood type (Fy^0) are due to historical events, the forced transport of hundreds of thousands of Africans to the New World during the seventeenth and eighteenth centuries. This illustrates why contemporary populations may not provide evidence of the correlation of a gene frequency and selected force. The distribution of Rh (cde) type in Europe and North Africa may indicate previous contact between groups living in these areas (the occupation of Spain and parts of southern Europe by North Africans during the seventh and eighth centuries). Numerous indigenous populations in the Americas today contain certain gene combinations because of their ancestors' being overrun by European colonists. The presence of several blood types and HLA markers gives evidence to this contact, just as the mtDNA sequences support east Asian origins.

The clines illustrated in the various figures describe the distribution of both monogenic and polygenic traits, and there are, as previously discussed, major distinctions between them. Morphological dimensions of complex phenotypes such as skin color or body size vary continuously, and each population or group usually grades imperceptibly into neighboring groups of a region. Rarely are there sharp, clear-cut divisions and smooth geographical distributions that may be plotted. In the case of monogenetic traits, population gene frequencies can and often do change rapidly, within one or two generations, as has been illustrated by the examples of island populations or small colonies. In addition, there are often steep differences between adjacent populations with a long history of occupancy, but minimal mate exchange. This is illustrated by the significant differences in blood-group frequencies between four tribes in central Australia who share adjacent boundaries but still have significant differences between them. Comparisons of one to another show differences in frequencies of ABO, MN, and Rh blood-group types by as much as 60 percent. Though continent-wide the cline of type A frequency showed a gradual decline from north to south, the effect of population boundaries is clearly demonstrated when the frequency dropped from 0.53 down to 0.13 from one tribal unit to an adjacent one (Birdsell, 1993). The probable cause of such a steep cline is the directional restriction of gene flow. Other steep changes are also recorded despite smooth directional averages for several genetic markers. Therefore, simple comparisons between trait distribution and selective forces are not always possible, since the larger overview of a distribution can often obscure significant differences. The population's size, its history, and mating patterns must be clearly defined.

Ethnic variations and their relationships to species averages are not only a matter of scale and perspective, but also of behavior and identity of the group under study. If we consider all those factors that cause changes in gene frequency—(1) mutation; (2) natural selection; (3) genetic drift; (4) migration or gene flow; and (5) breeding behavior—we then find that factors 1 and 2 act on certain alleles in unique ways. The first, mutation or error in DNA coding, is random and infrequent, providing the basis for all variation. Factor 2, natural selection, is determined by environmental conditions and a population's adaptation to them and is distributed geographically; and this distribution cuts across population boundaries. The other three factors are also important, but they are behaviorally determined, and they have an intense effect on the gene frequency from generation to generation. Through society's choice, effective breeding-population size may be restricted for a number of generations, or an adaptive innovation may cause a rapid expansion, affecting the gene-pool size. Such events will influence gene frequencies over the generations through genetic drift (factor 3). The decision to migrate or exchange mates with surrounding groups directs gene flow over the generations. Finally, the establishment of mating circles will direct gene exchange within a group, which may decide to limit or expand the network of mate choice. All societies do this to some extent by enforcing an incest taboo, proscribed matings between relatives.

Whatever the factors, we should recall that genes are not passed on one at a time, nor is an individual's fitness usually determined by a single gene. Biological fitness is a compromise between the interaction of all of one's gene products and the environments encountered during one's life cycle. These are important considerations when studying clinal distributions. The evidence of gene flow by itself is not descriptive of actual events because genes do not flow or "float around in space." They are transmitted as a group or an array by the chromosomes, and recombination of chromosomes is one of the key processes to offer variety between the generations. These several factors of behavior and basic genetics lend considerable support to the breeding-population concept—that group of people participating within the same circle of matings.

The clinal approach has its strengths as well, but only when used in conjunction with the actual basis for trait distribution through time and space—the population. Clinal distributions of gene frequencies cross population boundaries as result of natural selection, but the clines also represent directions of gene flow. Population size influences this gene flow as mate choice increases with density. No one approach to the study of the distribution of human variation is more efficient than another since major population movements or chance events from natural disasters can overwhelm the effects of natural selection. The results may be measured by human genetic diversity and its distribution, but this tells only part of the story because each generation differs from previous ones. The geographic pattern of gene variation is too complex and cannot be simplified into a few discrete groups. We must consider the adaptive significance or survival value of each trait in the context of the population and its history. We must pay heed to those conditions of environment and human adaptation that contributed to rapid increases in our species inter-spaced by sharp declines, a cycle to be repeated throughout our progress toward the level of over six billion people today.

chapter
9

Perspectives of Health and Human Diversity: Influences of the Race Concept

Studies of human biological variability can be made at several levels of abstraction from complex phenotypes to traits of simple inheritance and now at the level of the gene structure itself. The data from these studies may be viewed from a perspective of the species as a whole or partitioned into units as small as breeding populations or as broad as geographical divisions. Whichever unit is selected, comparisons of their biological diversity must take into account the forces that influence this diversity, whether behavior in the case of migrations and mating networks or the environmental elements that exert selective forces. No shortcuts, such as the use of race or ethnic group labels, are allowed if we are to understand disparities of health and disease rates among people. Nevertheless, after over a half century of rapid progress in genetic science, we still suffer from the influences of centuries' old racial typologies on biomedical research.

"I am a racially profiling doctor," proclaims a psychiatrist who describes a different treatment regime for his African American patients because, "they metabolize antidepressant drugs more slowly than Caucasians or Asians." She conceded, however, that not all are slow metabolizers (only about 40 percent), but race profiles were still used to adjust dosages and monitor treatment responses (Satel, 2002). This article, aimed at the general reader, was written in response to an editorial in a major medical journal that criticized "race-based" medicine (Schwartz, 2001:1393). The editorial went on to discuss the problems of the race concept just as I have considered in earlier chapters. Schwartz emphasized the error of attributing a "complex of physiological or clinical phenomenon to arbitrary aspects of external appearance." Schwartz made a convincing case against race profiling, but in the same journal a companion editorial on the next page was equally convincing in support of the use of a patient's phenotypic appearance (race) when selecting a treatment for heart failure (Wood, 2001:1394).

Wood described several well-known examples of inherited enzyme polymorphisms that affect the metabolism of drugs frequently used in the treatment of heart disease. Because of significant differences between whites, Asians, and blacks in their response to treatment, he concluded that racial differences were of practical importance for treatment of choice and "should alert physicians to the important underlying genetic determinants of drug response." Wood concluded that the identification of these genetic determinants should be an important extension of research into individual drug responses rather than relying on "external manifestations of race." Confusing, perhaps, but descriptive of the dilemma faced by a physician who must select the most effective treatment for a patient who is a member of a group whose drug reactions are reportedly different from a norm. Without the definitive genetic data, the option is a selection of a race/ethnic group identity with all of its shortcomings.

More than three years since these articles appeared, disparities of health and disease are even more frequently discussed and "race-based therapeutics" has become a central question in medical treatment (Bloche, 2004). Biomedical researchers dream of someday using individual genotypes to guide the choice of drug treatment. This Genomics Era, the study of an individual's genome to detect gene products that may affect certain diseases or influence reactions to drug treatments, has not yet arrived. The number of reports of differing drug reactions increase each year, but individual reactions are still grouped by the race or ethnic group of the patient.

A special section on "genomic medicine" in *Science* examined the possibilities of using an individualized approach in medical treatment and raised the question, "Are we there yet?" (2003:587–608). This question of identity of genetically influenced responses is still confused by usage of the race concept that continues to affect research design as well as treatment choices. What criteria for race labeling should be used: self-selection, region of origin, skin color, and so on, and how is the label to be applied? In the first article of the series on the need to check a person's genome before treatment with a new leukemia drug because of its toxicity, the author notes that about 10 percent of "Caucasians" have at least one "risky" gene (Marshall, 2003:589). This use of the classic race type should be noted in contrast to the contents of the third essay by Holden (2003:594) that urges caution in any use of race categorization despite the varying treatment responses. Until the promise of genomics is fulfilled, many biomedical scientists maintain, however, that race can serve as a useful, if crude, indicator of variability of diversity in drug responses.

Explaining disease disparity among these so-called racial groups depends on presumed differences of genetic factors among the racially defined patient populations. After all, disproportionate rates of several simply inherited diseases have been widely reported as I have discussed earlier; hemoglobin abnormalities, Tay-Sachs, cystic fibrosis, and so on, are some examples. Given such results, it would be logical to seek genetic explanations for variation in health and differing responses to treatment. For example, one-third of adult Americans of African descent suffer from high blood pressure; therefore we assume probable gene influence (see the section on hypertension below). This large American minority group also has ten times the rate of kidney failure, three times the incidence of cardiac hypertrophy, twice as many diabetics, and three times the mortality from heart attack. These disease rates and health outcomes are measured against the "white" majority. The implication is that "whites" not only provide an index group but are also the norm, or standard against which other groups are to be compared (Bradby, 2003:6).

Health professionals are well aware of these differences and act accordingly in their treatment of minorities, but there is less understanding of the causes of health disparities. These causes are complex and due to a variety of environmental and behavioral factors that can be measured by socioeconomic status (SES), and not by racial differences. Over sixty million Americans have one or more types of cardio-vascular disease, and while mortality has decreased, the disparity between SES levels has increased. Mortality risk factors relate to occupation, income and education, regardless of race. Yet, race is frequently considered a factor despite the growing recognition that the labels define composite groups of diverse origins. The Food and Drug Administration (FDA) recommended that researchers use "racial divisions specified by the Census Bureau . . . to ensure the consistency in evaluating potential differences in drug response."[1] This recommendation was thoroughly rebutted because race and ethnicity data alone are insufficient to predict variable drug response (Haga and Venter, 2003).

In studies of treatment responses and health outcome, the use of race and/or ethnicity is as much a proxy for social class as it is a marker of genetic diversity. However, the common usage of racial divisions continues when even most authors allow that race has little or no biological meaning, a fact frequently noted in epidemiological reports. The need to collect data on education, income, housing and family size is as important as the collection of pertinent genetic data. However, though there is an abundant reference to race or ethnicity, little is said about class. The labels serve as a measure of a group's exposure to social risk, which may account for health disparities in a race-conscious society.

How people live, what illness they suffer, and what they die of depends on much more than their genetic heritage, age, or gender; social class is also important. The focus on race has tended to obscure many of the environmental factors that affect our health and well-being. The use of race labels will continue to impede our understanding or explanation of the deterioration of the minority health, of why certain diseases place a heavier burden on ethnic minorities and the medically underserved. In this reference to the medically underserved, the meaning is clear—a disadvantaged group at the lower SES level. Even using race or ethnic group as a proxy for class is often difficult

---

[1]The standard categories recommended by the FDA for use in clinical trials are those used in the 2000 census: five racial and two ethnic categories, as discussed in Chapter 1.

because of varying definitions and changing boundaries. Recall the various changes in classifications of Mexican and South American people in the U.S. census until Hispanic was elevated to a separate category of it own in the year 2000 census.

Government classifications aside, race as a biological unit has been undergoing an ever-more critical scrutiny over the past decade with the rise of genomics and a heightened concern with human biodiversity, yet we continue to use race taxons as part of our scientific vocabulary. Thousands of publications can be found in the Index to Medical literature under the search terms "black," "white," and "Hispanic"; these publications encompass a range of race-based studies of physiological, biochemical variants, and clinical trials. Without going into the details of each of these studies, a reader might ask, "Do these authors assume that there is an inherent biological difference between white and nonwhite beyond the superficial differences of skin pigment?"

Black, white, Asian, or Hispanic are labels generally used as place holders in biomedical studies as crude markers of expected genetic differences between subjects of a study or patients undergoing treatment. Hence, we read frequently of higher or lower risks for a certain disease or adverse reactions to a certain drug therapy. These labels may, in fact, be a guide in a broad sense, but the variation between defined groups is seldom statistically significant because of small sample size and lack of control for confounding factors of the environment and lifestyle. Class differences, lifestyle changes, and a myriad of environmental factors strongly influence the diversity of human health and disease risk. This influence can and often does overwhelm many of the genomic factors. It is best to take a long view to gain a perspective of relative environment and genetic influences.

EPIDEMIOLOGICAL TRANSITION: THE DISTRIBUTION AND TYPE OF DISEASE

The health dimensions of our species are undergoing some critical changes reflecting environmental differences and should alter the ways in which we think of race and ethnic group risks. The major plagues of the past are no longer with us to the extent they were up to the sixteenth and seventeenth centuries when periodic epidemics caused mortality surges in which 30 to 50 percent of a population might be lost in a single year. Starting in the 1800s, we entered a period when fewer types of infectious diseases accounted for most illnesses and deaths each year. This change began what may be termed an "epidemiological transition" (Rockett, 1999). The *first stage of transition* was marked by periodic episodes of high mortality caused by outbreaks of infectious diseases like smallpox, cholera, typhoid, and a variety of acute respiratory diseases. One or another of these diseases in combination would spread throughout the poorly housed, poorly fed populations crowded into the growing cities of western Europe. The highest mortality was among infants and young children; life expectancy at birth was between 20 and 40 years of age. Throughout this period, average population increases were low and marked by periodic declines. Then gradual improvements in sanitation, housing, and living conditions in general reduced the impact of many of these infectious diseases and shifted the higher mortality rates to older age groups. Children were now more likely to survive to adulthood. This began a *second stage*, when pandemics declined, death rates fell, and average life expectancy at birth increased to 50 years of age. Most populations in Europe and North America remained at this epidemiological stage for nearly two centuries as gradual socioeconomic changes were made and improvements in health were gained.

Disease Epidemics and Selection in the Second Stage

The scourge of epidemics throughout human history that have caused wide fluctuation in population growth offers evidence of the probability that many of our genetic poly- morphisms today are the result of past natural selection. In Chapters 3 and 4, I gave examples of the probable disease resistance of certain genotypes of the ABO, HLA, and immunoglobins. Though these examples are mostly based on statistical correlations between disease and genotype, infectious diseases that had periodically killed thousands during past millennia should be seriously considered as probable agents of natural selection. Plague, cholera, typhus, smallpox, and typhoid, to mention a few of the major ones, have had dramatic effects on civilization throughout recorded history. Wars were won or lost, cities were abandoned, and civilizations fell because of epidemics. In past warfare, more casualties were often caused by disease than by bullets. One example is the louse-borne disease typhus, which, along with freezing weather and malnutrition, accounted for most of the deaths among Napoleon's troops in 1812 during their war with Russia. Another is typhoid fever that killed more Union soldiers during the American Civil War than died in all of the battles fought. In fact, of the 364,000 deaths, only 140,400 were from battle wounds; the remaining 224,000 fatalities were due to disease spread through the army encampments because of poor sanitation and polluted water supplies.

In addition to these episodes, there were even more lethal diseases to contend with in everyday life, and some populations proved to be more susceptible than others. After the decline of the bubonic plague in Europe, smallpox, or simply the pox, was the foremost threat to the human species, particularly among the inhabitants of the New World.

Smallpox.   The invasion of the Americas by Europeans more than 400 years ago demonstrated the effect of infectious diseases on peoples who had no history of previous contact and who, therefore, had low resistance. Millions of Native Americans died—an estimated 1.5 million in Mexico alone—and smallpox is believed to have been the main cause. This deadly viral disease, which killed even Europeans at a rate of one out of four infected, passed from village to village, from the time of its introduction in Vera Cruz in 1507. Eventually the pox extended northward into what is now Arizona and New Mexico. Entire populations in the Southwest died from epidemics even before they were visited by Europeans (McNeill, 1976). Similar experiences were suffered by Native Americans in the eastern half of the continent following the establishment of European colonies in the seventeenth century. Later, in the nineteenth century, periodic epidemics continued to occur among the populations of the Great Plains as Euro-Americans pushed westward across the Mississippi.

In modern times smallpox has been responsible for many deaths, even in those populations with a long history of contact with the disease. African populations continued to suffer from recurrence of epidemics; over 100,000 cases were reported in the 1940s. The increased use of a newly developed freeze-dried vaccine that did not require refrigeration gradually reduced the number and range of these outbreaks, but they still occurred over the next decade. There were an estimated 2.5 million cases in 1967, mainly in South America, Africa, and parts of south Asia, but enforcement of stringent vaccination regulations brought this number down to slightly more than 100,000 by 1972 (see Hopkins, 1983). No cases were reported for 1978, and the disease is now believed to have been eradicated entirely, but a constant watch is maintained by the World Health Organization.[2] This control of smallpox and other infectious diseases, a remarkable achievement of modern health science, should not be allowed to make us complacent, however. Eradication of smallpox is a medical milestone—but there remains a continuous struggle between humans and microbes; to maintain the low death rates enjoyed during the last three generations, perpetual vigilance is necessary (Dubos, 1968). This warning is underscored by several recent experiences with other deadly microbes.

Cholera.   A major cause of epidemics in the past and even today, cholera is spread by bacteria through contaminated food and water and has reappeared periodically, killing millions. Where crowded conditions exist, accompanied by poor sanitation, the population is at grave risk for infection from these bacteria. For example, 50,000 cases were reported in New York City in 1866, but there were only a few dozen reported in 1900. The provision of clean water and improved sanitation reduced the danger of recurrence in many areas. In the same year that cholera nearly disappeared from New York, nearly a million persons died of the disease in India. Since a major world epidemic in 1919, the disease has appeared sporadically throughout Africa and Asia. Spreading from a base in Indonesia, cholera broke out in a new epidemic in 1970, but intensive efforts by the World Health Organization brought it under control. Periodic outbreaks still reoccur, rapidly spreading cholera throughout much of the lesser developed world.

Sometimes cholera has appeared in areas previously free or with little contact with the disease. Between 1991 and 1995, cholera infected 595,000 persons in South America, a region that had previously been spared exposure to this disease. Starting in Peru, this disease spread over South America and into Mexico, with a reported 16,000 cases and 137 deaths in 1995; during this same year, Peru continued to experience over 22,000 cases. After this peak, the epidemic declined and has all but disappeared in the Americas with only 23 cases reported in 2002.

---

[2]The last case of smallpox occurred in Somalia on October 26, 1977. The patient, a 23-year-old hospital cook, made a complete recovery. In 1980 at the Thirty-third World Health Assembly meeting in Geneva, smallpox was declared officially erradicated from the planet.

Several countries of Africa also experienced high rates of cholera: Nigeria reported over 12,000 cases with 10 percent mortality in 1996. Africa continued to lead the world with a majority of the world total (81 percent in 1999). Outbreaks continued to occur throughout Asia, with Afghanistan reporting the greatest increase in 1998. The World Health Organization described these increases—at the same time noting the significant declines in Latin America (*Weekly Epidemiological Record*, 2003a).

Despite increases in some regions, the total world cases of 254,310 (1998) is far below the over half-million cases in 1995. The numbers have dropped even further to 142,311 cases in the fifty-two nations reporting in 2002. Several African nations account for 96 percent of these cases (137,866) and some reported increases. These examples illustrate how a major disease, a scourge from former times, can quickly reappear whenever conditions favor its spread as a new worldwide pandemic. The rise and fall of cholera are key indicators of social conditions and should serve to alert us to how fragile our control of the environment can be at times. Cholera knows no boundaries of geography or population group.

Recent Epidemiological Transitions

The health status of populations continues to undergo changes between generations, as it always has, but now the range of differences among populations is much broader than at any other time in our history. In the developed industrialized countries the major causes of death have now shifted to several chronic diseases like cancers and diseases of the heart and circulatory system. By contrast, most populations of the developing world remain in a middle transition between the infectious diseases of old and the newer chronic ones.

The *third stage* of the transition in the developed world began about 1900 and was marked by significant changes in the leading causes of death. Because of preventive measures, several infectious diseases were no longer threats to health in developed countries, though they have remained a problem in many of the developing countries. The incidence of gastrointestinal diseases, several childhood diseases, and tuberculosis (TB)—all once among the leading causes of death—have been reduced to insignificant levels in the developed nations. The major causes of death are now the chronic degenerative diseases of the heart and circulatory system and cancers as shown in the United States (Table 9-1). Several kinds of cancers and cardiovascular disease have steadily increased to replace tuberculosis and pneumonia as the two most frequent causes of death. By mid-twentieth century, life expectancy had increased to 65 years, and there was a greater risk of dying from one of several of the chronic degenerative diseases later in life. In the last two decades, new health threats have begun to appear in the form of chronic respiratory diseases, like emphysema and bronchitis, and these are becoming significant factors in the death rates of an aging population as more people live into the seventh decade with an average life expectancy of 77 years.

Early in the transition, clean water and more efficient waste disposal, along with improved housing, were major reasons for a decline in infectious disease. Inoculations and early medical diagnosis and treatment were additional contributing factors.

TABLE 9-1   AVERAGE ANNUAL DEATH RATES per 100,000 from Fifteen Leading Causes, United States, 1900 and 2001

1900		2001	
All Causes	1,755.0	All Causes	848.5
1. Tuberculosis	201.9	1. Diseases of heart	245.8
2. Influenza and pneumonia	181.5	2. Malignant neoplasms,	194.4
3. Diarrhea and enteritis	133.2	3. Cerebrovascular diseases	57.4
4. Diseases of heart	132.1	4. Chronic respiratory	43.2
5. Congenital malformations	91.8	5. Accidents (unintentional injuries)	35.7
6. Acute and chronic nephritis	89.0	6. Diabetes mellitus	25.1
7. Cerebral hemorrhage, embolism	75.0	7. Influenza and pneumonia	21.8
8. Bronchitis and bronchopneumonia	67.6	8. Alzheimer's	18.9
9. Cancer and other malignant tumors	63.0	9. Nephritis, nephrotic syndrome, and nephosis	13.8
10. Diphtheria	43.3	10. Septicemia	11.3
11. Typhoid and paratyphoid	35.9	11. Suicide	10.8
12. Cirrhosis of the liver	12.9	12. Chronic liver disease	9.5
13. Measles	12.5	13. Assault (homicide)	7.1
14. Whooping cough	12.1	14. Hypertension and renal disease	6.8
15. Diabetes mellitus	9.7	15. Pneumonitis due to solids and liquids	6.1

Source: *Statistical Abstract of the United States*, 1930, 1997; National Center for Health Statistics, *National Vital Statistics Record*, 2003.

Improved nutrition was also a factor, but some dietary changes and increases in food quantity have proved to be something of a mixed blessing. There are fewer cases of vitamin deficiencies or malnutrition. The numbers do not even come close to experiences of the nineteenth century; major vitamin deficiency diseases have been largely eradicated, along with protein-energy malnutrition. The problems are now mainly overnutrition and its consequences of obesity, diabetes, and cardiovascular problems. Overeating, high-fat consumption, and limited exercise are believed to be major contributing factors to cardiovascular diseases. The American Heart Association, for example, has recommended for years that Americans reduce total caloric intake and limit fat consumption and accompanied its recommendation with convincing statistics that show that high cholesterol and obesity contribute to heart disease. In sum, our changing lifestyle as a result of urbanization and the rise of industrialization and its pollution, together with tobacco smoking and overeating, have likely contributed to an increase in cardiovascular, lung, and cancer diseases.

The leading causes of death differ between the two groups of countries, the more developed (MDCs) and the lesser developed (LDCs). Whereas heart disease, cancer, and vascular disease head the list in the MDCs, gastroenteritis, pneumonia, and malarial diseases, aggravated by malnutrition, are the major causes of death in the LDCs. World Health Organization surveys show, however, that whenever people adopt the dietary habits and lifestyles of the more affluent nations, certain chronic diseases increasingly effect mortality rates among the wealthy.

Cardiovascular Diseases.   In the United States cardiovascular diseases of all types account for 31 percent of mortality, and in most of Europe these percentages are nearly as high. Certain developing countries are suffering an increase in coronary disease among the wealthier classes as they adopt Western lifestyles. As their incomes rise, so does their consumption of animal protein and fats together with an overabundance of total calories. The dietary influence is underscored by the experiences of several European populations during World War II. The incidence of coronary heart disease dropped to one-third of the prewar incidence in Finland and the Netherlands, but after the war, as nutrition returned to prewar levels, so did coronary heart disease, which reached a peak in many of the MDCs in the early 1970s and then began to decline. A realization of the importance of proper diet and exercise began to influence health, and several countries began to show a dramatic decrease. The United States reduced the rate of incidence of coronary heart disease from 470 per 100,000 population in 1975 to 245.8 per 100,000 in 2001.

A ranking of fifty-two nations in 1987 for mortality rates from all types of cardiovascular disease showed broad differences, from a low of 119.4 per 100,000 in Guatemala to a high of 449.7 in Romania (54 percent of the deaths from all causes). Other high rates were found throughout eastern Europe. By contrast, Finland, New Zealand, Northern Ireland, and Denmark were in the midrange of all types of cardiovascular diseases (36, 33, 39, and 18, respectively) but ranked at the top for death rates from coronary heart disease (47, 46, 52, and 42 respectively). The coronary heart mortality rate in Finland had dropped by 55 percent from its high in 1972. This was probably due to major changes in diet, emphasizing reduction in fat while increasing intakes of fruits and vegetables (Pietinen et al., 1996).

Considering only the MDCs, Japan has the third lowest mortality rate of any nation, whereas France is the fourth lowest for all cardiovascular diseases (*World Health Statistics Annual*, 1987 see also Polednak, 1989:67–72). These differences have generated numerous questions regarding behaviors that relate to health, as well as genetic influences. In all nations reporting health statistics by ethnic group, however, significant variation is seen between the ethnic groups.

In Finland, for example, a country with one of the higher coronary heart disease rates (1987), the Saami (Lapps) minority group had a significantly lower rate than the national average. Finns living in a region of northern Norway have higher coronary heart disease rates than Norwegians and Saami living in the same area. Careful studies of populations in another high-rate country, New Zealand, also reveal considerable ethnic group differences. Maori, the aboriginal inhabitants, had a higher rate than those of European descent; there was even a significant difference between Maori who followed the Mormon religion and those who did not. The Mormon Maori had the lower incidence, but an interesting aspect of the study was the finding that Maori women were at higher risk from coronary heart disease than Maori men, the reverse of results from many other studies that showed males at a higher risk (Prior et al., 1986).

Coronary heart diseases, with their debilitating sequel of reduced physical activity and risk of early death, are problems confronting all adults. The chance of developing heart disease increases with age with certain lifestyles and with some diets. In the many epidemiological studies, high-risk groups have been identified: Gender is the first distinction made—males are at greater risk than females. The second is by race, defined by black and white, and, sometimes, Hispanic. The list goes on to include the high-risk behaviors of smoking, the use of alcohol, and overeating. A familial factor—a history of heart disease in the family—is noted as well, but whether there are gene products affecting heart disease risk is not clear, though several possibilities have been proposed. The genes for the proteins of the apolipid complex are examples as described in Chapter 3. However, determination of race or ethnic-group risk as possible evidence of genetic factors is difficult because of similar responses of all groups to changes in lifestyles and diets. Though native diets of Polynesians, Asians, and Africans, for example, are quite different, their adoption of the modern Western diets and lifestyles cause the same sequel of health changes leading to increased risk of cardiovascular disease regardless of their apoprotein types. A similar example can be found among several American groups living at lower socioeconomic levels.

Hypertension.   On average, blood pressure tends to rise with age and with excess body weight, and it is higher in males than in females, at least among populations of the developed world. Though there is no clear-cut division between normal and high blood pressure, about 20 mmHg above 120/70 pressure of young adult males is considered mild hypertension.[3] Significant differences have been reported between socioeconomic and ethnic groups within a country. In the United States, African Americans—both males and females—have consistently higher pressures than averages for Euro-Americans. These differences have been attributed to dietary habits—consumption of fats and the frequent and heavy use of common table salt (sodium chloride), for example—and possibly genetic factors as well. It has been hypothesized that African Americans may be highly sensitive to sodium and less able to manage even moderate intakes. This hypothesis assumes their ancestors' genetic adaptation to low-sodium diets because their original homeland, West Central Africa, is a region low in available salt supplies (Wilson, 1986). This may be questioned on the grounds that there is wide variation of hypertension throughout African populations, as well as a wide range of salt availability.

A more likely explanation for hypertension in some ethnic minorities may be found in social factors. The frustration and tensions encountered in the daily lives of persons of lower socioeconomic status can add to anxiety and increased blood pressure. Attempts to link skin color (assumed to be a crude measure of African admixture)

---

[3]Blood pressure is measured by reference to the height of a column of mercury as is atmospheric pressure described in Chapter 6.

with blood pressure met with little success when corrections were made for socioeconomic level. Persons with darker skin did tend to have higher blood pressure, but only if those measured were in the lower economic and educational levels (Gleiberman et al., 1995). African Americans as well as other minority groups around the world encounter many stressful situations in their daily lives, and there is ample physiological evidence that anxiety and tension brought about by many causes can quickly elevate blood pressure. The measurement procedure itself is often a sufficient cause of anxiety.

The stresses of modern living certainly influence us all to some degree. Populations living in isolated rural communities frequently show lower average blood pressures than their relatives living in urban areas. When aboriginal peoples move to cities and adopt Western lifestyles, one of the earliest detectable physiological responses is increased blood pressure. This relocation effect has been measured in peoples as genetically diverse as Eskimos, New Guinea highlanders, Solomon Islanders, and Australian Aborigines. In their native environments, not only is there no hypertension, but there is also no increase in blood pressure with age, as is typically recorded for Europeans and persons of European ancestry. In addition, nomadic tribes of East Africa, normally with low pressure patterns, have increased blood pressure when they adopt a sedentary lifestyle. The same experience is shared by numerous other tribal groups throughout Africa (Hutt and Burkitt, 1986). A feature common among these low-blood-pressure communities is a low salt intake, while diverse ethnic groups on high-salt diets show a similar history of rising blood pressure with age. The salt intake level and blood pressure relationship is not as simple as once thought, however. Other factors, such as the intake of potassium and calcium, are influential; an increase in these elements in proportion to sodium lowers the salt-risk factor.

Regardless of the causes, hypertension is a serious risk factor in cardiovascular diseases (CVD), and together with diet (the rich, high-fat, high-protein diet of developed countries) effects an increase in the mortality from these diseases. The CVD rate has been declining during the past decade in the United States, partly because of the recognition of the influence of diet, an appreciation of the need for exercise, and earlier medical intervention. Cardiovascular mortality, however, remains at the top of the list of leading causes of death and is often referred to as a disease of affluence. The consumption of an excess of calories, through a refined-carbohydrate, high-fat diet, leads to a state of overnutrition and its disease sequel, as can be clearly demonstrated by the increases observed among developing countries when a segment of the population adopts a Western diet and sedentary lifestyle.

Cancer (Malignant Neoplasms).   A variety of malignant neoplasms are grouped under the term cancer because they have certain characteristics in common. A malignant neoplasm is formed when a collection of cells radically change their normal functions and begin to multiply rapidly in uncontrolled growth, which eventually leads to a spreading and an overcoming of healthy tissues in other parts of the body. There are 100 varieties of this disease, classified according to the site or organ in which they originate (lung, skin, breast, prostate, colon, and so on). Certain cancers are more lethal than others, and approximately 50 percent of malignancies may prove to be fatal. The fatality rate depends a great deal on the type of neoplasm, the length of time it had grown before detection, and, of course, the treatment. The cure rate of skin cancers (basal and squamous types) is close to 100 percent, whereas it is less than 50 percent for lung cancer and for the third type of skin cancer, melanoma. About 24 percent of deaths in the United States are due to malignant neoplasms, compared with the 40 percent caused by cardiovascular disease. Though heart-disease-related deaths leveled off in the 1990s and began to decline, deaths from cancer continued to climb; the rate increased by 6.3 percent between 1973 and 1992 (National Center for Health Statistics, 1999). There has been some success in bringing down rates of certain types of cancer, but the overall rate remains high. In the developing world, as urbanization and industrialization increase, cancer mortality is growing.

Causes of many cancers are still obscure—that is, the mechanisms that cause cells to become malignant are not known for certain, though there are several studies that point to a mutation in the somatic cells' DNA that energizes growth stimulation and receptor systems (Ames et al., 1995). Ionizing radiation from X-rays, nuclear power, or cosmic rays have long been known to have such mutagenic effects. In addition, persons who have been exposed to fallout from atomic testing have two to three times the national average for leukemia. Another source, ultraviolet rays from the sun, causes skin cancers, which occur most frequently in fairer skinned persons, usually on the backs of the hands and parts of the face. Skin cancer is more likely in those fair-skinned persons whose occupations keep them outdoors a good part of the day (see Chapter 5).

In addition to these mutagens, a number of environmental risk factors have been listed for different types of malignancies. Close correlations are seen between certain diets and cancers of the stomach and colon; between alcohol and esophagus, throat, and mouth cancer; and between tobacco smoke and lung cancer. A long list of organic chemicals and substances like asbestos fibers are also implicated as causes of cancers of the lung, liver, and bladder, especially because workers exposed to them through their occupations have an extremely high incidence of certain types of cancer (lung cancer among asbestos plant workers, for example). Cancers of the lung, large intestine, and breast cause about half of all cancer deaths. Lung cancer, described by Cairns (1975:69) as "a disease of the twentieth century," is closely related to cigarette smoking; the risk of lung cancer is fifty times greater in smokers than in nonsmokers. Many health officials have pointed out that if tobacco smoking were abolished, this form of cancer would be nearly eliminated, though air pollution remains a contributing cause. Further evidence is provided by the rising incidence of lung cancer among females, who, as a group, began to adopt the smoking habit some twenty to thirty years after the males. The rate among women was more than three times as great in 1985 as in 1950, whereas the male rate increased 2.7 times during this same period but is now decreasing. Though tobacco use in much of the developed world has declined over the past decade, especially in the United States, it is on the increase in many of the LDCs, especially throughout Asia. China now consumes one-quarter of the world's cigarette production. Lung diseases of all types are expected to increase, while a decline is already evident in the developed countries (Lopez, 1990).

Food habits are another likely cause of certain types of cancers. A diet high in meat and saturated fat, but low in cereals, especially unrefined, appears to be closely linked to cancer of the large intestine; a significant factor appears to be the low amount of dietary fiber in diets high in meat, fat, and refined carbohydrates. The distribution of colon cancer corresponds closely with dietary quality, and this form of cancer varies considerably between countries; the MDCs have the highest incidence (Burkitt, 1971). Because of this relationship of colon cancer to saturated fats in the diet, a great deal of attention has been directed to the fat and fiber content consumed by wealthy nations. The results have reinforced the earlier observations of dietary influences (Cohen, 1987). Note also the decline of Finnish heart disease rate concordant with the reduction of fat intake mentioned above.

The most frequent cancer in women, breast cancer, has a world distribution similar to that of colon cancer in males. Because this distribution closely follows dietary quality, it is possible that some factor(s) are lost in the refined diet. Women on refined diets lacking in whole grain have higher rates of breast cancer (American women, for example). Though the evidence is not all in yet, it seems that the element selenium and vitamin E may be the factors involved, because these substances are found in abundance in many whole grains but are mostly lost during the refining process. Test results have shown the antioxidant properties of selenium and vitamin E, which work to protect cell membranes from free radicals, oxidation byproducts of cell metabolism (Combs and Scott, 1977). The general functions of selenium in human nutrition are becoming better understood, as well as its influence on certain cancer sites (Levander, 1987). More recent large-scale studies of the effects of antioxidants (vitamin E and beta-carotene) show a significant reduction in gastric cancers, but there were different results in other patient populations (Antioxidants and Cancer Prevention; National Cancer Institute Web site, 7/28/04). These data, plus those gained from earlier studies, make a strong case for dietary effects on malignancy.

The environmental influence of diet is further supported by the example of Japanese women who migrated to Hawaii. Here, within two generations, their breast cancer rates were nearer those of Hawaiian women (80 per 100,000) than those in Japan (11 per 100,000). However, there is a growing number of genes that have been implicated in the susceptibility for the growth of certain types of tumors.

Though about 95 percent of breast and ovarian cancers are not inherited, mutations of tumor suppressor genes, BRCA 1 and BRCA 2, have been implicated in both types of cancers. Women with one or more mutations of these genes, and with a family history of cancer, have an increased probability of contracting the disease; their lifetime risk factor is 80 percent (calculated to age 80) compared to about 10 percent in the general population. Expressed by age group, the risk is 20 percent by age 40 and rises to 55 percent by age 65. Calculation of cancer predisposition of women with the BRCA mutations and without a family history of the disease is difficult to calculate, but one estimate is about 50 percent of the carriers remain cancer free. Nongenetic factors influence cancer risks and age of onset; pregnancy, hormones, diet, maintenance of normal weight, and exercise are the major influences (King et al., 2003).

TABLE 9-2 Cancer Incidence of U.S. Ethnic Groups (per 100,000 Population)

ETHNIC GROUP	LUNG	BREAST (F)	STOMACH	PROSTATE (M)	COLON
EuroA*	45.4	46.9	8.6	26.7	31.0
AfrA	62.5	40.2	15.4	46.1	11.7
Hispanic	34.3	54.1	15.7	—	—
Chinese (Calif.)	53.5	30.7	15.0	15.5	32.3
Chinese (Hawaian)	35.9	31.8	12.0	20.1	12.0
Japanese (Calif)	20.3	35.2	31.4	7.0	31.9
Japanese (Hawaian)	30.4	27.1	31.4	22.4	29.1

*EuroA = European American; AfrA = African American.

Source: Data selected from Polednak, 1989.

The preceding examples plus others suggest that many cancers, perhaps 70 to 95 percent, are environmentally determined (see Cairns, 1975; Mayer, 1983; Trichopoulos et al., 1996). The data on diet, the incidence of environmental pollutants, the use of alcohol, and smoking all point to this possibility. Additional evidence is provided by a comparison of ethnic groups who have migrated and adopted the diets of their new homelands. Japan has a very high rate of stomach cancer (75 per 100,000), while Japanese immigrants in California have a significantly lower incidence. The sons of immigrants have an even lower incidence, one that is much closer to that experienced by Americans of European ancestry (Table 9-2). The high frequency of stomach cancer in Japan may be due to a diet that contains large quantities of salt fish and pickled vegetables. Other groups with similar diets also have high rates of this disease—Iceland, Finland, and Norway, for example, where large quantities of dried, salted fish are eaten.

Further evidence of environmental effects on the course of the disease is offered by the increase of cancer incidence with age. Cairns described the population older than 60 years of age as the group at greatest risk. He reasoned that the longer one is exposed to carcinogenic factors, the greater the chance of developing the disease; the effects of many carcinogenic substances may not show up until twenty to forty years after exposure. With an increasing number of persons living into their eighties, a higher cancer rate is to be expected. Finally, the work environment has proved to contain many substances that are carcinogenic—but for many, the tumors will not appear until years later. Asbestos fibers, silicates in quartz dust, and polyvinyl chloride (a cause of liver cancer) lead the list of dangerous substances, which includes insecticides and organic solvents, many of which have been introduced into the environment too recently to allow us to understand their long-term biological effects fully.

Diabetes.   The disease diabetes mellitus is a complex syndrome principally characterized by the inability to maintain blood-sugar levels within a normal range. This condition of glucose intolerance has a variety of causes: the insufficiency of insulin (a pancreatic hormone regulating glucose levels); cellular insensitivity to the action of insulin; an excess of glucagon (another hormone of the pancreas); and a host of other factors, some caused by rare genetic defects of carbohydrate metabolism. The most frequent expressions of the disease are classified into two categories: type I, juvenile or insulin dependent (IDDM), and type II, an adult-onset form or noninsulin dependent (NIDDM). The juvenile or IDDM type is less frequent, only about 5 percent of all cases. Diabetic symptoms appear by adolescence or young adulthood and may be controlled principally by insulin injection. Juvenile diabetes is influenced by gene mutations within the HLA cluster on chromosome 6 that affects an autoimmune condition—a formation of antibodies that attack and destroy the insulin secreting cells of the pancreas. The 33 percent concordance rate between identical twins indicates that nongenetic factors influence gene expression.

Type II, NIDDM, is the most common form afflicting world populations, and high blood glucose levels with related symptoms usually appear after 40 years of age. There is some component of genetic susceptibility suggested by family and twin studies, but environmental factors, principally dietary, overwhelmingly determine the expression of the disease. With major dietary and lifestyle changes in many populations, type II diabetes has increased dramatically over the past decades and continues to rise (Harris, 1990). Because it has become a major health threat and is now one of the leading causes of death, the balance of the discussion will consider only this type of diabetes.

Once only the twenty-seventh most common cause of death, diabetes has now reached near-epidemic proportions and is the sixth most frequent cause of death in the United States. Though medical treatment has prevented the death rate from rising further, the number of diabetics has increased by 60 percent among Euro-Americans and 120 percent among African Americans. Today, there are approximately 18.2 million diabetics recorded in the United States, with hundreds of thousands of new cases added each year. Though 40 percent are 65 years and older, each year more newly reported diabetics are from younger age groups, even among children. Because a diabetic, over the years, gradually develops impaired circulation and is more prone to kidney failure, heart disease, and blindness by late middle age, and the number of people involved, the cost of diabetic-related illness and death is even higher than that from diabetes alone (Center for Disease Control, Fact Sheet, 2004).

Though there is some hereditary influence as noted above, this disease is closely linked to food choices, overnutrition, and reduced physical inactivity; diabetes distribution has followed the spread of Western diet and lifestyle. In DCs, as long as a half century ago, diabetes was found mainly among the wealthier classes in urban areas. For example, among the rich urban residents of India, diabetes was twice the rate of the rural poor. Further, though rare among Japanese women before the end of World War II, diabetes rose to become the eighth most frequent cause of death among this group. In Puerto Rico, though the general health of the population improved during the economic boom of the 1960s, diabetes rose from twelfth place to become the eighth most frequent cause of death (Eckholm, 1977).

Further evidence of the influence of dietary changes is provided by the experiences of populations like Australian Aborigines and several groups of Native Americans. The Tohono Otam (Papago) of Southern Arizona are especially predisposed to diabetes by middle age; more than 50 percent of the adults aged 45 to 65 were diagnosed as diabetic, which was a 50 percent increase since the epidemiological survey of 1965.

Environmental effects are clearly demonstrated when these Arizona natives are compared with their relatives living in Mexico. These Tohono Otam, separated only by an international border in the last 170 years, share the same gene pool intermarrying with the U.S. group, but they have five times less diabetes. Several other Native American groups also have significantly higher rates than the U.S. average (27.8 versus 6.3 percent for the national rate). In addition, other minorities suffer from higher rates: Hispanics, 8.2 percent with an estimated one-third of the population with undiagnosed diabetes. African Americans have twice the diabetic rate found among Euro-Americans, with females of both groups showing a higher rate than the males.

Among Australian Aborigines who have adopted Western diets (high in sugar and white flour), the incidence of diabetes has been found to be 10 percent compared with only 2.3 percent among a European population living near the Aborigine reserve where the study was carried out (Kirk et al., 1985). Throughout the Pacific, similar high diabetes rates are also reported for those Polynesians or Melanesians who have urbanized and adopted the Western diet, ceased to work as hard as they formerly did, and substantially increased their average body weight. People on the island of Nauru are a classic example of the detrimental health effects of a changing lifestyle. This small Pacific Island is populated by people with one of the world's highest diabetic rates, about 42.2 percent of the adults. The disease was unknown before 1945 but, following the mining of the island's rich phosphate deposits, the population's income rose to $34,000 per capita, another world record. With this new-found wealth they radically changed their living habits, purchasing all of the available goods of the developed world, from airplanes to motorcycles and especially imported foods. The result is near-universal obesity and a record incidence of diabetes (Zimmet, 1982).

No simple explanation for this dramatic difference between some population groups, for example, Pacific Islanders, Native Americans, and Europeans, will suffice. Dietary changes alone will not do. There is a probability, however, that certain populations are better adapted genetically to the type of diet humans had consumed for 99 percent of the species' existence, a diet highly variable in quantity with a large mixture of complex carbohydrates. Neel (1962, 1982) offered a hypothesis he called the "thrifty genotype" that could explain the food-storage capacity of certain peoples. He noted that hunters' and gatherers' diets range from "feast to famine," with times of scarcity alternating with times of plenty, when the people gorge themselves. During these times, persons with the physiological ability to convert and store the excess food as body fat are at an advantage. The surplus food energy enables them to endure the periodic episodes of starvation. Neel proposed that their insulin-producing beta cells in the pancreas are more sensitive to stimulus, and the insulin increased rapidly and aided in this energy storage. If such persons, however, continuously consumed large quantities of refined carbohydrates during a long period, as in the case of so many people today, they would exhaust their insulin-secreting potential by middle age. They would then become unable to regulate their blood-glucose levels within physiologically acceptable limits.

Such examples are offered by the populations described above, people who have changed from their aboriginal lifestyles and diets only within the last two centuries or less. These people, some Native Americans for example, began to consume a surplus of calories initiating a sequel of obesity and diabetes. Their quick response—rapid release of insulin and storage of energy—that served them in the past turned to a lethal disadvantage in modern times. Australian Aborigines and Pacific Islanders also provide examples that support the "thrifty genotype" hypothesis. Euro-Americans and Afro-Americans, far removed from hunting–gatherer lifestyles, do not fit this model as well, but these peoples still respond in a similar way to intakes of surplus calories. In fact, evidence gained from affluent classes of the developing world suggest that we all do to differing degrees. Are there genes involved that convey unique abilities of energy storage? At least five genes have been described, which, in mutated form disturb glucose metabolism, glycogen storage, insulin receptors, or the insulin molecular structure itself. But as any one of these influences only about 1 percent of type II diabetics, the balance are likely affected by multiple-gene factors; identical twin concordance is close to 100 percent. Expression of genetic propensity depends on nutritional factors, however.

Pacific Islanders come close to following the hunter–gatherer feast-or-famine model of physiological response to food surplus or scarcity, but not quite. Their long history of agriculture and fishing had ensured a reasonably dependable food supply. Another advantage of efficient energy storage was offered by Prior (1971), who suggested that Polynesians, famous for their long sea voyages in open canoes, were an example of a population who could rapidly become obese on a food surplus. This characteristic served them well in ancient times on the open ocean. Even in the tropical climate of the South Pacific, cold temperatures can be a problem when the sun goes down; the temperature drops rapidly and people in small outrigger canoes are exposed to cold winds, causing a rapid loss of body heat. Persons with thicker fatty layers were better insulated and thus protected from metabolic heat loss; such individuals would also have an excess of stored energy. With a steady diet of surplus calories today, this predisposition for rapid weight gain, once an advantage, now contributes to a high incidence of type II diabetes.

THE DEVELOPING WORLD AND EPIDEMIOLOGICAL TRANSITIONS

The rise of these several chronic diseases, among people of the MDCs discussed above, illustrates the impact of environment on human survival and, eventually, will influence the composition of the human genome. In the LDCs, where the growing populations are undergoing a rapid change in diet and lifestyle, the epidemiological transition is not yet complete. While some groups of the wealthier classes in the LDCs have entered the final phase, where the chronic diseases have risen to significant levels, infectious diseases still remain the leading causes of morbidity and mortality for the majority of the populations in the developing world. One-third of the fifty-one million deaths worldwide in 1993 were due to infectious diseases, and 99 percent of these deaths occurred in the LDCs. Most were caused by the "big four": acute respiratory infections, diarrheal diseases (the leading cause of death among children under five), TB, and malaria.

In the developed world, we live longer and suffer more diseases of late onset, and infectious diseases are no longer the threat to survival they were in the early 1900s. Such diseases now account for only about 1 percent of the total mortality. But as if to demonstrate that humans, wherever they live, are still at risk, several new virus strains of probable African origin have made periodic appearances, causing high mortality.

Hemorrhagic Fever

In recent years there have been numerous cases of new, deadly infections labeled Lassa, Ebola, and Marberg fever. The course of the infections, causing high fever and severe uncontrollable hemorrhaging, is usually short, with high mortality; the first recorded outbreak of the Ebola epidemic in Zaire in 1976 claimed 90 percent of the infected victims. A more recent epidemic in 1995 quickly killed 244 people, and only quick action by the health authorities prevented its spread to Zaire's capital 100 miles away. Ebola continues to be a threat, but African health authorities are more experienced and effective in preventing the virus's spread; the recent outbreak of 405 persons infected in Uganda (December 2000) was held to a mortality of 160; an outbreak of 17 cases in early 2004 was quickly controlled with only 6 fatalities.

Ebola and some of the other hemorrhagic viruses appear to be maintained within a primate "reservoir of disease" located in Central Africa with periodic outbreaks, but the precise sources are not known. What is documented, however, is that the viruses have been carried by infected travelers and monkeys imported for lab experiments. Sporadic outbreaks have occurred among laboratory workers in America and Europe that set off warnings of the threats from these new viruses. A readable but very alarming book, *The Hot Zone* by Richard Preston, describes some of the episodes of the transmission of these dangerous viruses. While the sudden appearances of these "hot" viruses attracted our fearful attention in the 1970s, another deadly organism had already spread around the world and was about to announce its presence as a new disease syndrome—AIDS.

HIV/AIDS

The acquired immune deficiency syndrome (AIDS) was first recognized as a disease syndrome among homosexual men and drug addicts in the United States in 1981. These individuals were diagnosed with respiratory and other infections that did not respond to treatment. About one-third of them also had a rare form of cancer, Kaposi's sarcoma. In general, they suffered from repeated opportunistic infections because of a suppressed immune system; the T cells of the lymphocytes (see Chapter 3), instead of increasing as they should, declined by as much as 50 percent when confronted by any of several infectious organisms. As the number of cases began to climb, an extensive search was made to isolate the agent that infected and gradually destroyed a major set of cells of the immune system. By 1983 HIV (human immuno-deficiency virus) was identified as the cause of AIDS, and it was being discovered in heterosexual populations in Europe, Africa, and Asia, as well as in North America. Spread by blood transfusions or blood-clotting products used by hemophiliacs (until 1986), and by heterosexual contact, AIDS presented the world with a newly recognized infectious disease of pandemic proportions.

The virus has a long latency period of seven to ten years before the disease symptoms appear. This permitted the near silent spread of HIV throughout the 1980s, but the virus has probably been around much longer, perhaps since the 1950s. Though its origins are obscure, HIV is believed to have spread undetected through Zaire and Zambia in the 1970s and then into Europe and the Western Hemisphere, infecting people in Belgium, France, Haiti, and the United States. Whatever its origins, the virus has been responsible for an increasing number of AIDS patients. Over 600,000 cases were reported by 1992 and the actual figure is believed to be closer to 2.5 million, with many nations under reporting. By 2003, there were 40 million people with HIV or AIDS and 3 million deaths. The scope of this new threat twenty-four years after its appearance is illustrated in Table 9-3. AIDS is one of the leading cause of death in many underdeveloped countries and millions of new cases are reported each year. HIV infection has remained a serious problem in the United States and is still one of the major causes of death though the rate has been reduced from the fifteenth leading cause in 1995 to the twenty-second in 2001.

Mortality from AIDS is much higher in sub-Saharan Africa; 1.5 million of 2.5 million deaths there in 1993 were attributed to AIDS. The rate was expected to increase, and twice the number of deaths were projected in the population than if the

TABLE 9-3   Global HIV-AIDS Epidemic

REGION	PEOPLE WITH HIV-AIDS	PERCENT ADULTS	NEW HIV CASES (2003)	AIDS DEATHS (2003)
Total	37,800,000	1.1	4,800,000	2,900,000
Africa (sub-Saharan)	25,000,000	7.5	3,000,000	2,200,000
Asia (south and east)	6,500,000	0.6	850,000	460,000
America (Latin)	1,600,000	0.6	200,000	84,000
Europe (Eastern and central Asia)	1,300,000	0.6	360,000	49,000
America (North)	1,000,000	0.6	44,000	16,000
Asia (East)	900,000	0.1	200,000	44,000
Europe (West)	580,000	0.3	20,000	6,000
Middle East and North Africa	480,000	0.2	75,000	24,000
Caribbean	430,000	2.3	52,000	35,000
Oceania	32,000	0.2	5,000	700

Source: 2004 Report on the Global AIDS Epidemic. Geneva: Joint United Nations Program on HIV/AIDS, July 2004.

disease had not been present (see Jamison and Hobbs, 1994). The 3 million new infections and the over 2 million deaths in 2003 proved that the projections of a decade ago were not exaggerated and world epidemiologists expect further increases.

These mortality rates, though alarming, are low by comparison to what the future may hold, given the increasing number of people around the world infected with HIV. Midyear, 2004, there were 40 million adults and children infected, and 95 percent of these live in LDCs. With a seemingly slow start two decades ago, no region has escaped the spread of this virus. Africa leads the world at present, with 64 percent of the world total, with over 2 million new cases each year, but Asia is catching up fast, with an estimated 13 million HIV carriers. Of these cases, China and Central Asia and India have the largest number. AIDS is already the leading cause of death in sub-Saharan Africa and the fourth leading cause worldwide (Steinbock, 2004; Weekly Epidemiological Record, 2003b). Given these increases and the probability that 50 percent of HIV-infected people will develop AIDS, mortality rates will further accelerate in this century.

A NEW WORLD, BUT OLD DISEASES

World environments, where people live, and what they do, have been undergoing rapid change. Starting from a technological base established during the Industrial Revolution of the eighteenth and nineteenth centuries, all of our systems of manufacturing, communications, and transportation have risen to new levels of efficiency, encouraging mass movements of people around the globe. Improvements in agricultural technology have boosted productivity, and developments in medical science have fostered a population explosion that has contributed to hundreds of millions more people than fifty years ago migrating and establishing new settlement patterns. In the process, there have been radical changes in human uses of space and an increased exploitation of environmental resources. Some of these changes have had a major impact on human survival and influence biological variability of regional populations.

First is the use of space that contributes to a redistribution of people, increasing population density. More and more people are migrating to expanding urban centers, especially in the developing countries. In 1976 there were 100 cities of a million or more in each of the two major world regions (developed and less developed). Since then, world urbanization has proceeded at a growth rate of about 4.5 percent per year in the LDCs, fed by a natural population increase and by rural-to-urban migration, compared with only 0.8 percent for the developed countries. This means that urban populations in the LDCs totaled 1.5 billion in 1990, and continued growth pushed this number to about 2.0 billion (or 40 percent of the total world population) in the year 2000, compared with the MDCs, which remained at 0.9 billion over this same period. The scale of increase may be comprehended if we note that cities like Lagos, Nigeria; Mexico City; and Bombay, India, have grown from under 3 million each in 1950 to over 17 million by 1998 (Brockerhoff, 2000). By comparison, London required over a century to grow from 1 to 8 million residents (Ashford, 1995).

The impact of this nearly 1 million people per week moving into urban areas is being felt throughout the world. The lack of adequate shelter, or safe drinking water, or sanitation for a third or more of the urban populations means that the health and very survival of hundreds of millions are threatened. The crowded conditions, poor diet, and lack of basic city services place such populations at risk of epidemic diseases, both old and new. Incidence of diarrheal diseases and the others of the "big four," (TB, acute respiratory, and malaria) already high, will probably rise, given the increased population densities and the polluted environments. Old diseases like typhoid, diphtheria, measles, and even typhus are already reappearing, as does cholera from time to time, spreading in a new world pandemic as discussed above. There is an occasional reappearance of plague like the 1994 outbreak in India, in which 6,000 people were infected (80 percent lived in urban shantytowns). Early diagnosis and fast action by public health officials, aided by antibiotics and insecticides, have usually contained the epidemics and have kept mortality to lower levels than in the past. Insect vectors are developing immunity to the more widely used insecticides, however, and many antibiotics are no longer effective in treatment of several types of infections.

Like the turning of the tide, as one writer described it, microbes that were once easily controlled by antibiotics have returned in newer, more virulent forms. Despite an announcement by the United States Surgeon General in 1969 that "we can close the book on infectious diseases," several major microbes have persisted and are now an even greater threat to human health. Staphylococcus bacteria, the cause of a variety of infections of the skin, internal organs, and bone, now exist in several immune strains. Gonorrheal bacteria have also developed strains resistant to penicillin, and even malarial parasites have evolved varieties that resist the standard drugs used to treat the disease. These all pose problems for medical treatment, but the greatest threat is from an old disease enemy—TB.

Once the number one cause of death among populations in European and American cities, TB declined to insignificant levels as improvements in housing, diet, and general health were made. The use of antibiotics contributed to a further decline in the number of active cases of TB reported. There was a steady decrease until 1985, when the number of new cases annually began to increase, rising 18 percent from 1985 to 1991, and the number has been climbing ever since with 20,000 new cases reported in 1997. The increase has been mainly among inner-city residents, mostly among those groups classified as nonwhites. The homeless, drug abusers, and AIDS patients are especially at risk. A substantial number of the new cases were caused by a new drug-resistant strain of bacteria.

A large number of us harbor the tuberculin bacterium (estimated to be about 34 percent of the world population) without symptoms of the active disease. As long as our general state of health is good and our immune system functions efficiently, we are able to prevent the growth and spread of the tuberculin organism. If our health declines and we are repeatedly exposed to infection, our immune system will be overchallenged, and then the bacteria will seize the opportunity and multiply rapidly. This has happened in AIDS patients and other groups of individuals who, because of economic circumstances or drug abuse, suffer from a decline in their general health. When treatment is sought, one or a combination of drugs are given. But in recent years a significant number of patients have failed to respond, and physicians have recognized that there is a new TB bacterium loose in the urban population. Drugs that had been used successfully since 1948 now fail to halt the progress of the disease. How widespread this multiple-drug-resistant (MDR) bacterium has become is not known, but its presence in many patients has alerted health officials, who are gravely concerned about the new wave of TB. What adds to the threat is the fact that persons carrying the HIV virus are at higher risk and, because of the long dormancy period of HIV, are likely to be a source of a rising case load of tuberculosis in the coming decades. The rise of drug-resistant strains of TB, as well as of several of the other major infectious organisms, set the stage for a twenty-first-century revival of epidemics caused by the old killers, as described by Laurie Garret in her books *The Coming Plague* and *Betrayal of Trust*, a later volume that reviewed the lack of preparedness of the world's health care systems.

Race and Disease, or Environment and Disease

Socially disadvantaged groups suffer the highest incidence and mortality from the return of these old diseases as they do from the new diseases. Their rate of infection is higher and they have a less favorable response to treatment. Explain it on the basis of their race, if you will, with an implication of genetic susceptibility to tuberculosis or AIDS. But considering our epidemiological experiences with the rise and fall of disease types and mortality, more probably, environmental factors are responsible. The transitions we have undergone over the last two centuries raise questions about the overreliance on a genetic explanation, especially when race is used as a proxy for some assumed genotype. What is a "race" anyway?

WHAT IS A RACE?

Studies of racial variation were often carried out by comparing look-a-likes, similarities of superficial phenotypes, as described earlier. Now, most often we are presented with descriptions of genetic variants whose frequencies differ between groups or races (labeled or defined by their phenotypes). So it is important to ask what is a race? Or who is black? Who is white? In our day-to-day encounters we might excuse a casual use of black, white, Asian, or African, and even Asian Indian may be acceptable. But for serious biological study or as group identity in the reporting of disease or mortality data a more precise meaning must be applied.

Blacks/African Americans

This color designation is most frequently used to identify peoples of African descent though it can just as accurately apply to populations in south Asia, Australia, and New Guinea. In practice, however, a classification of black means African or African American. Even so, this use of color/geographic designation of race encompasses a broad genetic heterogeneous cluster of thousands of populations.

First, African Americans are descendents of populations who have undergone over four hundred years of interbreeding with Europeans and some Native Americans. The average degree of European (Caucasian) genetic admixture in all African Americans is about 25 percent but varies widely among individuals and between regional populations. As described earlier, higher admixture is recorded in northern than in southern cities. Even within a single state, South Carolina, differences in rates are seen between regional groups; people living on some of the Barrier Islands off the coast have the least admixture (3.5 percent) and have retained more of their ancestral African culture and genes than other African Americans (Pollitzer, 1994). Other populations of South Carolina show a broad range of admixture, up to 50 percent in Columbia (Parra et al., 2001). These are averages, however, and many individuals possess a much higher admixture. Nevertheless, all are persons who will be classified as "black" by different agencies of the local, state, and federal government. How helpful will such a classification be for biomedical research? The answer, of course, is not much unless the research considers a bit of local history and regulations for recording race. Community standards and governmental regulations vary from state to state and change over time. Recall the example of the three brothers in Houma, Louisiana, who were each listed as a different race on their birth records (see Chapter 1).

To add to the complexity of genetic diversity studies, African immigration over the past decade has increased the number of foreign-born blacks from 4.9 percent (1990) to 6.7 percent in the year 2000. The rise in the number of African immigrants has made the label African American even less meaningful in the genomic sense. If a genetic or clinical study examines "blacks" in New York (foreign born, 30.2 percent), results will be certainly different from one conducted in South Carolina (foreign born, <1 percent) or in Minneapolis (foreign born, 16.2 percent). From the prospective of breeding populations or gene pools, each of these groups offers a different sample because of their diverse ancestry. Expand this to include other states, or regions whose "blacks" have different histories of geographic origin and descent, and one can appreciate the potential for distortion of results of any genetic studies that use "black" as a label and do not take into account such complexity of origin.

The issue of genetic contribution of recent African immigrants alerts us to this churning of America's black population, but there is additional genetic diversity because these new immigrants come from several regions of Africa. Garte (2002) reminds us that Africa contains many diverse environments. People of West Africa live under different selective pressures than people in Ethiopia, one people exposed to climates and disease organisms that are quite different than the other. Both population groups in the United States are classified as blacks, but they differ in many characteristics. As one example, Garte describes a gene that codes for an enzyme whose function is to detoxify certain plant alkaloids. A high percentage of Ethiopians have multiple alleles of this gene, probably enabling them to consume a greater variety of plants of high alkaloid content that they avoid except during times of food shortages. The frequency of these alleles is low (1 to 3 percent) in West African peoples as well as throughout most of the world's population. Examples of other regional differences are found in blood types, hemoglobins, and HLA types as discussed earlier.

So we should remember that continent of origin or skin color may not be a significant marker of genomic components.

Whites (Caucasians)/Euro-Americans

The "white" race has been used so randomly (as opposed to nonwhite) as a label that, like "black," it has lost genetic relevance. White is applied most frequently to Europeans or persons of European descent and is often interchanged with Caucasoid as if the labels were synonymous. First, European defines a continental group as does African, and, like African, there is a range of genetic diversity encompassed by over one-half a billion people. European populations extend from the British Isles eastward to the Ural mountains and genetic diversity is described by clines running east to west and north to south. The millions of people of European descent around the world, mostly in North America, are a heterogeneous lot who possess certain parts of the genetic array dispersed across the continent. Hence, people in the United States and Canada, descendants of eastern Europeans, significantly differ from those whose ancestors came from the British Isles or Scandinavia. Likewise, contrasts exist between Americans of Greek or Spanish descent, and even greater distinctions will be found between smaller, formerly isolated populations like the Basques of northwestern Spain or Saami of Finland. Europeans all, and described as a race (Caucasoid/white) if you will, but genetically differing to considerable degree.

Europeans, both continental and overseas (Canada, United States, Australia, et al.) are routinely, and without qualification, classified by government agencies as Caucasoid. The label is also used widely in scientific literature without any explanation because of the assumption that every reader knows the meaning of the term. However, there are difficulties when questions arise about the designation of people of western Asia or India, or North Africa because many populations in these regions are also labeled Caucasoid. Genetically, all of these, plus Europeans, are supposed to share a distant ancestry, and they do, but several of the easily perceived traits of size, form, and color do not fit the Caucasoid stereotype. There are dark-skinned people with European facial features, for example.

Look-a-likes can mislead as illustrated by a remark made by Henry Field during his studies among the Kish ("marsh Arabs") living south of Bagdad between the Tigris and Euphrates Rivers. He pondered that Arab facial features are so often Caucasoid in appearance that one may mistake him for a southern European, except for a deeper pigmentation (Field, 1935). Field was not the first, nor will he be the last, to be confused by racial typologies.

India's population offers a special challenge for biomedical studies because of its large and diverse population. Its over 1.2 billion people encompass most of the range of human diversity that has inspired writers to observe that, "Peoples of India include representatives of every human race." The people of the northern half to two-thirds of the country are like those of western Asia due to ancient migrations while, to the south and eastern parts of the country, there is a greater similarity to Southeast Asia. Interwoven throughout this vast population are significant signs of past contact with

China through expansions of Mongol empires. For over ten thousand years or more, migrations and interbreeding have mixed gene pools and obscured boundaries. Besides the mixing of the 200 or more genetic markers, the easily recognized phenotypes of color, size, and form have been rearranged.

When there are biological studies of India's peoples, there is always the question of classification. Eveleth and Tanner faced this problem in their collection of data from worldwide growth studies. They did not place India with Asians but grouped them as part of Indo-Mediterraneans with North Africans and people of the near East. They noted that their decision of placement within some defined group was complicated by Britain's recent and popular designation of Indians as Asian rather than Caucasians (Eveleth and Tanner, 1990). The selection of a meaningful population assignment may seem a small thing until one considers the comparative use of the data, such as measuring a child's growth progress against European or Asian standards (i.e., East Asian).

Studies of drug metabolizing enzymes require an even finer definition of group identity. Mutations of a gene for a protein that regulates triglyceride metabolism and hence increases the risk of cardiovascular disease were reported to be more frequent among Indian males living in the United States. Evaluation of drug treatments to lower this risk are proposed, or are in progress, on "South Asian Americans," "North Indian males," and "Asian Indians" depending on which of the studies is cited. How will any results be interpreted to aid in the understanding and prevention of heart disease in males who had little risk of heart disease in their native country but have a high probability in the United States? Again, the question of gene pool is obscured by use of race taxonomy. Comparing DNA markers (SNP) of the "Asian" sample to another high risk CVD group (African Americans) lends to the confusion (Holden, 2003:596).

Admixture: A Matter of "Blood"

We are required to enter our race/ethnic group on a variety of forms for census records, other government reports, and our health records. The label we choose depends on our experience, knowledge of close or distant relatives, and our appearance and self-image. Selection is mainly determined by law and local custom, however. If we do not make a choice, than someone else will based on the easily perceived traits we have discussed. In some states criteria are more specific. In Louisiana, for example, any person having one-thirty-second or less "Negro blood" shall not be described or designated as black or Afro-American. It followed that persons with greater than this prescribed amount would be designated as a black or African American. A stricter application of this law in the 1970s caused considerable controversy and a number of lawsuits to have the race designation changed on birth certificates of those who thought of themselves as "white" until they found that birth certificate copies showed otherwise. This episode of race documentation was discussed in a review of an unsuccessful suit against the state to have a race classification changed from black to white (Omi and Winant, 1986). Other states have similar regulations but usually rely on self-identification for census records, driver's license, and school records. The question often raised is why are race records so important that a governmental body goes to such length to define a degree of ancestry? If a person with a distant ancestor from Africa is "black," why then is not a person with a distant European ancestor a "white"? In Haiti they are, in fact, described in this way. Puerto Rico has given up on race labels. The fallacy of such an exercise is clear. It reverts to the old thinking of inheritance by "blood lines" and has nothing to do with a person's genetic complement.

One Drop Rule.   The schemes to define ancestry may be relevant to social issues, but not to questions of genetics, a fact that is seldom recognized (see Bennett, 1976). The "one drop rule"—a single black ancestor—makes a person black sociopolitically, but it does not guarantee a person a given portion of African genes. Genealogies only tell us of lines of descent, not what components of grandparental or great-grandparental genes we carry. This can easily be explained by reference to the laws of inheritance; the second law is one of independent assortment which reassorts the chromosomes when gametes are formed. We carry one-half of the chromosomes from each parent but do not possess an even assortment of chromosomes from their parents (our grandparents). Recall, again independent assortment. This means that the genes *are not evenly* distributed down through the generations in even proportions: parents ($\frac{1}{2}$ each), grandparents ($\frac{1}{4}$ each), great-grandparents ($\frac{1}{16}$), and so on. So, for genetic purposes, uses of black/white labels, regardless of degree of ancestral admixture, raises serious doubts about method and objectivity.

GENES, RACES, ENVIRONMENTS, AND DISEASES: SOME CONCLUSIONS

Health disparities between groups have been and continue to be explained largely by reference to race/ethnicity when socioeconomic factors should be considered. The epidemiological trends outlined above point to more environmental involvement than to some presumed racial identity and its implied propensity for certain diseases. The changing definitions of race/ethnicity and then a comparison against a "white" norm raises issues of who belongs in what group and, more important, what is the genetic composition of the group.

The sophisticated research into the structure and functions of the human genome still appears to rest on a simplistic premise about human diversity, that is, race. Skin color is not a marker of continent of origin, nor is it useful in determination of disease susceptibility. What color does is define a class or caste that fits into our preconceived images of inequality and can easily create a microclimate affecting the well-being of the "nonwhite" individual. Likewise, genes cannot accurately define a race in our scheme of dividing humankind into discrete units. Recall that 95 percent of human genetic variability is within these units of geographic races, while only 5 percent between them. This seeming paradox—greater difference within a race than between races—is a result of a broad sharing of genes throughout the human gene pool. There is no race-specific gene. Even the rarest, like Tay-Sachs that occurs at its highest frequency among

Ashkenazi Jews of eastern Europe, occurs in other populations (French Canadians and several Middle Eastern groups), albeit, at much lower frequencies. The same examples can be made for many other genotypes. These examples are increasing rapidly as additional populations are surveyed. Truly, we are more alike than different once we get beyond the superficial phenotypes.

The race concept has been described as useful for initial sorting or place holding, as a first step in locating the genes that cause a propensity for a metabolic abnormality or susceptibility to a disease. But without knowing the ancestry of the individuals under study or their genomic components, it becomes but an exercise in data manipulation. We continue to seek simple answers; we search for genes for everything, forgetting that a gene acts only within a certain context. Now that it is possible to examine an individual's genome, we should study gene influences by individual and not by some arbitrarily defined group. If you are going to study genes, then study genes. Blood transfusions are not made on the basis of race nor are organ transplants; there is careful typing of the ABO and HLA systems.

This brings us to a question of whether race should be discarded as obsolete or can the concept contribute to public health efforts, as one author put it (Reardon, 2005). This question is being raised more and more frequently among health professionals as genomics becomes more central to research and treatment as I discussed above. The issue of race in health and medical treatment is sensitive and very difficult. The examples of the lack of comprehension and misunderstanding of human diversity are numerous; a great many of these examples relate to forgetfulness of basic biology. In health research and clinical treatment the race concept remains pervasive, and assumptions based on typological thinking are many. Witness the problems encountered in epidemiological studies when the National Notifiable Diseases Surveillance System seeks to compare mortality and morbidity rates among races and ethnic groups. Nowhere are the difficulties of classification of human diversity more clear and more problematic. The reasoning often follows along these lines: If a person is a member of a definable race or ethnic group, then they are assumed to have all of the array of genetic attributes of that group and are at a higher risk for certain aliments because of what has been reported. Never mind that the method of classification may be suspect and the basic assumptions regarding heredity incorrect. In genetic studies, in epidemiology, and in medical treatment, seldom is the method of race or ethnic identification questioned. The trend has been to follow and accept the assumption that there are primary races of *Homo sapiens*, a view that has changed little over the generations.

The acceptance of this antiquated taxonomy is exemplified by recent discussions about the need to define the "genetics of race." Instead of recognizing that race is but a genetically open taxon, arbitrarily classifying a portion of the human species (a genetically closed unit), the expressed need is to list the genes possessed by Africans, Asians, Europeans, and so on. Human variability, again, may be explained by many factors. Racial profiling is not one of them.

chapter
10

Changing Dimensions of the Human Species

Viewed from an evolutionary perspective, our species has been extraordinarily successful. Not only have we increased in numbers and improved our adaptability, but we have also gained in the ability to alter environments to suit our needs. These environmental alterations and population increases have created a feedback system that has had a profound influence on biological variability and, in turn, places limits on our adaptive responses. The effectiveness of our behavior has contributed to an expansion and dispersal of humans around the globe, overcoming natural obstacles, breaking down older population boundaries, and establishing new ones while, at the same time, creating new dimensions of biological diversity.

Throughout the preceding chapters I have described our biological diversity and have considered the probable causes. Among these many causes relating to diversity is the increase in the variety of ways our species exploits natural resources. Development of technology and improved organization, for example, have aided human response to the forces of natural selection. The results have been dramatic during the past 10,000 years, the last 300 years in particular. Environments have been altered to fit human needs, but there are still many problems confronting us today. Natural selection is still operating, though, but in different forms, and it is continuing to shape the composition and diversity of human populations. The dimensions and scope of these ongoing processes require careful consideration, especially the increase in numbers of people and the burden these expanded populations place on natural resources. Demographic factors of this expansion exert a major influence on worldwide distribution of gene frequencies. Epidemiology—determination and distributions of disease—is also altered in each generation as new diseases gain influence while older ones decline as threats to human health as described in Chapter 9.

POPULATION SIZE AND GROWTH: HISTORICAL PERSPECTIVES

Our close ancestors, archaic *Homo sapiens*, probably numbered only a few hundred thousand at any given time, and population growth from generation to generation was painfully slow over tens of thousands of years. Throughout this period and including the time of appearance of modern *Homo sapiens*, we could not be judged to have been a very successful species. In fact, many other primate species far outnumbered us during these times. From this small number our species evolved and increased until, by the beginning of the Neolithic (the invention of agriculture), we had reached an estimated 5 million people. With the development of agriculture we passed beyond the era of slow growth and our numbers began to increase more rapidly. Even with this increase, however, it still took an average of 1,500 years for our species to double in number, an annual rate of increase (estimated at about 0.05 percent) that persisted over the next 8,000 years. From A.D. 1650, when the world contained approximately 500 million people, it now took only 200 years to increase to 1 billion (Table 10-1). From then on the annual rate of population growth accelerated; in the year 2004, our numbers increased by an annual rate of 1.3 percent. About 83 million new people are added each year, a significant increase from the 35 million added in 1950.

TABLE 10-1 World Population Size and Doubling Times

YEAR	POPULATION	DOUBLING TIME (YEARS)
8000 B.C.	5,000,000*	1,500
A.D. 1	250,000,000*	1,500
1650	545,000,000*	200
1850	1,171,000,000*	100
1950	2,486,000,000	50
1970	3,632,000,000	35
1975	4,000,000,000	36
1990	5,321,000,000	39
2004	6,396,000,000	53
2025	7,934,000,000**	53

*These are estimated population sizes and the time for a population to grow to double its size, given an estimated growth rate.

** Projected population size assuming continuation of current annual increases.

Source: Based on data from the Population Reference Bureau, 1975, 1990, and 2004; and Deevey, 1960.

Many factors have contributed to accelerated population growth since the Neolithic, and some are difficult to identify. A major influence, though, has been a production of a more dependable food supply. Early prehistoric hunters and gatherers probably had an ample food supply during most of the annual cycle that could have supported a much larger population, judging from studies of modern hunters. But seasonal changes, animal population fluctuations, or a bad weather cycle would create shortages. These times of scarcity kept population numbers below the carrying capacity of the environment that existed during the good times.[1] The major achievement of the agriculturists, beginning with the Neolithic, was an ability to produce and store a surplus of food, which enabled them to survive times of scarcity between harvests. This capability helped sustain a larger average number of people than had existed before the Neolithic.[2]

Another possible factor contributing to population growth was the radical change in lifestyles brought about by agricultural subsistence. During our nomadic hunting and gathering phase of existence, females could nurse only one child at a time; in addition, infants had to be breast fed for up to three years because of the lack of an adequate weaning food. This prolonged nursing period, plus the heavy workload and the frequent movement of camp sites, kept lean body mass high and contributed to reduced female fertility. In addition, infanticide probably played a role in keeping population increase to a minimum. There are reports that it was a common practice among recent hunting nomads to smother a newborn if the mother was still nursing an older sibling (Birdsell, 1981). The mother could carry a single infant and provide sufficient breast milk, but not the burden of a second infant. The effects of infanticide on fertility among nomadic hunters is still a much debated subject. Whatever the various causes, the result was a low fertility rate and small annual population increase for most of human existence.

By contrast, a major feature of life since the earliest advent of agriculture was the establishment of semipermanent settlements, and this more sedentary life had an important effect on female fertility. The less arduous existence encountered in a sedentary village, in contrast to a nomadic hunting life, reduced the strain on females and extended their reproductive period. The average number of births per woman during her lifetime increased from an average of four (reported among hunting nomads as recently as the 1960s) to six or even more, as in tropical horticultural groups today. With the advent of sedentary life, females were no longer forced to transport an infant while going about their daily round of food collecting over many miles of territory, as in former times. Improved infant care, suitable weaning foods, and increased nutrition reduced mortality, contributing to a greater number of children reaching adolescence.

---

[1]"Carrying capacity" is the estimated number of people who may be sustained by the resources contained in an environment when exploited by a given technology.

[2]Agriculturists were more or less successful producing surpluses to carry them through the years of crop failures, but not always. Many times during the Middle Ages and even into recent centuries, two or more successive years of poor crops resulted in famine and, together with epidemics, caused high mortality rates. A recent and interesting account of these episodes in Europe details the impact of crop failures on population (Ladurie, 1988).

Though settled village life had certain advantages, many new problems affecting human survival were created. Greater numbers of people living in close contact over long periods polluted their environment and water resources. This sustained a variety of insects and microorganisms that could readily be transferred from victim to victim, causing diseases that took a heavy toll on the population and shortened life expectancy. In early agricultural periods, judging from skeletal remains, there was a high mortality among young adults and adolescents; up to one-third or more of the skeletons found in many archaeological sites dating from this period were from children under 12.

Human existence, though improved since the days of the Paleolithic hunters, was still precarious for several millennia after the introduction of agriculture. This is demonstrated by the long doubling time until about A.D. 1. In later centuries there was an acceleration of population growth until by A.D. 1650, it took only 200 years for a population doubling (see Table 10-1). There has been much debate over the cause of this rate increase. For example, a question argued between archeologists and economists is whether a more dependable food supply contributed to an increase in numbers or did an increase in population provide the impetus to develop improved food-producing technology (see Boserup, 1981). Given the nature of the evidence and the long time periods involved, it is nearly fruitless to inquire about the antecedents to population growth at this early stage in our history. What we can be assured of is that growth did happen accompanied by or preceded by technological change. In more recent times we are on firmer ground.

By the nineteenth century we can point to improved sanitation and the control of infectious disease as major reasons for declining death rates, but in the seventeenth, eighteenth, and even the early decades of the nineteenth century, control of disease was probably not the single most important reason for growth. It is likely that increased efficiency in food production was more important. New food crops were introduced into Europe from the Americas. Plants like potatoes and corn, in particular, enabled agricultural production to increase radically because of their shorter growing season and a yield of a greater amount of calories per unit measure than the traditionally grown grains. The same amount of land planted in such crops could sustain many more people than possible previously; also, these New World crops could grow well on soils unsuitable for wheat and barley, the former staple European crops. Increased food supply plus the harnessing of a new energy source, coal, brought on a new era marked by population increase and industrialization.

Toward the end of the nineteenth century, after 100 years of Industrial Revolution,[3] many European populations had increased as much as 133 percent, and population pressures had reached the point at which millions from western Europe migrated to new lands. With this rapid expansion, the modern era began, and the conditions under which we live today were initiated. These modern living conditions,

---

[3]The term describes a rapid change in technology that occurred first in England and then in western Europe over a period of about 100 years (1760–1840). During this time, steam-powered machinery was developed and used in some of the earliest manufacturing. Driven by this new technology, the simple agrarian economy gave way to one based on manufacturing and export.

though varied and complex, have the capacity to change rapidly. Adaptation to changing environments, which in a previous period favored one group over another, influenced a shift in population size and reproduction rate within a few generations.

All populations of *Homo sapiens* were not affected equally, however, nor were the same selective forces present everywhere at the same time. While the technologically advanced societies were seeking new space, many, perhaps most, of the world's populations were living at pre-seventeenth-century levels. Africans and peoples of North and South America were less numerous in proportion to the carrying capacity of their lands than were Asians and Europeans. There was an 8 percent gain of Europeans (and persons of European origins in North America) between A.D. 1750 and 1900. Such gain brought Europeans up to 30 percent of the total world population, compared with only a 4 percent gain for India and China combined, which reduced their world proportion from 64 to 58 percent (Figure 10-1). Africa and the Middle East showed a net decline in proportion of the total world population. Considering earlier periods, if more reliable estimates were available for the Neolithic populations in Europe and the Middle East, disproportionate population gains would likely be demonstrated also. The point is, because growth is greater in some world regions than in others, some population boundaries expand, whereas others remain stable or may even contract. Changes in relative sizes of geographic groups likely occurred during most of our history as a species; certainly it has been and still remains a factor.

The experiences of many aboriginal people can serve to illustrate disproportinate population variations over time. Bands of hunting nomads were much more numerous

FIGURE 10-1 **World Regions, 1750–1950.** The populations in major world regions have grown disproportionately over the last two centuries, with Europe exceeding all others between 1750 and 1950. Even allowing for the wide range of error in these estimates, the changes in regional increases have been impressive.

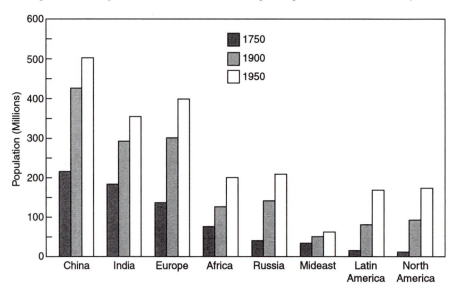

in the early Neolithic, and even outnumbered many sedentary agriculturists in some parts of the world. The hunters of southern Africa, the San, were probably once as numerous as Europeans, but competition with expanding agriculturists and pastoralists some 2,000 years ago forced them on to more and more marginal lands. In these harsh environments they could not sustain their numbers; they had to adapt to these new forms of subsistence, intermarry with the invaders, or perish. Some groups did and have left descendants who survive today, but many did not. The aboriginal peoples of Australia and North and South America had much the same experience, but in more recent times with the arrival of European colonists.

As Europeans have expanded and successfully occupied new areas of the world, hunters, pastoralists, and simple agriculturists have been all but destroyed, except for a few survivors living in isolated refuge areas, though exceptional areas, like New Guinea, have continued to sustain large and growing populations. The net result of expansion and contraction of the world's peoples during the Neolithic into recent times, and especially in the last 400 years, are some rather unique distributions and variations of populations. The hunters have all but disappeared except in a very few refuge areas, and even simple agriculturalists are only a fraction of their former number and are rapidly diminishing as their environments and resources are destroyed. By contrast, many other peoples have sustained a phenomenal growth rate over the last few generations.

FACTORS OF POPULATION CHANGE

A significant aspect of the phenomenal population growth in the last century has been the reduction in mortality rates while maintaining high birth rates. A great many factors influence human survival from birth to death and alterations in the social or physical environments are reflected in the numbers of people that survive to adulthood. Populations' growth and projections of size in future generations may be calculated by gain and loss of people at all ages and from all causes.

Birth and Death Rates

The number of newborns each year are entered as a crude birth rate (CBR) or births per thousand population. Likewise the total number of deaths each year are converted to a crude death rate (CDR) or deaths per thousand population. The CBR minus CDR gives the rate of natural increase (RNI), a percentage of gain in population size each year. The world population, in midyear 1972, had a loss of 3,782 million people dying at a rate of 13 per thousand (CDR), or a loss of 49 million people. These were replaced with 125 million since the CBR was 33; this was a net gain of 76 million people, a rate of natural increase of 2.0 percent (CBR−CDR). The crude birth rate was down to 21 in year 2004, but the death rate also declined to 9 for a difference of 12 (rounded off to 13) that gave a RNI of 1.3 percent. Though this rate is lower than it was in 1972, there was a net gain of 85 million because the world's population had grown to 6,067 million (6 billion, 67 million) in twenty-eight years.

When these rates and increases are compared for the entire world, significant differences are seen between regions. Africa increased its population by 2.4 percent in 2004, down slightly from 2.6 percent in 1972; Europe is actually declining by −0.1 percent compared to a slight gain of 0.7 percent in 1972; Latin America showed a decrease of from 2.8 to 1.6 percent. Latin American populations were still growing, but at a slower rate. Asia, with over half of the world's population, has also reduced its rate of annual increase by nearly 1 percent. Within each of these regions, there are major differences among the nations. Some countries have brought their birth rates down as death rates declined while other nations maintained high birth rates as deaths declined, leading to a higher RNI than the regional average. For example, Pakistan grew by 2.4 percent compared to 1.8 percent for the south central Asian region; India's growth was slightly less.

Infant Mortality

The demographic factor with the greatest influence on population size is infant-mortality rate, an influence well understood by every society. Infant-mortality rates have varied widely from ancient to recent times, and even slight changes have had major effects on the generations that followed. The lowering of infant mortality, together with improvement in maternal care, has radically driven up fertility rates (average number of live births per female living through their reproductive years).

In the United States today, more than 99 percent of all children born alive reach their thirteenth birthday, compared with only 50 percent who did so 100 years ago. This major demographic change is due primarily to a dramatic lowering of infant-mortality rates since the start of the twentieth century, followed by eradication of many of the childhood diseases affecting preadolescents. Western European countries have had the same experience. Table 10-2 shows comparative data on infant mortality for selected countries over the last one hundred years. Most MDCs have brought death rates down to less than 7 per 1,000 live births, whereas LDCs have maintained rates from 25 to 100 per 1,000 live births. All countries listed in this table have experienced a dramatic reduction of death rates during the past hundred years. The greatest decreases, however, have been among the industrialized MDCs.[4]

The United States, at the turn of the century, had an appallingly high infant-mortality rate that would be comparable to that of many of the LDCs twenty years ago, but this rate has now been reduced to 6.7 per 1,000. Still, most of the MDCs have lower infant-mortality rates. Seven of these countries listed in Table 10-2 have shown a 70 to 80 percent reduction in infant deaths since 1900. This reduction has been achieved through a variety of changes; improved diets, lessened female

---

[4]Classification of the MDCs and LDCs follows that of the United Nations—that is, the MDCs comprise all of Europe, North America (United States and Canada), Australia, New Zealand, and Japan. The rest of the world is regarded as LDCs or, in the new terminology, developing. The LDCs vary widely in population size and their economies cover an enormous range of gross national product or per capita incomes. For example, where would China or Mexico fit?

TABLE 10-2   Infant Mortality Rates of Selected Countries, 1898–2004 (deaths per 1,000 lives births)

COUNTRY	1898–1902	1918–22	1956–60	1980	2004
Sweden	98	65	17	8	2.8
Japan	155	172	36	8	3.0
Norway	88	—	20	9	3.4
Denmark	131	84	24	9	4.4
France	154	112	32	11	4.1
United Kingdom	152	85	23	11	5.3
Spain	190	158	49	16	3.7
United States	162	85	26	13	6.7
Italy	167	141	47	18	4.8
Hungary	204	—	—	24	7.3
Russia	—	—	81	31	13
Argentina	—	—	61	45	16.3
Mexico	—	—	76	70	25
Guatemala	—	—	95	76	25
Kenya	—	—	—	102	78
India	200	212	198	134	61
Nigeria	—	—	—	157	100

Source: Selected data from *World Population Data Sheet*, Population Reference Bureau, 1980, 2004; *Demographic Yearbook*, 1979.

workload, better maternal care, and control of infectious diseases have all contributed. By 1980, Sweden led the world in quality of infant health, a fact that is reflected in Sweden's having one of the lowest infant-mortality rates in the world. Because of the completeness of its health records extending back nearly two centuries, Sweden may be used as an example of what can be achieved in the field of infant health. From 250 per 1,000 infant deaths a century-and-a-half ago, the rate was reduced to 8 per 1,000 by 1980, which was thought to be the minimum that could be achieved, given the knowledge of fetal development. However, the rate has undergone a significant reduction since; a rate of 2.8 and 3.0 had been achieved in Sweden and Japan, respectively by the end of 2004 (a graphical comparison of sixteen MDCs is shown in Figure 10-2).

Where adequate data are available for comparison, mortality rates are seen to vary within a nation; urban centers with available medical services usually have lower rates than rural areas. In the United States, for example, the national IMR is 6.7, but the distribution is quite broad among the states. The highest IMR is recorded in the District of Columbia (10.6), Mississippi (10.5), and Louisiana (9.8) and the lowest rates (5.4 or less) are found in New Hampshire, Massachusetts, California, Utah, and Minnesota. What may account for these differences? Is it economics, religion, or that category so often applied to explain patterns of sociocultural differences—race and ethnicity— responsible? The degree of urbanization is also a consideration since residence patterns and population density influence access to health care.

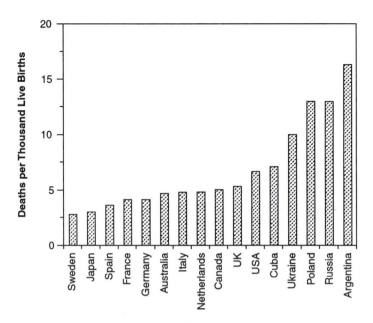

FIGURE 10-2   Infant Mortality Rates of Select Populations. (Source: Data selected from *World Population Data Sheet,* Population Reference Bureau, 2004.)

Encompassing all of these considerations are two closely interrelated factors, maternal ethnicity and socioeconomic position.[5] Studies of maternal health and infant mortality rates often emphasize the racial differences, noting the higher rates among Afro-Americans, Hispanic, and Native American groups. Significant ethnic group differences have been recorded ever since health statistics have been compiled. African Americans have the highest infant mortality of any ethnic group (16.8 versus 6.9 for Euro-Americans). A variety of explanations are offered—from lack of access to medical facilities, or failure to use them, to an average younger age at first pregnancy—but whatever the causes, significant differences have been recorded throughout the twenty-first century. Low-birth-weight infants are twice as frequent among Afro-Americans as among Euro-Americans just as is the rate of teenage pregnancies. These two conditions contribute to the higher infant mortality rate among this minority group. Seldom compared, however, are economics, education, household size, and place of residence. When these socioeconomic conditions are factored into the infant health equation, the differences between white (Euro-American) and nonwhite (Afro-American, Asian, and sometimes Hispanic) groups diminish. That is, if income levels, place of residence, and access to prenatal care are considered, than the ethnicity factor diminishes to insignificant levels. The differences among race/ethnic groups are frequently those of education and poverty.

---

[5]Ethnicity and/or race is often confused when demographic data are reported. As in the previous chapter, both labels of group identity are more of a proxy for social class than a definition of a biological unit.

Infant health relates not to ethnicity and poverty as much as to the delivery of quality health care. This has been made clear by the example of Sweden, the world's leader in prenatal care and one of the first countries to decrease infant mortality below ten per thousand. Sweden has admitted many immigrants from high IMR countries of eastern Europe and the Middle East over the last few decades. These people fill the many menial jobs in an advanced industrial society and they occupy the lowest socioeconomic status. Yet, their health, especially that of infants and children, is excellent and there has been no lowering of the national averages. Sweden's experience has demonstrated the importance of health care delivery, and it counters those arguments that have emphasized race and ethnicity as causal factors influencing infant health. Sweden achieved this low level of infant death through major innovations in prenatal care and obstetrical services; a countrywide network ensures that every woman is within an hour of a maternity health center, which offers free services. The Swedish experience indicates the importance of socioeconomic factors. The influence of social factors on fetal/maternal health is further illustrated by the higher rates of mortality among those many national minorities.

Maternal Health, Infant Mortality, and Natural Selection

Throughout the last few generations, as infant mortality has declined and maternal health has improved, childbirth-related deaths have been reduced rapidly. Maternal death rates of 320 per 100,000 a century ago in the developed world have decreased to around 10 per 100,000 today. The combined effects of lower infant and maternal-mortality rates were increased growth of population. Then family sizes began a decline in the MDCs to a point near or below replacement level. In the LDCs the story is somewhat different. High maternal-mortality rates persist, though the rates are probably much lower than they were a few generations ago, but firm data are lacking for LDCs. As shown in Table 10-3, there is a wide disparity between countries, and most have rates as high or higher than recorded in the developed world at the turn of the century. Further improvement in prenatal care and maternity services should reduce the risks of pregnancy and contribute to a rise in fertility rates. Family planning efforts, changing traditions, and more years of formal education for women have worked in some countries to lower fertility over the past decades, and this lowering of fertility should compensate for the increased numbers of women living through their reproductive years.

Maternal health, prenatal care, and race (actually socioeconomic class) are often cited as affecting maternal and newborn health. Mortality risks vary among ethnic minorities, which are generally higher than the national averages, with a slower decline of mortality rates. Poor diet, smoking, alcohol, and drug abuse are listed among other more serious influences, as well as teenage pregnancy. Teenagers, as a group, are less likely to be watchful of their health, and, especially if unmarried and with little family support, are less likely to seek prenatal care. The net result is, the higher the rate of unmarried adolescent pregnancies, the higher the rate of high-risk births and maternal deaths. In fact, United States data on these events

TABLE 10-3   Estimates of Maternal Mortality by Region

REGION	NUMBER OF MATERNAL DEATHS (THOUSANDS)	MATERNAL-MORTALITY RATE (PER 100,000 LIVE BIRTHS)
Africa	150	640
North	24	500
West	54	700
East	46	660
Central	18	690
Southern	8	570
Asia	308	420
West	14	340
South	230	650
Southeast	52	420
East	12	55
Latin America	34	270
Central	9	240
Caribbean	2	220
Tropical South	22	310
Temperate South	1	110
Oceania	2	100
Developing Countries	494	450
Developed Countries	6	30
World	500	390

Source: Adapted from *Population Today*, Population Reference Bureau, 1990.

show that those states with the highest percentage of low-birth-weight infants are those with the greatest number of teenage pregnancies, the lowest incomes, and the highest infant mortality.

The changes of maternal and infant health are altering the effects of selective forces acting on the human populations. A reduction of the selection against those genetic defects that contribute to early death or that affect infant susceptibility to disease will undoubtedly increase the genetic load in future populations. Likewise, improved maternity services enable many women to give birth to healthy infants when they might otherwise not have been able to because of hormonal deficiencies, poor general health, or defective pelvic structure (discussed earlier in the example of rickets influencing female growth).

Fertility and Fertility Rates

Critical to any population study is the consideration of fertility rates. The use of crude birth rate is helpful as an initial step, but for more accurate depiction of growth or growth potential, a measure of a population's fertility and female age composition is necessary. This measure is the average number of live births compared to the number of females living through their reproductive years. Since almost all births are to mothers between 15- and 49-years of age, this is considered as a standard age range for calculating fertility rates.

The total number of children born during the year to women in this age range is a relatively easy measure to obtain and is called the *general fertility rate* (GFR). It is calculated as the total number of births per thousand women ages 15 to 49. This ratio considers the age factor and allows for comparisons between populations so projection of the size of future generations may be made. The greater number of women within this age group, the greater the reproductive potential compared with those populations with a higher proportions of females of age groups above or below the reproductive life span.

Not all females live to reach the age of reproduction and others do not live long enough to complete their reproductive life span so fertility rates are measured by age-specific intervals. To facilitate these calculations, reproductive age span is divided into five-year intervals and the births per thousand women in each interval are listed. Typically, female fecundity (biological ability to conceive) is low for the first few years following menarche and then rises during young adulthood. A peak is reached somewhere between ages 20 and 29. It is during this middle period of reproductive life span when conception is most likely and when the highest fertility rates (marked by live births) occur in any population. After age 29 these rates decline rapidly as women approach menopause, but there are wide ranges of individual variation. Calculations of the number of births divided by the number of women in each interval is the fertility rate for that age interval. Adding the rates for all age intervals (15–49) yields a total fertility rate (TFR) for that population at that point in time.

Total fertility rate (TFR). The number of lifetime births per woman living through her reproductive period and reproducing at the average rate varies considerably over generations and among populations. In populations that do not practice any form of contraception the TFR ranges between 6 and 12 and has been described as a natural fertility rate. Actually some form of birth control is practiced by a majority of couples so rates are much lower; the ranges are from a low of 1.3 to a high of 6. The TFRs of most countries, even the LDCs, cluster between 2 and 3.5. Twenty-five years ago rates were much higher, but they have been reduced by active family planning programs and changes in female social status.

In examples of most of the LDCs, especially Latin America, there has been a downward trend in the fertility that began in the 1950s but which slowed somewhat by the 1970s. Then TFR decline resumed as progress was made in family planning. In just the past decade, Latin America declined from 4.5 to 2.6 TFR with increased contraception from 58 to 70 percent. Brazil, one of the largest developing countries, has made major advances in reducing fertility rates from over 6.2 (1950) down to 2.2 by 2004 as contraceptive use increased from near 0 to 76 percent. Because of its young population, however, Brazil still maintains a 1.3 percent rate of natural

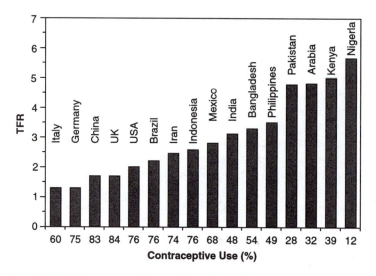

FIGURE 10-3   Contraceptive Use and Fertility Rates. Source: Adapted from *World Population Data Sheet*, Population Reference Bureau, 2004.

increase. Several of the smaller nations, Peru (TFR, 2.8), Bolivia (TFR, 3.8), Ecuador (TFR, 3.0), for example, have retained high fertility rates and their populations continue to grow at over 2 percent per year. Figure 10-3 plots national fertility of select countries against the percent of women using some form of contraception in 1990 and 2004.

Family planning for most African nations has not been as successful during this period of fertility transition over the past twenty-five years. The rate has remained at a high TFR of 5.1 which contributes to continued population growth. Egypt (3.2 TFR), Kenya (5.0 TFR), and Nigeria (5.7 TFR) continue to maintain high fertility despite economic improvement and some successes in family planning. Though governments are sensitive to the socioeconomic and demographic problems related to high fertility rates, growth continues because of the large proportion of the population under age 20. The largest of the African countries, Nigeria, Ethiopia, and the Congo, accounting for about one-third of all African peoples, have changed little from their high fertility rates of a decade ago. These three nations will be the major contributors to the continent's population, nearly doubling by about the year 2025 if current trends continue.

Muslim countries, with the exception of Indonesia, have continued to maintain high fertility while lowering mortality rates; the result has been large annual increases in population. Syria, Iraq, and Saudi Arabia, to select three examples, have maintained fertility rates of from 6.8 to 7.2 through most the 1990s and have only recently been declining. By contrast, Turkey and Indonesia have reduced their rates to 2.6 and 2.7, respectively. These differences by region, national religion, political orientation, plus the dramatic declines seen at certain periods raise the question of the primary causes of fertility rate variability among populations.

In addition to the biological variables affecting female fertility, religious and socioeconomic factors weigh heavily in the fertility transition of any nation. The strength of a nation's family planning program and the female's role in society are the principle influences, however. As traditional roles of women change and their status improves, there have been changes in reproductive rates. This is reflected by the fertility declines in nations as diverse as Brazil, Thailand, Jordan, and India. We have already mentioned certain of these factors in relation to infant mortality and similar relationships exist for fertility rates.

EMPOWERMENT OF WOMEN

It has been said in different ways by many writers that a measure of civilization is that civilization's treatment of women. This treatment was well described by a physician three-quarters of a century ago in a review of medical history. He stated that, "The care of child-bearing women is an index of the civilization of the community as a whole and not alone of the leaders of the civilization" (Haggard, 1929). This statement, made in the historical context of medical progress, has come to mean much more today with our concern with population sizes and future projections. Haggard, indirectly, calls attention to the important linkages between community, tribe, or national survival and the status of womanhood. As the decades have passed, we become more aware of these linkages and the importance of empowering women. The independent variable that directs future populations is the status of the female segment, especially those in their reproductive years.

Women's health, now merged into a category called reproductive health, was noted above as an important issue. This category encompasses the health and growth pattern of female children and their age at menarche, age at first pregnancy, maternal health, and access to means of birth spacing and prenatal care. Taken together, these factors influence a woman's reproductive lifespan and the number of children she will bear. But the issues are not just a matter of health, though it is of great importance. It is the question of options and choices that a young woman has during her reproductive years. It is the empowerment of women that guides future population growth.

Education

In making these choices, education stands out as a prime factor. The age at marriage and the number of children women will bear is closely correlated to the number of years she has spent in school. In the populations LDCs, women with no education have a fertility rate of between 5 and 7.1 in contrast to those who complete primary school (TFR of 3.6 to 6.7) and those who finish secondary school whose TFR drops to 2.5 to 4.5. The greatest percent of females enrolled in secondary school is in the MDCs which have the lowest TFR, and the highest TFR is among those populations

TABLE 10-4   Secondary School Enrollment (percent)*

COUNTRY OR REGION	1980		1990–1996	
	BOYS	GIRLS	BOYS	GIRLS
MDC	88	89	99	100
LDC	43	30	57	88
North Africa	47	29	63	57
Sub-Saharan Africa	19	10	29	23
Western Asia	49	31	63	48
South Central Asia	38	20	55	37
Southeast Asia	40	35	53	49
East Asia	59	45	77	70
Central America	46	42	56	57

*Percent is of those children of secondary school age.
Source: Data selected from Ashford, 2001.

with the lowest secondary school enrollments (Table 10-4). The increases in school attendance at all levels reduces the rate of female illiteracy, and as illiteracy declines so does fertility.

A special example is provided by Kerala, the state with the lowest infant mortality rate in India. In this predominantly agricultural economy of one of the poorest states, women enjoy a high status of property ownership, voting rights, and an equal access to education. One of the results has been India's highest female literacy rate (86 percent compared with the national rate of only 39 percent). Kerala is distinguished also by a lower fertility rate, 2.0 versus the national average of 3.9 in 1993 (see Visaria and Visaria, 1995).

Work Force.   The expansion of female education and women's increased entry into the work force outside of the home has significantly delayed age of marriage. This delay has contributed to the reduced births seen in several developing countries. South Korea declined from a TFR of 6.1 to 4.0 between 1960 to 1970, and then it declined further to 1.6 as average age of females at marriage rose from 18 to 24. The differences between Bangladesh and Sri Lanka are likewise attributable to an increased average age at marriage, 16 versus 25 (Merrick, 1986). Kerala also has, for Asia in general, a later age at marriage, 22, in contrast to the average of 18 years for India as a whole. Education and participation in the cash economy serve the additional function of communication and awareness of the alternatives offered by family planning. In sum, where females enjoy greater economic freedom, there is a lower infant mortality, a delay in marriage, lower fertility, and an increase in the proportion of unmarried women.

The developed world has undergone an even more striking change over the last fifty years. Women are spending more time in school than did their grandmothers and more are entering the labor force (as of 1995, 46 percent of the United States labor force were women compared to only 18 percent in 1900). They are marrying later and choose to have fewer children, or none at all. Sometimes the decisions are based on economic or social considerations as in the examples of the depressed economies of eastern Europe and Russia. Since 1990, conditions have improved, but marriages are still delayed and rates of unmarried are higher.

Economic Conditions and Choices.   Harsh living conditions, a lack of housing, and poor economic prospects tended to delay marriages and keep family size low as in the examples of some eastern European countries before the collapse of the USSR. These countries had higher mortality rates, shorter life expectancies and were among the earliest of the European countries where birth rates fell below replacement levels.

On the other hand, improved economic circumstances can also have similar results—delayed childbearing and a reduction in completed family size. Spain and Italy have significantly expanded their economies over the past decade, which has contributed to more opportunities for females and an improvement in their reproductive health status. More education and career options were open to females; selection from among these options led to later age at marriage and a preference for smaller family size. These decisions resulted in a TFR reduced from 2.6 to 1.2 (Spain) and from 1.9 to 1.2 (Italy) between 1980 to 2000. These examples serve to illustrate that fluctuations of population size between generations or among ethnic groups are the result of complex forces that can quickly alter demographic processes because of social or natural factors. The net effect is a wide range of differences not only among ethnic groups, but also between countries of the developed and less-developed regions.

In sum, educated women have smaller, healthier families, about half the number of children than those women lacking schooling. Furthermore, the time spent in school increases the age of first sexual experiences and delays marriage. Education increases literacy and knowledge of health practices, which allows for a broader range of options in lifestyle selection. It also enables greater participation in socioeconomic decisions. Such a trend, started a century ago in the industrialized world, is now well underway in the developing countries and the speed of change may be measured by the several factors of population changes. In the more developed world the improvement in female status in the past 100 years has advanced to the point of not only slowing population growth, but also in reducing its size.

Replacement Level

If women are reproducing at an average fertility rate of 2.1, there will be newborns added in sufficient numbers to maintain a stable population. However, this depends on several factors: population age composition, mortality rates, and social customs, as for example, age at first sexual union. Germany with its late age at marriage, a high number of unmarried, and low fertility over several decades, has a very small proportion of its population under age 15 (16 percent compared to 22 percent in the United States, or the 37 percent average for much of the lesser developed world). For Germany, a TFR greater than 2.1 will be necessary to sustain population size. Replacement level also depends on average life expectancy. A TFR slightly greater than 2.0 is required to compensate for deaths of infants and children and also to allow for the fact that not all women will live through their reproductive years. In populations with higher mortality rates, a TFR greater than 2.1 is needed. For example, Kenya, with a life expectancy of 49, would require an estimated replacement level of 2.25 in contrast to 2.06 for the United States with a life expectancy of 72 (male) and 79 (female) years at birth.

FERTILITY DIFFERENCES AND POPULATION COMPOSITION

In addition to the variation in mortality rates and fertility rates between various areas of the world, there are significant differences among socioeconomic classes and ethnic groups in each country. These differences plus immigration have contributed to changes in population composition of several nations during the past three generations and are likely to continue. But alterations in total fertility rates among socioeconomic classes and ethnic groups within any country are difficult to define or predict. Social statuses often shift, and fashions change as preferences for large or small families alter. The baby boom experience in the United States can serve as an example.[6] The increase in fertility occurred mainly among middle-class women (total fertility rate went from 2.1 to 3.7), which accounted for most of the rise in number of births that produced an increase of 18.2 percent in the U.S. population between 1947 and 1964. The situation is different now, with most groups showing low fertility levels, while rates among Hispanic women remain above the national average.

Ethnic Groups and Fertility

Mexican Americans, the largest group of Hispanics, lead in the number of births. The effects of this high fertility on ethnic composition and on overall fertility rate have been traced over the last twenty years in California. The proportion of women giving birth who are identified as Hispanic[7] increased from 20 percent to 44 percent since 1975; those classified as "non-Hispanic white" declined from 68 percent to below 38 percent, and the African American segment decreased from 9 percent to 8 percent of total births (Riche, 2000). The remaining ethnic groups, or "others" (Asian, Pacific Islanders, Native Americans) increased their share from 3 to 10 percent (Burke, 1995). This ethnic pattern of fertility rates has continued throughout the country over the past

---

[6]The baby boom is generally defined as the rise of birth rates during the post war era, generally set between 1946 and 1964. The peak was reached in 1957 and began to decline after 1960, continuing to drop through a "baby bust" period (1964–1975) as delays in family starts by the now-adult baby boomers reduced birth rates. After 1975 and through present times, an echo effect began to appear as the number of births rose, despite a lower fertility rate.

[7]Recall that these ethnic labels encompass a number of populations whose origins are quite different. The identification of people in a Hispanic or non-Hispanic group does not sort out the genetic and cultural diversity encompassed in each. Hence, Peruvians would be lumped together with Salvadorans for purposes of statistical collection without acknowledging major differences in their heritage.

decade. Fertility rates are on the decline among all groups as attitudes about family size change—a wish for more than two children is the exception. This change has been most notable among second- and third-generation Mexican Americans. The nation's majority group (White, non-Hispanic) has a TFR of 1.79 total and the Asian and Native American minorities are even lower at 1.62 and 1.7, respectively. African Americans have a TFR right at the national level of 2.0. Hispanics, 13 percent of Americans, are a young and growing group with 2.7 TFR, which makes up for the below replacement level of the majority.

Immigration and Ethnicity

The intake of about one million immigrants annually adds to America's population growth. Immigration is also contributing to a change in the diverse composition of the American population. Before 1960, Europe was the source of almost all immigrants entering the United States. Now a majority of the nearly one million legal immigrants admitted each year since 1980 are arriving from Latin American and Asian countries. Between 1960 and 1969, 40 percent came from Europe versus only 38 percent from Latin America; this ratio was more than reversed by the 1990s (to 13 and 51 percent). Asian immigrants accounted for only a small percentage in the 1960s but now enter at the rate of 30 percent of total annual immigrants. Add to this the number of illegals, mostly from Latin America, and it is easy to understand the projected changes in the ethnic composition of the country over the next half century (Figure 10-4). About one in three Americans will be members of what we now call ethnic minorities. By the time another half century

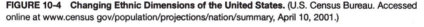

FIGURE 10-4 Changing Ethnic Dimensions of the United States. (U.S. Census Bureau. Accessed online at www.census gov/population/projections/nation/summary, April 10, 2001.)

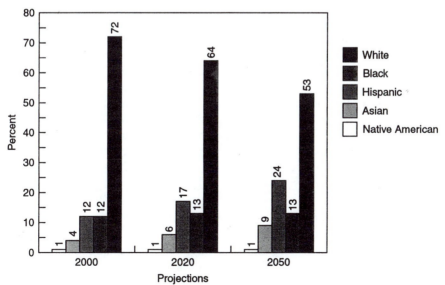

has passed the labels we use will have become obsolete and population groups and boundaries will have altered completely through economic change and intermarriage.

This is only a part of the story regarding population composition because immigration accounts for only 30 percent of the increase of the population in one of the few growing countries of the MDCs. The balance of increase in national population is due to natural increase, an excess of births over deaths. The U.S. population increases at the rate of 0.6 percent annually compared with only 0.1 percent in western Europe and 0.1 percent in Japan. Since fertility and immigration are higher among most of the ethnic minorities, it is easy, if one is a member of the majority, to fall into the trap of racial bias and deplore the changing ethnic makeup of the nation. But such anxiety should be tempered with the evidence of America's recent history. At the peak of immigration, between 1881 and 1920, when twenty-three million people were admitted, a cry went up warning of the ethnic makeup of these new immigrants. These new immigrants came from southern and eastern Europe in contrast to the original and later colonists, "the Old Americans" whose origins were western European. Despite the reactions at the time by the "old" Americans toward the new wave of immigrants, no harm came to the country; rather the reverse occurred. The economy expanded and the nation prospered with the growth of population and an increase in ethnic diversity.

European Examples of Fertility Rate Differences

Socioeconomic influences on decisions to have children are even more clearly illustrated by the rapidly changing conditions in Europe in the last twenty years; the lack of housing, low family income, and high inflation rates have caused many young couples to decide against having children, resulting in significant drops in fertility rates in many countries. Several eastern European countries have reduced their total fertility rate below replacement level (a TFR of 2.1), but some, like Romania and Poland, maintained a replacement level TFR of 2.1 until 1990, despite the hardships confronting young families. Since then, with the breakup of the eastern European communist block, these rates have dropped to 1.2 (Poland) and 1.2 (Romania). The TFR for the former Soviet Union was 2.5 in 1990, which was an average for the total population of 291 million people of diverse cultures. The religious beliefs and cultures of the central Asian republics included a tradition of large families, contributing to fertility rates two to three times the Russian average. Since the separation of the republics, Russia, Belarus, and the Ukraine record some of the lowest fertility rates in the world (TFR of 1.2 to 1.4), while the now independent central Asian republics have remained at or near their former high rates of 3.0.

DEMOGRAPHIC BALANCES

The major differences between world regions in their natural population increase over the last half century have been due to a dramatic lowering of death rates in the LDCs. When both birth and death rates were high, a reduction in only the death rates while maintaining a high birth rate would, of course, result in a rapid increase, as experienced by Africa, Asia, and Latin America since the 1950s. Countries of these regions with their rapidly growing populations are undergoing a stage of the *demographic transition*. Demographers use this term to describe a transition in the growth potential of a population. In past centuries, relatively stable populations were maintained with little net increase between the generations because a high birth rate was counterbalanced by a high death rate, the *first demographic phase*. Such populations begin to change when they enter the *second phase* of the demographic transition by dramatically reducing death rates through various health measures (usually associated with improved sanitation, innoculations), while births still remain high. In this phase there will be a high natural increase (a surplus of births over deaths) that will continue until a new balance is reached by a reduction in births. This *third phase* of the demographic transition is entered when birth rates begin to decline until replacement equals or barely exceeds loss, and the population approaches a zero-population-growth condition. European countries have reached this phase, and the United States and Canada are approaching it.

A critical factor for population stability is the length of time required for the completion of this demographic transition in the LDCs. Though many of the LDCs have made significant reductions in birth rates over the past twenty-five years, they still remain at a level that locks the countries in a demographic phase 2, many populations will double in size in slightly more than a generation. Mexico, for example, had a natural increase of 2.1 percent in 2004, an annual increase that added over 2 million people that year. If continued at this rate, Mexico will have a projected population of 131 million by 2025. A number of other countries, especially in Africa and Asia, continue to grow and will probably double in size within the next generation.

Rapid-growth countries have younger age structures, as illustrated by the population pyramid for Mexico, where persons born between 1981 and 1996 make up 36 percent of the population, in contrast to 22 percent in the United States (a slow-growth nation). Sweden is an example of a no-growth nation; each age segment between birth and 60 years is nearly equal in size (Figure 10-5). These differentials of age-group sizes between developed and developing countries become even broader in some large fast-growth nations; 44 percent of Nigeria's 137 million people are under 15 years of age, Mexico has 44, Bangladesh 37, and India 36 percent. The MDCs have maintained the proportion of children under age 15 at about 20 percent since 1950, while this age group has nearly doubled in the developing countries and may even rise further in some.

Population Momentum

These "young" fast-growing populations will continue to increase for decades even after replacement levels have been reached because of what might be termed a reproductive momentum. Just as the United States population did not stop growing when its fertility rate dropped below replacement level because of the large numbers of women in their reproductive years, the LDCs will continue to grow well past the

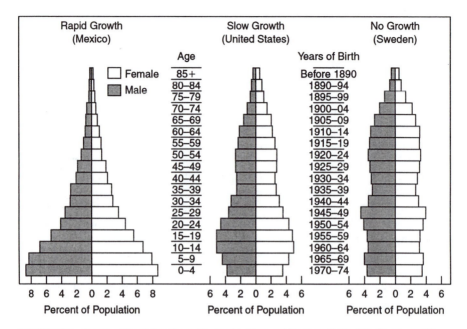

FIGURE 10-5   Age-Sex Population Pyramids: Rapid, Slow, and No-Growth Models. (Courtesy of the Population Reference Bureau, Inc., Washington, DC, 1990.)

middle of the twenty-first century. Indonesia had 600,000 more births in 2004 than twenty years ago when the TFR was nearly twice as high. Because of the age distribution, even with a further decline in fertility, Indonesia will likely grow from 218 to 275 million within twenty-five years. Significant population increases are also probable for several other countries like Brazil and Egypt that will continue to grow through a momentum of the shear size of their reproductive age groups, a size that is a result of the last generation's high fertility.

India, with its large size and continued high fertility, will approach China in population size and surpass it by 200 million within fifty years. Bangladesh's remarkable achievement in the reduction of its TFR within a single decade has brought down the number of births despite its young population and demonstrates what can be achieved. Countries like Nigeria, Ethiopia, and Pakistan continue on a rapid growth path with both high fertility and a young population. Each will add 50 percent or more to its population within two decades. Comparisons of age structure and fertility history of several of the world's largest nations show that the absolute number of births will remain nearly the same or even increase despite fertility declines.

Dependency Ratio

A population is not simply a matter of the number of individuals. We pass through a series of stages in our life cycle from birth to death, and we fullfill different biological

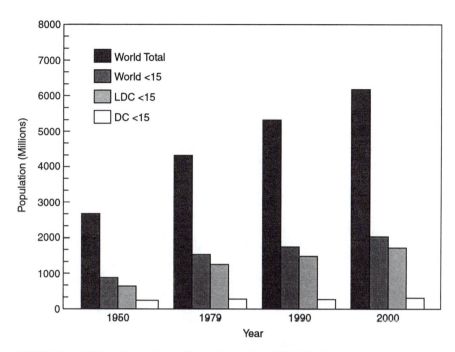

FIGURE 10-6   Children Younger Than Fifteen Years of Age, 1950–2000. (Data selected from Population Reference Bureau, 1990, 2000.)

and social roles at each stage. Therefore, a population's age structure is an important determiner of a society's present and future needs and may be measured by a *dependency ratio*. This is the ratio between the productive portion of the population, set typically between 15 and 64 years, and the dependent age groups—those individuals younger than 15 years and older than 64 years. The larger the dependent group, the larger will be the dependency ratio (DR). Populations in the LDCs have a very high dependency ratio compared to the MDCs because of the large numbers of children under 15 years.

Comparisons between slow-growth and rapid-growth countries show a wide difference in the DR for the under age 15 group (Figure 10-6). These figures are based on estimates provided by the Population Reference Bureau but do not consider the probable use of child labor, which, of course, would reduce the size of the dependent group. Even allowing for this, the dependency ratios are high among the LDCs, whose poorer economies are less able to support such a burden of dependents. Most importantly, this large proportion of children provides a potential for high reproduction rates as the children reach maturity and are a source for rapid population growth in the future.

Baby Boom

Changes in population structure will affect the economy, the environment, and the social institutions of the LDCs in diverse ways. One way of gauging the impact of rapid growth on a nation's resources is to consider the structural and social dislocation created by high birth rates over short periods. Within less than a generation of high fertility and rapid population growth, persons of the same age cohort (born within a given time period) have to be accommodated by educational and socioeconomic systems. For example, in the United States, the group born during the baby boom period followed the age cohort born during the *Depression years* (1929 to 1941), when fertility rates were close to replacement level.

This baby boom has resulted in a 75-million-person bulge in America's population, which has contributed to major stresses on social institutions and sociocultural changes as they have passed through the life cycle. First, it was the hospitals and then the educational facilities that bore the burden as this large cohort moved through childhood and entered the next phase. College enrollments shot up, and many more persons entered the labor market in the 1970s than in previous decades. As this birth cohort entered adulthood, delayed marriages and smaller families were the favored choices, so the "boomers" were followed by a smaller age cohort because of decreased birthrates (fertility below 2.1). Because of the large numbers of women in their reproductive years, however, there was a short period of increased births despite the group's low fertility rate. This created an increase in the childhood cohort, an echo effect in the 1980s, which may be over now as the older baby boom women leave their prime childbearing years.

In the United States, we have witnessed and recorded some major stresses on our social system—in particular, reduced numbers of job opportunities and an increased demand for housing, education, and medical care. Magnify these problems many times and consider the effects on LDCs. The LDCs, with more than one-third of their total population under 15 years of age, must find ways of meeting the needs of childhood, and then later, the economy must be expanded to offer employment as this large age cohort enters adulthood. This critical cohort of under 20-year-olds has reached over 2 billion in the LDC. About 400 million are in the 15 to 19 age range, but with the under 15 group at about one-third of the total population, the critical cohort will be expanding each year.

There has been a wide variation in experience in coping with this burden, depending on the nation, its resources, government, and social institutions. Expanding industry has worked for some, while migration or seasonal labor has more often been the source of job opportunities for others.

The Geriatric Boom or the "Graying Effect"

Rapid transition from high to low fertility can also cause problems for future generations as did high productivity rates of baby booms. In the case of China, the two decades of enforcement of a rigorous one-child family policy worked to bring down the rate of natural increase from 1.2 percent in 1980 to 0.6 in 2004. This policy, though unevenly enforced across the country, was eased by 1996 and supplemented with large-scale family planning efforts. These programs reduced TFR to below replacement levels in less than a generation, satisfying national goals to reduce growth of the one-billion-plus population. The long-term effects of this abrupt decline, the disruption of age distribution, are just becoming recognized, however. The large cohort of citizens 65 and older, those born during times of rapid population growth, will face an old age with only a small number of productive citizens, the children born during the family reduction stage. With an age top-heavy pyramid expected, China will face a shortage of workers to support the elderly, a result of what can be called a demographic dilemma—how to control population without a major dislocation of its age structure.

A similar experience is already being confronted in the slow-growth nations of Europe. Japan, after a generation of near or below replacement level fertility, will also soon have the problems caused by an imbalance of age distribution. Only 15 percent of Japan's population is below age 15, the lowest in the world. Simply, there will be too many pensioners supported by too few wage earners, a prospect that continues to arouse arguments about pension fund solvency over the next twenty-five years.

The aging of the post-World War II cohort in the developed nations is a prime cause for concern. With many now in middle age and soon to reach retirement, the developed nations with low birth rates have fewer young workers to take their places in the work force. The shortfall varies between countries but will continue to widen as the population ages without replacement. The recent discussions over social security in the industrialized world, especially in the United States, emphasize that there are now six to eight workers for each retiree, a ratio that will decline to about three to one by mid-century. The increase of average population age will also place a burden on services for the elderly over the next few decades as this proportion (over 65 years) of the dependency ratio rises. The effects of a "graying" of the work force are already being felt in western Europe, which is becoming more dependent on immigrant labor; most are coming from North Africa and the Middle East, much to the distress of those ultranationalists who would keep their nation "pure" and free of foreigners. This final stage in the human life cycle illustrates, as did the other stages, the impact that disproportionate age groups can have on a society.

There is no escape from this impact; the numbers are clear, the people are here, and plans must be made to cope with the dislocation caused by the demands and stresses of population age imbalance. We only partially escaped disaster centuries before by moving people about through major voluntary and forced migration. Now with a crowded planet, there is no place to go. Major regional changes of population sizes and reordering of ethnic composition are continuing rapidly.

REGIONAL CHANGES OF WORLD POPULATIONS

The future, if growth projections are reasonably accurate, will see an even greater change in the distribution of the world's peoples (Figure 10-7). The growth trends of two centuries ago have been reversed. Those countries with a larger industrial base, a higher per capita income, and more technological resources now have a much slower projected growth rate than the less-developed areas of the world.

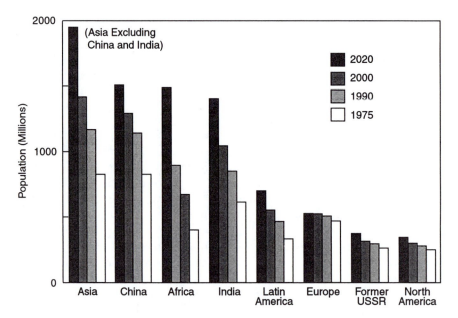

FIGURE 10-7   Regional Populations, 1975–2020. Given the current growth rates of major world regions, the projections for the year 2020 will place Asia and Africa far ahead of the other regions. Latin American will nearly double in size in contrast to those areas that experience only slow growth (Europe, North America, and Russia, the former USSR). (Data selected from Population Reference Bureau, 1990, 2000.)

The majority of the more than 6 billion people in the world in the year 2004 lived in these LDCs. There are an estimated 81 percent of the world's population in the LDCs, a significant increase from the 66 percent living in these regions of the world in 1950. If China's 1.3 billion population is not counted as part of the LDC group because of the country's rapid development, then the LDC percent drops to 60.8 percent of the world's total. The MDCs are expected to continue to grow, but very slowly, a natural increase of only about 0.1 percent per year. The LDCs have reduced their 1975 rate of 2.1 percent but still increase their populations by 1.5 percent per annum. At this rate their doubling time will be 47 years in contrast to the 124- to 500-year doubling time for North America and Europe. If China, now with a rate of natural increase of 0.6 percent and a doubling time of 116 years, is excluded from the calculations, then the LDC doubling time shortens to 39 years.

Replacement Migration

The natural increase (births over deaths) in the MDCs will not be sufficient to maintain a stable population or even a slowly growing one as the future unfolds. Europe is projected to decline from 728 million (2004) to 668 million (2050) with the greatest loss in eastern and southern Europe. Though its numbers will be nearly the same over this period, western Europe will confront demographic problems because of the increase in the proportion of the elderly. The population shortfall over the next fifty years and the shortage of workers will require an infusion of immigrants to fill the economic needs of many, if not most, of the developed countries. Not only will this infusion of migrants aid the developed nations, but it will also relieve some of the pressures from a growing population in the developing countries.

The four largest countries of the European Union (EU) (France, Germany, Italy, and the UK) need to increase the numbers of immigrants to maintain their work force. Using data from 1995 as a bench mark, these countries, 66 percent of the total of the European Union's population, absorbed 237,000 immigrants. This number increased to about 400,000 by 2004 but will have to be increased 1 million annually if labor needs are to be met. To balance the age proportions and to meet social needs as well—that is, pay for social security/pensions— an estimated 8 million will be needed annually (World Watch, 2004). Germany alone would require 3.4 million new immigrants each year to cover the gap between worker availability and economic needs. If added up over the years to 2050, this means the addition of a number of foreigners equal to twice the German population in 2004. Similar projections can be made for the other three countries, whose stable or declining populations require a greater dependence on foreign workers.

These nations, and probably no nation, would accept such massive imports of foreign workers. A nation would rather increase the birth rate of its own nationals. In fact, efforts are being made to encourage women to have more children. Bonuses are offered, child care, and maternity leave are made available, but since the recognition of the "demographic time bomb," no improvement has been seen. Aside from increasing birth rates there is no simple answer, and even if fertility rises significantly, it will be years before the economic benefits would be realized. In the meantime, the immigrant populations reproduce at twice the rate, or more, of the host countries. This is reflected in the school population; 22 percent of French schoolchildren are Muslims whose parents migrated from North Africa. Similar experiences are reported for other EU countries, which makes for rather difficult and tense social relationships given language, religion, and cultural barriers, to say nothing of the superficial biological differences.

Parts of eastern and southern Europe are in even worse shape; populations in Russia, Poland, and Ukraine will decrease between 16 and 20 percent over the next forty years. Russia has been described as a "sick and shrinking nation" whose population will decline by 18 percent. Life expectancy has decreased for both male and female to the lowest of the developed nations, while Russian's infant mortality rate is the highest. Not only are eastern European populations declining, but also the young people are leaving in large numbers for jobs in the West. Those with advanced education and marketable skills are in demand and their emigration further adds to their nation's decline. The United States, on the other hand, has been able to maintain a near stable, but slow growing population. This has been due principally to the million-plus immigrants admitted annually, mostly from Latin America.

In sum, people are on the move. North Africans to Europe, West Africans to the United States, eastern Europeans to the West, Latin Americans and Chinese to North America are some examples of the major ones. The direction of migration has been largely from the less LDCs to the more MDCs for the obvious economic reasons. More frequently the pressure of population growth has been the motivating factor coupled with the labor needs of the host countries. Sometimes the migration is temporary, sometimes permanent, legal or illegal. But whatever the reasons, our perspectives of human distribution and national and ethnic boundaries have to be reconsidered.

When in their new homelands, the migrants may cling to their native cultures and languages for a time, but the attractions of the past diminish with each generation. The young acquire a new language and lose their old, the prospect of intermarriage becomes a reality, and popular culture gains a stronger influence leading to assimilation. These factors, of course, will vary widely between immigrant communities and the effects will be expressed differently in each. Economics and education will play a major role in this expression, as well as the nation in which the minority lives, be it one of the EU countries, United States, or Canada. Biology, the physical appearance of the migrant, will also affect assimilation and can feed an already festering xenophobia.

We read frequently of the anti-immigrationists' emotional outbursts that declare against the dangers to the nation of taking in foreign peoples. Strong anti-immigration movements have risen periodically against one or another group; the Irish, Jews, Chinese, or Italians, and so on, have been targets in the past. Now alarms are raised about the "swamping" of American culture by the influx of Latinos (mainly Mexicans), and Asians. We forget how times change and how our xenophobia passes as the "old Americans" became accustomed to the newcomers and they to us as we learned that immigration is what keeps the country growing. Europe's resistance to immigrants has far surpassed any prejudice exhibited by America now or in the past, however.

Europe's anti-immigration stance has been focused in several directions. German neo-nazi gangs regularly attack Turks, people who have lived and worked in Germany for at least a generation. As more eastern Europeans—Poles, Bosnians, Albanians, and so on—enter the country, they too have felt discrimination and have come under attack. In France, it is the North African Arabs who bear the brunt of French xenophobia. In Spain, there are periodic surges of violence against Moroccans brought in to work the farms for less than a minimum wage. Most have entered illegally and their cheap labor has set the scene for so much violence against foreigners—what one writer described as "Europe's powder keg." All together, some 20 to 24 million Muslims live in Europe and their lot has not been made any easier since the 9/11 terrorist attacks. Throughout Europe, they are feeling hostility and hatred, but families have lived there for many years and are now into the second and third generation. This is home and they know no other life. These people plus some 20 million sub-Saharan Africans (blacks) has caused a "Fortress Europe" mentality, a resistance to any further intruders threatening European culture.

Britain has had its own special problems. Having allowed entry of so many people from its former colonies in Asia, Africa, and the Caribbean, it now finds itself confronted with race problems. The early conflicts generated by the presence of

Pakistani and Indian refugees have now escalated into full-scale riots involving other groups as well. This time it is often the second generation, the sons of the earlier immigrants. The nation has become a multi-ethnic society of diverse cultures, languages, and, yes, of color. These attributes of the immigrant society developing since World War II have stimulated political backlash as well as the occasional riot. The National Front Party has gained in voter popularity and offers such statements as, ". . . multiracial societies are inherently unstable, and creating them is stupid." This is part of Europe's rejection of immigrants who look different, speak different, and seemingly compete for housing, welfare, and/or jobs. The arrival and permanent residence of so many over the past fifty years has influenced a rightward shift of political parties. There has been definite ethnic change in Europe whose need of the labor provided by these immigrants does not make their presence any easier to bear. The arguments pro and con and the complaints and stories about the threats to society, however complex the issues, are still couched in racist terms.

We read frequent statements that express this racism in terms of "browning of America," or the country will be "mostly nonwhite by mid century," or "immigration will have a swamping effect." Such sentiments are typical of many of the alarmist statements made by anti-immigration lobbies here and in Europe. "Keep out the alien hordes" is the watch word now as it was nearly a century ago in America. For Europe, large-scale immigration is more recent, but the sentiments are much the same: maintain the traditions and status quo. But, no matter, change is coming as fertility rates drop and working-age populations decline faster than total population over the next generation.

There are now 6.4 billion people occupying virtually every environment on the planet and we are on the move—from country to country and most often into cities as humans become more urbanized than ever. Population boundaries change and are then reformed, and the process is repeated. As people move about and new breeding populations are formed, gene flow patterns are altered. The old ethnic labels do not apply easily and population identity is now much more difficult.

The diverse group we call Hispanics differs in many ways from their cousins left behind; they have evolved in their traditions and as well as genetic composition. Turks and Moroccans in Europe also form new population units that set them apart from the native lands of their parents or grandparents. Likewise, Asians and Africans in America undergo changes. Traditions and languages change, but what is most important in the alteration of mating circles as each generation differs from the last and especially from the founding population. The younger generation will see to that change as mate choices widen and parental influences weaken. The rate of inter-ethnic marriages increases over time though the rates vary widely between groups. As such marriages increase, it becomes more and more difficult to rely on simple labels of ethnicity. So what's the problem then? A matter of color or a matter of the way we think about ourselves?

A Matter of "Color"

Many discussions of human variability and most attempts to classify human differences end up incorporating, at some point, a color code of sorts. Black and white, or nonwhite and sometimes brown are the colors of choice that often direct a discussion of comparisons of populations or ethnic groups. The U.S. Census Bureau elevated an ethnic group, Hispanic, to "race" status, but with the qualifier that a Hispanic person be listed as white or nonwhite. A reporter writing about research into the complexities of the human genome and its medical application, described the "black" geneticist whom he, the white reporter, was interviewing (Wheelwright, 2005). The interview ranged over a broad area of human genomics research and how this emerging field would change medical treatment by recognition of our genetic diversity. They talked of the lack of black participants in these studies, referred to black race and, though allowing that there is no direct connection between racial group and anything in the human genome, the article continued to discuss race. In fairness to reporter and scientist they both acknowledged the vagueness of traditional race terminology and its racist implications. Still black and white color coding was used in discussion of health disparities.

Genomics of Race

Because of the continued confusion over human diversity, a number of major genetics journals have recently published extensive reviews that examine the influence of race concepts on genomic research. For example, one paper argues that traditional race categories cannot accommodate individual uniqueness nor can these socially defined categories explain health disparities in terms of genetic factors (Royal and Dunston, 2004). Another noted the significant factor in comparative studies of the human genome is that the accuracy of interpretation of ancestry depends on the number of DNA markers used. The authors make the point that population history is a most important consideration because the accuracy of ancestral identification declines with degree of admixture and in geographically intermediate populations, for example, the Middle East (Tishkoff and Kidd, 2004).

These two papers cited offer a sample of the twelve published in a special supplement, "Genetics for the Human Race" (*Nature Genetics*, 2004). This supplement examines the validity of the race concept and explores the several false assumptions about correlations of gene diversity and classifications. Though each paper is written by authors of different research backgrounds and start from different perspectives, they all reach the same point—the doubt that color and/or race are useful concepts for biomedical studies.

RACES, TYPES, AND ETHNIC GROUPS: WHERE ARE WE?

So where are we in the study of human biological diversity in the first decade of this new century with all the achievements in biological and genetic studies? What do we know and what are the possible applications of these recently acquired data?

First, race is but a label we append to a population grouping with some physical characteristics that have some genetic components. These components of size, shape, and color together with special morphological features of head and face are all multifactorial traits, the result of several gene products interacting under environmental influences to produce what we can see or measure. This gives individuals and their relatives a similarity of appearance that has led to, or caused, a social group to be established. The group is then a social construct to set in order what we perceive as our mental image of mankind. The concept of race is not founded on a biological reality, but the concept is a means by which we divide humans into convenient units of discussion, comparison for political purposes, or for scientific study. Now, with a closer, more detailed understanding of human genetics we can no longer treat a few or many races as natural units.

There is no gene for race identification, that is, there is no marker that is unique to a particular race (race used in the classic sense). Gene frequencies cross populations, as well as continental boundaries, as we have shown. The differences in frequencies of certain DNA markers may be useful in identifying region of origin if all the person's grandparents came from the same locale. If a person's ancestral trail leads through diverse grandparental stock, then the probability of defining origin by DNA markers drops significantly; the greater the admixture, the lower the probability.

There is no black disease. Sickle cell was labeled as such until its distribution became better described and related to malaria. The discovery of this and several other abnormal hemoglobins in numerous populations outside of Africa has put an end to the black disease label. Likewise, other diseases described as specific to Africans have been discarded after a more thorough analysis. The higher diabetic rate, or hypertension, or heart disease relate more to lifestyle than to genetics. Likewise, there is no disease specific to the white race, or Asian race, but only a variation of environmental responses that may or may not have some genetic component. Determining reactions to drug treatment by race, the genomics' hope of the twenty-first century is but a dream as long as there is confusion over genes and racial types. The misguided advocacy of the study of the genetics of race is an example of this confusion.

Second, besides race being an artificial construct, color is useless as a criterion or label. Black, as a designation of a race or type, encompasses several geographical populations. The hundreds of millions in Africa, millions more in India and throughout Southeast Asia, together with the island populations of New Guinea and Melanesia are included in the black category. What about the few thousand remaining Australian Aborigines, and where do the African descendents in the New world fit into this color scheme? If the black type brings together a confusing array of populations, then white, generally used as a synonym for Causcasian, offers almost as much confusion. The people of the Middle East are lumped together with North Africans, Northern Indians, and Europeans. Where does it stop or, rather, where does it begin? We forget that skin color is just that, a matter of degree of pigmentation related to ancestral distribution relative to the incidence of solar radiation.

Nowhere is it more futile and harder to justify the use of color labels then in the health sciences. Both in the clinic and in drug research, simplistic black and white labels are used to classify the subjects or patients based on their self-identification. The basic assumption is that these labels are important indicators of some underlying significant genetic factor that influences the course of a disease or the treatment of choice. This foundation of assumptions about racial units and health goes back centuries, but now we see Hispanic and Asian, or brown added as racial categories to be considered. Would we want to record blood type by skin color, or decide on a tissue match for transplants by the donor's and recipient's color? Inheritance of the thousands of antigens in our system is a complex process determined by many gene complexes and not by skin pigmentation.

Third, what about racial origins? There is really no agreed-upon definition of race, though there have been many attempts as I described in the first chapter. But however defined, the race concept implies a real natural origin—a special creation of a few types. The many discoveries of fossil humans and near-humans whose remains are distributed over vast distances from China to Europe and from Africa to Southeast Asia have proven the special creation of racial types wrong.

Recall that race/subspecies was and still is determined on a basis of morphological differences defined centuries ago. Why or how these subspecies taxons apply today is a major question. Why should these seventeenth- and eighteenth-century perspectives of human division apply at all? The race concept is but a social construct as noted above and based on knowledge of the known world five hundred years ago. The concept of race began as folklore—people are different—and was then raised to a scientific level by Linneaus and his contemporaries, who bolstered their racial divisions with careful measurements of skeletal remains. But then this rudimentary science of race descended back into folklore as Europeans colonized the globe. The earlier studies of human variability were used to justify the subjugation of native peoples. This application of the race concept to arrange people into higher or lower orders was a reversion or a descent back into folklore.

The rediscovery of Mendelian genetics in 1900 initiated a new era in human studies and returned the race concept to a scientific level. Now we could talk of blood types, of dominant and recessive genes, and eventually of gene frequencies. Comparisons of populations on the basis of the frequencies of certain blood-group antigens enabled a more scientific approach to race, or so it was argued. But the use of these markers, though they helped sort out some population relationships, was still based on assumptions about human types. Sometimes the application of blood-group genes for population comparisons could lead to improbable conclusions as when the same combinations of blood-group frequencies were found in both a sample of Germans living in Hamburg, Germany, and a Bantu population in Central Africa. These two samples could not be representative of the same race type, of course. All this similarity showed was that the use of gene markers for determining a race type was as fallible as skull measurements.

We have moved several steps beyond these early days of defining people and their ancestry by skull shape or blood type. We are in a new generation of scientific achievement now and are not prone to the same typological thinking and mistakes as in the past, or are we? The human genome has been identified by sequencing the 3 billion bases in our DNA, and the 30,000 genes that function to code for the synthesis of the body's proteins. Great advances have been made in the description of these genes and their products. All this has raised the study of human diversity to a high, in fact, to a peak of scientific achievement in the study of human diversity. So why partition people into a few units that we call races and then try to explain them (the racial divisions)? We have the technology to deal with human diversity at the individual level as measured by genome, gene, or phenotype. Why be bound and limited by thinking at the seventeenth-century level when we can rise to new scientific heights for a much broader view of our species in its glorious diversity and place in the biological world.

References

ANONYMOUS. 2004. "Antioxidants and cancer prevention: Questions and answers. *National Cancer Inst.* On line www.Cancer.gov., updated:28 July 2004.

ANONYMOUS. 2004. *Report on the Global AIDS Epidemic.* Joint United Nations Program on HIV AIDS. July 2004.

ANONYMOUS. 1996. "Statement on Race." *Am. J. Phys. Anthropol.* 101(4):569–570.

ABBIE, A. A. 1967. "Book review: *The Living Races of Man.*" *Current Anthrop.*, 8:113–114.

ABBIE, A. A. 1975. *Studies in Physical Anthropology.* Vols. I and II. Canberra: Australian Institute of Aboriginal Studies, RRS5.

AIRD, I., H. H. BENTALL, and J. A. F. ROBERTS. 1953. "A relationship between cancer of the stomach and the ABO groups." *Br. Med. J.*, 1:799–801.

ALLEN, J., et al. 2004. "The structure of the human brain." *Am. Scientist*, 92:246–253.

ALLISON, A. C. 1954. "Protection afforded by sickle-cell trait against malarial infection." *Br. Med. J.*, 1:290–294.

American Association of Physical Anthropologists'. 1996. "Statement on Biological aspects of race." *Am. J. of Phys. Anthrop.* 101:569–570.

AMES, B. N., L. S. GOLD, and W. C. WILLETT. 1995. "The causes and prevention of cancer." *Proceedings of the National Academy of Sciences*, 92(12):5258–5265.

ANDERSON, W. F. 2000. "The best of times, the worst of times." *Science*, 288:627–620.

ANDREASEN, N. C., M. FLAUM, V. SWAYZE, et al. 1993. "Intelligence and brain structure in normal individuals." *Am. J. Psychiatry*, 150:130–134.

ANGEL, J. L. 1966. "Porotic hyperostosis anemias, malarias and marshes in prehistoric eastern Mediterranean." *Science*, 153:760–763.

ANTONARAKIS, S. E., C. D. BOEHM, G. R. SERJEANT, C. E. THESIAN, G. J. DOVER, and H. H. KAZAZIAN. 1984. "Origin of the B^S-globin gene in Blacks: The contribution of recurrent mutation or gene conversion or both." *Proceedings of the National Academy of Sciences*, 81: 853–856.

ASHFORD, L. S. 1995. New Perspectives on Population: Lessons from Cairo. *Population Bulletin*, 50(1). Washington, DC: Population Reference Bureau, Inc.

ASHFORD, L. S. 2001. "New population policies: Advancing women's health and rights." Population Bulletin, 56(1): 3–44.

AUGER, F., et al. 1980. "Anthropometry of circumpolar populations." In: *The Human Biology of Circumpolar Populations*, ed. F. A. Mila. Cambridge, MA: Cambridge Univ. Press. pp. 213–235.

AWADALLA, P., A. EYRE-WALKER AND J. M. SMITH 1999. "Linkage disequilibrium and recombination in Hominid mitochondrial DNA." *Science*, 286:2524–2525.

BAKER, J. R. 1974. *Science, Racism and Social Darwinism: A Review of Race*. London: Oxford University Press.

BAKER, P. T. 1997. The Raymond Pearl Memorial Lecture, 1996, "The eternal triangle-genes, phenotype, and environment." *Am. J. of Human Biology*, 9:93–101.

BALLEW, C. et al. 1989. "High altitude hematology: Paradigm or enigma? In *Human Population Biology*, ed. M. A. Little and J. D. Haas. New York: Oxford University Press.

BARNICOT, N. A. 1957. "Human pigmentation." *Man*, 57(144):114–120.

BARNICOT, N. A. 1964. "Taxonomy and variation in modern man." In *The Concept of Race*, ed. Ashley Montagu. New York: Free Press.

BARRETT, M. J., and T. BROWN. 1971. "Increase in average height of Australian Aborigines. *Medical J. of Australia*, 2(23):1169–1172.

BARZUN, J. 1965. *Race: A Study in Superstition*. New York: Harper & Row.

BASU, A. 1969. "The Pahira: A population genetical survey." *Am. J. Phys. Anthrop.*, 31:399–416.

BAYOUMI, R. A. L., N. SAHA, A. S. SALIH, A. E. BAKKAR, and G. FLATZ. 1981. "Distribution of the lactase phenotypes in the population of the Democratic Republic of The Sudan." *Hum. Genetics*, 57:279–28.

BEALL, C. M. et al. 1997. "Ventilation and hypoxic ventilatory reponse of Tibetan and Aymara high altitude natives." *Am. J. Phys. Anthrop.*, 104:427–447.

BEALL, C. M. et al. 1998. "Hemoglobin concentration of high-altitude Tibetans and Bolivian Aymara." *Am. J. Phys. Anthrop.*, 106:385–400.

BEALL, C. M. et al. 1999. "Percent of oxygen saturation of arterial hemoglobin among Bolivian Aymara at 3,900–40,000 m." *Am. J. Phys. Anthrop.*, 108:41–51.

BEALS, K. L., C. L. SMITH, and S. M. DODD. 1984. "Brain size, cranial morphology, climate, and time machines." *Current Anthrop.*, 25(3):301–330.

BELICH, J. 1986. *The New Zealand Wars*. Auckland: Auckland University Press.

BENNETT, J. W. 1976. "Dianne Ward versus Director of the Bureau of Vital Statistics, Lousiana State Health Department." *Perspectives in Biology and Medicine* (Summer): 582–592.

BEUTLER, E. 1983. "Glucose-6-phosphate dehydrogenase deficiency." In *The Metabolic Basis of Inherited Disease*, ed. J. B. Stanbury, J. B. Wyngaarden, D. S. Fredrickson, J. Goldstein, and M. Brown, 5th ed. New York: McGraw-Hill. pp. 1629–1653.

BEUTLER, E., R. J. DERN, and C. L. FLANAGAN. 1955. "Effect of sickle-cell trait on resistance to malaria." *Br. Med. J.*, 1:1189–1191.

BIERCE, A. 1978. *The Devil's Dictionary*. Owings Mills, MD: Stemmer House Publishers.

BINDON, J. R., and P. T. BAKER. 1985. "Modernization, migration and obesity among Samoan adults." *Annals of Human Biology*, 12:67–76.

BIRDSELL, J. B. 1981. *Human Evolution: An Introduction to the New Physical Anthropology*. Boston: Houghton Mifflin.

BIRDSELL, J. B. 1993. *Microevolutionary Patterns in Aboriginal Australia: A Gradient Analysis of Clines*. New York: Oxford University Press.

BLOCHE, G. M. 2004. "Race-based therapeutics." *New Eng. J. Medicine*, 315:2035–2037.

BLOCK, D., and E. MOORE, 1986. *Advantages and Disadvantage*. Hillsdale, NJ: Lawrence Erlbaum.

BLOCK, N. J., and G. DWORKIN, eds. 1976. *The IQ Controversy*. New York: Pantheon, Random House.

BOAS, F. 1911. *The Mind of Primitive Man*. New York: Macmillan.

BOAS, F. 1940a. "The relations between physical and social anthropology." In *Race, Language and Culture*. New York: Free Press.

BOAS, F. 1940b. "Age changes and secular changes in anthromopometric measurements." *Am. J. Phys. Anthrop.*, 26:63–68.

BODMER, J. G., L. J. KENNEDY, J. LINDSAY, and A. M. WASIK. 1987. "Applications of serology and the ethnic distribution of three locus HLA haplotypes." *Brit. Med. Bulletin*, 43(1):94–121.

BODMER, W. F., and L. L. CAVALLI-SFORZA. 1976. *Genetics, Evolution and Man.* San Francisco: W. H. Freeman.

BOGIN, B. 1999. "Patterns of human growth. In *Cambridge Studies in Biological and Evolutionary Anthropology,* 2nd ed. Cambridge: Cambridge University Press, pp. 39–94.

BOGIN, B. 2001. *The Growth of Humanity.* New York: Wiley-Liss.

BOSERUP, E. 1981. *Population and Technological Change: A Study of Long Term Trends.* Chicago: University of Chicago Press.

BOUCHARD, T. J., JR., D. T. LYKKEN, N. L. SEGAL, and K. J. WILCOX. 1986. "Development in twins reared apart: A test of the chronogenetic hypothesis." In *Human Growth: A Multidisciplinary Review,* ed. A. Demirjian and M. Brault. London and Philadelphia: Taylor & Francis.

BOUCHARD, T. J., JR., D. T. LYKKEN, M. MCGUE, N. L. SEGAL, and A. TELLEGEN. 1990. "Sources of human psychological differences: The Minnesota study of twins reared apart." *Science,* 250:223–228.

BOWCOCK, A. M., J. M. HEBERT, J. L. MOUNTAIN, J. R. KIDD, J. ROGERS, K. K. KIDD, and L. L. CAVALLI-SFORZA. 1991. "Study of an additional 58 DNA markers in five human populations from four continents." *Gene Geography,* 5:151–173.

BOWCOCK, A. M., C. BUCCI, J. M. HEBERT, J. R. KIDD, K. K. KIDD, J. S. FRIEDLAENDER, and L. L. CAVALLI-SFORZA. 1987. "Study of 47 DNA markers in five populations from four continents." *Gene Geography,* 1:47–64.

BOWER, B. 2003. "Harvesting intelligence." *Science News,* 163:293–294.

BOWMAN, J. E. 1977. "Genetic screening programs and public policy." *Phylon,* 38:117–142.

BOYD, W. C. 1950. *Genetics and the Races of Man.* Boston: Little, Brown.

BOYD, W. C. 1963a. "Genetics and the human race." *Science,* 140:1057–1065.

BOYD, W. C. 1963b. "Four achievements of the genetical method in physical anthropology." *Am. J. Phys. Anthrop.,* 65:243–252.

BRACE, C. L. 1962. "Cultural factors in the evolution of the human dentition." In *Culture and the Evolution of Man,* ed. M. F. Ashley Montagu. New York: Oxford University Press.

BRACE, C. L. 1995. *The Stages of Human Evolution.* 5th ed. Upper Saddle River, NJ:Prentice Hall.

BRACE, C. L. 2000. *Evolution in an Anthropological View.* Walnut Creek, CA: Altamura Press.

BRACE, C. L., et al. 1993. "Clines and Clusters versus 'Race,' A test in Ancient Egypt and the case of a death on the Nile." *Yearbook of Physical Anthrop.,* 36:1–31.

BRACE, C. L., et al. 2001. "Old World sources of the first New World human inhabitants: A comparative craniofacial view." *PNAS,* 98(17):10017–10022.

BRADBY, H. 2003. "Describing ethnicity in health research." *Ethnicity and Health,* 8(1):5–13.

BRANDA, R. F., and J. W. EATON. 1978. "Skin color and nutrient photolysis: An evolutionary hypothesis." *Science,* 201:625–626.

BRIMELOW, P. 1995. *Alien Nation: Common Sense About America's Immigration Disaster.* New York: Random House.

BROCKERHOFF, M. P. 2000. "An Urbanizing World." *Population Bulletin,* 55(3). Washington DC: Population Reference Bureau.

BROWN, K. 2000. "The business of the human genome." *Scientific Am.,* 283(1):50–55.

BROWN, T. 1978. "Tooth emergence in Australian Aboriginals." *Annals of Human Biology,* 5(1):41–54.

BROWN, T. and G. C. TOWNSEND. 1982. "Adolescent growth in height of Australian Aboriginals analysed by the Preece-Baines function: A longitudinal study." *Annals of Human Biology,* 9(6):495–505.

BRUES, A. M. 1977. *People and Races.* New York: Macmillan.

BUCHI, E. C. 1968. "Somatic groups composing the modern population of India." In *Proceedings of Eighth International Congress of Anthropological and Ethniological Sciences.* Uno Park, Tokyo, Japan. Science Council of Japan. pp 154–162.

BUETTNER-JANUSCH, J. 1966. *Origins of Man.* New York: John Wiley.

BUETTNER-JANUSCH, J. 1973. *Physical Anthropology: A Perspective.* New York: John Wiley.

BURKE, B. M. 1995. "Mexican immigrants shape California's fertility future." *Population Today* (September): 4–5.

BURKITT, D. F. 1971. "Epidemiology of cancer of the colon and rectum." *Cancer,* 28:3–13.

BURNHAM, S. 1985. *Black Intelligence in White Society.* Anthens, GA: Social Science Press.

CAIRNS, J. 1975. "The cancer problem." *Scientific American,* 233(5):64–78.

CALLEGARI-JACQUES, S. M., F. M. SALZANO, J. CONSTANS, and P. MAURIERES. 1993. "Gm haplotype distribution in Amerindians: Relationship with geography and language." *Am. J. Phys. Anthrop.*, 90:427–444.

CANN, R. L. 1987. "In search of Eve." *The Sciences*, 27:30–37.

CANN, R. L. 1988. "DNA and human origins." *Annual Review of Anthrop.*, 17:127–143.

CANN, R. L. and J. K. LUM 2004. "Dispersal ghosts in Oceania." *Am. J. of Hum. Biol.*, 16:440–451.

CARPENTER, K. J. 1986. *The History of Scurvy and Vitamin C.* Cambridge: Cambridge University Press.

CAVALLI-SFORZA, L. 1969. "Genetic drift in an Italian population." In *Readings from Scientific American— Biological Anthropology.* San Francisco: W. H. Freeman.

CAVALLI-SFORZA, L. L., ed. 1986. *African Pygmies.* New York: Academic Press.

CAVALLI-SFORZA, L. L., A. MORONI, and G. ZEI. 2004a. *Consanguinity, Inbreeding, and Genetic Drift in Italy.* Princeton: Princeton University Press.

CAVALLI-SFORZA, L. L. 2004b. "Diversity Project takes time but reaps reward." *Nature*, 428:467.

CAVALLI-SFORZA, L. L., J. R. KIDD, K. K. KIDD, C. BUCCI, A. M. BOWCOCK, B. S. HEWLETT, and J. S. FRIEDLAENDER. 1986. "DNA markers and genetic variation in the human species." *Cold Spring Harbor Symposia on Quantitative Biology*, 50:411–417.

CAVALLI-SFORZA, L. L., P. MENOZZI, and A. PIAZZA. 1994. *The History and Geography of Human Genes.* Princeton, NJ: Princeton University Press.

Center for Disease Control. 2004. Diabetes Awareness Month, November. Online: www. cdc. gov/omh/ highlights/2004/Nov04.htm.

CHAGNON, N. A. 1983. *Yanomamo: The Fierce People.* 3rd ed, New York: Holt, Rinehart & Winston.

CHAGNON, N. A., J. V. NEEL, L. WEITKAMP, H. GHRSHOWITZ, and M. AYRES. 1970. "The influence of cultural factors on the demography and pattern of gene flow from the Makiritare to the Yanomama Indians." *Am. J. Phys. Anthrop.*, 32:339–349.

CHAKRABORTY, R., and K. K. KIDD. 1991. "The utility of DNA typing in forensic work." *Science*, 254:1735–1739.

CHAKRAVARTI, A., and R. CHAKRABORTY. 1978. "Elevated frequency of Tay-Sachs disease among Ashkenazic Jews unlikely by genetic drift alone." *Am. J. Hum. Genetics*, 30:256–261.

CHAN, V., T. K. CHAN, F. F. CHEBAB, and D. TODD. 1987. "Distribution of beta-thalassemia mutations in South China and their association with haplotypes." *Am. J. Hum. Genetics*, 41:678–685.

CHASE, A. 1977. *The Legacy of Malthus: The Social Costs of the New Scientific Racism.* New York: Knopf.

COHEN, L. A. 1987. "Diet and cancer." *Scientific American*, 257:42–48.

COHEN, P. 2000. "Lights, Camera, Action." *New Scientist*, 20 (May), p. 18.

COMAS, J. 1960., *Manual of Physical Anthropology.* Springfield. IL: Charles C Thomas.

COMBS, G. F. J. R., and M. L. SCOTT. 1977. "Nutritional interrelationships of vitamin E and selenium," *Bio. Science*, 27 (7):467–473.

COON, C. S. 1962. *The Origin of Races.* New York: Knopf.

COON, C. S. 1965. *The Living Races of Man.* New York: Knopf.

COON, C. S., S. M. GARN, and J. B. BIRDSELL. 1950. *Races: A Study of the Problems of Race Formation in Man.* Springfield, IL: Charles C Thomas.

COOPER, D. N., and J. SCHMIDTKE. 1986. "Diagnosis of genetic disease using recombinant DNA." *Hum. Genetics*, 73:1–11.

COPEMAN, R. et al. 1975. "The health of the Aboriginal children of Cunnamulla, Western Queensland." *Medical J. of Australia*, Special Suppl. 13:5–6.

COUZIN, J. 2004. "Consensus emerges on Hap map Strategy." *Science*, 304:671–672.

CRAVENS, H. 1978. *The Triumph of Evolution: American Scientists and the Heredity-Environment Controversy, 1900, 1941.* Philadelphia: University of Pennsylvania Press.

CURTIN, P. D. 1969. *The Atlantic Slave Trade.* Milwaukee: University of Wisconsin Press.

DARLINGTON, C. D. 1969. *The Evolution of Man and Society.* New York: Simon & Schuster.

DARWIN, C. 1871. *The Descent of Man and Selection in Relation to Sex.* Reprint, 1965. New York: Random House, Modern Library.

DAS,. M. K. 1995. "Sickle cell gene in central India; Kinships and geography. *Am. J. Human Biol.*, 7:565–573.

DAUSSET, J. W. and J. COLOMBANI. 1972. *Histocompatibility Testing.* Copenhagen: Munksgaard.

DAVIES, K. 2001. *Cracking the Genome. Inside the Race to Unlock Human DNA.* New York: Free Press.

DEAN, G. 1963. *The Porphyrias: A Story of Inheritance and Environment.* Philadelphia: J. B. Lippincott.

DEEVEY, E. S., JR. 1960. "The human population." *Scientific American,* 203:28–36.

Demographic Yearbook. 1977. New York: United Nations.

Demographic Yearbook. 1979. New York: United Nations.

Demographic Yearbook. 1990. New York: United Nations.

Demographic Yearbook. 1995. New York: United Nations.

DE MONTELLAGNO, B. R. O. 1993. "Melanin, Afrocentricity, and pseudoscience." *Yearbook of Physical Anthropology,* 36:33–58.

DIGEST OF EDUCATION STATISTICS. 1999. Chapter 2, "Elementary and Secondary Education." Online: NCES.ed.gov/pubs.com.

DILL, D B., et al. 1964. *Handbook of Physiology.* Vol. 4. Washington, DC American Physiology Society.

DOBZHANSKY, T. 1944. "On species and races of living and fossil man." *Am. J. Phys. Anthrop.,* 2:251–265.

DOBZHANSKY, T. 1962. *Mankind Evolving: The Evolution of the Human Species.* New Haven and London: Yale University Press.

DOBZHANSKY, T. 1968. *Science and the Concept of Race.* New York: Columbia University Press.

DOBZHANSKY, T. 1976. "The myths of genetic predestination and of tabula rasa." *Perspectives in Biology and Medicine,* 19(2):156–170.

DOLPHIN, D., and R. POULSON. 1989. *Glutathione: Chemical, Biochemical and Medical Aspects: Part B.* New York: John Wiley.

DUBOS, R. 1968. *Man Adapting.* New Haven: Yale University Press.

DUSTER, T. 1990. *Backdoor to Eugenics.* New York: Routledge.

DUTTA, R., et al. 2002. "Patterns of genetic diversity at the nine forensically approved. STR loci in the Indian populations." *Human Biol.,* 74(1):33–49.

EATON, J. W., and J. A. GAVAN. 1965. "Sensitivity to P-T-C among primates." *Am. J. Phys. Anthrop.,* 23:381–388.

ECKHOLM, E. P. 1977. *The Picture of Health.* New York: W. W. Norton.

EDELSTEIN, S. J. 1986. *The Sickled Cell: From Myths to Molecules.* Cambridge, MA: Harvard University Press.

ELLISON, P. T. 1998. "Sexual Maturation." In *Human Growth and Development,* ed. S Ulijaszek, F. E. Jhonston, and M. A. Preece. Cambridge: Cambridge Up Press. pp 227–229.

ENSMINGER, J. 1990. *Personal Communication.* St. Louis MO: Washington University.

ERHARDT, C. L. 1973. "Worldwide distribution of sickle cell disease: A consideration of available data." In *Sickle Cell Disease: Diagnosis, Management, Education and Research,* ed. H. Abramsom, J. F. Bertles, and D. I. Withers. St. Louis MO: Mosby.

ERICKSON, D. 1992. "Genes to order." *Scientific American,* 266:112–114.

ETKIN, N. L., and J. W. EATON. 1983. Abstract: "Blood bankers, viruses and ABO blood groups." *Am. J. Phys. Anthrop.,* 60 (2):192.

EVELETH, P. B., and J. M. TANNER. 1976. *Worldwide Variation in Human Growth,* Cambridge: Cambridge University Press.

EVELETH, P. B., and J. M. TANNER. 1990. *Worldwide Variation in Human Growth,* 2nd ed. New York: Cambridge University Press.

EXCOFFIER, L., B. PELLEGRINI, A. SANCHEZ-MAZAS, C. SIMON, and A. LANGANEY. 1987. "Genetics and history of Sub-Saharan Africa," *Yearbook of Physical Anthropology,* 30:151–194. New York: Alan Liss.

FABER, M. 1989. "Ultraviolet radiation." In *Nonionizing Radiation Protection,* 2nd ed., M. J. Suess and D. A. Benwell-Morison. WHO Regional Publications European Series #25.

FALLOWS, J. 1989. *More Like Us.* Boston: Houghton Mifflin.

FELSENSTEIN, J. 1973. "Maximum-likelihoods estimation of evolutionary trees from continuous characters." *Am. J. Hum. Genetics,* 25:471–492.

FENTON, F. D. 1859. *Aboriginal Inhabitants of New Zealand.* Auckland: W. C. Wilson.

FERNANDEZ, C. A. 1992. "La Raza and the melting pot: A comparative look at multiethnicity." In *Racially Mixed People in America,* ed. M. P. P. Root. Newbury Park, CA: Sage. pp. 126–143.

FIELD, H. 1935. "Arabs of Central Iraq: Their history, ethnology and physical characters. *Field Museum, Anthropology Memoirs*. Vol. IV. Chicago: Field Museum of Natural History.

FINCHER, C. et al. 2004. "Racial disparities in coronary heart disease: A sociological view of medical literature in physican bias." *Ethnicity and Disease*, 14:360–361.

FLATZ, G., J. N. HOWELL, J. DOENCH, and S. D. FLATZ. 1982. "Distribution of physiological adult lactase phenotypes, lactose absorber and malabsorber, in Germany." *Hum. Genetics*, 62:152–157.

FLYNN, J. R. 1984. "The mean IQ of Americans: Massive gains 1932 to 1978." *Psychological Bulletin*, 95(1):29–51.

FOGEL, R. W., and S. L. ENGERMAN. 1984. *Time on the Cross: The Economics of American Negro Slavery*. Lanham, New York: University Press of America.

FOLK, G. E. 1974 *Textbook of Environmental Physiology*. Philadelphia: Lea Febriger

FOWDEN, L., et al., eds. 1981. *Trace Element Deficiency: Metabolic and Physiological Consequences*. U. K.: London Royal Society.

FRANCISCUS, R. G., and J. C. LONG. 1991. "Variation in human nasal height and breadth." *Am. J. Phys. Anthrop.*, 85:419–427.

FRASER, S., ed. 1995. *The Bell Curve Wars*. New York: HarperCollins.

FRAYER, D. W., M. H. WOLPOFF, A. G. THORNE, F. H. SMITH, and G. G. POPE. 1993. "Theories of modern human origins: The paleontological test." *Am. Anthrop.*, 95(1):14–50.

FREELAND, S. J., and L. D. HURST. 2004. "Evolution encoded." *Scientific Am.*, (April) Vol. 290:84–91.

FRIEDLAENDER, J. S., ed. 1987. *The Solomon Islands Project: A Long-Term Study of Health, Human Biology and Culture Change*. Oxford: Oxford University Press.

FRISANCHO, A. R. 1995. *Human Adaptation and Accommodation*. Ann Arbor: University of Michigan Press.

FRISANCHO, A. R., and P. T. BAKER. 1970. "Altitude and growth: A study of the patterns of physical growth of a high altitude Peruvian Quechua population." *Am. J. Phys. Anthrop.*, 32:209–221.

FRISCH, R. 1988. "Fatness and fertility." *Scientific American*, 258(3):88–95.

FRISCH, R. E. 1990 "Body fat, menarche, fatness and fertility." *Progress in Reproductive Biology and Medicine*, 14:1–26.

GADJUSEK, D. C. 1964. "Factors governing the genetics of primitive human populations." *Cold Spring Harbor Symposia in Quantitative Biology*, 29:121–135.

GALTON, F. 1869. *Hereditary Genius*. Republished 1962. London: Macmillan.

GAMBOA, R. et al. 2001. "Influence of the apolipoprotein in E polymorphism on plasma lipoproteins in a Mexican population." *Human Biol*, 73(6):835–843.

GANONG, W. F. 2003. *Review of Medical Physiology*, 21st ed. Norwalk, CT: Appleton & Lange.

GARN, S. M., ed. 1960. *Readings on Race*. Springfield, IL: Charles C Thomas.

GARN, S. M. 1961. *Human Races*. Springfield, IL: Charles C Thomas.

GARRETT, L. 1994. *The Coming Plague*. New York: Penguin Books.

GARRETT, L. 2000. *Betrayal of Trust*. New York: Hyperion.

GARROD, A. 1902. "Inborn errors of metabolism." *Lancet*, 2:1616–1619.

GARTE, S. 2002. "The racial genetics paradox in biomedical research and public health." *Public Health Reports*, 117:421–425.

"Genomic Medicine," 2003. Special Section, *Science*, Vol. (302) October 24, 587–608.

GERARD, G., D. VITRAC, J. LE PENDU, A. MULLER, and R. ORIOL. 1982. "H-deficient blood groups (Bombay) of Reunion island." *Am. J. Hum. Genetics*, 34:937–947.

GIBLETT, E. R. 1969. *Genetic Markers in Human Blood*. Philadelphia: F. A. Davis.

GILL, P., A. J. JEFFREYS, and D. J. WERRETT. 1985. "Forensic applications of DNA fingerprints." *Nature*, 318:577.

GLASS, B. 1955. "On the unlikelihood of significant admixture of genes from the North American Indians in the present composition of the Negroes of the United States." *Am. J. Hum. Genetics*, 7(4):368–385.

GLASS, B., M. S. SACKS, E. F. JAHN, and C. HESS. 1952. "Genetic drift in a religious isolate: An analysis of the causes of variations in blood group and other gene frequencies in a small population." *American Naturalist*, 86:145–159.

GLEIBERMAN, E. et al. 1995. "Skin color, measurements of socioeconomic status, and blood pressure among blacks. In Erie County." *Annal. of Human Biol.*, 22:69–78.

GLBORIA-BOTTINI, F., G. GERLINI, A. AMANTE, R. PASCONE, and E. BOTTINI. 1992. "Diabetic pregnancy: Evidence of selection on the Rh blood group system." *Human Biology*, 64:81–87.

GOODFIELD, J. 1977. *Playing God: Genetic Engineering and the Manipulation of Life.* New York: Random House.

GORING, C. 1919. *The English Convict: A Statistical Study.* Montclair, NJ: Patterson Smith.

GOULD, S. J. 1978. "Morton's ranking of races by cranial capacity." *Science,* 200:503–509.

GOULD, S. J. 1983. *The Mismeasure of Man.* New York; W. W. Norton.

GOULD, S. J. 1994. "Curveball." *The New Yorker,* Nov. 28, 1994.

GOULD. S. J. 1995. "Curveball." In *The Bell Curve Wars,* ed. S. Fraser. New York: HarperCollins. pp. 11–22.

GREENE, L. S. 1993. "G6PD deficiency as protection against falciparum malaria: An epidemiologic critique of population and experimental studies." *Yearbook of Phys. Anthrop.* 36: 153–178.

GRESKA, L., and C. M. BEALL 1989: "Development of chest size and lung function at high altitude." In *Human Population Biology: A Transdisciplinary Science,* ed. M. A. Little and J. D. Haas. New York: Oxford University Press.

HAGA, S., and J. C. VENTER. 2003. "FDA races in wrong direction." *Science* 301 (July 25): 466.

HAGGARD, H. W. 1929. *Devils, Drugs and Doctors.* New York: Harper.

HAKOMORI, S. I. 1986. "Glycosphingolipids." *Scientific American,* 254:44–53.

HALLER, J. S., JR. 1971. *Outcasts from Evolution: Scientific Attitudes of Racial Inferiority, 1859–1900.* Urbana: University of Illinois Press.

HALPRIN, M., and A, OHKAWARA. 1967. "Human pigmentation: The role of glutathione". In: *Advances in Biology of Skin,* Vol. 8, ed. B. W. Montagna and J. Her. New York: Pergamon Press. pp 241–251.

HAMMER, M. F., T. KARAFET, A. RASANAYAGAM, et al. 1998. "Out of Africa and back again: Nested cladistic analysis of human Y chromosome variation." *Mol. Biol. Evol.* 15(4): 427–441.

HANSEN, J. D., et al. 1993 "Hunter-gatherer to pastoral way of life: Effects of the transition on health, growth, and nutritional status." *Suid-Afrikaanse Tydskrif vir Wetenskap* 89:559–564.

HARRIS, H. 1980. *The Principles of Human Biochemical Genetics,* 3rd ed. Amsterdam: Elsevier/North Holland.

HARRIS, M. I. 1990. "Noninsulin-dependent diabetes mellitus in black and white Americans." *Diabetes/ Metabolism Reviews,* 6(2): 71–90.

HARRISON, G.1978. *Mosquitoes, Malaria and Man: A History of the Hostilities since 1880.* New York: E. P. Dutton.

HARRISON, G. A. 1975. "Pigmentation." In *Human Variation and Natural Selection,* ed. D. F. Roberts. *Symposia of the Society for the Study of Human Biology,* Vol. XII, pp. 179–194. London: Taylor and Francis.

HARRISON, G. A., J. M. TANNER, D. R. PILBEAM, and P. T. BAKER. 1988. *Human Biology: An Introduction to Human Evolution, Variation, Growth, and Adaptability,* 3rd ed. New York and Tokyo: Oxford University Press.

HARRISON, R., and W. MONTAGNA. 1973. *Man,* 2nd ed. Englewood Cliffs, NJ: Prentice Hall.

HAUSMAN, A J., and E. N. WILMSEN 1985. "Economic change and secular trends in the growth of San children." *Human Biology,* 57: 563–571.

HAUSPIE, R. C., and C. SUSANNE. 1998. "Genetics and child growth." In *The Cambridge Encyclopedia of Human Growth and Development,* S. J. Ulijaszek, F. E. Johnston, and M. A. Preece. New York: Cambridge University Press. pp 124–128.

HAWKES, NIGEL, 1979. "Tracing Burt's Descent to Scientific Fraud." *Science,* August 17.

HEARNSHAW, L. S. 1979. *Cyril Burt: Psychologist.* London: Hodder and Stoughton.

HERRNSTEIN, R. J., and C. MURRAY. 1994. *The Bell Curve: Intelligence and Class Structure in American Life.* New York: Free Press.

HETZEL, B. S. 1993. "The iodine deficiency disorders." In *Iodine Deficiency in Europe: A Continuing Concern,* ed. F. Delange, J. T. Gunn, and D. Glioner. New York: Plenum Press. pp. 25–31.

HEYWOOD, P. F. 1983. "Growth and nutrition in Paua New Guinea." *J. of Human Evolution,* 122:133–143.

HIERNAUX, J. 1964. "The concept of race and the taxonomy of mankind." In *The Concept of Race,* ed. Ashley Montagu. New York: Free Press.

HIERNAUX, J. 1966a. "Peoples of Africa from 22° N to the Equator." In *The Biology of Human Adaptability,* ed. Paul T. Baker. Oxford: Clarendon Press.

HIERNAUX, J. 1966b. "Human biological diversity in Central Africa." *Man,* 1(3):287–306.

HIERNAUX, J. 1977. "Long-term biological effects of human migration from the African savanna to the equatorial forest: A case study of human adaptation to a hot and wet climate." In *Population Structure and Human Variation,* ed. G. A. Harrison. New York: Cambridge University Press. pp. 187–217.

HILL, A. V. S. 1986. "The population genetics of alpha thalassemia and the malaria hypothesis." *Cold Spring Harbor Symposia on Quantitative Biology*, 51: 489–498.

HILL, A. V. S., and J. S. WAINSCOAT. 1986. "The evolution of the alpha and beta-globin gene clusters in human populations." *Hum. Genetics*, 74:16–23.

HILL, A. V. S., et al. 1992. "Molecular analysis of HLA-B53 and resistance to severe malaria." *Nature* 360:434–439.

Historical Statistics of the United States, Colonial Times to 1957. 1960. Washington, DC: U.S. Department of Commerce, Bureau of Census.

HOFF, C. J., and E. ABELSON. 1976. "Fertility." in Man in the Andes, ed. P. Baker and M. Little. London: Hutchinson and Rose.

HOLDEN, C, 2003. "Race and Medicine." *Science*, 302:595–596.

HOOTON, E. A. 1946. *Up From the Ape*. New York: Macmillan.

HOOTON, E. A., and C. W. DUPERTIUS. 1955. *The Physical Anthropology of Ireland*. Peabody Museum of Archaeology and Ethnology, Vol. XXX, Nos. 1–2. Cambridge, MA: Harvard University.

HOPKINS, D. R. 1983. *Princes and Peasants: Smallpox in History*. Chicago: University of Chicago Press.

HOUGHTON, P. 1996. *People of the Great Ocean: Aspects of Human Biology of the Early Pacific*. Cambridge: Cambridge University Press.

HOWELLS, W. 1973. *The Pacific Islanders*. New York: Scribner's.

HULSE, F. S. 1957. "Some factors influencing the relative proportions of human racial stocks." *Cold Spring Harbor Symposia in Quantitative Biology*, 22:33–45.

HULSE, F. S. 1971. *The Human Species*. New York: Random House.

"Human Genome Variation and Race." 2004. Special issue. *Nature Genetics*, 36:1–60. Online: October 26.

HUTT, M. S. R., and D. P. BURKITT. 1986. *The Geography of Non-Infectious Disease*. Oxford: Oxford University Press.

HUXLEY, J. S., and A. C. HADDON. 1935. *The Europeans: A Survey of Racial Problems*. London: Johnathan Cape.

IBRAIMOV, A. I. 1991, "Brief communications: Cerumen phenotypes in certain populations of Eurasia and Africa." *Am. J. Phys. Anthropol.*, 84:209–211.

JABLONSKI, N. G., and G. CHAPLIN. 2000 "The evolution of human skin coloration." *J. Human Evol.* 39:57–106.

JABLONSKI, N. G., and G., CHAPLIN. 2003. "Skin Deep." *Scientific Am.* 13(2):72–79.

JACKSON, F. L. C. 1993. "The influence of dietary cyanogenic glycosides from cassava on human metabolic biology and mircoevolution." In *Tropical Forests, People and Food*, eds. C. M. Hladik et al. Paris: UNESCO and the Parthenon Publishing Group. pp. 321–338.

JACOBY, R., and N. GLAUBERMAN, eds. .1995. *The Bell Curve Debate*. New York: Times Book.

JAMISON, E., and F. HOBBS. 1994. *World Population Profile: 1994*. Bureau of the Census. Report WP/94. Washington, DC: U.S. Govt. Printing Office.

JEFFREYS, A. J. 1989. "Molecular biology and human evolution." In *Human Origins*, ed. J. R. Durans. Oxford: Clarendon Press. pp. 27–51.

JEFFREYS, A. J., V. WILSON, and S. L. THEIN. 1985. "Hypervariable 'minisatellite' regions in human DNA." *Nature*, 314:67–73.

JENSEN, A. R. 1969. "How much can we boost IQ and scholastic achievement?" In *Environment, Heredity, and Intelligence*. Cambridge, MA: Harvard Educational Review.

JENSEN, A. R. 1971. "Can we and should we study race differences?" In *Race and Intelligence*, ed. C. L. Brace, G. R. Gamble, and J. T. Bond. Washington, DC: American Anthropological Association.

JONES, A., and W. F. BODMER. 1974. *Our Future Inheritance: Choice or Chance*. Oxford: Oxford University Press.

JONES, S. 1992. "Bottlenecks in Evolution." In *The Cambridge Encyclopedia of Human Evolution*, ed. S. Jones, R. Martin, and D. Pilbeam, pp. 281–283.

JONES, S. 2003. *Y: The Descent of Man*. Boston, and New York. Houghton Mufflin Co.

JONWA, A 1992. "Bottlenecks in Evolution." In *The Cambridge Encyclopedia of Human Evolution*, Cambridge: Cambridge University Press. pp. 281–283.

JORDE, L. B. et al. 2000. "The distribution of human genetic diversity: A comparison of mitochondrial, autosomal, and Y-chromosome data." *Am. J. Genetics*, 66:979–988.

KAMIN, L. J. 1974. *The Science and Politics of IQ.* Hillsdale, NJ: Erlbaum.

KAN, Y. W., and A. M. DOZY. 1978. "Polymorphism of DNA sequence adjacent to the human beta-globin structural gene: Relationship to sickle mutation." *Proceedings of the National Academy of Science*, 75:5631–5635.

KELSO, A. J., T. SIFFERET, and A. THIEMAN 1995. "Do type B women have more offspring?: An instance of asymmetrical selection at the ABO bloodgroup locus." *Am. J. Human Biol.* 7:41–44.

KENNEDY, W. A., V. VAN DE RIET, and J. C. WHITE. 1963. "A Normative Sample of Intelligence and Achievement of Negro Elementary School Children in Southeastern United States." Chicago: Monographs of the Society for Research on Child Development, 28, No. 6.

KEVLES, D. J. 1995. *In the Name of Eugenics.* Cambridge, MA: Harvard University Press.

KHOURY, M. J., T. H. BEATY, C. A. NEWILL, et al. 1986. "Genetic-environmental interactions in chronic airways obstruction." *International J. Epidemiology*, 15:64–71.

KIDD, J. R., F. L. BLACK, K. M. WEISS, I. BALAZS, and K. K. KIDD. 1991. "Studies of three Amerindian populations using nuclear DNA polymorphisms." *Human Bio.*, 63(6):775–794.

KIDD, J. R., K. K. KIDD, and K. M. WEISS. 1993. "Human genome diversity initiative." *Human Bio.*, 65(1):1–6.

KIDD, K., and J. R. KIDD. 1996. "A nuclear perspective on human evolution." In *Molecular Biology and Human Evolution*, ed. A. J. Boyce and C. G. M. Mascie-Taylor. Cambridge: Cambridge University Press.

KING, M. C., et al. 2003. "Breast and Ovarian cancer risks due to inherited mutation BRCA1 and BRCA2." *Science* 302:643–646.

KIRK, R. L., S. W. SERJEANTSON, H. KING, and P. ZIMMET. 1985. "The genetic epidemiology of diabetes mellitus." In *Diseases of Complex Etiology in Small Populations: Ethnic Differences and Research Approaches*, ed. R. Chakraborty and E. J. E. Szathmary. New York: Alan R. Liss.

KLINEBERG, O. 1935. *Race Differences.* New York: Harper.

KNOWLER, W. C., D. J. PETTITT, M. F. SAAD, and P. H. BENNETT. 1990. "Diabetes mellitus in the Pima Indians: Incidence, risk factors and pathogenesis." *Diabetes/Metabolism Reviews*, 6(1):1–27.

KOMLOS, J., ed. 1995. *The Biological Standard of Living on Three Continents. Further Explorations in Anthropolometric History.* Boulder, CO: Westview Press.

KONOTEY-AHULU, F. I. D. 1982. "Ethics of aminocentesis and selective abortion for sickle cell disease." *Lancet*, 1:38–39.

KOSTYU, D. D., C. L. OBER, D. V. DAWSON, M. GHANAYEM, S. ELIAS, and A. O. MARTIN. 1989. "Genetic analysis of HLA in the U.S. Schmiedenleut Hutterites." *Am. J. Hum. Genetics*, 45:261–269.

KROEBER, A. 1917. "The superorganic." *Am. Anthropol.*, 19:163–213.

KROGMAN, W. M. 1972. *Child Growth.* Ann Arbor: University of Michigan Press.

KUROKI, Y., T. IWAMOTO, J. LEE, et al. 1999. "Spermatogenic ability is different among males in different Y chromosome lineage." *J. Hum. Genet*, 44:2289–292.

LABIE, B., et al. 1986. "The genetic origin of the variability of the phenotypic expression of the Hb S gene." In *Genetic Variation and Its Maintenance*, ed. D. F. Roberts and G. F. Stefano. Cambridge, MA: Cambridge University Press. pp. 149–155.

LADURIE, E. L. 1988. *Times of Feast, Times of Famine: A History of Climate Since the Year 1000.* New York: Farrar, Straus & Giroux.

LAMPL, M. et al. 1978. "The effects of protein supplementation on the growth and skeletal maturation of New Guinea School children." *Annals of Human Biology* 5(3):219–227.

LANE, C. 1999 "The tainted sources of the Bell Curve." In *Race and IQ*, expanded ed., ed. A. Montagu. New York: Oxford University Press. pp. 408–424.

LEATHERMAN, T. L., J. W. CAREY, and R. B. THOMAS. 1995. "Socioeconomic change and patterns of growth in the Andes." *Am. J. Phys. Anthropol.*, 97: 307–321.

LE BLANC, J. 1975. *Man in the Cold.* Springfield, IL: Charles C Thomas.

LEFFELL, D. J., and D. E. BRASH. 1996. "Sunlight and skin cancer." *Scientific American.* 275(1):52–59.

LEONARD, W. R., T. L. LEATHERMAN, J. W. CAREY, and R. B. THOMAS. 1990. "Contributions of nutrition versus hypoxia to growth in rural Andean populations." *Am. J. of Human Biol.* 2:613–626.

LEVANDER, O. A. 1987. "A global view of human selenium nutrition." *Annual Review of Nutrition*, 7:227–250.

LEWONTIN, R. C. 1972. "The apportionment of human diversity." In *Evolutionary Biology*, Vol. 6, ed. T. Dobzhansky, M. K. Hecht, and W. C. Steers. New York: Appleton-Century-Crofts.

LEWONTIN, R. C. 1974. *Genetic Basis of Evolutionary Change.* New York: Columbia University Press.

LEWONTIN, R. C., S. ROSE, and L. KAMIN. 1984. *Not in Our Genes.* New York: Pantheon Books.

LITTLE, M. A. et al. 1983 "Cross-sectional growth of nomadic Turkana pastoralists." *Human Biology* 55(4):811–830.

LIVINGSTONE, F. B. 1958. "Anthropological implications of sickle cell gene distribution in West Africa." *Am. Anthropol.*, 60:533–562.

LIVINGSTONE, F. B. 1963. "Blood groups and ancestry: A test case from the New Guinea highlands." *Current Anthrop.*, 4:541–542.

LIVINGSTONE, F. B. 1964. "On the nonexistence of human races." In *The Concept of Race*, ed. Ashley Montagu. New York: Free Press.

LIVINGSTONE, F. B. 1967. "*Abnormal Hemoglobins in Human Populations.* Chicago: Aldine.

LIVINGSTONE, F. B. 1984. "The Duffy blood groups, vivax malaria, and malarial selection in human populations. A review." *Human Bio.*, 56:413–425.

LIVINGSTONE, F. B. 1985. *Frequencies of Hemoglobin Variants.* New York: Oxford University Press.

LIVINGSTONE, F. B. 1989. "Who gave whom hemoglobin S: The use of restriction site haplotype variation for the interpretation of the evolution of the beta^S-globin gene." *Am. J. Human Biology*, 2:289 302.

LOEHLIN, J. C., G. LINDZEY, and J. N. SPUHLER. 1975. *Race Differences in Intelligence.* San Francisco: W. H. Freeman.

LOGAN, W. H. G., and R. KRONFELD. 1933. "Development of the human jaws and surrounding structures from birth to the age of fifteen years." *J. Am. Dent. Assoc.*, 20:379.

LOOMIS, F. W. 1970. "Rickets." *Scientific American*, 223(6):77–91.

LOPEZ, A. D. 1990. "Causes of death: An assessment of global patterns of mortality around 1985." *World Health Statistics Quarterly*, 43(2):91–104.

LOURIE, J. A., and T. TAUFA. 1986. "The Ok Tedi health and nutrition project, Papua New Guinea: Physique, growth and nutritional status of the Wopkaimin of the Star Mountains." *Annals of Human Biology*, 13(6):517–536.

LOWREY, G. H. 1978. *Growth and Development of Children.* 7th ed. Chicago: Year Book Medical Publishers.

LUDMAN, M. D., G. A. GRABOWSKI, J. D. GOLDBERG, and R. J. DESNICK. 1986. "Heterozygote detection and prenatal diagnosis for Tay-Sachs and Type 1 Gaucher Diseases." In *Genetic Disease: Screening and Management*, ed. T. P. Carter and A. M. Willey. New York: Alan R. Liss. pp. 19–48.

LYNN, R. 1978. "Ethnic and racial differences in intelligence. International comparisons." In *Human Variation: The Biopsychology of Age, Race, and Sex*, ed. R. T. Osborne, C. E. Noble, and N. Weyl. New York: Academic Press.

MACEACHERN, S. 2000. "Genes, tribes, and African history." *Current Anthrop.*, 41(3): 357–384.

MACFARLANE, W. V. 1976. "Aboriginal paleophysiology." In *The Origin of Australians*, ed. R. L. Kirk and A. G. Thorne. pp 183–194., Canberra: Australian Institute of Aboriginal Studies.

MACKINTOSH, N. J. 1986. "The biology of intelligence." *Brit. Psychology*, 77:1–18.

McCOWN, T. D., and K. A. R. KENNEDY, eds. 1972. *Climbing Man's Family Tree: A Collection of Major Writings on Human Phylogeny 1699 to 1971.* Englewood Cliffs, NJ: Prentice Hall.

McCRACKEN, R. D. 1971. "Lactase deficiency: An example of dietary evolution." *Current Anthrop.*, 12(4–5): 479–500.

McFALLS, J. A. JR. 2003. "Population: A Lively Introduction." *Population Bulletin*, 58 (December):4.

McKUSICK, V. A. 1967. "The ethnic distribution of disease in the United States." *J. Chronic Diseases*, 20:115–118.

McKUSICK, V. A. 1978. *Mendelian Inheritance in Man.* 5th ed. Baltimore and London: John Hopkins University Press.

McKUSICK, V. A. 1994. *Mendelian Inheritance in Man: A Catalog of Human Genes and Genetic Disorders.* Baltimore and London: Johns Hopkins University Press.

McNEILL, W. H. 1976. *Plagues and Peoples.* New York: Anchor Press/Doubleday.

MANGE, A. P., and E. J. MANGE. 1990. *Genetics: Human Aspects.* 2nd ed. Sunderland, MA: Sinauer Assoc.

MARSHALL, E. 2003. "Preventing toxicity with a gene test." *Science*, 302:588–590.

MASCIE-TAYLOR, G. G., and M. A. LITTLE 2004. "History of migration studies in biological anthropology." *Am. J. Human Biol.*, 16:365–378.

MATSUNAGA, E., and Y. HIRAIZUMI. 1962. "Prezygotic selection in ABO blood groups." *Science*, 135:432–434.

MAYER, J. D. 1983. "The role of spatial analysis and geographic data in the detection of disease causation." *Social Science Medicine*, 17: 1213.

MAYESKE, G. W. 1971. *On the Explanation of Racial-Ethnic Group Differences in Achievement Test Scores.* Washington, DC: Office of Education, U. S. Department of Health, Education and Welfare.

MAYR, E. 1963. *Animal Species and Evolution.* Cambridge, MA: Belknap Press.

MAYR, E. 1982. *The Growth of Biological Thought: Diversity, Evolution, and Inheritance.* Cambridge, MA: Belknap Press.

MAYR, E. 1988. *Toward a New Philosophy of Biology.* Cambridge, MA: Belknap Press.

MAZESS. R. B. 1975. "Human Adaptation to high altitude." In *Physiological Anthropology*, ed. A. Damon. New York: Oxford University Press. pp 167–209.

MEINDL, R. S. 1987. "Hypothesis: A selective advantage for cystic fibrosis." *Am. J. Phys. Anthrop.*, 74:39–45.

MERCER, J. 1972. *Labeling the Mentally Retarded.* Berkeley: University of California Press.

MERIMEE, T. J., and D. L. RIMOIN. 1986. "Growth hormone and insulin-like growth factors in the western pygmy." In *African Pygmies*, ed. L. L. Cavalli-Sforza. New York: Academic Press, pp. 167–177.

MERRICK, T. W. 1986. "World population in transition." *Population Bulletin, Vol. 41*, Population Reference Bureau.

MINTON, H. L. 1988. *Lewis M Terman: Pioneer in Psychological Testing.* New York: New York University Press.

MOLNAR, S. 1971. "Human tooth wear, tooth function and cultural variability." *Am. J. Phys. Anthrop.*, 34:175–190.

MOLNAR, S. 1996. "Book Review: *The Bell Curve: Intelligence and Class Structure in American Life.* R. J. Herrnstein and C. Murray. New York: Free Press." *Current Anthrop.*, 37:S165–S168.

MOLNAR, S., and I. M. MOLNAR 2000. *Environmental Change and Human Survival.* Upper Saddle River, N.J.: Prentice-Hall.

MONTAGU, M. F. A. 1960. *An Introduction to Physical Anthropology.* 3rd ed. Springfield, IL: Charles C Thomas.

MONTAGU, M. F. A. 1964. "Discussion and criticism on the race concept." *Current Anthrop.*, 5:37.

MOORE, D. S. 2003. *The Dependent Gene. The Fallacy of "Nature vs. Nurture."* New York: Henry Holt and Co.

MOORE, L. G., et al. 1998 "Human adaptation to high altitude: Regional and life cycle perspectives." *Yearbook of Physical Antrhopology, Suppl. 27*, Vol. 41.

MORGANTI, G. 1959. "Distributions of blood groups in Italy." In *Medical Biology and Etruscan Origins*, ed. G. E. W. Wolstenholme and C. M. O'Connor. Ciba Foundation Symposium, London. Boston: Little, Brown.

MORTON, N. E. 1958. "Empirical risks in consanguineous marriages: Birth weight, gestation time, and measurements of infants." *Am. J. Hum. Genetics*, 10:344–349.

MORTON, N. E. 1961. "Morbidity of children from consanguineous marriages." *Progr. Med. Genetics*, 1:261–291.

MOURANT, A. E. 1954. *Distribution of the Human Blood Groups.* Oxford: Blackwell Scientific Publications.

MOURANT, A. W. 1983. *Blood Relations: Blood Groups and Anthropology.* New York: Oxford University Press.

MOURANT, A. E., A. C. KOPEC, and K. DOMANIEWSKA-SOBCZAK. 1978. *Blood Groups and Diseases: A Study of Associations of Diseases with Blood Groups and Other Polymorphisms.* New York: Oxford University Press.

MOURO, I., Y. COLIN, B CHERIF-ZAHAR, J. CARTRON, and C. LE VAN KIM. 1993. "Molecular genetic basis of the human Rhesus blood group system." *Nature Genetics* 5:62–65.

MYEROWITZ, R., and N. G. HOGIKYAN. 1987. "A deletion involving Alu sequences in the b hexosaminidase—a chain gene of French Canadians with Tay-Sachs disease." *J. Biological Chemistry*, 262:15396–15399.

National Academy of Sciences. 1980. *Recommended Dietary Allowances*, 9th ed. Food and Nutrition Board, National Research Council.

National Academy of Sciences. 1989. *Recommended Dietary Allowances*, 11th ed. Washington. D. C.

National Center For Health Statistics (NCHS). 1999. *National Vital Statistics Report*, 47(25). Washington, DC: U. S. Govt. Printing office.

National Center For Health Statistics. 2003. *National Vital Statistics Record*, No. 52. Washington, DC: U. S. Govt. Printing Office.

NEEL, J. V. 1962. "Diabetes mellitus; a 'thrifty' genotype rendered detrimental by progress?" *Am. J. Hum. Genetics*, 14:353–362.

NEEL, J. V. 1970. "Lessons from a 'primitive' people." *Science*, 170:815–822.

NEEL, J. V. 1982. "The thrifty genotype revisited." In *The Genetics of Diabetes Mellitus*, ed. J. Kobberling and R. Tattersall. London: Academic Press.

NEEL, J. V. 1994. *Physician to the Gene Pool*. New York: John Wiley.

NEWMAN, M. T. 1953. "The application of ecological rules to the racial anthropology of the aboriginal New World." *Amer. Anthropol*, 55:311–37

NICHOLS, E. K. 1988. *Human Gene Therapy*. Cambridge, MA: Harvard University Press.

NICHOLS, P. O., and V. E. ANDERSON. 1973. "Intellectual performance, race and socioeconomic status." *Social Biology*, 20 (4):367–374.

OGBU, J. U. 1978. *Minority Education and Caste: The American System in Cross-Cultural Perspective*. New York: Academic Press.

OHASHI, J. et al. 2000 "Analysis of HLA-DRBI polymorphism in the Gidra of Papua New Guinea." *Human Biology*, 72(2) 337–347.

OMI, M., and H. WINANT. 1986. *Racial Formation in the U. S. from the 1960s to the 1980s*. New York: Routledge and Kegan Paul.

OMOTO, K. 1987. "Population genetic studies in the Philippines." *Man and Culture in Oceania*, Special Issue: 33–40.

OPPENHEIMER, S. J., D. R. HIGGS, D. J. WEATHERALL, J. BARKER, and R. A. SPARK. 1984. "Alpha-thalassemia in Papua New Guinea." *Lancet*, I:424–426.

OREL, V. 1984 *Mendel*, Oxford. Oxford University Press.

OVED, Y. 1988. *Two Hundred Years of American Communes*. New Brunswick and Oxford· Transaction Books.

OWEN, M., and M. C. O'DONOVAN. 2003. "Schizophrenia and genetics." In *Behavioral Genetics in the Postgenomic Era*, ed. R. Plomin et al. Washington, DC: American Psychological Assoc. pp 463–480.

PAKKENBERG, H., and J. VOIGT. 1964. "Brain weight of the Danes." *Acta Anat.*, 56(4):297–307.

PARRA, E. J. et al. 2001. "Ancestral proportion and admixture dynamics in geographically defined African Americans living in South Carolina." *Am. J. of Phys. Anthropol.* 114:18–29.

PARRA, F. C. 2003. "Color and genomic ancestry in Brazilians." *Proc. Natl. Academy Science*, 100:177–182.

PARRA, E. J. J. C. TEIXEIRA RIBEIRO, J. L. B. CAEIRO, and A. RIVEIRO. 1995. "Genetic structure of the population of Cabo Verde (West Africa: Evidence of substantial European admixture)." *Am. J. of Phys. Anthropol.*, 97:381–389.

PASTORE, N. 1978. "The Army intelligence tests and Walter Lippman." *J. History of Behavioral Sciences*, 14:316–327.

PAULING, L., H. A. ITANO, S. J. SINGER, and I. C. WELLS. 1949. "Sickle cell anemia, a molecular disease." *Science*, 110:543–548.

PEACH, C., and J. C. MITCHELL. 1988. "Marriage distance and ethnicity." In *Human Mating Patterns*, ed. C. G. N. Mascie-Taylor and A. J. Boyce. Cambridge: Cambridge University Press. pp. 31–45.

PENNISI, E. 2000 "Finally, the book of life and instructions for navigating it." *Science* 288:2304–2307.

PETRAKIS, N. L., K. T. MOLOHON, and D. J. TEPPER. 1967. "Cerumen in American Indians: Genetic implications of sticky and dry types." *Science*, 158:1192–1193.

PIAZZA, A. et al. 1985. "Genetics and population structure of four Sardinian villages. *Ann. Human Genet.* 49:47–63.

PIETINEN, P., E. VARIAINEN, R. SEPPANEN, A. ARO, and P. PUSKA. 1996. "Changes in diet in Finland from 1972 to 1992. *Prev. Med.*, 25(3):243–250.

PIETRUSEWSKY, M. 1990. "Craniofacial variation in Australasian and Pacific populations." *Am. J. Phys. Anthrop.*, 82:319–340.

PLOMIN, R. 1989. "Environment and genes: Determinants of behavior." *Am. Psychologist*, 44(2):105–111.

PLOMIN, R. et al. 2003. "Behavioral genetics in the post genomic era." Washigton, DC: American Psychological Assoc.

POLEDNAK, A. P. 1989. *Racial and Ethnic Differences in Disease*. New York: Oxford University Press.

POLLARD, K. M., and W. P. O'HARE. 1999. "America's Racial and Ethnic Minorities." *Population Bulletin*, 54(3). Washington DC: Population Reference Bureau.

POLLITZER, W. S. 1958. "The negroes of Charleston (S.C.): A study of hemoglobin types, serology, and morphology." *Am. J. Phys. Anthrop.*, 16:241–263.

POLLITZER, W. S. 1972. "The physical anthropology and genetics of marginal people of the southeastern United States." *Am. Anthrop.*, 74(3):719–734.

POLLITZER, W. S. 1994. "Ethnicity and human biology." *Am. J. Human Bio.*, 6:3–11.

POLLITZER, W. S., R. M. MENEGAZ-BOCK, and J. C. HERION. 1966. "Factors in the microevolution of a triracial isolate." *Am. J Hum. Genetics*, 18(1):26–38.

POPULATION REFERENCE BUREAU. 1975. *World Population Data Sheet.* Washington, DC: Population Reference Bureau.

POPULATION REFERENCE BUREAU. 1980. *World Population Data Sheet.* Washington, DC: Population Reference Bureau.

POPULATION REFERENCE BUREAU. 1990. *World Population Data Sheet.* Washington, DC: Population Reference Bureau.

POPULATION REFERENCE BUREAU. 1996. *World Population Data Sheet.* Washington, DC: Population Reference Bureau.

POPULATION REFERENCE BUREAU. 2000. *World Population Data Sheet.* Washington, DC: Population Reference Bureau.

POPULATION REFERENCE BUREAU. 2004. *World Population Data Sheet.* Washington, DC: Population Reference Bureau.

POPULATION TODAY. 1990. Vol. 18(5). Washington DC: Population Reference Bureau.

POWARS, D. R. 1994. "Sickle cell disease in nonblack persons." *J. Am. Med. Assoc.*, 271(23):1885.

PRESTON, R. 1994. *The Hot Zone.* New York: Random House.

PRICHARD, J. C. 1826. *Researches into the Physical History of Mankind*, 2nd ed. 2 vols. London: John and Arthur Arch.

PRIOR, I. A. M. 1971. "The price of civilization." *Nutrition Today*, 6(4):2–11.

PRIOR, I. A. M. et al. 1986. "Cardiovascular epidemiological studies in New Zealand and the Pacific and the Tokelau Island migrant study." *Research Review.* Medical Research Council of New Zealand.

PROCTOR, R. N. 1988. *Racial Hygiene: Medicine Under the Nazi* Cambridge, MA: Harvard University Press.

PROTA, G. 1989 "Melanin and pigmentation." In *Glutathione: Chemical, Bochemical and Medical Aspects. Part B*, ed. D. Dolphin and R. Poulson. New York: John Wiley & Sons. pp. 441–464.

QUEVEDO, W. C., JR., T. B. FITZPATRICK, and K. JIMBOW. 1985. "Human skin color: Origin, variation and significance." *J. Hum. Evol.*, 14:43–56.

RACE, R. R., and R. SANGER. 1975. *Blood Groups in Man.* 6th ed. Philadelphia: F. A. Davis.

RAMEY, C. T., D. MACPHEE, and K. O. YEATES. 1982. "Preventing developmental retardation: A general systems model." In *How and How Much Can Intelligence Be Increased*, eds. D. K. Detterman and R. J. Sternberg. Norwood, NJ: Ablex.

REARDON, J. 2005. *Race to the Finish: Identity and Governance in an Age of Genomics.* Princeton NJ: Princeton University Press.

REED, T. E. 1969. "Caucasian genes in American Negroes." *Science*, 165:762–768.

RELETHFORD, J. H. 2000. "Human skin color diversity is highest in sub-Saharan African populations. *Human Biol.* 12 (5) 773–780.

RELETHFORD, J. H. 2003. *Reflections of Our Past.* Boulder CO: Westview Press.

RICKLAN, D. E., and P. V. TOBIAS, 1986. "Unusually Low Sexual Dimorphism of Endocranial Capacity in a Zulu Cranial Series." *Am. J. Phys. Anthrop.*, 71(3): 285–294.

RICHE, M. 2000. "America's Diversity and Growth: Signpost of the 21st Century." *Population Bulletin* 55(2). Washington, DC: Population Reference Bureau.

RIDLEY, M. 2003. *Nature VIA Nurture.* New York: Harper Collins.

RIPLEY, W. Z. 1899. *The Races of Europe.* New York: Appleton.

ROBERTS, D. F. 1978. *Climate and Human Variability.* 2nd ed. Menlo Park, CA: Cummings.

ROBERTS, L. 2000. "SNP mappers confront reality and find it daunting." *Science*, 287: 1898–1899.

ROBERTSON, G. G. 1966. "Developmental anatomy." In *Morris Human Anatomy*, 12th ed., ed. B. J. Anson. New York: McGraw-Hill.

ROBINS, A. H. 1991. *Biological Perspectives on Human Pigmentation*. New York: Cambridge University Press.

ROCKETT, I. R. H. 1999. "Population and Health: An Introduction to Epidemiology." *Population Bulletin*, 2nd ed., Vol. 54, no. 4., Washington, DC: Population Reference Bureau.

RODE, A., and R. J. SHEPHARD. 1984. "Growth, development and acculturation—a ten year comparison of Canadian Inuit children." *Human Biology*, 56(2): 217–230.

ROGERS, A. R. et. al. 2004. "Genetic Variation at the MCiR locus and the time since the loss of human body hair." *Current Anthropol.* 45(1):105–108.

ROITT, I. M. 1988. *Essential Immunology*, 6th ed. Oxford: Blackwell Scientific Publications.

ROSNER, F. 1977. *Medicine in the Bible and Talmud*. New York: Yeshiva University Press.

ROYAL, C. D. M., and G. M., DUNSTON. 2004. "Changing the paradigm from 'race' to human genome variation." *Nature Genetics*, 36:55–57.

RUSHTON, J. P. 1992. "Cranial capacity related to sex, rank, and race in a stratified random sample of 6, 325 U.S. military personnel." *Intelligence*, 16:401–413.

RUSHTON, J. P. 1995. *Race, Evolution and Behavior: A Life-history Perspective*. New Brunswick, NE: Transaction Publishers.

RUSHTON, J. P., and C. D. ANKNEY. 1996. "Brain size and cognitive ability: Correlations with age, sex, social class, and race." *Psychonomic Bulletin and Review*, 3(1): 21–36.

SAHI, T. 1978a. "Intestinal lactase polymorphisms and dairy foods." *Hum. Genetics*, Suppl. 1: 115–123.

SAHI, T. 1978b. "Intestinal lactase polymorphisms and dairy foods." International Titisee Conference, October 1977. *Hum. Genetics*, 50: 107–143.

SANTOS, S. E. B., J. D. RODRIGUES, A. K. C. RIBEIRO-DOS SANTOS, and M. A. ZAGO. 1999. "Differential contribution of indigenous men and women to the formation of an urban population in the Amazon region as revealed by mtDNA and Y-DNA." *Am. J. Phys Anthropol.*, 109: 175–180.

SATEL, S. 2002. "I am a Racially Profiling Doctor." *New York Times*, 5 May, pp. 56–58.

SCARR., S. 1981. "Toward a more biological psychology." In *Science and the Question of Human Equality*, ed. M. S. Collins, I. W. D. Wainer, and T. A. Bremner. Boulder, CO: Westview.

SCARR, S., and R. A. WEINBERG. 1978. "Attitudes, interests and IQ". *Human Nature*, 1(4): 29–36.

SCARR, S., and R. A. WEINBERG. 1983. "The Minnesota adoption studies: Genetic differences and malleability." *Child Development*, 54: 260–267.

SCARR-SALAPATEK, S. 1971. "Race, social class and IQ." *Science*, 174: 1285–1295.

SCHAEFER, O. 1970. "Pre- and post-natal growth acceleration and increased sugar cosumption Canadian Eskimos." *Canadian Medical Assoc. J.*, 103: 1059–1068.

SCHAEFER, O. 1981. "Eskimos (Inuit)." In *Western Diseases: Their Emergence and Prevention*. Cambridge MA: Harvard University Press. pp. 113–128.

SCHIFF, M., and R. LEWONTIN. 1986. *Education and Class: The Irrelevance of IQ Genetic Studies*. Oxford: Clarendon Press.

SCHOUR, I., and M. MASSLER. 1944. "Development and growth of teeth." In *Oral Histology and Embryology*, ed. B. Orban. St. Louis MO: C. V. Mosby.

SCHROEDER, W. A., and E. S. MUNGER. 1990. "Sickle cell anemia, genetic variations, and the slave trade to the United States." *Journal of African History*, 31: 163–180.

SCHULL, W. J., and J. V. NEEL. 1965. *The Effects of Inbreeding on Japanese Children*. New York: Harper & Row.

SCHURR, T. G. 2000. "Mitochondrial DNA and the peopling of the New World." *American Scientist*, 88: 246–263.

SCHURR, T. G., and S. T. SHERRY. 2004. "Mitochondrial DNA and Y chromosome diversity and the peopling of the Americas. Evolutionary and demographic evidence." *Am. J. Human Biol.*, 16: 420–439.

SCHWARTZ, R. S. 2001. "Racial profiling. in medical research." *New England J. Medicine*, 344: 1392–1393.

SCHWIDETZKY, I., and F. W. RÖSING. 1982. "European population of the high and late medieval period (1000–1500)—comparative statistical studies on historical physical anthropology." *Human-Biol. Budapest* 10: 39–47.

SCIENCE. 2003. *Genomic Medicine.* Vol. 302, October 24.

SERJEANTSON, S. W. 1984. "Migration and admixture in the Pacific." *J. Pacific History,* 19(3): 160–171.

SERJEANTSON, S. W., R. L. KIRK, and P. B. BOOTH. 1993. "Linguistics and genetic differentiation in New Guinea." *J. Human Evol.,* 12: 77–92.

SHAPIRO, H. L. 1942. "The anthropometry of Puka Puka." *Anthrop. Papers Mus. Nat. His.,* 38: 141–169.

SHEPHARD, R., and A. RODE. 1996. *The Health Consequences of Modernisation. Evidence from Circumpolar Peoples.* Cambridge: Cambridge University Press.

SHOCKLEY, W. 1972. "Dysgenics, geneticity, raceology: A challenge to the intellectual responsibility of educators." *Phi Delta Kappan,* 53(5): 297–307.

SINISCALCO, M., L. L. BERNINI, G. FILIPPI, B. LATTE, P. MEERA KHAN, S. PIOMELLI, and M. RATTAZZI. 1966. "Population genetics of haemoglobin variants, thalassemia and glucose-6-phosphate dehydrogenase deficiency with particular reference to the malaria hypothesis." *Bulletin World Health Org.,* 34: 379–393.

SKALETSKY, H. T. KURODA-KAWAGUCHI, P. MINX et al. 2003. "The male specific region of the human Y chromosome is a mosaic of discrete sequence classes." *Nature,* 423: 825–837.

SLOTKIN, J. S. 1965. *Readings in Early Anthropology.* New York: Viking Fund Publications in Anthropology, No. 40.

SMAGILK, P. 2000. "Genetic diversity project fights for its life." *Nature,* 404: 212.

SOUTHERN, E. M. 1975. "Detection of specific sequences among DNA fragments separated by gel electrophoresis." *J. Mol. Biol.,* 98: 503–517.

SPICKARD, P. R. 1992. "The illogic of American racial categories." In: *Racially Mixed People in America,* ed. M. P. Root. Newbury Park, CA: Sage Publications.

SPRITZ, R. A., and V. J. HEARING. 1994. "Genetic disorders of Pigmentation." In *Advances in Human Genetics.* ed. H. HARRIS, K. KIRSCHHORN. New York: Plenum Press. 22: 1–19.

SPUHLER, J. N. 1988. "Evolution of mitochondrial DNA in monkeys, apes, and humans." *Yearbook of Physical Anthropol.,* 31:15–48.

SPUHLER, J. N., and G. LINDZEY. 1967. "Racial differences in behavior." In *Behavior Genetic Analysis,* ed. Jerry Hirsch. New York: McGraw-Hill.

STARKE, L., ed. 1996. *Vital Signs 1996.* New York: W. W. Norton.

Statistical Abstract of the United States. 1930. Washington, DC: U.S. Government Printing Office.

Statistical Abstract of the United States. 1995. 115th ed. Washington, DC: U.S. Government Printing Office.

Statistical Abstract of the United States. 1997. 117th ed. Washington, DC. U.S. Government Printing Office.

STEEGMAN, A. T. 1975. "Human adaptation to cold." In *Physiological Anthropology,* ed. A. Damon. New York: Oxford University Press. pp. 130–162.

STEINBOCK. R. 2004. "The AIDS epidemic in 2004." *N Eng. J. Medicine,* 351(2):115.

STEPAN, N. 1982. *The Idea of Race in Science: Great Britain 1800–1960.* Hamden, CO: Archon Books.

STERN, C. 1973. *Principles of Human Genetics,* 3rd ed. San Francisco: W. H. Freeman.

STIGLER, S. M. 1986. *The History of Statistics: The Measurement of Uncertainty before 1900.* Cambridge, MA: Belknap Press.

STOCKING, G. W., JR., ed. 1973. *Researches into the Physical History of Man.* Chicago: University of Chicago Press.

STOKSTAD, E. 2003. "The vitamin D deficit." *Science,* 302:1886.

STRINGER, C. B. 1993. "New views on modern human origins." In *The Origin and Evolution of Humans and Humanness,* ed. D. T. Rasmussen. Boston: Jones and Bartlett. pp. 75–94.

STRINGER, C. B., and R. MCKIE. 1996. *African exodus: The Origins of Modern Humanity.* London: Jonathan Cape.

SWINDLER, D. R. 1962. *The Racial Study of the West Nakanai.* University Museum, University of Pennsylvania. Museum Monographs.

SZATHMARY, E. 1985. "Peopling of North America: Clues from genetic studies." In *Out of Asia: Peopling the Americas and the Pacific,"* ed. R. Kirk and E. Szathmary. Canberra: *The Journal of Pacific History,* Inc., Australian National University.

SZATHMARY, E. J. E. 1993. "Genetics of Aboriginal North Americans." *Evolutionary Anthroyp.,* 1(6):202–220.

TANNER, J. M. 1962. *Growth at Adolescence.* Oxford: Blackwell Scientific Publications.

TANNER, J. M. 1973. "Growing up." In *Readings from Scientific American, Biological Anthropology.* San Francisco: W. H. Freeman.

TANNER, J. M. 1981. *A History of the Study of Human Growth.* Cambridge: Cambridge University Press.

TANNER, J. M. 1986. "Growth as a mirror of the condition of society: Secular trends and class distinctions." In *Human Growth. A Multidisciplinary Review,* ed. A. Demirjian and M. Brault Dubue. London and Philadelphia: Taylor & Francisa. pp 3–34.

TARTAGLIA, M. R. et al 1995. "Genetic hereogeneity among the Hindus and their relationships with other 'Caucasoid' populations" New data on Punjab-Haryana and Rajasthan Indian states." *Am. J. Phys. Anthropl.,* 98:257–273.

TEMPLETON, A. R. 1985. "The phylogeny of the hominoid primates: A statistical analysis of the DNA hybridization data." *Mol. Biol. Evol.,* 2:420–433.

TEMPLETON, A. R., 2002. "Out of Africa and back Again" *Nature,* 416:45–51.

THOMAS, M. G. et al 2000. "Y chromosomes traveling south: The Cohen Modal Haplotype and the origins of the Lemba the "Black Jews of Southern Africa" *Am. J. Genet.* 66:674–686.

THORNE, A. G., and M. H. WOLPOFF. 1992. "The multiregional evolution of humans." *Scientific American,* 266(4):76–83.

THURSTONE, L. L. 1940. "Current issues in factor analysis." *Psychological Bulletin,* 37:189–236.

TISHKOFF, S. A., and K. K. KIDD. 2004. "Implications of biogeography of human populations for 'race' and medicine." *Nature Genetics,* 36:521–527.

TISHKOFF, S. A., E. DIETZSCH, W. SPEED, A. J. PAKTIS, J. R. KIDD, K. CHEUNG, B. BONNE-TAMIR, A. S. SANTACHIARA-BENERECETTI, P. MORAL, M. KRINGS, S. PAABO, M. WATSON, N. RISCH, T. JENKINS, and K. K. KIDD. 1996. "Global patterns of linkage disequilibrium at the CD4 locus and modern human origins." *Science,* 271:1380–1387.

TOBIAS, P. V. 1970. "Brain size, grey matter and race—fact or fiction." *Am. J. Phys. Anthrop.,* 32:3–26.

TOBIAS, P. V. 1971. *The Brain in Hominid Evolution.* New York and London: Columbia University Press.

TOBIAS, P. V. 1975. Anthropometry among disadvantaged peoples. Studies in Southern Afrcia." In *Biosocial Interrelations in Population Adaptation,* ed. E. S. WATTS, F. E. JOHNSTON, G. W. LASKER. The Hague and Paris: Mouton. Publishers. pp. 287–305.

TOBIAS. P. F., ed. 1978. *The Bushman, San Hunters and Herders of Southern Africa.* Cape Town and Petoria: Human and Rosseau.

TRICHOPOULOS, D., F. P. LI, and D. J. HUNTER. 1996. "What causes cancer?" *Scientific American,* 275(3):80–87.

TRANTER, N. L. 1985. *Population and Society 1750–1940.* London and New York: Longman.

TRAVIS, J. 2004. "Code Breakers." *Science News,* 65:106–107.

TURNER, C. G., II. 1985. "The dental search for Native American origins." In *Out of Asia: Peopling the Americas and the Pacific,* ed. R. KIRK and E. SZATHMARY. Canberra: The Journal of Pacific History, Inc., Australian National University.

TURNER, C. G., II. 1990. "Major features of Sundadonty and Sinodonty, including suggestions about East Asian microevolution, population history, and late Pleistocene relationships with Australian Aboriginals." *Am. J. Phys. Anthrop.,* 82:295–317.

ULIJASZEK, S. 1998. "Growth in infancy and pre-adolescence. In *The Cambridge Human Growth and Development,* JOHNSTON & PREECE. ed. New York: Cambridge University Press. pp. 373–374.

ULIJASZEK, S. et al. 1987. "Mining, modernisation, and dietary change among the Wopkaimin of Papua New Guinea." *Ecology of Food and Nutrition,* 220:143–156.

U. S. Department of Health and Human Services. 1985. *Diabetes in America.* NIH Publications No. 85-1468.

U. S. Department of Health and Human Services. 1989. *Monthly Vital Statistics Report,* Vol. 38, No. 5. Washington, DC.

UNDERHILL, P. A., L. JIN, A. A. LIN, et al. 1997. "Detection of numerous Y chromosome biallelic polymorphisms by denaturing high-performance liquid chromatography" (letter) (see Comments). *Genome Res.,* 7(10):996–1005.

VIETH, R. 1999. "Vitamin D supplementation, 25-hydroxy vitamin D concentrations, and safety." *Am. J. Clinical Nutrition,* 69:842–856.

VISARIA, L., and P. VISARIA. 1995. "India's population in transition." *Population Bulletin,* Vol. 50. Washington, DC: Population Reference Bureau.

VOGEL, F. 1968. "Anthropological implications of the relationship between ABO blood groups and infections." *Proceedings of the Eighth International Congress of Anthropological and Ethnological Sciences,* 1:365–370.

VOGEL, F. 1975. "ABO blood groups, the HL-A system and diseases." In *The Role of Natural Selection in Human Evolution*, ed. F. M. SALZANO. New York: American Elsevier.

VOGEL, F., and A. G. MOTULSKY. 1986. *Human Genetics: Problems and Approaches*, 2nd ed. Berlin, Heidelberg, New York, Tokyo: Springer-Verlag.

VON BONIN, G. 1963. *The Evolution of the Human Brain*. Chicago: University of Chicago Press.

WALSH, R. J. 1963. "Variations of melanin pigmentation of the skin in some Asian and Pacific peoples." *J. Royal Anthropological Inst.*, 93, pt. 1:126–133.

WAMBAUGH, J. 1989. *The Blooding*. New York: Perigord Press.

WASHBURN, S. L. 1964. "The study of race." In *The Concept of Race*, ed. A. Montagu. New York: Free Press of Glencoe.

WATSON, J. D. 1980. *The Double Helix: A Personal Account of the Discovery of the Structure of DNA*. New York: Norton.

WATSON, J. D. 1987. *Molecular Biology of the Gene*. 4th ed. Menlo Park CA: W. A. Benjamin Cummings.

WATTENBERG, B. J. 1985. *The Birth Dearth*. New York: Pharos Books.

WATTENBERG, B. J. 2004. *Fewer: How the New Demorgraphy of Depopulation Will Shape Our Future*. Chicago: Ivan R. Dee.

WEIDENREICH, FRANZ. 1947. "Facts and speculations concerning the origin of Homo sapiens." *Am. Anthrop.*, 49(2):135–151.

WEINBERG, R. A. 1989. "Intelligence and IQ. Landmark issues and great debates." *Am. Psychologist*, 44(2):98–104.

WEISS, K. M. 1993. *Genetic Variation and Human Disease: Principles and Evolutionary Approaches*. Cambridge: Cambridge University Press.

WEITZ, C. A. et al. 2000 "Growth of Qinghai Tibetans living at three different high altitudes." *Am. J. of Phys. Anthropol.*, 111(1):69–88.

WHEELWRIGHT, J. 2005. "Human study thyself." *Discover*. pp. 39–45.

WILLIAMS, J. 2003. "Dementia and genetics." In *Behavioral Genetics in the Postgenomic Era*, ed. R. PLOMIN, J. DEFRIES, I. W. CRAIG, and A. P. McGUFFIN. Washington DC: American Psychological Assoc. pp. 503–527.

WILLIAMS, R. C. 1985. "HLA II: The emergence of the molecular model for the human major histocompatibility complex." *Yearbook of Physical Anthrop.*, 28:79–95.

WILLIAMS, R. J. 1956. *Biochemical Individuality*. New York: John Wiley.

WILLIAMS, R. L. 1974. "The silent mugging of the black community." *Psychology Today*, 7:32–41.

WILSON, A. C., and R. L. CANN. 1992. "The recent African genesis of humans." *Scientific American*, 266(4):68–73.

WILSON, T. W. 1986. "History of salt supplies in West Africa and blood pressures today." *Lancet*, 1:784–786.

WITKIN, H. A., et al. 1976. "Criminality in XYY and XXY men." *Science*, 193:547–555.

WITKOP, C. J., JR., W. C. QUEVEDO, JR., T. B. FITZPATRICK, and R. A. KING. 1989. "Albinism." In *The Metabolic Basis of Inherited Disease*, 6th ed. Vol. II, ed. C. R. SCRIVER, A. L. BEAUDET, W. S. SLY, and D. VALLE. New York: McGraw-Hill. pp. 2905–2947.

WOLPOFF, M. H. 1968. "Climatic influences on the skeletal nasal aperture." *Am. J. Phys. Anthrop.*, 3:405–424.

WOLPOFF, M. H. 1996. *Human Evolution*. New York: McGraw-Hill.

WOLPOFF, M. H. 1999. *Paleoanthropology*, 2nd ed. Boston: McGraw-Hill.

WOLPOFF, M. H. 2000. "Multiregional, not multiple origins." *Am. J. Phys. Anthropol.*, 112:129–136.

WOOD, A. 2001. "Racial differences in the response to Drugs—Pointers to genetic differences." *New Eng. J. of Medicine* 344(18):1393–1396.

WOOD, C. S. 1974. "Preferential feeding of anopheles gambiae mosquitoes on human subjects of blood group O: A relationship between the ABO polymorphism and malaria vectors." *Human Biology*, 46(3):385–404.

Weekly Epidemiological Record, 2003a. "Cholera, 2002," 78(31):269–276. Geneva: *World Health Organization*.

Weekly Epidemiological Record, 2003b. "Global situation of the HIV/AIDS pandemic, end of 2003," 78(4):417–423. Geneva: World Health Organization.

Weekly Epidemiological Record, 2004. "Tuberculosis fact sheet," 79(13):125–127. Geneva: World Health Organization.

WORLD HEALTH STATISTICS ANNUAL. 1978. Geneva.

WORLD HEALTH STATISTICS ANNUAL. 1979. Geneva.

WORLD HEALTH STATISTICS ANNUAL. 1987. Geneva.

World Watch. 2004. "Population and its discontents." Special Issue, 17(5), September/October.

WU, C. 2000 "Mosquito magnets." *Science News*, (157):268–270.

WU, J. et al. 2002. "Characterization of apolipoprotein E. genetic variations in Taiwanese. Association with coronary heart disease and plasma lipid levels." *Human Biol.* 74 (1):25–31.

WYNDHAM, C. H 1966. "Southern African ethnic adaptation to temperature and exercise." In: *The Biology of Human Adaptability* P. T. Baker and J. S. Weiner. Oxford. Clarendon Press.

YAMAMOTO. F., et al. 1990. "Molecular genetic basis of the histo-blood group ABO system". *Nature*, 345:229–233.

YOUNG, J. B. 1971. *An Introduction to the Study of Man.* London: Oxford University Press.

ZAGO, M. A., M. S. FIGUEIREDO, and S. H. OGO, 1992. "Bantu B^S cluster haplotype predominates among Brazilian blacks." *Am. J. Phys. Anthrop.*, 88:295–298.

ZALLEN, B. T. 2000. "U.S. gene therapy on crisis." *Trends in Genetics*, 16(6);272–275.

ZEMEL, B., and C. JENKINS. 1989. "Dietary change and adolescent growth among the Bundi (Gendespeaking) people of Papua New Guinea." *Am. J. of Human Biology*, 1:709–718.

ZIMMET, P. 1982. "Review articles: Type 2 (non-insulin-dependent) diabetes. An epidemiological overview." *Diabetologia*, 22:399–411.

Glossary

adaptation Response to environmental conditions by adjustments of physiological processes or behavior to improve an organism's chance of survival; may be shortterm (functional), sometimes referred to as acclimatization, or a longterm response of a population's genetic variability that is affected by natural selection over several generations.

age cohorts Individuals who share a common demographic attribute; most frequently, members of the same age group.

agglutination The clinging together of cells caused by the attraction of antibodies and antigens, as in the case of blood cells with specific antibodies.

albumin A type of simple, soluble protein distributed throughout the tissue fluids.

allele Alternate genetic forms of the same locus.

amino acids Small organic compounds, containing the amino group, that are combined to form protein compounds.

anthropometry The measurement of human body form.

antibodies Protein molecules in the blood serum that will react with foreign proteins and protect against invading organisms.

antigen A substance capable of stimulating the production of an antibody; or inherited antigen forms, such as those of the red blood cell—the blood groups.

assortative mating The preferential selection of a mate with a particular trait or attribute; most frequently seen in positive assortative mating.

autosome All chromosomes except the sex chromosomes, X and Y.

biodeterminism Attributing certain behaviors to particular races or ethnic groups, behaviors that presumably exist because of some inherited traits.

brachycephalic Describes a short, broad-shaped head whose breadth is approximately 80 percent or more of its length.

breeding population A group of individuals who are potentially interbreeding, who occupy a local area, and who make up a basic unit of our species.

brow ridge The ridge of bone over the eyes.

carpals Wrist bones.

cartilage A dense, firm, but flexible connective tissue that is the major part of most of the skeleton and that calcifies at various stages of growth.

centromere The part of the chromosome where the chromatids are joined.

cephalic index   The ratio of the breadth to the length of the head or skull.

cerumen   The waxy substance secreted by glands in the external ear.

chiasma   Crossing over of chromatids of homologous chromosomes during an early stage of meiosis.

chromatid   One of the two strands that make up the chromosome.

chromosome   The darkly staining rod-shaped structure, located in the nucleus of a cell, that is composed of DNA molecules.

clinal distribution   Traces the geographical range of phenotypic or genetic characteristics of our species.

coefficient of inbreeding   The probability of like alleles from a common ancestor. The coefficient is higher, for example, in matings of first cousins (1/16) than in second cousins (1/64).

collagen   A fibrous protein that is the chief constituent part of connective tissue and bone.

congenital defect   A defective organ, system, or anatomical structure that is present at birth.

consanguineous   Genetic relative; related because of a common ancestor.

cormic index   The ratio of sitting height to standing height that shows the proportion of body height due to the head and trunk.

corneum   Outer layer of the epidermis.

correlation   The degree of correspondence between two measurements.

cranial capacity   The volume of the skull; used to estimate brain volume.

craniology   A science dealing with variations in size, shape, and proportions of skulls among *Homo sapiens.*

crossover   The exchange of genetic material between homologous chromosomes when in synapse during meiosis.

culture   The learned behavioral pattern that *Homo sapiens* uses to manipulate the environment.

Darwinian fitness   States characteristic of those who produce the most offspring.

deme   *See* breeding population.

demographic transition   A transition in the growth potential of a population.

demography   The study of a population's growth, size, and composition.

deoxyribonucleic acid (DNA)   A large organic molecule composed of two intertwined strands of similar units, nucleotides; each nucleotide contains an organic base, deoxyribose sugar, and a phosphate molecule.

dependency ratio   The ratio between the economically productive portion of the population and the dependent age groups, usually taken as those under 15 and over 65 years.

dermis   Inner layer of skin where the blood vessels, nerves, glands, and hair follicles are located.

diaphysis   The shaft of long bones.

diploid number   The number of chromosomes in all cells except a germinal cell.

distal   Referring to the direction away from the point of attachment of a limb.

DNA   *See* deoxyribonucleic acid.

dolichocephalic   Describes a long, narrow head whose breadth is 75 percent or less of its length.

dominant inheritance   One allele is dominant to another and, in the heterozygote, will cause the expression of the trait.

dysgenic   Those factors that reduce hereditary qualities; frequently applied to the preservation in the gene of defective traits through modern medical treatment of the affected individual; the opposite of eugenics.

effective breeding population   That proportion of the population who are in their reproductive years.

electrophoresis   A method of separating proteins by applying an electric charge to a solution of proteins.

embryo   Organism during the first eight weeks of gestation of in utero development of *Homo sapiens.*

endemic   The continuous presence of a disease in a community; often used in reference to a disease like malaria that continually infects a tropical population on a year-round basis.

endogamy   Inbreeding within a certain social unit, population, or deme.

endonucleases   Enzymes that break bonds at specific nucleotide sites along strands of DNA or RNA.

enzyme   A protein catalyst that causes a chemical reaction to occur in a living organism.

epidemiology   The study of the distribution and causes of a disease.

epidermis   Outer layer of skin; a tissue of four layers.

epiphysis   The portion of bone that develops from secondary centers of ossification and remains separate throughout the period of bone growth; the ends of the long bones connected to the main shaft, the diaphysis.

erythroblastosis fetalis   The hemolytic blood disease of the newborn in which the blood cells of an Rh1 infant are destroyed by maternal antibodies from an Rh- mother.

erythrocytes   Red blood cells.

ethnic group   A group of persons who share the same language and customs and who identify with certain recent origins.

eugenics   Efforts to improve the human species by controlled breeding.

evolution   Change in gene frequency of a population through time; descent with modification.

exogamy   Matings between members of different social groups, populations, or demes; outbreeding.

exon   The segments of DNA that are transcribed into mRNA that are then translated into a polypeptide chain.

fetus   Human organism from eight weeks of development until birth.

fitness   *See* Darwinian fitness.

forensic anthropology   Facts relating an individual's age, sex, and probable ethnic identity that may be applied to legal problems; most often this involves identification of skeletal remains.

founders' effect   Establishment of a new population by a few original migrants or "founders" whose genetic composition may be an aberrant sample of the gene pool of the large population from which it migrated.

gametes   Germ cells, either ova or sperm.

gamma globulin   A serum protein consisting of antibodies that act as a defense against infection.

gene   That region of the DNA molecule that contains the nucleotide sequence code for the production of a polypeptide chain relayed by a messenger RNA.

gene flow   Exchange of genetic material between populations due to dispersion of gametes through interbreeding.

genetic disease   An inherited disorder, usually caused by recessive alleles but sometimes by dominants.

genetic drift   Refers to chance events that alter gene frequencies in small breeding populations; the reduction in gene frequency is due to a sampling error because of a small number of matings.

genetic load   The total frequency of a population's lethal or sublethal genes that may affect an individual's growth, development, health, or chance of survival.

genotype   Actual genetic composition of an organism; the pair of alleles at a locus of homologous chromosomes determined at conception.

globulins   A major group of proteins in blood plasma that include alpha, beta, and gamma globulins.

haploid   Refers to the number of chromosomes in sperm or ova (twenty-three) that is one-half the number of a somatic cell (forty-six).

haplotypes   A series or combination of closely linked loci.

haptoglobin   A protein in the serum portion of blood whose function is to bind with free hemoglobin to prevent its excretion.

Hardy-Weinberg equilibrium   A mathematical formula stating the proportions between alleles within a stable population.

hemoglobin   Red respiratory protein making up more than 90 percent of the protein of a red cell and functioning to transport oxygen to the tissues of the body.

hemolysis   The bursting apart of a red blood cell, releasing its products into the blood plasma.

heritability   That proportion of variation of a trait in a population that is due to the variation of genotypes.

heterozygote   A pair of different alleles.

homeostasis   Maintenance of an equilibrium of various metabolic functions in the body.

hominid   The primate family taxon that includes *Homo sapiens* and extinct ancestral forms such as the Australopithecines.

homologous   Having a likeness in structure.

Homo sapiens   The human species; genus *Homo*, species *sapiens*.

homozygote   A pair of identical alleles.

hypoxia   Less than normal levels of oxygen in air, blood, or tissues; also refers to a general physiological state in response to low levels of atmospheric oxygen, particularly among persons at higher elevations.

incest taboo   Matings forbidden between certain classes of relatives.

intron   A noncoding region of DNA that is transcribed but excised from mature mRNA.

isolate   A population or group of populations that maintain a high degree of breeding isolation from other groups because marriages with outsiders are forbidden or restricted.

karyotype   The distinctive array of chromosomes; the size and shape of a species' chromosomes seen at metaphase of cell division.

keratin   A protein; the major constituent of the outer skin layers.

Law of Independent Assortment   Two traits, simultaneously considered, will sort and recombine independently of each other; Mendel's second law.

Law of Independent Segregation   Traits are transmitted as discrete units that do not blend with or contaminate each other: Mendel's first law.

linkage   Two or more genes located at loci close to one another on a chromosome.

locus   A chromosome position or space for the coded unit of the gene.

mandible   The lower jaw; the bone containing the lower teeth.

matrilocal   The settlement pattern in which adult males leave to marry outside of their natal community while the females remain.

maxilla   Bone of the major portion of the face; contains the teeth and upper jaw.

meiosis   Process of cell division and chromosome replication in germinal cells followed by cell fission and reduction in chromosome number.

melanin   Dark pigment granules of the skin and hair of animals and of structures of plants.

melanocytes   Pigment cells of the skin.

menarche   The onset of menstruation; the first menstrual period.

Mendelian ratio   The ratio of genotypes of homozygote and heterozygote combinations.

mesocephalic   Describes an intermediate head shape between brachycephalic (broad headed) and dolichocephalic (long headed).

metacarpals   The bones of the hands connecting the phalanges with the carpals (bones of the wrist).

microevolution   Alteration in the frequency of occurrence of certain genes that persists throughout generations.

mitosis   Cell division that occurs in somatic cells producing two identical daughter cells.

molecular clock   An estimate of the time since divergence of two related species from a common ancestor by comparison of certain molecular structures or DNA fragments.

monogenic   Single gene traits as contrasted with traits determined by two or more genes (polygenic).

mutation   A change in the genetic code; a change in the sequence of base pairs of the DNA molecule.

nasal index   A ratio of the width to the length of the nose.

natal   Associated with one's birth; applied to location, native or community, where one's birth took place.

natural selection   Due to certain natural conditions in the environment, some individuals, because of their genetic endowment, produce more offspring who, in turn, reproduce at a higher rate than do other individuals. Through this process the less well adapted are gradually reduced in number over the generations.

Neolithic   The "New Stone Age," a period beginning approximately 10,000 to 12,000 years ago when *Homo sapiens* began to domesticate plants and, later, animals. A major feature of the Neolithic is the sedentary lifestyle that it encouraged.

orthognathic   Straight faced; the teeth and supporting bone in the anterior part of the face lie close to a line drawn between the chin and the brow.

osteomalacia   Failure of the collagen of the newly formed bone to mineralize. A similar condition in children and juveniles is referred to as rickets.

pandemic   A disease affecting a large number of people dispersed over a wide geographic area.

patrilocal   The settlement pattern in which females leave to marry outside of their natal community while the males remain.

penetrance   The frequency of expression of the phenotype; some genes are expressed less than 100 percent of the time, so they have a low penetrance.

phalanges   The long bones of the fingers and toes.

phenotype   The trait expressed as a result of the interaction of the environment and genotype.

photolysis   The destruction of chemical compounds by light; usually in reference to the ultraviolet range.

plasma   The yellowish fluid part of the blood containing nutrients, many proteins, and the red and white blood cells.

pleiotropic   Genes that influence the expression of more than one trait.

polygenic   Multiple genes that influence a single trait.

polymorphic   Describes variability between individuals within a population.

polytypic   Describes variability between populations.

porphyrins   Complex pigment molecules widely dispersed in plants and animals. Examples in humans are heme (of hemoglobin), bile, and cytochrome.

prognathic Having forward protrusion of the midfacial region due primarily to large teeth and robust dental arches.

race A geographically and culturally determined collection of individuals who share in a common gene pool and are similar in many characteristics (also referred to as a subspecies).

random mating Matings that occur without regard to genotype.

recessive inheritance A trait determined by a pair of recessive alleles.

recombination The formation of new combinations of linked genes by crossover between parts of homologous chromosomes during meiosis.

RFLP Restriction fragment length polymorphisms of DNA molecules produced by nucleotide specific enzymes (endonucleases).

ribonucleic acid (RNA) A single-strand molecule of organic bases, sugars (ribose), and phosphates; used to translate the coded sequence of the DNA (RNA) or carry amino acids to the sites of protein synthesis (1RNA).

ribosomes These small spherical structures in the cell cytoplasm are made up of proteins and RNA and are the site for protein synthesis.

rickets A bone disease of young children and juveniles in which their rapidly growing bones fail to mineralize properly; the bones—especially the weight-bearing ones—easily bend or may become distorted.

RNA *See* ribonucleic acid.

sampling error A change in gene frequencies within a population that is due to an error caused by the small size of the effective breeding population.

secular trend A trend continuing for a long term or over a generation.

sex-linked Describes a trait determined by a gene carried on the sex chromosomes, usually the X-chromosome.

sexual dimorphism Refers to the difference in form or size in males and females.

shovel-shaped incisor Incisor tooth that has thickened margins on the lingual surface (tongue side of the tooth).

somatology The science that deals with the body, its form, and function; usually applied to comparative studies of body forms of different ethnic groups.

species Groups of interbreeding organisms reproductively isolated from other such groups.

steatopygia An excessive accumulation of fat and probably fibrous tissue in the buttocks; particularly in evidence among females of certain ethnic groups such as the Bushmen and Hottentots of southern Africa.

subspecies A grouping of individuals or populations who share a number of characteristics in common; frequently geographically limited.

synapsis The pairing of homologous chromosomes during the anaphase stage of meiosis.

syndrome The group or aggregate of symptoms associated with any disease or abnormal condition; for example, Down syndrome, a group of physical and neurological deformities appearing in a person with an extra chromosome of the twenty-first pair.

transferrins A group of iron-binding proteins found in the serum portion of blood.

trisomy The diploid number plus one, as in the example of a Down syndrome person with 47 chromosomes.

twins (dizygotic) Twins who are developed from a pair of fertilized ova and who are no more identical in their genotypes than siblings; also called fraternal twins.

twins (monozygotic) Twins developed from a cleavage of a single fertilized ovum; hence, they have identical genotypes; identical twins.

variance The measure of the dispersion of values about a population mean.

zygomatic arches Cheekbones.

zygote The fertilized egg.

Index